Lecture Notes in Computer Sc   T0238024

Commenced Publication in 1973
Founding and Former Series Editors:
Gerhard Goos, Juris Hartmanis, and Jan van Leeuwen

Thomas Eiter   Leonid Libkin (Eds.)

Database Theory –
ICDT 2005

10th International Conference
Edinburgh, UK, January 5-7, 2005
Proceedings

 Springer

Volume Editors

Thomas Eiter
Technische Universität Wien
Institut für Informationssysteme
Favoritenstr. 9-11, 1040 Wien, Österreich
E-mail: eiter@kr.tuwien.ac.at

Leonid Libkin
University of Toronto
Department of Computer Science
6, King's College Road, Pratt Building
Toronto, Ontario M5S 3H5, Canada
E-mail: libkin@cs.toronto.edu

Library of Congress Control Number: Applied for

CR Subject Classification (1998): H.2, F.1.3, F.4.1, I.2.1, H.4, F.2, H.3

ISSN 0302-9743
ISBN 3-540-24288-0 Springer Berlin Heidelberg New York

Springer is a part of Springer Science+Business Media

springeronline.com

© Springer-Verlag Berlin Heidelberg 2005
Printed in Germany

Typesetting: Camera-ready by author, data conversion by Scientific Publishing Services, Chennai, India
Printed on acid-free paper   SPIN: 11366843   06/3142   5 4 3 2 1 0

Preface

This volume collects the papers presented at the 10th International Conference on Database Theory, ICDT 2005, held during January 5–7, 2005, in Edinburgh, UK.

ICDT (`http://alpha.luc.ac.be/~lucp1080/icdt/`) has now a long tradition of international conferences, providing a biennial scientific forum for the communication of high-quality and innovative research results on theoretical aspects of all forms of database systems and database technology. The conference usually takes place in Europe, and has been held in Rome (1986), Bruges (1988), Paris (1990), Berlin (1992), Prague (1995), Delphi (1997), Jerusalem (1999), London (2001), and Siena (2003) so far. ICDT has merged with the Symposium on Mathematical Fundamentals of Database Systems (MFDBS), initiated in Dresden in 1987, and continued in Visegrad in 1989 and Rostock in 1991.

ICDT had a two-stage submission process. First, 103 abstracts were submitted, which were followed a week later by 84 paper submissions. From these 84 submissions, the ICDT Program Committee selected 24 papers for presentation at the conference. Most of these papers were "extended abstracts" and preliminary reports on work in progress. It is anticipated that most of these papers will appear in a more polished form in scientific journals.

The proceedings also contain three invited papers by David Maier, Michael Schwartzbach, and Moshe Vardi. The Best Newcomer Award, for the best submission written solely by authors who had never published in earlier ICDT proceedings, was given by the program committee to Albert Atserias for his paper *"Conjunctive Query Evaluation by Search Tree Revisited."*

We would like to thank a number of people who made ICDT 2005 a successful event. First of all, the authors who submitted papers, the members of the program committee for their efforts in reviewing and selecting the papers, the external referees for their help, and, importantly, Andrei Voronkov for supplying his marvelous PC Expert conference submission management system. A great thanks is owed to Peter Buneman and his organizing committee for hosting the conference, and to Marcelo Arenas and Wenfei Fan for running the conference website. Last but not least, we are very grateful to the sponsors, the United Kingdom National e-Science Centre and the Digital Curation Centre, for their support.

January 2005
Thomas Eiter
Leonid Libkin

Organization

ICDT 2005 was organized by the the School of Informatics, University of Edinburgh and the UK National e-Science Centre.

Organizing Committee

Peter Buneman (University of Edinburgh, UK, chair)
Marcelo Arenas (University of Toronto, Canada, publicity)
Lee Callaghan (UK National e-Science Centre, UK)
Yrsa Roca Fannberg (University of Edinburgh, UK)
Wenfei Fan (Bell Laboratories, USA, publicity)
Dyane Goodchild (University of Edinburgh, UK)
Gill Maddy (UK National e-Science Centre, UK)

Program Co-chairs

Thomas Eiter (Vienna University of Technology, Austria)
Leonid Libkin (University of Toronto, Canada)

Program Committee

Lars Arge (Duke University, USA)
Catriel Beeri (Hebrew University of Jerusalem, Israel)
Michael Benedikt (Bell Laboratories, USA)
Leopoldo Bertossi (Carleton University, Canada)
Nicole Bidoit (Université Paris Sud, France)
Giuseppe De Giacomo (Università di Roma "La Sapienza", Italy)
Wenfei Fan (Bell Laboratories, USA)
Nicola Leone (Università della Calabria, Italy)
Jerzy Marcinkowski (Wroclaw University, Poland)
Yossi Matias (Tel Aviv University, Israel)
Gultekin Özsoyoglu (Case Western Reserve University, USA)
Rajeev Rastogi (Bell Laboratories, USA)
Ken Ross (Columbia University, USA)
Thomas Schwentick (Marburg University, Germany)
Kyuseok Shim (Seoul National University, South Korea)
Eljas Soisalon-Soininen (Helsinki University, Finland)
Bernhard Thalheim (Kiel University, Germany)
Jan Van den Bussche (Limburg University, Belgium)
Victor Vianu (University of California at San Diego, USA)
Andrei Voronkov (Manchester University, UK)
Peter Widmayer (ETH Zürich, Switzerland)

External Referees

Pankaj Agarwal
Suleyman Fatih Akgul
Marcelo Arenas
Denilson Barbosa
Pablo Barceló
Roy Bartsch
Monica Caniupan
Aleksander Binemann-Zdanowicz
Philip L. Bohannon
Vladimir Braverman
Loreto Bravo
Francesco Buccafurri
Ali Cakmak
Toon Calders
Andrea Cali
Diego Calvanese
Stefano Ceri
Jan Chomicki
Jaehyok Chong
Meir Cohen
Anuj Dawar
Alin Deutsch
Gunar Fiedler
Floris Geerts
Georg Gottlob
Gianluigi Greco
Michael Greenwald
Nadav Grosshaug
Sariel Har-Peled
Jayant Haritsa
Giovambattista Ianni
Mohammed Khazal Jaber
Chulyun Kim
Mustafa Kirac
Hans-Joachim Klein
Christoph Koch
Domenico Lembo
Maurizio Lenzerini
Lipyeow Lim
Jan Lindström
Maarten Marx
Yariv Matia

Vincent Millist
Tova Milo
Alan Nash
Apostol Natsev
Kobbi Nissim
Matthieu Objois
Kenneth Oksanen
Luigi Palopoli
Yannis Papakonstantinou
Hyoungmin Park
Gerald Pfeifer
Kerttu Pollari-Malmi
Nattakarn Ratprasartporn
Riccardo Rosati
Riku Saikkonen
Peter Sanders
Ulrike Sattler
Vladimir Sazonov
Francesco Scarcello
Klaus-Dieter Schewe
Peggy Schmidt
Luc Segoufin
Gabby Shainer
Kyoung Shin
Dan Suciu
Injae Sung
Wieslaw Szwast
Murat Tasan
Lidia Tendera
Giorgio Terracina
Jukka Teuhola
David Toman
Hans Tompits
Tomasz Truderung
Jerzy Tyszkiewicz
Daniel Urieli
Jan Vahrenhold
Piotr Wieczorek
Wanhong Xu
Ke Yi
Hai Yu

Table of Contents

Invited Papers

Regular Papers

Session: Query Languages and Types

Session: Multi-dimensional Data Processing

Session: Algorithmic Aspects

Session: Privacy and Security

Session: Logic and Databases

Session: Query Rewriting

Session: Query Processing, and Data Streams

Model Checking for Database Theoreticians

Moshe Y. Vardi *

Rice University
Houston, TX, USA
vardi@cs.rice.edu
http://www.cs.rice/edu/~vardi

Abstract. Algorithmic verification is one of the most successful applications of automated reasoning in computer science. In algorithmic verification one uses algorithmic techniques to establish the correctness of the system under verification with respect to a given property. Model checking is an algorithmic-verification technique that is based on a small number of key ideas, tying together graph theory, automata theory, and logic. In this self-contained talk I will describe how this "holy trinity" gave rise to algorithmic-verification tools, and discuss its applicability to database verification.

1   Introduction

The recent growth in computer power and connectivity has changed the face of science and engineering, and is changing the way business is being conducted. This revolution is driven by the unrelenting advances in semiconductor manufacturing technology. Nevertheless, the U.S. semiconductor community faces a serious challenge: chip designers are finding it increasingly difficult to keep up with the advances in semiconductor manufacturing. As a result, they are unable to exploit the enormous capacity that this technology provides. The International Technology Roadmap for Semiconductors suggests that the semiconductor industry will require productivity gains greater than the historical 20% per-year to keep up with the increasing complexity of semiconductor designs. This is referred to as the "design productivity crisis". As designs grow more complex, it becomes easier to introduce flaws into the design. Thus, designers use various validation techniques to verify the correctness of the design. Unfortunately, these techniques themselves grow more expensive and difficult with design complexity. As the validation process has begun to consume more than half the project design resources, the semiconductor industry has begun to refer to this problem as the "validation crisis".

Formal verification is a process in which mathematical techniques are used to guarantee the correctness of a design with respect to some specified behavior. Algorithmic formal-verification tools, based on *model-checking technology* [17, 51, 64, 70], have enjoyed a substantial and growing use over the last few years, showing an ability to discover

---

* Supported in part by NSF grants CCR-9988322, CCR-0124077, CCR-0311326, IIS-9908435, IIS-9978135, EIA-0086264, and ANI-0216467, by BSF grant 9800096, by Texas ATP grant 003604-0058-2003, and by a grant from the Intel Corporation.

T. Eiter and L. Libkin (Eds.): ICDT 2005, LNCS 3363, pp. 1–16, 2005.

subtle flaws that result from extremely improbable events [18]. While until recently these tools were viewed as of academic interest only, they are now routinely used in industrial applications, resulting in decreased time to market and increased product integrity [48]. It is fair to say that algorithmic verification is one of the most successful applications of automated reasoning in computer science [19].

The main thrust of database theory has traditional focused on data models, queries, and database design, cf. [52, 8, 2]. The dynamic aspects of databases, cf. [58, 57, 73], received somewhat less attention by database theoreticians [59]. Almost no attention was given to the verification perspective. This has started to change over the last few years, driven to a large extent by the confluence of data and the Web [1]. Recent database-theory papers that address the verification perspective include [3, 36, 65, 21].

Our goal in this paper is to offer a basic introduction to the theory of algorithmic verification. A second purpose is to expose the reader to the automata-theoretic approach to algorithmic verification. The automata-theoretic approach uses the theory of automata as a unifying paradigm for system specification, verification, and synthesis [76, 25, 47, 71, 46]. Automata enables the separation of the logical and the algorithmic aspects of reasoning about systems, yielding clean and asymptotically optimal algorithms. The automata-theoretic framework for reasoning about finite-state systems has proven to be very versatile. Automata are the key to techniques such as on-the-fly verification [28], and they are useful also for modular verification [41], partial-order verification [29, 75], verification of real-time and hybrid systems [33, 22], and verification of open systems [5, 42]. Many decision and synthesis problems have automata-based solutions and no other solution for them is known [24, 63, 44]. Automata-based methods have been implemented in industrial automated-verification tools (c.f., COSPAN [31] and SPIN [34]). While the application of automata theory to database theory goes back to the 1980s, cf. [66], it is only recently that they have become a popular tool [55, 56].

The outline of the paper is as follows. We first describe in Section 2 the automata-theoretic approach to the verification of finite-state systems with respect to linear-time properties. This uses Büchi automata as the basic working tool. We then describe in Section 3 the automata-theoretic approach to the verification of context-free systems with respect to (branching-time) μ-calculus properties. This uses alternating two-way tree automata as the basic working tool. In Section 4 we discuss the application of these techniques to the verification of database systems. We conclude with a discussion in Section 5.

2   Finite-State Systems

The first step in formal verification is to come up with a *formal specification* of the system under verification, consisting of a description of the desired behavior. One of the more widely used specification languages for systems is *temporal logic* [62]. Two possible views regarding the nature of time induce two types of temporal logics [49]. In *linear* temporal logics, time is treated as if each moment in time has a unique possible future. Thus, linear temporal logic formulas are interpreted over linear sequences and we regard them as describing a behavior of a single computation of a system. In *branching* temporal logics, each moment in time may split into various possible futures. Accordingly, the structures over which branching temporal logic formulas are interpreted can be viewed as infinite computation trees, each describing the behavior of the possible computations of a nondeterministic program. We focus on linear time in this section, and on branching time in the next section. For a discussion of linear vs. branching time, see [69].)

In the linear temporal logic LTL, formulas are constructed from a set $Prop$ of atomic propositions using the usual Boolean connectives as well as the unary temporal connective X ("next"), F ("eventually"), G ("always"), and the binary temporal connective U ("until"). For example, the LTL formula $G(request \rightarrow F\ grant)$, which refers to the atomic propositions $request$ and $grant$, is true in a computation precisely when every state in the computation in which $request$ holds is followed by some state in the future in which $grant$ holds. The LTL formula $G(request \rightarrow (request\ U\ grant))$ is true in a computation precisely if, whenever $request$ holds in a state of the computation, it holds until a state in which $grant$ holds is reached.

LTL is interpreted over *computations*, which can be viewed as infinite sequences of truth assignments to the atomic propositions; i.e., a computation is a function $\pi : I\!N \rightarrow 2^{Prop}$ that assigns truth values to the elements of $Prop$ at each time instant (natural number). For a computation π and a point $i \in I\!N$, the notation $\pi, i \models \varphi$ indicates that a formula φ holds at the point i of the computation π. For example, $\pi, i \models X\varphi$ iff $\pi, i+1 \models \varphi$, and and $\pi, i \models \varphi U \psi$ iff for some $j \geq i$, we have $\pi, j \models \psi$ and for all k, $i \leq k < j$, we have $\pi, k \models \varphi$. We say that π *satisfies* a formula φ, denoted $\pi \models \varphi$, iff $\pi, 0 \models \varphi$. The connectives F and G can be defined in terms of the connective U: $F\varphi$ is defined as **true** $U\varphi$, and $G\varphi$ is defined as $\neg F\neg\varphi$.

Systems can be described in a variety of formal description formalisms. Regardless of the formalism used, a system can be abstractly viewed as a *labeled transition graph*, i.e., as a structure of the form $M = (W, W_0, R, L)$, where W is the set of states that the system can be in, $W_0 \subseteq W$ is the set of initial states of the system, $R \subseteq W^2$ is a transition relation that indicates the allowable state transitions of the system (we typically assume that T is *total*; that is, every state has at least one R-successor), and $L : W \rightarrow 2^{Prop}$ assigns truth values to the atomic propositions in each state of the system. A labeled transition graph is essentially a Kripke structure, the standard model for *modal logic* [35]. Our focus in this section is on *finite* labeled transition graphs; that is, W is required to be finite. A *path* in M that *starts at* u is a possible infinite behavior of the system starting at u, i.e., it is an infinite sequence $u_0, u_1 \ldots$ of states in W such that $u_0 = u$, and $u_i R u_{i+1}$ for all $i \geq 0$. The sequence $L(u_0), L(u_1) \ldots$ is a *computation* of M that *starts at* u. It is the sequence of truth assignments visited by the path, The *language* of M, denoted $L(M)$ consists of all computations of M that start at a state in W_0. Note that $\mathcal{L}(M)$ can be viewed as a language of infinite words over the alphabet 2^{Prop}. $\mathcal{L}(M)$ can be viewed as an abstract description of a system, describing all possible "traces". We say that M *satisfies* an LTL formula φ if all computations in $\mathcal{L}(M)$ satisfy φ, that is, if $\mathcal{L}(M) \subseteq models(\varphi)$. When M satisfies φ we also say that M is a model of φ, which explain why the technique is known as *model checking* [18].

One of the major approaches to algorithmic verification is the *automata-theoretic approach*. The key idea underlying the automata-theoretic approach is that, given an LTL formula φ, it is possible to construct a finite-state automaton A_φ on infinite words that accepts precisely all computations that satisfy φ. The type of finite automata on infinite words we consider is the one defined by Büchi [10]. A *Büchi automaton* is a tuple $A = (\Sigma, S, S_0, \rho, F)$, where Σ is a finite alphabet, S is a finite set of states, $S_0 \subseteq S$ is a set of initial states, $\rho : S \times \Sigma \rightarrow 2^S$ is a nondeterministic transition function, and $F \subseteq S$ is a set of accepting states. A *run* of A over an infinite word $w = a_1 a_2 \cdots$, is a sequence $s_0 s_1 \cdots$, where $s_0 \in S_0$ and $s_i \in \rho(s_{i-1}, a_i)$ for all $i \geq 1$. A run $s_0, s_1, \ldots$ is *accepting* if there is some accepting state that repeats infinitely often, i.e., for some $s \in F$ there are infinitely many i's such that $s_i = s$. The infinite word w is *accepted* by A if there is an accepting run of A over w. The *language* of infinite words accepted by A is denoted $\mathcal{L}(A)$. The following fact establishes the correspondence between LTL and Büchi automata [71] (for a tutorial introduction for this correspondence, see [67]):

Theorem 1. *Given an LTL formula φ, one can build a Büchi automaton $A_\varphi = (\Sigma, S, S_0, \rho, , F)$, where $\Sigma = 2^{Prop}$ and $|S| \leq 2^{O(|\varphi|)}$, such that $\mathcal{L}(A_\varphi)$ is exactly the set of computations satisfying the formula φ.*

A detailed proof of Theorem 1 is out of the scope of this paper. The intuition is that a state of the automaton A_φ is simply a set of subformulas of φ. The automaton that reads a computation π in state P checks that π satisfies all formulas in P. Initial states of A_φ contain φ. The transition relation of A_φ checks the correctness of the temporal connectives. For example, if the current state contains $X\psi$ then the next state contains ψ. Dealing with the U connective is a bit more complicated. If the current state contains $\theta U \psi$, then either the current state contains also ψ or the next state contains $\theta U \psi$. This enables the "fulfillment" of $\theta U \psi$ to be postponed forever, which is prevented by the acceptance condition of A_φ.

The correspondence provided by Theorem 1 enables a reduction of the verification problem to an automata-theoretic problem as follows [70]. Suppose that we are given a finite labeled transition graph M and an LTL formula φ. We check whether $\mathcal{L}(M) \subseteq$ models(φ) as follows: (1) construct the automaton $A_{\neg\varphi}$ that corresponds to the *negation* of the formula φ, (2) take the *cross product* of the transition graph M and the automaton $A_{\neg\varphi}$ to obtain an automaton $A_{M,\varphi}$, such that $\mathcal{L}(A_{M,\varphi}) = \mathcal{L}(M) \cap \mathcal{L}(A_{\neg\varphi})$, and (3) check whether the language $\mathcal{L}(A_{M,\varphi})$ is nonempty, i.e., whether $A_{M,\varphi}$ accepts *some* input.

Theorem 2. *Let M be a finite labeled transition graph and φ be an LTL formula. Then M satisfies φ iff $\mathcal{L}(A_{M,\varphi}) = \emptyset$.*

The emptiness test of Büchi automata can be done efficiently [26, 71].

Proposition 1. *Checking for a given Büchi automaton A whether $\mathcal{L}(A) = \emptyset$ can be done in time that is linear in the size of A.*

Proof. Let $A = (\Sigma, S, S_0, \rho, F)$ be the given automaton. Let $G_A = (S, E)$ be a directed graph, where $E = \{\langle s, t \rangle : t \in \rho(s, a) \text{ for some } a \in \Sigma\}$. It is easy to see that $\mathcal{L}(A)$ is nonempty iff there are states $s \in S_0$ and $t \in F$ such that t is connected, or equal, to s in G_A, and t is connected to itself in G_A. Thus, A is nonempty if G_A has a reachable nontrivial strongly connected component that intersects F non-trivially.

(In fact, the nonemptiness problem for Büchi automata is NLOGSPACE-complete [71].)

If $\mathcal{L}(A_{M,\varphi})$ is empty, then the design is correct. Otherwise, the design is incorrect and the word accepted by $\mathcal{L}(A_{M,\varphi})$ is an incorrect computation. Model-checking tools use efficient algorithms for checking emptiness of Büchi automata [20] to check emptiness of $\mathcal{L}(A_{M,\varphi})$. In case of nonemptiness, the incorrect computation is presented to the user as a finite trace, possibly followed by a cycle. Thus, once the automaton $A_{\neg\varphi}$ is constructed, the verification task is reduced to automata-theoretic problems, namely, intersecting automata and testing emptiness of automata, which have highly efficient solutions [67]. Furthermore, using data structures that enable compact representation of very large state space makes it possible to verify designs of significant complexity [11].

The linear-time framework is not limited to using LTL as a specification language. ForSpec is a recent extension of LTL, designed to address the need of the semiconductor industry [7]. There are those who prefer to use automata on infinite words as a specification formalism [71]; in fact, this is the approach of COSPAN [47]. In this approach, we are given a design represented as a finite transition graph M and a property represented by a Büchi (or a related variant) automaton P. The design is correct if all computations in $\mathcal{L}(M)$ are accepted by P, i.e., $\mathcal{L}(M) \subseteq \mathcal{L}(P)$. This approach is called the *language-containment* approach. To verify M with respect to P, we: (1) construct the automaton P^c that *complements* P, (2) take the product of the transition graph M and the automaton P^c to obtain an automaton $A_{M,P}$, and (3) check that the automaton $A_{M,P}$ is nonempty. As before, the design is correct iff $A_{M,P}$ is empty. Thus, the verification task is again reduced to automata-theoretic problems, namely intersecting and complementing automata and testing emptiness of automata. As complementing Büchi automata is harder than complementing automata on finite words, cf. [45], tools that work directly with automata require the user to provide the complementary automaton P^c [47, 34]. For an automata-theoretic approach to branching-time model checking of finite-state systems, see [46]. In the next section we describe an automata-theoretic approach to branching-time model of context-free systems.

3 Context-Free Systems

An important research topic in algorithmic verification during the 1990s has been the application of model checking to infinite-state systems. Notable successes in this area has been the application of model checking to real-time and hybrid systems, cf. [32, 50]. Another active thrust of research is the application of model checking to *infinite-state sequential systems*. These are systems in which a state carries a finite, but unbounded, amount of information, e.g., a pushdown store. The origin of this thrust is the important result that the monadic second-order theory of *context-free graphs* is decidable [53]. As the complexity involved in that decidability result is non-elementary, researchers sought decidability results of elementary complexity. This started with development of an exponential-time algorithm for model-checking formulas in the *alternation-free* μ-calculus with respect to context-free graphs [13]. The μ-calculus is modal logic augmented with least and greatest fixpoint operators [38]. It is an expressive logic, which subsumes LTL. (The alternation-free μ-calculus, in which alternation of least and greatest fixpoint operators is not allow, does not subsume LTL [40].) Researchers then went on to extend this result to the full μ-calculus, on one hand, and to more general graphs on the other hand. See [12] for a survey and [15, 61] for some recent extensions. In this section we describe an automata-theoretic framework for reasoning about context-free systems [43].

It is not obvious that the automata-theoretic approach is applicable for effective reasoning about infinite-state systems. The reason, essentially, lies in the fact that the automata-theoretic techniques involve constructions in which the state space of the system directly influences the state space of the automaton (e.g., when we take the product of a specification automaton with the graph that models the system). On the other hand, the automata we know to handle algorithmically, e.g., test emptiness, have finitely many states. The key insight, which enables us to overcome this difficulty, and which is implicit in all previous decidability results in the area of infinite-state sequential systems, is that in spite of the somewhat misleading terminology (e.g., "context-free graphs"), the classes of infinite-state graphs for which decidability is known can be described by finite-state automata. This is explained by the fact the the states of the graphs that model these systems can be viewed as nodes in an infinite tree and transitions between states can be expressed by finite-state automata. As a result, automata-theoretic techniques can be used to reason about such systems. In particular, we show that the analysis of such systems can be reduced to the emptiness problem for *alternating two-way tree automata*, which is known to be decidable in exponential time [68].

3.1   Labeled Rewrite Systems

Here we extend the notion of transition graph to allow infinitely many states. We are interested, however, in infinite systems with finitary representations. A *rewrite system* is a triple $\mathcal{R} = \langle V, R, x_0 \rangle$, where V is a finite alphabet, R is a finite set of rewrite rules, to be defined below, and $x_0 \in V^*$ is an initial word. In a *context-free* rewrite system, each rewrite rule is a pair $\langle A, x \rangle \in V \times V^*$. The rewrite system $\mathcal{R}$ together with a labeling $L : V^* \to 2^{Prop}$ induces the labeled transition graph $G_{\mathcal{R}} = (V^*, \{x_0\}, \rho_{\mathcal{R}}, L)$, where $\langle x, y \rangle \in \rho_{\mathcal{R}}$ if there is a rewrite rule in R whose application on x results in y. Formally, if $\mathcal{R}$ is a context-free rewrite system, then $\rho_{\mathcal{R}}(A \cdot y, x \cdot y)$ if $\langle A, x \rangle \in R$. A labeled transition graph that is induced by a context-free rewrite system is called a *context-free graph*. Such graphs model the call graphs of systems with recursive procedures [4]. (To fully model call graphs of such systems one needs to consider *pushdown graphs*, which slightly generalize context-free graphs [14, 72]. We restrict attention here to context-free graphs for simplicity sake.) We define the *size* $|R|$ of R as the space required in order to encode the rewrite rules in R. Thus, in the case of a context-free rewrite system, $|R| = \sum_{\langle A, x \rangle \in R} |x|$.

The rewrite rules provide us with a finite representation of a transition relation over an infinite state space. We also need to represent the labeling L is a finitary manner. We consider here *regular state properties*, where each property $p \in Prop$ is associated with a NFA $\mathcal{U}_p$ over V, describing the set of states (words in V^*) in which p holds. Thus, $L(w) = \{p : w \in \mathcal{L}(\mathcal{U}_p)\}$. We say that L is a *regular labeling*. The size $|L|$ of the regular labeling L is $\sum_{p \in Prop} |\mathcal{U}_p|$.

3.2   Alternating Two-Way Automata

Given a finite set Υ of directions, an Υ-*tree* is a set $T \subseteq \Upsilon^*$ such that if $v \cdot x \in T$, where $v \in \Upsilon$ and $x \in \Upsilon^*$, then also $x \in T$. The elements of T are called *nodes*, and the empty word ε is the *root* of T. For every $v \in \Upsilon$ and $x \in T$, the node x is the *parent* of $v \cdot x$. Each node $x \neq \varepsilon$ of T has a *direction* in Υ. The direction of the root is the symbol $\bot$ (we assume that $\bot \notin \Upsilon$). The direction of a node $v \cdot x$ is v. We denote by $dir(x)$ the direction of node x. An Υ-tree T is a *full infinite tree* if $T = \Upsilon^*$. A *path* π of a tree T is a set $\pi \subseteq T$ such that $\varepsilon \in \pi$ and for every $x \in \pi$ there exists a unique $v \in \Upsilon$ such that $v \cdot x \in \pi$. Note that our definitions here reverse the standard definitions (e.g., when $\Upsilon = \{0, 1\}$, the successors of the node 0 are 00 and 10 (rather than 00 and 01)[1].

Given two finite sets Υ and Σ, a *Σ-labeled Υ-tree* is a pair $\langle T, V \rangle$ where T is an Υ-tree and $V : T \rightarrow \Sigma$ maps each node of T to a letter in Σ. When Υ and Σ are not important or clear from the context, we call $\langle T, V \rangle$ a labeled tree. We say that an $((\Upsilon \cup \{\bot\}) \times \Sigma)$-labeled Υ-tree $\langle T, V \rangle$ is *Υ-exhaustive* if for every node $x \in T$, we have $V(x) \in \{dir(x)\} \times \Sigma$.

Alternating automata on infinite trees generalize nondeterministic tree automata and were first introduced in [54]. Here we describe alternating *two-way* tree automata. For a finite set X, let $\mathcal{B}^+(X)$ be the set of positive Boolean formulas over X (i.e., boolean formulas built from elements in X using $\land$ and $\lor$), where we also allow the formulas **true** and **false**, and, as usual, $\land$ has precedence over $\lor$. For a set $Y \subseteq X$ and a formula $\theta \in \mathcal{B}^+(X)$, we say that Y *satisfies* θ iff assigning **true** to elements in Y and assigning **false** to elements in $X \setminus Y$ makes θ true. For a set Υ of directions, the *extension* of Υ is the set $ext(\Upsilon) = \Upsilon \cup \{\varepsilon, \uparrow\}$ (we assume that $\Upsilon \cap \{\varepsilon, \uparrow\} = \emptyset$). We view an element $(c, q) \in ext(\Upsilon) \times Q$ as an instruction to move in direction c into state q. An *alternating two-way automaton* over Σ-labeled Υ-trees is a tuple $\mathcal{A} = \langle \Sigma, Q, q_0, \delta, F \rangle$, where Σ is the input alphabet, Q is a finite set of states, $\delta : Q \times \Sigma \rightarrow \mathcal{B}^+(ext(\Upsilon) \times Q)$ is the transition function, $q_0 \in Q$ is an initial state, and F specifies the acceptance condition.

A run of an alternating automaton $\mathcal{A}$ over a labeled tree $\langle \Upsilon^*, V \rangle$ is a labeled tree $\langle T_r, r \rangle$ in which every node is labeled by an element of $\Upsilon^* \times Q$. A node in T_r, labeled by (x, q), describes a copy of the automaton that is in the state q and reads the node x of Υ^*. Note that many nodes of T_r can correspond to the same node of Υ^*; there is no one-to-one correspondence between the nodes of the run and the nodes of the tree. The labels of a node and its successors have to satisfy the transition function. Formally, a run $\langle T_r, r \rangle$ is a Σ_r-labeled Γ-tree, for some set Γ of directions, where $\Sigma_r = \Upsilon^* \times Q$ and $\langle T_r, r \rangle$ satisfies the following:

1. $\varepsilon \in T_r$ and $r(\varepsilon) = (\varepsilon, q_0)$.
2. Consider $y \in T_r$ with $r(y) = (x, q)$ and $\delta(q, V(x)) = \theta$. Then there is a (possibly empty) set $S \subseteq ext(\Upsilon) \times Q$, such that S satisfies θ, and for all $\langle c, q' \rangle \in S$, there is $\gamma \in \Gamma$ such that $\gamma \cdot y \in T_r$ and the following hold:
   - If $c \in \Upsilon$, then $r(\gamma \cdot y) = (c \cdot x, q')$.
   - If $c = \varepsilon$, then $r(\gamma \cdot y) = (x, q')$.
   - If $c = \uparrow$, then $x = v \cdot z$, for some $v \in \Upsilon$ and $z \in \Upsilon^*$, and $r(\gamma \cdot y) = (z, q')$.

Thus, ε-transitions leave the automaton on the same node of the input tree, and $\uparrow$-transitions take it up to the parent node. Note that the automaton cannot go up the root of the input tree, as whenever $c = \uparrow$, we require that $x \neq \varepsilon$.

---

[1] As will get clearer in the sequel, the reason for that is that rewrite rules refer to the prefix of words.

A run $\langle T_r, r \rangle$ is *accepting* if all its infinite paths satisfy the acceptance condition. We consider here *parity* acceptance conditions [25]. A parity condition over a state set Q is a finite sequence $F = \{F_1, F_2, \ldots, F_m\}$ of subsets of Q, where $F_1 \subseteq F_2 \subseteq \ldots \subseteq F_m = Q$. The number m of sets is called the *index* of $\mathcal{A}$. Given a run $\langle T_r, r \rangle$ and an infinite path $\pi \subseteq T_r$, let $inf(\pi) \subseteq Q$ be such that $q \in inf(\pi)$ if and only if there are infinitely many $y \in \pi$ for which $r(y) \in \Upsilon^* \times \{q\}$. That is, $inf(\pi)$ contains exactly all the states that appear infinitely often in π. A path π satisfies the condition F if there is an even i for which $inf(\pi) \cap F_i \neq \emptyset$ and $inf(\pi) \cap F_{i-1} = \emptyset$. An automaton accepts a labeled tree if and only if there exists a run that accepts it. We denote by $\mathcal{L}(\mathcal{A})$ the set of all Σ-labeled trees that $\mathcal{A}$ accepts. The automaton $\mathcal{A}$ is *nonempty* iff $\mathcal{L}(\mathcal{A}) \neq \emptyset$.

Theorem 3. *Given an alternating two-way parity tree automaton $\mathcal{A}$ with n states and index k, we can check the nonemptiness of $\mathcal{A}$ in time exponential in nk* [68].

3.3 Alternating Graph Automata

In the previous subsection we described alternating automata on trees. It is technically convenient to adapt this definition to automata on graphs. We need to deal with the difficulty that the success of a node in a graph do not have a well-defined direction. Let $next = \{\varepsilon, \Box, \Diamond\}$. An alternating automaton on labeled graphs (*graph automaton*, for short) [37, 22, 74] is a tuple $\mathcal{S} = (\Sigma, Q, q_0, \delta, F)$, where Q, q_0, and F are as in alternating two-way automata, and $\delta : Q \times \Sigma \to \mathcal{B}^+(next \times Q)$ is the transition function. Intuitively, when $\mathcal{S}$ is in state q and it reads a node s of G, fulfilling an atom $\langle \Diamond, q' \rangle$ (or $\Diamond q'$, for short) requires $\mathcal{S}$ to send a copy in state q' to *some* successor of s. Similarly, fulfilling an atom $\Box q'$ requires $\mathcal{S}$ to send copies in state q' to *all* successors of s. Finally, fulfilling an atom $\langle \varepsilon, q' \rangle$ requires $\mathcal{S}$ to send a copy in state q' to s itself. Thus, graph automata cannot distinguish between the various successors of a node and treat them in an existential or universal way.

Like runs of alternating two-way automata, a run of a graph automaton $\mathcal{S}$ over a labeling G with nodes W, initial node s_0, and labeling L is a labeled tree in which every node is labeled by an element of $W \times Q$. A node labeled by (s, q), describes a copy of the automaton that is in the state q of $\mathcal{S}$ and reads the node s of G. Formally, a run starting at a node s_0 is a Σ_r-labeled Γ-tree $\langle T_r, r \rangle$, where Γ is an arbitrary set of directions, $\Sigma_r = W \times Q$, and $\langle T_r, r \rangle$ satisfies the following:

1. $\varepsilon \in T_r$ and $r(\varepsilon) = (s_0, q_0)$.
2. Consider $y \in T_r$ with $r(y) = (s, q)$ and $\delta(q, L(s)) = \theta$. Then there is a (possibly empty) set $S \subseteq next \times Q$, such that S satisfies θ, and for all $\langle c, q' \rangle \in S$, the following hold:
   - If $c = \varepsilon$, then there is $\gamma \in \Gamma$ such that $\gamma \cdot y \in T_r$ and $r(\gamma \cdot y) = (s, q')$.
   - If $c = \Box$, then for every successor s' of s, there is $\gamma \in \Gamma$ such that $\gamma \cdot y \in T_r$ and $r(\gamma \cdot y) = (s', q')$.
   - If $c = \Diamond$, then there is an successor s' of s and $\gamma \in \Gamma$ such that $\gamma \cdot y \in T_r$ and $r(\gamma \cdot y) = (s', q')$.

A run $\langle T_r, r \rangle$ is *accepting* if all its infinite paths satisfy the acceptance condition. The graph G is accepted by $\mathcal{S}$ if there is an accepting run on it. We denote by $\mathcal{L}(\mathcal{S})$ the set of all graphs that $\mathcal{S}$ accepts. We denote by $\mathcal{S}^q = (\Sigma, Q, \delta, q, F)$ the automaton $\mathcal{S}$ with q as its initial state.

We use graph automata as our specification language. We say that a labeled transition graph G satisfies a graph automaton S, denoted $G \models S$, if S accepts G. It is known [37, 22, 74] that graph automata are as expressive as μ-calculus. In particular, we have the following.

Theorem 4. *Given a μ-calculus formula ψ, of length n and alternation depth k, we can construct a graph parity automaton S_ψ such that $\mathcal{L}(S_\psi)$ is exactly the set of graphs satisfying ψ. The automaton S_ψ has n states and index k.*

In particular, an LTL formula ψ of length n can be translated into an equivalent graph automaton with $2^{O(n)}$ states and index 2 [71].

3.4   Model Checking of Context-Free Graphs

In this section we present an automata-theoretic approach to model-checking of context-free transition systems. Consider a labeled transition graph $G = (V^*, \{v_0\}, \rho_R, L)$, induced by a rewrite system $\mathcal{R} = \langle V, R, x_0 \rangle$ and a regular labeling L. Since the state space of G is the full V-tree, we can think of each transition $\langle z, z' \rangle \in \rho_R$ as a "jump" from the node z of the V-tree to the node z'. Thus, if $\mathcal{R}$ is a context-free rewrite system and we are at node $A \cdot y$ of the V-tree, a transition takes us to nodes $x \cdot y$, for $\langle A, x \rangle \in R$. Technically, this means that we first move up to the parent y of $A \cdot y$, and then move down along x. Such a navigation through the V-tree can be easily performed by two-way automata.

Theorem 5. *Given a context-free rewrite system $\mathcal{R} = \langle V, R, v_0 \rangle$, regular labeling L, and a graph automaton $S = \langle 2^{Prop}, Q, \delta, q_0, F \rangle$, we can construct an alternating two-way parity automaton $\mathcal{A}$ over $(V \cup \{\bot\})$-labeled V-trees such that $\mathcal{L}(\mathcal{A})$ is not empty iff $G_\mathcal{R}$ satisfies S. The automaton $\mathcal{A}$ has $O(|Q| \cdot (|R| + |L|) \cdot |V|)$ states, and has the same index as S.*

Proof. The automaton $\mathcal{A}$ checks that the input tree is V-exhaustive (that is, each node is labeled by its direction). As such, $\mathcal{A}$ can learn from labels it reads the state in V^* that each node corresponds to. The transition function of $\mathcal{A}$ then consults the rewrite rules in R in order to transform an atom in $next \times Q$ to a chain of transitions that spread copies of $\mathcal{A}$ to the corresponding nodes of the full V-tree.

Before we define $\mathcal{A}$ we need also to deal with the difficulty that the graph automaton S expects input symbols in 2^{Prop}, but the labeling L defines the label implicitly: $L(x) = \{p : x \in \mathcal{L}(\mathcal{U}_p)\}$. Thus, when $\mathcal{A}$ wants to simulate S in a node x, it guess a set $P \subseteq Prop$ and then checks that $L(x) = P$. For each proposition $p \in Prop$, we have an NFA $\mathcal{U}_p$. We can assume with out loss of generality that the state spaces of different NFAs are disjoint. Thus, we can assume that there is an NFA $\mathcal{U} = \langle V, N, N_0, \rho, H \rangle$, where for every $p \in Prop$ there is some state $n_p \in N$ such that $\mathcal{L}(\mathcal{U}_p) = \mathcal{L}(\mathcal{U}^{n_p})$. To check that $L(x) = P$, $\mathcal{A}$ has to simulate $\mathcal{U}$. We simulate $\mathcal{U}$ by means of a two-way alternating tree automata. Since we need to check that $p \in L(x)$ for $p \in P$ and $p \notin L(x)$ for $p \notin P$, we each state $n \in N$ we need two states n^+ and n^-. Let $N^\pm = \bigcup_{n \in N} \{n^+, n^-\}$.

We define $\mathcal{A} = (V \cup \{\bot\}, Q', \eta, q_0', F')$ as follows:

- $Q' = Q \times tails(\mathcal{R}) \times (V \cup \{\bot, \#\}) \cup N^{\pm}$, where $tails(\mathcal{R}) \subseteq V^*$ is the set of all suffixes of words $x \in V^*$ for which there is $A \in V$ such that $\langle A, x \rangle \in R$. Intuitively, when $\mathcal{A}$ visits a node $x \in V^*$ in state $\langle q, y, A \rangle$, it checks that $G_{\mathcal{R}}$ with initial state $y \cdot x$ is accepted by $\mathcal{S}^q$. In particular, when $y = \varepsilon$, then $G_{\mathcal{R}}$ with initial state x (the node currently being visited) needs to be accepted by $\mathcal{S}^q$. In addition, if $A \neq \#$, then $\mathcal{A}$ also checks that $dir(x) = A$. States of the form $\langle q, \varepsilon, A \rangle$ are called *action states*. From these states $\mathcal{A}$ consults δ and R in order to impose new requirements on the exhaustive V-tree. States of the form $\langle q, y, A \rangle$, for $y \in V^+$, are called *navigation states*. From these states $\mathcal{A}$ only navigates downwards y to reach new action states. On its way, $\mathcal{A}$ also checks the V-exhaustiveness of the input tree. The states in $N^{\pm}$ are used to simulate $\mathcal{U}$. Positive copies of N are used to simulate $\mathcal{U}$ positively, while negative copies of N are used to simulate $\mathcal{U}$ negatively.
- In order to define $\eta : Q' \times (V \cup \{\bot\}) \to \mathcal{B}^+(ext(V) \times Q')$, we first define the function $apply_R : next \times Q \times (V \cup \{\bot\}) \to \mathcal{B}^+(ext(V) \times Q')$. Intuitively, $apply_R$ transforms atoms participating in δ, together with a letter $A \in V \cup \{\bot\}$, which stands for the direction of the current node, to a formula that describes the requirements on $G_{\mathcal{R}}$ when the rewrite rules in R are applied to words of the form $A \cdot V^*$. For $c \in next$, $q \in Q$, and $A \in V \cup \{\bot\}$, we define

$$apply_R(c, q, A) = \begin{cases} \langle \varepsilon, (q, \varepsilon, A) \rangle & \text{if } c = \bullet, \\ \bigwedge_{\langle A, y \rangle \in R} \langle \uparrow, (q, y, \#) \rangle & \text{If } c = \square. \\ \bigvee_{\langle A, y \rangle \in R} \langle \uparrow, (q, y, \#) \rangle & \text{If } c = \Diamond. \end{cases}$$

(We take empty conjunctions as **true**, and take empty disjunctions as **false**.)

In order to understand the function $apply_{\mathcal{R}}$, consider the case $c = \square$. When $\mathcal{S}$ reads the state $A \cdot x$ of the input graph, fulfilling the atom $\square q$ requires $\mathcal{S}$ to send copies in state q to all the successors of $A \cdot x$. The automaton $\mathcal{A}$ then sends to the node x copies that check whether all the states $y \cdot x$, with $\rho_{\mathcal{R}}(A \cdot x, y \cdot x)$, are accepted by $\mathcal{S}$ with initial state q. Now, for a formula $\theta \in \mathcal{B}^+(next \times Q)$, the formula $apply_R(\theta, A) \in \mathcal{B}^+(ext(V) \times Q')$ is obtained from θ by replacing an atom $\langle c, q \rangle$ by the atom $apply_R(c, q, A)$.

We can now define η for all $A \in V \cup \{\bot\}$ as follows.

- $\eta(\langle q, \varepsilon, A \rangle, A) = \eta(\langle q, \varepsilon, \# \rangle, A) =$

$$\bigvee_{P \subseteq Prop} \left(\bigwedge_{p \in P} \langle \varepsilon, n_p^+ \rangle \wedge \bigwedge_{p \notin P} \langle \varepsilon, n_p^- \rangle \wedge apply_R(\delta(q, P), A) \right).$$

- $\eta(\langle q, B \cdot y, A \rangle, A) = \eta(\langle q, B \cdot y, \# \rangle, A) = (B, \langle q, y, B \rangle)$.
- $\eta(n^+, A) = \bigvee_{m \in \rho(n, A)} \langle \uparrow, m^+ \rangle$ and $\eta(n^-, A) = \bigwedge_{m \in \rho(n, A)} \langle \uparrow, n^- \rangle$. Also, $\eta(n^+, \bot) = $ **true** if $n \in H$, $\eta(n^+, \bot) = $ **false** if $n \notin H$, $\eta(n^-, \bot) = $ **false** if $n \in H$, and $\eta(n^-, \bot) = $ **true** if $n \notin H$.

Thus, in action states, $\mathcal{A}$ reads the direction of the current node and applies the rewrite rules of $\mathcal{R}$ in order to impose new requirements according to δ. In navigation states, $\mathcal{A}$ needs to go downwards $B \cdot y$ and check that the nodes it comes across on its way are labeled by their direction. For that, $\mathcal{A}$ proceeds only with the direction of the current node (maintained as the third element of the state), and sends to direction B a state whose third element is B. Note that since we reach states with $\#$ only with upward transitions, $\mathcal{A}$ visits these states only when it reads nodes x that have already been read by a copy of $\mathcal{A}$ that does check whether x is labeled by its direction. When $\mathcal{A}$ is in a state of $N^{\pm}$, it simulate $\mathcal{U}$, going up the tree.

- $q'_0 = \langle q_0, x_0, \bot \rangle$. Thus, in its initial state $\mathcal{A}$ checks that $G_{\mathcal{R}}$ with initial state x_0 is accepted by $\mathcal{S}$ with initial state q_0. It also checks that the root of the input tree is labeled with $\bot$.
- F' is obtained from F by replacing each set F_i by the set $F_i \times tails(R) \times (V \cup \{\#\})$.

Theorem 6. *The model-checking problem for a context-free system* $\mathcal{R} = \langle V, R, v_0 \rangle$ *with regular labeling* L *and a graph automaton* $\mathcal{S} = \langle 2^{Prop}, Q, \delta, q_0, F \rangle$, *can be solved in time exponential in* nk, *where* $n = |Q| \cdot (|R| + |L|) \cdot |V|$ *and* k *is the index of* $\mathcal{S}$.

Together with Theorem 4, we can conclude with an EXPTIME bound also for the model-checking problem of μ-calculus formulas matching the lower bound in [72]. What about LTL specifications? Recall that that there is an exponential blow-up in going from LTL formulas to graph automata. Thus, Theorem 6 yields a doubly exponential model-checking algorithm. It is known, however, that model checking context-free graphs with respect to LTL specifications can be done in exponential time [9, 27]. An automata-theoretic approach to model checking LTL properties of context-free systems in described in [39].

4   Model Checking for Databases

An examination of the framework presented in the previous two sections reveals two important features. First, it assume that states can be modeled propositionally. Second, it assume that that the desired behavior can be specified in linear or branching temporal logic. Though these assumption might be applicable in some settings, cf. [36], neither of these assumptions seems appropriate for database systems in general. For example, a basic desirable properties of database transactions in *serializability* [58, 57, 73], which cannot be specified in standard temporal logic [60]. For an algorithmic treatment of serializability verification, see [6].

More fundamentally, one would expect the state of a database system to be modeled relationally rather than propositionally. That is, if we want a labeled transition graph $M = (W, W_0, R, L)$ to model a database system, then the labeling L should assign to each state w a relational structure $L(w)$. Such structures would correspond to relational Kripke structures, which serves as models for for first-order modal logic [35]. Verification of such models was explored in [3, 65, 21]. The parameters studied in this paper are, for example, how the set W_0 of initial states is defined, how the transition relation R is defined, and what specification language is used. In general, of course, the verification problem is undecidable, but under various restrictions the problem is decidable. An obvious example of such a restriction is restricting the cardinality of the relational structures in the range of the labeling L. Under such a cardinality restriction, as there are only finitely many such relational structures, relational transition graphs are in essence propositional transition graphs.

A more interesting restriction is to limit the specification language to ∀LTL, the *universal closure* of LTL. In this logic, formulas are constructed from a atomic formulas (including equality), using Boolean as well as temporal connectives. Sentences are obtained by quantifying universally over all variables in a formula. For example, the LTL formula $(\forall x)G(request(x) \rightarrow F\ grant(x))$, is true in a computation precisely when every state in the computation in which $request(x)$ holds is followed by some state in the future in which $grant(x)$ holds. The logic ∃LTL is the dual of ∀LTL, where variables are quantified existentially. One of the major result in [65] is that under appropriate restrictions on W_0 and R, model checking ∀LTL properties of relational transition graphs is decidable. Underlying this result is the observation that validity of ∀LTL sentences, or, dually, satisfiability of ∃LTL sentences is decidable. This is shown in [65] via a reduction to the existential fragment of *transitive-closure logic* [23]. An easier way to see that satisfiability of ∃LTL sentences is decidable is to observe that the reduction to Büchi automata still applies (see also [16]). Again, the intuition is that a state of the automaton A_φ is simply a set of subformulas of φ. The automaton that reads a computation π in state P checks that π satisfies all formulas in P. Initial states of A_φ contain φ. The transition relation of A_φ checks the correctness of the temporal connectives.

5   Concluding Remarks

Database technology is emerging as one of the key technologies in the global information infrastructure. While 15 years ago databases were used mostly for business data processing, databases today are used in a vast array of applications, such as computer-aided design, decision support systems, e-commerce, expert systems, geographical information systems, multimedia, and the like. Database systems use highly complex transaction management systems [30]. This complexity is expected to grow with the coming confluence of database systems and web services [36]. While no one disputes the importance of gaining confidence in the correctness of such systems, research on database verification is nascent. We hope that this paper would serve to stimulate interest in this important area.

References

1. S. Abiteboul, P. Buneman, and D. Suciu. *Data on the Web: from Relations to Semistructured Data and XML*. Morgan Kaufmann, San Mateo, CA, 2000.
2. S. Abiteboul, R. Hull, and V. Vianu. *Foundations of databases*. Addison-Wesley, 1995.
3. S. Abiteboul, V. Vianu, B.S. Fordham, and Y. Yesha. Relational transducers for electronic commerce. *J. Comput. Syst. Sci.*, 61(2):236–269, 2000.
4. R. Alur, K. Etessami, and M. Yannakakis. Analysis of recursive state machines. In *Proc. 13th Int'l Conf. on Computer Aided Verification*, volume 2102 of *Lecture Notes in Computer Science*, pages 207–220. Springer-Verlag, 2001.

5. R. Alur, T.A. Henzinger, and O. Kupferman. Alternating-time temporal logic. In *Proc. 38th IEEE Symp. on Foundations of Computer Science*, pages 100–109, Florida, October 1997.
6. R. Alur, K.L. McMillan, and D. Peled. Model-checking of correctness conditions for concurrent objects. *Information and Computation*, 160(1-2):167–188, 2000.
7. R. Armoni, L. Fix, A. Flaisher, R. Gerth, B. Ginsburg, T. Kanza, A. Landver, S. Mador-Haim, E. Singerman, A. Tiemeyer, M.Y. Vardi, and Y. Zbar. The ForSpec temporal logic: A new temporal property-specification logic. In *Proc. 8th International Conference on Tools and Algorithms for the Construction and Analysis of Systems*, volume 2280 of *Lecture Notes in Computer Science*, pages 296–211, Grenoble, France, April 2002. Springer-Verlag.
8. P. Atzeni and V. De Antonellis. *Relational Database Theory*. Benjamin/Cummings, 1993.
9. A. Bouajjani, J. Esparza, and O. Maler. Reachability analysis of pushdown automata: Application to model-checking. In *Proc. 8th Conference on Concurrency Theory*, volume 1243 of *Lecture Notes in Computer Science*, pages 135–150, Warsaw, July 1997. Springer-Verlag.
10. J.R. Büchi. On a decision method in restricted second order arithmetic. In *Proc. Internat. Congr. Logic, Method. and Philos. Sci. 1960*, pages 1–12, Stanford, 1962. Stanford University Press.
11. J.R. Burch, E.M. Clarke, K.L. McMillan, D.L. Dill, and L.J. Hwang. Symbolic model checking: 10^{20} states and beyond. *Information and Computation*, 98(2):142–170, June 1992.
12. O. Burkart, D. Caucal, F. Moller, and B. Steffen. Verification over infinite states. In J. Bergstra, A. Ponse, and S.A. Smolka, editors, *Handbook of Process Algebra*, pages 545–623. Elsevier, 2001.
13. O. Burkart and B. Steffen. Model checking for context-free processes. In *Proc. 3rd Conference on Concurrency Theory*, volume 630 of *Lecture Notes in Computer Science*, pages 123–137. Springer-Verlag, 1992.
14. O. Burkart and B. Steffen. Composition, decomposition and model checking of pushdown processes. *Nordic J. Comut.*, 2:89–125, 1995.
15. T. Cachat. Higher order pushdown automata, the caucal hierarchy of graphs and parity games. In *Proc. 30th International Colloqium on Automata, Languages, and Programming*, volume 2719 of *Lecture Notes in Computer Science*, pages 556–569, Eindhoven, The Netherlands, June 2003. Springer-Verlag.
16. J. Chomicki and D. Niwinski. On the feasibility of checking temporal integrity constraints. *J. Comput. Syst. Sci.*, 51(3):523–535, 1995.
17. E.M. Clarke, E.A. Emerson, and A.P. Sistla. Automatic verification of finite-state concurrent systems using temporal logic specifications. *ACM Transactions on Programming Languages and Systems*, 8(2):244–263, January 1986.
18. E.M. Clarke, O. Grumberg, and D. Peled. *Model Checking*. MIT Press, 1999.
19. E.M. Clarke and J.M. Wing. Formal methods: State of the art and future directions. *ACM Computing Surveys*, 28:626–643, 1996.
20. C. Courcoubetis, M.Y. Vardi, P. Wolper, and M. Yannakakis. Memory efficient algorithms for the verification of temporal properties. *Formal Methods in System Design*, 1:275–288, 1992.
21. A. Deutsch, L. Sui, and V. Vianu. Specification and verification of data-driven web services. In *Proc. 23rd ACM Symp. on Principles of Database Systems*, pages 71–82, 2004.
22. M. Dickhfer and T. Wilke. Timed alternating tree automata: the automata-theoretic solution to the TCTL model checking problem. In *Automata, Languages and Programming*, volume 1644 of *Lecture Notes in Computer Science*, pages 281–290, Prague, Czech Republic, 1999. Springer-Verlag, Berlin.
23. H.D. Ebbinghaus and J. Flum. *Finite Model Theory*. Perspectives in Mathematical Logic. Springer-Verlag, 1995.
24. E.A. Emerson and C. Jutla. The complexity of tree automata and logics of programs. In *Proc. 29th IEEE Symp. on Foundations of Computer Science*, pages 328–337, White Plains, October 1988.

25. E.A. Emerson and C. Jutla. Tree automata, μ-calculus and determinacy. In *Proc. 32nd IEEE Symp. on Foundations of Computer Science*, pages 368–377, San Juan, October 1991.

26. E.A. Emerson and C.-L. Lei. Temporal model checking under generalized fairness constraints. In *Proc. 18th Hawaii International Conference on System Sciences*, North Holywood, 1985. Western Periodicals Company.

27. A. Finkel, B. Willems, and P. Wolper. A direct symbolic approach to model checking pushdown automata. In F. Moller, editor, *Proc. 2nd International Workshop on Verification of Infinite States Systems*, 1997.

28. R. Gerth, D. Peled, M.Y. Vardi, and P. Wolper. Simple on-the-fly automatic verification of linear temporal logic. In P. Dembiski and M. Sredniawa, editors, *Protocol Specification, Testing, and Verification*, pages 3–18. Chapman & Hall, August 1995.

29. P. Godefroid and P. Wolper. A partial approach to model checking. *Information and Computation*, 110(2):305–326, May 1994.

30. J. Gray and A. Reuter. *Transaction Processing: Concepts and Techniques*. Morgan Kaufmann, 1993.

31. R.H. Hardin, Z. Har'el, and R.P. Kurshan. COSPAN. In *Computer Aided Verification, Proc. 8th International Conference*, volume 1102 of *Lecture Notes in Computer Science*, pages 423–427. Springer-Verlag, 1996.

32. T.A. Henzinger, P.-H Ho, and H. Wong-Toi. A user guide to HYTECH. In *Tools and algorithms for the construction and analysis of systems*, volume 1019 of *Lecture Notes in Computer Science*, pages 41–71. Springer-Verlag, 1995.

33. T.A. Henzinger, O. Kupferman, and M.Y. Vardi. A space-efficient on-the-fly algorithm for real-time model checking. In *Proc. 7th Conference on Concurrency Theory*, volume 1119 of *Lecture Notes in Computer Science*, pages 514–529, Pisa, August 1996. Springer-Verlag.

34. G.J. Holzmann. The model checker SPIN. *IEEE Trans. on Software Engineering*, 23(5):279–295, May 1997. Special issue on Formal Methods in Software Practice.

35. G.E. Hughes and M.J. Cresswell. *A New Introduction to Modal Logic*. Routledge, London, 1996.

36. R. Hull, M. Benedikt, V. Christophides, and J. Su. E-services: a look behind the curtain. In *Proc. 22rd ACM Symp. on Principles of Database Systems*, pages 1–14, 2003.

37. D. Janin and I. Walukiewicz. Automata for the modal μ-calculus and related results. In *Proc. 20th International Symp. on Mathematical Foundations of Computer Science*, Lecture Notes in Computer Science, pages 552–562. Springer-Verlag, 1995.

38. D. Kozen. Results on the propositional μ-calculus. *Theoretical Computer Science*, 27:333–354, 1983.

39. O. Kupferman, N. Piterman, and M.Y. Vardi. Model checking linear properties of prefix-recognizable systems. In *Proc. 14th International Conference on Computer Aided Verification*, volume 2404 of *Lecture Notes in Computer Science*, pages 371–385. Springer-Verlag, 2002.

40. O. Kupferman and M.Y. Vardi. Freedom, weakness, and determinism: from linear-time to branching-time. In *Proc. 13th IEEE Symp. on Logic in Computer Science*, pages 81–92, June 1998.

41. O. Kupferman and M.Y. Vardi. Modular model checking. In *Proc. Compositionality Workshop*, volume 1536 of *Lecture Notes in Computer Science*, pages 381–401. Springer-Verlag, 1998.

42. O. Kupferman and M.Y. Vardi. Robust satisfaction. In *Proc. 10th Conference on Concurrency Theory*, volume 1664 of *Lecture Notes in Computer Science*, pages 383–398. Springer-Verlag, August 1999.

43. O. Kupferman and M.Y. Vardi. An automata-theoretic approach to reasoning about infinite-state systems. In *Proc. 12th International Conference on Computer Aided Verification*, volume 1855 of *Lecture Notes in Computer Science*, pages 36–52. Springer-Verlag, 2000.

44. O. Kupferman and M.Y. Vardi. Synthesis with incomplete informatio. In *Advances in Temporal Logic*, pages 109–127. Kluwer Academic Publishers, January 2000.
45. O. Kupferman and M.Y. Vardi. Weak alternating automata are not that weak. *ACM Trans. on Computational Logic*, 2001(2):408–429, July 2001.
46. O. Kupferman, M.Y. Vardi, and P. Wolper. An automata-theoretic approach to branching-time model checking. *Journal of the ACM*, 47(2):312–360, March 2000.
47. R.P. Kurshan. *Computer Aided Verification of Coordinating Processes*. Princeton Univ. Press, 1994.
48. R.P. Kurshan. Formal verification in a commercial setting. In *Proc. Conf. on Design Automation (DAC'97)*, volume 34, pages 258–262, 1997.
49. L. Lamport. Sometimes is sometimes "not never" - on the temporal logic of programs. In *Proc. 7th ACM Symp. on Principles of Programming Languages*, pages 174–185, January 1980.
50. K. G. Larsen, P. Petterson, and W. Yi. UPPAAL: Status & developments. In *Computer Aided Verification, Proc. 9th International Conference*, volume 1254 of *Lecture Notes in Computer Science*, pages 456–459. Springer-Verlag, 1997.
51. O. Lichtenstein and A. Pnueli. Checking that finite state concurrent programs satisfy their linear specification. In *Proc. 12th ACM Symp. on Principles of Programming Languages*, pages 97–107, New Orleans, January 1985.
52. D. Maier. *The Theory of Relational Databases*. Computer Science Press, Rockville, Md., 1983.
53. D.E. Muller and P.E. Schupp. The theory of ends, pushdown automata, and second-order logic. *Theoretical Computer Science*, 37:51–75, 1985.
54. D.E. Muller and P.E. Schupp. Alternating automata on infinite trees. *Theoretical Computer Science*, 54:267–276, 1987.
55. F. Neven. Automata, logic, and XML. In *16th International Workshop on Computer Science Logic*, volume 2471 of *Lecture Notes in Computer Science*, pages 2–26, Edinburgh, Scotland, September 2002. Springer-Verlag.
56. F. Neven. Automata theory for xml researchers. *SIGMOD Record*, 31(3):39–46, 2002.
57. N. Goodman P.A. Bernstein, V. Hadzilacos. *Concurrency Control and Recovery in Database Systems*. Addison-Wesley, 1987.
58. C. Papadimitiou. *Theory of Database Concurrency Control*. Computer Science Pr., 1986.
59. C.H. Papadimitriou. Database metatheory: Asking the big queries. In *Proc. 14th ACM Symp. on Principles of Database Systems*, pages 1–10, 1995.
60. D. Peled, S. Katz, and A. Pnueli. Specifying and proving serializability in temporal logic. In *Proc. 6th IEEE Symp. on Logic in Computer Science*, pages 232–244, 1991.
61. N. Piterman and M. Vardi. Micro-macro stack systems: A new frontier of decidability for sequential systems. In *18th IEEE Symposium on Logic in Computer Science*, pages 381–390, Ottawa, Canada, June 2003. IEEE, IEEE press.
62. A. Pnueli. The temporal logic of programs. In *Proc. 18th IEEE Symp. on Foundation of Computer Science*, pages 46–57, 1977.
63. A. Pnueli and R. Rosner. On the synthesis of a reactive module. In *Proc. 16th ACM Symp. on Principles of Programming Languages*, pages 179–190, Austin, January 1989.
64. J.P. Queille and J. Sifakis. Specification and verification of concurrent systems in Cesar. In *Proc. 5th International Symp. on Programming*, volume 137 of *Lecture Notes in Computer Science*, pages 337–351. Springer-Verlag, 1981.
65. M. Spielmann. Verification of relational transducers for electronic commerce. *J. Comput. Syst. Sci.*, 66:40–65, 2003.
66. M.Y. Vardi. Automata theory for database theoreticians. In *Proc. 8th ACM Symp. on Principles of Database Systems*, pages 83–92, 1989.

67. M.Y. Vardi. An automata-theoretic approach to linear temporal logic. In F. Moller and G. Birtwistle, editors, *Logics for Concurrency: Structure versus Automata*, volume 1043 of *Lecture Notes in Computer Science*, pages 238–266. Springer-Verlag, Berlin, 1996.

68. M.Y. Vardi. Reasoning about the past with two-way automata. In *Proc. 25th International Coll. on Automata, Languages, and Programming*, volume 1443 of *Lecture Notes in Computer Science*, pages 628–641. Springer-Verlag, Berlin, July 1998.

69. M.Y. Vardi. Branching vs. linear time: Final showdown. In *Proc. Tools and Algorithms for the Construction and Analysis of Systems (TACAS)*, volume 2031 of *Lecture Notes in Computer Science*, pages 1–22. Springer-Verlag, 2001.

70. M.Y. Vardi and P. Wolper. An automata-theoretic approach to automatic program verification. In *Proc. 1st Symp. on Logic in Computer Science*, pages 332–344, Cambridge, June 1986.

71. M.Y. Vardi and P. Wolper. Reasoning about infinite computations. *Information and Computation*, 115(1):1–37, November 1994.

72. I. Walukiewicz. Pushdown processes: games and model checking. In *Proc. 8th International Conference on Computer Aided Verification*, volume 1102 of *Lecture Notes in Computer Science*, pages 62–74. Springer-Verlag, 1996.

73. G. Weikum and G. Vossen. *Transactional Information Systems: Theory, Algorithms, and the Practice of Concurrency Control*. Morgan Kaufmann, 2001.

74. T. Wilke. CTL^+ is exponentially more succinct than CTL. In C. Pandu Ragan, V. Raman, and R. Ramanujam, editors, *Proc. 19th conference on Foundations of Software Technology and Theoretical Computer Science*, volume 1738 of *Lecture Notes in Computer Science*, pages 110–121. Springer-Verlag, 1999.

75. B. Willems and P. Wolper. Partial-order methods for model checking: From linear time to branching time. In *Proc. 11th Symp. on Logic in Computer Science*, pages 294–303, New Brunswick, July 1996.

76. P. Wolper, M.Y. Vardi, and A.P. Sistla. Reasoning about infinite computation paths. In *Proc. 24th IEEE Symp. on Foundations of Computer Science*, pages 185–194, Tucson, 1983.

The Design Space of Type Checkers for XML Transformation Languages

Anders Møller* and Michael I. Schwartzbach

BRICS**, University of Aarhus
{amoeller, mis}@brics.dk

A bstract. We survey work on statically type checking XML transformations, covering a wide range of notations and ambitions. The concept of *type* may vary from idealizations of DTD to full-blown XML Schema or even more expressive formalisms. The notion of *transformation* may vary from clean and simple transductions to domain-specific languages or integration of XML in general-purpose programming languages. Type annotations can be either explicit or implicit, and type checking ranges from exact decidability to pragmatic approximations.

We characterize and evaluate existing tools in this design space, including a recent result of the authors providing practical type checking of full unannotated XSLT 1.0 stylesheets given general DTDs that describe the input and output languages.

1   Introduction

XML is an established format for structured data, where each document is essentially an ordered labeled tree [8]. An XML *language* is a subset of such trees, typically described by formalisms known collectively as *schemas*. Given a schema S, we use $\mathcal{L}(S)$ to denote the set of XML trees that it describes. Several different schema formalisms have been proposed: the original DTD mechanism that is part of the XML specification [8], more expressive schemas such as XML Schema [39], RELAX NG [13], or DSD2 [33], and various tree automata formalisms [21, 14].

Many different languages have been devised for specifying transformations of XML data, covering a wide range of programming paradigms. Several such languages have type systems that aim to statically catch runtime errors that may occur during transformations, but not all consider the overall problem of type checking the global effect: given a transformation T, an input schema S_{in} and an output schema S_{out}, decide at compile time if

$$\forall X \in \mathcal{L}(S_{in}) : T(X) \in \mathcal{L}(S_{out})$$

The input and output language may of course be the same. Notice that schemas here act as types in the programming language. Also, we use the notion of *type checking* in a general sense that also covers techniques based on dataflow analysis.

---

* Supported by the Carlsberg Foundation contract number ANS-1507/20.
** Basic Research in Computer Science (www.brics.dk), funded by the Danish National Research Foundation.

In this paper we describe the design space of XML transformation languages and their type checkers, and survey a representative collection of examples: XDuce [21], XACT [27], XJ [17], XOBE [24], JDOM [23], JAXB [37], HaXml [42], Cω [31, 4], *tree transducers* [32, 30], and XQuery [5]. Furthermore, we present a preliminary report on a novel point in the design space: a flow-based type checker for the full XSLT 1.0 language [34].

XML transformations are motivated by different usage scenarios: queries on XML databases generate results that are again XML data; XML documents are presented in XHTML or XSL-FO versions; translations are performed between different dialects of XML languages; and views or summaries of XML publications are automatically extracted. A major contributing factor to the success of XML is the ability to unify such diverse tasks in a single framework. While the various languages we survey certainly have different sweet spots, it is reasonable to expect that they should each support most of the above scenarios.

2   Aspects of XML Transformation Languages

Languages for programming XML transformations may be characterized in many different ways. A major distinction, which is actually relevant for any kind of application domain, is between *domain-specific languages (DSLs)* and *general purpose languages (GPLs)* [41].

A **GPL** is an ordinary programming language, like Java or C++. One approach for obtaining integration of XML is using a library that allows construction and deconstruction of XML values and provides support for parsing and unparsing. Another approach is *data binding*, which represents XML data through native types of the programming language, often guided by schemas and manually specified mappings. Since XML documents are ordinary data values in the language, there is no special syntax or analysis of XML manipulations.

A DSL is a specially designed language that supports domain-specific values and operations. A DSL may be either *stand-alone* or *embedded*.

A **stand-alone DSL** is designed and implemented from scratch with its own tailor-made compiler or interpreter. This allows the highest degree of exploitation of domain-specific knowledge for both syntax, analysis, and implementation. Stand-alone DSLs have two obvious downsides: First, it is expensive to implement a language from scratch (though there is much active research in lowering the cost) and it is difficult to provide as complete an infrastructure as, say, the Java language libraries. Second, potential users have a steep learning curve, even though DSLs are often designed to resemble other known languages. For XML transformations, a stand-alone DSL will have some kind of XML trees as native values.

An **embedded DSL** is based on a GPL with a framework for XML programming. The domain-specific parts consist of specialized syntax and analysis. The domain-specific syntax, typically for XML constants and navigation in XML data, may be provided through a preprocessor that desugars the DSL syntax into GPL syntax. At runtime, the DSL operations are then handled by a GPL library.

The domain-specific program analysis may be performed at the DSL source code level, on the desugared code, or it may exploit a GPL analysis. Compared to a stand-alone DSL, having the foundation of a GPL makes it easier to interact with other systems, for example, communicate on the Web or access data bases through the use of preexisting libraries. It also makes it simpler to integrate non-XML computations into the XML processing, for example, complex string manipulations or construction of XML data from non-XML data or vice versa.

The distinction between these categories can be blurry: a GPL may be extended with XML-like features to allow better data binding, or a DSL for XML processing may be extended to become a GPL. We shall call these approaches **XML-centric GPLs**.

Another distinguishing aspect of an XML transformation language is its **expressiveness**. All GPLs are clearly Turing complete, but some embedded DSLs are designed to express only a limited class of transformations. The benefit of a restricted language is twofold: First, if only certain transformations are required, then a specialized syntax makes their programming easier. Second, a restricted language may be subjected to more precise analysis.

It is important to distinguish between two different kinds of Turing completeness: the ability to perform arbitrary computations on representations of XML trees vs. the ability to perform arbitrary computations on some encoding of the integers. Some stand-alone DSLs are only Turing complete in the latter sense. Also, an embedded DSL may be Turing incomplete in the XML sense, even though the underlying GPL is Turing complete in the traditional sense. A common example is a language where element names and attribute names cannot be generally computed but only chosen among constants that appear in the program. However, such a restriction might not be a limitation in practice since schemas written in existing schema languages can only define fixed sets of such names anyway.

A well-known aspect of any language is its **paradigm**. For the purpose of this paper, we shall merely distinguish roughly between *imperative* languages, which have explicit mutable state, and *declarative* languages, which are without side-effects and often have implicit control flow. The most widely used GPLs are imperative, but most stand-alone DSLs are declarative.

The languages we consider apply an abundance of different **models of XML data**. Some treat XML as *mutable* tree structures, whereas others view them as being *immutable*. Of course, this aspect is closely related to the language paradigm. Mutability is natural in an imperative language; however, immutability has many advantages, in particular with respect to type checking, and can be beneficial even in languages where data is generally mutable. In approaches that involve data binding for GPLs, XML data is represented using the underlying data model, in object-oriented languages by mapping schema types into classes and XML data into objects.

These different models may involve varying mechanisms for constructing XML data and for navigating through or deconstructing the data. One approach is to perform direct tree manipulation where construction and navigation is on the level of individual XML tree nodes, perhaps with a term language for constructing tree fragments from constants and dynamically evaluated expressions. Deconstruction and navigation might also be based on *pattern matching* or on XPath expressions. Another variant is to model XML data as *templates*, which are tree structures with gaps that can be substituted with other values.

Finally, the **quality of the implementation** of a language may obviously vary. We will distinguish between three levels: First, an *industrial strength* implementation scales to real-life applications and has a robust infrastructure of support and documentation. Second, a *prototype* is provided by a research group, has been shown to work on moderately sized examples, and is only sporadically supported. Finally, *theoryware* is an implementation whose feasibility has been established in a research paper but for which little practical experience exists. Note that many prominent software tools have taken the full trip from theoryware over prototype to industrial strength.

3   Aspects of XML Type Checking

Independently of the above aspects, the type checking capabilities of an XML transformation language may be characterized.

First of all, an XML transformation language may of course be entirely unchecked, which means that all errors will be observed during runtime. For the other languages, we will distinguish between *internal* and *external* type checking.

Internal type checks aim at eliminating runtime errors during execution. For a GPL framework, this property is mainly inherited from the underlying language, and XML operations throwing their own kinds of exceptions are generally beyond the scope of the type system. For an embedded DSL, the type system of the underlying language will perform its own checks, while a separate analysis may perform additional checks of XML operations. One example of this is to verify that when the program navigates to, say, a given attribute of an element, then such an attribute is guaranteed to exist according to the schema. For a stand-alone DSL, a domain-specific type checker is often integrated into the compiler.

External type checks aim at validating the overall behavior of the XML transformation: that an XML tree belonging to the language of an input schema is always transformed into an XML tree belonging to the language of an output schema. For a GPL framework, this will require a global program analysis of the underlying language. This is often also true for an embedded DSL, but the restrictions imposed by the domain-specific syntax may make this task considerably simpler. For a stand-alone DSL, the external type check may also require a program analysis, but often it will be possible to express external type checks in terms of internal type checks if the schemas can be mapped to the domain-specific types.

The types of the XML data must be specified in some **type formalism**. A simple choice is DTD or the closely related formalism of *local tree grammars* [35]. A more ambitious choice is to use general *regular (unranked) tree languages*, corresponding to bottom-up tree automata [36]. Another approach is to use the full XML Schema language or other advanced schema languages used in real-life development projects. Finally, for GPL frameworks and embedded DSLs, the types will be characterized as *native* if they are effectively those of the underlying language. Approaches that rely on schema languages such as DTD or XML Schema most often tacitly ignore uniqueness and reference constraints (that is, ID/IDREF in DTD and key/keyref/unique in XML Schema), since these aspects of validity seem exceedingly hard to capture by type systems or dataflow analysis, and also usually are regarded as secondary features compared to the structural aspects of schemas.

Some type checkers use **type annotations**, which are part of the language syntax and explicitly state the expected or required types of variables and expressions. Annotations may be mandatory, meaning that certain language constructs must be given explicit types. Some languages require annotation of every XML variable, whereas others have a more light use of annotations, for example at input and output only. Heavy use of type annotations has both pros and cons. Type annotations may make the task of the type checker easier since less inference is needed. Also, one may argue that explicit types make the code more comprehensible since its intention is made more clear. On the other hand, the types being involved in XML processing can be quite complicated and writing explicit types might be viewed as an annoying extra burden on the programmer. Also, explicit types may incur a *rigid* type checker where type correctness must be obeyed at every program point. The consequences might be that XML trees can only be built strictly bottom-up, and that sequences of updates that gradually convert data from one type to another are not possible to type check. We discuss these issues further in the next section.

For Turing complete languages, type checking is an undecidable problem. For internal type checks, the decision problem is to determine the absence of certain runtime errors. For external type checks, the decision problem is to determine if the input language is transformed into the output language. Thus, type systems must approximate the answers to these problems. We will characterize the **precision** of both the internal and the external type checking capabilities according to the levels of guarantees being provided: The typical solution is to devise a static type checking algorithm that *conservatively* (that is, soundly but not completely) decides if the desired properties hold. Thus, any type checker will unfairly reject some programs, which is a common experience of most programmers. Another solution is to apply a *pragmatic* type checker which attempts to catch as many errors as possible, but which may generate both false positives and false negatives (in other words, it is neither sound nor complete). Note that even conservative internal type checkers usually ignore certain kinds of runtime errors, the classical examples being division by zero and null pointer dereferences. Also, approaches belonging to the pragmatic category can be sound if certain unchecked assumptions are adhered to. Of course, for non-Turing complete languages, it might also be feasible to guarantee *exact* answers.

The theoretical **complexity** of the type checking algorithm is also a relevant aspect. However, the asymptotic complexity of an algorithm is not always a true measure of its experienced running time (for example, ML type inference is exponential but runs smoothly in practice). A related aspect is the **modularity** of the type checking. A highly modular approach is more likely to scale to large programs. Some algorithms analyze each operation individually; if each operation type checks, then the entire program type checks. Others involve whole-program type inference or dataflow analysis using fixed-point iteration. Naturally, this aspect depends on the use of type annotations described above: high modularity is correlated with heavy use of annotations.

Finally, as for the transformation implementation, we will characterize the **type checking implementation**; for some languages, the transformation implementation is much more developed than the type checker. The **availability** of implementations is also interesting, where we distinguish between *open source*, free *binary* distributions, *commercial* products, and implementations that seem *unavailable*.

4   Points in the Design Space

The above discussions allow us to provide a succinct profile of a given XML transformation language and its type checker. For each language, we look into the following aspects (however, some are not applicable to all examples):

Language Type: Is the language a GPL library, a data-binding framework, a stand-alone DSL, an embedded DSL, or an XML-centric GPL? In case of a stand-alone DSL, is it imperative or declarative? Is it Turing complete?

Model for XML Data: Is XML data mutable or immutable? How is XML data constructed and deconstructed?

Type Formalism: Which formalism is used as types?

Annotations: How much does the approach depend on explicit types in the programs?

Precision: Is the type system exact, conservative, or pragmatic? Which guarantees are given when a program type checks? This aspect is relevant for both internal and external type checks. For conservative systems, is the precision acceptable in practice or are too many semantically correct programs rejected by the type checker?

Complexity: What is the theoretical complexity of the type checking process (if known)? Of course, this aspect must be evaluated together with the modularity aspect. Also, observed behavior in practice may appear very different.

Modularity: What is the granularity of the type checking? This ranges from individual operations to whole-program analyses.

Implementation Quality and Availability: What is the quality of implementations of the transformation language and of the type checker? Is their source code available?

Additionally, we will try to relate each language with the most closely related ones to investigate the similarities and essential differences.

4.1   XDuce

XDuce was the first programming language with type checking of XML operations using schemas as types [21]. It is a simplistic language that has provided the foundation for later languages, in particular XTATIC and CDuce, which we briefly mention below, and has also influenced the design of XQuery (see Section 4.10) and the popular schema language RELAX NG [13].

Language Type: XDuce is a declarative stand-alone DSL. It can also be characterized as a first-order pure functional language. Its intention has been to investigate type-safe integration of XML into programming languages, not to be a full fledged programming language. The original description of the language did not include attributes, but this has been amended in a later version [19]. It is Turing complete, with the exception that it cannot compute element names and attribute names dynamically.

Model for XML Data: Since the language is pure, XML data is obviously treated as immutable trees. Construction of values is expressed as tree terms. Navigation and deconstruction is based on a mechanism of *regular expression pattern matching* [20] – a combination of regular expressions and ML-style pattern matching that is closely connected with the type system.

Type Formalism: The type system of XDuce is based on the notion of *regular expression types*, which corresponds to the class of regular tree languages. The most essential part of the type system is the subtyping relation, which is defined by inclusion of the values represented by the types (this is also called *structural* subtyping).

Annotations: XDuce requires explicit type annotations for both function arguments and return values; however it provides local type inference for pattern matching operations, which means that many pattern variables do not need annotations.

Precision: The type checker of XDuce is conservative: a program that passes type checking is guaranteed to transform valid input into valid output. Regarding internal checking, various properties of pattern matching operations are checked: exhaustiveness (that at least one clause always matches), irredundancy (every clause can match some value), and unambiguity (that unique bindings are always obtained). Since the type formalism is decidable there exist programs that are semantically correct but where appropriate type annotations are not expressible, but such problematic programs have not been described in the XDuce papers.

Complexity: Since subtyping is based on automata language inclusion, the complexity of type checking—including the local type inference and the checks of pattern matching operations—is exponential time complete. Nevertheless, the algorithm being used appears efficient in practice [22].

Modularity: Since no global type inference or fixed-point iteration is involved, the approach is highly modular.

Implementation Quality and Availability: An open source prototype is available. This implementation focuses on type checking and analysis of patterns, not on runtime efficiency.

A key to the success of XDuce is the clean mathematical foundation of regular expression types. However, a number of issues remain. First, the current design does not handle unordered content models although these are common in real-life schemas. Second, the regular expression pattern matching mechanism can in some situations be too low-level, for example, for navigating deep down XML tree structures, processing data iteratively, or performing almost-identity transformations. Ongoing work aims to provide higher-level pattern matching primitives [18]. Third, devising an efficient runtime model for the language is challenging; for example, pattern matching may involve exponential time or space algorithms [29].

Other issues are being addressed in descendants of XDuce: XTATIC [15] aims to integrate the main ideas from XDuce into C$^\sharp$ (and can hence be categorized as an embedded DSL). As a part of making the technologies available in a mainstream language, efficient runtime representation of the XML data is also considered [16]. The CDuce language [3] goes another direction by extending XDuce towards being an XML-centric functional GPL by adding features, such as higher-order functions and variations of pattern matching primitives. Additionally, parametric polymorphism is being considered.

4.2   XACT

XACT [27, 26] has roots in the language JWIG, which is a Java-based language for development of interactive Web services [10, 7]. JWIG contains a template-based mechanism for dynamic construction of HTML/XHTML pages and includes a static program analysis that checks for validity of the pages; in XACT this mechanism has been generalized to full XML transformations.

Language type: XACT is an embedded DSL, with Java as host language. As XDuce, it is Turing complete but cannot compute element names and attribute names dynamically.

Model for XML data: This language uses a variant of immutable trees called *templates*, which are XML tree fragments with named *gaps* appearing in element contents or attributes. Values can be filled into these gaps in any order and at any time, and conversely, subtrees can be replaced by gaps in order to remove or replace data. Constant templates are written in an XML syntax. The main operations are the following: `plug` constructs a new value by inserting XML templates or strings into the gaps of the given name; `select` takes an XPath expression as argument and returns an array of the selected subtrees; `gapify` also takes an XPath expression as argument but in contrast to `select` it replaces the addressed subtrees by gaps of a given name; `setAttribute` inserts or replaces attributes selected using XPath; and `setContent` similarly replaces element content. In addition, there are methods for importing and exporting XML values to other formats, such as strings, streams, or JDOM documents. Note that a major difference to the XDuce family of languages is that XACT relies on XPath for navigation in XML trees.

Type formalism: The static guarantees in XACT are obtained through the use of a dataflow analysis that exploits a formalism called *summary graphs*, which approximatively tracks the operations on templates in the program. DTD is used for input and output types; however, the analyzer does permit the stronger schema language DSD2 [33] for the output types. The asymmetry arises since the input type must be translated into a summary graph, while the final check of the output type uses a separate algorithm that tests inclusion of summary graphs into DSD2 schemas. It is theoretically possible to map also a DSD2 schema into a summary graph accepting the same language (ignoring as usual uniqueness and pointer constraints), but this has not been implemented yet.

Annotations: Being based on dataflow analysis, the annotation overhead is much lighter than in most other techniques. Types, that is, references to DTDs, are specified only at input and at designated analysis points (typically at output).

Precision: The analysis is conservative, that is, a program that passes the analysis cannot produce invalid XML at runtime. The analyzer also performs some internal checks: that `plug` operations never fail (by attempting to plug templates into attribute gaps), and that XPath expressions used in the other XML operations can potentially select nonempty node sets. The main practical limitations of the analysis precision are caused by the facts that the current implementation employs a monovariant and path-insensitive analysis and that all field variables are treated flow insensitively (to ensure soundness).

Complexity: The analysis has polynomial complexity.

Modularity: The approach has poor modularity since it performs fixed-point iteration over the entire program. Nevertheless, it appears reasonably efficient in practice [27].

Implementation quality and availability: An open source prototype is available. The analyzer handles the full Java language. The runtime representation has been crafted to obtain good performance despite operating on immutable structures. [26]

Although less mathematically elegant, the template-based mechanism in XACT can be more flexible to program with than the XDuce model. First, using the `plug` operation, templates with gaps can be passed around as first-class values. Gaps may be filled in any order and computed templates can be reused; in the XDuce family of languages, trees must be constructed bottom-up. Second, the use of XPath appears powerful for addressing deeply into XML trees; several other languages have chosen XPath for the same purpose, as described in the following sections. Third, the `gapify` operation makes it easy to make almost-identity transformations without explicitly reconstructing everything that does not change.

Despite the differences between the XDuce and XACT approaches, there is a connection between the underlying formalisms used in the type checkers: as shown in [9], the notions of summary graphs and regular expression types are closely related.

Current work on the XACT project aims to obtain a closer integration with the new generics and iteration features that have been introduced in Java 5.0.

4.3   XJ

The development of the XJ [17] language aims at integrating XML processing closely into Java using XML Schema as type formalism.

Language type: XJ is an embedded DSL using Java as host language.

Model for XML data: XML data is represented as mutable trees. Construction of XML data is performed at the level of individual nodes. It is dynamically checked that every node has at most one parent. Subtrees are addressed using XPath. Updating attribute values or character data is likewise expressed using XPath, whereas insertion and deletion of subtrees involving elements are expressed with special `insert` and `delete` operations.

Type formalism: Types are regular expressions over XML Schema declarations of elements, attributes, and simple types. Thus, the type system has two levels: regular expression operators and XML Schema constructions. Subtyping on the schema level is defined by the use of type derivations (extensions and restrictions) and substitution groups in the schemas: if A is derived from B or is in the substitution group of B, then A is defined to be a subtype of B. In other words, this is a *nominal* style of subtyping. Subtyping on the regular expression level is defined as regular language inclusion on top of the schema subtyping. Coercions are made between certain XML types and normal Java types, for example between `int` of XML Schema and `int` of Java, or between Kleene star and `java.lang.List`.

Annotations: All XML variable declarations must be annotated with types.

Precision: The type checker is in the pragmatic category because updates require runtime checks due to potential aliasing. Also, not all features in XML Schema are accounted for by the type system, an example being facet constraints. Updates involving XPath expressions that evaluate to multiple nodes result in runtime errors.

Complexity: Since subtyping relies on inclusion between regular expressions, complexity is exponential in the size of the regular expressions being used.

Modularity: Due to the heavy use of annotations, each operation can be checked separately, which leads to a high degree of modularity.

Implementation quality and availability: A prototype implementing parts of the system has been made (in particular, type checking of updates of complex types is not implemented). This prototype has not been available to us.

The authors of [17] acknowledge the fact that the type checker of XJ can be too rigid. Since the values of a variable at all times must adhere to its type and this type is fixed at the variable declaration, it is impossible to type check a sequence of operations that temporarily invalidate the data. A plausible example is constructing an element and inserting a number of mandatory attributes through a sequence of updates.

A problem with the nominal style of subtyping is that a given XML value is tied too closely with its schema type. Imagine a transformation (inspired by the addrbook example from [21]), which creates a telephone book document from an address book document by extracting the entries that have telephone numbers. That is, the output language is a subset of the input language, the only difference being that telephone elements are mandatory in the content model of person elements in the output. Since the nominal type system treats the two versions of person elements as unrelated, an XJ transformation must explicitly reconstruct all person elements instead of merely removing those without a telephone element.

4.4 XOBE

The XOBE language [24] has been developed with similar goals as XJ and has many similarities in the language design; however, the type checking approach appears closer to that of XDuce.

Language type: XOBE is an embedded DSL using Java as host language.

Model for XML data: XML data is represented as mutable trees. (It is not explicitly stated in the available papers on XOBE that the XML trees are mutable, however an example program in [24] strongly suggests that this is the case.) Construction of XML trees is written in an XML-like notation with embedded expressions (unlike XJ). Subtrees are addressed using XPath expressions.

Type formalism: The underlying type formalism is *regular hedge expressions*, which corresponds to the class of regular tree languages that, for instance, XDuce also relies on. From the programmer's point of view, XML Schema can be used as type formalism, but features of XML Schema that go beyond regularity are naturally not handled by the type checker. It is not clear how the type derivation and substitution group features of XML Schema are handled, but it might be along the lines suggested in [35].

Annotations: XOBE requires explicit type annotations on every XML variable declaration.

Precision: The main ingredient of the type checker is checking subtype relationship for assignment statements. Since mutable updates are possible and the potential aliases that then may arise are apparently ignored (unlike in the XJ approach which relies on runtime checks), the XOBE type checker is unsound and hence belongs in the pragmatic category. However, if assuming that problematic aliases do not arise, type checking is conservative. When XML Schema is used as type formalism, certain kinds of constraints that are expressible in XML Schema, such as number of occurrences and restricted string types, are handled by runtime checks.

Complexity: The complexity of checking subtype relationship is exponential.

Modularity: As with XJ, the modularity of type checking is high.

Implementation quality and availability: A binary-code prototype is available (but, at the time of writing, with minimal documentation).

As in XJ, integrating XML into a GPL using mutable trees as data model and XPath for addressing subtrees is a tempting and elegant approach. However, two crucial problems remain: it appears infeasible to ensure soundness of the type checker when aliasing and updates can be mixed, and the type checker can be too rigid as noted above.

4.5   JDOM

As as baseline, we include JDOM [23] – a popular approach that does not perform any type checking for validity of the generated XML data but only ensures well-formedness. In return, it is simple, offers maximal flexibility and performance, and is widely used. JDOM is developed as a Java-specific alternative to the language independent DOM [1].

Language type: JDOM is a GPL library (for Java).

Model for XML data: XML data is represented as mutable trees (in particular, nodes must have unique parents). The library contains a plethora of operations for performing low-level tree navigation and manipulation and for importing and exporting to other formats. Additionally, there is built-in support for evaluating XPath location path expressions.

Type formalism: Well-formedness comes for free with the tree representation, but JDOM contains no type system (in addition to what Java already has).

Implementation quality and availability: JDOM has an open source industrial strength implementation.

Compared to the other approaches mentioned in this paper, DOM and JDOM are generally regarded as low-level frameworks. They are often used as foundations for implementing more advanced approaches.

4.6   JAXB

Relative to DOM/JDOM, Sun's JAXB framework [37] and numerous related projects [6] can be viewed as the next step in integrating XML into GPL programming languages.

Language type: JAXB is a data binding framework for Java.

Model for XML data: Schemas written in the XML Schema language are converted to Java classes that mimic the schema structure. XML data is represented as objects of these classes. Conversion between textual XML representation and objects is performed by `marshall` and `unmarshall` operations. The mapping from schemas to classes can be customized either via annotations in the schema or in separate binding files.

Type formalism: JAXB relies on the native Java type system. Note that, in contrast to JDOM, this representation is able to obtain static guarantees of certain aspects of validity because the binding reflects many properties of the schemas. Full XML Schema validation is left as a runtime feature.

Annotations: No special annotations are needed in the Java code.

Precision: The approach is pragmatic due to the significant impedance mismatch between XML schema languages and the type system of Java. Using a customized binding, this mismatch can be alleviated, though. Nevertheless, there is no automatic translation from DTD, XML Schema, or the more idealized schema languages that provides precise bindings.

Implementation quality and availability: JAXB has several (even open source) industrial strength implementations.

Data binding frameworks are a commonly used alternative to the DOM/JDOM approach. Still, they constitute a pragmatic approach that cannot provide the static guarantees of conservative frameworks.

4.7   HaXml

If the host language has a more advanced type system, then data binding may be more precise. An example of that is the HaXml [42] system, which uses Haskell as host language. HaXml additionally contains a generic library like JDOM, which we will not consider here.

Language type: HaXml is a data binding framework for Haskell.

Model for XML data: DTDs are converted into algebraic types using a fixed strategy.

Type formalism: HaXml uses the native Haskell types.

Annotations: Type annotations are optional.

Precision: The Haskell type checker is conservative and generally acknowledged to have good precision. For the XML binding, however, the lack of subtyping of algebraic types rejects many natural programs. On the other hand, the presence of polymorphism allows a different class of useful programs to be type checked.

Complexity: The type checker of Haskell is exponential.

Modularity: Modularity is excellent, since Haskell supports separate compilation.

Implementation quality and availability: The Haskell compiler has industrial strength implementations.

In [38] different binding algorithms for Haskell are discussed, enabling more flexible programming styles while trading off full DTD validity.

4.8   Cω

The Cω language (formerly known as Xen) is an extension of C$^\sharp$ that aims at unifying data models for objects, XML, and also databases [4, 31]. This goes a step beyond data binding.

Language type: Cω is an XML-centric GPL based on the C$^\sharp$ language.

Model for XML data: The mutable data values of C$^\sharp$ are extended to include immutable structural sequences, unions, and products on top of objects and simple values. XML trees are then encoded as such values. XML templates may be used as syntactic sugar for the corresponding constructor invocations. A notion of *generalized member access* emulates simple XPath expressions for navigation and deconstruction.

Type formalism: The $C\omega$ type system similarly supports structural sequence, union, and product types. There is no support for external types, but the basic features of DTD or XML Schema may be encoded in the type system.

Annotations: $C\omega$ requires ubiquitous type annotations, as does $C^\sharp$.

Precision: The $C\omega$ type checker appears somewhat restrictive, since the notion of subtyping is not semantically complete: two types whose values are in a subset relation are not necessarily in a subtype relation. This means that many programs will be unfairly rejected by the type checker. For example, an `addrbook` with mandatory `telephone` elements cannot be assigned to a variable expecting an `addrbook` with optional `telephone` elements.

Complexity: The complexity is not stated (but appears to be polynomial given the simple notion of subtyping).

Modularity: The type system is highly modular as that of the underlying $C^\sharp$ language.

Implementation quality and availability: The language is available in a prototype implementation.

$C\omega$ solves a more ambitious problem than merely type checked XML transformations, and many of its interesting features arise from the merger of different data models.

4.9   Tree Transducers

XML has a mathematical idealization as ordered labeled trees and schemas may be modeled as regular tree languages. Corresponding to this view, XML transformations may be seen as some notion of *tree transducers*. Two representative examples are TL transformers [30] and k-pebble transducers [32].

Language type: Tree transducers are declarative stand-alone DSLs. Actually, they are generally presented simply as 5-tuples with alphabets and transition functions. The languages are not Turing complete but still capture many central aspects of other transformation languages.

Model for XML data: XML data is immutable. Attributes must be encoded as special nodes, and attribute values and character data are ignored. Construction is performed node by node. Navigation and pattern matching is in the k-pebble approach performed by tree walking and in the TL approach by evaluating formulas in monadic second-order logic.

Type formalism: Types are general regular tree languages.

Annotations: Only the input and output types are specified.

Precision: These classes of tree transducers are particularly interesting, since their type checking problems are decidable. The k-pebble transducers may be viewed as low-level machines, while TL transformers provide a more succinct declarative syntax.

Complexity: The type checking algorithms are hyperexponential.

Modularity: Tree transducers are closed under composition, which provides a simple form of modular type checking.

Implementation quality and availability: The type checking algorithms have not been implemented and are thus pure theoryware. However, non-elementary algorithms on tree automata have previously been seen to be feasible in practice [28].

This work fits into a classical scenario where practical language design and theoretical underpinnings inspire each other. Type checking algorithms for Turing complete languages will become ever more precise and formalisms with decidable type checking will become ever more expressive, but the two will of course never meet.

4.10   XQuery

XQuery is the W3C recommendation for programming transformations of data-centric XML [5] (currently with the status of working draft). As XML trees may been seen to generalize relational databases tables, the XQuery language is designed to generalize the SQL query language.

Language type: XQuery is a Turing complete declarative stand-alone language. Like XDuce, it is also a first-order pure functional language.

Model for XML data: XML data is treated as immutable trees. Future extensions plan to generalize also the update mechanisms of SQL, but the query language itself continues to operate on immutable data. Nodes of trees also have a physical identity, which means that fragments may be either identical or merely equal as labeled trees. A term language is used for constructing values, and XPath is used for deconstruction and pattern matching.

Type formalism: The input and output types are XML Schema instances. Internally, types are tree languages with data values, corresponding to single-type tree grammars. Input/output types are mapped approximately into internal types, and the subtyping is structural (unlike XJ). Most of XML Schema fits into this framework [35].

Annotations: Variables, parameters, and function results have type annotations that by default denote a type containing all values.

Precision: The internal type checker is conservative and based on type rules. Some XQuery constructions are difficult to describe, and the designers acknowledge that some type rules may need to be sharpened in later versions [14]. While XQuery unlike most other transformation languages handle computed element and attribute names, it should be noted that the corresponding type rule must pessimistically assume that any kind of result could arise. The external type checker is strictly speaking pragmatic. The unsoundness arises because XML Schema is only mapped approximately into internal types. To achieve a conservative external type checker, the mapping of the input language should produce an upper approximation and the mapping of the output language a lower approximation. The current mapping apparently meets neither criterion. The practical precision of the type checking algorithm is as yet unknown.

Complexity: The type checking algorithm is exponential.

Modularity: The type checker is in a sense modular, since functions may be type checked separately against their type annotations. However, since the type system lacks analogies of principal type schemes, a single most general choice of type annotations does not exist.

Implementation quality and availability: XQuery is available in several prototype implementations, both commercial and open source. Only a single prototype supports type checking. Industrial strength implementations are being undertaken by several companies.

XQuery will undoubtedly fulfill its goal as an industrial XML standard. In that light, its strong theoretical foundation is a welcome novelty.

4.11   Type Checking XSLT

XSLT 1.0 is the current W3C recommendation for programming transformations of document-centric XML [12]. There is no associated type checker, but in a recent project we have applied the summary graph technology from XACT to create a flow-based external type checker [34]. This tool has been designed to handle a real-life situation, thus the full XSLT 1.0 language is supported.

Language type: XSLT is a declarative stand-alone DSL. It is Turing complete [25], but only in the encoded sense. Even though computed element and attribute names are allowed, there are several XML transformations that cannot be expressed, primarily because XSLT transformations cannot be composed. For example, a transformation that sorts a list of items and alternatingly colors them red and blue cannot be programmed in XSLT.

Model for XML data: XML data is treated as immutable trees. Templates are used as a term language (in a declarative fashion, unlike the template mechanism in XACT). Navigation is performed using XPath.

Type formalism: XSLT 1.0 is itself untyped, but our tool uses summary graphs for internal types. External types are DTDs. The output type may in fact be a DSD2 schema, as in XACT.

Annotations: Our tool works on ordinary XSLT stylesheets, thus only the input and output type must be specified.

Precision: The analysis is conservative. At present, no internal type checks are performed, but we obtain the required information to catch XPath navigation errors and detect dead code. The external type checker has been tested on a dozen scenarios with XSLT files ranging from 35 to 1,353 lines and DTDs ranging from 8 to 2,278 lines. Most of these examples originate from real-life projects and were culled from the Web. In a total of 3,665 lines of XSLT, the type checker reported 87 errors. Of those, 54 were identified as real problems in the stylesheets, covering a a mixture of misplaced, undefined, or missing elements and attributes, unexpected empty contents, and wrong namespaces. Most are easily found and corrected, but a few seem to indicate serious problems. The 33 false errors fall in two categories. A total of 30 are due to insufficient analysis of string values, which causes problems when attribute values are restricted to NMTOKEN in the output schema. A variation of the string analysis presented in [11] may remedy this. The remaining 3 false errors are caused by approximations we introduce and would require sophisticated refinements to avoid. Another important measure of the achieved precision is that the generic identity transformation always type checks.

Complexity: The algorithm is polynomial and appears reasonably efficient in practice. The largest example with 1,353 lines of XSLT, 104 lines of input DTD, and 2,278 lines of output DSD2 schema (for XHTML) ran in 80 seconds on a typical PC (constructing a summary graph with more than 26,000 nodes).

Modularity: The type checker is based on whole-program analysis and thus is not modular.

Implementation quality and availability: XSLT 1.0 has of course many industrial strength implementations. The type checker is implemented as a prototype, which we are currently developing further.

The analysis has several phases. First, we desugar the full XSLT syntax into a smaller core language using only the instructions `apply-templates`, `choose`, `copy-of`, `attribute`, `element`, and `value-of`. The transformation has the property that the type check of the original stylesheet may soundly be performed on the reduced version instead.

Second, we perform a control flow analysis finding for each `apply-templates` instruction the possible target `template` rules. This reduces to checking that two XPath expressions are *compatible* relative to a DTD, which is challenging to solve with the required precision. We use a combination of two heuristic algorithms, partly inspired by a statistical analysis of 200,000 lines of real-life XSLT code written by hundreds of different authors.

Third, a summary graph that soundly represents the possible output documents is constructed based on the control flow graph and the input DTD. The main challenge here is to provide sufficiently precise representations of content sequences in the output language.

Finally, the resulting summary graph is compared to the output schema using the algorithm presented in [10].

There have been other approaches to type checking XSLT stylesheets [40, 2], but our tool is the first working implementation for the full language.

5   Conclusion

Many different programming systems have been proposed for writing transformations of XML data. We have identified a number of aspects by which these systems and their type checking capabilities can be compared. The approaches range from integration of XML into existing languages to development of language extensions or entirely new languages. Some aim for soundness where others are more pragmatic. Additionally, we have presented a brief overview of a novel approach for type checking XSLT 1.0 stylesheets and have shown how this fits into the design space of XML type checkers. An extensive description of this approach is currently in preparation [34].

The variety of approaches indicates that the general problem of integrating XML into programming languages with static guarantees of validity has no canonical solution. Nevertheless, some general observations can be made:

- A fundamental issue seems to be that real-life schema languages are too far from traditional type systems in programming languages.
- The choice of using an immutable representation is common, even in imperative languages. (We have seen the problems that arise with mutability and aliasing).
- It is common to rely on type annotations on all variable declarations. This improves modularity of type checking but is an extra burden on the programmer.
- Many type checkers appear restrictive in the sense that they significantly limit the flexibility of the underlying language. One example is type systems that are not structural; another is rigidity that enforces a programming style where XML trees are constructed purely bottom-up.
- Irrespectively of the type checker, it is important that the language is flexible in supporting common XML transformation scenarios. For example, variants of template mechanisms can be convenient for writing larger fragments of XML data. Also, XPath is widely used for addressing into XML data.
- In many proposals, runtime efficiency is an issue that has not been addressed yet. Also, handling huge amounts of XML data seems problematic for most systems.
- A claim made in many papers is that high theoretical complexity does not appear to be a problem in practice. Nevertheless, it is unclear how well most of the proposed type checking techniques work on real, large scale programming projects.

Overall, the general problem is challenging and far from being definitively solved, and we look forward to seeing the next 700 XML transformation languages and type checking techniques.

Acknowledgments

We thank Claus Brabrand and Christian Kirkegaard for useful comments and inspiring discussions.

References

1. Vidur Apparao et al. Document Object Model (DOM) level 1 specification, October 1998. W3C Recommendation. http://www.w3.org/TR/REC-DOM-Level-1/.
2. Philippe Audebaud and Kristoffer Rose. Stylesheet validation. Technical Report RR2000-37, ENS-Lyon, November 2000.
3. Veronique Benzaken, Giuseppe Castagna, and Alain Frisch. CDuce: An XML-centric general-purpose language. In *Proc. 8th ACM International Conference on Functional Programming, ICFP '03*, August 2003.
4. Gavin Bierman, Erik Meijer, and Wolfram Schulte. The essence of data access in Cω. Technical report, Microsoft Research, 2004. http://research.microsoft.com/Comega/.

5. Scott Boag et al. XQuery 1.0: An XML query language, November 2003. W3C Working Draft. http://www.w3.org/TR/xquery/.
6. Ronald Bourret. XML data binding resources, September 2004. http://www.rpbourret.com/xml/XMLDataBinding.htm.
7. Claus Brabrand, Anders Møller, and Michael I. Schwartzbach. The <bigwig> project. *ACM Transactions on Internet Technology*, 2(2):79–114, 2002.
8. Tim Bray, Jean Paoli, C. M. Sperberg-McQueen, Eve Maler, and Franois Yergeau. Extensible Markup Language (XML) 1.0 (third edition), February 2004. W3C Recommendation. http://www.w3.org/TR/REC-xml.
9. Aske Simon Christensen, Anders Møller, and Michael I. Schwartzbach. Static analysis for dynamic XML. Technical Report RS-02-24, BRICS, May 2002. Presented at Programming Language Technologies for XML, PLAN-X '02.
10. Aske Simon Christensen, Anders Møller, and Michael I. Schwartzbach. Extending Java for high-level Web service construction. *ACM Transactions on Programming Languages and Systems*, 25(6):814–875, November 2003.
11. Aske Simon Christensen, Anders Møller, and Michael I. Schwartzbach. Precise analysis of string expressions. In *Proc. 10th International Static Analysis Symposium, SAS '03*, volume 2694 of *LNCS*, pages 1–18. Springer-Verlag, June 2003.
12. James Clark. XSL transformations (XSLT), November 1999. W3C Recommendation. http://www.w3.org/TR/xslt.
13. James Clark and Makoto Murata. RELAX NG specification, December 2001. OASIS. http://www.oasis-open.org/committees/relax-ng/.
14. Denise Draper et al. XQuery 1.0 and XPath 2.0 formal semantics, November 2002. W3C Working Draft. http://www.w3.org/TR/query-semantics/.
15. Vladimir Gapayev and Benjamin C. Pierce. Regular object types. In *Proc. 17th European Conference on Object-Oriented Programming, ECOOP'03*, volume 2743 of *LNCS*. Springer-Verlag, July 2003.
16. Vladimir Gapeyev, Michael Y. Levin, Benjamin C. Pierce, and Alan Schmitt. XML goes native: Run-time representations for Xtatic, 2004.
17. Matthew Harren, Mukund Raghavachari, Oded Shmueli, Michael Burke, Vivek Sarkar, and Rajesh Bordawekar. XJ: Integration of XML processing into Java. Technical Report RC23007, IBM Research, 2003.
18. Haruo Hosoya. Regular expression filters for XML, January 2004. Presented at Programming Language Technologies for XML, PLAN-X '04.
19. Haruo Hosoya and Makoto Murata. Validation and boolean operations for attribute-element constraints, October 2002. Presented at Programming Language Technologies for XML, PLAN-X '02.
20. Haruo Hosoya and Benjamin C. Pierce. Regular expression pattern matching for XML. *Journal of Functional Programming*, 13(4), 2002.
21. Haruo Hosoya and Benjamin C. Pierce. XDuce: A statically typed XML processing language. *ACM Transactions on Internet Technology*, 3(2), 2003.
22. Haruo Hosoya, Jerome Vouillon, and Benjamin C. Pierce. Regular expression types for XML. *ACM Trans. on Programming Languages and Systems*, 2004. To appear.
23. Jason Hunter and Brett McLaughlin. JDOM, 2004. http://jdom.org/.
24. Martin Kempa and Volker Linnemann. On XML objects, October 2002. Presented at Programming Language Technologies for XML, PLAN-X '02.
25. Stephan Kepser. A proof of the Turing-completeness of XSLT and XQuery. Technical report, SFB 441, University of Tübingen, 2002.
26. Christian Kirkegaard, Aske Simon Christensen, and Anders Møller. A runtime system for XML transformations in Java. In *Proc. Second International XML Database Symposium, XSym '04*, LNCS 3186. Springer-Verlag, 2004.

27. Christian Kirkegaard, Anders Møller, and Michael I. Schwartzbach. Static analysis of XML transformations in Java. *IEEE Trans. on Software Engineering*, 30(3):181–192, March 2004.
28. Nils Klarlund, Anders Møller, and Michael I. Schwartzbach. MONA implementation secrets. *International Journal of Foundations of Computer Science*, 13(4):571–586, 2002. World Scientific Publishing Company.
29. Michael Y. Levin. Compiling regular patterns. In *Proc. 8th ACM SIGPLAN International Conference on Functional Programming, ICFP '03*, August 2003.
30. Sebastian Maneth, Alexandru Berlea, Thomas Perst, and Helmut Seidl. XML type checking with macro tree transducers. Tech. Rep. TUM-I0407, TU Munich, 2004.
31. Erik Meijer, Wolfram Schulte, and Gavin Bierman. Programming with rectangles, triangles, and circles. In *Proc. XML Conference and Exposition, XML '03*, December 2003.
32. Tova Milo, Dan Suciu, and Victor Vianu. Typechecking for XML transformers. *Journal of Computer and System Sciences*, 66, February 2002. Special Issue on PODS '00, Elsevier.
33. Anders Møller. Document Structure Description 2.0, December 2002. BRICS, Department of Computer Science, University of Aarhus, Notes Series NS-02-7. Available from http://www.brics.dk/DSD/.
34. Anders Møller, Mads Østerby Olesen, and Michael I. Schwartzbach. Static validation of XSL Transformations, 2004. In preparation.
35. Makoto Murata, Dongwon Lee, and Murali Mani. Taxonomy of XML schema languages using formal language theory. In *Proc. Extreme Markup Languages, August 2001*.
36. Frank Neven. Automata, logic, and XML. In *Proc. 16th International Workshop on Computer Science Logic, CSL '02*, September 2002.
37. Sun Microsystems. JAXB, 2004. http://java.sun.com/xml/jaxb/.
38. Peter Thiemann. A typed representation for HTML and XML documents in Haskell. *Journal of Functional Programming*, 12(5):435–468, 2002.
39. Henry S. Thompson, David Beech, Murray Maloney, and Noah Mendelsohn. XML Schema part 1: Structures, May 2001. W3C Recommendation. http://www.w3.org/TR/xmlschema-1/.
40. Akihiko Tozawa. Towards static type checking for XSLT. In *Proc. ACM Symposium on Document Engineering, DocEng '01*, November 2001.
41. Arie van Deursen, Paul Klint, and Joost Visser. Domain-specific languages: An annotated bibliography. *ACM SIGPLAN Notices*, 35(6):26–36, June 2000.
42. Malcolm Wallace and Colin Runciman. Haskell and XML: Generic combinators or type-based translation? In *Proc. 4th ACM SIGPLAN International Conference on Functional Programming, ICFP '99*, September 1999.

Semantics of Data Streams and Operators

David Maier[1], Jin Li[1], Peter Tucker[2], Kristin Tufte[1], and Vassilis Papadimos[1]

[1] Portland State University, Computer Science Department, Portland, OR, 97207
{maier, jinli, tufte, vpapad}@cs.pdx.edu
[2] Whitworth College, Spokane, WA 99251
ptucker@whitworth.edu

Abstract. What does a data stream mean? Much of the extensive work on query operators and query processing for data streams has proceeded without the benefit of an answer to this question. While such imprecision may be tolerable when dealing with simple cases, such as flat data, guaranteed physical order and element-wise operations, it can lead to ambiguities when dealing with nested data, disordered streams and windowed operators. We propose *reconstitution functions* to make the denotation and representation of data streams more precise, and use these functions to investigate the connection between monotonicity and nonblocking behavior of stream operators. We also touch on a reconstitution function for XML data. Other aspects of data stream semantics we consider are the use of punctuation to delineate finite subsets of a stream, adequacy of descriptions of stream disorder, and the formal specification of windowed operators.

1 Introduction

Data streams arise in many application domains, such as sensor processing, network monitoring and financial analysis. Streams from different domains could mean quite diverse things: a discrete signal, an event log, a combination of time series. Most work on algorithms and architectures for data stream management, however, never defines what a stream means. Thus it is hard to judge whether the definition of a particular stream operator is sensible. The default seems to be that a stream operator should behave like the pipelined version of a relational operator, but that may be inappropriate if the stream denotes something other than an unbounded relation, or if the representation the stream uses is different from the usual serialization of a finite table. When new operators are introduced, such as windowed versions of *group-by* and *join*, the situation becomes even fuzzier, especially if the semantics of the operator depends on the physical presentation order of items in the data stream.

In this paper, we propose *reconstitution functions* as a means to make precise the denotation and representation of a data stream. A reconstitution function is applied incrementally to prefixes of a stream to give successive approximations of its denotation. While generally we do not expect to actually apply a reconstitution function to a stream, it is useful in specifying the correct behavior of

T. Eiter and L. Libkin (Eds.): ICDT 2005, LNCS 3363, pp. 37–52, 2005.

a stream analogue of an existing operator over the denotation domain. Reconstitution functions also prove useful in examining the subtle interplay between monotonicity and non-blocking behavior in stream operators.

We also consider additional semantics that may be available about the content or physical presentation of data streams, and discuss stream *punctuation* as one means to make such additional information available to stream operators and queries. One aspect we cover at more length is disorder in data streams. We explore some of the existing proposals for describing the expected disorder in a data stream. From our own investigations of disorder, we point out two areas in which disorder descriptions could be enhanced, namely non-uniform disorder, and statistical distributions of item displacement.

Our final topic is the semantics of windowed operators: operators that manipulate a data stream by decomposing it into a sequence of finite subsets and processing each subset in turn. Many such operators are defined in operational terms, which can make them sensitive to the physical presentation order of a stream. We propose a formal semantics for window definition that appears able to capture the underlying semantics of almost all window operators proposed to date. That semantics is independent of the physical order of a stream, and hence can describe the expected behavior of a window operator in the presence of disorder, and also leads to operator implementations with no internal buffering.

2   Stream Denotation and Representation

As we pointed out in the introduction, the proper interpretation of a stream might vary from application to application, but papers on data streams do not always make clear what interpretation they use. Even where the interpretation is provided, it can be somewhat confusing. For example, Law et al. [LWZ04] view data streams as "bags of append-only ordered tuples," or, alternatively, as "unbounded append-only bags of elements" when there is an explicit timestamp associated with each tuple. Such definitions conflate the kind of structure a stream denotes (an unbounded sequence?) with a particular representation (tuples with timestamps) with the function for recovering one from another (append). There are several questions left unanswered here. Are the timestamps considered part of the content of stream items — and thus, for example, available in selection conditions — or do they simply serve to define an order on the stream? Is the order total, or can two tuples have the same timestamp? Might the bag of tuples be viewed as a set by ignoring duplicates? The answers to such questions are important in evaluating whether or not a proposed stream operator is reasonable.

We think it important to distinguish the *denotation* of a stream from the particular *representation* of the denotation that the stream uses. The denotation is an abstract interpretation of what the stream means as a mathematical structure in some domain, whereas the representation is a particular encoding being used for elements of that domain. For example, a stream might be viewed as denoting a sequence of (finite) relation states over a common schema $R : [r_1(R),$

$r_2(R)$, $r_3(R)$, ...]. Let us assume for concreteness that the individual relations are unordered sets. There are many ways a stream could represent such a relation sequence:

(a) as the concatenation of serializations of the r_i (similar to the Rstream function of CQL [AW04R]);
(b) as a list of tuple-index pairs, where $\langle t, j \rangle$ indicates $t \in r_j$;
(c) as a serialization of r_1, followed by a series of "delta" tuples that indicate updates to make to obtain r_2, r_3, etc.;
(d) as a "replacement sequence," where some attribute A is treated as a key, and arriving tuple t replaces any existing tuple with the same $t(A)$-value to form a new relation state;
(e) as a "broadcast disk" format [AA95], where the state of a single r_i might be repeated multiple times;
(f) as an "overlapped window" encoding, in which each subsequence of 50 tuples represents a relation state in the sequence.

Clearly there are many other possible representations and variants for the relation-sequence denotation. Properly reflecting the behavior of an operation from the denotation domain in a stream operator requires consideration of the representation being used. Consider, for example, component-wise selection. That is, the desired outcome is $[\sigma_C(r_1), \sigma_C(r_2), \sigma_C(r_3), \ldots]$ for some selection condition C. For representations (a) – (e), one can apply the condition C individually to the items in an input stream S to get an output stream that represents the result. (There may be issues with representation (a) if σ_C selects away all tuples in some r_i, depending on how successive serializations are delimited.) However, applying C itemwise to a stream using representation (f) will not give the correct result, unless the output stream adopts a different representation.

As another example, consider a stream of sensor readings from, say, a temperature probe. We might view such a stream as denoting a discrete signal with a regular sampling rate (which in turn approximates a continuous physical measurement in the environment). A temperature stream might represent such a signal in several different ways:

(a) as a sequence of readings, one for each sampling point;
(b) as a sequence of changes in temperature from the previous sampling point;
(c) as a sequence of reading-timestamp pairs, with a pair included only if the reading differs from the previous reading included.

Representation (c) might be desirable for logistical considerations, such as power conservation, but it may require care in implementing certain operations. For example, if the average of two signals is the desired output, one needs to deal with the situation where there are long pauses in one stream because the temperature has not changed.

We also note that a single data stream might be viewed more than one way. That is, it can be construed with different denotations by interpreting it using different representations. Consider a stream of stock-trade items of the form `<ticker, time, shares, price>`. We can consider this stream as denoting a relation sequence, using the replacement-sequence representation (a) above with `ticker` as the key. Each item in the stream produces a new relation state in the sequence. An alternative view is that the trade stream denotes a relation sequence of recent trades, using representation (f) above. A third interpretation is that the stream denotes a collection of time series of prices, one for each different stock. Each item in the stream extends one of these time series. Observe that conversions between these different denotation values might be a no-op on the stream itself — just a change in the representation used to interpret it.

3   Reconstitution Functions

The notions of denotation and representation are useful for thinking about the semantics of a given stream, but are not necessarily precise enough yet for use in proofs of operator correctness or query equivalence. As a practical matter, the denotations we have used as examples are potentially infinite structures giving meaning to a whole stream, whereas there is a general desire to treat streams incrementally. We thus propose *reconstitution functions* as a mechanism for expressing and reasoning about stream semantics and representations. One can view a reconstitution function as constructing successive approximations to the denotation of a stream from successive finite prefixes of that stream. Consider streams with items of type $\mathbf{T}$, and let $\mathbf{D}$ be the desired domain of interpretation. A reconstitution function *reconst* for type $\mathbf{stream(T)}$ will map each prefix P (of type $\mathbf{sequence(T)}$) of a stream into $\mathbf{D}$: $reconst(P) = d \in \mathbf{D}$. We give some example reconstitution functions below.

The Insert Reconstitution Function: If the domain of interpretation is $\mathbf{bag(T)}$, then a reconstitution function *ins* that starts with an empty bag and inserts each successive stream item is appropriate:

$$ins([]) = \varnothing$$
$$ins(P : i) = insert(i, ins(P)).$$

Here we use $[]$ for the empty sequence, and $P : i$ to denote sequence P extended by item i.

The Insert-Unique Reconstitution Function: If the intended domain of interpretation for a stream is $\mathbf{set(T)}$, then we can define a reconstitution function ins_u that checks for duplicates:

$$ins_u([]) = \varnothing$$
$$ins_u(P : i) = \text{if } i \notin ins_u(P) \text{ then } insert(i, ins_u(P)) \text{ else } ins_u(P).$$

The Insert-Replace Reconstitution Function: Here we assume that each item in the stream has a component A that is treated as a key, and define a reconstitution function ins_r that guarantees only the most recent item with a given key is included:

$$ins_r([]) = \varnothing$$
$$ins_r(P : i) = insert(i, \{j \mid j \in ins_r(P) \wedge j.A \neq i.A\}).$$

The Insert-Replace-Collect Reconstitution Function: The ins_r reconstitution function yields the final state resulting from applying all the items in the stream. If the desired domain of interpretation is sequences of states (that is, type **sequence(set(T))**), similar to the relation-sequence example of Section 2, we can use the ins_{rc} reconstitution function to collect successive states:

$$ins_{rc}([]) = []$$
$$ins_{rc}(P : i) = ins_{rc}(P) : ins_r(P : i).$$

Remarks:

1. All the examples of reconstitution functions above are *incremental*: Each can be cast in the form $reconst(P : i) = g(reconst(P), i)$ for some function g. We do not require this property for a reconstitution function, but it may prove to have useful consequences. However, there are situations where a non-incremental reconstitution function is called for. For example, for some of the representations for relation sequences in Section 2, it might be that $reconst(P)$ only returns that part of the relation sequence for which it can construct complete relation states.

2. Note that if $reconst$ returns a sequence, $reconst(P)$ need not be a prefix of $reconst(P : i)$, even though P is a prefix of $P : i$. For example $reconst$ might sort according to some component A: $reconst(P) = sort_A(P)$.

3. The element type **T** of the stream need not be the element type in the domain of interpretation (though in the examples above they are the same). For example, Hammad et al. [HG04] have some stream items with "negative" flags that cancel previous normal items in the stream. Presumably, the reconstitution of such a stream would not contain any negative items.

4. If $reconst(P) = d$, we will sometimes write $const(d) = P$. We caution that this notation is informal, however. There may in fact be more than one P where $reconst(P) = d$, or no such P at all. That is, there can be values in the domain of interpretation **D** that are not the reconstitution of any stream.

5. The condition for a stream operator *sop* being the on-line analogue of an operation *dop* over the domain **D** is given by the commutative diagram in Figure 1. We note that the reconstitution function need not be constant throughout a query.

6. We see from the examples above that presentation order of items in a stream is sometimes significant for a reconstitution function (ins_r and ins_{rc}) and sometimes not (ins and ins_u). The question arises whether applications where stream order is not important show up in practice much. We think the more common case is that order does convey part of the semantics of a data stream, but that the other case does arise. Consider, for example, a stream of URLs arising from a web crawl. While some aspects of the crawl process, or posting times of pages, might influence the order of URLs in the stream, most applications will treat it as an unordered collection. There are also cases where there are some global aspects of order in a stream, but locally order is not significant. For example, consider the stream of network packets

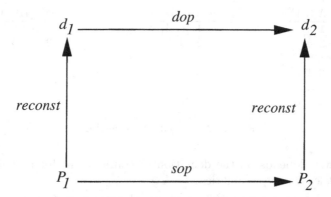

F ig.1. A stream operator as an on-line analogue of a domain operator

passing through a router. The denotation might be a collection of sessions under various protocols, where each session is a sequence of messages. However, the packets for a given message might not be in order, because of taking different routes or being retransmitted.

4   Monotonicity, Reconstitution and Non-blocking Operators

We are using reconstitution functions to study the connection between monotonicity of a domain operation and the existence of a non-blocking stream analogue, particularly for hierarchically structured data such as XML. Several papers [ST97, LWZ04] have singled out monotone relational operators (such as *select, join, dupelim*), as they are easy to carry over to stream counterparts. This connection relies on the common reconstitution functions for relational data, typically ins or ins_u. For a monotone relational operator rop, $r_1 \subseteq r_2 \implies rop(r_1) \subseteq rop(r_2)$. If $const(rop(r_1)) = U_1$ (that is, $ins(U_1) = rop(r_1)$), then we can find a sequence U_2 such that $const(rop(r_2)) = U_1 : U_2$. That is, the representation for $rop(r_1)$ is a prefix of the representation for $rop(r_2)$. Thus a stream analogue sop for rop can emit $const(rop(ins(P)))$ in response to prefix P of a stream, and know that $const(rop(ins(P : i)))$ will extend that response.

We note, however, that the definition of monotone depends on the definition of containment. The appropriate definition is fairly clear for relations (tuple subset), but there are alternatives when considering hierarchical data such as nested relations and XML. Consider the relational operation $nest_B$, which nests B-values of a relation based on equality of values on the remaining attributes. Consider relation r containing the first three tuples of Figure 2(a) (in bold type). Then $nest_B(r) = v$, where nested relation v is given in Figure 2(b). Let r^+ be the relation in Figure 2(a) with the fourth tuple included. Then $nest_B(r^+) = w$, for w in Figure 2(c). The question is now whether $nest_B$ is monotone. Specifically, is $v \subseteq w$?

r(A B)	v(A {B})	w (A {B})
1 c	1 {c, d}	1 {c, d}
2 e	2 {e}	2 {e, f}
1 d		
2 f		
(a)	(b)	(c)

F ig.2. Monotonicity of nesting

The answer depends on the definition of containment for nested relations. There are at least two possibilities:

1. Containment is simply tuple subset, in which case $v \not\subseteq w$, since $\langle 2, \{e\}\rangle$ is not in w. Hence $nest_B$ is not monotone.
2. Containment is subsumption. Thus $v \subseteq w$, because every tuple in v is subsumed by some tuple in w. In particular, $\langle 2, \{e\}\rangle$ is subsumed by $\langle 2, \{e, f\}\rangle$, and $nest_B$ is monotone.

Suppose we choose the second definition, where nest is monotone. Can we derive a non-blocking stream version of that operation? Doing so requires an appropriate choice of reconstitution function. Let us call the proposed stream operator *snest*, and consider how we want it to behave. We want $snest(P)$ to be a prefix of $snest(P : i)$, and, of course, $reconst(snest(P : i))$ should subsume $reconst(snest(P))$. If upon receiving $\langle 2, f\rangle$, *snest* emits $\langle 2, \{f\}\rangle$, then the simple *ins* reconstitution function will not give the desired relationships. However, if the reconstitution function performs a deep union [BDT99] with the cumulative result and combines $\langle 2, \{f\}\rangle$ with $\langle 2, \{e\}\rangle$ to form $\langle 2, \{e, f\}\rangle$, we will satisfy the conditions. Alternatively, *snest* could maintain state and emit $\langle 2, \{e, f\}\rangle$ upon receiving $\langle 2, f\rangle$. In that case, we need a "subsume-replace" reconstitution function that overwrites $\langle 2, \{e\}\rangle$ with $\langle 2, \{e, f\}\rangle$.

A particular case of interest to us is streams of XML. If a stream of XML elements simply denotes a sequence of independent documents, then not much new mechanism is needed beyond what is used for flat data items in a stream. On the other hand, we may want to view an XML stream as a series of fragments that constitute a single XML document. We have been working on a deep-union-like operator for XML we call *merge* [TM01]. The *merge* operator is logically performing a lattice-join of two XML documents in a subsumption lattice. One use we have for *merge* is a reconstitution-like structural aggregation operator called *accumulate*. The *accumulate* operator successively merges in XML fragments with a base document, called an *accumulator*, and makes the accumulator available to further query-processing steps. For example, in Figure 3(a) we have an accumulator for auction data that is grouping bids under their appropriate items. (This example is based on the XMark benchmark [XM03].) Figure 3(b) shows a new bid coming in as an XML element, and Figure 3(c) is the result of merging that element into the accumulator. The behavior of the merge operator is modulated by a *merge template*, which in essence indicates which lattice we are using to define the lattice-join. In the example of Figure 3, the merge template would indicate,

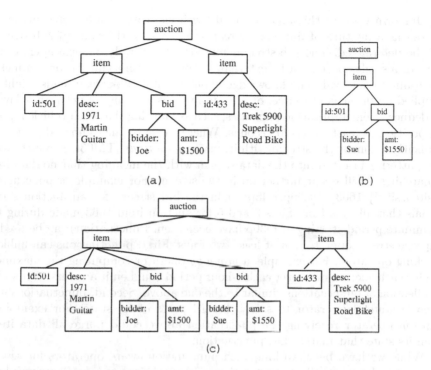

Fig.3. Illustration of the *merge* operator showing (a) initial accumulator, (b) a fragment to be merged, and (c) the resulting accumulator

for instance, that the merge process should combine corresponding `<item>` elements, but create new `<bid>`, `<bidder>`, and `<amt>` elements, as opposed, say, to creating a new element in the accumulator for each `<item>` element added.

5   Additional Stream Semantics

There may be information known about a stream in addition to its denotation and representation, related to its content or presentation order, that is useful for query processing. Some examples on content are whether or not the stream contains duplicates, and if some subset of attributes forms a key (that is, there are no duplicate values over these attributes). Another example, for a stream with a relation-sequence denotation, is whether there is a constant bound on the size of the relation states. For instance, if the stream contains position reports on a fleet of vehicles, and each relation state consists of the most recent report on each vehicle, then the size of any state is at most the number of vehicles n. Such information can be useful in determining whether a query has bounded state requirements or not [BB02]. Information on the physical presentation of streams is useful as well, such as if the stream is ordered on a particular attribute, or whether there is limited skew among the arrival times of items on different streams [BU04].

Our own work in this area has dealt with the case where a stream can be viewed as a mixture of finite sub-streams, and where the ends of sub-streams can be determined. The sub-streams may occur naturally, for example, all the bids for a single auction, or be externally imposed, such as all sensor readings in a ten-minute interval. The knowledge about when a sub-stream ends might be supplied by the stream source, or arise from measurements of network delay, or be deduced from application semantics, such as knowing that each vehicle reports its position at least every 20 seconds. Where we have such knowledge, we can explicitly augment the stream with it, via *punctuations* [TM03]. A punctuation is a pattern p inserted into the data stream with the meaning that no data item i matching p will occur further on in the stream. For example, a punctuation $\langle\{\text{site3}, \text{site5}\}, 1663, *, [6:30\text{p}, 6:45\text{p}], *\rangle$ in the bid stream for an auction server signals that all bids from Sites 3 and 5 for auction item 1663 made during the 15-minute period starting at 6:30p have been seen. Punctuations can be used to improve stream operators in at least two ways. First, punctuations can unblock blocking operators. For example, a *group-by* operator computing the maximum bid for each auction item over each 1-hour period could emit answers after seeing a collection of punctuations similar to the one above. Second, punctuations may allow a stateful operator to safely discard parts of its state. For example, a *dupelim* operator receiving the punctuation above could purge all data items from its state that match that punctuation.

While we have been working with punctuation-aware operators for several years now, there are still many questions and extensions to investigate. We have a good understanding of how single operators can exploit punctuation. However, we are less far along in understanding when particular punctuation helps a given query, or, a more challenging problem, starting from a query, determining what punctuation, if any, would benefit the query [TMS03].

Currently our punctuation marks the end of a sub-stream. We believe there may also be advantages to "forward-looking" punctuation that describes data that will appear further on in a stream. We are also starting to investigate the notion of a *deterministic stream*: a stream in which for any possible data item i, one is guaranteed to eventually see either i or a punctuation matching i. Another variation we are considering is where a bound is known on the amount of unpunctuated data (items at a given instant with no corresponding punctuation received). Reasoning with such information could lead to bounds on the amount of state a query needs. Finally, our current implementation of punctuation is for flat data, though the underlying query engine handles general XML [NDM]. Punctuation for XML data is still an open area.

6   Disorder in Streams

Disorder in data streams can arise from many sources, such as stream items being routed by different paths in a network, or combining streams that are out of synch. A stream may have multiple natural orders, such as start time and end time of a network flow, and cannot be sorted on both simultaneously. There are also algorithms for stream operators that produce disordered output, such as windowed multi-join [HF03]. In order to deal with disorder in stream query processing, it is useful to have some description of the expected or maximum disorder in a stream. There have been several proposals in this regard. Some describe disorder operationally, that is, in terms of what kind of operation will restore order. An example is the order specifications of Aurora [AC03], which say how much buffer space is needed to sort the stream (or partitioned sub-streams of it) on a particular attribute. Other disorder descriptions express the maximal displacement of any item from its correct position. The displacement is usually measured from a "high-water mark," and expressed either as a number of items or as a difference in the ordering attribute. For example, consider the stream of bid items in Figure 4, where we are considering order on bid time (the fourth column). We see that item i_4 is out of order. It is displaced by 2 items from its correct position (between items i_1 and i_2) and by 3 seconds based on the value of the *time* attribute. Examples of this maximum-displacement approach to describing disorder include *slack* in the early versions of the Aurora system [C02] and the *banded-increasing* property of the Gigascope project [CJ02]. The *k-ordering* [BU04] and *out-of-order generation* [SW04] constraints of the STREAM project are similar.

$$
\begin{array}{ll}
i_1 & \langle \text{site3}, 1663, \text{b420}, 3\text{:}15\text{:}32, \$11.50 \rangle \\
i_2 & \langle \text{site2}, 7287, \text{b812}, 3\text{:}15\text{:}35, \$8.00 \rangle \\
i_3 & \langle \text{site5}, 1663, \text{b173}, 3\text{:}15\text{:}36, \$12.50 \rangle \\
i_4 & \langle \text{site1}, 1601, \text{b662}, 3\text{:}15\text{:}33, \$65.00 \rangle \\
i_5 & \langle \text{site3}, 1663, \text{b420}, 3\text{:}15\text{:}38, \$13.00 \rangle \\
\end{array}
$$

. . .

Fig. 4. A disordered auction stream

While such disorder descriptions are useful, our own investigations have shown that they are somewhat limited in their expressive power. First, they assume that the disorder bound is constant across the stream. Figure 5 shows netflow records from a router in the Abilene Network Observatory [Abi], ordered by the sequence in which they were emitted, and showing the start time of each netflow. (A netflow record summarizes packet traffic between two $\langle \text{IP}, \text{port} \rangle$-pairs.) We have termed such a stream *block sorted*, and it is clear no items are displaced across block boundaries.

A second issue is that existing descriptions focus on the maximum disorder, rather than the average displacement or a distribution of displacements. Consider Figure 6, which shows the observation time of the 8th packet in a network flow, ordered by the start time of each flow, for a network trace gathered by the PMA project [PMA]. While one packet is significantly displaced (perhaps a retransmission), the rest occur in a close band of their desired position. We refer to such a sequence as *band disordered*. It would be useful to have some statistical characterization of such disorder, so, for example, one could estimate how the accuracy of a query is affected by a given cutoff on late items.

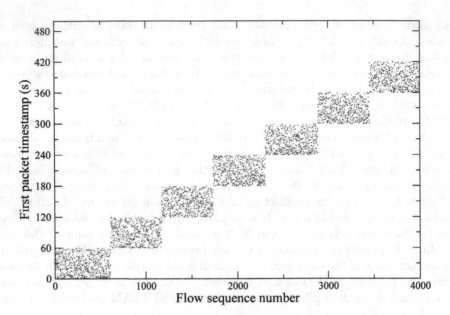

Fig.5. Block-sorted disorder

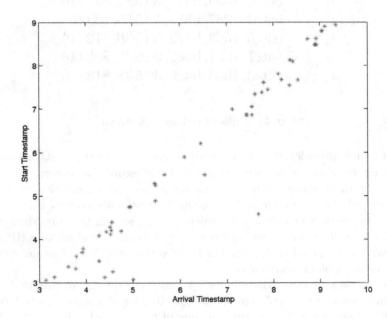

Fig.6. Band disorder

We note that any disorder descriptions of these kinds can be used to generate punctuations in a data stream, marking the end of particular subsets of data. For example, if a stream is known to be bound by a slack of 20 seconds, a *punctuate* operator can insert a punctuation of the form $\langle *, *, *, t - 20s, * \rangle$

when it sees an item with bid time t. (However, it likely would not insert a punctuation based on every item, but less frequently, based on the needs of the query.)

7   Windowed Operators

Another area where semantics of streams is still a bit fuzzy is windowed operators. One way to modify a blocking or stateful operator to work with data streams is to change it from considering the totality of a stream to instead operating over a series of finite subsets of the stream. (There are other ways to modify such an operator. For example, a blocking aggregate such as sum can be converted to report a "running sum" after each input item.) The most studied windowed operators are *group-by* (aggregation) [AW04, C04, SH98, AC03] and *join* [HF03, KNF03, HAK03, GO03].

Windowed operators predate their current use in data streams. A WINDOW construct over stored data appears in SQL 1999 [SQL99]. In fact, the CQL formulation for windows draws from the SQL counterpart [ABW03]. There has been a considerable range of proposals on how to define windowed operators, based, for example, on whether one end or both of the window moves (and in which direction), the size of the window (its *range*), how much and how often it moves (its *slide*), and where it is located relative to the current point in the stream (its *offset*). The range, slide and offset can be denominated in terms of a number of items, or a quantity or duration of some attribute. In the case that the window range is expressed by a number of items, and the operator partitions the stream (such as a group-by aggregation), there are variants where the range is applied to the whole stream or separately to each partition. The windowing attribute can be a sequence number, an internally assigned arrival timestamp, or a value supplied by the stream source.

We see some semantic problems, however. Most approaches to windows are described in terms of the physical presentation of the stream, rather than its denotation, often on an operator-by-operator basis [AC03]. Such operational definitions can lead to problems when the stream appears out of order with respect to the windowing attribute. We have been developing a formal approach to window specifications that is independent of physical stream order [LMP04]. In our approach, the various window extents that arise as a window slides over a stream are each given an explicit *window identifier* (*window id*), and an *extent* function defines the stream items that are associated with each window id. Our approach assumes that windows are always defined against an explicit attribute W, though in practice W might be a sequence number or timestamp supplied by the stream management system.

For illustration, consider window specifications having the form [RANGE r, SLIDE u], where r and u are quantities compatible with the domain of W. For example, if the domain of W is time, then a possible specification is [RANGE $30s$, SLIDE $10s$], which defines window extents of length 30 seconds, spaced every 10 seconds.

The functions that define window extents are expressed in terms of the collection I of items in input stream S. The window function gives the set of window ids for a particular specification. In our illustration,

$$windows(I, r, u) = \{0, 1, 2, \ldots\}.$$

Here the set of window ids does not depend in the stream contents, nor the range and slide parameters, but it may for other window types. The *extent* function determines the items associated with each window extent. In our illustration, for $w \in windows$,

$$extent(I, w, r, u) = \{i \in I \mid w \cdot u \leq i.W \leq w \cdot u + r\}.$$

(This definition is slightly simplified; in general, it must account for the boundary conditions at stream startup.)

We have found this approach quite expressive, being able to capture many flavors of windows mentioned in the literature: landmark, tumbling, slide-by-tuple, partitioned, etc. Moreover, it has led to a class of algorithms for windowed aggregates that often outperform approaches based on intra-operator buffering. Our approach requires an inverse, *wids*, for the *extent* function, giving the set of window ids of window extents that a given item appears in. In our running illustration,

$$wids(I, i, r, u) = \{w \mid \lceil i.W/u \rceil - 1 < w \leq \lceil (i.W + r)/u \rceil - 1\}.$$

(Again, this definition is simplified.) Our approach uses a *bucket* operator to extend each stream item with its associated window ids. The resulting output can then be fed to a *group-by* operator that treats the window id as just another grouping attribute. We rely on punctuation (also supplied by *bucket*) to keep the aggregation unblocked.

There are still several issues we are investigating with our window semantics. One is to classify window specifications in terms of properties of their *wids* functions. In the example above, *wids* is "context-free" in the sense that it can be applied by *bucket* to each stream item in isolation. Other window specifications, such as slide-by-tuple with a time-interval range require *bucket* to be stateful. A second area of investigation is the interaction of windowing with reconstitution. Suppose *wind* is a reconstitution function that interprets a stream as a sequence of window extents using an interval-based range and slide, and that we are interested in applying operations window-by-window to such a sequence (the usual situation). In some cases, the appropriate stream analogue is easy to come by. For example, with selection, we have

$$\sigma(wind(P)) = wind(\sigma(P)).$$

If we consider a window based on tuple count, in contrast, the equality no longer holds. Other operators are more challenging. With duplicate elimination

$$dupelim(wind(P)) \neq wind(dupelim(P))$$

even with an interval-based window. In fact, as far as we can determine, there is no function g such that

$$dupelim(wind(P)) = wind(g(P)).$$

The result of $dupelim(wind(P))$ must be a stream with a different reconstitution function, perhaps one with positive and negative tuples, or using explicit window ids.

8 Conclusions

We hope we have taken at least a small step towards answering the question *What do data streams mean?* There are still many gaps and rough edges here. While we think reconstitution functions are a useful device for capturing datastream semantics, it is not yet tested whether they can deal with the range of data streams seen in practice, or are helpful in proving properties of stream operators. Reconstitution functions help clarify for us the requirements for a non-blocking stream version of a monotone domain operator, and suggest approaches for reconstitution of streams of XML fragments. However, we would like to find ways to encode more general updates in an XML stream, such as deletions. Playing with punctuations has been fun, but the problems are getting harder, such as proving space bounds on stream queries. Having more expressive descriptions for stream disorder is just the starting point. The real challenge is to use them to manage tradeoffs between query latency, accuracy and space usage. Finally, the alert reader will have noted we have not yet integrated reconstitution functions with our semantics for windows. So do something about it.

Acknowledgements

This work was supported by NSF grant IIS 0086002. We thank Ted Johnson for his insights on sources of disorder, and the Abilene Observatory for access to network monitoring data.

References

[AC03]   D. Abadi, D. Carney, U. Cetintemel, M. Cherniack, C. Convey, S. Lee, M. Stonebraker, N. Tatbul, S. Zdonik. Aurora: a new model and architecture for data stream management. *VLDB Journal (12)2: 120-139, August 2003.*

[Abi]   The Abilene Observatory. http://abilene.internet2.edu/observatory.

[AA95]   S. Acharya, R. Alonso, M. Franklin, and S. Zdonik. Broadcast Disks: Data Management for Asymmetric Communication Environments. In *Proceedings of ACM SIGMOD International Conference on Management of Data (SIGMOD 95).* San Jose, CA, June 1995.

[ABW03]   A. Arasu, S. Babu and J. Widom. *The CQL Continuous Query Language: Semantic Foundations and Query Execution* Stanford University Technical Report, Oct. 2003

[AW04]   A. Arasu, J. Widom. Resource Sharing in Continuous Sliding-Window Ag-
          gregates. In *Proceedings of the 30th International Conference on Very Large
          Databases (VLDB 2004)*, Toronto, Canada, September 2004.

[AW04R]   A. Arasu, J. Widom. A Denotational Semantics for Continuous Queries over
          Streams and Relations. *SIGMOD Record* 33(3), September 2004.

[BB02]   B. Babcock, S. Babu, M. Datar, R. Motwani, and J. Widom. Models and
          Issues in Data Stream Systems. In *Proceedings of the 21st ACM Symposim
          on Principles of Database Systems (PODS 2002)*, Madison, Wisconsin, June
          2002

[BU04]   S. Babu, U. Srivastava, and J. Widom. Exploiting k-Constraints to Reduce
          Memory Overhead in Continuous Queries over Data Streams. *ACM Trans-
          actions on Database Systems*, 29(3):545-580, September 2004.

[BDT99]   P. Buneman, A. Deutsch, and W.C. Tan. A Deterministic Model for
          Semistructured Data. In *Proceedings of the Workshop on Query Process-
          ing for Semistructured Data and Non-Standard Data Formats*, Jerusalem,
          Israel, January 1999.

[C02]   Carney, D., *et al.* Monitoring Streams - A New Class of Data Management
          Applications. In *Proceedings of the 28th International Conference on Very
          Large Databases (VLDB 2002)*, Hong Kong, China, August 2002.

[C04]   Cormode, G., *et al.* Holistic UDAFs at streaming speeds. In *Proceedings of
          the 2004 ACM SIGMOD International Conference on the Management of
          Data (SIGMOD 2004)*, Paris, France, June 2004.

[CJ02]   C. Cranor, T. Johnson, O. Spatscheck. *How to Query Network Traffic Data
          Using Data Streams*, unpublished manuscript, 2002.

[GO03]   L. Golab, M. Tamer Özsu. Processing Sliding Window Multi-Joins in Con-
          tinuous Queries over Data Streams. In *Proceedings of the 29th Interna-
          tional Conference on Very Large Databases (VLDB 2003)*, Berlin, Germany,
          September 2003.

[SQL99]   P. Gulutzan and T. Pelzer. *SQL-99 Complete, Really*. CMP Books, 1999.
          ISBN: 0-87930-568-1

[HG04]   M. Hammad, T. Ghanem, W. Aref, A. Elmagarmid and M. Mokbel. Effi-
          cient Pipelined Execution of Sliding-Window Queries Over Data Streams.
          Purdue University Department of Computer Sciences Technical Report CSD
          TR#03-035, June 2004.

[HF03]   M. Hammad, M. Franklin, W. Aref, and A. Elmagarmid. Scheduling for
          shared window joins over data streams. In *Proceedings of the 29th Interna-
          tional Conference on Very Large Databases (VLDB 2003)*, Berlin, Germany,
          September 2003.

[HAK03]   M. Hammad, W. Aref, and A. Elmagarmid. Stream Window Join: Tracking
          Moving Objects in Sensor-Network Databases. In *Proceedings of the 15th
          International Conference on Scientific and Statistical Database Management
          (SSDBM 2003)* Cambridge, MA, July 2003.

[KNF03]   J. Kang, J. Naughton and J. Viglas. Evaluating Window Joins over Un-
          bounded Streams. In *Proceedings of the 19th International Conference on
          Data Engineering (ICDE 2003)*, Bangalore, India, March 2003.

[LWZ04]   Y. Law, H. Wang, C. Zaniolo. Query Languages and Data Models for
          Database Sequences and Data Streams. In *Proceedings of the 30th Interna-
          tional Conference on Very Large Databases (VLDB 2004)*, Toronto, Canada,
          September 2004.

[LMP04] J. Li, D. Maier, V. Papadimos, P. A. Tucker and K. Tufte. *Evaluating Window Aggregate Queries over Streams*. OGI Technical Report, available from http://www.cse.ogi.edu/~jinli/papers/WinAggrQ.pdf, May 2004.

[NDM]   J. Naughton, D. DeWitt, D. Maier. *et al.* The Niagara Internet Query System. http://www.cs.wisc.edu/niagara.

[PMA]   Passive Measurement and Analysis project. San Diego Supercomputer Center. http://pma.nlanr.net/PMA.

[ST97]   J. Shanmugasundaram, K. Tufte, D. DeWitt, J. Naughton, D. Maier, Archtecting a Network Query Engine for Producing Partial Results. *Lecture Notes in Computer Science, Vol. 1997/2001 The World Wide Web and Databases; Third International Workshop WebDB 2000, Dallas TX, May 2000, Selected Papers*, Springer-Verlag Publishers 2001.

[SW04]   U. Srivastava and J. Widom. Flexible Time Management in Data Stream Systems. In *Proceedings of the 2004 ACM Symposium on Principles of Database Systems (PODS 2004)*, Paris, France, June 2004.

[SH98]   M. Sullivan and A. Heybey. Tribeca: A system for managing large databases of network traffic. In *Proceedings of the USENIX Annul Technical Conference*, New Orleans, Louisiana, June 1998.

[TM03]   P. A. Tucker, D. Maier, T. Sheard and L. Fegaras. Exploiting Punctuation Semantics in Continuous Data Streams. *Transactions on Knowledge and Data Engineering*, 15(3):555-568, May, 2003

[TMS03] P. A. Tucker, D. Maier and T. Sheard. Applying Punctuation Schemes to Queries over Continuous Data Streams. *IEEE Data Engineering Bulletin*, 26(1):33 40, March, 2003

[TM01]   K. Tufte and D. Maier. Aggregation and Accumulation of XML Data. *IEEE Data Engineering Bulletin* 24(2):34-39, June 2001.

[XM03]   XMark Benchmark. http://www.xml-benchmark.org/

Conjunctive Query Evaluation by Search Tree Revisited

Albert Atserias[*]

Universitat Politècnica de Catalunya, Barcelona, Spain
atserias@lsi.upc.es

Abstract. The most natural and perhaps most frequently used method for testing membership of an individual tuple into a conjunctive query is based on search trees. We investigate the question of evaluating conjunctive queries with a time-bound guarantee that is measured as a function of the size of the minimal search tree. We provide an algorithm that, given a database D, a conjunctive query Q, and a tuple t, tests whether $Q(t)$ holds in D in time bounded by $(sn)^{O(\log k)}(sn)^{O(\log\log n)}$, where n is the size of the domain of the database, k is the number of bound variables of the conjunctive query, and s is the size of the optimal search tree. In many cases of interest, this bound is significantly smaller than the $n^{O(k)}$ bound provided by the naive search-tree method. Moreover, our algorithm has the advantage of guaranteeing the bound for any given conjunctive query. In particular, it guarantees the bound for queries that admit an equivalent form that is much easier to evaluate, even when finding such a form is an NP-hard task. Concrete examples include the conjunctive queries that can be non-trivially folded into a conjunctive query of bounded size or bounded treewidth. All our results translate to the context of constraint-satisfaction problems via the well-publicized correspondence between both frameworks.

1   Introduction and Summary of Results

The foundational work of Chandra and Merlin [CM77] identified the class of conjunctive queries in relational database systems as an important and fundamental class of queries that are repeatedly "asked in practice". These are the queries of first-order logic that are built from atomic formulas by means of conjunctions and existential quantification only. Thus, the generic conjunctive query takes the form

$$(\exists x_1)\cdots(\exists x_k)(R_1 \wedge \ldots \wedge R_q)$$

where $R_1, \ldots, R_q$ are atomic formulas built from the relations of the database with the variables $x_1, \ldots, x_k$. Alternatively, it is known that the class of conjunctive queries coincides with the class of queries of the relational algebra that use selection, projection, and join only. Conjunctive queries may also have free

---

[*] Partially supported by CICYT TIC2001-1577-C03-02.

T. Eiter and L. Libkin (Eds.): ICDT 2005, LNCS 3363, pp. 53–67, 2005.

variables, but for the sake of simplicity we will focus on Boolean conjunctive queries in this introduction.

Evaluating conjunctive queries is such a common task that it is no surprise that a huge amount of work has focused on its algorithmic and complexity-theoretic aspects. The most obvious algorithm is perhaps the one that exhaustively checks for the existence of an assignment of values to the variables in such a way that all relations in the body of the query (the quantifier-free part) are satisfied. Obviously, if the domain of the database has cardinality n, this algorithm takes time roughly n^k, which is exponential in the number of variables of the query. But, can we do better?

Unfortunately, unless P = NP, we cannot expect an algorithm that is polynomial in both n and k since the problem is NP-complete. This was already noticed by Chandra and Merlin [CM77]. To make things worse, more recent work on the parameterized complexity of query languages by Papadimitriou and Yannakakis [PY99] indicates that the situation might be even more dramatic. Namely, we cannot even expect an algorithm that, while arbitrarily complex in k, remains polynomial in n. Thus, we cannot expect an algorithm of complexity $2^{2^k} n^2$, say, unless certain widely believed assumptions in complexity theory are violated. These theoretical results indicate that the algorithmic problem is just too hard to be addressed in its wider generality.

Luckily, the situation in real database applications is not as catastrophic. Conjunctive queries that are asked in practice usually have some structure that makes them more tractable. The paradigmatical example is the class of *acyclic* conjunctive queries identified by Yannakakis [Yan81]. These are the conjunctive queries whose underlying hypergraph is acyclic, that is, the hypergraph that has the variables of the query as vertices, and the tuples of the variables appearing in the atomic formulas as hyperedges, is acyclic. Yannakakis showed that such queries could be evaluated in polynomial time by an efficient dynamic programming technique. The exact complexity of acyclic conjunctive queries was later studied in [GLS98], and generalized in several other directions [CR97, KV00]. The most interesting generalization is perhaps the one based on treewidth, to which we will get back later.

1.1   Search Trees and Backtracking Algorithms

Let us return now to the most obvious algorithm that checks for all possible assignments of values to the variables. Clearly, this algorithm can be modestly improved by a backtracking algorithm that considers the variables one-at-a-time and backtracks whenever the current partial assignment forces the body of the query to be either false because some atomic formula is falsified, or true because all atomic formulas are satisfied. Such a search-based pruning algorithm can be remarkably fast in certain cases, especially if a good heuristic is used for choosing the next splitting variable. As a matter of fact, backtracking is probably the most frequently used method for solving constraint satisfaction problems, which is essentially the same problem as conjunctive query evaluation as noticed by Kolaitis and Vardi [KV00], and is well-known by now.

This leads immediately to the concept of search tree which is a key concept in our paper. A search tree is an n-ary tree that is produced by such a backtracking procedure for an arbitrary choice of variables at each branch. Here, n is the cardinality of the domain of the database. Notice that search trees provide an enumeration of all possible solutions for the bound variables of the query since we backtrack even when the body of the query is satisfied. This permits us capturing the notion of optimal search-space through the concept of *minimal search tree*. Intuitively, the size of the minimal search tree for a given instance provides an ideal benchmark against which all search-based algorithms should be compared. For example, a backtracking algorithm that spends time $O(n^k)$ on an instance admitting a search tree of size $O(kn)$ should be considered inefficient: it spends much more time than what is, in principle, necessary. Clearly, we would prefer an algorithm whose running time is bounded by a modest function of the size of the minimal search tree. The ideal case would be an algorithm that is polynomial in that quantity.

The idea of comparing the efficiency of an algorithm with the size of the minimal search tree originates in the field of propositional proof complexity, and, as far as we know, was not considered before in the fields of database theory and constraint-satisfaction problems. In proof complexity, the efficiency of a proof-search algorithm on a given propositional tautology is compared with respect to the size of its minimal proof in the proof system. A proof system admitting a proof-search algorithm that runs polynomially in the minimal proof is called *automatizable* [BPR00]. The connection shows up when the proof system under consideration is tree resolution and the instance is an unsatisfiable propositional formula F in conjunctive normal form. In that case, a minimal proof becomes a minimal search tree for the constraint-satisfaction instance given by F, by simply turning it upside down (see also [BKPS02]).

1.2   Results of This Paper

The main contribution of this paper is the observation that the concepts and techniques that were developed for automatizability of tree resolution carry over, to some extent, to the more general case of conjunctive query evaluation and constraint-satisfaction problems. By adapting an algorithm that was developed for tree resolution, we exhibit an algorithm for conjunctive query evaluation whose complexity is bounded by a non-trivial function of the size of the minimal search tree.

More concretely, we provide an algorithm that, given a database $\mathbf{A}$ of cardinality n, a tuple $\mathbf{a}$ of $\mathbf{A}$, and a conjunctive query Q with k bound variables, determines whether the Boolean conjunctive query $Q(\mathbf{a})$ holds in $\mathbf{A}$ in time that is polynomial in $(sn)^{\log k}(sn)^{\log \log n}$, where s is the size of the minimal search tree for testing whether $Q(\mathbf{a})$ holds in $\mathbf{A}$. While we do not achieve the desired polynomial bound on s, we note that the running time of our algorithm is remarkably good, compared to the obvious n^k bound, when the minimal search tree is small.

Then we go on to analyze our algorithm. We first consider the class of conjunctive queries whose underlying graph is a tree, or is similar to a tree in the sense of having small treewidth. We note that if $Q(\mathbf{a})$ has treewidth w and does not hold on $\mathbf{A}$, then the size of the minimal search tree is bounded by $n^{(w+1)\log k}$. Surprisingly perhaps, the hypothesis that $Q(\mathbf{a})$ does not hold on $\mathbf{A}$ seems essential for our proof. Nonetheless, this does not prevent us from showing that our algorithm works correctly for *any* query of bounded treewidth in time $n^{O((\log k)^2)} n^{\log \log n}$. Indeed, if the algorithm does not stop within the prescribed time bound, then we know that $Q(\mathbf{a})$ holds in $\mathbf{A}$, although the algorithm gives no clue why.

It follows from this discussion that for queries of known treewidth w, our algorithm can be used for deciding whether $Q(\mathbf{a})$ holds in $\mathbf{A}$ within a time-bound that is far better than the worst case n^k, when k is large. Obviously, our bound is also far worse than the $O(|Q|n^w)$ bound of the known ad-hoc algorithms for evaluating queries of treewidth w [GLS98, KV00]. It is quite interesting, nonetheless, that our algorithm achieves a non-trivial bound in that case despite it is not specialized for that purpose. As a matter of fact, our algorithm does not even compute a tree-decomposition of the query!

Another remarkable consequence is the following. In their seminal paper [CM77], Chandra and Merlin showed that for every conjunctive query there is a minimal equivalent query, unique up to isomorphism, that can be obtained from the original one by identifying variables and deleting atomic formulas (see Theorem 12 and the discussion preceding it in [CM77]). In turn, Chandra and Merlin showed that finding such a minimal equivalent query is NP-hard. More recently, Dalmau, Kolaitis, and Vardi [DKV02] noticed that the problem remains NP-hard even when the minimal equivalent query is of constant size (and in particular has bounded treewidth). Thus, on the one hand, queries whose minimal equivalent query has bounded size admit search trees of size $n^{O(1)}$ on databases on which they fail. The reason for this is that the minimal equivalent query is a subquery, so a search tree for the minimal query is also a search tree for the query itself, when the query evaluates to false. On the other hand, there is no efficient way of finding such a minimal equivalent query since the problem is NP-hard. Hence, it is perhaps surprising that, on those instances, our algorithm achieves complexity $n^{O(\log k)}$ without ever worrying about minimal equivalent queries at all.

Finally, we also provide some lower bounds on the size the minimal search trees for certain conjunctive queries of interest. First, it is relatively easy to show that the minimal search trees for the conjunctive query expressing the existence of a k-clique on graphs of size n may require n^{k-3} nodes. Second, it requires a slightly more contrived argument showing that the minimal search trees for the conjunctive query expressing the existence of a path of length k on graphs of size n may require $n^{\log k - 3}$ nodes. This result shows that the $n^{(w+1)\log k}$ upper bound for queries of treewidth w is essentially optimal. This is because the path-of-length-k query has treewidth 1. Quite remarkably, our algorithm behaves in time polynomial in $n^{(\log k)^2}$ on such queries, which is nearly optimal with respect to search-tree size.

2   Preliminaries and Definitions

Databases, structures, and conjunctive queries We view databases as finite structures over finite relational vocabularies with constants. A relational vocabulary with constants σ is a set of relation symbols, each of a specified positive arity, and a set of constant symbols. A σ-structure, or database, consists of a domain A, a relation $R^{\mathbf{A}} \subseteq A^r$ for each relation symbol R in σ of arity r, and an individual $c^{\mathbf{A}} \in A$ for each constant symbol c in σ. Structures are denoted by $\mathbf{A} = (A, R_1^{\mathbf{A}}, \ldots, R_t^{\mathbf{A}}, c_1^{\mathbf{A}}, \ldots, c_d^{\mathbf{A}})$, where $R_1, \ldots, R_t$ are the relation symbols of σ, and $c_1, \ldots, c_d$ are the constant symbols of σ.

Atomic formulas are formulas of the form $R(x_1, \ldots, x_r)$ where R is a relation symbol of arity r, and $x_1, \ldots, x_r$ are first-order variables or constants. A conjunctive query is a formula of the form $(\exists z_1) \ldots (\exists z_k)\psi$, where $z_1, \ldots, z_k$ are first-order variables, and ψ is a conjunction of atomic formulas. The quantifier-free part ψ is called the body. The variables $z_1, \ldots, z_l$ are called bound variables. The rest of variables of ψ are called free variables. The total size of a conjunctive query is the number of atomic formulas in ψ. Let Q be an atomic formula with free variables $x_1, \ldots, x_l$. If $\mathbf{A}$ is a σ-structure and $\mathbf{a} = (a_1, \ldots, a_l)$ is a tuple of $\mathbf{A}$, we write $\mathbf{A} \models Q(\mathbf{a})$ if viewing x_i as a constant interpreted by a_i satisfies Q in $\mathbf{A}$ in the standard sense of first-order logic.

Treewidth. Let $\mathbf{G} = (V, E)$ be a finite graph. A tree-decomposition of $\mathbf{G}$ is a pair $(\{X_i : i \in I\}, T = (I, F))$ with $\{X_i : i \in I\}$ a family of subsets of V, one for each node of T, and T is a tree such that:

1. $\bigcup_{i \in I} X_i = V$
2. for all edges $(v, w) \in E$, there exists an $i \in I$ with $\{v, w\} \subseteq X_i$
3. for all $i, j, k \in I$: if j is on the path from i to k in T, then $X_i \cap X_k \subseteq X_j$.

The width of a tree-decomposition is $\max_{i \in I} |X_i| - 1$. The treewidth of $\mathbf{G}$ is the minimum width over all possible tree-decompositions of $\mathbf{G}$.

The treewidth of a σ-structure $\mathbf{A}$ is the treewidth of its Gaifman graph, that is, the graph whose set of vertices is A, and whose edges relate each pair of vertices that appear together in some tuple of the relations of $\mathbf{A}$. The Gaifman graph of a conjunctive query Q is the graph whose set of vertices is the set of variables of Q, and whose edges relate every pair of variables that appear together in an atomic formula (note that constants are ignored here). The treewidth of a conjunctive query is the treewidth of its Gaifman graph.

Search Trees. Let $\mathbf{A}$ be a finite σ-structure with universe $A = \{a_1, \ldots, a_n\}$. Let $f : V \to A$ be a partial mapping of the first-order variables to the universe A of $\mathbf{A}$. Extend f to the constant symbols of σ in the natural way. Let $R(x_1, \ldots, x_k)$ be an atomic formula. If $x_i \in \mathrm{Dom}(f)$ for every $i \in \{1, \ldots, k\}$, we say that f decides R. If f decides R and $(f(x_1), \ldots, f(x_k)) \in R^{\mathbf{A}}$, we say that f satisfies R. If f decides R and $(f(x_1), \ldots, f(x_k)) \notin R^{\mathbf{A}}$, we say that f falsifies R. Let $\psi(x_1, \ldots, x_k)$ be a conjunction of atomic formulas. We say that f satisfies ψ if it satisfies every atomic formula in ψ. We say that f falsifies ψ if it falsifies some atomic formula in ψ. In those cases we say that f decides ψ. Otherwise, we say that f does not decide ψ.

A search tree for $\psi(x_1, \ldots, x_k)$ in $\mathbf{A}$ is a labeled rooted tree (T, L) whose nodes are labeled by partial assignments $f : V \to A$, and for which the following conditions are satisfied:

1. If v is the root of T, then $L(v)$ is the empty partial assignment $\emptyset$.
2. If v is an internal node of T, then $L(v)$ does not decide ψ.
3. If v is a leaf of T, then $L(v)$ decides ψ.
4. If v is an internal node of T and $L(v) = f$, then there exists an $x \notin \text{Dom}(f)$ such that v has exactly n successors $v_1, \ldots, v_n$ such that $L(v_j) = f \cup \{(x, a_j)\}$ for every $j \in \{1, \ldots, n\}$.

The variable x that is guaranteed to exist in clause 4 will be denoted by $x(v)$. We say that $x(v)$ is the splitting variable at node v. Notice that there may be several search trees for a given conjunction of atomic formulas and a given finite structure. A search tree for ψ in $\mathbf{A}$ is minimal if every other search tree for ψ in $\mathbf{A}$ is at least as large in size. For a finite σ-structure $\mathbf{A}$, a tuple $\mathbf{a}$ of $\mathbf{A}$, and a conjunctive query Q, a search tree for testing whether $\mathbf{A} \models Q(\mathbf{a})$ is a search tree for the body of $Q(\mathbf{a})$.

3   Booleanization and Algorithm

The purpose of this section is to develop the algorithm that achieves the promised performance. Let us start by announcing the result:

Theorem 1. *Let σ be a relational vocabulary of maximum arity r and cardinality t. There exists a deterministic algorithm that, given a finite σ-structure $\mathbf{A}$ of cardinality n, a conjunctive query Q with k bound variables and total size q, and a tuple $\mathbf{a}$ from $\mathbf{A}$, determines whether $\mathbf{A} \models Q(\mathbf{a})$ in time polynomial in q, t, n^r, k, and $(sn)^{\log k}(sn)^{\log \log n}$, where s is the size of a smallest search tree for testing whether $\mathbf{A} \models Q(\mathbf{a})$.*

The proof of this theorem requires some preparation. The first thing we do is a *Booleanization* of the problem that will simplify the design and the analysis of the algorithm. Let $A = \{a_1, \ldots, a_n\}$ be the universe of $\mathbf{A}$. Each element of the universe $a_i \in A$ can be encoded by a string of $\log n$ bits. In turn, by using this encoding, each relation on A of arity r can be identified with a relation on the Boolean domain $\{0, 1\}$ of arity $r \log n$ in the most obvious way. For a finite σ-structure $\mathbf{A}$, let $\mathbf{A}^{(n)}$ denote its Booleanization; that is, the universe of $\mathbf{A}^{(n)}$ is $\{0, 1\}$, and each relation of $\mathbf{A}$ of arity r is encoded in the obvious way into a relation of $\mathbf{A}^{(n)}$ of arity $r \log n$. For an r-tuple $\mathbf{a}$, let $\mathbf{a}^{(n)}$ be the $r \log n$-tuple encoding $\mathbf{a}$ over $\{0, 1\}$.

The Booleanization can also be carried out over a conjunctive query. If Q is a conjunctive query with k bound variables, its Booleanization $Q^{(n)}$ is the conjunctive query with $k \log n$ bound variables that results from using $\log n$ new variables for each original variable in Q, and replacing the atomic formulas by their Booleanization. The following Lemma is obvious.

Lemma 1. *Let* $\mathbf{A}$ *be a finite* σ*-structure of cardinality* n, *let* $\mathbf{a}$ *be a tuple of* $\mathbf{A}$, *and let* Q *be a conjunctive query. Then* $\mathbf{A} \models Q(\mathbf{a})$ *if and only if* $\mathbf{A}^{(n)} \models Q^{(n)}(\mathbf{a}^{(n)})$. *Moreover, if there exists a search tree for testing whether* $\mathbf{A} \models Q(\mathbf{a})$ *of size* s, *then there exists a search tree for testing whether* $\mathbf{A}^{(n)} \models Q^{(n)}(\mathbf{a}^{(n)})$ *of size* $2sn$.

Proof: Take the search tree for $\mathbf{A} \models Q(\mathbf{a})$ and replace each internal node by a complete binary tree of height $\log n$. This blows up the tree by a factor of at most $2n$. $\square$

The Booleanization allows us focus on the Boolean case, which is nothing else but a generalized satisfiability problem. Now we can apply the techniques that were developed for propositional logic and tree resolution [BP96, BKPS02].

Let $\mathbf{A}$ be a Boolean σ-structure, that is, a σ-structure with Boolean domain $A = \{0, 1\}$. Let $\mathbf{a}$ be a tuple of $\mathbf{A}$, and let Q be a conjunctive query. The algorithm takes a partial assignment $f : V \to A$ as parameter and performs as follows: First, the algorithm checks whether f decides the body of $Q(\mathbf{a})$, in which case it returns the leaf-tree that consists of a single node labeled by f. Otherwise, for every variable $x \notin \text{Dom}(f)$ and every value $a \in \{0, 1\}$, the algorithm calls recursively itself on input $f \cup \{(x, a)\}$. These recursive calls are run in parallel, either by executing one step from each in parallel rounds, or by applying a doubling technique that executes 2^i steps of each call, sequentially, for increasing values of i. As soon as one of the recursive calls terminates, say, the one with input $f \cup \{(x, a)\}$, the rest of calls are aborted except for $f \cup \{(x, 1 - a)\}$ which is run to completion. Let T_a and T_{1-a} be the search trees returned by the only two recursive calls that are run to completion. The output is the search tree (f, T_0, T_1); that is, the search tree whose root is labeled by f, whose left subtree is T_0, and whose right subtree is T_1.

Lemma 2. *Let* σ *be a relational vocabulary of maximum arity* r *and cardinality* t. *Let* $\mathbf{A}$ *be a Boolean* σ*-structure, let* $\mathbf{a}$ *be a tuple of* $\mathbf{A}$, *and let* Q *be a conjunctive query with* k *bound variables and total size* q. *The algorithm, when run with parameter* $f = \emptyset$, *returns a search tree testing whether* $\mathbf{A} \models Q(\mathbf{a})$. *Moreover, if there exists such a search tree of size* s, *then the algorithm runs in time polynomial in* q, t, 2^r, k *and* $s^{\log k}$.

Proof: The correctness of the algorithm is easily proved by induction on k. For the running time we proceed as follows. Let ψ be the body of Q. Let $T(i, s)$ be the minimum upper bound to the running time of the algorithm for every f such that $|\text{Dom}(f)| \geq k - i$ and the smallest search tree for $\psi[\mathbf{a}, f]$ has size at most s. When $i = 0$, the running time of the algorithm is bounded by some value c that depends on σ and Q only. More precisely, we can take c to be linear in $qt2^r$. Consider now the case $i > 0$. Consider a smallest search tree of size at most s. If $s \leq 1$, the running time is again bounded by c, since necessarily, $\emptyset$ decides $\psi[\mathbf{a}, f]$. If $s \geq 2$, one of its two subtrees has size at most $s/2$. It follows that at least one of the $2i$ recursive calls terminates after at most $T(i - 1, s/2)$ steps. Each parallel round takes di steps to execute for some constant d. The other recursive call that is left will take at most $T(i-1, s)$ steps to complete. All in all, the running time of the algorithm is bounded by

$$T(i, s) \le c + diT(i-1, s/2) + T(i-1, s),$$

if $i \ge 1$ and $s \ge 2$, and $T(i, s) \le c$ if either $i = 0$ or $s \le 1$. For solving this recurrence we expand the last term repeatedly, until we reach $T(0, s) \le c$, and obtain

$$T(i, s) \le c(i+1) + d \sum_{j=1}^{i} jT(j-1, s/2).$$

Now we use the fact that $T(j, s/2) \le T(j+1, s/2)$ which follows directly from the definition of T, and obtain

$$T(i, s) \le c(i+1) + di^2 T(i, s/2).$$

Solving this recurrence of a single variable s is now a routine task. The solution satisfying equality is

$$c \left[(i+1) \frac{(di^2)^{\log s+1} - 1}{di^2 - 1} + (di^2)^{\log s} \right].$$

Noting that $(di^2)^{\log s} = s^{2 \log i + \log d}$ and recalling that c is linear in $qt2^r$, we see that the running time $T(k, s)$ is bounded by a polynomial in q, t, 2^r, k and $s^{\log k}$. ⌐

With this Lemma in hand we are ready to prove Theorem 1.

Proof of Theorem 1: It suffices to Booleanize σ, **A**, Q and **a**, and run the algorithm that we just described for the Boolean case. By Lemma 1, if $\mathbf{A} \models Q(\mathbf{a})$ has a search tree of size s, then $\mathbf{A}^{(n)} \models Q^{(n)}(\mathbf{a}^{(n)})$ has a search tree of size $2sn$. On the other hand, the number of bound variables of $Q^{(n)}$ becomes $k \log n$, and the maximum arity of the Booleanization of σ becomes $r \log n$. The result follows by plugging these values into the bounds of Lemma 2. □

Let us note that, the way we described it, the algorithm does not produce a search tree for $\mathbf{A} \models Q(\mathbf{a})$. This is because it is not necessarily possible to convert a search tree for $\mathbf{A}^{(n)} \models Q^{(n)}(\mathbf{a}^{(n)})$, which is what the algorithm gives, into a search tree for $\mathbf{A} \models Q(\mathbf{a})$, while preserving the bounds. Let us note, however, that a search tree for $\mathbf{A}^{(n)} \models Q^{(n)}(\mathbf{a}^{(n)})$ gives all the essential information. We do not know whether it is possible to have an algorithm with similar performance that avoids the Booleanization and produces a search tree for $\mathbf{A} \models Q(\mathbf{a})$.

4   Search Trees for Queries of Bounded Treewidth

The aim of this section is to investigate the size of search trees for conjunctive queries whose underlying graph is a tree or is similar to a tree in the sense of having small treewidth. The key to the argument is that graphs of treewidth w have separators of size $w + 1$.

Definition 1. *A p-separator of a graph $\mathbf{G} = (V, E)$ is a set $U \subseteq V$ such that each connected component of $\mathbf{G} - U$ contains at most p vertices.*

The following fact is known about the relationship between treewidth and separator size (see [Bod98, Theorem 19]).

Lemma 3. *Let $\mathbf{G}$ be a graph of cardinality n. If the treewidth of $\mathbf{G}$ is at most w, then $\mathbf{G}$ has a $\frac{1}{2}(n - w)$-separator of size at most $w + 1$.*

We use this fact in the proof of the following Theorem. The proof of this result makes use of an idea that Moshe Vardi shared with the author.

Theorem 2. *Let σ be a relational vocabulary of maximum arity r and cardinality t. Let $\mathbf{A}$ be a finite σ-structure of cardinality n, let $\mathbf{a}$ be a tuple of $\mathbf{A}$, and let Q be a conjunctive query with k bound variables. If $Q(\mathbf{a})$ has treewidth at most w and $\mathbf{A} \not\models Q(\mathbf{a})$, then there exists a search tree for testing whether $\mathbf{A} \models Q(\mathbf{a})$ of size $n^{(w+1)\log k}$.*

Proof: We proceed by induction on k. If $k = 0$ then the claim is obvious because the search tree has size 1 (we convey here that $\log 0 = 0$). Consider the case $k > 0$. Assume that $Q(\mathbf{a})$ has treewidth at most w and $\mathbf{A} \not\models Q(\mathbf{a})$. Let $\mathbf{G}$ be the Gaifman graph of $Q(\mathbf{a})$. Since $\mathbf{G}$ has treewidth at most w, it has a $\frac{1}{2}(k - w)$-separator $S = \{z_1, \ldots, z_l\}$ of size at most $w + 1$. Let $Q'(z_1, \ldots, z_l)$ be the conjunctive query that results from $Q(\mathbf{a})$ when the variables in S are left free. Since S is a $\frac{1}{2}(k - w)$-separator of $\mathbf{G}$, we may assume that $Q'(z_1, \ldots, z_l)$ is the conjunction of several conjunctive queries $Q'_1(z_1, \ldots, z_l), \ldots, Q'_d(z_1, \ldots, z_l)$ with at most $\frac{1}{2}(k - w)$ bound variables each. Since $\mathbf{A} \not\models Q(\mathbf{a})$, we have $\mathbf{A} \not\models Q'(f(z_1), \ldots, f(z_l))$ for every partial assignment f for which $\mathrm{Dom}(f) = S$. In turn, necessarily $\mathbf{A} \not\models Q'_i(f(z_1), \ldots, f(z_l))$ for some $i \in \{1, \ldots, d\}$. Let $i(f) \in \{1, \ldots, d\}$ be such that $\mathbf{A} \not\models Q'_{i(f)}(f(z_1), \ldots, f(z_l))$. Notice that the number of bound variables of $Q'_{i(f)}$ is less than $\frac{1}{2}k < k$. We apply the induction hypothesis and obtain a search tree for testing whether $\mathbf{A} \models Q'_{i(f)}(f(z_1), \ldots, f(z_l))$ of size $n^{(w+1)\log(k/2)}$. The search tree for $\mathbf{A} \models Q(\mathbf{a})$ can now be built by first querying the $l \leq w + 1$ variables in the separator S, in sequence, and then, for each partial assignment f at the leaves of this partial search tree, plugging in the search tree for testing whether $\mathbf{A} \models Q'_{i(f)}(f(z_1), \ldots, f(z_l))$ that is given by the induction hypothesis. The size of the resulting tree is bounded by

$$n^{w+1} \cdot n^{(w+1)\log(k/2)} \leq n^{(w+1)\log k}$$

as was to be shown. □

In Section 5 we will show that the bound provided by Theorem 2 is essentially optimal even when the underlying graph of the query is a very simple tree. It is important to notice the extra hypothesis $\mathbf{A} \not\models Q(\mathbf{a})$ in Theorem 2. As a matter of fact, we do not know whether the hypothesis is necessary. In other words, we do not know if conjunctive queries of bounded treewidth always have search trees of size $n^{O(\log k)}$.

There is one important consequence of Theorem 2 that is worth noticing. Fix a relational vocabulary σ of maximum arity r and cardinality t. Suppose we run the algorithm of Section 3 on a σ-structure $\mathbf{A}$ of cardinality n and a query $Q(\mathbf{a})$ with k bound variables, total size q, and treewidth at most w. Let $s = n^{(w+1)\log k}$. By Theorem 1 and Theorem 2, we know that if $\mathbf{A} \not\models Q(\mathbf{a})$, then the algorithm finishes in a number of steps that is a fixed polynomial of q, t, n^r, k, and $(sn)^{\log k}(sn)^{\log\log n}$, and reports so. Consequently, if the algorithm does not succeed in finishing within that number of steps, we can conclude that $\mathbf{A} \models Q(\mathbf{a})$, although we get no clue why.

It follows from this discussion that for queries of known treewidth, our algorithm can be used for deciding whether $\mathbf{A} \models Q(\mathbf{a})$ within a time-bound that is far better than the worst case n^k, when k is large. Obviously, our bound is also far worse than the $O(qn^w)$ bound of the known ad-hoc algorithms for evaluating queries of bounded treewidth [GLS98, KV00]. As discussed in the introduction, this is interesting because our algorithm is not special purpose for bounded treewidth queries.

5   Bounds on Search-Tree Size

In this section we prove lower bounds for the minimal search trees for particular queries of interest. The first lower bound is relatively easy, but we include the proof as a warm-up for the second, which is more difficult. The second lower bound shows that the $n^{(w+1)\log k}$ bound for queries of treewidth w in Theorem 2 is essentially optimal.

5.1   Lower Bound for the General Case

Consider the vocabulary of graphs $\sigma = \{E\}$, where E is a binary relation symbol. For $k \geq 2$, let CLIQUE_k be the conjunctive query expressing the existence of a k-clique. More specifically, CLIQUE_k is the following conjunctive query:

$$(\exists x_1)\cdots(\exists x_k)\left(\bigwedge_{i\neq j} E(x_i, x_j)\right).$$

We aim for a family of graphs $\mathbf{H}_n$ for which the size of the minimal search trees for testing whether $\mathbf{H}_n \models \text{CLIQUE}_k$ is nearly as large as it can be.

The graph $\mathbf{H}_n$ that we need is the complete $(k-1)$-partite graph with all color-classes of cardinality n. More precisely, the set of vertices of $\mathbf{H}_n$ is

$$V_n = \{(i, u) : 1 \leq i \leq k-1, 1 \leq u \leq n\},$$

and the set of edges of $\mathbf{H}_n$ is

$$E_n = \{((i, u), (j, v)) : 1 \leq i, j \leq k-1, 1 \leq u, v \leq n, i \neq j\}.$$

Each set of vertices of the form $\{(i, u) : 1 \leq u \leq n\}$ is called a color-class. Clearly, $\mathbf{H}_n$ does not contain any k-clique, so the query CLIQUE_k does not hold on $\mathbf{H}_n$. Note that $\mathbf{H}_n$ has kn vertices in total, and CLIQUE_k has k bound variables. Hence, the obvious upper bound for any search tree is $(kn)^k$. We see next that when n is much bigger than k, then this is essentially the best one can do. The proof is quite simple but we give it as it will serve as a warm-up for a more difficult proof in the next section.

Theorem 3. *Every search tree for testing whether* $\mathbf{H}_n \models CLIQUE_k$ *has at least* n^{k-3} *nodes.*

Proof: The idea of the proof is to describe an adversary argument that, given a purported search tree of size less than n^{k-3}, finds a leaf that is labeled by a partial assignment that does not decide the body of CLIQUE_k. Since this contradicts the definition of search tree, no such search tree can exist.

Suppose that (T, L) is a search tree testing whether $\mathbf{H}_n \models \text{CLIQUE}_k$. We construct a path $q_0, q_1, \ldots$ through T, starting at the root, with the following properties:

1. $L(q_j)$ does not decide the body of CLIQUE_k.
2. The subtree rooted at q_j has size less than n^{k-3-j}.

The idea behind the construction is to set $x(q_j)$ to a node of a different color-class; for example, we hope to set $x(q_j)$ to a node in color-class $j + 1$. Let q_0 be the root of T. Suppose next that $q_0, \ldots, q_j$ have already been defined, and that q_j is not a leaf. We claim that among the n vertices in color-class $j + 1$, there must exist at least one, say $(j + 1, u)$, for which the subtree rooted of q_j labeled by $L(q_j) \cup \{(x(q_j), (j + 1, u))\}$ has size less than $n^{k-3-j-1}$. Indeed this is the case since otherwise the size of the subtree rooted at q_j would be at least $n \cdot n^{k-3-j-1} = n^{k-3-j}$ which contradicts the inductive construction. Let q_{j+1} be any of these successors.

Notice that after a certain number of steps m no larger than $k - 3$, we will reach a leaf q_m because the size of the subtree will become less than 2. It remains to be seen that our construction guarantees that the label $L(q_m)$ of this leaf does not decide the body of CLIQUE_k. However, this is clear from the construction because the partial assignment that is built assigns each variable to a different color-class. Therefore, $L(q_m)$ does not falsify any atomic formula, and it cannot satisfy all either because its domain is not all $\{x_1, \ldots, x_k\}$. Hence, $L(q_m)$ does not decide the body of CLIQUE_k as was to be shown. $\square$

5.2   Lower Bound for the Bounded Treewidth Case

Consider the vocabulary of directed graphs $\sigma = \{E\}$, where E is a binary relation symbol. For $k \geq 2$, let $\text{PATH}_k(x, y)$ be the conjunctive query expressing the existence of a path of length k from x to y. More specifically, $\text{PATH}_k(x, y)$ is the following conjunctive query:

$$(\exists x_1) \cdots (\exists x_{k-1})(E(x, x_1) \wedge E(x_1, x_2) \wedge \ldots \wedge E(x_{k-2}, x_{k-1}) \wedge E(x_{k-1}, y)).$$

It is trivially seen that the treewidth of $\text{PATH}_k(x, y)$ is one because the underlying Gaifman graph is a path, and hence a tree. We aim for a family of directed graphs $\mathbf{G}_n$, with two distinguished nodes s and t, for which the size of the minimal search trees for testing whether $\mathbf{G}_n \models \text{PATH}_k(s,t)$ nearly matches the upper bound provided by Theorem 2. Moreover, we will choose our graphs so that the hypothesis $\mathbf{G}_n \not\models \text{PATH}_k(s,t)$ in that theorem is satisfied.

The construction of the directed graphs $\mathbf{G}_n$ is as follows. The set of vertices of $\mathbf{G}_n$ is

$$V_n = \{(i,u) : 1 \le i \le k-1, 1 \le u \le n\} \cup \{s,t\}.$$

The vertices of the type (i,u) need to be thought as arranged into $k-1$ levels of n vertices each. We call them middle vertices. The source vertex s is at level 0 and the target vertex t is at level k. Each middle vertex (i,u) at level i is connected precisely to the vertices at level $i+1$ whose second components have the same parity as u. The source s is connected precisely to the vertices at level 1 whose second component is even, and the target t is connected precisely to the vertices at level $k-1$ whose second component is odd. More formally, the arcs of $\mathbf{G}_n$ are

$$E_n = \{((i,u),(i+1,v)) : 1 \le i \le k-2, \ 1 \le u,v \le n, \ u \equiv v \ (\text{mod } 2)\} \cup$$
$$\{(s,(1,u)) : 1 \le u \le n, \ u \equiv 0 \ (\text{mod } 2)\} \cup$$
$$\{((k-1,u),t) : 1 \le u \le n, \ u \equiv 1 \ (\text{mod } 2)\}.$$

It is readily seen from the definition, that there is no path of length k from s to t in $\mathbf{G}_n$. In other words, $\mathbf{G}_n \not\models \text{PATH}_k(s,t)$. This is because the only middle vertices reachable from s are those whose second component is even, and the only middle vertices that reach t are those whose second component is odd.

Theorem 4. *For $n \ge k/2 \ge 2$, every search tree for testing whether $\mathbf{G}_n \models$ PATH$_k(s,t)$ has at least $n^{\log k - 3}$ nodes.*

Proof: As in Theorem 3, the idea of the proof is again to describe an adversary argument. For simplicity we assume that n is an even number; the general case is similar. Suppose that (T,L) is a search tree testing whether $\mathbf{G}_n \models \text{PATH}_k(s,t)$. Before we start the argument we need some terminology. Every internal node q of T has an associated level $l(q)$ in $\{1,\ldots,k-1\}$ defined as follows. Let $x(q) = x_i$; that is, x_i is the splitting variable at node q. Then we define $l(q) = i$.

We construct a path $q_0, q_1, \ldots$ through T, starting at the root, with the following properties:

1. $L(q_j)$ does not decide the body of PATH$_k(s,t)$.
2. The subtree rooted at q_j has size less than $2^j n^{\log k - 3 - j}$.

Each internal q_j will also have an associated parity $p_j \in \{0,1\}$ that will be defined on the fly. Let q_0 be the root of T. The parity p_0 is defined 0 if $2l(q_0) < k$ and 1 otherwise. Intuitively, p_0 is 0 if level $l(q_0)$ is closer to level 0 than to level k. Suppose next that $q_0, \ldots, q_j$ and $p_0, \ldots, p_j$ have already been defined, and that q_j is not a leaf. First we define the parity p_{j+1} as follows. Intuitively, p_{j+1} will be defined in such a way that the minimum distance, in terms of number of levels, between any two elements of different parity in the sequence is at most halved. More formally, consider the level $l(q_j) = i$ of q_j and the level i' in $\{l(q_0), \ldots, l(q_{j-1}), 0, k\}$ that minimizes $|i' - i|$ (break ties arbitrarily). If $i' = 0$, let $p_{j+1} = 0$. If $i' = k$, let $p_{j+1} = 1$. Otherwise, let j' be such that $i' = l(q_{j'})$, and let $p_{j+1} = p_{j'}$. Next we define q_{j+1}. We claim that among the $n/2$ middle vertices at level i whose second component is congruent to p_{j+1} mod 2, there must exist at least one, say (i, u), for which the subtree rooted at the successor of q_j labeled by $L(q_j) \cup \{(x(q_j), (i, u))\}$ has size less than $2^{j+1} n^{\log k - 3 - j - 1}$. Indeed this is the case because otherwise the size of the subtree rooted at q_j would be at least

$$\frac{n}{2} \cdot 2^{j+1} n^{\log k - 3 - j - 1} = 2^j n^{\log k - 3 - j}$$

which contradicts the inductive construction. Let q_{j+1} be any of these successors.

Notice that after a certain number of steps m no larger than $\log k - 2$, we will reach a leaf q_m because the size of the subtree will become less than 2. It remains to be seen that our construction guarantees that the label $L(q_m)$ of this leaf does not decide the body of $\text{PATH}_k(s, t)$. Consider the sequence $q_0, \ldots, q_m$. To every internal q_j in the path there corresponds a vertex of $\mathbf{G}_n$, namely, the image of the variable $x(q_j)$ under $L(q_{j+1})$. Let $v_0, \ldots, v_{m-1}$ be the corresponding sequence of vertices in $\mathbf{G}_n$. Note that, by construction, each v_j is a middle vertex of the form $(l(q_j), u)$ and the parity p_j coincides with the parity of its second component u. Let us define $v_m = s$, $v_{m+1} = t$, $p_m = 0$, and $p_{m+1} = 1$. We claim that any two vertices in $\{v_0, \ldots, v_{m+1}\}$ that belong to consecutive levels are connected by an arc. In order to see this, it suffices to note that the shortest distance between any pair of elements of different parity in the sequence is at least $k/2$ when $j = 0$, and is at most halved when going from j to $j + 1$. Therefore, by $j = \log k - 2$, the shortest distance between any pair of elements of different parity is at least 2. Hence, any two consecutive vertices have the same parity, so are connected by an arc. Hence, $L(q_m)$ does not falsify any atomic formula, and it cannot satisfy all either because its domain is not all $\{x_1, \ldots, x_{k-1}\}$. Hence, $L(q_m)$ does not decide the body of $\text{PATH}_k(s, t)$ as was to be shown. $\square$

6   Conclusions

We have proposed a new way of measuring the complexity of algorithms for conjunctive query evaluation, or equivalently, for constraint-satisfaction problems. The concept of minimal search tree tries to capture the notion of optimal search space for search-based pruning algorithms. As discussed in the introduction, measuring the complexity of the algorithm as a function of the minimal search tree is an idea that originates in propositional proof complexity. By adapting an automatization algorithm for tree resolution that was developed in that context, we were able to provide an algorithm that achieves a remarkable theoretical performance. What remains to be seen is whether the idea can lead to practical algorithms with reasonable behavior.

Our work also suggests several technical open problems. First, our algorithm provides a search tree for the Booleanization, but as we discussed, it is not clear that such a search tree can be converted to a search tree for the original conjunctive query. It would be nice to investigate this further. Second, proving the bounds on search-tree size for bounded treewidth queries seemed to require the hypothesis $\mathbf{A} \not\models Q(\mathbf{a})$. We do not know whether it is really needed.

Open Problem. Find bounds on the maximum search-tree size of conjunctive queries of bounded treewidth on structures on which they hold. More concretely: Do conjunctive queries with k variables and bounded treewidth have search trees of size $n^{O(\log k)}$ on structures of cardinality n on which they hold? If not, repeat for bounded pathwidth.

Another interesting direction to follow, that looks related to this work, is to establish the precise relationship between the CSP refutations developed in [AKV04] and the refutations provided by the search trees when $\mathbf{A} \not\models Q(\mathbf{a})$. It seems that the techniques that were developed for proof complexity should be useful here. Ideally, it would be nice to move back and forth and apply techniques from one area to the other.

Acknowledgments. I am grateful to José L. Balcázar and Roberto Nieuwenhuis for fruitful discussions, and also to a referee for comments. I am also grateful to Moshe Vardi for providing useful pointers and for the discussion of ideas related to Theorem 2.

References

[AKV04]   A. Atserias, Ph. G. Kolaitis, and M. Vardi. Constraint propagation as a proof system. To appear in proceedings of CP 2004, 2004.

[BKPS02] P. Beame, R. Karp, T. Pitassi, and M. Saks. The efficiency of resolution and Davis-Putnam procedures. *SIAM Journal of Computing*, pages 1048–1075, 2002.

[Bod98]   H. L. Bodlaender. A partial k-arboretum of graphs with bounded treewidth. *Theoretical Computer Science*, 209:1–45, 1998.

[BP96]   P. Beame and T. Pitassi. Simplified and improved resolution lower bounds. In *37th Annual IEEE Symposium on Foundations of Computer Science*, pages 274–282, 1996.

[BPR00]   M. L. Bonet, T. Pitassi, and R. Raz. On interpolation and automatization for Frege systems. *SIAM Journal of Computing*, 29(6):1939–1967, 2000. A preliminary version appeared in FOCS'97.

[CM77]   A. K. Chandra and P. M. Merlin. Optimal implementation of conjunctive queries in relational databases. In *9th Annual ACM Symposium on the Theory of Computing*, pages 77–90, 1977.

[CR97]   C. Chekuri and A. Rajaraman. Conjunctive query containment revisited. In *6th International Conference on Database Theory*, volume 1997 of *Lecture Notes in Computer Science*, pages 56–70, 1997.

[DKV02]   V. Dalmau, Ph. G. Kolaitis, and M. Y. Vardi. Constraint satisfaction, bounded treewidth, and finite variable logics. In *8th International Conference on Principles and Practice of Constraint Programming (CP)*, volume 2470 of *Lecture Notes in Computer Science*, pages 310–326. Springer, 2002.

[GLS98]   G. Gottlob, N. Leone, and F. Scarcello. The complexity of acyclic conjunctive queries. In *39th Annual IEEE Symposium on Foundations of Computer
Science*, pages 706–715, 1998.

[KV00]   Ph. G. Kolaitis and M. Y. Vardi. Conjunctive-query containment and constraint satisfaction. *Journal of Computer and System Sciences*, 61(2):302–
332, 2000.

[PY99]   C. H. Papadimitriou and M. Yannakakis. On the complexity of database
queries. *Journal of Computer and System Sciences*, 58(3):407–427, 1999.

[Yan81]   M. Yannakakis. Algorithms for acyclic database schemes. In *7th International Conference on Very Large Data Bases*, pages 82–94, 1981.

Which XML Schemas Admit 1-Pass Preorder Typing?

Wim Martens[1], Frank Neven[1], and Thomas Schwentick[2]

[1] Limburgs Universitair Centrum
Universitaire Campus
B-3590 Diepenbeek, Belgium
{wim.martens, frank.neven}@luc.ac.be
[2] Philipps Universität Marburg
Fachbereich 12, Mathematik und Informatik
tick@informatik.uni-marburg.de

Abstract. It is shown that the class of regular tree languages admitting one-pass preorder typing is exactly the class defined by restrained competition tree grammars introduced by Murata et al. [14]. In a streaming context, the former is the largest class of XSDs where every element in a document can be typed when its opening tag is met. The main technical machinery consists of semantic characterizations of restrained competition grammars and their subclasses. In particular, they can be characterized in terms of the context of nodes, closure properties, allowed patterns and guarded DTDs. It is further shown that deciding whether a schema is restrained competition is tractable. Deciding whether a schema is equivalent to a restrained competition tree grammar, or one of its subclasses, is much more difficult: it is complete for EXPTIME. We show that our semantic characterizations allow for easy optimization and minimization algorithms. Finally, we relate the notion of one-pass preorder typing to the existing XML Schema standard.

1 Introduction

XML (eXtensible Markup Language) constitutes the basic format for data exchange on the Web [4]. For many applications, it is important to constrain the structure of documents by providing a schema specified in a schema language. The most common schemas are *Document Type Definitions (DTDs)*. A DTD is basically a set of rules of the form $a \to r$, where a is a tag name and r is a regular expression. A document is *valid* with respect to a DTD if each element labeled with a has a sequence of children whose tags match r. We view an XML document as a tree in the way indicated by Figure 1.

Unfortunately, DTDs are limited in various ways. A particular limitation is that the type of an element can only depend on its tag but not on its context. As an example, in Figure 1 it is not possible to assign different types to discount DVDs and non-discount DVDs while retaining the same tag.

XML Schema Definitions (XSDs) is the standard proposed by the World Wide Web consortium (W3C) to answer the shortcomings of DTDs [5]. In database

T. Eiter and L. Libkin (Eds.): ICDT 2005, LNCS 3363, pp. 68–82, 2005.

theory, the latter are modeled by extended context-free grammars, the former by unranked regular tree languages [2]. Such regular tree languages can be represented by specialized DTDs (SDTDs) [16] allowing to assign types a^i to elements with tags a (cf. Definition 2). The rules are of the form $a^i \to r$ where r is a regular expression over types, i.e., the rules constrain, for each element type, the sequence of types of sub-elements. In our example, regular DVDs could get the type dvd^1, discount DVDs the type dvd^2 (cf. Section 2.2). A tree is then valid w.r.t. an SDTD if there is an assignment of types matching the rules of the grammar. The enlarged flexibility of SDTDs requires an additional algorithmic task: besides simply checking validity it will often be necessary to compute a matching assignment. We refer to this as *typing*.

The goal of the present paper is to identify the largest class of SDTDs which can be typed in a streaming fashion. In other words, when processing an XML document as a stream of opening and closing tags, the type of each element should be uniquely determined when the opening tag is met. We will refer to this as *1-pass preorder typing*. The latter can be an important first step in processing streaming XML data. On top of this information, e.g., subscription queries can be defined (e.g., *inform me if there are new discounted dvds*) and their evaluation can be optimized.

Note that a document is valid w.r.t. an SDTD if all elements can be correctly typed. Hence, 1-pass preorder typing implies 1-pass (preorder) validation, but not vice versa. Indeed, consider the SDTD consisting of the rules $a^0 \to b^1 + b^2$, $b^1 \to c$ and $b^2 \to d$, defining the finite tree language $\{a(b(c)), a(b(d))\}$. This language can easily be validated via an algorithm making a preorder traversal through the input tree, but does not admit preorder typing: the type of the b-element cannot be determined without looking at its child.

Murata, Lee and Mani [14] proposed[1] two restrictions of SDTDs, *single-type* and *restrained competition*, which guarantee 1-pass preorder typing. An SDTD is *single-type* if for each rule $a^i \to r$ and each tag b at most one type b^j occurs in r. It is *restrained competition* if there is no rule $a^i \to r$ for which there exist strings $wb^j u$ and $wb^k v$ in $L(r)$ with $j \neq k$. Clearly, both restrictions assure 1-pass preorder typing. However, from the definition of these restrictions it is not immediately clear whether they are the weakest possible to ensure 1-pass preorder typing. More importantly, a precise semantical characterization providing insight in fundamental properties of these classes remained open.

Contributions. It turns out that an SDTD admits 1-pass preorder typing if and only if its trimmed version (i.e., without useless symbols) is restrained competition. So, a regular tree language admits 1-pass preorder typing if and only if it be described by a restrained competition SDTD. Therefore, restrained competition SDTDs might be a good basis for an XML schema language ex-

---

[1] Actually, they defined these classes in the slightly different framework of regular tree grammars. We use SDTDs here to simplify proofs. Nevertheless, w.r.t. defining tree languages, the two formalisms are equally expressive and one can be translated into the other efficiently in a straightforward manner.

tending XSDs without losing the ability of efficient parsing. Interestingly, for this purpose no further restriction to one-unambiguous regular expressions [3] is necessary. We discuss this further in Section 7.

Starting from this, we study the classes of tree languages which can be described by restrained-competition SDTDs and single-type SDTDs, respectively. The next contribution is a set of semantical characterizations of these classes. The main parameter in these characterizations is the dependency of the type of a node on the context of the node in the document. In particular, we prove that a regular tree language can be defined by (1) a single-type SDTD if and only if the type of each node only depends on the sequence of tags on the path from the root to the node; and, (2) a restrained competition SDTD if and only if the type of each node only depends on the tags of the nodes on the path from the root to the node *and their left siblings*. The other characterizations are in terms of closure properties, allowed patterns and guarded DTDs.

Next, we turn to algorithmic issues. Two algorithmic problems immediately arise from the above. Given an SDTD **d**, (1) is **d** a DTD, single-type SDTD or restrained competition SDTD, and (2) is there a DTD, single-type SDTD or restrained competition SDTD **d'** describing the same tree language as **d**? The first question is trivial for DTDs and single-type SDTDs. We prove that it is in NLOGSPACE for restrained competition SDTDs. The second question turns out to be much harder: in all three cases it is complete for EXPTIME. Furthermore, the algorithm is constructive. That is, if **d** is in fact in the desired class, an equivalent DTD, single-type SDTD or restrained competition SDTD **d'** is constructed.

Our semantical characterizations lead to easy optimization and minimization algorithms. Whereas the inclusion problem is EXPTIME-complete for general SDTDs (even with one-unambiguous regular expressions [13]) it follows from our characterizations that these problems are in PSPACE for restrained competition SDTDs and even in PTIME if it is additionally required that the regular expressions are one-unambiguous. We show that, in contrast to general SDTDs (cf. Section 5.2), for every tree language definable by restrained competition grammars, there exists a unique minimal restrained competition grammar that describes it. Moreover, this minimal grammar can be computed in polynomial time.

We conclude with an observation on post-order typing. Although in general, arbitrary SDTDs do not admit 1-pass preorder typing, we show that for each regular tree language there is an SDTD which allows *1-pass postorder typing*, i.e., a parsing algorithm that determines a type of an element when it reaches its closing tag. That every SDTD allows 1-pass *validation* was already observed by Segoufin and Vianu [18].

Related Work. Brüggemann-Klein, Murata, and Wood study unranked regular tree languages as a formal model for XML schema languages [2]. In particular, they prove that the latter model is equivalent to the morphic image of tree-local tree languages. Papakonstantinou and Vianu [16] formalize the latter as the more manageable specialized DTDs which are used in this paper. Murata et al. [14] provided a taxonomy of XML schema languages in terms of restrictions on grammars which are equivalent to specialized DTDs. In particular, they propose

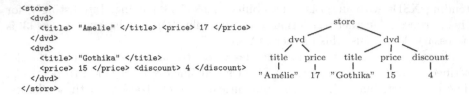

```
<store>
  <dvd>
    <title> "Amelie" </title> <price> 17 </price>
  </dvd>
  <dvd>
    <title> "Gothika" </title>
    <price> 15 </price> <discount> 4 </discount>
  </dvd>
</store>
```

Fig. 1. An example of an XML document and its tree representation

to formalize DTDs, XML Schema, and Relax NG [24] as local, single-type, and arbitrary regular tree grammars, respectively. They also introduce the notion of restrained competition and show that these are 1-pass preorder typeable but do not discuss optimality or give any semantical characterizations.

The organization of the paper is as follows. In Section 2 we define the various classes of SDTDs and the properties by which we characterize them. The actual characterizations are given in Section 3. In Section 4 the complexity of the basic decision problems is addressed. In Section 5, we discuss optimization and minimization algorithms. Section 6 shows that every regular tree language allows 1-pass postorder typing. We discuss our results in Section 7.

2   Definitions

2.1   Trees and Tree Languages

For our purposes, an XML document is basically a sequence of opening and closing tags, properly nested. As usual, we identify XML documents with their corresponding trees. The domain $\mathrm{Dom}(t)$ of a tree t is the set of its nodes, represented in a fixed way by sequences of numbers. The empty sequence ε represents the root. The n children of a node u are named $u1, \ldots, un$ in the order given by the document. Nodes carry labels from alphabet Σ of tags. We denote the label of v in t by $\mathrm{lab}^t(v)$. The set of all unranked Σ-trees is denoted by $\mathcal{T}_\Sigma$. A *tree language* is a set of trees. For a gentle introduction into trees, tree languages and tree automata we refer to [15].

2.2   XML Schema Languages

Definition 1. A *DTD* is a pair (d, s_d) where d is a function that maps Σ-symbols to regular expressions and $s_d \in \Sigma$ is the start symbol. We usually simply denote (d, s_d) by d. A tree t *is valid w.r.t.* d (or *satisfies* d) if its root is labeled by s_d and, for every node with label a, the sequence $a_1 \cdots a_n$ of labels of its children is in $L(d(a))$. By $L(d)$ we denote the set of trees that satisfy d.

A simple example of a DTD defining the inventory of a store is the following:

$$\text{store} \rightarrow \text{dvd dvd}^* \qquad \text{dvd} \rightarrow \text{title price(discount} + \varepsilon)$$

Definition 2 ([16, 17]). A *specialized DTD* (SDTD) is a 4-tuple $\mathbf{d} = (\Sigma, \Sigma',$ $(d, s_d), \mu)$, where Σ' is an alphabet of *types*, (d, s_d) is a DTD over Σ' and μ is a mapping from Σ' to Σ. A tree t is *valid w.r.t.* $\mathbf{d}$ (or satisfies $\mathbf{d}$) if $t = \mu(t')$ for some $t' \in L(d)$ (where μ is extended to trees). Again, we denote the set of trees defined by $\mathbf{d}$, by $L(\mathbf{d})$. We denote by $(\mathbf{d}, a^i)$ the specialized DTD $\mathbf{d}$, where we replace the DTD (d, s_d) by (d, a^i).

The class of tree languages defined by SDTDs corresponds precisely to the regular (unranked) tree languages [2]. For ease of exposition, we always take $\Sigma' = \{a^i \mid 1 \leq i \leq k_a, a \in \Sigma, i \in \mathbb{N}\}$ for some $k_a \in \mathbb{N}$ and set $\mu(a^i) = a$. We refer to the label a^i of a node (or sometimes also to i) in t' as its *state* or *type*. We say that an SDTD $\mathbf{d}$ is *trimmed* if d has no unreachable rules and that there exists no $a^i \in \Sigma'$ for which $L((d, a^i)) = \emptyset$. Note that $L((d, a^i))$ contains trees over alphabet Σ', whereas $L((\mathbf{d}, a^i))$ contains Σ-trees. In the remainder of the paper, we assume that all SDTDs are trimmed. We note that trimming an SDTD is PTIME-complete. A simple example of an SDTD is the following:

$$\text{store} \rightarrow (\text{dvd}^1 + \text{dvd}^2)^* \text{dvd}^2 (\text{dvd}^1 + \text{dvd}^2)^*$$
$$\text{dvd}^1 \rightarrow \text{title price} \qquad \text{dvd}^2 \rightarrow \text{title price discount}$$

Here, dvd^1 defines ordinary DVDs while dvd^2 defines DVDs on sale. The rule for store specifies that there should be at least one DVD on discount.

Murata et al. [14] argue that the expressiveness of SDTDs corresponds to the XML schema language Relax NG, while the single-type SDTDs defined next correspond to XML Schema.

Definition 3. A *single-type SDTD* (SDTDst) is an SDTD $(\Sigma, \Sigma', d, \mu)$ in which in no regular expression $d(a)$ two types b^i and b^j with $i \neq j$ occur.

The above defined SDTD is not single type as both dvd^1 and dvd^2 occur in the rule for store. An example of a single-type SDTD is given next:

$$\text{store} \rightarrow \text{regulars discounts}$$
$$\text{regulars} \rightarrow (\text{dvd}^1)^* \qquad \text{discounts} \rightarrow \text{dvd}^2 (\text{dvd}^2)^*$$
$$\text{dvd}^1 \rightarrow \text{title price} \qquad \text{dvd}^2 \rightarrow \text{title price discount}$$

Although there are still two element definitions dvd^1 and dvd^2, they can only occur in a different context. The next class was defined in [14] because it still allows 1-pass preorder typing.

Definition 4. A regular expression r *restrains competition* if there are no strings $wa^i v$ and $wa^j v'$ in $L(r)$ with $i \neq j$. An SDTD is *restrained competition* (SDTD^{rc}) iff all regular expressions occurring in rules restrain competition.

An example of a restrained competition SDTD that is not single-type is given next:

$$\text{store} \rightarrow (\text{dvd}^1)^* \text{ discounts } (\text{dvd}^2)^*$$
$$\text{discounts} \rightarrow \varepsilon \qquad \text{dvd}^1 \rightarrow \text{title price} \qquad \text{dvd}^2 \rightarrow \text{title price discount}$$

The classes of tree languages defined by the grammars introduced above are included as follows: DTD $\subsetneq$ SDTDst $\subsetneq$ SDTD^{rc} $\subsetneq$ SDTD [14].

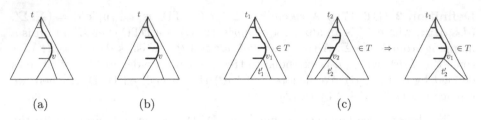

(a)   (b)   (c)

Fig. 2. Illustration of notions introduced in Section 2.3. Figures 2(a) and 2(b) illustrate the ancestor-string (anc-str) and ancestor-sibling string (anc-sib-str) of v. Figure 2(c) illustrates the notion of ancestor-sibling-guarded subtree exchange

2.3   Ancestor- and Ancestor-Sibling-Patterns

Finally, we define the notions that will be used in our semantical characterizations. Let t be a tree and v be a node. By ch-str$^t(v)$ we denote the string formed by the children of v, i.e., lab$^t(v1) \cdots$ lab$^t(vn)$ if v has n children. Usually we omit the superscript t. By anc-str$^t(v)$ we denote the string formed by the labels on the path from the root to v, i.e., lab$^t(\varepsilon)$lab$^t(i_1)$lab$^t(i_1 i_2) \cdots$ lab$^t(i_1 i_2 \cdots i_k)$ where $v = i_1 i_2 \cdots i_k$. By l-sib-str$^t(v)$ we denote the string formed by the labels of the left siblings of v, i.e., lab$^t(u1) \cdots$ lab$^t(uk)$ where $v = uk$. By anc-sib-str$^t(v)$ we denote the string l-sib-str$^t(\varepsilon)\#$l-sib-str$^t(i_1)\# \cdots \#$l-sib-str$^t(i_1 i_2 \cdots i_k)$ formed by concatenating the left-sibling strings of all ancestors starting from the root. We assume that $\# \notin \Sigma$. Note that the final symbol of anc-str$^t(v)$ and anc-sib-str$^t(v)$ is always the label of v.

Definition 5. We say that a specialized SDTD $\mathbf{d} = (\Sigma, \Sigma', d, \mu)$ has *ancestor-based types* if there is a (partial) function $f : (\Sigma \cup \{\#\})^* \to \Sigma'$ such that, for each tree $t \in L(\mathbf{d})$ the following holds: (1) there is a unique tree $t' \in L(d)$ with $\mu(t') = t$; and (2) for each node $v \in \text{Dom}(t)$, the label of v in t' is $f(\text{anc-str}^t(v))$. We say $\mathbf{d}$ *has ancestor-sibling based types* if the same holds with anc-str$^t(v)$ replaced by anc-sib-str$^t(v)$.

By $t_1[u \leftarrow t_2]$ we denote the tree obtained from a tree t_1 by replacing the subtree rooted at $u \in \text{Dom}(t_1)$ by t_2. By subtree$^t(u)$ we denote the subtree of t rooted at u.

Definition 6. We say that a tree language T is *closed under ancestor-guarded subtree exchange* if the following holds. Whenever for two trees $t_1, t_2 \in T$ with nodes $u_1 \in \text{Dom}(t_1)$ and $u_2 \in \text{Dom}(t_2)$ it holds that anc-str$^{t_1}(u_1) = $ anc-str$^{t_2}(u_2)$ implies $t_1[u_1 \leftarrow \text{subtree}^{t_2}(u_2)] \in T$. We call it *closed under ancestor-sibling-guarded subtree exchange* if the same property holds with anc-sib-str$^{t_1}(u_1) = $ anc-sib-str$^{t_2}(u_2)$ as precondition of the implication. Figure 2 illustrates the just defined notions.

Definition 7. An *ancestor-guarded DTD* $\mathbf{d}$ is a pair (d, s_d) where $s_d \in \Sigma$ is the start symbol as in a DTD. But in contrast to a DTD, d is a finite set of triples (r, a, s), where $a \in \Sigma$ and r and s are regular expressions. If there are triples

(r, a, s) and (r', a, s') in d then $L(r)$ and $L(r')$ are disjoint. A tree t satisfies $\mathbf{d}$ if for every node $v \in \text{Dom}(t)$ the following holds. If anc-str(v) matches r and lab$(v) = a$ there must be a triple (r, a, s) in d and ch-str(v) must match s.

An *ancestor-sibling-guarded DTD* is defined in the same way with the difference that r has to be matched by anc-sib-str(v).

Definition 8. Let $P_{\text{anc}}(t) = \{\text{anc-str}(v)\#\text{ch-str}(v) \mid v \in t\}$ and $P_{\text{anc-sib}}(t) = \{\text{anc-sib-str}(v)\#\text{ch-str}(v) \mid v \in t\}$. Let T be a set of trees. We say that T *can be characterized by ancestor-based patterns*, if there is a regular string language L such that, for every tree t, we have that $t \in T$ if and only if $P_{\text{anc}}(t) \subseteq L$. We say T *can be characterized by ancestor-sibling-based patterns* if the same holds with $P_{\text{anc}}(t)$ replaced by $P_{\text{anc-sib}}(t)$.

3   Semantic Characterizations of Single-Type and Restrained Competition SDTDs

In this section, we first show that an SDTD is restrained competition if and only if it allows for 1-pass preorder typing. Afterwards, as an intermediate step, we characterize the regular tree languages definable by single-type SDTDs. Finally, we characterize the class of tree languages which can be described by restrained competition SDTDs.

3.1   Schemas with 1-Pass Preorder Typing

It follows from Theorem 12 that in restrained competition SDTDs the type of a node only depends on its ancestor-sibling string. However, in an SDTD which admits 1-pass preorder typing the type of a node might depend on all parts of the tree which occur before the node. We formalize this notion via SDTDs with preceding based types. Nevertheless, it will turn out that these two notions are identical.

For a tree t and a node v we denote by preceding$^t(v)$ the tree resulting from t by removing everything below v, all right siblings of v's ancestors and of v, and their respective subtrees (cf. Figure 3). We define the term *preceding-based types* in analogy to Definition 5 with preceding$^t(v)$ in place of anc-str$^t(v)$.

Expressed in a different way, the type of an element only depends on the prefix of the XML document ending with its opening tag.

Theorem 9. *A trimmed SDTD* $\mathbf{d}$ *has preceding based types if and only if it is restrained competition.*

Proof sketch. The "if"-part of the statement is obvious. We sketch the "only if". Actually, it is easy to show that every trimmed SDTD $\mathbf{d}$ with ancestor-sibling based types is restrained competition. Otherwise, a counterexample could be constructed in a straightforward manner (cf. Theorem 12). It can also be

Fig. 3. From left to right: a tree t, preceding$^t(v)$ and preceding-subtree$^t(v)$

shown by contraposition that each SDTD with preceding based types already has ancestor-sibling based types.   □

Hence, we immediately obtain the following:

Corollary 10. *Restrained competition SDTDs are exactly those SDTDs which admit 1-pass preorder typing.*

3.2 Ancestor Based Schemas

In this subsection, we characterize single-type SDTDs in terms of the ancestor axis. In the following theorem we assume that all the trees in language T have the same root label.

Theorem 11. *For a regular tree language T the following are equivalent:*

(a) T is definable by a single-type SDTD;
(b) T is definable by an SDTD with ancestor-based types;
(c) T is closed under ancestor-guarded subtree exchange;
(d) T can be characterized by ancestor-based patterns; and,
(e) T is definable by an ancestor-guarded DTD.

Proof. We show the following sequence of implications. (a) $\Rightarrow$ (e) $\Rightarrow$ (d) $\Rightarrow$ (b) $\Rightarrow$ (c) $\Rightarrow$ (a). We only give the necessary constructions.

(a) $\Rightarrow$ (e): Let T be defined by a single-type SDTD $\mathbf{d} = (\Sigma, \Sigma', (d, s_d), \mu)$ with $\bot \notin \Sigma'$. Let A be a DFA over Σ with state set $Q = \Sigma' \cup \{\bot\}$ and let $\delta(a^i, b)$ equal the unique b^j occurring in $d(a^i)$ if such a symbol exists, otherwise $\bot$. Note that the single-type property ensures that A is deterministic.

Let $\mathbf{d}' = (d', s_d)$ be the guarded DTD with all triples $(r_{a,i}, a, \mu(d(a^i)))$, where $r_{a,i}$ is a regular expression describing the set $\{w \mid \delta^*(s_d, w) = a^i\}$ of strings which bring A into state a^i. Of course, the languages $L(r_{a,1}), \ldots, L(r_{a,k_a})$ are all disjoint where $\{a^1, \ldots, a^{k_a}\}$ are the symbols mapped to a by μ.

(e) $\Rightarrow$ (d): Let T be defined by the ancestor-guarded DTD $\mathbf{d} = (d, s_d)$. Then T can be characterized by the set $L = \{ua\#v \mid ua \in L(r), v \in L(s), (r, a, s) \in d\}$.

(d) $\Rightarrow$ (b): Let T be characterized by ancestor-based patterns using the language L. Let $A = (\Sigma, Q, \delta, s, F)$ be a DFA for L. Let $\mathbf{d} = (\Sigma, \Sigma', d, \mu)$ be defined as follows. Σ' is the set of all pairs (a, q), where $a \in \Sigma$ and $q \in Q$. We let $d((a, q))$ be a regular expression describing all strings $(b_1, q_1) \cdots (b_n, q_n)$, for which A accepts $\#b_1 \cdots b_n$ when started from state q and $q_i = \delta(q, b_i)$, for every $i \leq n$.

(b) ⇒ *(c)*: Let T be defined by a SDTD $\mathbf{d} = (\Sigma, \Sigma', d, \mu)$ with ancestor-based types. Let t_1, t_2 be in T and let u_1 and u_2 be nodes in t_1 and t_2, respectively, with anc-str$^{t_1}(u_1)$ = anc-str$^{t_2}(u_2)$. Let t'_1 and t'_2 be the unique trees in $L(d)$ with $\mu(t'_1) = t_1$ and $\mu(t'_2) = t_2$. As the labels of u_1 in t'_1 and the label of u_2 in t'_2 are determined by anc-str$^{t_1}(u_1)$ = anc-str$^{t_2}(u_2)$, they are the same. Hence, by replacing the subtree rooted at u_1 in t'_1 with the subtree rooted at u_2 in t'_2 we get a tree $t' \in L(d)$. Therefore, $\mu(t') = t_1[u_1 \leftarrow \text{subtree}^{t_2}(u_2)]$ is in T, as required.

(c) ⇒ *(a)*: The idea of the proof is as follows. In a sense, we close a given SDTD $\mathbf{d}$ for T with respect to the single-type property. Assume, e.g., that the regular expression $d(a^i)$ contains two different types b^j and b^k. Then, we replace all occurrences of b^j and b^k by a new type $b^{\{j,k\}}$ obtaining a single-type expression with respect to b. Of course, we now need a new rule with $b^{\{j,k\}}$ on the left-hand side. This rule should capture the union of $d(b^j)$ and $d(b^k)$. By applying this step inductively, we arrive at an SDTD $\mathbf{d_1}$ which is single-type but uses types of the form b^S, for $S \subseteq \{1, \ldots, k_b\}$ where $\{1, \ldots, k_b\}$ are the types of b in Σ'. In a second step we prove that $L(\mathbf{d_1}) = T$ unless T fails to fulfill (c).

Let T be a tree language defined by an SDTD $\mathbf{d} = (\Sigma, \Sigma', d, \mu)$. Let the alphabet Σ'_1 consist of all symbols a^S, where $S \subseteq \{1, \ldots, k_a\}$. We extend this notation to sets $C \subseteq \Sigma'$ in a natural way. We write a^C for the type a^S with $S = \{i \mid a^i \in C\}$. For example, for $C = \{a^1, a^2, b^1, b^3\}$, a^C is the type $a^{\{1,2\}}$. For a regular expression r over Σ' and $C \subseteq \Sigma'$ let r^C denote the expression which is obtained from r by replacing every symbol a^i by a^C.

We define the SDTD $\mathbf{d_1} = (\Sigma, \Sigma'_1, d_1, \mu_1)$ as follows. For each symbol a^S, $\mu_1(a^S) = a$, and $d_1(a^S) = \bigcup_{i \in S} d(a^i)^{C(a^S)}$, where $C(a^S)$ is the set of all b^j in $\bigcup_{i \in S} d(a^i)$. For instance, for $S = \{1, 2\}$, $d(a^1) = a^1 b^1(a^2 + b^1)$ and $d(a^2) = (a^3 + b^3)a^1$, $d_1(a^S)$ equals the expression $(a^{\{1,2,3\}} b^{\{1,3\}} (a^{\{1,2,3\}} + b^{\{1,3\}})) + ((a^{\{1,2,3\}} + b^{\{1,3\}})a^{\{1,2,3\}})$.

Note that in $d_1(a^S)$, for each symbol $b \in \Sigma$, there is at most one symbol of the form $b^{S'}$, hence $\mathbf{d_1}$ is a single-type SDTD. It can be shown that, if $L(\mathbf{d}) \neq L(\mathbf{d_1})$, the language T is not closed under ancestor-guarded subtree exchange. By contraposition we get that (c) implies (a).   □

It should be noted that an analogous characterization can be easily obtained for DTDs by replacing *ancestor* by *parent*. The equivalence between (c) and (a) is then already obtained in [16].

3.3   Ancestor-Sibling Based Schemas

Finally, we consider restrained competition SDTDs and show that their tree languages can be characterized in terms of the ancestor and left-sibling axis. We again assume that all the trees in language T have the same root label.

Theorem 12. *For a regular tree language T the following are equivalent:*

(a) T is definable by a restrained competition SDTD;
(b) T is definable by an SDTD with ancestor-sibling-based types;

(c) T is closed under ancestor-sibling-guarded subtree exchange;
(d) T can be characterized by ancestor-sibling-based patterns; and
(e) T is definable by an ancestor-sibling-guarded DTD.

Proof. Again we show (a) $\Rightarrow$ (e) $\Rightarrow$ (d) $\Rightarrow$ (b) $\Rightarrow$ (c) $\Rightarrow$ (a).

(e) $\Rightarrow$ (d), (d) $\Rightarrow$ (b), (b) $\Rightarrow$ (c): These proofs are almost word for word the same as for Theorem 11. Only *ancestor* has to be replaced by *ancestor-sibling*.

(c) $\Rightarrow$ (a): The proof is similar as but a bit more involved than the corresponding proof in Theorem 11. Let T be a tree language defined by a SDTD $\mathbf{d} = (\Sigma, \Sigma', d, \mu)$.

Let, for each state a^i of $\mathbf{d}$, $A_{a,i} = (Q_{a,i}, \Sigma', \delta_{a,i}, s_{a,i}, F_{a,i})$ be an NFA for $L(d(a^i))$. W.l.o.g. we assume that the sets $Q_{a,i}$ are pairwise disjoint and that for every state in each $A_{a,i}$ a final state is reachable.

Let Σ'_1 be defined as in the proof of Theorem 11. We define, for each $a^S \in \Sigma'_1$ a DFA $A_{a,S} = (Q_{a,S}, \Sigma'_1, \delta_{a,S}, s_{a,S}, F_{a,S})$ as follows.

- $Q_{a,S} = \{q^\perp\} \cup \bigcup_{i \in S} 2^{Q_{a,i}}$;
- $s_{a,S} = \bigcup_{i \in S} \{s_{a,i}\}$;
- $F_{a,S} = \{B \in Q_{a,S} \mid B \cap F_{a,i} \neq \emptyset, i \in S\}$;
- In order to define $\delta_{a,S}$, let $B \in Q_{a,S}$ and $b \in \Sigma$. We set $S' := \{j \mid \delta_{a,i}(p, b^j) \neq \emptyset, i \in S, j \leq k_b, p \in B\}$ and $\delta_{a,S}(B, b^{S'}) := \bigcup_{i,p,j} \delta_i(p, b^j)$, where the latter union is over all $i \in S$, $p \in B$ and $j \leq k_b$. For all other sets S'', we set $\delta_{a,S}(B, b^{S''}) := q^\perp$.

Intuitively, $A_{a,S}$ can be seen as obtained in two steps from $\mathbf{d}$. First, we take the product of the power set automata of the $A_{a,i}$, $i \in S$. Then, for each symbol b, for each state of this intermediate automaton, all outgoing edges with label of the form b^j are combined into one transition which ends in the (component wise) union of the all possible target states. The transition is labeled by b to the union of all outgoing b-labels.

We now define the SDTD $\mathbf{d}_1 = (\Sigma, \Sigma'_1, d_1, \mu_1)$, where, for each a and S, $d_1(a^S)$ is a regular expression corresponding to $A_{a,S}$.

Note that each $d_1(a^S)$ has restrained competition. Indeed, as $A_{a,S}$ is deterministic, for each string w, $A_{a,S}$ enters a unique state. Furthermore, for each $b \in \Sigma$ there is only one outgoing transition of the form $b^{S'}$ that can lead to acceptance.

(a) $\Rightarrow$ (e): Let T be defined by a restrained competition DTD $\mathbf{d} = (\Sigma, \Sigma', d, \mu)$. For each symbol a^i in Σ', let $A_{a,i} = (Q_{a,i}, \Sigma', \delta_{a,i}, s_{a,i}, F_{a,i})$ be a DFA for $d(a^i)$. We can modify $A_{a,i}$ such that it has exactly one state $q^\perp$ from which no accepting state is reachable and such that it has no unreachable states (possibly besides $q^\perp$). From the restrained competition property it immediately follows that in $A_{a,i}$, for each state q, if $\delta(q, b^j) = q_1$, $\delta(q, b^k) = q_2$, $q_1 \neq q_2$ and $j \neq k$ then q_1 or q_2 must be $q^\perp$. We require that the sets $Q_{a,i}$ are pairwise disjoint.

From these DFAs over the extended alphabet Σ' we construct a DFA $A = (Q_A, \Sigma, s_A, \delta_A, F_A)$ as follows. The set Q_A consists of all pairs (q, b), where $q \in Q_{a,i}$, for some a^i, and $b \in \Sigma' \cup \{\#\}$. Intuitively, q is the current state of an automaton $A_{a,i}$ and b is the last extended symbol or type that has been identified.

The initial state s_A of A is $(s_{a,i}, \#)$ for the initial symbol a^i of d. The transition function δ_A is defined as follows. For each $q \in Q_{a,i}$, $c \in \Sigma'$ and $b \in \Sigma$ we let $\delta_A((q,c),b) = (\delta_{a,i}(q,b^j),b^j)$, for the unique j with $\delta_{a,i}(q,b^j) \neq q^{\perp}$, if such a j exists. Otherwise, $\delta_A((q,c),b) = (q^{\perp}, \#)$. Furthermore, we let $\delta_A((q,b^j),\#) = (s_{b,j}, \#)$. We set $F_A = \{q \mid q \in F_{a,i}\}$.

Now we are ready to define the ancestor-sibling guarded DTD $\mathbf{d}'$. It consists of all triples (r, a, s), for which there is a state (q, a^i) of A, such that r describes the set of strings w with $\delta_A^*(s_A, w) = (q, a^i)$ and s is $\mu(d(a^i))$. $\qquad \Box$

4   Complexity of Basic Decision Problems

As the definition of a DTD and single-type SDTD is syntactical in nature, it can be immediately verified by an inspection of the rules whether an SDTD is in fact a DTD or a single-type SDTD.

Theorem 13. *It is decidable in* NLOGSPACE *for an SDTD* $\mathbf{d}$ *whether it is restrained competition.*

We study the complexity of determining whether a tree language, given by an SDTD, can be defined by a DTD, a single-type or a restrained competition SDTD, respectively.

Theorem 14. *Each of deciding whether an SDTD has an equivalent DTD, single-type SDTD or restrained competition SDTD is* EXPTIME-*complete.*

Proof sketch. In all three cases, the lower bound is obtained by a reduction from the universality problem for non-deterministic tree automata [19].

The exponential time upper bounds for the single-type and restrained competition cases can be obtained by performing the constructions in the proofs (c) $\Rightarrow$ (a) in Theorems 11 and 12. Both the construction of the SDTD and checking equivalence with the original one can be done in exponential time. For DTDs a similar construction is in polynomial time but the equivalence check still needs exponential time. $\qquad \Box$

5   Applications of the Semantical Characterizations

5.1   Inclusion and Equivalence of Schemas

Decision problems like testing for inclusion or equivalence of schema languages often occur in schema optimization or as basic building blocks of algorithms for typechecking or type inference [8, 11, 12, 16, 22]. In general these problems are PSPACE and EXPTIME-complete for DTDs and SDTDs, respectively [21, 19]. The XML specification, however, restricts regular expressions in DTDs to be deterministic [4] (sometimes also called 1-unambiguous [3]).

Theorem 15. *Given two restrained competition SDTDs* $\mathbf{d_1}$ *and* $\mathbf{d_2}$, *deciding whether (a)* $L(\mathbf{d_1}) \subseteq L(\mathbf{d_2})$, *and whether (b)* $L(\mathbf{d_1}) = L(\mathbf{d_2})$ *is* PSPACE-*complete in general, and* PTIME-*complete if* $\mathbf{d_1}$ *and* $\mathbf{d_2}$ *use deterministic regular expressions.*

This result strongly contrasts with our results in [13], where we show that even for very simple non-deterministic regular expressions these decision problems are intractable, and with the case of arbitrary SDTDs with deterministic regular expressions, for which inclusion and equivalence test are EXPTIME-complete.

5.2   Minimization of SDTDs

In strong contrast to ranked trees, there are unranked regular tree languages for which there is no unique minimal deterministic bottom-up tree automaton. Moreover, minimization can not be obtained by the standard translation to the ranked case. Using the characterizations of Section 3, we obtain that when content models are represented by DFAs rather than by regular expressions, every restrained competition SDTD can be minimized in polynomial time and this minimal SDTD is unique up to isomorphism.

Theorem 16. *Every restrained competition (single-type) SDTD can be minimized in* PTIME. *This minimal SDTD is unique up to isomorphism.*

6   Subtree Based Schemas

From what was presented so far an obvious question arises. What happens if we soften the requirement that the type of an element has to be determined when its *opening* tag is visited? What if instead it has to be computed when the *closing* tag is seen? It turns out that every regular tree language has a SDTD which allows such 1-pass *postorder* typing. Furthermore, the SDTDs used for this purpose can be defined as straightforward extensions of restrained competition SDTDs.

Definition 17. An SDTD $d = (\Sigma, \Sigma', d, \mu)$ is *extended restrained competition* iff for every regular expression r occurring in a rule the following holds: whenever there are two strings wa^iv and wa^jv' in $L(r)$ with $i \neq j$, then $L((\mathbf{d}, a^i)) \cap L((\mathbf{d}, a^j))$ is empty.

For a tree t and a node v we denote by preceding-subtree$^t(v)$ the tree resulting from t by removing all right siblings of v and its ancestors together with the respective subtrees (cf. Figure 3).

Definition 18. We say that a specialized SDTD $\mathbf{d} = (\Sigma, \Sigma', d, \mu)$ *has preceding-subtree based types* if there is a (partial) function $f : \mathcal{T}_\Sigma \times \text{Dom} \to \Sigma'$ such that, for each tree $t \in L(\mathbf{d})$ the following holds: (1) there is a unique tree $t' \in L(d)$ with $\mu(t') = t$, and (2) for each node $v \in \text{Dom}(t)$, the label of v in t' is $f(\text{preceding-subtree}^t(v), v)$.

Stated in terms of XML documents, the type of an element depends on the prefix of the document which ends with the closing tag of the element. The following result shows that all regular tree languages admit 1-pass postorder typing. We assume that all the trees in language T have the same root label.

Theorem 19. *For a tree language T the following are equivalent:*

(a) T is definable by an extended restrained competition SDTD;
(b) T is definable by an SDTD with preceding-subtree-based types;
(c) T is regular.

Proof sketch. The directions (a) $\Rightarrow$ (c) and (b) $\Rightarrow$ (c) are trivial. The proof of the opposite directions uses the fact that regular languages can be validated by deterministic bottom-up automata.   □

In the SDTD used in the proof the type of each element actually only depends on its subtree. This should be compared with the previous characterizations where the type depended on the upper context. These issues are further discussed in Section 7.

Note that not every SDTD is extended restrained competition. The SDTD **d** defined by $r \to (a^1 + a^2)$, $a^1 \to b + c + \varepsilon$, and $a^2 \to c + d + \varepsilon$ is *not* extended restrained competition, as $\{\varepsilon, c\} \subseteq L((\mathbf{d}, a^1)) \cap L((\mathbf{d}, a^2))$.

We conclude by noting that extended restrained competition is a tractable notion.

Theorem 20. *It is decidable in* PTIME *for an SDTD* **d** *whether it is extended restrained competition.*

7   Conclusion

The results of this paper show that its initial question has a simple answer. The regular tree languages which admit 1-pass preorder typing are exactly those which can be described by a restrained competition SDTD.

From the proof of Theorem 12 (c) $\Rightarrow$ (a) it further follows that for each such language a very simple and efficient typing algorithm exists. It is basically a deterministic pushdown automaton with a stack the height of which is bounded by the depth of the document. For each opening tag it pushes one symbol, for each closing tag it pops one. Hence, it only needs a constant number of steps per input symbol. In particular, it works in linear time in the size of the document. It should be noted that such automata have been studied in [18] and [9] in the context of streaming XML documents. The subclass of the context-free languages accepted by such automata has recently been studied in [1].

Further, the paper shows that restrained competition SDTDs can be efficiently recognized (in NLOGSPACE but also in quadratic time) and that from an SDTD without the restrained competition property an equivalent one with the property can effectively (though not efficiently, in general) be constructed if it exists at all.

The 1-pass preorder typing constraint can be seen as a generalization of the determinism constraint on content models of DTDs (Appendix E in [4]) to XSDs. In the case of DTDs, the meaning of a tag is determined by the position in the matching regular expression. The determinism constraint then specifies that this meaning should be computed independent of the tags occurring to the right of the current tag. Similarly, in the context of XML Schema, the meaning of a tag corresponds to its type and should be computed independent of the remainder of the nodes.

Brüggemann-Klein and Wood gave a clean formalization for the concept of determinism needed for DTDs in terms of 1-unambiguous regular expressions [3]. Intuitively, a regular expression is 1-unambiguous if, when processing the input from left to right, it is always determined which symbol in the expression matches the next input symbol. Just as Brüggemann-Klein and Wood contributed to the formal underpinnings of DTDs, our characterization contributes to the foundation of XML Schema by providing a complete notion for 1-pass preorder typeable schemas.

How do these results relate to existing standards? The XML Schema specification requires XSDs to be single-type (end of Section 4.5 in [6] and the Element Declarations Consistent constraint in Section 3.8.6 in [7]) and regular expressions (after dropping the superscripts describing the types) to be deterministic or 1-unambiguous [3] (cf. Section 3.8.6 of [7], Unique Particle Attribution). Although such schemas are always restrained competition, it is easy to prove that they do not capture the complete class of 1-pass preorder typeable schemas. Indeed, from a 1-ambiguous regular language a restrained competition expression can be easily constructed by giving to each symbol the same superscript. The results in the present paper, therefore, indicate that replacing the Element Declarations Consistent and Unique Particle Attribution constraints by the single requirement that regular expressions are restrained competition allows for a larger expressive power without (essential) loss in efficiency. Indeed, for both classes, validation and typing is possible in linear time, allowed schemas can still be recognized in quadratic time and an allowed schema can be constructed in exponential time, if one exists [3]. The latter would also eliminate the heavily debated restriction to 1-unambiguous regular expressions (cf., e.g., pg 98 of [23] and [10, 20]).

On the negative side, both 1-unambiguous expressions and restrained competition expressions lack a comprehensive syntactical counterpart. Whether such an equivalent syntactical restriction exists remains open. It would also be interesting to find syntactic restrictions which imply an efficient construction of an equivalent restrained competition SDTD.

We already mentioned that Murata, Lee, and Mani showed that DTD $\not\subseteq$ SDTDst $\not\subseteq$ SDTD^{rc} $\not\subseteq$ SDTD. They exhibited concrete tree languages that are in one class but not in the other. Our semantical characterizations provide a toolbox to show inexpressibility for arbitrary tree languages. For instance, using the closure of restrained-competition SDTDs under ancestor-guarded subtree exchange, it is immediate that SDTD^{rc} cannot define the set of all Boolean tree-shaped circuits evaluating to true.

Acknowledgments

We thank Geert Jan Bex, Christoph Koch, Nicole Schweikardt, Luc Segoufin and Stijn Vansummeren for helpful discussions.

References

1. R. Alur and P. Madhusudan. Visibly pushdown languages. In *STOC 2004*, pages 202-211, 2004.
2. A. Brüggemann-Klein, M. Murata, and D. Wood. Regular tree and regular hedge languages over unranked alphabets: Version 1, april 3, 2001. Technical Report HKUST-TCSC-2001-0, The Hongkong University of Science and Technology, 2001.
3. A. Brüggemann-Klein and D. Wood. One-unambiguous regular languages. *Information and Computation*, 142(2):182–206, 1998.
4. World Wide Web Consortium. Extensible Markup Language (XML). http://www.w3.org/XML.
5. World Wide Web Consortium. XML Schema. http://www.w3.org/XML/Schema.
6. World Wide Web Consortium. XML Schema Part 0: Primer. http://www.w3.org/TR/xmlschema-0/.
7. World Wide Web Consortium. XML Schema Part 1: Structures. http://www.w3.org/TR/xmlschema-1/.
8. H. Hosoya and B. C. Pierce. XDuce: A statically typed XML processing language. *ACM Transactions on Internet Technology (TOIT)*, 3(2):117–148, 2003.
9. C. Koch and S. Scherzinger. Attribute grammars for scalable query processing on XML streams. In *DBPL*, pages 233–256, 2003.
10. M. Mani. Keeping chess alive - Do we need 1-unambiguous content models? In *Extreme Markup Languages*, Montreal, Canada, 2001.
11. W. Martens and F. Neven. Typechecking top-down uniform unranked tree transducers. In *ICDT 2003*, pages 64–78, 2003.
12. W. Martens and F. Neven. Frontiers of tractability for typechecking simple XML transformations. In *PODS 2004*, pages 23–34, 2004.
13. W. Martens, F. Neven, and T. Schwentick. Complexity of decision problems for simple regular expressions. In *MFCS 2004*, pages 889–900, 2004.
14. M. Murata, D. Lee, and M. Mani. Taxonomy of XML schema languages using formal language theory. In *Extreme Markup Languages*, Montreal, Canada, 2001.
15. F. Neven. Automata, logic, and XML. In *CSL 2002*, pages 2–26. Springer, 2002.
16. Y. Papakonstantinou and V. Vianu. DTD inference for views of XML data. In *PODS 2000*, pages 35–46. ACM Press, 2000.
17. Y. Papakonstantinou and V. Vianu. Incremental validation of XML documents. In *ICDT 2003*, pages 47–63. Springer, 2003.
18. L. Segoufin and V. Vianu. Validating streaming XML documents. In *PODS 2002*, pages 53–64. ACM Press, 2002.
19. H. Seidl. Deciding equivalence of finite tree automata. *SIAM Journal on Computing*, 19(3):424–437, 1990.
20. C. M. Sperberg-McQueen. XML Schema 1.0: A language for document grammars. In *XML 2003 - Conference Proceedings*, 2003.
21. L. J. Stockmeyer and A. R. Meyer. Word problems requiring exponential time: Preliminary report. In *STOC 1973*, pages 1–9, 1973.
22. D. Suciu. Typechecking for semistructured data. In *DBPL 2001*, 2001.
23. E. van der Vlist. *XML Schema*. O'Reilly, 2002.
24. E. van der Vlist. *Relax NG*. O'Reilly, 2003.

The Pipelined Set Cover Problem

Kamesh Munagala[1,*], Shivnath Babu[2,**], Rajeev Motwani[2,***],
and Jennifer Widom[2,†]

[1] Computer Science Department, Duke University
kamesh@cs.duke.edu
[2] Computer Science Department, Stanford University
{shivnath, rajeev, widom}@cs.stanford.edu

Abstract. A classical problem in query optimization is to find the optimal ordering of a set of possibly correlated selections. We provide an abstraction of this problem as a generalization of set cover called *pipelined set cover*, where the sets are applied sequentially to the elements to be covered and the elements covered at each stage are discarded. We show that several natural heuristics for this NP-hard problem, such as the greedy set-cover heuristic and a local-search heuristic, can be analyzed using a linear-programming framework. These heuristics lead to efficient algorithms for pipelined set cover that can be applied to order possibly correlated selections in conventional database systems as well as data-stream processing systems. We use our linear-programming framework to show that the greedy and local-search algorithms are 4-approximations for pipelined set cover. We extend our analysis to minimize the l_p-norm of the costs paid by the sets, where $p \geq 2$ is an integer, to examine the improvement in performance when the total cost has increasing contribution from initial sets in the pipeline. Finally, we consider the *online* version of pipelined set cover and present a competitive algorithm with a logarithmic performance guarantee. Our analysis framework may be applicable to other problems in query optimization where it is important to account for correlations.

1 Motivation

A common operation in database query processing is to find the subset of records in a relation that satisfy a given set of selection conditions. To execute this operation efficiently, a query processor prefers to determine the optimal order in which to evaluate the individual selection conditions, so we call this operation *pipelined filters* [2, 4, 12, 18]. Optimality in pipelined filters is usually with respect to minimizing the total processing time [4, 12].

---

 * Part of this work was done while the author was at Stanford University supported by NIH 1HFZ465.
 ** Supported by NSF under grants IIS-0118173 and IIS-9817799.
 *** Supported in part by NSF Grants IIS-0118173 and EIA-0137761, NSF ITR Award Number 0331640, and grants from Microsoft and Veritas.
 † Supported by NSF under grants IIS-0118173 and IIS-9817799.

T. Eiter and L. Libkin (Eds.): ICDT 2005, LNCS 3363, pp. 83–98, 2005.
© Springer-Verlag Berlin Heidelberg 2005

For example, consider a relation packets, where each record contains the header and an initial part of the payload of network packets logged by a network router. Suppose a query needs to compute the subset of packets where each record r in the result satisfies the following three conditions:

1. p_1: destPort $= 80$, where destPort is the destination port field of r.
2. p_2: $domain$(destAddr) $=$ "yahoo.com", where destAddr is the destination address field of r, and $domain$ is a function that returns the Internet domain name of an address passed as input.
3. p_3: The payload of r contains the regular expression "^[^\\n]*HTTP/1.*" [9].

A query processor might use three selection operators on packets, denoted O_{p_1}, O_{p_2}, and O_{p_3}, to evaluate these three conditions respectively. In this case the query processor might choose to apply O_{p_1} first on each record in packets so that O_{p_2} and O_{p_3} need only process records that are selected by O_{p_1}. Since both O_{p_2} and O_{p_3} involve complex functions, applying either of them before O_{p_1} could increase the total processing time by orders of magnitude. Further, the query processor may choose to process O_{p_2} before O_{p_3}, since packets selected by O_{p_1} are also likely to be selected by O_{p_3}. As this example shows, it is important to choose a good, if not the optimal, order for applying the selection operators on the records of the input relation. Also note that both the expected fraction of records selected (the *selectivity*) and the record-processing time of each selection operator must be taken into account.

Suppose the selection conditions are independent; that is, the selectivity s of any operator O among the records that O processes is independent of the operators that appear before O in the order. Under this assumption, computing the order that minimizes total processing time is easy: We simply order the operators in nonincreasing ratio of $1 - s$ and the record-processing time. Most previous work on the selection-ordering problem and on related problems make the independence assumption and use this ordering technique [4, 12, 18, 23].

The independence assumption reduces the complexity of finding the optimal order, but it is often violated in practice [6, 25]. It can be shown that when the independence assumption does not hold, the total processing time can be $O(n)$ times worse than optimal when n operators are ordered in nonincreasing ratio of $1 - s$ and the record-processing time. Without the independence assumption, the problem is NP-hard. Previous work [17, 22, 23] on ordering of dependent (correlated) operators either uses exhaustive search—which requires selectivity estimates for an exponentially large number of operator subsequences—or proposes simple heuristics with no provable performance guarantees for the solution obtained. As databases are being extended to manage complex data types such as multimedia and XML, the use of expensive selection conditions are becoming frequent, making the problem of ordering dependent selections even more important [4, 12]. The pipelined filters problem also captures restricted types of relational joins and combinations of joins and selections; see [2].

Pipelined filters can be formulated as a generalization of the classical set cover problem [13, 15]: The relation represents the elements to be covered, and each selection operator is a set which drops (or covers) a certain number of records (or elements). The sets are applied sequentially to the elements to be covered, with each set removing the elements that it covers from further processing; the cost of applying a set depends linearly on the number of elements that are still not covered when the set is applied. The solution desired is an ordering of the sets that minimizes the total cost of applying the sets sequentially. We call this problem *pipelined set cover*, the key difference with classical set cover being the cost function. The mapping from pipelined filters to pipelined set cover is straightforward: the operators map to the sets, and the operator ordering, or *pipeline*, maps to the ordering of the sets.

2 Our Contribution

Pipelined set cover has been considered previously in a non-database context by Feige et al. [11] and by Cohen and Kaplan [7]. They show that the uniform cost version of this problem is MAX-SNP hard and develop a greedy 4-approximation algorithm for the uniform cost version. In addition to showing the application of pipelined set cover to classical optimization problems in database and data-stream processing, we extend previous work significantly in this paper, as follows.

2.1 Approximation Algorithms for Pipelined Set Cover

We provide two approximation algorithms for pipelined set cover, one based on the greedy heuristic for classical set cover and another based on an intuitive local-search heuristic. (In separate work we have implemented both algorithms efficiently in a data-stream processing system [2].) Using a different and more general analysis technique from previous work, we show that both these algorithms are 4-approximations, even when the linear cost function depends on the set. This relatively new analysis technique is based on formulating the worst-case performance of the algorithms as linear programs. (This technique was first used by Jain, Mahdian, and Saberi to analyze the performance of a dual-fitting algorithm for facility location [14].) This technique has several advantages. In addition to bounding the approximation ratio, the linear program can be used to analyze running time, e.g., the rate of convergence of the local search heuristic. The linear program gives new insights about the approximation algorithms, with strong implications for query optimization: The bound on approximation depends on the number of sets (operators) n; for $n \leq 20$, this bound ≤ 2.35. Furthermore, this technique can be used to analyze other algorithms for pipelined set cover, including a simple *move-to-front* algorithm which can be implemented very efficiently.

We can view our problem as minimizing the l_1-norm of the vector of the number of elements processed (or the cost paid) by each set. The classical set cover problem can be viewed as minimizing the l_0-norm[1]—it gives a cost to

---

[1] Of course, technically speaking, there is no such norm. However, we can adopt the view that the set cover objective function is minimizing a Hamming measure, which is sometimes treated as a substitute for the l_0-norm [8].

any set that is independent of the number of elements it processes, so long as that set processes at least one element. For set cover, the performance of the greedy algorithm is logarithmic [13, 15, 24], and this approximation factor is optimal [10], assuming $P \neq NP$. The approximation ratio improves to 4 for our l_1-norm formulation, where the cost of each set is weighted by the number of elements it processes. A natural question to ask is what happens to the approximation ratio when the goal is to minimize the l_p-norm of the costs paid by the sets, for integers $p \geq 2$. As p increases, this formulation gives increasing weight to sets at the start of the pipeline that process more elements. The intuition is that the performance of the greedy algorithm should improve with increasing p, and it should reach the optimal solution when we are minimizing the l_∞-norm. Since the objective function is nonlinear, linear programming techniques fail to apply. We develop a Lagrangian-relaxation analysis technique for $p \geq 2$ to show that the approximation ratio of the greedy algorithm is $9^{\frac{1}{p}}$ when the processing costs are uniform (independent of the set), and that local search is a $4^{\frac{1}{p}}$-approximation when the processing costs are nonuniform. The improvement in performance of greedy confirms the intuition that as we skew the total cost in favor of the initial sets chosen, greedy's performance should improve for uniform processing costs.

2.2   Online Pipelined Set Cover

Our original motivation for defining and analyzing pipelined set cover came from our work on processing pipelined filters in a data-stream query processor [2]. A stream, as opposed to a relation, is a continuous unbounded flow of records arriving at a stream-processing system [1]. Example streams include network packets, stock tickers, and sensor observations. Pipelined filters are common in stream processing, e.g., `packets` may be a stream in our example query introduced at the beginning of this section. Another common example of pipelined filters in stream processing is a join of a stream S with a set of relations $R_1, R_2, \ldots, R_k$: For each record s arriving in S, we need to find $R_i' \subseteq R_i$, $1 \leq i \leq k$, such that each record $r_i \in R_i'$ satisfies $r_i.A = s.A$ where A is a field that is common among $S, R_1, R_2, \ldots, R_k$. (We have defined a restricted version of the problem for succinctness [2].) The join output for s is the set of concatenated records $s \cdot r_1 \cdot r_2 \cdots r_k$ for each combination of $r_1 \in R_1', r_2 \in R_2', \ldots, r_k \in R_k'$. If any of the R_i''s are empty, then s produces no join output and we say that s is *dropped*. For processing the join efficiently, we must order $R_1, R_2, \ldots, R_k$ for computing $R_1', R_2', \ldots, R_k'$ such that records in S that get dropped eventually consume minimal processing time. Note that the processing required for records that are not dropped is independent of the ordering.

Pipelined filters over data streams motivate the *online* version of pipelined set cover. In online pipelined set cover, some number of elements arrive at each time step. Our online algorithm has to choose an ordering of the sets in advance at every time step, and process the incoming elements according to this ordering. The performance of our online algorithm is compared against the performance of the best possible offline algorithm that does not change its ordering for the entire course of the request sequence. For online pipelined set cover, we present an $O(\log n)$ competitive algorithm for the uniform cost case, where n is the number of sets. This algorithm can be extended to an $O(\log n + \log \frac{c_{max}}{c_{min}})$ competitive algorithm for the nonuniform cost case, where c_{max} is the largest per-element processing cost among all sets, and c_{min} is the smallest such cost.

2.3   Implementation

In a companion paper [2], we describe our implementation of some of the approximation algorithms for pipelined set cover proposed in this paper for optimizing pipelined filters in a Data Stream Management System [20]. We propose and evaluate techniques to compute selectivity estimates of operator subsequences needed by our approximation algorithms with minimal overhead, as part of query processing itself. While previous work [22, 23] on provably good algorithms for dependent pipelined filters required selectivity estimates for an exponentially large number of operator subsequences, our algorithms require only $O(n^2)$ estimates. (In a conventional database setting, a sample of records from the input relation can be used to estimate these selectivities with low overhead [3, 19].) Furthermore, because data and arrival characteristics of streams can change over time, in [2] we introduce adaptive versions of the algorithms that modify orderings as statistics change, converging on the static solution when statistics do not change. The need to adapt forces us to optimize the pipeline continuously, which motivates the low-overhead heuristics we consider such as greedy and local search.

2.4   Organization

The rest of the paper is organized as follows:

- Section 3 presents the formal problem statement. In Section 4, we introduce and use our linear-programming framework to analyze the greedy set cover algorithm applied to pipelined set cover.
- We move on to local search heuristics in Section 5, showing that our analysis technique carries over to this case, leading to bounds not only on the approximation ratio, but also on the rate of convergence. In the full version [21] we describe simpler implementations of the local search algorithm using limited amount of state, and analyze the resulting performance degradation.
- In Section 6, we present a Lagrangian-relaxation method for analyzing the performance of the greedy and local search algorithms when we optimize the l_p-norm of the cost paid by the sets. The detailed analysis of the local search heuristic, showing that it is a $4^{\frac{1}{p}}$-approximation, is relegated to the full version [21].
- We finally present the online algorithm and its analysis in Section 7.

We omit a separate section on related work because of space constraints. However, related work is referenced appropriately in all sections in the paper.

3   Preliminaries

We are given a set cover instance with n elements denoted $U = \{e_1, e_2, \ldots, e_n\}$, and a collection of sets $A = \{S_1, S_2, \ldots, S_k\}$. Set S_i has a *processing cost* per unit element of c_i. Let $\pi(A)$ denote the set of all possible orderings (permutations) of the sets $S_1, S_2, \ldots, S_k$. The goal is to choose an ordering of the sets, $(S_{p_1}, S_{p_2}, \ldots, S_{p_k}) \in \pi(A)$, so as to minimize the *pipelined cost*:

$$\sum_{i=1}^{k} c_{p_i} |U - \cup_{j=1}^{i-1} S_{p_j}|$$

This cost reflects the cost of a sequence of selection operations in a relational schema, and the goal is to find the optimal such sequence of operations. If the c_i's are equal, we call the instance *uniform*. Note that in this formulation, each element can have a weight associated with it, so that the size of a set is simply the sum of the weights of the elements. We call this problem the *Pipelined Set Cover* problem. Feige et al [11] show that this problem does not admit to better than a 4 approximation unless $P = NP$.

4   Greedy Algorithm

We now analyze the greedy set cover algorithm for this problem. At step i, let n denote the total number (weight) of uncovered elements. Let n_j be the number (respectively weight) of uncovered elements that get covered by set j. We choose the set that minimizes the *cost ratio* $\frac{c_j n}{n_j}$. The uniform cost version of this algorithm was analyzed in [11] and in [7]. We provide a different analysis that handles nonuniform costs which are important in databases since different operators in a pipeline can have different costs.

We can formulate the worst-case performance of greedy as a linear program. Consider any optimal solution whose sets are pipelined $\{O_1, O_2, \ldots, O_k\}$. Suppose we scale down the problem size by scaling down the weights of the elements so that the pipelined cost of the optimal solution is 1. Without loss of generality, assume that the sets in the optimal solution are disjoint, else O_i denotes the residual part of the set after the application of $O_1, \ldots, O_{i-1}$. We denote $|O_i|$ by a_i, and the processing cost of O_i by c_{oi}. The cost of the optimal solution is:

$$OPT = \sum_{i=1}^{k} \left(a_i \cdot \sum_{s=1}^{i} c_{os} \right)$$

Let us denote the sets chosen by greedy as $\{G_1, G_2, \ldots, G_k\}$. Again, assume without loss of generality that they are disjoint, else G_i denotes the residual part of the set after application of $G_1, \ldots, G_{i-1}$. Let $b_{ij} = |O_i \cap G_j|$, so that $a_i = \sum_{j=1}^{k} b_{ij}$. Let the processing cost of G_j be c_{gj}. The cost of greedy is:

$$GREEDY = \sum_{j=1}^{k} \left(\sum_{r=1}^{j} c_{gr} \cdot \sum_{s=1}^{k} b_{sj} \right)$$

Since greedy maximizes the weight of uncovered elements at each time, we have for every stage j of greedy and every set O_i of OPT, the cost ratio of the residual part of O_i after $j-1$ stages of greedy must be at least the cost ratio of G_j. This gives us:

$$\frac{\sum_{s=1}^k b_{sj}}{c_{gj}} \geq \frac{\sum_{r=j}^k b_{ir}}{c_{oi}}$$

We can now formulate the worst possible approximation ratio that greedy can achieve as the following linear program:

$$\text{maximize } \sum_{j=1}^k \left(\sum_{r=1}^j c_{gr} \cdot \sum_{s=1}^k b_{sj} \right), \text{ subject to:}$$

$$\sum_{i=1}^k (\sum_{s=1}^i c_{os} \cdot \sum_{r=1}^k b_{ir}) \leq 1$$
$$c_{gj} \cdot \sum_{r=j}^k b_{ir} \leq c_{oi} \cdot \sum_{s=1}^k b_{sj} \qquad \forall i,j$$
$$b_{ij} \geq 0 \qquad \forall i,j$$

For all the processing costs being uniform, we can compute the precise worst-case ratios. For $k = 20$, the worst-case ratio is 2.35. For $k = 100$, this climbs to 2.61, and for $k = 200$, this is around 2.80.

The upper bound on this approximation ratio for any possible value of the processing costs would be an upper bound on the worst-case performance of the greedy algorithm. For this purpose, we take the dual of this linear program:

$$\text{minimize } \gamma, \text{ subject to:}$$

$$\gamma \sum_{s=1}^i c_{os} + \sum_{r=1}^j \alpha_{ir} c_{gr} \geq \sum_{s=1}^k \alpha_{sj} c_{os} + \sum_{r=1}^j c_{gr} \qquad \forall i,j$$
$$\alpha_{ij} \geq 0 \qquad \forall i,j$$

By linear programming duality, for any choice of the processing costs, the objective function value for *any* feasible solution for the dual problem would be an upper bound on the optimal solution to the primal problem for those processing costs. The maximum of this value over all possible choices of the processing costs would therefore be a bound on the worst-case approximation ratio for the greedy algorithm.

Fix a choice of the processing costs. We show that there is a feasible solution to the dual with $\gamma = 4$. Let $P_i = \sum_{s=1}^i c_{os}$ and $Q_j = \sum_{r=1}^j c_{gr}$. We set $\alpha_{ij} = 2$ if $P_i \leq \frac{Q_j}{2}$ and 0 otherwise. For any i, j, if $P_i \leq \frac{Q_j}{2}$, then $\sum_{r=1}^j \alpha_{ir} c_{gr} \geq 2(Q_j - 2P_i) = 2Q_j - 4P_i$. This implies $4\sum_{s=1}^i c_{os} + \sum_{r=1}^j \alpha_{ir} \geq 4P_i + 2Q_j - 4P_i = 2Q_j$. In the other case, if $P_i > \frac{Q_j}{2}$, then $\sum_{r=1}^j \alpha_{ir} c_{gr} = 0$, implying $4\sum_{s=1}^i c_{os} + \sum_{s=1}^j \alpha_{is} = 4P_i \geq 2Q_j$. We also have for all j, $\sum_{s=1}^k \alpha_{sj} c_{os} \leq 2\frac{Q_j}{2} = Q_j$, implying $\sum_{r=1}^j c_{gr} + \sum_{s=1}^k \alpha_{sj} c_{os} \leq 2Q_j$. We have for all i, j:

$$4 \sum_{s=1}^i c_{os} + \sum_{r=1}^j \alpha_{ir} c_{gr} \geq \sum_{s=1}^k \alpha_{sj} c_{os} + \sum_{r=1}^j c_{gr}$$

Our choice of α_{ij} forms a feasible solution for the dual with an objective value of $\gamma = 4$ for every choice of values for the processing costs. Therefore, the greedy algorithm always has an approximation ratio of at most 4.

Theorem 1. *The greedy algorithm is a 4-approximation to the pipelined set cover problem.*

4.1 Approximate Greedy Algorithm

At every step, suppose the greedy algorithm does not pick the best set, but any set that covers a fraction $\sigma \leq 1$ times as many elements covered by the best possible set (for the case with uniform processing costs). We can express the worst case of this algorithm as a similar linear program, and derive an approximation ratio of $\frac{4}{\sigma}$. The argument generalizes naturally to the case with arbitrary processing costs and yields the same approximation ratio. The parameter σ was useful in our implementation [2] to avoid pipeline *thrashing*: we do not want to change the current ordering unless we detect a set (operator) that covers a significant fraction more of the elements at some earlier stage in the pipeline than the current set (operator) at that position.

5 Local Search

We will now analyze the following local search heuristic: We start with an arbitrary complete pipeline. We insert a set into the pipeline (in other words, move it up the pipeline) if it improves the cost of the solution. We repeat till no insert operation improves the cost of the solution. As before, we denote the residual part of the ith set in the optimal solution by O_i, and the residual part of the jth set in the current solution by L_j.

Let the processing cost of set O_i be c_{oi} and the cost of set L_j be c_{lj}. Let $Q_j = \sum_{r=1}^{j} c_{lr}$ and $P_i = \sum_{s=1}^{i} c_{os}$. Define $Q_0 = 0$.

We will show that local search is a $(4 + \epsilon)$-approximation. As before, we can formulate the problem as a linear program. The constraint to enforce is that inserting O_i at position j does not help the current solution:

$$\sum_{r=1}^{k} \left(Q_r \sum_{s=1}^{k} b_{sr} \right) \leq \sum_{r=1}^{j-1} \left(Q_r \sum_{s=1}^{k} b_{sr} \right) + \sum_{r=j}^{k} \left((c_{oi} + Q_{j-1})b_{ir} + (c_{oi} + Q_r) \sum_{\substack{s=1 \\ s \neq i}}^{k} b_{sr} \right)$$

This simplifies to:

$$\sum_{r=j}^{k} (Q_r - Q_{j-1})b_{ir} \leq c_{oi} \sum_{r=j}^{k} \sum_{s=1}^{k} b_{sr}$$

We can now write the linear program as:

$$\text{maximize} \quad \sum_{j=1}^{k} \left(Q_j \sum_{i=1}^{k} b_{ij} \right)$$

subject to:

$$\sum_{r=j}^{k}(Q_r - Q_{j-1})b_{ir} \le c_{oi}\sum_{r=j}^{k}\sum_{s=1}^{k}b_{sr} \qquad \forall i,j$$
$$\sum_{i=1}^{k}(P_i\sum_{j=1}^{k}b_{ij}) \le 1$$
$$b_{ij} \ge 0 \qquad\qquad\qquad \forall i,j$$

We now take the dual of this program:

$$\text{minimize } \gamma$$

subject to:

$$\gamma P_i + \sum_{r=1}^{j}(Q_j - Q_{r-1})\alpha_{ir} \ge Q_j + \sum_{r=1}^{j}\sum_{s=1}^{k}\alpha_{sr}c_{os} \qquad \forall i,j$$
$$\alpha_{ij}, \gamma \ge 0 \qquad\qquad\qquad \forall i,j$$

For every i, let $z(i)$ denote the first value j such that $Q_j \ge 2P_i$. We set $\alpha_{iz(i)} = 2$. For every other j, we set $\alpha_{ij} = 0$. Therefore, $\sum_{r=1}^{j}(Q_j - Q_{r-1})\alpha_{ir} \ge 2(Q_j - 2P_i)$ for all j. In addition, $\sum_{r=1}^{j}\sum_{s=1}^{k}\alpha_{sr}c_{os} \le Q_j$ for all j. Therefore, $\gamma = 4$ is feasible for the dual.

5.1   Convergence Analysis

We now examine the number of iterations required by local search. Suppose the current solution is an M-approximation to the optimal solution. We will compute the smallest amount by which the approximation factor improves with the best possible local move. This can be formulated as the following linear program (note that M is not a variable):

$$\text{minimize } A$$

subject to:

$$\sum_{r=j}^{k}(Q_r - Q_{j-1})b_{ir} \le A + c_{oi}\sum_{r=j}^{k}\sum_{s=1}^{k}b_{sr} \qquad \forall i,j$$
$$\sum_{j=1}^{k}(\sum_{j=1}^{k}Q_j\sum_{i=1}^{k}b_{ij}) \ge M$$
$$\sum_{i=1}^{k}(P_i\sum_{j=1}^{k}b_{ij}) \le 1$$
$$b_{ij} \ge 0 \qquad\qquad\qquad \forall i,j$$

We take the dual as before, and set $\alpha_{iz(i)} = \frac{1}{k}$. This yields a dual value of $\frac{M-4}{2k}$. Therefore, the reduction in approximation ratio is $\frac{M-4}{2k}$.

Fix any $\epsilon > 0$. Suppose we stop when we achieve an approximation ratio of $(4 + \epsilon)$. It is easy to start with a solution of cost at most $nk \cdot OPT$. Therefore, the number of iterations is at most $2k\log\frac{nk}{\epsilon}$. We have therefore shown:

Theorem 2. *The local search heuristic produces a $(4 + \epsilon)$-approximation in $O(k\log\frac{nk}{\epsilon})$ operations.*

We provide simpler implementations of the local search algorithm using limited amount of state, and show the degradation in performance in the full version.

6   Extensions to Higher l_p Norms

Consider the problem of finding a pipeline $S_{t_1}, S_{t_2}, \ldots, S_{t_k}$ which minimizes the l_p-norm $(p \geq 1)$:

$$\left(\sum_{i=1}^{k} (c_{t_i} |U - \cup_{j=1}^{i-1} S_{t_j}|)^p \right)^{\frac{1}{p}}$$

We will analyze the greedy and local search algorithms for this cost function. Note that the greedy algorithm gives a $O(\log n)$-approximation for classical set cover which be viewed as seeking to minimize an l_0-norm (see Footnote 1), as the cost of a set is independent of the number of elements it processes, as long as it is nonzero. When $p = 1$, the cost of a set is weighted by the number of elements it processes (so that initial sets in the ordering are more important), and this ratio goes down to 4. Clearly, the greedy algorithm could have an approximation ratio as bad as $\frac{c_{max}}{c_{min}}$ for the l_∞-norm, as the cost of the first set chosen dominates. We will consider the *uniform* case where $c_i = 1$ for all i, and show that for integers $p \geq 2$ the approximation ratio for the greedy algorithm is at most $9^{\frac{1}{p}}$, using a Lagrangian-relaxation analysis. This proves the intuitive claim that the performance of the greedy algorithm improves as we skew the objective function more and more in favor of the initial sets in the ordering. The analysis can be tightened by a better choice of constants; our only goal here is to show that the performance ratio improves dramatically with increasing p. We leave the problem of computing the approximation ratio for arbitrary monotone cost functions as an interesting open problem.

We will analyze the local search heuristic in the full version and show that it is a $4^{\frac{1}{p}}$-approximation minimizing the l_p-norm for the nonuniform case when $p \geq 1$ is an integer.

Consider the objective function of the form $\sum_{i=1}^{k} |U - \cup_{j=1}^{i-1} S_{t_j}|^p$. For this case, the worst-case performance of greedy can be formulated as a nonlinear program:

$$\text{maximize} \quad \sum_{j=1}^{k} \left(\sum_{i=1}^{k} \sum_{r=j}^{k} b_{ir} \right)^p$$

subject to:

$$\sum_{i=1}^{k} (\sum_{s=i}^{k} \sum_{r=1}^{k} b_{sr})^p = 1$$
$$\sum_{r=j}^{k} b_{ir} \leq \sum_{s=1}^{k} b_{sj} \qquad \forall i, j$$
$$b_{ij} \geq 0 \qquad \forall i, j$$

We now write the Lagrangian relaxation of this formulation, using nonnegative α_{ij} and γ:

$$\sum_{j=1}^{k} \left(\sum_{i=1}^{k} \sum_{r=j}^{k} b_{ir} \right)^p + \gamma \left(1 - \sum_{i=1}^{k} \left(\sum_{s=i}^{k} \sum_{r=1}^{k} b_{sr} \right)^p \right) + \sum_{i,j} \alpha_{ij} \left(\sum_{s=1}^{k} b_{sj} - \sum_{r=j}^{k} b_{ir} \right)$$

Given any setting of the b_{ij}, we will find a setting for the α_{ij} and γ so that the Lagrangian is at most 9. We will use a simple method for setting the variables – we will ensure that the coefficients for all the b_{ij} variables in the Lagrangian are negative or zero. If this were true for $\gamma = 9$, we would be able to easily establish a 9-approximation. Let $L_{ij} = \sum_{r=j+1}^{k} \sum_{s=i}^{k} b_{sr}$. We set $\alpha_{ij} = 3pL_{ij}^{p-1}$ if $i \leq \frac{j}{3}$, and 0 otherwise.

We will now compute the coefficient of a general term of the form $b_{i_1 j_1}^{p_1} b_{i_2 j_2}^{p_2} \cdots b_{i_t j_t}^{p_t}$, where $p_1 + p_2 + \ldots + p_t = p$. Let $i = \min(i_1, i_2, \ldots, i_t)$ and $j = \min(j_1, j_2, \ldots, j_t)$. Let b_{im_i} and $b_{m_j j}$ be the relevant terms. The relevant nonzero terms are present in the following sum; note that there are more terms, but these would make the sum only smaller.

$$\sum_{j=1}^{k} \left(\sum_{i=1}^{k} \sum_{r=j}^{k} b_{ir} \right)^p - \gamma \left(\sum_{i=1}^{k} \left(\sum_{s=i}^{k} \sum_{r=1}^{k} b_{sr} \right)^p \right) - \sum_{r=1}^{j} \alpha_{ir} b_{im_i} + \sum_{s=1}^{k} \alpha_{sj} b_{m_j j}$$

Let $H = \frac{p!}{p_1! p_2! \cdots p_t!}$. The coefficient from the first two terms in the summation is $H(j - 9i)$. Let $n(j)$ denote the sum of the exponents of the terms in the product $b_{i_1 j_1}^{p_1} b_{i_2 j_2}^{p_2} \ldots b_{i_t j_t}^{p_t}$ of the form b_{sj}. The coefficient of the product depends on whether $n_j = 1$ or not. Let $n(i) \geq 1$ denote the total power of terms in the product of the form b_{ir}. We consider four cases:

Case 1: If $n(j) = 1$ and $i \leq j/3$, the coefficient is: $-3H \times n(i) \times \max(j - 3i - 1, 0) + 3H \times \frac{i}{3} \leq H(9i - 2j + 3) \leq H(9i - j)$, as $j \geq 3$ in this case.

Case 2: If $n(j) = 1$ and $i > j/3$, the coefficient is: $3H \times \frac{i}{3} \leq H(3i) \leq H(9i - j)$.

Case 3: If $n(j) > 1$ and $i \leq j/3$, the coefficient is: $-3H \times n(i) \times \max(j - 3i - 1, 0) \leq H(9i + 3 - 3j) \leq H(9i - j)$ since $j \geq 3$ for this case.

Case 4: If $n(j) > 1$ and $i > j/3$, the coefficient is $0 \leq H(9i - j)$.

Therefore, in all cases, the net coefficient of $b_{i_1 j_1}^{p_1} b_{i_2 j_2}^{p_2} \ldots b_{i_t j_t}^{p_t}$ is negative or zero, showing that the primal problem has objective value at most 9. We have therefore proved the following theorem:

Theorem 3. *The greedy algorithm is a $9^{\frac{1}{p}}$-approximation for minimizing the l_p-norm (for integer $p \geq 1$) of the costs in the uniform cost model.*

7   Online Problem

We now consider the pipelined set cover problem in the online setting which arises in data-stream processing [1]. At each time step, the algorithm is presented with a collection of elements. The algorithm has to choose an ordering of the sets without knowledge of these newly-arriving elements, and use this ordering to process the elements. The goal is to be competitive against the best possible algorithm that does not change its ordering for the entire request sequence.

We will begin by assuming that the incoming elements are chosen from a domain containing a relatively small number of distinct elements $\{e_1, e_2, \ldots, e_d\}$.

This assumption will be dropped in Section 7.3. Each element $e_i \in \{e_1, e_2, \ldots, e_d\}$ is dropped by zero or more sets, not dropped by the others, and this behavior does not change over time. In the rest of this section, we will use the phrase "count of elements till time t" to refer to the vector $\{s_{e_1}, s_{e_2}, \ldots, s_{e_d}\}$ where s_{e_i} is the number of times the element e_i has arrived till t time steps. "Count of elements at time t" is defined similarly.

We give an $O(\log n)$ competitive algorithm for the uniform cost version of online pipelined set cover, where n is the number of sets. Our algorithm uses a technique introduced by Kalai and Vempala in [16]. (Our algorithm and proof extend to the case with arbitrary processing costs; we omit the discussion because of space constraints.) The basic idea behind this technique is the observation that if we knew the counts of the elements at time t in advance, then using the optimal solution for the counts till time t to process the elements at time t, for all t, gives the optimal solution for the online case. Since we do not know the counts at time t in advance, we use the counts till time $t - 1$. To prevent the adversary from being malicious, we add a large random value to these counts. The first argument is that adding randomness does not affect the cost of the solution too much, provided the randomness is "small". The second argument is that for any choice of the counts at time t, the expected cost of the solution we pick will be good, since the distribution of the counts till $t - 1$ with randomness and till time t with randomness are almost identical, if the randomness is sufficiently "large". The analysis framework from [16] can be used to find the optimal amount of randomness to add. The only catch is that for approximation algorithms, this analysis works only for algorithms that provide a lower bound on the cost of the optimal solution, and provide approximation guarantees on the cost of processing every element against the fractional cost of processing the same element. (The reason for this condition can be found in [16].) The greedy and local search algorithms from Sections 4 and 5 respectively, do not provide per element guarantees, so they cannot be used here.

As a first step, we need a technique to lower bound the optimal solution for a certain set of counts. We do this by writing a linear program. Suppose the count for element e is s_e. We have a variable x_{ij} which is set to 1 if set S_i is placed in position j. We also have a variable y_{ej} which is 1 if element e passes through j stages of the pipeline. We have the following integer programming constraints:

$$
\begin{aligned}
\sum_j x_{ij} &= 1 & \forall\, S_i \\
\sum_i x_{ij} &= 1 & \forall\, j \\
y_{ej} &\geq 1 - \sum_{j' \leq j} \sum_{e \in S_i} x_{ij'} & \forall\, e, j \\
x_{ij}, y_{ej} &\in \{0, 1\} & \forall\, S_i, j, e
\end{aligned}
$$

The optimal solution minimizes the objective function:

$$
\text{Objective Function} = \sum_{e,j} s_e y_{ej}
$$

7.1   Offline Solution

We first present an offline randomized rounding algorithm for the problem, and then show how to convert it to an online algorithm. We solve the linear relaxation of the integer program described above. For each position j, we pick $2 \log n$ sets independently at random, the probability of picking set S_i at each trial being equal to x_{ij}. We repeat this for every j. If a set gets picked more than once, we place it at the earliest position at which it got picked. Note that we pick $2 \log n$ sets for each position, which implies the solution is "stretched" by the same factor. We therefore pay a cost of $2 \log n$ per element (instead of unit cost) for each position j.

Lemma 1. *For any element e, let z_{ej} denote the indicator variable showing element e "survived" until position j. If $y_{ej} < 0.25$, then:*

$$\Pr[z_{ej} = 1] \leq \frac{1}{n^{1.5}}$$

Proof. An element survives if none of the sets containing it are picked at that or the previous positions. We divide the picking of the sets into $3 \log n$ independent trials, in each of which we pick one set per position. Consider element e and position j. For one of the trials, the probability that no set containing it was picked is at most $(1 - \frac{1 - y_{ej}}{j})^j \leq \exp(y_{ej} - 1)$. If this experiment is repeated $2 \log n$ times, the probability that no set was picked is at most $\exp(-2(1 - y_{ej}) \log n) \leq \frac{1}{n^{1.5}}$ assuming $y_{ej} < 0.25$.

It is easy to bound the cost of the solution now. In expectation, if $y_{ej} > 0.25$, we pay a cost of $2 \log n$ for that stage with probability 1. Otherwise, we pay a cost of $2 \log n$ with probability $\frac{1}{n^{1.5}}$. Since an element can pass through at most n sets, the contribution to the expected cost from the second set of terms is negligible. Therefore, we have a $O(\log n)$ approximation algorithm. Note that the guarantee holds for the processing cost of every element versus its fractional processing cost.

7.2   Online Solution

We convert this offline algorithm to an online algorithm exactly as in [16]. Let s_{et} denote the count for element e given the input at time t. Let p_{et} denote a number chosen uniformly at random in $[0, \frac{\sqrt{t}}{\delta}]$, where δ is a function of the input [16]. Set $S_{et} := \sum_{t'=0}^{t-1} s_{et'} + p_{et}$. Note that we do not know s_{et}, and therefore can only compute the sum till time $t - 1$. We find the solution using S_{et} as the counts in the above integer program, and use this solution at time t. Using the same proof idea as in [16], it is easy to show that since this algorithm provides a $O(\log n)$ approximation to the fractional cost of every element, it converges to within $O(\log n)$ of optimal fixed offline solution with an additive error of $O(\sqrt{T})$ at time T. In other words, in the limit as $T \to \infty$, the cost of this algorithm converges to within $O(\log n)$ of the cost of the optimal offline solution.

7.3   Incomplete Information Model

So far we assumed that the incoming elements are chosen from a small domain so that we can keep track of the counts of the arrived elements. We now drop this assumption and show that our algorithm from above can be used unchanged in this case except now we use sampling-based estimates instead of the actual counts of the elements. We sample the incoming elements with probability $\frac{1}{n^2}$. For each element e in the sample, we pass e through all n sets to categorize e such that elements that are dropped by exactly the same sets belong to a specific category. This sampling process gives us an estimate of the counts of elements till time t. We use this estimate to find the optimal online solution for the remaining elements using the algorithm described previously. The sampled elements, which are processed by all the sets, usually add little extra overhead to the overall cost; see [2]. Furthermore, by Chernoff bounds, if $T \gg n$, the estimates of the large counts converge to the true values, and therefore, the error due to sampling is negligible. Details are omitted for lack of space.

8   Conclusions and Future Work

We identified the relevance of pipelined set cover to query optimization and presented efficient approximation algorithms for this NP-Hard problem. We also considered the online version of pipelined set cover and presented a competitive algorithm with a logarithmic performance guarantee. An interesting open problem is to incorporate precedence constraints on the sets that are required to handle non-commutative operators. Natural extensions of the algorithms mentioned in this paper do not yield constant factor approximations to this variant. While we focused on a single pipeline, an interesting avenue for future work is to consider approximation algorithms for optimizing a set of pipelines, which, e.g., is applicable in a publish-subscribe setting [5]. If the pipelines are optimized independently in such a setting, e.g., using the greedy algorithm from Section 4, then the resulting overall plan may be far from optimal because it misses opportunities for sharing computation using operator sequences that are common among the pipelines.

Acknowledgments

We would like to thank Pankaj Agarwal, Arvind Arasu, Arpita Ghosh, Chandra Nair, Serge Plotkin, and Jun Yang for helpful discussions.

References

1. B. Babcock, S. Babu, M. Datar, R. Motwani, and J. Widom. Models and issues in data stream systems. In *Proc. of the 2002 ACM Symp. on Principles of Database Systems*, pages 1–16, June 2002.

2. S. Babu, R. Motwani, K. Munagala, I. Nishizawa, and J. Widom. Adaptive ordering of pipelined stream filters. In *Proc. of the 2004 ACM SIGMOD Intl. Conf. on Management of Data*, 2004.

3. S. Chaudhuri, R. Motwani, and V. Narasayya. Random sampling for histogram construction: How much is enough? In *Proc. of the 1998 ACM SIGMOD Intl. Conf. on Management of Data*, pages 436–447, June 1998.

4. S. Chaudhuri and K. Shim. Optimization of queries with user-defined predicates. *ACM Transactions on Database Systems*, 24(2):177–228, 1999.

5. J. Chen, D. DeWitt, F. Tian, and Y. Wang. NiagaraCQ: A scalable continuous query system for internet databases. In *Proc. of the 2000 ACM SIGMOD Intl. Conf. on Management of Data*, pages 379–390, May 2000.

6. S. Christodoulakis. Implications of certain assumptions in database performance evaluation. *ACM Transactions on Database Systems*, 9(2):163–186, 1984.

7. E. Cohen, A. Fiat, and H. Kaplan. Efficient sequences of trials. In *Proc. of the 2003 Annual ACM-SIAM Symp. on Discrete Algorithms*, 2003.

8. G. Cormode, M. Datar, P. Indyk, and S. Muthukrishnan. Comparing data streams using hamming norms (how to zero in). In *Proc. of the 2002 Intl. Conf. on Very Large Data Bases*, pages 335–345, August 2002.

9. C. Cranor, T. Johnson, O. Spataschek, and V. Shkapenyuk. Gigascope: A stream database for network applications. In *Proc. of the 2003 ACM SIGMOD Intl. Conf. on Management of Data*, pages 647–651, June 2003.

10. U. Feige. A threshold of ln n for approximating set cover. *Journal of the ACM*, 45:634–652, 1998.

11. U. Feige, L. Lovász, and P. Tetali. Approximating min-sum set cover. *Algorithmica*, 2004.

12. J. Hellerstein. Optimization techniques for queries with expensive methods. *ACM Transactions on Database Systems*, 23(2):113–157, 1998.

13. D. Hochbaum, editor. *Approximation Algorithms for NP-Hard Problems*. PWS Publishing Company, Boston, MA, 1997.

14. K. Jain, M. Mahdian, and A. Saberi. A new greedy approach for facility location problems. In *Proc. of the 2002 Annual ACM Symp. on Theory of Computing*, May 2002.

15. D. Johnson. Approximation algorithms for combinatorial problems. *Journal of Computer and System Sciences*, 9:256–278, 1974.

16. A. Kalai and S. Vempala. Efficient algorithms for the online decision problem. In *Proc. of 16th Conf. on Computational Learning Theory*, 2003.

17. A. Kemper, G. Moerkotte, and M. Steinbrunn. Optimizing boolean expressions in object-bases. In *Proc. of the 1992 Intl. Conf. on Very Large Data Bases*, pages 79–90, August 1992.

18. R. Krishnamurthy, H. Boral, and C. Zaniolo. Optimization of nonrecursive queries. In *Proc. of the 1986 Intl. Conf. on Very Large Data Bases*, pages 128–137, August 1986.

19. Y. Ling and W. Sun. An evaluation of sampling-based size estimation methods for selections in database systems. In *Proc. of the 1995 Intl. Conf. on Data Engineering*, pages 532–539, March 1995.

20. R. Motwani, J. Widom, and et al. Query processing, resource management, and approximation in a data stream management system. In *Proc. of the 2003 Conf. on Innovative Data Systems Research*, pages 245–256, January 2003.

21. K. Munagala, S. Babu, R. Motwani, and J. Widom. The pipelined set cover problem. *Stanford University Database Group Technical Report 2003-65*, 2003.

22. L. Reinwald and R. Soland. Conversion of limited-entry decision tables to optimal computer programs I: Minimum average processing time. *Journal of the ACM*, 13(3):339–358, 1966.
23. K. Ross. Conjunctive selection conditions in main memory. In *Proc. of the 2002 ACM Symp. on Principles of Database Systems*, June 2002.
24. A. Srinivasan. Improved approximations of packing and covering problems. In *Proc. of the 1995 Annual ACM Symp. on Theory of Computing*, pages 268–276, June 1995.
25. M. Stillger, G. Lohman, V. Markl, and M. Kandil. LEO - DB2's LEarning Optimizer. In *Proc. of the 2001 Intl. Conf. on Very Large Data Bases*, pages 9–28, September 2001.

Well-Definedness and Semantic Type-Checking in the Nested Relational Calculus and XQuery
Extended Abstract

Jan Van den Bussche[1], Dirk Van Gucht[2,*], and Stijn Vansummeren[1,**]

[1] Limburgs Universitair Centrum, Diepenbeek, Belgium
{jan.vandenbussche, stijn.vansummeren}@luc.ac.be
[2] Indiana University, Bloomington, Indiana, USA
vgucht@cs.indiana.edu

Abstract. Two natural decision problems regarding the XML query language XQuery are well-definedness and semantic type-checking. We study these problems in the setting of a relational fragment of XQuery. We show that well-definedness and semantic type-checking are undecidable, even in the positive-existential case. Nevertheless, for a "pure" variant of XQuery, in which no identification is made between an item and the singleton containing that item, the problems become decidable. We also consider the analogous problems in the setting of the nested relational calculus.

1 Introduction

Much attention has been paid recently to XQuery, the XML query language currently under development by the World Wide Web Consortium [5, 9]. Unlike in traditional query languages, expressions in XQuery can have an undefined meaning (i.e., these expressions produce a run-time error). As an example, consider the following variation on one of the XQuery use cases [7]:

```
<bib> {
  for $b in $bib/book
  where $b/publisher = "Springer-Verlag"
  return element{$b/author}{$b/title}
} </bib>
```

This expression should create for each book published by Springer-Verlag a node whose name equals the author of the book, and whose child is the title of the book. If there is a book with more than one `author` node however, then the result of this expression is undefined because the first argument to the element constructor must be a singleton list.

This leads us to the natural question whether we can solve the *well-definedness problem* for XQuery: given an expression and an input type, check whether the

---

* Supported by NSF Grant IIS-0082407.
** Research Assistant of the Fund for Scientific Research - Flanders (Belgium).

T. Eiter and L. Libkin (Eds.): ICDT 2005, LNCS 3363, pp. 99–113, 2005.

semantics of the expression is defined for all inputs adhering to the input type. This problem is undecidable for any computationally complete programming language, and hence also for XQuery. Following good programming language practice, XQuery therefore is equipped with a static type system (based on XML Schema [4, 18]) which ensures "type safety" in the sense that every expression which passes the type system's tests is guaranteed to be well-defined. Due to the undecidability of the well-definedness problem, such type systems are necessarily incomplete, i.e., there are expressions which are well-defined, but not well-typed.

Can we find fragments of XQuery for which the well-definedness problem is decidable? In this paper we will study *Relational XQuery* (RX), a set-based fragment of XQuery where we omit recursive functions, only allow the child axis, take a value-based point of view (i.e., we ignore node identity), and use a type system similar to that of the nested relational or complex object data model [1, 6, 19]. We regard RX as the "first-order database fragment" of XQuery.

Even for RX, the well-definedness problem is still undecidable, due to two features which allow us to simulate the relational algebra: quantified expressions and type switches. Surprisingly, however, well-definedness remains undecidable for RX without these features, which we call positive-existential RX or PERX for short.

The core difficulty here is due to the fact that in the XQuery data model an item is identified with the singleton containing that item [11]. In a set-based model this identification becomes difficult to analyze, since $\{i, j\}$ is a singleton if and only if $i = j$. Since, as shown in the example above, there are expressions which are undefined on non-singleton inputs, this implies that in order to solve the well-definedness problem, one also needs to solve the equivalence problem. Indeed, we will see that the equivalence problem for PERX is undecidable.

Nevertheless, for a "pure" variant of PERX, in which no identification is made between an item and the singleton containing that item, well-definedness becomes decidable. We actually prove this result not for pure PERX itself, but for PENRC: the positive-existential fragment of the *nested relational calculus* [6, 19], which is well-known from the complex object data model, and whose well-definedness problem is interesting in its own right.

All our results hold not only for well-definedness, but also for *semantic type-checking*: given an expression, an input type and an output type, check whether the expression always returns outputs adhering to the output type on inputs adhering to the input type.

In the main body of the paper we will work in a set-based data model. Considering that the real XML data model is list-based, at the end of the paper we will discuss how and if our results transfer to a list-based or bag-based setting.

Related Work. The semantic type-checking problem has already been studied extensively in XML-related query languages [2, 3, 13, 14, 15, 17]. In particular, our setting closely resembles that of Alon et al. [2, 3] who, like us, study the problem in the presence of data values. In particular they have shown that (un)decidability depends on the expressiveness of both the query language and the type system. While the query language of Alon et al. can simulate PERX, our results do not follow immediately from theirs, since their type system is incompatible with ours [16].

2 Relational XQuery

In what follows we will need to define various query languages. In some definitions it will help to talk abstractly about a query language. To this end, we define a *query language* Q as a tuple $(V, T, E, [\![.]\!])$ where V is a set of *values*; T is a set of *types*; E is a set of *expressions*; and $[\![.]\!]$ is the interpretation function giving a semantics to types and expressions. The set V is also referred to as the data model.

We assume to be given an infinite set $\mathcal{X} = \{x, y, \dots\}$ of *variables*. Every expression e has associated with it a finite set $FV(e) \subseteq \mathcal{X}$ of *free variables*. An *environment* on e is a function $\sigma : FV(e) \to V$ which associates to each $x \in FV(e)$ a value $\sigma(x) \in V$. A *type assignment* on e is a function $\Gamma : FV(e) \to T$ which associates to each $x \in FV(e)$ a type $\Gamma(x) \in T$. If ρ is an environment (or a type assignment), and v is a value (respectively a type), then we write $x : v, \rho$ for the environment (respectively type assignment) ρ' with domain $dom(\rho) \cup \{x\}$ such that $\rho'(x) = v$ and $\rho'(y) = \rho(y)$ for $y \neq x$. Intuitively, environments describe the input to expressions, and type assignments describe their type.

Every type τ is associated with a set $[\![\tau]\!]$ of values. An environment σ is *compatible with* a type assignment Γ, denoted by $\sigma \in \Gamma$, if they have the same domain and $\sigma(x) \in [\![\Gamma(x)]\!]$ for all x. Every expression e has associated with it a (possibly partial) computable function $[\![e]\!]$ which associates environments on $FV(e)$ to values in V. We call $[\![e]\!]$ the *semantics* of e.

In order not to burden our notation we will identify types and expressions with their respective interpretations, and write for example $e(\sigma)$ for $[\![e]\!](\sigma)$.

2.1 Relational XQuery Data Model

In this section we define a set-based fragment of the XQuery data model [11] called the *Relational XQuery (RX) data model*. We take a value-based point of view (i.e., we ignore node identity), focus on data values, element nodes and data nodes (known as text nodes in XQuery), and abstract away from the other features in the XQuery data model such as attributes.

We assume to be given a recursively enumerable set $\mathcal{A} = \{a, b, \dots\}$ of *atoms*. An *item* is an atom or a *node*. A node is either an *element node* $\langle a : N \rangle$ or a *data node* $\langle a \rangle$, where $a \in \mathcal{A}$ and N is a finite set of nodes (N is called the content of the element node). An *RX-value*, finally, is any finite set of items. Note that, as in the XQuery data model, atoms can only occur at the "top level" of a value. Inside element nodes they must be encapsulated in a data node.

An *RX-type* τ is a term generated by the following grammar:

$$\tau ::= \mathbf{coll}(\iota) \mid \mathbf{single}(\iota)$$
$$\iota ::= \mathbf{atom} \mid \nu \mid \iota \cup \iota$$
$$\nu ::= \mathbf{data} \mid \mathbf{elem}(\gamma) \mid \nu \cup \nu$$
$$\gamma ::= \mathbf{coll}(\nu) \mid \mathbf{single}(\nu)$$

Here, τ ranges over types, ι ranges over item types, ν ranges over node types, and γ ranges over node content types. An RX-type denotes a set of RX-values:

- **data** denotes the set of all data nodes,
- **elem**(γ) denotes the set of all element nodes $\langle a : N \rangle$ for which N is in the denotation of γ,
- **atom** denotes the set $\mathcal{A}$ of all atoms,
- $\iota_1 \cup \iota_2$ denotes the union of the denotations of ι_1 and ι_2,
- **coll**(ι) denotes the set of all finite sets over the denotation of ι, and
- **single**(ι) denotes the set of all singletons over the denotation of ι.

Note that every γ is also a τ, and hence the denotation of terms produced by γ is subsumed in the definition above.

An *RX-kind* κ is a term generated by the following grammar:

$$\kappa ::= \mathbf{atom} \mid \mathbf{data} \mid \mathbf{elem} \mid \kappa \cup \kappa$$

An RX-kind denotes a set of items, which can be the set of all atoms, the set of all data nodes, the set of all element nodes, or the union of the denotations of two kinds.

Discussion. The type system we have defined above is quite simple. Types merely indicate the many-or-one cardinality of a value, and the kinds of items that can appear in it. Only values of a fixed maximal nesting height can be described in our type system. This is justified because the expressions in the XQuery fragment RX we will work with in this paper can look only a fixed number of nesting levels down anyway. Also, it is a public secret that most XML documents in practice have nesting heights at most five or six, and that unbounded-depth nesting is not needed for many XML data processing tasks.

The presence of the **single** type constructor is justified by the fact that an item i is identified with the singleton set $\{i\}$ in the XQuery data model [11]. Consequently, an XQuery expression in which the input is always expected to be a string actually receives singleton strings as inputs. Its input type would therefore be **single(atom)** in our setting.

Our types also do not specify anything about the names of element nodes, but this is an omission for the sake of simplicity; we could have added node types of the form **elem**$_a(\gamma)$, with a the atom that must be the name of the element node, without sacrificing any of the results we present in this paper.

2.2   Relational XQuery Syntax and Semantics

A *Relational XQuery expression* is an expression generated by the following grammar:

$$
\begin{aligned}
e ::= \; & x \\
& \mid \; text\{e\} \mid elem\{e\}\{e\} \mid data(e) \mid name(e) \mid children(e) \\
& \mid \; () \mid e, e \mid for \; x : \kappa \; in \; e \; return \; e \\
& \mid \; if \; e \; eq \; e \; then \; e \; else \; e \mid if \; e = \emptyset \; then \; e \; else \; e \mid if \; e \in \tau \; then \; e \; else \; e
\end{aligned}
$$

Here, e ranges over RX-expressions, x ranges over variables, τ ranges over RX-types and κ ranges over RX-kinds. The *free variables* of e are defined in the usual way, and will be denoted by $FV(e)$.

The semantics of RX is parameterized by two "oracle" functions:

- *content*, which maps element nodes to atoms; and
- *concat*, which maps finite sets of atoms to atoms.

We further define the following (partial) functions on values:

- $data(v) = \{a \mid a \in v\} \cup \{a \mid \langle a \rangle \in v\} \cup \{content(\langle a : N \rangle) \mid \langle a : N \rangle \in v\}$,
- $name(v)$, which is $\{a\}$ if v is a singleton element node $\{\langle a : N \rangle\}$; $concat(v)$ if v is empty; and undefined otherwise.
- $children(v)$, which is undefined if there is some atom in v, and otherwise returns

$$\bigcup \{N \mid \langle a : N \rangle \in v\}.$$

- $construct(v, w)$ which is undefined if $data(v)$ is not a singleton atom $\{a\}$; and returns $\langle a : N \rangle$ otherwise, where N is obtained from w by replacing every atom in w by a corresponding data node:

$$N = \{\langle a \rangle \mid a \in w\} \cup \{i \mid i \in w, i \text{ is a node}\}.$$

Let e be an RX-expression and let σ be an RX-environment on e.[1] The *semantics* $e(\sigma)$ of e under σ can now be inductively defined as follows:

$$x(\sigma) = \sigma(x)$$
$$text\{e\}(\sigma) = \{\langle concat(data(e(\sigma)))\rangle\}$$
$$elem\{e_1\}\{e_2\}(\sigma) = \{construct(e_1(\sigma), e_2(\sigma))\}$$
$$data(e)(\sigma) = data(e(\sigma))$$
$$name(e)(\sigma) = name(e(\sigma))$$
$$children(e)(\sigma) = children(e(\sigma))$$
$$()(\sigma) = \emptyset$$
$$e_1, e_2(\sigma) = e_1(\sigma) \cup e_2(\sigma)$$
$$for\ x : \kappa\ in\ e_1\ return\ e_2 = \bigcup \{e_2(x : \{i\}, \sigma) \mid i \in e_1(\sigma) \cap \kappa\}$$

$$(if\ e_1\ eq\ e_2\ then\ e_3\ else\ e_4)(\sigma) = \begin{cases} e_3(\sigma) & \text{if } data(e_1(\sigma)) = data(e_2(\sigma)) = \{a\}, \\ & \text{with } a \text{ an atom} \\ e_4(\sigma) & \text{if } data(e_1(\sigma)) = \{a\}, \\ & data(e_2(\sigma)) = \{b\}, \\ & \text{with } a \text{ and } b \text{ atoms, } a \neq b \end{cases}$$

$$(if\ e_1 = \emptyset\ then\ e_2\ else\ e_3)(\sigma) = \begin{cases} e_2(\sigma) & \text{if } e_1(\sigma) = \emptyset \\ e_3(\sigma) & \text{otherwise} \end{cases}$$

$$(if\ e_1 \in \tau\ then\ e_2\ else\ e_3)(\sigma) = \begin{cases} e_2(\sigma) & \text{if } e_1(\sigma) \in \tau \\ e_3(\sigma) & \text{otherwise} \end{cases}$$

---

[1] Recall from the beginning of this section that σ assigns an RX-value to each free variable of e.

Note that $e(\sigma)$ is not necessarily defined: this models the situations in which XQuery expression evaluation produces a run-time error. Specifically, $e(\sigma)$ can become undefined for the following reasons:

- $e = elem\{e_1\}\{e_2\}$, and $data(e_1(\sigma))$ is not a singleton atom. (This can only happen if $e_1(\sigma)$ is not a singleton.)
- $e = name(e')$, and $e'(\sigma)$ is not the empty set, or not a singleton element node.
- $e = children(e')$, and $e'(\sigma)$ contains an atom.
- $e = if\ e_1\ eq\ e_2\ then\ e_3\ else\ e_4$, and $data(e_1(\sigma))$ is not a singleton atom, or $data(e_2(\sigma))$ is not a singleton atom. (This can only happen if $e_1(\sigma)$ respectively $e_2(\sigma)$ is not a singleton.)

Relation to XQuery. The RX query language corresponds to a set-based version of XQuery [5, 9] where we have omitted recursive functions, literals, arithmetic expressions, generalized and order comparisons, and only allow the children axis. We have replaced XQuery quantified expressions by the emptiness test (which is equivalent in expressive power), and have moved kind tests from XQuery step expressions to the "for" expression. As an example, the XQuery step expression $x/child :: text()$ can be expressed in RX as

$$for\ z : \textbf{data}\ in\ children(x)\ return\ z.$$

The "oracle" functions *concat* and *content* model features which are present in XQuery, but which are clumsy to take into account in our data model. For example *name* applied to the empty sequence returns the empty string in XQuery. Furthermore, applying *data* to a singleton element node in XQuery returns the "string content" of the node. This is (roughly speaking) a concatenation of all atoms (converted to strings) encountered in a depth-first left-to-right traversal of the node's content.

3   Well-Definedness and Semantic Type-Checking

As we have noted in Section 2.2, the semantics $e(\sigma)$ of RX-expression e under environment σ can be undefined. This leads us to the following definition.

Definition 1. *The well-definedness problem for a query language Q consist of checking, given a Q-expression e and a Q-type assignment Γ on e: whether $e(\sigma)$ is defined for every $\sigma \in \Gamma$. In this case we say that e is well-defined under Γ.*

A problem which is related to well-definedness is the *semantic type-checking* problem:

Definition 2. *The semantic type-checking problem for a query language Q consist of checking, given a Q-expression e, a Q-type assignment Γ on e such that e is well-defined under Γ, and a Q-type τ: whether $e(\sigma) \in \tau$ for every $\sigma \in \Gamma$. In this case we say that τ is an output type for e under Γ.*

4 Undecidability Results

We will show that well-definedness for RX is undecidable, even for a quite restricted fragment. Our results do not depend on the particular interpretation given to the oracle functions *concat* and *content*.

Let us begin by defining RX$^-$ as the fragment of RX where

- we disallow data node construction expressions of the form *text*$\{e\}$;
- we disallow data extraction expressions of the form *data*(e); and
- we disallow kind tests, or equivalently, we only allow the use of the single "universal" kind **atom** $\cup$ **data** $\cup$ **elem**.

An RX$^-$-expression e is *positive existential* if it does not contain *emptiness tests* of the form *if* $e_1 = \emptyset$ *then* e_2 *else* e_3, or *type switches* of the form *if* $e_1 \in \tau$ *then* e_2 *else* e_3. We denote the language of all positive-existential RX$^-$ expressions by PERX$^-$, and we will mention specific features added back to PERX$^-$ in square brackets. Thus, PERX$^-$[empty] includes emptiness tests, and type switches are included in PERX$^-$[type].

Proposition 1. *Type switches can be used to simulate emptiness tests, i.e. PERX$^-$[empty] is a semantic subset of PERX$^-$[type].*

Indeed, *if* $e_1 = \emptyset$ *then* e_2 *else* e_3 can be expressed as follows:

$$if \ (for \ x \ in \ e_1 \ return \ elem\{a\}\{()\}) \in \mathbf{coll(data)} \ then \ e_2 \ else \ e_3$$

The following proposition is not surprising, and parallels earlier results on semistructured query languages such as StruQL [10]:

Proposition 2. *PERX$^-$[empty] can simulate the relational algebra. Concretely, for every relational algebra expression ϕ over database schema $\mathbf{S}$, there exists a PERX$^-$[empty]-expression e_ϕ and a type assignment $\Gamma_{\mathbf{S}}$, such that*

- e_ϕ *is well-defined under $\Gamma_{\mathbf{S}}$, and,*
- e_ϕ *evaluated on an encoding of database D equals an encoding of $\phi(D)$.*

Consequently, satisfiability (i.e., nonempty output on at least one input) is undecidable for PERX$^-$[empty] (and thus for RX$^-$), because it is undecidable for the relational algebra. Since the expression

$$for \ x \ in \ e \ return \ elem\{()\}\{()\}$$

is well-defined if, and only if, e is unsatisfiable, we obtain:

Corollary 1. *Well-definedness for PERX$^-$[empty] (and thus RX) is undecidable.*

What is perhaps more surprising is that without emptiness test, we remain undecidable:

Theorem 1. *Well-definedness for PERX⁻ is undecidable.*

Proof (Crux). The proof goes by reduction from the implication problem for functional and inclusion dependencies, which is known to be undecidable [1, 8].

Let Σ be a set of functional and inclusion dependencies, and let ρ be an inclusion dependency. We show in the full version of this paper that we can construct two expressions e_1 and e_2, a type assignment Γ and a node content type γ, such that

- e_1 and e_2 are well-defined under Γ,
- γ is an output type for e_1 and e_2 under Γ, and,
- $e_1(\sigma) = e_2(\sigma)$ for every $\sigma \in \Gamma$ if, and only if, ρ is implied by Σ.

Consequently, the expression $name(elem\{a\}\{e_1\}, elem\{a\}\{e_2\})$ is well-defined under Γ if, and only if, ρ is implied by Σ.   □

As a corollary to the proof, we note:

Corollary 2. *Equivalence of PERX⁻ expressions is undecidable.*

We further derive:

Corollary 3. *Semantic type-checking for PERX⁻ is undecidable.*

Indeed, referring to the above proof sketch of Theorem 1, e_1 and e_2 are equivalent if, and only if, $(elem\{a\}\{e_1\}, elem\{a\}\{e_2\})$ has output type **single(elem(γ))**.

We remark that to establish undecidability of well-definedness we do not need singleton types. For undecidability of semantic type-checking, we do.

5   Pure RX

In the XQuery data model, an item i is identified with the singleton $\{i\}$ [11]. With this identification, it is indeed natural to let, e.g., $name(e)$ be undefined when $e(\sigma)$ is a set with more than one element. As we have seen in the previous Section, it is exactly this behavior that causes well-definedness to be undecidable.

So let us define a version of RX, called *pure RX*, which does not explicitly identify an item i with $\{i\}$. We will show in Section 6 that well-definedness and semantic type-checking for the positive-existential fragment of pure RX is decidable.

A *pure RX-value* is an item or a set of items. A *pure RX-type* τ is a term generated by the following grammar:

$$\tau ::= \mathbf{coll}(\iota) \mid \iota \mid \tau \cup \tau$$
$$\iota ::= \mathbf{atom} \mid \nu \mid \iota \cup \iota$$
$$\nu ::= \mathbf{data} \mid \mathbf{elem}(\nu_1 \cup \cdots \cup \nu_k)$$

Here, τ ranges over types, ι ranges over item types, ν ranges over node types, and $k \geq 0$.

A *pure RX-type* denotes a set of pure RX-values:

- **data** denotes the set of all data nodes,
- **elem**$(\nu_1 \cup \cdots \cup \nu_k)$ denotes the set of all element nodes $\langle a : N \rangle$ for which N is a finite set over the union of the denotations of $\nu_1, \ldots, \nu_k$.
- **atom** denotes the set $\mathcal{A}$ of all atoms,
- $\tau_1 \cup \tau_2$ denotes the union of the denotations of τ_1 and τ_2, and,
- **coll**(ι) denotes the set of all finite sets over the denotation of ι.

Note that since every ι is also a τ, the denotation of $\iota_1 \cup \iota_2$ is subsumed by the definition above.

The syntax of *pure RX* is obtained from the syntax of RX by adding a singleton constructor expression (e), and by replacing RX-types in type switch expressions by pure RX types.

In order to give the semantics of pure RX, we define the following (partial) functions on pure RX-values.

- $data'(v) = \{a \mid a \in v\} \cup \{a \mid \langle a \rangle \in v\}$
- $name'(v)$, which is a if v is an element node $\langle a : N \rangle$, and is undefined otherwise.
- $children'(v)$, which is undefined if there is some atom in v, and otherwise returns

$$\bigcup \{N \mid \langle a : N \rangle \in v\}.$$

- $construct'(v, w)$ which is undefined if v is not an atom, and returns $\langle v : N \rangle$ otherwise where N is obtained from w by replacing every atom in w by a corresponding data node:

$$N = \{\langle a \rangle \mid a \in w\} \cup \{i \mid i \in w, i \text{ is a node}\}$$

The semantics of pure RX is then defined as follows:

$$x(\sigma) = \sigma(x)$$

$$text\{e\}(\sigma) = \langle a \rangle \quad \text{if } e(\sigma) = a$$

$$elem\{e_1\}\{e_2\}(\sigma) = construct'(e_1(\sigma), e_2(\sigma))$$

$$data(e)(\sigma) = data'(e(\sigma))$$

$$name(e)(\sigma) = name'(e(\sigma))$$

$$children(e)(\sigma) = children'(e(\sigma))$$

$$()(\sigma) = \emptyset$$

$$(e)(\sigma) = \{e(\sigma)\} \quad \text{if } e(\sigma) \text{ is an item}$$

$$e_1, e_2(\sigma) = e_1(\sigma) \cup e_2(\sigma)$$

$$for\ x : \kappa\ in\ e_1\ return\ e_2 = \bigcup \{e_2(x : i, \sigma) \mid i \in e_1(\sigma) \cap \kappa\}$$

$$(if\ e_1\ eq\ e_2\ then\ e_3\ else\ e_4)(\sigma) = \begin{cases} e_3(\sigma) & \text{if } e_1(\sigma), e_2(\sigma) \in \mathcal{A} \text{ and } e_1(\sigma) = e_2(\sigma) \\ e_4(\sigma) & \text{if } e_1(\sigma), e_2(\sigma) \in \mathcal{A} \text{ and } e_1(\sigma) \neq e_2(\sigma) \end{cases}$$

$$(if\ e_1 = \emptyset\ then\ e_2\ else\ e_3)(\sigma) = \begin{cases} e_2(\sigma) & \text{if } e_1(\sigma) = \emptyset \\ e_3(\sigma) & \text{otherwise} \end{cases}$$

$$(if\ e_1 \in \tau\ then\ e_2\ else\ e_3)(\sigma) = \begin{cases} e_2(\sigma) & if\ e_1(\sigma) \in \tau \\ e_3(\sigma) & otherwise \end{cases}$$

Note that again $e(\sigma)$ is not necessarily defined. Specifically, $e(\sigma)$ can become undefined for the following reasons:

- $e = text\{e'\}$, and $e'(\sigma)$ is not an atom,
- $e = elem\{e_1\}\{e_2\}$, and $e_1(\sigma)$ is not an atom,
- $e = name(e')$, and $e'(\sigma)$ is not an element node,
- $e = children(e')$, and $e'(\sigma)$ contains an atom,
- $e = (e')$, and $e'(\sigma)$ is not an item,
- $e = e_1, e_2$, and $e_1(\sigma)$ is not a set or $e_2(\sigma)$ is not a set,
- $e = for\ x : \kappa\ in\ e_1\ return\ e_2$, and $e_1(\sigma)$ is not a set or $e_2(x : i, \sigma)$ is not a set for some $i \in e_1(\sigma) \cap \kappa$, or,
- $e = if\ e_1\ eq\ e_2\ then\ e_3\ else\ e_4$, and $e_1(\sigma)$ or $e_2(\sigma)$ is not an atom.

Pure PERX

Well-definedness and semantic type-checking for the entire pure RX remains undecidable due to the presence of the emptiness test and type switch expressions. Let us define *pure PERX* as the fragment of pure RX in which these expressions are disallowed.

6   Decidability Results

In this section we will show that well-definedness and semantic type-checking for pure PERX are decidable. In fact, we will solve the corresponding problems for the nested relational calculus (NRC): the well-known standard query language for nested relations and complex objects. Indeed, this language remains fundamental and its study remains interesting in its own right. As we will see, pure PERX can be simulated by the positive-existential fragment of NRC (extended with kind-tests).

6.1   Nested Relational Calculus

An *NRC-value* is either an atom, a pair of NRC-values, or a finite set of NRC-values. Note that we allow sets to be heterogeneous. If $v = (v_1, v_2)$, then we write $\pi_1(v)$ for v_1 and $\pi_2(v)$ for v_2.

An *NRC-type* τ is a term generated by the following grammar:

$$\tau ::= \emptyset \mid \mathbf{atom} \mid \tau \times \tau \mid \tau \cup \tau \mid \mathbf{coll}(\tau)$$

An NRC-type *denotes* a set of NRC-values:

- $\emptyset$ denotes the empty set,
- **atom** denotes the set $\mathcal{A}$ of all atoms,
- $\tau_1 \times \tau_2$ denotes the cartesian product of the denotations of τ_1 and τ_2,

- $\tau_1 \cup \tau_2$ denotes the union of the denotations of τ_1 and τ_2, and,
- $\mathbf{coll}(\tau)$ denotes the set of all finite sets over the denotation of τ.

An *NRC-kind* κ is a term generated by the following grammar:

$$\kappa ::= \mathbf{atom} \mid \mathbf{coll} \mid \kappa \times \kappa \mid \kappa \cup \kappa$$

An NRC-kind denotes a set of NRC-values, which can be the set of all atoms, the set of all finite sets of values, the cartesian product of the denotation of two kinds, or the union of the denotation of two kinds.

The *positive existential nested relational calculus* (PENRC) is the set of all expressions generated by the following grammar:

$$
\begin{aligned}
e ::=\ & x \\
\mid\ & (e, e) \mid \pi_1(e) \mid \pi_2(e) \\
\mid\ & \emptyset \mid \{e\} \mid e \cup e \mid \bigcup e \mid \{e \mid x \in e\} \\
\mid\ & e = e\ ?\ e\ :\ e
\end{aligned}
$$

Here e ranges over expressions, and x ranges over variables. The PENRC with kind tests, denoted by PENRC[kind] is the PENRC extended with one additional expression:

$$e ::= \cdots \mid e \in \kappa\ ?\ e\ :\ e$$

Here, κ ranges over NRC kinds. The *free variables* of e are defined in the usual way, and will be denoted by $FV(e)$.

If e is a PENRC[kind]-expression and σ is an NRC-environment on e, then the *semantics* $e(\sigma)$ of e under σ is inductively defined as follows:

$$
\begin{aligned}
x(\sigma) &= \sigma(x) \\
(e_1, e_2)(\sigma) &= (e_1(\sigma), e_2(\sigma)) \\
\pi_1(e)(\sigma) &= \pi_1(e(\sigma)) \\
\pi_2(e)(\sigma) &= \pi_2(e(\sigma)) \\
\emptyset(\sigma) &= \emptyset \\
\{e\}(\sigma) &= \{e(\sigma)\} \\
(e_1 \cup e_2)(\sigma) &= e_1(\sigma) \cup e_2(\sigma) \\
(\bigcup e)(\sigma) &= \bigcup e(\sigma) \\
\{e_2 \mid x \in e_1\}(\sigma) &= \{e_2(x : v, \sigma) \mid v \in e_1(\sigma)\} \\
(e_1 = e_2\ ?\ e_3\ :\ e_4)(\sigma) &= \begin{cases} e_3(\sigma) & \text{if } e_1(\sigma), e_2(\sigma) \in \mathcal{A} \text{ and } e_1(\sigma) = e_2(\sigma) \\ e_4(\sigma) & \text{if } e_1(\sigma), e_2(\sigma) \in \mathcal{A} \text{ and } e_1(\sigma) \neq e_2(\sigma) \end{cases} \\
(e_1 \in \kappa\ ?\ e_2\ :\ e_3)(\sigma) &= \begin{cases} e_2(\sigma) & \text{if } e_1(\sigma) \in \kappa \\ e_3(\sigma) & \text{otherwise} \end{cases}
\end{aligned}
$$

Note that $e(\sigma)$ can be undefined. For example $\pi_1(x)(\sigma)$ is undefined when $\sigma(x)$ is not a pair, and $(x \cup y)(\sigma)$ is undefined when $\sigma(x)$ is not a set. Hence, we can also study the well-definedness problem for PENRC[kind].

It is easy to see that well-definedness for full NRC: PENRC extended with an emptiness test, is undecidable. Indeed, it is well known that NRC can simulate the relational algebra [6].

6.2   Simulating RX in NRC

Formally, a *simulation* of a query language Q in a query language Q' is a function $enc : V_Q \to V_{Q'}$ such that

- for every type $\tau \in T_Q$ there exists a type $\tau' \in T_{Q'}$ such that $v \in \tau$ if and only if $enc(v) \in \tau'$, and
- for every expression $e \in E_Q$ there exists an expression $e' \in E_{Q'}$ such that
  1. $e(\sigma)$ is defined if and only if $e'(enc(\sigma))$ is defined, and
  2. if $e(\sigma)$ is defined, then $enc(e(\sigma)) = e'(enc(\sigma))$.

A simulation is *effective* if τ' can be computed from τ and e' can be computed from e.

Lemma 1. *Pure PERX can be effectively simulated in PENRC[kind].*

Proof (Crux). Consider the encoding function enc for which

$$enc(a) = a \qquad\qquad enc(\langle a \rangle) = ((a,a), \emptyset)$$
$$enc(\langle a : N \rangle) = (a, enc(N)) \qquad\qquad enc(v) = \{enc(i) \mid i \in v\}$$

Then enc is an effective simulation. It is easy to find τ' by induction on τ. Furthermore, e' can be constructed by induction on e. To illustrate this, let us write $e_1 \in \kappa \to e_2$ for $e_1 \in \kappa ? e_2 : \pi_1(\emptyset)$. Intuitively, this expression will be used to verify that the input to e' is an encoding of a legal input to e. Otherwise, we become undefined.

We can now for example simulate $text\{e\}$ by $e' \in \mathbf{atom} \to ((e',e'), \emptyset)$. We can simulate $elem\{e_1\}\{e_2\}$ by

$$e_1' \in \mathbf{atom} \to (e_1', \{x \in \mathbf{atom} ? ((x,x), \emptyset) : x \mid x \in e_2'\}).$$

And we can simulate $children(e)$ by $\bigcup\{\pi_2(x) \mid x \in e'\}$. $\square$

Corollary 4. *If the well-definedness or semantic type-checking problem is decidable for PENRC[kind], then it is also decidable for pure PERX.*

6.3   Well-Definedness for PENRC[kind]

Consider the following expression:

$$e = \{\{z = y ? \pi_1(z) : y \mid y \in x\}) \mid x \in R\},$$

and let the environment σ be defined by

$$\sigma(R) = \{\{a, b\}, \{c\}, \{a, b, d\}\}\} \qquad \sigma(z) = d.$$

Since there is a set in $\sigma(R)$ which contains $\sigma(z)$, we will need to evaluate $\pi_1(\sigma(z))$ at some point, which is undefined. Hence, $e(\sigma)$ is undefined. Note that we do not need all elements in $\sigma(R)$ to reach the state where $e(\sigma)$ becomes undefined. Indeed, e is also undefined on the small environment σ' where $\sigma'(R) = \{\{d\}\}$ and $\sigma'(z) = d$.

We generalize this observation in the following general property. Here, we say that an environment σ is in the set $\mathcal{E}_k$ if every set occurring in $\sigma(x)$ has cardinality at most k for every $x \in dom(\sigma)$.

Lemma 2 (Small Model Property for Undefinedness). *Let e be a positive existential NRC[kind] expression, let Γ be a type assignment on e, and let σ be an environment compatible with Γ such that $e(\sigma)$ is undefined. There exists a natural number l which can be computed from e alone, and an environment $\sigma' \in \mathcal{E}_l$ compatible with Γ, such that $e(\sigma')$ is also undefined.*

We obtain:

Corollary 5. *The well-definedness problem for PENRC[kind] is decidable.*

Indeed, up to isomorphism (and expressions cannot distinguish isomorphic inputs) there are only a finite number of different input environments in $\mathcal{E}_l$ compatible with Γ. So we can test them all to see if there is a counterexample to well-definedness.

Also for semantic type-checking we have:

Lemma 3 (Small Model Property for Semantic Type-Checking). *Let e be a PENRC[kind] expression, let Γ be a type assignment on e such that e is well-defined under Γ, and let τ be a type. Let σ be an environment compatible with Γ such that $e(\sigma) \notin \tau$. There exists a natural number l which can be computed from e and τ alone, and an environment $\sigma' \in \mathcal{E}_l$ compatible with Γ, such that also $e(\sigma') \notin \tau$.*

Corollary 6. *Semantic type-checking for PENRC[kind] is decidable.*

6.4   Equivalence and Satisfiability

The above decidability results are quite sharp, because *equivalence* of PENRC expressions is undecidable. This can be proven in a similar way as Theorem 1. Of course, containment is then also undecidable. Levy and Suciu [12] have shown that a "deep" form of containment (known as simulation) is decidable for PENRC.

Another important problem is satisfiability. For example, the XQuery type system generates a type error whenever it can deduce that an expression which is not the empty set expression itself always returns the empty set. As noted in Section 4, satisfiability is undecidable for PERX⁻[empty]. For pure PERX, and PENRC[kind], however, satisfiability can be solved using the small model property for semantic type-checking. Indeed, a PENRC[kind] expression e is unsatisfiable under Γ if, and only if, $\mathbf{coll}(\emptyset)$ is an output type for e under Γ. We point out that, at least for PENRC without union and kind-tests, decidability of satisfiability already follows from the work of Levy and Suciu cited above.

7   Lists and Bags

In this paper we have focused our attention on a set-based abstraction of XQuery. The actual data model of XQuery is list-based however, and hence it is natural to ask how our results transfer to such a setting.

Let us denote by $\mathrm{RX}^{\mathrm{list}}$ the list-based version of RX, which can be obtained from RX as follows. The list-based RX data model is obtained by replacing "set" in the definition of the RX data model by "list". The list-based semantics of an expression is obtained from the set-based semantics by replacing every set operator by the corresponding list operator (i.e., empty set becomes empty list, union becomes concatenation, and so on). We can similarly define the bag-based version of RX, which we will denote by $\mathrm{RX}^{\mathrm{bag}}$.

We can still simulate the relational algebra in the list- and bag-based versions of PERX$^-$[empty] and PERX$^-$[type]. Hence, well-definedness and semantic type-checking for these languages is undecidable. It is an open problem however whether well-definedness and semantic type-checking in the list- and bag-based versions of PERX$^-$ remains undecidable. Indeed, our undecidability proof depends heavily on the fact that set union is idempotent, which is not the case for list concatenation and bag union.

We can also consider a list-based and bag-based version of PENRC[kind], to which our decidability results transfer. Hence, well-definedness and semantic type-checking are decidable for pure PERX^{list} and pure PERX^{bag}.

References

1. Serge Abiteboul, Richard Hull, and Victor Vianu. *Foundations Of Databases.* Addison-Wesley, 1995.
2. Noga Alon, Tova Milo, Frank Neven, Dan Suciu, and Victor Vianu. Typechecking XML views of relational databases. *ACM Transactions on Computational Logic*, 4(3):315–354, 2003.
3. Noga Alon, Tova Milo, Frank Neven, Dan Suciu, and Victor Vianu. XML with data values: typechecking revisited. *Journal of Computer and System Sciences*, 66(4):688–727, 2003.
4. Paul V. Biron and Ashok Malhotra. *XML Schema Part 2: Datatypes.* W3C Recommendation, May 2001.
5. Scott Boag, Don Chamberlin, Mary F. Fernández, Daniela Florescu, Jonathan Robie, and Jérôme Siméon. *XQuery 1.0: An XML Query Language.* W3C Working Draft, November 2003.
6. Peter Buneman, Shamim A. Naqvi, Val Tannen, and Limsoon Wong. Principles of programming with complex objects and collection types. *Theoretical Computer Science*, 149(1):3–48, 1995.

7. Don Chamberlin, Peter Fankhauser, Daniela Florescu, Massimo Marchiori, and Jonathan Robie. *XML Query Use Cases*. W3C Working Draft, November 2003.
8. Ashok K. Chandra and Moshe Y. Vardi. The implication problem for functional and inclusion dependencies is undecidable. *SIAM Journal on Computing*, 14(3):671–677, 1985.
9. Denise Draper, Peter Fankhauser, Mary F. Fernández, Ashok Malhotra, Kristoffer Rose, Michael Rys, Jérôme Siméon, and Philip Wadler. *XQuery 1.0 and XPath 2.0 Formal Semantics*. W3C Working Draft, February 2004.
10. Mary F. Fernández, Daniela Florescu, Alon Levy, and Dan Suciu. Declarative specification of Web sites with Strudel. *The VLDB Journal*, 9:38–55, 2000.
11. Mary F. Fernández, Ashok Malhotra, Jonathan Marsh, Marton Nagy, and Norman Walsh. *XQuery 1.0 and XPath 2.0 Data Model*. W3C Working Draft, November 2003.
12. Alon Y. Levy and Dan Suciu. Deciding containment for queries with complex objects (extended abstract). In *Proceedings of the Sixteenth ACM SIGACT-SIGMOD-SIGART symposium on Principles of Database Systems*, pages 20–31. ACM Press, 1997.
13. Wim Martens and Frank Neven. Typechecking top-down uniform unranked tree transducers. In *Database Theory - ICDT 2003*, volume 2572 of *Lecture Notes in Computer Science*, pages 64–78. Springer-Verlag, 2003.
14. Wim Martens and Frank Neven. Frontiers of tractability for typechecking simple xml transformations. In *Proceedings of the Twenty-third ACM SIGACT-SIGMOD-SIGART Symposium on Principles of Database Systems*, pages 23–34. ACM Press, 2004.
15. Tova Milo, Dan Suciu, and Victor Vianu. Typechecking for XML transformers. In *Proceedings of the Nineteenth ACM SIGMOD-SIGACT-SIGART Symposium on Principles of Database Systems*, pages 11–22. ACM Press, 2000.
16. Frank Neven. Personal communication, May 2004.
17. Dan Suciu. Typechecking for semistructured data. In *Database Programming Languages, 8th International Workshop, DBPL 2001, Revised Papers*, volume 2397 of *Lecture Notes in Computer Science*, pages 1–20. Springer-Verlag, 2001.
18. Henry S. Thompson, David Beech, Murray Maloney, and Noah Mendelsohn. *XML Schema Part 1: Structures*. W3C Recommendation, May 2001.
19. Limsoon Wong. *Querying nested collections*. PhD thesis, University of Pennsylvania, 1994.

First Order Paths in Ordered Trees

Maarten Marx

Informatics Institute University of Amsterdam

Abstract. We give two sufficient conditions on XPath like languages for having first order expressivity, meaning that every first order definable set of paths in an ordered node-labeled tree is definable in that XPath language. They are phrased in terms of expansions of navigational (sometimes called "Core") XPath. Adding either complementation, or the more elegant conditional paths is sufficient. A conditional path is an axis relation of the form (`one_step_axis::n[F]`)$^+$, denoting the transitive closure of the relation expressed by `one_step_axis::n[F]`. As neither is expressible in navigational XPath we also give characterizations in terms of first order logic of the answer sets and the sets of paths navigational XPath can define. The first in terms of a suitable two variable fragment, the second in terms of unions of conjunctive queries.

1 Introduction

[11] showed how a simple addition to Core XPath led to expressive completeness: every first order definable set of nodes in an XML tree is definable as the answer set of an expression //[fexpr] in which the filter expression is generated by the following grammar:

$$
\begin{aligned}
\mathsf{step} \quad &::= \mathsf{self} \mid \mathsf{child} \mid \mathsf{parent} \mid \mathsf{right} \mid \mathsf{left} \\
\mathsf{locpath} \quad &::= \mathsf{step::ntst[fexpr]} \mid (\mathsf{step::ntst[fexpr]})^+ \\
\mathsf{fexpr} \quad &::= \mathsf{locpath} \mid \mathsf{not}\ \mathsf{fexpr} \mid \mathsf{fexpr}\ \mathsf{and}\ \mathsf{fexpr}.
\end{aligned}
$$

Here ntst is a node test consisting of a tag name or the wild card ∗. The steps correspond to the four basic steps in an ordered tree. The semantics is as with standard Core XPath [5], with $(\cdot)^+$ interpreted as the transitive closure.

Although the choice of the syntax can be motivated by its close relation to temporal logic with since and until, it may still seem rather ad hoc. Moreover the result is really about the expressive power of filter expressions, rather than about location paths. In this paper we present additional evidence for the great expressive power of the construction (step::ntst[fexpr])$^+$, and obtain an expressive completeness result for location paths. Extensive motivation for such a result can be found in [1].

In the above definition it was not needed to close the location path expressions under composition (the '/') and union (the '|'). This is because we dealt with filter expressions only. When defining paths in a tree they are obviously needed. So in the following, assume that the language is closed under these two operations as well. We show that

T. Eiter and L. Libkin (Eds.): ICDT 2005, LNCS 3363, pp. 114–128, 2005.

1. any extension of Core XPath which is closed under complementation can define every first order definable set of paths;
2. the above defined language (called Conditional XPath) is closed under complementation, whence first order complete for expressing paths.

The first result states a sufficient condition for an XPath dialect having full first order expressivity. The second states that very little is needed to achieve it: allow unions and compositions of path expressions, and allow transitive closure of the simplest location path step::ntst[fexpr]. The first result is a corollary of a more general result which states that the class of ordered trees has the three variable property: every first order formula in at most three free variables is equivalent (on this class) to a first order formula in at most three free and bound (possibly reused) variables.

These results are about expansions of Core XPath. This language was defined by Gottlob, Koch and Pichler [5] as the logical core of XPath 1.0. Core XPath is strictly weaker than Conditional XPath, so the question remains which fragment of first order logic is picked out by Core XPath. It turns out that this is a very natural one indeed:

1. The answer sets definable in Core XPath are exactly those definable with first order formulas $\phi(x)$ which use only two (free and bound) variables in a signature with predicates corresponding to the *child, descendant* and *following_sibling* relations.
2. The paths definable in Core XPath are exactly those which can be defined by unions of conjunctive queries consisting of the *child, descendant* and *following_sibling* relations and unary first order formulas as in item 1.
3. Core XPath is closed under intersection but not under complementation.

We thus give a precise characterization of both Core and Conditional XPath, both in terms of defining answer sets and sets of paths. For general related work, we refer to [11] and to the conclusions. Specific relations are given in the running text.

The paper is organized as follows. Section 2 introduces the needed definitions. Section 3 contains all results and some of the more easy proofs. Section 4 is devoted to the proof of the most important result: closure of Conditional XPath under complementation. We motivate our work in the conclusion. To give complete proofs of the results presented here takes at least another 15 pages, which we don't have. This work has a number of interesting connections with temporal logic. These connections, together with further related work and fairly complete proofs are in the full version of the paper, which is available from the author. For related work, see also [11, 13]. We note that the expressive completeness result for Conditional XPath's answer sets (shown in [11]) follows from the result presented here, but not conversely. The results about Core XPath have been presented at the Twente workshop on Database Management [13]. They are included here in order to give a complete picture.

2   Navigational XPath

We use an XPath syntax which is better suited for mathematical manipulation and easier to read when formulas tend to get large. (And they will. . .) The relation with the official W3C syntax should be clear.

XPath languages are two sorted languages, defined by mutual recursion. There are formulas denoting sets of nodes (called *node wffs*), and formulas denoting a binary relation between nodes (called *path wffs*). An XPath *step* is one of the following four atomic relation symbols

$$\text{step} ::= \text{child} \mid \text{parent} \mid \text{right} \mid \text{left}.$$

We define Core XPath and Conditional XPath. They differ only in the operations allowed on path wffs. Let some set of (propositional) variables be fixed. They are denoted by p_i. We do not put any restriction on the number of variables in our language. The node wffs are generated by

$$\text{node\_wff} ::= p_i \mid \top \mid \langle \text{path\_wff} \rangle \mid \neg \text{node\_wff} \mid \text{node\_wff} \wedge \text{node\_wff}.$$

Here $\top$ denotes the predicate which always evaluates to true. The path wffs of Core XPath are generated by

$$\text{path\_wff} ::= \text{step} \mid \text{step}^+ \mid ?\text{node\_wff} \mid \text{path\_wff}/\text{path\_wff} \mid \text{path\_wff} \cup \text{path\_wff}.$$

The path wffs of Conditional XPath differ only in that we allow $(\text{step}/?\text{node\_wff})^+$ instead of just step^+. We call this construction a *conditional path* and the language derives its name from it. The main purpose of conditional paths is to define an until like relation. For instance, the relation between a node n and it's descendant n' at which A holds, and for which at all nodes strictly in between n and n' B holds is defined by

$$(\text{child}/?B)^*/\text{child}/?A.$$

Here and elsewhere we use R^* as an abbreviation of $R^+ \cup ?\top$, denoting the transitive reflexive closure of R. We use variables R, S, T for path wffs and A, B, C for node wffs. The differences with the standard XPath syntax are small. Our node wffs correspond to XPath's filter expressions. Our formulas $?\text{node\_wff}$ (called *tests*) mean the same as XPath's self:: $*$ [node_wff]. We abolished the two different tests on nodes in XPath, and capture node tests as follows:

$$\text{axis}::A[F] \equiv \text{axis}:: * [\text{self}::A \wedge F] \equiv \text{axis}/?(A \wedge F).$$

To make the language context-free, we use $\langle \text{path\_wff} \rangle$ inside node wffs instead of just path_wff. For axis one of step, step^+, $(\text{step}/?A)^+$, we often write axis?node_wff instead of axis/?node_wff. Just as in XPath, we consider these expressions as the basic expressions of the language. The relation between the just defined language and XPath 1.0 is exemplified in Table 1 in which some expressions in our notation are given also as equivalent XPath expressions.

Table 1. Equivalent XPath 1.0 and Core XPath expressions

child :: p_i	child$/?p_i$
child :: p_i[descendant :: *]	child$/?p_i/?\langle$child$^+\rangle$) or child$/?(p_i \wedge \langle$child$^+\rangle$))
/descendant :: p_i	$?\neg\langle$parent$\rangle/$child$^+/?p_i$
child :: *	child
self :: p_i[child]	$?(p_i \wedge \langle$child$\rangle$))
preceding :: p_i	parent$^*/$left$^+/$child$^*/?p_i$.

The semantics of XPath expressions is given with respect to *node labeled sibling ordered trees*[1] (trees for short). Each node in the tree is labeled with a set of primitive symbols from some alphabet. Sibling ordered trees come with two binary relations, the child relation, denoted by $R_\downarrow$, and the immediate_right_sibling relation, denoted by $R_\rightarrow$. Together with their inverses $R_\uparrow$ and $R_\leftarrow$ they are used to interpret the axis relations. We denote such trees as first order structures $(N, R_\downarrow, R_\rightarrow, P_i)_{i\in\omega}$.

Remark 1. Unlike in most of the literature on XPath we do not restrict the class of structures to trees corresponding to XML documents. So our trees can be infinitely deep, infinitely branching and may contain multiple atomic labels at each node. All our results apply to document trees as well. This is because our theorems are of the following form: for every first order formula ϕ, there is an XPath expression α such that on all trees, the denotations of ϕ and α coincide.

Remark 2. Although we borrowed the name Core XPath from [5], our language is slightly more expressive, due to the availability of the left and right axis relations. Arguably, these must be available in an XPath dialect which calls itself *navigational*.

Given a tree $\mathfrak{M}$ and an expression R, the denotation or meaning of R in $\mathfrak{M}$ is written as $[\![R]\!]_{\mathfrak{M}}$. As promised, path wffs denote sets of pairs, and node wffs sets of nodes. Table 2 contains the definition of $[\![\cdot]\!]_{\mathfrak{M}}$. The equivalence with the W3C syntax and semantics (cf., e.g., [5,18]) should be clear.

Let us spell out the semantics of the conditional axis relation, as it does not occur in standard navigational XPath. The path wff (child$?A)^+$ denotes all pairs (n, n') for which there exists a finite sequence of nodes $n = n_1 \dots n_k = n'$ $(k > 1)$ such that for all i, n_{i+1} is a child of n_i and A is true at all n_j $(j > 1)$. As an example of its expressive power, consider the *next frontier node* relation which holds between leaves which are consecutive in document order. Let us use the following abbreviations:

$$\text{leaf} = \neg\langle\text{child}\rangle, \quad \text{first} = \neg\langle\text{left}\rangle, \quad \text{last} = \neg\langle\text{right}\rangle.$$

---

[1] A sibling ordered tree is a structure isomorphic to $(N, R_\downarrow, R_\rightarrow)$ where N is a set of finite sequences of natural numbers closed under taking initial segments, and for any sequence s, if $s \cdot k \in N$, then either $k = 0$ or $s \cdot k - 1 \in N$. For $n, n' \in N$, $nR_\downarrow n'$ holds iff $n' = n \cdot k$ for k a natural number; $nR_\rightarrow n'$ holds iff $n = s \cdot k$ and $n' = s \cdot k + 1$.

Table 2. The semantics of Core and Conditional XPath

$$[\![p_i]\!]_{\mathfrak{M}} = \{n \mid \mathfrak{M} \models P_i(n)\}$$
$$[\![\top]\!]_{\mathfrak{M}} = \{n \mid n \in \mathfrak{M}\}$$
$$[\![\langle R \rangle]\!]_{\mathfrak{M}} = \{n \mid \exists n', (n, n') \in [\![R]\!]_{\mathfrak{M}}\}$$
$$[\![\neg A]\!]_{\mathfrak{M}} = \{n \mid n \notin [\![A]\!]_{\mathfrak{M}}\}$$
$$[\![A \wedge B]\!]_{\mathfrak{M}} = [\![A]\!]_{\mathfrak{M}} \cap [\![B]\!]_{\mathfrak{M}}.$$

$$[\![\mathsf{child}]\!]_{\mathfrak{M}} = R_{\downarrow}$$
$$[\![\mathsf{parent}]\!]_{\mathfrak{M}} = [\![\mathsf{child}]\!]_{\mathfrak{M}}^{-1}$$
$$[\![\mathsf{right}]\!]_{\mathfrak{M}} = R_{\rightarrow}$$
$$[\![\mathsf{left}]\!]_{\mathfrak{M}} = [\![\mathsf{right}]\!]_{\mathfrak{M}}^{-1}$$

$$[\![R^+]\!]_{\mathfrak{M}} = [\![R]\!]_{\mathfrak{M}}^{+} \; (= [\![R]\!]_{\mathfrak{M}} \cup ([\![R]\!]_{\mathfrak{M}} \circ [\![R]\!]_{\mathfrak{M}}) \cup ([\![R]\!]_{\mathfrak{M}} \circ [\![R]\!]_{\mathfrak{M}} \circ [\![R]\!]_{\mathfrak{M}}) \cup \ldots)$$
$$[\![?A]\!]_{\mathfrak{M}} = \{(n, n) \mid n \in [\![A]\!]_{\mathfrak{M}}\}$$
$$[\![R/S]\!]_{\mathfrak{M}} = [\![R]\!]_{\mathfrak{M}} \circ [\![S]\!]_{\mathfrak{M}}$$
$$[\![R \cup S]\!]_{\mathfrak{M}} = [\![R]\!]_{\mathfrak{M}} \cup [\![S]\!]_{\mathfrak{M}}.$$

Then the next frontier node relation is definable as the path wff

$$?\mathsf{leaf}/[?\neg\mathsf{last} \cup (?\mathsf{last}/\mathsf{parent})^+]/\mathsf{right}/(\mathsf{child}?\mathsf{first})^*/?\mathsf{leaf}. \qquad (1)$$

Here $(?\mathsf{last}/\mathsf{parent})^1$ abbreviates $?\mathsf{last}/(\mathsf{parent}?\mathsf{last})^*/\mathsf{parent}$. We finish with a useful result. For R a path wff, define the *converse* of R, denoted by R^{-1} with meaning $[\![R^{-1}]\!]_{\mathfrak{M}} = \{(n', n) \mid (n, n') \in [\![R]\!]_{\mathfrak{M}}\}$.

Proposition 1. *The path wffs of both Core and Conditional XPath are closed under taking converses.*

3 First Order Characterizations of XPath

This section contains all our results: first order characterizations of both the node wffs and the path wffs of Core and Conditional XPath, as well as sufficient conditions for first order expressivity.

Let FO^{tree} denote the first-order language over the signature with binary predicates $\{R_{\downarrow}, R_{\rightarrow}\}$ and countably many unary predicates P_i. FO^{tree} is interpreted on ordered trees in the obvious way: $R_{\downarrow}$ is interpreted by the transitive closure of the child relation, and $R_{\rightarrow}$ is interpreted by the transitive closure of the right-sibling relation. Note that both one step relations are first order definable from $R_{\downarrow}$ and $R_{\rightarrow}$.

3.1 Sets of Nodes

The answer set of an XPath path expression R consists of the range of R, or the nodes which are reachable from some node by R [5, 3]. The main result of [11] stated that every first order definable set of nodes is definable as the answer set of some Conditional XPath path expression. Here we give a characterization of Core XPath's expressions as the two variable fragment[2] of first order logic in an expanded signature. In FO^{tree} we can define the one step axis relations from the transitive relations using three variables[3]. With two variables this is not possible, hence we should expand the signature with relations $R_\downarrow$ and $R_\rightarrow$ corresponding to the child and to the right-sibling axis, respectively. Let FO_2^{tree} denote the restriction of FO^{tree} in this expanded signature to the two variable fragment.

Theorem 1. [13] *(1) The answer sets of Core XPath path expressions are exactly the sets definable in FO_2^{tree}.*
(2) FO_2^{tree} formulas in one free variable and Core XPath's node wffs are equally expressive.

The hard direction follows more or less directly from the argument used to show a similar statement for linear orders —characterizing temporal logic with only unary temporal connectives— by Etessami, Vardi and Wilke [4]. The proof shows that a similar statement holds for the version of Core XPath of Gottlob, Koch and Pichler [5] which does not have the right- and left-sibling axis but just their transitive closures. That language can define each set definable in FO_2^{tree} without the right-sibling relation.

Proof. Because the path wffs of Core XPath are closed under taking inverses, for every path wff R there exists a node wff A such that the answer set of R equals the denotation of A in every model. Thus we need only work with the node wffs and only prove the second equivalence in the theorem. By the standard translation well known from modal logic each node wff translates into a one free variable FO_2^{tree} formula (cf., [17] which takes care to use only two variables). The translation is just the definition from Table 2 written in first order logic. This takes care of the easy direction.

   For the other direction, let $\phi(x)$ be a first order formula. We want a node wff A such that for every tree $\mathfrak{M}$, $\{n \mid \mathfrak{M} \models \phi(n)\} = [\![A]\!]_{\mathfrak{M}}$. The proof is a copy of the one for linear temporal logic in [4] (Theorem 1). The only real change needed is in the set of order types: they are given in the left hand side of Table 3, together with the needed translations (A' denotes the translation of A).

Remark 3. The answer sets of the path wffs of both Core and Conditional XPath have a first order characterization. An interesting question is how the sizes of the first order formulas and their corresponding equivalent XPath node wffs compare. For conditional XPath, the blow up is non elementary and this is unavoidable [11]. For Core XPath, it is much better. The blow up is "only" single exponential, which is also unavoidable [4]. The difference can be explained as

---

[2] With the two variable fragment we mean the set of formulas in which at most two variables may occur. Variables might be reused. Thus $\exists y \exists z (x R_\downarrow y \wedge y R_\downarrow z \wedge P(z))$ is not in the two variable fragment, but it is equivalent to $\exists y (x R_\downarrow y \wedge \exists x (y R_\downarrow x \wedge P(x)))$ which is equivalent to the node wff $\langle \text{child}^+/\text{child}^+/?P\rangle$.

[3] For instance, $x\text{child}y$ is defined as $x R_\downarrow y \wedge \neg\exists z(x R_\downarrow z \wedge z R_\downarrow y)$.

Table 3. Order types and their translations

$\tau(x,y)$	$\exists y(\tau(x,y) \wedge A(y))$
$x = y$	A'
$x\, R_\downarrow\, y$	$\langle \text{child?}A' \rangle$
$y\, R_\downarrow\, x$	$\langle \text{parent?}A' \rangle$
$x\, R_\rightarrow\, y$	$\langle \text{right?}A' \rangle$
$y\, R_\rightarrow\, x$	$\langle \text{left?}A' \rangle$
$x\, R_\Rightarrow\, y \wedge \neg x\, R_\rightarrow\, y$	$\langle \text{right/right}^+?A' \rangle$
$y\, R_\Rightarrow\, x \wedge \neg y\, R_\rightarrow\, x$	$\langle \text{left/left}^+?A' \rangle$
$x\, R_\Downarrow\, y \wedge \neg x\, R_\downarrow\, y$	$\langle \text{child/child}^+?A' \rangle$
$y\, R_\Downarrow\, x \wedge \neg y\, R_\downarrow\, x$	$\langle \text{parent/parent}^+?A'. \rangle$

follows. For Core XPath, we translate first order formulas in at most two variables into Core XPath wffs, which are again (equivalent to) first order formulas in at most two variables. For Conditional XPath, *every* first order formula (in one free variable) translates to a Conditional XPath node wff, which is (equivalent to) a first order formula in at most three variables.

3.2 Sets of Paths

In the previous section we characterized the node sets that can be defined in XPath. (Defined either by means of a node wff, or equivalently as the answer set of a path wff). We next characterize path sets. It is known that on finite linear orders not every first order definable set can be defined using just two variables, even in the signature expanded with the child relation. Whence there are sets of nodes which are not definable in Core XPath, by the previous theorem. The following example goes back to Kamp [10]: the set of all nodes x such that

$$\exists y(x \textbf{ descendant } y \wedge A(y) \wedge \forall z((x \textbf{ descendant } z \wedge z \textbf{ descendant } y) \rightarrow B(z))). \quad (2)$$

Note that this set is expressible in Conditional XPath. By the node wff

$$\langle (\text{child?}B)^*/\text{child?}A \rangle.$$

It is also expressible in Core XPath expanded with a complementation operator $\overline{(\cdot)}$ on path wffs. The semantics of complementation is the standard boolean one: $[\![\overline{R}]\!]_{\mathfrak{M}} = \{(n,n') \mid (n,n') \notin [\![R]\!]_{\mathfrak{M}}\}$. Note that this operation is defined on *path wffs*, so it has nothing to do with the boolean negation $\neg$ which is only defined on *node wffs*. The set defined by (2) is also defined by the node wff

$$\langle \text{child}^+?A \ \cap \ \overline{\text{child}^+/?\neg B/\text{child}^+} \rangle,$$

where $\cap$ is defined as usual from union and complementation.

Definition 1. *We say that an XPath language $\mathcal{L}$ is first order complete for path sets if for every FO^{tree} formula $\phi(x,y)$ there exists an $\mathcal{L}$ expression R such that for all trees $\mathfrak{M}$, $\{(n,n') \mid \mathfrak{M} \models \phi(n,n')\} = [\![R]\!]_{\mathfrak{M}}$.*

Theorem 2. *1. Any expansion of Core XPath which is closed under complementation is first order complete for path sets.*
  2. Conditional XPath is closed under complementation, whence first order complete for path sets.

The proof of the second part will be sketched in the next section. The first part of the theorem is a corollary of a more general result:

Theorem 3. *Let C be the class of sibling ordered trees. Then, on C, every FO^{tree} formula in at most 3 free variables is equivalent to a FO^{tree} formula in the same signature which uses at most 3 free and bound variables.*

This theorem can be shown using Ehrenfeucht–Fraïssé pebble games from [9]. The first part of Theorem 2 can now be derived as follows.

Proof. Let L be an expansion as in the Theorem. Then L can express every binary relation expressible in Tarski's relation algebras. Tarski's relation algebras are algebras of the form $(A, \cup, \overline{(\cdot)}, \circ, (\cdot)^{-1}, \epsilon)$ with A a set of binary relations, and the operators have the standard set theoretic meaning. As the atoms of Core XPath are closed under $^{-1}$, the language is closed under it. ϵ is definable as $?\top$. The formalism of Tarski's relation algebras is equally expressive as FO_3^2, first order logic in a signature with at most binary relations symbols in which every formula contains at most three free and bound (possibly reused) variables and at most two free variables [16]. The desired result now follows from Theorem 3.

Remark 4. It is tempting to think that the three variable property for ordered trees is derivable from results about trees and CTL like languages, perhaps in case of finite trees. This is partly due to inconsistent terminology, partly because all notions are closely related. [8] give a clear picture of these notions and their relations and especially the relations that do not exist. In particular they show that the three variable property is strictly stronger than the property which says that every *sentence* is equivalent to a sentence in just three variables (called H-dimension). Also, the fact that there is an finite number of "one dimensional temporal connectives" with which we can express every first order formula $\phi(x)$ is independent from the three (in fact k) variable property. Such a set was established implicitly in [11]. That result does indeed imply that every FO^{tree} formula in *one* free variable is equivalent to a Conditional XPath node wff, whence to an FO^{tree} formula in at most three variables. Unfortunately, from this we cannot derive the same thing for formulas in *two* free variables.

We finish the section with a characterization of Core XPath's path wffs. For *positive* Core XPath (without negation but with disjunction of node wffs), such a characterization is provided in [1] and in [6]. It is exactly positive existential first order logic (of course in the signature expanded with the child and right-sibling relation).[4] The node wffs of Core XPath *with* negation have been characterized in Theorem 1. We can combine these results using a relaxation of positive existential first order logic, reminiscent of the Carin language [7].

---

[4] [1] does not consider the horizontal axis relations, but their proof is easily adjusted.

Definition 2. *A first order Core XPath query is a formula of the form*

$$Q(x,y) :- \bigvee_i \bigwedge (R_1^i \wedge \ldots \wedge R_n^i \wedge A_1^i \wedge \ldots \wedge A_m^i), \qquad (3)$$

in which the A_j^i are FO_2^{tree} formulas in one free variable, and the R_j^i are atomic formulas in the signature $\{R_{\Downarrow}, R_{\Rightarrow}, R_{\downarrow}, R_{\rightarrow}, =\}$

An example is

$$Q(x,y) : -z\,R_{\Downarrow}\,x, z\,R_{\Rightarrow}\,z', z'\,R_{\Downarrow}\,y, P_1(z), \forall x(y\,R_{\downarrow}\,x \rightarrow P_2(x)),$$

which is equivalent to the XPath expression

$$\mathsf{parent}^+?P_1/\mathsf{right}^+/\mathsf{child}^+?\neg\langle\mathsf{child}?\neg P_2\rangle.$$

So these are like unions of usual conjunctive queries, except that properties may contain negations.

Theorem 4. [13] *Every first order Core XPath query is equivalent to a Core XPath path wff and conversely.*

4   Closure Under Complementation

In this section we prove Theorem 2. Recall that in order to prove Theorem 2, we must find, given an arbitrary Conditional XPath path wff R, a Conditional XPath path wff R' which is equivalent to the complement of R. The proof is divided into a number of lemmas. The proof itself is not very difficult, but consists of a great number of small steps. The dependencies between the different lemmas are given in Figure 1.

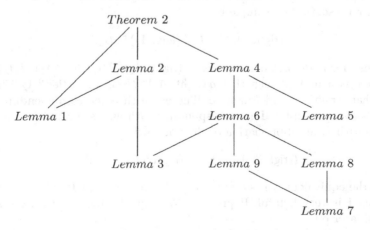

Fig. 1. Dependencies within the proof of Theorem 2

Table 4. Separating $(\mathsf{right}?A_1)^+?B_1/(\mathsf{left}?A_2)^+?B_2$

case	equivalent path wff
$a\,\mathsf{right}^+\,b$	$(\mathsf{right}?A_1)^+?(A_2 \wedge B_2 \wedge E)$
$a = b$	$?(A_2 \wedge B_2 \wedge E)$
$b\,\mathsf{right}^+\,a$	$?(A_2 \wedge E)/(\mathsf{left}?A_2)^+?B_2.$

In the first lemma, R is brought into a shape which is easier to handle. We need a bit of terminology. An *atom* is a path wff of the form $\mathsf{step}?A$, or $(\mathsf{step}?B)^+?A$. A *test* is a path wff of the form $?A$. A *basic composition* is a test followed by a sequence of atoms separated by $/$'s. We call an atom *down* if it is of the form $\mathsf{down}?A$, or $(\mathsf{down}?B)^+?A$. Analogously, we define atoms being *up*, *right*, and *left*. A path wff *has form* T if it is a test. It has form D, U, R, L if it is a basic composition of down, up, right or left atoms, respectively. We say that a basic composition is *separated* if it has one of the following forms:

$$D, \quad U, \quad U^*/R/D^*, \quad U^*/L/D^*. \tag{4}$$

Here we use $U^*/R/D^*$ as an abbreviation for the forms U/R, R, R/D, $U/R/D$, and similarly for $U^*/L/D^*$.

The syntactic notion of separated composition has a semantic counterpart. On every tree, every wff of the form D is a subrelation of child^+ (or $\mathsf{descendant}$ in XPath terminology). Similarly, wffs of the form U, $U^*/R/D^*$ and $U^*/L/D^*$ are subrelations of parent^+ ($\mathsf{ancestor}$), $\mathsf{parent}^*/\mathsf{right}^+/\mathsf{child}^*$ ($\mathsf{following}$) and $\mathsf{parent}^*/\mathsf{left}^+/\mathsf{child}^*$ ($\mathsf{preceding}$), respectively.

Lemma 1. *Every path wff is equivalent to a union of tests and separated basic compositions.*

The proof of the lemma consists of an case analysis of all compositions of two atoms. A representative example is

$$(\mathsf{right}?A_1)^+?B_1 \ / \ (\mathsf{left}?A_2)^+?B_2.$$

Suppose, for nodes a, b in some tree, $a\,(\mathsf{right}?A_1)^+?B_1/(\mathsf{left}?A_2)^+?B_2\,b$ holds. Then there is a node c such that $a\,(\mathsf{right}?A_1)^+?B_1\,c$ and $c\,(\mathsf{left}?A_2)^+?B_2\,b$. It follows that $a\,\mathsf{right}^+\,c$ and $b\,\mathsf{right}^+\,c$. There are three cases, depending on the relation between a and b. The corresponding path wffs are given in Table 4 for each case with E an abbreviation of the node wff

$$\langle(\mathsf{right}?(A_1 \wedge A_2))^+/\mathsf{right}?(B_1 \wedge A_1)\rangle.$$

Thus the equivalent wff is a union of a T, an L and an R wff.

Lemma 1 is very helpful. It provides for a quick proof of two results which are useful later on.

Lemma 2. *Conditional XPath path wffs are closed under intersection.*

Lemma 3. *Let $Q(x, y)$ be a conjunctive query consisting of down atoms and a test $x?Ax$. $Q(x, y)$ is such that it implies $x\,\text{child}^+ y$ and for all existentially quantified variables z, $x\,\text{child}^+ z$ and $z\,\text{child}^+ y$. Then there exists an equivalent Conditional XPath path wff which is a union of basic compositions of form D. The same result holds for up, left and right atoms.*

Lemmas 1 and 2 reduce the task of proving Theorem 2 to showing

Lemma 4. *The complement of each separated basic composition is definable as a Conditional XPath path wff.*

The proof of Lemma 4 consists of an easy and a hard part, separated in Lemma 5 and 6, which are shown below.

PROOF OF THEOREM 2.2.   Let R be a path wff. Then by Lemma 1 $R \equiv \bigcup_i R_i$, with the R_i tests and separated basic compositions. Whence $\overline{R} \equiv \bigcap_i \overline{R_i}$. By Lemma 2, the path wffs are closed under intersection. The complement of a test $?A$ is equivalent to $?\neg A \cup \text{not\_equal}$ with the latter abbreviating

$$\text{child}^+ \cup \text{parent}^+ \cup \text{parent}^*/\text{left}^+/\text{child}^* \cup \text{parent}^*/\text{right}^+/\text{child}^*.$$

By Lemma 4 each complement of a separated basic composition is equivalent to a path wff. Hence the theorem.   QED

We rewrote the path wffs into separated basic compositions because it helps to reduce the reasoning to "lines" or "strings". For example, consider a path wff of the form U. Now if in a tree $a\,\overline{U}\,b$ holds, we can break into two cases:

- a is not below b;
- a is below b, but not $a\,U\,b$.

The first case is easy to express (using the partition again). The second is harder but, as U is a composition of up atoms, *we only need to reason about the elements in between a and b*. That is, we need to reason about a line segment. But not all separated path wffs are of this simple form, consisting of one direction. The next lemma however states that complements of these can be defined using complements of the uni-directed forms.

Lemma 5. *The complement of each separated basic composition is definable from path wffs and formulas of the form*

$$(\text{child}^+ \cap \overline{D}), \quad (\text{parent}^+ \cap \overline{U}), \quad (\text{right}^+ \cap \overline{R}), \quad and \quad (\text{left}^+ \cap \overline{L}). \tag{5}$$

As an example, consider a path wff of the form U/R. The other forms are handled using the same argument. Then

$$\overline{U/R} \equiv (\overline{\text{parent}^+/\text{right}^+} \cap \overline{U/R}) \ \cup \ (\text{parent}^+/\text{right}^+ \cap \overline{U/R}). \tag{6}$$

Since $\models U/R \subseteq \text{parent}^+/\text{right}^+$, the first disjunct is equivalent to $\overline{\text{parent}^+/\text{right}^+}$, which is equivalent to

$$\text{child}^* \cup \text{parent}^*/\text{left}^+/\text{child}^* \cup \text{parent}^+ \cup \text{right}^+/\text{child}^* \cup \text{parent}^+/\text{right}^+/\text{child}^+. \tag{7}$$

For the second disjunct, we use the following equation:

$$\mathsf{parent}^+/\mathsf{right}^+ \cap \overline{U/R} \equiv (\mathsf{parent}^+ \cap \overline{U})/\mathsf{right}^+ \cup \mathsf{parent}^+/(\mathsf{right}^+ \cap \overline{R}). \quad (8)$$

The left to right direction is a validity for all relations. The other direction is not, but it holds because the models are trees.

All the preparation has been done, we can start the real work. We just have to define the relations in (5) as Conditional XPath path wffs.

Lemma 6. *Each relation in* (5) *is definable as a Conditional XPath path wff.*

We will define these relations as conjunctive queries of the form specified in Lemma 3. This is sufficient by that Lemma. We use the fact (Proposition 1) that Conditional XPath is closed under conversion (denoted by R^{-1}) to reduce the number of cases to two. Consider $\mathsf{parent}^+ \cap \overline{U}$. Then

$$\mathsf{parent}^+ \cap \overline{U} \equiv ((\mathsf{parent}^+ \cap \overline{U})^{-1})^{-1} \equiv ((\mathsf{parent}^+)^{-1} \cap \overline{U^{-1}})^{-1} \equiv \bigcap (\mathsf{child}^+ \cap \overline{D})^{-1}.$$

The last equivalence holds because the converse of a composition of form U is a union of compositions of form D. We can similarly relate the L and R forms. By Proposition 1 path wffs are closed under $(\cdot)^{-1}$, thus it is sufficient to show the lemma for $\mathsf{child}^+ \cap \overline{D}$ and $\mathsf{right}^+ \cap \overline{R}$. The argument is identical in both cases. For concreteness, we consider the case for down compositions.

Let R be of the form $\mathsf{child}^+ \cap \overline{D}$. All our arguments are semantical, thus assume xRy holds, for x, y nodes in an arbitrary model.

To reduce the number of cases, we use a notion well known from temporal logic. For A, B node wffs, define the path wff $\mathsf{until}(A, B)$ with the semantics

$$x\,\mathsf{until}(A, B)\,y \iff xR_{\Downarrow}y \wedge A(y) \wedge \forall z(x\,R_{\Downarrow}\,z\,R_{\Downarrow}\,y \to B(z)).$$

Please note that $\mathsf{until}(A, B)$ is a path wff, whence denotes a set of pairs, unlike its use in temporal logic. Temporal logic is a *one-sorted* formalism, containing only node wffs. The until formula from temporal logic, denoting a set of points is of course expressed in our formalism as $\langle \mathsf{until}(A, B) \rangle$.

Both down atoms are expressible as an until formula: $\mathsf{child}?A \equiv \mathsf{until}(A, \neg\top)$ and $(\mathsf{child}?B)^+?A \equiv \mathsf{until}(A \wedge B, B)$. Thus it is sufficient to show how to define $\mathsf{child}^+ \cap \overline{?C/R}$, for R a composition of until formulas, and C an arbitrary test. We call such formulas *until wffs*. In order to increase readability we use $<$ and $\leq$ instead of child^+ and child^*, respectively. We define complementation by a case distinction. The first case is when there is only one atom:

$$< \cap \overline{?C/\mathsf{until}(A, B)} \equiv ?\neg C/< \cup ?C/</?\neg A \cup ?C/</?\neg B/</?A. \quad (9)$$

For the case with more atoms we make a further case distinction. Let $R = S/\mathsf{until}(A, B)$, where S is a composition of until wffs. Then

$$< \cap \overline{R} \equiv (\overline{S/<} \cap < \cap \overline{R}) \cup (S/< \cap < \cap \overline{R}). \quad (10)$$

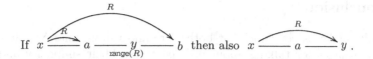

If $x \xrightarrow{R} a \underset{\text{range}(R)}{\underline{\quad\quad} y \quad\quad} b$ then also $x \xrightarrow{R} a \quad\quad y$.

Fig. 2. Lemma 7 in a picture

As $\models \overline{S/<} \subseteq \overline{S/\text{until}(A,B)}$, the first disjunct is simply equivalent to $< \cap \overline{S/<}$. Lemma 9 shows how to define such expressions.

Now we explain how to define $S/< \cap < \cap \overline{R}$, the second disjunct in (10). Suppose x and y stand in this relation. Then $x < y$ and there is a z such that xSz and $z < y$. Let z' be the *last* between x and y such that xSz'. Then we must enforce $z'\overline{\text{until}(A,B)}y$, which we can by (9). But that is enough, because suppose to the contrary that there is a z such that xSz and $z\text{until}(A,B)y$ and $z < z' < y$. From the last two conjuncts we obtain that $z'\text{until}(A,B)y$, a contradiction. So if we can express that

$$(x, z) \text{ is the largest subinterval in } (x, y) \text{ which is in } S, \qquad (11)$$

we have defined the second disjunct.

To summarize, for $R = S/\text{until}(A,B)$, the expression $< \cap \overline{R}$ is equivalent to the union of $< \cap \overline{S/<}$ and a formula expressing $\exists z((11) \wedge z(< \cap \overline{\text{until}(A,B)})y)$. (9) defines $< \cap \overline{\text{until}(A,B)}$ as a path wff. Lemmas 8 and 9 define (11) and $< \cap \overline{S/<}$, respectively.

The statement (11) is a first order formula in three free variables. As we need it quite a lot, we make an abbreviation. For S an until wff, define $\max(S, x, z, y)$ as the ternary relation $x < z < y \wedge xSz \wedge \neg\exists w(z < w < y \wedge xSw)$. In defining both $\overline{S/<}$ and the $\max$ predicate we use a crucial lemma. For R a path wff, let $\text{range}(R)$ be the node wff which is true at a point x iff there exists a point y such that yRx holds. These node wffs are definable in Conditional XPath, using conversion: $\text{range}(R) \equiv \langle R^{-1} \rangle$.

Lemma 7. *Let R be an until wff. For all points x, y, a, b, such that $x < a \leq y \leq b$, if xRa and xRb and $\text{range}(R)y$, then also xRy. See Figure 2.*

The proof is by induction on the number of /'s in R.

Lemma 8. *For R an until wff, $\max(R, x, z, y)$ is definable as a Conditional XPath path wff.*

Lemma 9. *For R an until wff, $< \cap \overline{R/<}$ is definable as a Conditional XPath path wff.*

For both lemmas, the definitions are given inductively on the number of /'s in R. Lemma 7 is used in the inductive case.

5   Conclusion

The results make us conclude that both Core and Conditional XPath are very natural languages for talking about ordered trees. Their simplicity and visual attractiveness make them suitable candidates for a user-friendly alternative to first order logic. The expressive completeness result for paths is very important, as arguably the relations in Conditional XPath are still "drawable". With drawable we mean that one can make an intuitive picture which exactly captures the meaning of the query. Composition and union are obviously drawable, whereas intersection and negation are not. The conditional step $(\mathsf{step}?A)^+$ is also drawable using ellipsis. Of course one should not draw the filter expressions, but just indicate them with formulas attached to nodes in the drawings.

In this context it is interesting to note a repetition in history. The natural class of models in computational linguistics is the class of finite ordered trees. In the beginning of the field of model theoretic syntax Monadic Second Order Logic was invariably used to reason about these structures [15]. Later, formalisms based on modal logic were proposed as alternatives. Arguments for the alternatives were both based on computational complexity (which is lower both for model checking and theorem proving) and on "naturalness" of expressing properties (in this case of grammars). In fact, both Core and Conditional XPath have their roots in the nineties: [2] and [14] define isomorphic variants of the filter expressions of Core and Conditional XPath, respectively.

From a theoretical point of view, Conditional XPath is not harder than Core XPath: the query evaluation problem is still solvable in time $O(|Q| \cdot |D|)$, with $|Q|$, $|D|$, the sizes of the query and the data, respectively [12].

Its easy syntax, visual attractiveness, and low complexity combined with its expressive completeness make Conditional XPath an excellent candidate for succeeding XPath 1.0.

Acknowledgments

Maarten Marx was supported by the Netherlands Organization for Scientific Research (NWO), under project number 612.000.106. Thanks are due to Loredana Afanasiev, David Gabelaia, Evan Goris, Jan Hidders, Sanjay Modgil, Maarten de Rijke, Thomas Schwentick, Yde Venema and Petrucio Viana.

References

1. M. Benedikt, W. Fan, and G. Kuper. Structural properties of XPath fragments. In *Proceedings. ICDT 2003*, 2003.
2. P. Blackburn, W. Meyer-Viol, and M. de Rijke. A proof system for finite trees. In H. Kleine Büning, editor, *Computer Science Logic*, volume 1092 of *LNCS*, pages 86–105. Springer, 1996.
3. World-Wide Web Consortium. XML path language (XPath): Version 1.0. http://www.w3.org/TR/xpath.html.

4. K. Etessami, M. Vardi, and Th. Wilke. First-order logic with two variables and unary temporal logic. In *Proc. LICS'97*, pages 228–235, 1997.
5. G. Gottlob, C. Koch, and R. Pichler. Efficient algorithms for processing XPath queries. In *VLDB'02*, 2002.
6. G. Gottlob, C. Koch, and K. Schulz. Conjunctive queries over trees. In *Proceedings of PODS*, pages 189–200, 2004.
7. A. Halevy and M. Rousset. Combining horn rules and description logics in CARIN. *Artificial Intelligence*, 104:165–209, 1998.
8. I. Hodkinson and A Simon. The k-variable property is stronger than H-dimension k. *Journal of Philosophical Logic*, 26:81–101, 1997.
9. N. Immerman and D. Kozen. Definability with bounded number of bound variables. In *Proceedings of the Symposium of Logic in Computer Science*, pages 236–244, Washington, 1987. Computer Society Press.
10. J.A.W. Kamp. *Tense Logic and the Theory of Linear Order*. PhD thesis, University of California, Los Angeles, 1968.
11. M. Marx. Conditional XPath, the first order complete XPath dialect. In *Proceedings of PODS'04*, pages 13–22, 2004.
12. M. Marx. XPath with conditional axis relations. In *Proceedings of EDBT'04*, volume 2992 of *LNCS*, pages 477–494, 2004.
13. M. Marx and M. de Rijke. Semantic characterizations of XPath. In *TDM'04 workshop on XML Databases and Information Retrieval.*, Twente, The Netherlands, June 21, 2004.
14. A. Palm. Propositional tense logic for trees. In *Sixth Meeting on Mathematics of Language.* University of Central Florida, Orlando, Florida, 1999.
15. J. Rogers. *A Descriptive Approach to Language Theoretic Complexity*. CSLI Press, 1998.
16. A. Tarski and S. Givant. *A Formalization of Set Theory without Variables*, volume 41. AMS Colloquium publications, Providence, Rhode Island, 1987.
17. M. Vardi. Why is modal logic so robustly decidable? In *DIMACS Series in Discrete Mathematics and Theoretical Computer Science 31*, pages 149–184. American Math. Society, 1997.
18. P. Wadler. Two semantics for XPath. Technical report, Bell Labs, 2000.

An Abstract Framework for Generating Maximal Answers to Queries*

Sara Cohen[1] and Yehoshua Sagiv[2]

[1] Faculty of Industrial Engineering and Management,
Technion—Israel Institute of Technology,
Technion City, Haifa 32000, Israel
sarac@ie.technion.ac.il
[2] The Selim and Rachel Benin School of Engineering and Computer Science,
The Hebrew University of Jerusalem,
Jerusalem 91904, Israel
sagiv@cs.huji.ac.il

Abstract. A framework for modeling query semantics as graph properties is presented. In this framework, a single definition of a query automatically gives rise to several semantics for evaluating that query under varying degrees of incomplete information. For example, defining natural joins automatically gives rise to full disjunctions. Two of the proposed semantics have incremental-polynomial-time query-evaluation algorithms for all types of queries that can be defined in this framework. Thus, the proposed framework generalizes previous definitions of semantics for incomplete information and improves previous complexity results for query evaluation.

1 Introduction

Incomplete data has always been perceived as a source of difficulty, due to the need to develop special semantics and query-evaluation algorithms. Over the years, different approaches for dealing with incomplete data have been developed. Some approaches deal with null values in the database itself and investigate the problem of computing answers that are true in all possible worlds, e.g., [11, 13]. Other approaches deal with null values that arise during query evaluation (e.g., when a tuple from one relation cannot be joined with any tuple from another relation) and investigate the problem of computing partial or maximal, rather than complete answers. The outerjoin is an early example of an operator for computing partial answers to join queries. [4] proposed full disjunctions as a clear semantics for maximal answers to join queries. [14] characterized when full disjunctions can be computed by outerjoins. [8] proposed several semantics for maximal answers to queries over semistructured data and investigated the complexity of query evaluation. For two of the semantics of [8], maximal answers can be computed in polynomial time in the size of the input and the output,

---

* This work was supported by the Israel Science Foundation (Grant 96/01).

T. Eiter and L. Libkin (Eds.): ICDT 2005, LNCS 3363, pp. 129–143, 2005.
© Springer-Verlag Berlin Heidelberg 2005

and the same is true for full disjunctions, which were shown to be a special case of one of those two semantics [10]. But the goal of finding appropriate semantics for maximal answers and developing query-evaluation algorithms seemed to be dependent on the specific query language at hand. For example, [2] gave a semantics and a query-evaluation algorithm for maximal answers to queries that generate relations from XML documents.

In this paper, we develop an abstract framework that automatically gives rise to several semantics that allow varying degrees of incomplete data in maximal answers to queries. In particular, we identify two semantics for which query evaluation is in incremental polynomial time (a complexity measure introduced by [7]). One of these two semantics admits all maximal answers that are structurally consistent with the given query. The second semantics requires, in addition, that maximal answers satisfy all the query conditions involving variables that are assigned non-null values. Our results essentially mean that one formulation of a query suffices for an efficient evaluation of that query under different circumstances of incomplete data. We show that earlier work [4, 8, 9, 15, 2] can be cast in our framework and the result is twofold. First, earlier work can be extended to more general types of queries. Second, we improve earlier complexity results for query evaluation and also give new complexity results.

2   Graphs and Graph Properties

In our abstract framework, we model queries, databases and answers as graphs. Semantics are modeled as graph properties. Hence, this section is devoted to defining graphs, graph properties and the *maximal P-subgraphs problem*.

Graphs. A *graph* $G = (V, E, r)$ consists of *(1)* a finite set of *vertices* V, *(2)* a set of *edges* $E \subseteq V \times V$ *and (3)* a *root* r such that $r \in V \cup \{\bot\}$. We say that G is *rooted* if *(1)* $r \neq \bot$ *and (2)* every vertex in G is reachable via a directed path from r. We say that G is *connected* if its underlying undirected graph is connected. Observe that every rooted graph is connected. However, a connected graph need not be rooted.

A graph G' is an *induced subgraph* of a graph G, written $G' \sqsubseteq G$, if *(1)* G' is derived from G by deleting some of the vertices of G (and the edges incident on these vertices) *and (2)* G' has the same root as G, if the root of G is among the vertices of G', and has $\bot$ as its root otherwise. We write $G' \sqsubset G$ if $G' \sqsubseteq G$ and G' is not equal to G.

Graph Properties. A *graph property* $\mathcal{P}$ is a possibly infinite set of graphs. For example, "is a clique" is a graph property that contains all graphs that are cliques. In this paper, we only consider properties $\mathcal{P}$ such that verifying whether a graph G is in $\mathcal{P}$ can be done in polynomial time.

We consider several types of graph properties. A graph property $\mathcal{P}$ is *hereditary* if $\mathcal{P}$ is *closed* with respect to induced subgraphs, i.e., whenever $G \in \mathcal{P}$, every induced subgraph of G is also in $\mathcal{P}$. A graph property $\mathcal{P}$ is *connected hereditary* if *(1)* all the graphs in $\mathcal{P}$ are connected *and (2)* $\mathcal{P}$ is closed with respect to connected induced subgraphs. Finally, $\mathcal{P}$ is *rooted hereditary* if *(1)* all the graphs in $\mathcal{P}$ are rooted *and (2)* $\mathcal{P}$ is closed with respect to rooted induced subgraphs.

Many graph properties are hereditary [5], e.g., "is a clique" and "is a forest." Note that "is a clique" is also connected hereditary. However, "is a clique" is not rooted hereditary, since it contains graphs that do not have roots. Some properties are connected hereditary, but not hereditary or rooted hereditary, such as "is a tree," which contains a graph G if the underlying undirected graph of G is a tree. Note that G is not necessarily rooted. Hence, "is a tree" is not rooted hereditary. The property "is a rooted clique" is rooted hereditary.

The Maximal $\mathcal{P}$-Subgraphs Problem. Let G be a graph and $\mathcal{P}$ be a property. (The graph G is not necessarily in $\mathcal{P}$.) We say that G' is a $\mathcal{P}$-*subgraph* of G if $G' \sqsubseteq G$ and $G' \in \mathcal{P}$. The set of $\mathcal{P}$-subgraphs of a graph G is denoted $\mathcal{P}(G)$.

We say that G' is a *maximal $\mathcal{P}$-subgraph* of G if G' is a $\mathcal{P}$-subgraph of G and there is no $\mathcal{P}$-subgraph G'' of G, such that $G' \sqsubset G''$. We use $\mathcal{P}^{\mathrm{MAX}}(G)$ to denote the set of maximal $\mathcal{P}$-subgraphs of G. The *maximal $\mathcal{P}$-subgraphs problem* is: Given a graph G, find the set $\mathcal{P}^{\mathrm{MAX}}(G)$.

3   Abstract Framework

The results in this paper are not dependent on a specific query language, type of a database, or semantics. Hence, we present an abstract framework that can be used to model many different queries, databases and semantics. Throughout this paper, we will discuss well-known types of queries, databases and semantics and show how they relate to our framework. In order to avoid confusion, we will use the terms *query graph*, *data graph* and *graph semantics* to refer to a query, database and semantics, respectively, in our framework.

Data Graphs and Query Graphs. A *data graph* is a tuple $D = (V, E, r, l_V, l_E)$, such that *(1)* (V, E, r) is a graph, *(2)* l_V is a *vertex-labeling function* that associates each vertex in V with a label *and (3)* l_E is an *edge-labeling function* that associates each edge in E with a label. The vertices of a data graph D are also called *data items* and are denoted with the letter d.

Query graphs have constraints defined on their vertices and their edges. A *vertex constraint* is a mapping c^v that associates every pair (d, D), such that d is a vertex in the data graph D, with the value TRUE or FALSE. An *edge constraint* is a mapping c^e that associates every triple (d, d', D), such that d and d' are vertices in the data graph D, with the value TRUE or FALSE.[1] Our complexity results hold only for vertex constraints and edge constraints that can be decided in polynomial time.

Intuitively, a vertex constraint resembles a selection condition, since it is applied to a single data item. An edge constraint resembles a join condition, since it is applied to a pair of data items. However, our vertex and edge constraints are much more expressive than standard selection and join conditions, since they

---

[1] The data graph D does not necessarily contain the edge (d, d').

can take the entire D into consideration. For example, a vertex constraint can associate a pair (d, D) with TRUE if the label of d is greater than the average value of all the labels of vertices in D.

Queries may also constrain the structure of their answers. A *structural constraint*, denoted s, is simply one of the letters C, R or N, where: C indicates that answers should be connected, R indicates that answers should be rooted and N imposes no constraint on the structure of query answers.

A *query graph* is a tuple $Q = (V, E, r, C_V, C_E, s)$, such that *(1)* (V, E, r) is a graph, *(2)* C_V is a *vertex-constraint function* that associates each vertex v in V with a vertex constraint c^v, *(3)* C_E is an *edge-constraint function* that associates each edge e in E with an edge constraint c^e and *(4)* s is a structural constraint. The vertices of a query graph Q are also called *variables* and are denoted with the letter q.

There may be different ways to model various types of databases and queries as data graphs and query graphs, respectively. We present some examples.

Example 1 (Data Graphs). Consider an XML document X. The document X can be modeled as a rooted data graph D_X in a straightforward manner, by defining D_X as the graph that reflects the nesting structure of X.

There are many potentially interesting ways to model a relational database $\mathcal{R}$ as a data graph $D_{\mathcal{R}}$. One option is to define $D_{\mathcal{R}} = (V, E, r, l_V, l_E)$ where *(1)* V contains a vertex d_t for each tuple t in a relation $R \in \mathcal{R}$, *(2)* $E = \emptyset$, *(3)* the root r is $\perp$, and *(4)* $l_V(d_t) = (N, t)$ where N is the name of the relation containing the tuple t, for each vertex $d_t \in V$. Note that we do not have to define l_E, since E is empty.

For example, consider the relational database $\mathcal{R}_1$ in Figure 1. The graph $D_{\mathcal{R}_1}$ also appears in the same figure. In $D_{\mathcal{R}_1}$, we use L, M and E as a shorthand for Location, Manages and Employee, respectively.   □

Example 2 (Query Graphs). Even queries that lack an inherent graph structure can be modeled as graphs. For example, consider the relational-algebra join-query $R_1 \bowtie \cdots \bowtie R_n$, where R_i $(1 \leq i \leq n)$ is a relation. This may be modeled as a query graph $Q = (V, E, r, C_V, C_E, s)$ in the following manner:

- V contains a vertex q_i for each relation R_i,
- there is an edge (q_i, q_j) in E if the relations R_i and R_j share some common attributes,
- the root r is $\perp$,
- C_V maps each vertex q_i to the vertex constraint that assigns TRUE to (d_t, D) if the tuple t belongs to the relation R_i, and FALSE otherwise,
- C_E maps each edge (q, q') to the edge constraint that assigns TRUE to $(d_t, d_{t'}, D)$ if the tuples t and t' are join consistent, and FALSE otherwise,
- $s =$ C.

The query graph Q_1 for Employee $\bowtie$ Location $\bowtie$ Manages appears in Figure 1. The edges in Q_1 are undirected, since $(q_i, q_j) \in E$ if and only if $(q_j, q_i) \in E$.   □

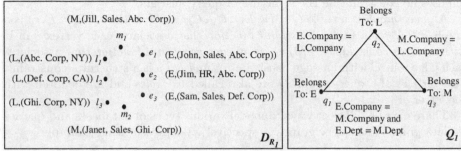

Location			Employee		
Company	Addr	EName	Dept	Company
Abc Corp.	NY	John	Sales	Abc Corp.
Def Corp.	CA	Jim	HR	Abc Corp.
Ghi Corp.	NY	Sam	Sales	Def Corp.

Manages		
MName	Dept	Company
Jill	Sales	Abc Corp.
Janet	Sales	Ghi Corp.

Fig. 1. The relational database $\mathcal{R}_1$, the data graph $D_{\mathcal{R}_1}$ and the query graph Q_1

Assignment Graphs and Partial Assignments. Recall that the vertices in a data graph D are data items and the vertices in a query graph Q are variables. Informally, an answer for Q over D is a set of pairs of the form (q_i, d_j), indicating that the variable q_i is assigned the data item d_j. We formalize this idea by introducing *assignments graphs* that are graphs containing all possible assignments of variables to data items, such that the assignments are consistent with the vertex constraints and the edge constraints of the query graph.

Formally, consider a query graph $Q = (V_Q, E_Q, r_Q, C_V, C_E, s)$ and a data graph $D = (V_D, E_D, r_D, l_V, l_E)$. The *assignment graph* for Q and D, denoted $Q \otimes D$, is defined as (V, E, r), where

- V is the set of pairs $(q, d) \subseteq V_Q \times V_D$ such that the result of applying $C_V(q)$ to (d, D) is TRUE,
- there is an edge $\big((q, d), (q', d')\big) \in E$ if there is an edge $(q, q') \in E_Q$ and the result of applying $C_E(q, q')$ to (d, d', D) is TRUE,[2] *and*
- the vertex r is defined as (r_Q, r_D) if $(r_Q, r_D) \in V$ and as $\bot$, otherwise.

Let Q be a query graph and let D be a data graph. A *partial assignment* A for Q over D is an induced subgraph of $Q \otimes D$ such that A does not contain two vertices (q, d) and (q', d'), where $q = q'$ and $d \neq d'$. Intuitively, this restriction states that a variable in Q is assigned at most one data item in D.[3]

Several special types of partial assignments are of interest. Let A be a partial assignment for Q over D. We say that A is *vertex complete* if for each vertex q

---

[2] Actually, we should write $C_E((q, q'))$. For clarity, we omit the extra parenthesis here and throughout this paper.

[3] Our partial assignments resemble the assignment graphs of [10]. However, their edges are defined in a somewhat different fashion.

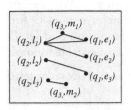

Full Disjunction				
Company	Addr	Dept	EName	MName
Abc Corp.	NY	Sales	John	Jill
Abc Corp.	NY	HR	Jim	⊥
Def Corp.	CA	Sales	Sam	⊥
Ghi Corp.	NY	Sales	⊥	Janet

Fig. 2. The assignment graph $Q_1 \otimes D_{\mathcal{R}_1}$ and the full disjunction of the relations in $\mathcal{R}_1$

in Q, there is a d in D such that (q,d) is in A. We say that A is *edge complete* if for every pair of vertices (q,d) and (q',d') in A, if there is an edge (q,q') in Q, then there is an edge $((q,d),(q',d'))$ in A. Finally, A is *structurally consistent* with Q if A satisfies the structural constraint of Q.

The following example demonstrates different types of partial assignments.

Example 3 ('The assignment graph $Q_1 \otimes D_{\mathcal{R}_1}$). Consider the query graph Q_1 and data graph $D_{\mathcal{R}_1}$, which appear in Figure 1. The assignment graph $Q_1 \otimes D_{\mathcal{R}_1}$ appears in Figure 2. Consider the partial assignments A_1, A_2, A_3 and A_4 defined as the induced subgraphs of $Q_1 \otimes D_{\mathcal{R}_1}$ that contain the sets of vertices S_1, S_2, S_3 and S_4, respectively:

$$S_1 = \{(q_1, c_1), (q_2, l_1), (q_3, m_1)\} \qquad S_3 = \{(q_1, e_2), (q_2, l_1)\}$$
$$S_2 = \{(q_1, e_2), (q_2, l_1), (q_3, m_1)\} \qquad S_4 = \{(q_1, e_2), (q_3, m_1)\}$$

Note that A_1 is vertex complete and edge complete, and A_2 is vertex complete, but is not edge complete (since there is no edge $((q_1, e_2), (q_3, m_1))$ in A_2). The partial assignment A_3 is edge complete, but is not vertex complete. Finally, A_4 is neither vertex complete nor edge complete. Note that A_1, A_2 and A_3 are strucurally consistent with Q_1. The partial assignment A_4 is not strucurally consistent with Q_1, since A_4 is not connected. □

Graph Semantics. We give a formal account of a graph semantics. Our framework is defined so as to capture varied methods for dealing with incomplete information. When complete information is unavailable, it may not be possible to completely satisfy a query graph over a data graph. Hence, we will consider graph semantics that allow answers that maximally satisfy a query.

A *graph semantics* S is a *parameterized graph property*, i.e., for each query graph Q and data graph D, $S[Q,D]$ is a graph property, with the following restriction: If $A \in S[Q,D]$, then $A \sqsubseteq Q \otimes D$ is a partial assignment for Q over D. Note that $S[Q,D]$ does not necessarily contain all partial assignments for Q over D. If $A \in S[Q,D]$, then we say that A is a *partial answer* for Q over D under the graph semantics S. The set of *maximal answers* for Q over D under a graph semantics S is $S^{\text{MAX}}[Q,D]$, i.e., the set of maximal graphs in $S[Q,D]$. Observe that using our formulation, the problem of computing all maximal answers for Q over D under a graph semantics S is simply a special case of the maximal $\mathcal{P}$-subgraphs problem, defined in Section 2.

A graph semantics can contain any set of partial assignments. We present several natural graph semantics. We show later on that common semantics are often special cases of these graph semantics. Let Q be a query graph and let D be a data graph. We define the graph semantics $\mathcal{S}_{\text{VES}}$, $\mathcal{S}_{\text{VS}}$, $\mathcal{S}_{\text{ES}}$ and $\mathcal{S}_{\text{S}}$ as follows:

- $\mathcal{S}_{\text{VES}}[Q, D]$ contains all partial assignments in $Q \otimes D$ that are vertex complete, edge complete and structurally consistent with Q.
- $\mathcal{S}_{\text{VS}}[Q, D]$ contains all partial assignments in $Q \otimes D$ that are vertex complete and structurally consistent with Q.
- $\mathcal{S}_{\text{ES}}[Q, D]$ contains all partial assignments in $Q \otimes D$ that are edge complete and structurally consistent with Q.
- $\mathcal{S}_{\text{S}}[Q, D]$ contains all partial assignments in $Q \otimes D$ that are structurally consistent with Q.

Common methods for query evaluation easily lend themselves to the formalisms presented above, as demonstrated in the following examples.

Example 4 (Joins). Let Q be a query graph that represents a join query $R_1 \bowtie \cdots \bowtie R_n$, as defined in Example 2, and let D be a data graph that represents a relational database $\mathcal{R}$, as defined in Example 1. It is not difficult to show that there is a one-to-one correspondence between the graphs in $\mathcal{S}_{\text{VES}}^{\text{MAX}}[Q, D]$ and the tuples resulting from applying $R_1 \bowtie \cdots \bowtie R_n$ to $\mathcal{R}$.

Intuitively, if $A \in \mathcal{S}_{\text{VES}}^{\text{MAX}}[Q, D]$, then A is a partial assignment of variables (that range over the relations appearing in the query) to tuples in the relations. The definition of the vertex conditions of Q ensures that variables are assigned tuples in the relations that they represent. The edge conditions of Q, along with the fact that $\mathcal{S}_{\text{VES}}$ only contains partial assignments that are edge complete, ensures that every pair of tuples in the assignment is join consistent. Finally, the fact that $\mathcal{S}_{\text{VES}}$ only contains vertex complete assignments ensures that A corresponds to the join of *all* relations mentioned in the query.

As an example, observe that the only partial assignment in $\mathcal{S}_{\text{VES}}^{\text{MAX}}[Q_1, D_{\mathcal{R}_1}]$ is the graph A_1 (from Example 3). This graph corresponds to the only tuple in the natural join of Location, Employee and Manages.   □

Example 5 (Full Disjunctions). When dealing with incomplete information, the join operator is often replaced with the full-disjunction operator. The full-disjunction operator is a natural extension of the outerjoin operator to an arbitrary number of relations. Full disjunctions were introduced by [4]. The complexity of evaluating a full disjunction of relations was studied in [14, 10].

Two relations are *connected* if they share a common attribute. A set of relations $R_1, \ldots, R_n$ is *connected* if it forms a connected graph (when creating a vertex for each R_i and placing an edge between R_i and R_j if they are connected). The *full disjunction* [14] of $R_1, \ldots, R_n$, is the set of tuples t over the attributes of $R_1, \ldots, R_n$, such that

1. t is the join of some collection of join-consistent tuples from a connected subset of the relations $R_1, \ldots, R_n$, padded with null values, and
2. There is no additional relation among the R_i's with a tuple that is join consistent with t.

We use $FD(R_1, \ldots, R_n)$ to denote the query that computes the full disjunction of a given set of relations $R_1, \ldots, R_n$.

Consider, for example, the relational database $\mathcal{R}_1$ in Figure 1. The full disjunction of the relations in $\mathcal{R}_1$ appears in Figure 2. Note that the result contains null values (denoted $\perp$) where no information is available. For example, in the second tuple of the result, there is a null value in the MName column, since there is no tuple, in the relation Manages, that contains information about the manager of the HR department in Abc Corp.

We now show how full disjunctions can be expressed in our framework. A relational database is represented as a data graph $D_\mathcal{R}$, as described in Example 1. A query $FD(R_1, \ldots, R_n)$ is represented as a query graph Q in the same manner that a join query is represented (see Example 2). Hence, the query graph Q_1 in Figure 1 also represents the query $FD(\text{Employee}, \text{Location}, \text{Manages})$.

It is not difficult to show that there is a one-to-one correspondence between graphs in $\mathcal{S}_{\text{ES}}^{\text{MAX}}[Q, D_\mathcal{R}]$ and tuples in the result of $FD(R_1, \ldots, R_n)$. In particular, note that partial assignments in $\mathcal{S}_{\text{ES}}[Q, D_\mathcal{R}]$ are connected (because of the strucural constraint in Q), and hence, they represent sets of connected tuples. For example the second tuple of the full disjunction in Figure 2 corresponds to the induced subgraph A_3 (from Example 3) that contains the vertices (q_1, e_2) and (q_2, l_1). Note that A_3 is a maximal $\mathcal{S}_{\text{ES}}$-subgraph in the assignment graph $Q_1 \otimes D_{\mathcal{R}_1}$, i.e., $A_3 \in \mathcal{S}_{\text{ES}}^{\text{MAX}}[Q_1, D_{\mathcal{R}_1}]$. □

4   Complexity Classes

We have shown that the problem of computing maximal answers, for a query graph Q, a data graph D and a graph semantics $\mathcal{S}$, is a special case of the more general maximal $\mathcal{P}$-subgraphs problem. Hence, it is of importance to analyze the complexity of the maximal $\mathcal{P}$-subgraphs problem, since it will immediately shed light on our query-evaluation problem.

The maximal $\mathcal{P}$-subgraphs problem cannot be solved in polynomial time, in the general case. This follows from the fact that sometimes the size of $\mathcal{P}^{\text{MAX}}(G)$ is exponential in the size of G. Hence, exponential time may be needed just to print the output. This phenomenon is quite similar to the problem that arises when analyzing query-evaluation time. It is well-known that for many types of queries the number of tuples in the result may be exponential in the size of the input (i.e., the query and database). Hence, *input-output complexity* is of interest when analyzing query evaluation [17].

Under input-output complexity, the complexity of a problem is analyzed as a function of its input and output. We say that a problem is in the complexity class PIO if it can be solved in polynomial time under input-output complexity. For most classes of queries, query evaluation is not in PIO. For example, the evaluation of a join of relations cannot usually be performed in polynomial time under input-output complexity, since it is NP-complete to determine whether the result of a join is nonempty [12]. Much effort has been put into finding classes of queries for which evaluation is in PIO. For such classes of queries, query evaluation can be considered "inherently easy," since evaluation is only polynomially longer than reading the input and printing the output. For example, for the class of acyclic joins [17] and for the class of queries with bounded variable size [16], query evaluation is in PIO. Recently, it has also been shown that evaluating a full disjunction is in PIO [10].

Another complexity class that is of interest when dealing with problems that may have large output (e.g., query evaluation and the maximal $\mathcal{P}$-subgraphs problem) is *incremental polynomial time* [7], or PINC for short. Formally, a problem is in PINC if k output items of the problem can be returned in polynomial time in the input and k, for all k.[4] Observe that PTIME $\subseteq$ PINC $\subseteq$ PIO. The class PINC is of interest when the user is interested in optimizing query-evaluation time for retrieval of the first k tuples, as opposed to optimizing for overall time. (Many commercial database systems allow the user to specify the option of optimizing the retrieval of the first k tuples.) This is particularly useful when the user reads the answers as they are delivered, or is only interested in looking at a small portion of the total answer. If query evaluation is in PIO, but not in PINC, the user may have to wait exponential time until the entire output is created, before viewing a single tuple. Interestingly, the algorithm for acyclic joins in [17] is in PINC, although this is not explicitly stated in that paper.

5   Efficiently Evaluating a Query

In this section, we present some known results about the complexity of the maximal $\mathcal{P}$-subgraphs problem. These results are used in order to analyze the complexity of query evaluation for the natural semantics presented in Section 3.

5.1   Complexity of the Maximal $\mathcal{P}$-Subgraphs Problem

Let $\mathcal{P}$ be a graph property. Suppose that we want to show that the maximal $\mathcal{P}$-subgraphs problem is in PIO. To do this, we must devise an algorithm that, when given any graph G, produces $\mathcal{P}^{\text{MAX}}(G)$, in polynomial time in the input (i.e., G) and the output (i.e., $\mathcal{P}^{\text{MAX}}(G)$). For many properties $\mathcal{P}$, it is difficult to find such an algorithm, since an arbitrary graph G must be dealt with. A naive algorithm will create the set of graphs $\mathcal{P}(G)$, and then remove the graphs that are not maximal. However, this is clearly too expensive to be desirable. Our task of finding an appropriate algorithm is even more difficult if we actually want to show that the maximal $\mathcal{P}$-subgraphs problem is in PINC. Hence, we focus on a version of the maximal $\mathcal{P}$-subgraphs problem that is restricted in its input. It is often easier to show that this version is in PIO or in PINC.

Let G be a graph and $\mathcal{P}$ be a property. We use $G - v$ to denote the induced graph of G that contains all vertices other than v. We say that G *almost satisfies* $\mathcal{P}$ if there is a vertex v in G, such that $G - v \in \mathcal{P}$. The *restricted maximal $\mathcal{P}$-*

---

[4] Note that no ordering is imposed on the output, and hence, these are arbitrary items.

subgraphs problem is: Given a graph G that almost satisfies $\mathcal{P}$, find all maximal $\mathcal{P}$-subgraphs of G.

The following result appears in [3] and presents a sufficient condition for the maximal $\mathcal{P}$-subgraphs problem to be in PINC.

Theorem 1. *Let $\mathcal{P}$ be a hereditary, rooted-hereditary or connected-hereditary graph property. If the restricted maximal $\mathcal{P}$-subgraphs problem is in PTIME, then the maximal $\mathcal{P}$-subgraphs problem is in PINC.*

Note that even if the restricted maximal $\mathcal{P}$-subgraphs problem is in PTIME, the maximal $\mathcal{P}$-subgraphs problem may not be in PTIME. For example, consider the property $\mathcal{P}_{\text{clique}}$, which contains all graphs that are cliques. There may be an exponential number of maximal $\mathcal{P}_{\text{clique}}$-subgraphs for a given graph. However, if G almost satisfies $\mathcal{P}_{\text{clique}}$, then there are at most two maximal $\mathcal{P}_{\text{clique}}$-subgraphs for G. Hence, the restricted maximal $\mathcal{P}_{\text{clique}}$-subgraphs problem is in PTIME, but the maximal $\mathcal{P}_{\text{clique}}$-subgraph is only in PINC, and not in PTIME.

5.2   Special Cases of the Maximal $\mathcal{P}$-Subgraphs Problem

Our graph semantics are parameterized graph properties, where the parameters are the query and the database. Thus, Theorem 1 (which deals with graph properties that are not parameterized) does not immediately yield results on the complexity of query evaluation. However, it is straightforward to generalize this theorem to parameterized properties. In this subsection, we analyze the complexity of query evaluation for the natural graph semantics defined in Section 3.

Semantics that allow only vertex-complete answers are often of high computational complexity. For the special case of $\mathcal{S}_{\text{VS}}^{\text{MAX}}[Q, D]$, where Q has the structural constraint N, the problem of generating all maximal answers is in PINC. For all other cases, query evaluation for $\mathcal{S}_{\text{VES}}$ and $\mathcal{S}_{\text{VS}}$ is not in PINC or in PIO, unless P=NP.

Theorem 2. *The problem of determining nonemptyness of $\mathcal{S}_{\text{VES}}^{\text{MAX}}[Q, D]$ is NP-complete. The problem of determining nonemptyness of $\mathcal{S}_{\text{VS}}^{\text{MAX}}[Q, D]$ is is NP-complete when the structural constraint of Q is either R or C.*

Query evaluation for $\mathcal{S}_{\text{ES}}$ or $\mathcal{S}_{\text{S}}$ can be performed efficiently. The proof for Theorem 3 follows from *(1)* a generalization of Theorem 1 for parameterized graph properties *and (2)* a proof that the restricted maximal $\mathcal{P}$-subgraphs problem (for an appropriately defined property $\mathcal{P}$) is in PTIME. We omit the details of the proof due to lack of space. Note that in the following theorem, the input consists of Q and D.

Theorem 3. *Let $\mathcal{S}$ be either $\mathcal{S}_{\text{ES}}$ or $\mathcal{S}_{\text{S}}$. Let Q be a query graph and let D be a data graph. The problem of generating $\mathcal{S}^{\text{MAX}}[Q, D]$ is in PINC.*

There is a special case in which query evaluation for $\mathcal{S}_{\text{VES}}$ is efficient. This follows directly from Theorem 3.

Corollary 1. *Let Q be a query graph and let D be a data graph. If all partial assignments in $\mathcal{S}_{\mathrm{ES}}^{\mathrm{MAX}}[Q, D]$ are vertex complete, then the problem of computing $\mathcal{S}_{\mathrm{VES}}^{\mathrm{MAX}}[Q, D]$ is in PINC.*

A similar result holds for $\mathcal{S}_{\mathrm{VS}}^{\mathrm{MAX}}$ if all partial assignments in $\mathcal{S}_{\mathrm{S}}^{\mathrm{MAX}}$ are vertex complete. A special case of Corollary 1 is the known fact that evaluation of acyclic joins is in PINC [17].

6   Generating Maximal Answers

In this section, we consider several semantics that have been proposed in order to deal with incomplete information. We briefly discuss how these semantics can be modeled in our abstract framework, and give the complexity results that are implied by these modelings.

6.1   Relational Databases: Full Disjunctions

Recall full-disjunction queries, introduced in Example 5. The problem of evaluating the full disjunction of γ-acyclic relations was shown to be in PIO [14]. In the general case, computing full disjunctions was also shown to be in PIO [10]. The algorithm in [10] cannot be used to show that the problem of evaluating a full disjunction is in PINC. However, this follows from Theorem 3 and from the fact that full disjunctions can be expressed using the graph semantics $\mathcal{S}_{\mathrm{ES}}$.[5]

Corollary 2. *Let $R_1, \ldots, R_n$ be relations. The problem of computing the full disjunction of $R_1, \ldots, R_n$, i.e., of evaluating $FD(R_1, \ldots, R_n)$, is in PINC.*

The following was observed by [10]. First, full disjunctions can be generalized by allowing constraints other than equality between attributes. Second, this generalization remains in PIO. Using our framework, it is easy to see that such extensions remain in PINC. All that is required is to associate the edges of a query with edge constraints that are different from equality of attributes. In addition, it is possible to allow more general vertex constraints. Query evaluation remains in PINC, as long as the vertex and edge constraints chosen are verifiable in PTIME. These types of extensions of full-disjunction queries are of importance when querying heterogeneous data sources, where *(1)* query variables may take values from several different relations *and (2)* it may be unlikely that string equality will hold between different values that denote the same entity (e.g., different character strings may actually denote the same address).

6.2   XML Databases

The hierarchical structure of an XML document is naturally modeled as a rooted data graph. Such data graphs are often trees, but may also contain cycles because

---

[5] Note that subsumption of tuples in our framework is defined in terms of object identities. For full disjunctions, tuple subsumption was defined in terms of values. These two notions of subsumption coincide for our modeling of full disjunctions.

of ID/IDREFs or XLinks. Queries against XML are often defined as graphs, and thus, lend themselves naturally to our framework. We consider several different methods that have been presented in the past, for evaluating queries flexibly against XML, and show how they can be modeled in our framework.

Weak Semantics and Or-Semantics. In [8], databases and queries are modeled as rooted, directed graphs with labeled edges. We write vlu to denote the fact that there is an edge from v to u labeled with l.

We quote from [8] two different semantics for evaluating their queries over a database. Let μ be a partial assignment of the vertices in a query Q to the vertices of a database D. The assignment μ *satisfies* the edge vlu in Q if *(1)* μ is defined on v and u, *and (2)* there is an edge from $\mu(v)$ to $\mu(u)$ in D that is labeled with l. Satisfaction of an edge is extended to satisfaction of a path π in the natural way, i.e., μ satisfies π if it satisfies every edge in π.

A partial assignment μ is an OR-*matching* if

- μ assigns the root of the query to the root of the database;
- for every vertex q, such that $\mu(q)$ is defined, there is a path π from the root of the query to q, such that μ satisfies π.

The OR-matching μ is also a *weak matching* if whenever μ is defined for q and q' and the query contains an edge qlq', then μ satisfies qlq'.

The problems of computing all maximal weak matchings and of computing all maximal OR-matchings, for a given query and database, were shown to be in PIO [8, 10]. It is not difficult to show that these problems are in PINC, by modeling their queries and databases in our framework. Weak semantics can be modeled using $\mathcal{S}_{ES}$ and OR-semantics can be modeled using $\mathcal{S}_{S}$. Hence, Corollary 3 follows from Theorem 3. Actually, the queries of [8] can be extended without affecting the PINC complexity by allowing more general vertex constraints and edge constraints. For example, edge constraints can require the existence of a path between two vertices, instead of requiring the existence of an edge.

Corollary 3. *Given a query and a database, the problems of generating all maximal* OR-*matchings and all maximal weak matchings are in* PINC.

Tree Pattern Relaxations. [15, 1, 6] consider the problem of answering *relaxed versions* of a given query, against a given database. Their queries and databases are trees (and not general graphs). The main focus of their work is on *(1)* defining a metric for measuring how exactly an answer satisfies a query *and (2)* presenting efficient algorithms that find the best k results, according to their metrics. Although the algorithms were shown to work well experimentally, no theoretical bounds on the runtime of the algorithms were presented. We discuss how relaxed queries from [15] can be modeled in our framework. Relaxed queries from [1, 6] can be modeled similarly.

In [15], XML documents are rooted trees whose vertices have *types*. Queries are called *tree patterns* and are a special type of rooted trees *(1)* whose vertices have types *and (2)* whose edges are either *pc-edges* (parent-child edges) or *ad-edges* (ancestor-descendent edges). An *exact answer* for a tree pattern T with respect to a database is a rooted subtree of the database that satisfies all the constraints implied by the tree pattern. Formally, this requires that *(1)* each pc-edge in T is mapped to an edge in the database, *(2)* each ad-edge in T is mapped to a directed path in the database, *and (3)* each vertex q in T is mapped to a vertex d in the database, such that the type of d is a subtype of that of q.

A *relaxation* of a tree pattern T is the result of one or more of the following actions: *(1)* replace a pc-edge in T with an ad-edge, *(2)* remove a leaf vertex from T, *(3)* make a node a child of its grandparent instead of its parent, *(4)* replace the type t of a vertex in T with a supertype of t. An *approximate answer* for T is an exact answer to any relaxation of T. We can model tree patterns in our framework by defining query graphs that correspond to tree patterns, appropriately, and by using the semantics $\mathcal{S}_{\mathrm{ES}}^{\mathrm{MAX}}$. Corollary 4 follows.

Corollary 4. *Let T be a tree pattern and let D be a database. The problem of finding all maximal approximate answers for T with respect to D is in* PINC.

Interconnections. In [2], databases are labeled, directed, rooted trees. A simple method was presented for determining whether two vertices in a database are *interconnected*, i.e., meaningfully related. The *interconnection graph I* for a database is a graph that has the same vertices as in the database, and an edge between interconnected vertices. A query consists of a series of XPath expressions $\pi_1, \ldots, \pi_n$. Two semantics for query evaluation were considered.

Consider a query $\pi_1, \ldots, \pi_n$ and a database with an interconnection graph I. A partial assignment μ from $\pi_1, \ldots, \pi_n$ to vertices in the database is a *reachably-interconnected matching* (resp., *completely-interconnected matching*) if *(1)* μ maps each path π_i to a vertex that satisfies π_i and *(2)* the induced subgraph of I that contains the vertices in the image of μ is connected (resp., a clique).

It was shown [2] that the following problems are in PIO: finding all maximal reachably-interconnected matchings and finding all maximal completely-interconnected matchings. Using our framework, we can show that these problems are in PINC, by *(1)* using an appropriate modeling of queries and databases, *and (2)* choosing $\mathcal{S}_{\mathrm{ES}}$ (resp., $\mathcal{S}_{\mathrm{S}}$) to model completely-interconnected matchings (resp., reachably-interconnected matchings). As before, the queries from [2] can be extended by allowing more general constraints while retaining their PINC complexity.

Corollary 5. *Given a database and query, the problems of finding all maximal completely-interconnected matchings and of finding all maximal reachably-interconnected matchings are in* PINC.

Flexible Semantics. [9] considered the problem of answering a query in a flexible fashion, by allowing permutations of the vertices in a query. Formally, their databases and queries are rooted, labeled, directed graphs. Flexible semantics were presented for query evaluation. A complete assignment μ from the vertices in a query to the vertices in a database is a *flexible matching* if for every edge qlq' in the query, *(1)* $\mu(q')$ has an incoming edge with the label l and *(2)* there is either a directed path from $\mu(q)$ to $\mu(q')$ or vice-versa.

Flexible matchings can be modeled in our framework by defining query graphs appropriately and by using the semantics $\mathcal{S}_{VES}$. Although [9] did not consider *partial flexible matchings*, these can easily be allowed by using the graph semantics $\mathcal{S}_{ES}$ (to derive a combination of flexible and weak matchings) or by using $\mathcal{S}_S$ (to derive a combination of flexible and OR-matchings). In both cases, query evaluation is in PINC.

Corollary 6. *The problems of generating all maximal flexible* OR-*matchings and all maximal flexible weak matchings, for a database and a query, are in* PINC.

7   Conclusion

The main contributions of this paper are as follows. First, an abstract framework for modeling queries, databases and semantics was presented. In our framework, semantics are modeled as graph properties. Hence, results for the maximal $\mathcal{P}$-subgraphs problem can be used in order to analyze the problem of efficient query evaluation. Second, we presented the natural semantics $\mathcal{S}_{ES}$ and $\mathcal{S}_S$ that can be used for any type of query. These graph semantics can be efficiently evaluated. Third, we showed that previously studied semantics coincide with $\mathcal{S}_{ES}$ and $\mathcal{S}_S$. This allowed us to improve upon previously known complexity results for query evaluation (i.e., PINC complexity instead of PIO). Fourth, using our modeling techniques, it is easy to extend existing semantics for inexact (e.g., maximal, approximate, interconnected or flexible) answers by incorporating more general vertex and edge constraints, without affecting the complexity of query evaluation.

An interesting problem for future research is that of efficiently returning query answers in ranking order, for some ranking scheme. Note that the complexity class PINC is of interest in this context, while PIO is not of interest, since PIO algorithms may wait until all answers are generated before returning a single answer. Using Theorem 2, it is easy to show that the problem of returning results in size order in not in PINC, even for the semantics $\mathcal{S}_{ES}$ and $\mathcal{S}_S$. It is of importance to discover other ranking schemes that can be efficiently computed and to find special efficient cases of ranking by size.

References

1. S. Amer-Yahia, L.V.S. Lakshmanan, and S. Pandit. FleXPath: flexible structure and full-text querying for xml. In *Proc. 2004 ACM SIGMOD International Conference on Management of Data*, 2004.
2. S. Cohen, Y. Kanza, and Y. Sagiv. Generating relations from XML documents. In *Proc 9th International Conference on Database Theory*, 2003.
3. S. Cohen and Y. Sagiv. Generating all maximal solutions for hereditary, connected-hereditary and rooted-hereditary graph properties, 2004. Corr ID: cs.DS/0410039.
4. C. Galindo-Legaria. Outerjoins as disjunctions. In *Proc. 1994 ACM SIGMOD International Conference on Management of Data*, 1994.
5. M.R. Garey and D.S. Johnson. *Computers and Intractability: A Guide to the Theory of NP-Completeness*. Freeman, San Francisco, 1979.

6. S. Guha, H.V. Jagadish, N. Koudas, D. Srivastava, and T. Yu. Approximate xml joins. In *Proc. 2002 ACM SIGMOD International Conference on Management of Data*, 2002.
7. D.S. Johnson, C.H. Papadimitriou, and M. Yannakakis. On generating all maximal independent sets. *Information Processing Letters*, 27(3):119–123, 1988.
8. Y. Kanza, W. Nutt, and Y. Sagiv. Queries with incomplete answers over semistructured data. In *Proc. 18th Symposium on Principles of Database Systems*, 1999.
9. Y. Kanza and Y. Sagiv. Flexible queries over semistructured data. In *Proc. 20th Symposium on Principles of Database Systems*, 2001.
10. Y. Kanza and Y. Sagiv. Computing full disjunctions. In *Proc. 22nd Symposium on Principles of Database Systems*, 2003.
11. L. Libkin. A semantics-based approach to design of query languages for partial information. In *Semantics in Databases*, 1995.
12. D. Maier, Y. Sagiv, and M. Yannakakis. On the complexity of testing implications of functional and join dependencies. *J. ACM*, 28(4):680–695, 1981.
13. A.O. Mendelzon and G.A. Mihaila. Querying partially sound and complete data sources. In *Proc. 20th Symposium on Principles of Database Systems*, 2001.
14. A. Rajaraman and J.D. Ullman. Integrating information by outerjoins and full disjunctions. In *Proc. 15th Symposium on Principles of Database Systems*, 1996.
15. D. Srivastava S. Amer-Yahia, S. Cho. Tree pattern relaxation. In *Proc. 8th International Conference on Extending Database Technology*, 2002.
16. M.Y. Vardi. On the complexity of bounded-variable queries. In *Proc. 14th Symposium on Principles of Database Systems*, 1995.
17. M. Yannakakis. Algorithms for acyclic database schemas. In *Proc. 7th International Conference on Very Large Data Bases*, 1981.

Optimal Distributed Declustering Using Replication

Keith B. Frikken

CERIAS and Department of Computer Sciences, Purdue University,
Recitation Building, 656 Oval Drive, West Lafayette IN 47907
Telephone: (765)-496-6767
kbf@cs.purdue.edu

Abstract. A common technique for improving performance for database query retrieval is to decluster the database among multiple disks so that retrievals can be parallelized. In this paper we focus on answering range queries over a multidimensional database, where each of its dimensions are divided uniformly to obtain tiles which are placed on different disks; there has been a significant amount of research for determining how to place the records on disks to minimize the retrieval time. Recently, the idea of using replication (i.e., placing records on more than one disk) to improve performance has been introduced. When using replication there are two goals: i) to minimize the retrieval time and ii) to minimize the scheduling overhead it takes to determine which disk obtains a specific record when processing a query. The previously known replicated declustering schemes with low retrieval times are randomized; and one of the primary advantages of randomized schemes is that they balance the load evenly among the disks for large queries with high probability. In this paper we introduce a new class of replicated placement schemes called the shift schemes that are: i) deterministic, ii) have retrieval performance that is comparable to the randomized schemes, iii) have a strictly optimal retrieval time for all large queries, and iv) have a more efficient query scheduling algorithm than those for the randomized placements. Furthermore, we display experimental results that suggest that the shift schemes have stronger average performance (in terms of retrieval times) than the randomized schemes.

1   Introduction

A typical bottleneck for answering queries in a database is I/O; to reduce the effect of this bottleneck, data can be declustered onto multiple disks to facilitate parallel retrieval. In a multi-dimensional database, such as a GIS or a spatio-temporal database, the dimensions can be tiled uniformly to form a grid. When answering a range query in such a grid, only the tiles that contain part of the query need to be retrieved. In such an environment, the goal of a placement scheme is to place the tiles onto disks in such a way that the average range query is answered as efficiently as possible (i.e., minimizing the number of parallel rounds of retrieval). A placement scheme is optimal for a query if at most

T. Eiter and L. Libkin (Eds.): ICDT 2005, LNCS 3363, pp. 144–157, 2005.

$\lceil$ (# of tiles)/(# of disks) $\rceil$ tiles are retrieved from any single disk. However, it was shown in [2] that even in two dimensions this cannot be done for all range queries in a grid except in a few limited circumstances. There is a large amount of work that attempts to be "close" to optimal (a subset of which is [2, 5, 6, 7, 8, 11, 12, 13, 15, 17, 18, 19, 20, 21]). If the database is treated like a grid and the disks as colors, then this can be stated as a grid coloring problem. For the rest of the paper we use "record" and "tile" synonymously, and likewise use "declustering" and "coloring" interchangeably.

To improve performance further, the usage of replication (i.e. placing each tile on multiple disks) [4, 9, 10, 12, 18, 19, 21] has been introduced. When replication is used, each tile in a query can be retrieved from multiple places, which allows greater flexibility when answering the query. When using replication there are two questions: i) which disk to retrieve each tile from and ii) how to use replication to improve performance. A general replicated scheduling algorithm exists that requires $O(rm^2)$ computation where m is the number of disks and r is the level of replication. The previously known replicated declustering schemes with low retrieval time are randomized and have a large query scheduling time. In this paper we introduce a new class of replicated placement schemes called the shift schemes that are: i) deterministic, ii) have comparable retrieval performance to randomized schemes, iii) have a strictly optimal retrieval time for all large queries (this is the first class of schemes that guarantees this property that the author is aware of), and iv) have an efficient query scheduling algorithm.

The outline of this paper is as follows: Section 2 discusses previous work in distributed database declustering, in Section 3 the shift schemes are introduced (for a level of replication of 2), a proof of their optimality bound is given, and a scheduling algorithm is presented. Section 4 contains generalizations of the shift schemes to levels of replication larger than two and discuss the performance of the schemes with disk failures. Section 5 contains experimental data showing the performance of the shift schemes, and Section 6 concludes the paper.

2   Related Work

Given a multi-dimensional database with each dimension divided uniformly to form tiles which are placed on different disks, the retrieval of records during query processing can be parallelized. As is usual in this area, we assume that retrieving a tile from a database requires a constant fixed amount of time regardless of the tile and that query borders are on tile boundaries. The query retrieval time in such a system is the time that it takes to retrieve the maximum number of tiles in the query that are stored on the same disk. The problem of placing the records so that the response times for range queries is minimized has been well studied; this section presents a survey of this work.

Given a database declustered onto k disks and a range query Q_m containing m tiles, let the retrievals from each disk be represented by $R_0, \ldots, R_{k-1}$. Let $rt(Q_m)$ represent the retrieval time for Q_m (this is $\max_{i=0}^{k-1} R_i$). A query Q_m is said to be retrieved optimally if $rt(Q_m) = \lceil \frac{m}{k} \rceil$. A coloring is said to be strictly optimal if all queries can be retrieved optimally. It was shown in [2] that strictly optimal colorings are impossible except in a few limited circumstances. To quantify how far a scheme is from optimal, let the additive error of a query Q_m be the value $(rt(Q_m) - \lceil \frac{m}{k} \rceil)$. The additive error of the coloring scheme is the maximum additive error over all range queries. In this paper we define another similar metric, the surplus of a query Q_m. The surplus for a query Q_m is defined by $\sum_{i=0}^{k-1} \max\{R_i - \lceil \frac{m}{k} \rceil, 0\}$; note that the surplus is the sum of the additive error of all disks. Similar to the additive error, the surplus of a coloring is the maximum value of the surplus over all queries. Several schemes have been developed to minimize the additive error including: Disk Modulo (DM) [11], Fieldwise eXclusive (FX) or [15], the cyclic schemes (including RPHM, GFIB, and EXH) [17], GRS [7], a technique developed by Atallah and Prabhakar [5], several techniques based on discrepancy theory [8, 20] (for an introduction to discrepancy theory see [16]), and many other schemes.

We now review a class of schemes called the Latin Hypercube Disk Modulo (LHDM) schemes [13]. An LHDM scheme is a coloring scheme that is defined in the following manner: Given a Latin Hypercube with each dimension of size k with a lookup function $L(x_1, \ldots, x_d)$ that returns the color in the range $[0, k)$ at tile $x_1, \ldots, x_d$. Recall that a Latin Hypercube has one instance of each color in any k tiles in a single dimension. The coloring function C for an LHDM scheme is $C(x_1, \ldots, x_d) = L(x_1 \bmod k, \ldots, x_d \bmod k)$. Many coloring schemes are instances of the LHDM scheme, including: Disk Modulo(DM), Fieldwise exclusive-or (FX) for powers of 2, the cyclic schemes, GRS, and many other schemes. The LHDM schemes have a nice property, which is that a query with dimension lengths $n_1, \ldots, n_d$ has the same additive error as a sub-query with dimension lengths $(n_1 \bmod k), \ldots, (n_d \bmod k)$; this is because any k consecutive tiles in any dimension have exactly one instance of each color. This result also holds for the surplus, and a natural consequence is that the additive error (surplus) for any LHDM scheme is bounded.

It was shown in [20] that the additive error for k colors in two dimensions is $\Omega(\log k)$, and that in $d(\geq 3)$ dimensions it is $\Omega(\log^{\frac{d-1}{2}} k)$. In two dimensions, schemes have been developed (Atallah and Prabhakar's scheme, GRS, and schemes based in discrepancy theory [5, 20]) that have a provable upper bound of $O(\log k)$ on additive error. For higher dimensions $d(\geq 3)$, two schemes are given in [8] with additive error $O(\log^{(d-1)} k)$, which are the schemes with the lowest proven asymptotic bound on additive error for higher dimensions. A recent trend has been to use replication [4, 9, 10, 12, 18, 19, 21] to improve performance. When using replication there are two questions that arise: i) given a query on a set of tiles which disk should retrieve each tile and ii) how to use replication to improve performance. It was shown in [10] that any replicated scheme for a query Q_m can be scheduled in $O(rm^2)$ time where r is the level of replication. The first schemes in this are were for general queries (i.e., not only for range queries). One of the first attempts at replication was the chained declustering [14], this scheme defined a primary and backup disk. And if a record has a primary disk of i, then the backup disk was $(i + 1 \bmod k)$, and thus this scheme formed a chain. It was shown in [3], that the there is an algorithm that can test if a query can be answered with at most K tiles per disk in linear time. However, the strongest mechanisms (to date) place the disks on two random disks, this is called Random Duplicate Allocation (RDA). In [18, 19] it was proven that if tiles are stored on two random disks then the probability of requiring more than ($\lceil \frac{m}{k} \rceil$ +1) retrievals from a single disk for a random query Q_m approaches 0 as the number of disks gets large. Recently, it was shown in [1] that if $m \geq ck \log k$ for large enough c that the query can be scheduled in strictly optimal time with high probability, and an algorithm that runs in time $\Delta k^{O(1)}$ that computes an optimal scheduling algorithm with high probability (where Δ is the imbalance of a non-replicated randomized scheme).

The above work does not take into account the previous work on non-replicated coloring schemes. Recently, there has been an attempt to merge the two techniques. In [21] replication was used to achieve optimal solutions for up to 15 disks. A strictly optimal scheme, called Complete Coloring (CC), for any number of disks by storing all tiles on all disks was introduced in [12, 21]. Recently [4, 9], there has been an effort to develop schemes that have small additive error, but that also have an efficient retrieval algorithm. We outline three such schemes:

1. A grouping scheme where the disks are placed into groups of size r (r is the level of replication) and the grid is colored with groups. The scheduling algorithm for this case has computation complexity $O(m)$ [4, 9] using only one-pass over the records.
2. Using a base scheme that is a strong non-replicated scheme and then placing each tile on $r - 1$ random disks. The scheduling algorithm for this coloring is $O(m + k^2\epsilon^2)$, where ϵ is the additive error of the base scheme [9].
3. This is the same as the previous scheme except that the scheduling algorithm is greedy and is done in $O(m)$ time [9].

3   Our Contribution

The primary contribution of this paper is a new type of replicated scheme called the shift schemes, which are a combination of a generalized version of chained declustering and non-replicated coloring schemes. The strongest schemes in the past have been randomized, and these schemes have the nice property that as a query gets large, the probability that the scheme performs well is high. The shift schemes are deterministic schemes with this property; specifically, we show that any query with at least $k(k-1)\epsilon$ tiles can be scheduled in a strictly optimal fashion (for a level of replication of 2). Surprisingly, this bound also holds if a single disk fails. While this bound is not as strong as the bound for RDA, we give experimental results that show that the shift schemes perform better than RDA and GRS with RDA. Also, this bound also holds if there is a disk failure. Furthermore, the shift schemes can be scheduled in $O(m+k \log \epsilon)$ (which is faster than the randomized algorithms, note that while a greedy GRS-RDA algorithm requires only $O(m)$ time our scheme performs substantially better at balancing the schemes load); it is worth noting that many shift schemes in two dimensions, will be scheduled in $O(m + k \log \log k)$ time.

4   Shift Coloring Schemes

In this section we introduce the shift schemes for declustering. In this section we introduce the shift schemes for a level of replication equaling two; we discuss extending the shift schemes to higher levels of replication in Section 5. We define the scheme in Section 4.1, we then prove that an upper bound for the largest query that cannot be retrieved optimally in Section 4.2, in Section 4.3 we discuss an efficient scheduling algorithm, and then in Section 4.4 we improve the bound on the maximum non-optimal query.

4.1   Definition of the Shift Schemes

We now introduce the class of replicated coloring schemes with level of replication two, called the shift schemes. Instead of being a specific method, this is a general technique for extending a non-replicated coloring scheme into a "strong" replicated coloring scheme. The first color for this scheme is defined by any non-replicated coloring scheme (which we call the base scheme); we let $f : [0, \infty)^d \to [0, k-1)$ represent this function (d is the dimension of the grid and k is the number of disks). The second color is determined by a shift value s, where $gcd(s, k) = 1$, and the second color of a tile T is $(f(T) + s \bmod k)$ (note that when $s = 1$ this is the chained declustering). We now give an example of a shift scheme for a 5 by 5 grid in Figure 1 with its base scheme being RPHM with 5 colors (i.e., $f(x, y) = x + 2y \bmod 5$ and the coordinate $(0,0)$ is the top left corner) with a shift value of 3.

0,3	1,4	2,0	3,1	4,2
2,0	3,1	4,2	0,3	1,4
4,2	0,3	1,4	2,0	3,1
1,4	2,0	3,1	4,2	0,3
3,1	4,2	0,3	1,4	2,0

Fig. 1. Example Shift Scheme

The intuition behind the shift schemes is that when there is a surplus for the query we would like to be able to shift tiles from the disk with surplus to disks with a shortage of tiles for the query. By choosing a shift value that is relatively prime to the number of disks it is possible to create a chain between any two disks. Thus if there are enough tiles at each disk to create enough such chains to balance all surplus values then the query can be answered optimally. Furthermore, the shift schemes have two interesting properties:

- For large queries, the shift schemes are strictly optimal (assuming that the base scheme has a bounded additive error). More specifically, if given a base scheme for k colors that has a maximum additive error ϵ, then any query with more than $k(k-1)(2\epsilon+1)$ tiles will be strictly optimal. This is proven in Section 4.2. After defining the scheduling algorithm for the shift schemes it is possible to refine the bound on the maximum non-optimal query to $k(k-1)(\epsilon)$. We present this analysis in Section 4.4.

- It is possible to schedule a query with m records in $O(m + k\log\epsilon)$ time (which is substantially better than the general retrieval algorithm that is $O(m^2)$), where ϵ is the additive error of the base scheme for the query. This is discussed in Section 4.3.

4.2   Performance of Shift Schemes

The primary result in this section is Theorem 1, which states that any query in a d-dimensional grid colored with shift scheme for k colors with $m \geq k(k-1)(2\epsilon+1)$ tiles (where ϵ is the maximum additive error of the base scheme used) can be scheduled in an optimal fashion.

Before we prove this theorem we need to define a *block*. Given a query Q in a database declustered over k disks using a shift scheme, a *block* is any k tiles where the base scheme retrieves exactly one tile from each disks. Note that the tiles of a block do not need to be located near each other. Also, the number of non-overlapping blocks in a query is $\min\{R_0, \ldots, R_{k-1}\}$, where R_i is the number of tiles retrieved from disk i in the base scheme.

Lemma 1. *Given a block for a shift scheme and any two disks $i, j \in [0, k)$: $i \neq j$ there is a schedule for the block such that the retrieval times for each disk (denoted by $R_0, \ldots, R_{k-1}$) are:*

$$R_q = \begin{cases} 0 & : \quad q = i \\ 2 & : \quad q = j \\ 1 & : \quad otherwise \end{cases}$$

Proof: The shift scheme defines a permutation on the disks; this permutation is $0, s, 2s, \ldots, (k-1)s$, where s is the shift value. Since $gcd(s, k) = 1$, this is a cyclic permutation (i.e., it is a chain). For this proof we assume $s = 1$, but this proof easily extends to any s. To obtain the desired schedule we use the second color (defined by the shift value) for tiles with initial disks $i, i+1, \ldots, j-1$ where the math is modulo k, and use the initial color for all other tiles. Since $i \neq j$, the number of tiles retrieved from disk i will be 0, the number of tiles retrieved from disk j will be 2, and all other disks will retrieve one tile.   □

Example: Suppose we are given a block in Figure 1; the colors of the block would be $(0,3),(1,4),(2,0),(3,1)$, and $(4,2)$. The cyclic permutation defined by the shift is 0,3,1,4,2. Suppose we need to shift a value from disk 4 to disk 3. Using the technique of the previous proof we shift values from tiles with base disks 4, 2, and 0. Thus the scheduling for this block would be (bold entries are the disks that retrieve the tiles): $(0,\mathbf{3}),(1,\mathbf{4}),(\mathbf{2},0),(\mathbf{3},1)$, and $(\mathbf{4},2)$. Notice that two tiles are retrieved from disk 3, no tiles are retrieved from disk 4, and a single tile is retrieved from the other disks.

Corollary 1. *Given a query Q in a grid declustered with a shift scheme, where the base scheme has retrieval times for Q from each disk as $R_0, R_1, \ldots, R_{k-1}$*

and has a surplus of s, then if $\min\{R_0, R_1, \ldots, R_{k-1}\} \geq s$, *there is a schedule for the shift scheme that is strictly optimal.*

Proof: Since $\min\{R_0, R_1, \ldots, R_{k-1}\} \geq s$, there is at least s non-overlapping blocks in the query. Thus by Lemma 1, each of these blocks can fix a unit of surplus; therefore the surplus can be shifted to disks with a shortage.   □

Example: Suppose we have a database declustered over five disks using a shift scheme with shift value $s = 1$. Furthermore, suppose there is a query with retrieval times for the base scheme as (1,2,3,2,2). Clearly, a locally optimal scheme for this solution would have retrieval time 2, and thus the surplus is 1, which is larger than the minimum number of tiles from each disk. Thus, by the previous Corollary there is an optimal schedule for the shift scheme. To balance the load a tile needs to be shifted from disk 2 to disk 0, which can be done by shifting a tile (i.e., by retrieving from the second disk) from disk 2, 3, and 4. The new retrieval times would be (1+1,2,3-1,2+1-1,2+1-1) or equivalently (2,2,2,2,2). This situation is depicted in the following figure.

0,1	1,2	1,2	2,3	2,3
2,3	3,4	3,4	4,0	4,0

0	1	1	2	2
3	3	4	4	0

Fig. 2. Example above, before and after scheduling

Theorem 1. *Any query* Q_m *with at least* $k(k-1)(2\epsilon+1)$ *tiles on a grid with* k *colors that is declustered using a shift scheme where the base scheme has maximum additive error* ϵ *can be answered in a strictly optimal fashion.*

Proof: Since the maximum additive error is ϵ, the maximum number of tiles retrieved from a single disk (in the base coloring) is $\lceil \frac{m}{k} \rceil + \epsilon$. Thus the surplus must be bounded by $(k-1)\epsilon$. Let $R_0, R_1, \ldots, R_{k-1}$ be the number of tiles retrieved from each disk in the base scheme, then:

$\min\{R_0, R_1, \ldots, R_{k-1}\}$
$\geq m - (k-1)(\lceil \frac{m}{k} \rceil + \epsilon)$
$\geq m - (k-1)(\frac{m}{k} + 1 + \epsilon)$
$= \frac{m}{k} - (k-1) - (k-1)\epsilon$
$\geq (k-1)(2\epsilon+1) - (k-1) - (k-1)\epsilon$ (since $m \geq k(k-1)(2\epsilon+1)$)
$= (k-1)\epsilon$.

Thus the $\min\{R_0, R_1, \ldots, R_{k-1}\}$ is larger than the surplus and by Corollary 1, this query has an optimal retrieval schedule.   □

This bound is not as strong as the bounds for randomized colorings, but there are many reasons to believe that this bound is not tight, including:

1. While it is theoretically possible that given a coloring scheme with an additive error of ϵ that the surplus is $(k-1)\epsilon$ it is much smaller in practice.
2. In many cases a single block could fix more than one surplus value.
3. The number of blocks in a query is likely to be larger than its lower bound that is established above.

4.3   Scheduling of the Shift Schemes

In this section we present an algorithm for scheduling queries for the shift schemes. The algorithm given in [10] can be used to schedule the queries with m tiles in $O(m^2)$ time. However, in this section we present an algorithm which schedules query retrieval in $O(m + k \log \epsilon)$ time, where ϵ is the additive error of the base scheme. Note that if the base scheme is GRS, Atallah and Prabhakar's scheme (for powers of 2), or the schemes based on the Corput set, then in 2 dimensions $\epsilon = O(\log k)$, and thus the scheduling algorithm runs in time $O(m + k \log \log k)$. Furthermore, if the scheme in [20] us used for $d(\geq 3)$ dimensions (where the additive error for k colors is $O(\log^{d-1} k)$) the retrieval time would be $O(m + kd \log \log k)$.

It requires $O(m)$ time to build an array of how many tiles are retrieved by each disk if the base scheme is used. The algorithm in [3] can be used to test if specific retrieval schedule time is possible in $O(k)$ time. And since the minimum retrieval time is in the ranges from $\lceil \frac{m}{k} \rceil$ to $\max\{R_0, \dots, R_{k-1}\}$, and this range is of size equal to the additive error of the base scheme (call it ϵ). Thus a binary search can be used to find the optimal schedule in time $O(m + k \log \epsilon)$. We now give an overview of the scheme presented by [3]. Essentially the algorithm starts at a disk and shifts the minimum number of tiles to the subsequent that will make the current disk no larger than the desired threshold. It then processes the subsequent disk, and continues till it reaches the first disk again. If at any time a disk attempts to shift more tiles than it has, then the algorithm returns false. Upon reaching the first disk, it is known that all other disks are optimal (the first one may not be) and so the algorithm proceeds for a second loop.

4.4   A Refined Analysis of the Maximum Non-optimal Area

The algorithm defined in the previous section, gives insight into a more refined analysis of the maximum non-optimal query. The only time that there is not an optimal retrieval schedule is if the number of tiles shifted to a disk plus the number of tiles that the disk retrieves from the base scheme exceed the optimal retrieval time (i.e., $\lceil \frac{m}{k} \rceil$). Suppose that $m \geq k(k-1)\epsilon$ (ϵ is the additive error of the base scheme), then $\lceil \frac{m}{k} \rceil \geq (k-1)\epsilon$. Thus, the optimal retrieval time is larger than any possible value being shifted into a disk. Thus for any disk with at least $\lceil \frac{m}{k} \rceil$ tiles is balanceable. Suppose that a disk has $\lceil \frac{m}{k} \rceil - c$ tiles (where $c > 0$). In this case the disk can absorb up to c surplus values, and thus this disk would also be balanceable. Therefore, the surplus is balanceable. Thus if there are at least $k(k-1)\epsilon$ tiles in the query, then there is an optimal retrieval.

We now outline some consequences of the above result:

1. If the base scheme is GRS [7] or the scheme proposed by Atallah and Prabhakar [5], then any maximum query without an optimal schedule is $O(k^2 \log k)$ for two dimensions.
2. If the base scheme is the scheme proposed by Chen et. al [8], then for $d(\geq 3)$ dimensional grids the maximum query without an optimal schedule is $O(k^2 \log^{d-1} k)$.

3. If the scheme is GRS for two dimensions, then for $k \leq 94$ any query with at least $2k(k-1)$ tiles can be answered optimally, and for $k \leq 550$ any query with at least $4k(k-1)$ tiles can be answered optimally. This is a natural consequence of the fact the GRS has a maximum additive error of 2 for $k \leq 94$ and of 4 for $k \leq 550$ [7].

5   Generalizing the Shift Schemes

In this section we look at several generalizations of the shift schemes including: i) a generalized way of defining the schemes (Section 5.1), ii) extending the schemes to higher levels of replication (Section 5.2), and iii) analyzing what happens when a disks fail (Section 5.3).

5.1   Permutations

For simplicity the shift schemes were described using an shift value to form a chain between any two sets of disks. A more general way of defining the schemes is to define such a chain with an arbitrary permutation of the disks. In such a situation, when the first color of a tile is x, then the second color is x's successor in the permutation (with wrap-around of course). This is clearly a generalization of the shift schemes; also, the properties of the shift schemes carry over to these permutation schemes.

5.2   Higher Levels of Replication

The shift schemes can easily be extended to higher levels of replication. When the level of replication is 2, we use a non-replicated coloring scheme (call it f) and a permutation of the colors (as discussed in Section 5.1). The colors for a tile T were $f(T)$ and $f(T)$'s successor in the permutation. The natural generalization to a level of replication r is to assign the first color to be $f(T)$ and that the remaining colors be $f(T)$'s $r-1$ successors in the permutation. This scheme has several interesting properties (the details will be in the full version of the paper):

1. Queries can be scheduled in time $O(m + rk \log \epsilon)$. This is done with a similar algorithm to the one outlined in Section 4.3.
2. A block can fix $r-1$ surplus values, and thus if each disk retrieves at least $\lceil \frac{(k-1)\epsilon}{r-1} \rceil$ tiles for a specific query, then that query can be answered in strictly optimal fashion.

5.3   Survivability

Another use of replication is to have resilience against disk failures; clearly if the shift schemes with level of replication r is used then the system can still answer all queries is $r-1$ disks fail. Furthermore, as long as r consecutive disks in the permutation do not fail then all queries can be answered; where as in the randomized case if r disk fail then with high probability there will be a tile that cannot be retrieved. However, we would like to know something about the performance of the scheduling algorithm as well as the retrieval times. The only other work in this area was in [9]. We make several claims below for the case where $r = 2$ and the number of failed disks is 1.

1. The queries can be scheduled in time $O(m + k \log \epsilon)$ using a simple modification to the scheduling algorithm.
2. Any query with at least $(k)(k-1)(\epsilon)$ tiles will be strictly optimal (this is proven below). Somewhat surprisingly this is same as the bound without disk failures. This does not imply that the schemes behave the same when a disk fails, because: i) when a disk fails the optimal retrieval time is greater (it is $\lceil \frac{m}{k-1} \rceil$ instead of $\lceil \frac{m}{k} \rceil$), and ii) the bound may not be tight for either case.

Theorem 2. *If given a query Q_m where $m > k(k-1)(\epsilon)$, then there is an optimal schedule for Q_m even if a single disk fails.*

Proof: First we claim that if $m \geq (k)(k-1)(\epsilon)$, then $\lceil \frac{m}{k-1} \rceil \geq \lceil \frac{m}{k} \rceil + \epsilon$. Thus after the disk fails, if you ignore the tiles on the failed disk, all other disks will retrieve at most $\lceil \frac{m}{k-1} \rceil$ tiles. However, to retrieve the tiles from the failed disk these must be shifted to its backup disk, which could cause a surplus of tiles at this disk. The rest of the proof continues similarly to the analysis in Section 4.4. □

6   Experiments

In this section we outline the results of two experiments:

- Experiment #1: How do you choose a strong shift value?
- Experiment #2: How well do the shift schemes perform in two and three dimensions compared to randomized schemes?

Like [9], we use the GRS scheme as our base scheme. Our comparison metric is the average deviation above the optimal retrieval time. To be more precise, our metric is given a set of queries Q we compute $\frac{\sum_{Q_m \in Q} rt(Q_m) - \lceil \frac{m}{k} \rceil}{|Q|}$. Clearly, a scheme with a lower average would have stronger average performance. Furthermore, one expects that randomized placements would be strongest on average as the law of large numbers would work in their favor. The average is computed by uniformly selecting a large number of queries with side length chosen uniformly from some range. We perform experiments for two dimensions for 32, 64, and 128 disks as well as for three dimensions for 32 disks.

6.1   Experiment #1

For 32 disks there are 16 possible shift values; these are all odd values in the range [0,31]. Figure 3 shows the average deviation for specific ranges of query sizes, note that the best two entries per range are highlighted (or more if ties exist). The diagram has a few interesting properties: i) the average deviation is similar for shift value s and $32 - s$ and ii) it appears as 7 and 25 are the strongest shift values for a GRS shift scheme with 32 colors. Further experimentation showed that these shift values were the strongest in similar tests for three dimensions. We now attempt to give intuition to these numbers. It is better to have a shift value that makes the second disk be "far away" in the grid from the base color; this is because values that are far away are unlikely to both be in surplus. As expected shifts of 7 and 25 lead to a second value that is far away from the base value. Similar experiments showed that strong shift values for 64 and 128 disks in two dimensions are 19 and 99 respectively.

s	[1,11]	[2,12]	[3,13]	[4,14]	[5,15]	[6,16]	[7,17]	[8,18]	[9,19]	[10,20]
1	0.1198	0.1264	0.1398	0.1314	0.1021	0.1162	0.093	0.0656	0.0473	0.031
3	0.0409	0.0385	0.0382	0.0391	0.0177	0.0111	0.0104	0.0025	**0.0**	**0.0**
5	0.0334	0.0314	0.0316	0.0284	0.0085	0.0084	0.0083	0.0023	**0.0**	**0.0**
7	**0.0249**	**0.0234**	**0.0226**	**0.0231**	**0.0058**	**0.0014**	**0.0004**	**0.0002**	**0.0**	**0.0**
9	0.044	0.044	0.0466	0.0363	0.0194	0.017	0.0155	0.0096	**0.0**	**0.0**
11	0.0775	0.0687	0.0683	0.0609	0.0323	0.0332	0.0155	0.0081	0.0026	0.0014
13	0.0854	0.0777	0.0809	0.0644	0.0258	0.0258	0.0135	0.0051	0.0028	0.0005
15	0.0571	0.0484	0.0517	0.0365	0.0201	0.0072	0.0042	**0.0002**	**0.0**	**0.0**
17	0.0587	0.0483	0.0523	0.0367	0.0203	0.0073	0.0042	**0.0001**	**0.0**	**0.0**
19	0.0868	0.0768	0.081	0.0638	0.026	0.0256	0.0134	0.0051	0.0027	0.0004
21	0.0777	0.0688	0.0675	0.0603	0.0316	0.0339	0.0157	0.0074	0.0026	0.0015
23	0.0444	0.0442	0.0465	0.0367	0.0196	0.0176	0.0151	0.0102	**0.0**	**0.0**
25	**0.0252**	**0.0236**	**0.0221**	**0.0236**	**0.0058**	**0.0012**	**0.0006**	**0.0002**	**0.0**	**0.0**
27	0.033	0.0312	0.0323	0.0288	0.0085	0.0086	0.0080	0.0024	**0.0**	**0.0**
29	0.0409	0.0386	0.0381	0.0391	0.0176	0.0111	0.0105	0.0026	**0.0**	**0.0**
31	0.1208	0.1247	0.141	0.1317	0.1025	0.1147	0.0929	0.0648	0.0467	0.0319

Fig. 3. Performance of various shift values for different query ranges

6.2   Experiment #2

In this section we compare various schemes with a level of replication two. More specifically we looked at the RDA scheme (where each tile is on two random unique disks), the GRS-RDA scheme (where the first color is the GRS scheme) and the second is random value, and the shift schemes with shift values 7, 19, and 99 for 32, 64, 128 disks respectively. Our comparison was based on looking at 1000 queries that were generated uniformly with side lengths chosen from $[x, x + 10]$. Clearly, a scheme with a lower average deviation from optimal (i.e. number of records/number of disks) would be desired. We performed the comparisons for two dimensions (for 32, 64, and 128 disks) and three dimensions (for 32 disks) (see Figure 4). Clearly, the results show that the shift schemes perform better in this situation than the randomized schemes.

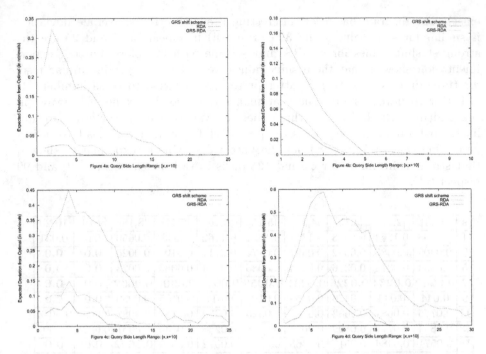

Fig. 4. Experimental Results: 4a) Average Deviation from Optimal (for 2-D), 32 disks, 4b) Average Deviation from Optimal (for 3-D), 32 disks, 4c) Average Deviation from Optimal (for 2-D), 64 disks, and 4d) Average Deviation from Optimal (for 2-D), 128 disks

7   Conclusions

In this paper a class of replicated schemes was introduced called the shift schemes. These schemes have several interesting properties including: i) they are deterministic, ii) any query with at least $k(k-1)\epsilon$ tiles can be retrieved in an optimal fashion, iii) queries can be scheduled in time $O(m + k\log\epsilon)$, and iv) if a single disk fails, then any query with at least $k(k-1)\epsilon$ tiles can be retrieved in an optimal fashion. Previously known replicated schemes use randomization and require more expensive query scheduling algorithms. We show that the shift schemes have stronger performance than the randomized schemes in many cases when the level of replication is two; we show this even for the case where the metric is average performance, which one might intuitively expect to be the randomized placements strongest case. Future directions for this work include:

1. A better analysis of the maximum non-optimal retrievable query.
2. A more detailed analysis of the survivability of the shift schemes.
3. A more detailed analysis of techniques for choosing strong shift values.

Acknowledgments. The authors would like to thank Mikhail Atallah for many useful discussions as well as the anonymous reviewers for their useful comments and suggestions on this paper.

References

1. C. R. A. Czumaj and C. Scheideler. Perfectly Balanced Allocation. In *7th International Workshop on Randomization and Approximation Techniques in Computer Science (RANDOM'03)*, pages 240–251, 2003.
2. K. Abdel-Ghaffar and A. E. Abbadi. Optimal Allocation of Two-dimensional Data. In *International Conference on Database Theory*, pages 409–418, 1997.
3. J. Aerts, J. Korst, and S. Egner. Random Duplicate Storage for Load Balancing in Multimedia Servers. *Information Processing Letters*, 76(1–2):51–59, 2000.
4. M. Atallah and K. Frikken. Replicated Parallel I/O without Additional Scheduling Costs. In *Proceedings of 14th Intl. Conf. on Database and Expert Systems Application (DEXA 2003, LNCS 2736)*, pages 223–232.
5. M. J. Atallah and S. Prabhakar. (Almost) Optimal Parallel Block Access to Range Queries. In *Proceedings of the nineteenth ACM SIGMOD-SIGACT-SIGART symposium on Principles of database systems*, pages 205–215. ACM Press, 2000.
6. R. Bhatia, R. Sinha, and C.-M. Chen. Hierarchical Declustering Schemes for Range Queries. In *In 7th Int'l Conf. on Extending Database Technology*, 2000.
7. R. Bhatia, R. K. Sinha, and C.-M. Chen. Declustering using Golden Ratio Sequences. In *ICDE*, pages 271–280, 2000.
8. C.-M. Chen and C. T. Cheng. From Discrepancy to Declustering: Near-optimal Multidimensional Declustering Strategies for Range Queries. In *Proceedings of the twenty-first ACM SIGMOD-SIGACT-SIGART symposium on Principles of database systems*, pages 29–38. ACM Press, 2002.
9. C.-M. Chen and C. T. Cheng. Replication and Retrieval Strategies of Multidimensional Data on Parallel Disks. In *Proceedings of the twelfth international conference on Information and knowledge management*, pages 32–39. ACM Press, 2003.
10. L. T. Chen and D. Rotem. Optimal Response Time Retrieval of Replicated Data (extended abstract). In *Proceedings of the thirteenth ACM SIGACT-SIGMOD-SIGART symposium on Principles of database systems*, pages 36–44. ACM Press, 1994.
11. H. Du and J. Sobolewski. Disk Allocation for Cartesian Product Files on Multiple Disk Systems. *ACM Transactions on Database System*, pages 82–101, 1982.
12. K. Frikken, M. Atallah, S. Prabhakar, and R. Safavi-Naini. Optimal Parallel I/O for Range Queries through Replication. In *Proceedings of 13th Intl. Conf. on Database and Expert Systems Application (DEXA 2002, LNCS 2453)*, pages 669–678.
13. B. Himatsingka, J. Srivastava, J.-Z. Li, and D. Rotem. Latin Hypercubes: A Class of Multidimensional Declustering Techniques, 1994.
14. H.-I. Hsiao and D. DeWitt. A new Availability Strategy for Multiprocessor Database Machines. In *Proceedings of Data Engineering*, pages 456–465, 1990.
15. M. H. Kim and S. Pramanik. Optimal File Distribution for Partial Match Retrieval. In *Proceedings of the 1988 ACM SIGMOD international conference on Management of data*, pages 173–182. ACM Press, 1988.
16. J. Matousek. *Geometric discrepancy, an illustrated guide*. Springer-Verlag, 1999.
17. S. Prabhakar, K. Abdel-Ghaffar, D. Agrawal, and A. E. Abbadi. Cyclic Allocation of Two-Dimensional Data. In *14th International Conference on Data Engineering*, pages 94–101, 1998.

18. P. Sanders. Reconciling Simplicity and Realism in Parallel Disk Models. In *Proceedings of the twelfth annual ACM-SIAM symposium on Discrete algorithms*, pages 67–76. ACM Press, 2001.
19. P. Sanders, S. Egner, and J. Korst. Fast Concurrent Access to Parallel Disks. In *Proceedings of the eleventh annual ACM-SIAM symposium on Discrete algorithms*, pages 849–858. ACM Press, 2000.
20. R. K. Sinha, R. Bhatia, and C.-M. Chen. Asymptotically Optimal Declustering Schemes for Range Queries. *Lecture Notes in Computer Science*, 1973:144–??, 2001.
21. A. Tosun and H. Ferhatosmanoglu. Optimal Parallel I/O using Replication. Technical Report OSU-CISRC-11/01-TR26, 2001.

When Is Nearest Neighbors Indexable?

Uri Shaft[1] and Raghu Ramakrishnan[2]

[1] Oracle Corporation, 500 Oracle Parkway, Redwood Shores, CA 94065 USA
`uri.shaft@oracle.com`
[2] University of Wisconsin–Madison, 1210 W. Dayton St., Madison, WI 53706, USA

Abstract. In this paper, we consider whether traditional index structures are effective in processing unstable nearest neighbors workloads. It is known that under broad conditions, nearest neighbors workloads become *unstable*–distances between data points become indistinguishable from each other. We complement this earlier result by showing that if the workload for your application is unstable, you are not likely to be able to index it efficiently using (almost all known) multidimensional index structures. For a broad class of data distributions, we prove that these index structures will do no better than a linear scan of the data as dimensionality increases.

Our result has implications for how experiments should be designed on index structures such as R-Trees, X-Trees and SR-Trees: Simply put, experiments trying to establish that these index structures scale with dimensionality should be designed to establish *cross-over points*, rather than to show that the methods scale to an arbitrary number of dimensions. In other words, experiments should seek to establish the dimensionality of the dataset at which the proposed index structure deteriorates to linear scan, for each data distribution of interest; that linear scan will eventually dominate is a given.

An important problem is to analytically characterize the *rate* at which index structures degrade with increasing dimensionality, because the dimensionality of a real data set may well be in the range that a particular method can handle. The results in this paper can be regarded as a step towards solving this problem. Although we do not characterize the rate at which a structure degrades, our techniques allow us to reason directly about a broad class of index structures, rather than the geometry of the nearest neighbors problem, in contrast to earlier work.

1 Introduction

Many published solutions to the nearest neighbors problem follow a common pattern. First, a multidimensional index structure is presented. The index structure specification consists of three parts:

Structural Specification. This specification describes the form of the index structure. For example, an R-Tree is a hierarchical structure, each node is described by a hyper-rectangle and all items in a node are contained in the node's hyper-rectangle.

T. Eiter and L. Libkin (Eds.): ICDT 2005, LNCS 3363, pp. 158–172, 2005.

Construction Algorithm. This specification describes how to build the index structure given data points. This can be either a bulk-loading algorithm or dynamic insertion and deletion.

Search Algorithm. This algorithm describes how to search for the nearest neighbor given a query point.

Once the index structure has been described, the next step is to show that its performance improves on prior art, in particular, that it is a significant improvement over doing a linear scan of all data points. In almost all cases it is clear that the method scales with an increase in data size. The difficulty lies in scaling with dimensionality. Experiments to show such scaling study a series of workloads that differ in the number of dimensions. For example, a common experiment is to choose a data size (say, 100,000 data points) and a data distribution (usually uniform). Then, the experimenter varies the number of dimensions (typically from two dimensions to about twenty) and plots the performance on a graph.

In this paper we present a mathematical analysis of such experiments. We show that the performance of a multidimensional index structure will converge with increasing dimensionality to the performance of a linear scan of the data, under quite broad conditions. Our result is applicable for a wide range of data distributions, and for almost all known multidimensional index structures. Furthermore, we do not rely on the index construction algorithm or the search algorithm, but only on the structural specification of the index. Thus, the result is robust. For example, clever techniques for bulk-loading might mitigate the problem, but linear scan will nonetheless dominate as dimensionality increases.

In related work, Beyer et al. [3] studied the geometry of the nearest neighbors problem. For a wide range of data distributions, they showed that pairs of data points become indistinguishable, in terms of the distance between them, as dimensionality increases. They describe such data distributions as "unstable". The result in this paper complements the Beyer et al. result by showing that (most) multidimensional index structures are no better than linear scan for unstable data distributions as dimensionality increases. While this is to be expected, perhaps, the number of papers that claim scalability of index structures with increasing dimensionality suggests that this is a point worth establishing rigorously. We hope there will be two practical consequences for experimental studies of multidimensional index structures:

1. An emphasis on the rate at which methods deteriorate with increasing dimensions.
2. Characterization of data distributions for which a given method indeed scales with dimensionality. Obviously, they would have to fall outside the class of distributions for which our results apply.

We also hope that the insight provided into index structures by our result will enable the design of new structures that deteriorate more slowly with dimensionality, for a wider class of data distributions than currently known structures.

The rest of the paper is structured as follows. Section 2 describes the main result of the paper, the *Nearest Neighbors Indexing Theorem*. Section 3 contains the proof of the theorem. Section 4 contains a short discussion about rate of convergence. Section 5 contains a discussion about the importance of the result, a short survey of related work, and a few directions for future work.

2   The Nearest Neighbors Indexing Theorem

In this section we present the nearest neighbors indexing theorem. Before we present the theorem we need to introduce two important concepts:

Convex Description Index Structures. The theorem characterizes this class of index structures.

Series of Workloads with Vanishing Variance. This is our formal description of workloads.

The theorem deals with the expected performance of a convex description index structure when used for indexing a series of workloads with vanishing variance. The theorem states that under such circumstances, the expected performance of the index structure will converge to the performance of a linear scan of the data. In other words, the average number of data points retrieved by the indexing structure will converge to the total number of points in the data set, as we advance in the series of workloads (e.g., increase dimensionality).

The rest of the section is structured as follows: Section 2.1 contains the definition of convex description index structures. Section 2.2 contains the definition of series of workloads with vanishing variance. Section 2.3 contains the formal definition of the theorem.

2.1   Convex Description Index Structures

Almost all known multidimensional index structures share a common structure: Data points are collected into buckets (or pages) and we save on query processing time by eliminating some buckets from consideration using some summary information which is pre-computed for each bucket. For example, an R-Tree [6] stores data points in leaf pages (the buckets). The summary information for the bucket is the *minimal bounding rectangle (MBR)* of the data in the bucket. In this description, we ignored the hierarchical structure of the R-Tree. Likewise, the following definition of a *Convex Description Index Structure* does not use much more than the idea of buckets with summary information. It is therefore independent of the hierarchical organizations that differentiate several index structures, and applies to a broad range of indexing techniques.

Definition 1. *A* Convex Description Index Structure *has the following properties:*

1. *All data points are distributed to buckets. Some points may be in multiple buckets (redundancy is permitted), and each point must be in at least one bucket. Each bucket must contain at least two points.*

2. *Each bucket has an associated description which is a convex region of the data space, called the* boundary *of the bucket. All data points in a bucket must be in the associated convex region.*
3. *During query processing we fetch entire buckets and consider all data points in them. We are not allowed to fetch only some data points from a bucket.*
4. *During query processing, the decision to fetch a bucket is done only based on the boundary of the bucket. When query processing ends, the only buckets that are not fetched are the buckets which we can prove to not contain any query results.*

Let us consider the R-Tree as an example of a convex description index structure.

1. Data points are distributed to leaf pages (buckets). Each data point is in exactly one bucket. It is usually the case that an R-Tree contains more than one point in each leaf page. However, a dynamic R-Tree may have a leaf page with one data point due to deletions. Our theoretical results can be easily extended to include such structures, but due to lack of space we leave this to the reader. Intuitively, having leaf pages with a single data point means that the R-Tree is not optimal both in usage of space and in query performance (i.e., we should be able to construct a better performing R-Tree for the same data set without the leaf pages with single data points).
2. The boundary of each leaf page is an MBR, which is a convex region of space.
3. We fetch entire pages only, and process all items in a page once it is fetched.
4. Suppose that we process a nearest neighbors query Q and return a result point X. Consider a bucket B (leaf page) of the R-Tree. If the distance of Q and the MBR of B (i.e., $d(Q, MBR(B))$) is lower than the distance of Q to its nearest neighbor X, then we must have fetched B during query processing. Not fetching B under the circumstances means B could contain a data point closer to Q than X; i.e., X may not be the nearest neighbor–an invalid assumption since query processing ended.
   Therefore, the only buckets we do not fetch satisfy $d(Q, MBR(B)) ¿ d(Q, X)$. In other words, we do not fetch a bucket only if we can prove it does not contain a valid result.

What are other convex description index data structures? Obviously, all variants of R-Trees qualify, since the variants differ only in the construction algorithms and not in any characteristic we used in our definition. These variants include the R-+Tree [11], the R-*Tree [1] and the X-Tree [2]. Other examples are variants of the KDB-Tree [10], the SS-Tree [14], the SR-Tree [8] and the TV-Tree [9].

Examples of index structures that are not convex description index structures are probabilistic structures (e.g., P-Sphere Trees [5] and multidimensional hash indexing [4]) and the projection index structures (e.g., see [13]). It is easy to show (using different arguments) that P-Sphere Trees do not scale with dimensionality for workloads with vanishing variance (for any distance metric). P-Sphere Trees are designed to work only when the spread is high.

2.2   Series of Workloads with Vanishing Variance

Scalability experiments are performed on a series of workloads $W_1, W_2, \ldots$ We usually construct the workloads such that only one parameter varies from one workload to the next. In this paper we focus on varying the number of dimensions. A single workload W consists of the following items:

S : A set of all possible data objects. In this paper we limit S to vectors in a Euclidean metric space.

F : A distribution function over the space S. We use this probability distribution to sample data points and query points from S.

n : The number of data points to sample for each experiment.

d : The distance function. In this paper we limit ourselves to the Euclidean distance:

$$d(X, Y) \equiv ||X, Y|| = \sqrt{\sum_{i=1}^{m} |x_i - y_i|^2}$$

For example, the most commonly used series of workloads in the literature uses uniform data. The universe of workload W_m (called S_m) is the unit cube in m dimensions. The data and query distribution is the uniform distribution over S_m. n is kept constant for all W_m (a typical number is 100,000). The distance function is the Euclidean distance. A typical experiment will sample some of the workloads in the series and repeat some performance experiments for each workload.

Before we get to vanishing variance we need to define the distance distribution of a workload. Suppose W is a workload with universe S, data distribution F and distance metric d. Let X and Y be two independent random variables with the F distribution (in probability theory notation: $X, Y \sim_{\text{iid}} F$). The distance between the two points $D = d(X, Y)$ is a random variable. The domain of D is the non-negative real numbers. We call the probability distribution of D *the distance distribution of* W.

Beyer et al. [3] identify an important class of series of workloads, which we call *series of workloads with vanishing variance* (it is not named in [3]). They show that a such a series of workloads exhibits "instability"–the spread between distances diminishes and eventually all points have the same distance from each other. We use the same property in our theorem.

Definition 2. *A series of workloads* $W1, W2, \ldots$ *with distance distributions* D_1, $D_2, \ldots$ *has vanishing variance if there exists* $\alpha > 0$ *such that*

$$\lim_{m \to \infty} var\left(\frac{D_m^\alpha}{\mathbf{E}\left[D_m^\alpha\right]}\right) = 0$$

In other words, we have vanishing variance if the magnitude of the variance in the distance distribution becomes insignificant compared to the magnitude of the mean distance.

Beyer et al. [3] show many examples of such a series of workloads. The most common one is the uniform data experiment. It turns out that any distribution that is applied independently to all dimensions exhibits vanishing variance. Beyer et al. show other cases where the different dimensions have different distributions, correlation, and even change with mean and variance. They show, using multiple examples, that this data model is very robust. We will not repeat the discussion presented in [3].

2.3   The Theorem

The nearest neighbors indexing theorem is about the performance of certain index structures when applied to certain workloads. Before we get to the actual theorem we need to specify how we measure performance. Suppose W is a workload with universe $\mathcal{S}$, data distribution F, and size n. The performance of an index structure $\mathcal{I}$ over the workload W is a random variable designating the number of data points retrieved by the search algorithm of $\mathcal{I}$. We denote this random variable by N. We are usually concerned with the average performance of the search algorithm–the expected value of N, denoted by $\mathbf{E}[N]$.

Informally, we estimate $\mathbf{E}[N]$ by (conceptually) constructing the index repeatedly for different data sets (that follow the distribution F), evaluating a nearest neighbors query using the index, and counting the number of data points retrieved. More precisely, we can describe the distribution of N by describing how to sample N using that distribution. To sample one value of N we sample n independent data points using the distribution F (the points are $x_1, .., x_n$). Then, we create an index I for the data set. Next, we sample one query point q using the data distribution F. Finally, we run the search algorithm over I and count how many data points were retrieved during query execution. The value of $\mathbf{E}[N]$ can be estimated by repeating this process and taking the average of the sampled values.

An alternative algorithm for computing nearest neighbors is linear scan of the data set. The number of points retrieved, i.e., its performance using our cost metric, is a constant n (the number of data points).

Our measure of performance, which is the number of data points retrieved, favors the index structure over a linear scan of the data:

1. We expect a linear scan of the data to consist of sequential I/O if the data is not in memory. Thus, fetching the same number of points is likely to be more efficient than the random reads incurred using an index structure. This is not reflected in our cost metric.
2. We also expect disk pages to have maximal occupancy. It is often the case that page occupancy is significantly lower than 100% for index structures, leading to more page I/Os for the same number of data points retrieved. This is not reflected in our cost metric.
3. We ignore extra costs associated with an index structure (e.g., the internal nodes in an R-Tree).

These approximations are acceptable since our goal is to show that linear scan dominates convex description index structures, even with a cost metric that favors the latter.

Nearest Neighbors Indexing Theorem: *Let $W_1, W_2, ..$ be a series of workloads with vanishing variance and constant size n. Let $\mathcal{I}$ be a convex description* *index structure and denote the performance of $\mathcal{I}$ over workload W_m as N_m. Then* $\lim_{m\to\infty} \mathbf{E}[N_m] = n$.

3   Proof of the Nearest Neighbors Indexing Theorem

We prove the NN indexing theorem in two main steps. First, we define a new type of random variable called *spread* and show that it converges to a constant. Second, we show that the convergence of the spread implies the convergence of the performance of the index structure to the performance of linear scan.

Definition 3. *The spread C of a workload W is a random variable obtained by the following process:*

- *We take a sample of $n+1$ independent points using the data distribution F. The points are $X_1, .., X_{n+1}$.*
- *We define the minimum and maximum of distances between all pairs of distinct points as:*

$$DMIN = \min\{d(X_i, X_j)\,|\,1 \le i \ne j \le n+1\}$$

$$DMAX = \max\{d(X_i, X_j)\,|\,1 \le i \ne j \le n+1\}$$

- *The spread is: $C = DMAX/DMIN$*

In other words, the spread is the ratio between the maximum and minimum of all distances of distinct pairs of points among the sample of $n+1$ points. We choose $n+1$ points since an experiment contains n data points and one query point. When the spread is the constant 1 ($C = 1$), all distances in that workload are the same. Our first step is to show that the series of spreads created by a series of workloads with vanishing variance converges to the constant 1. This step is almost identical to the instability theorem (and its proof) described by Beyer et al. [3]. The second step in our proof of the NN indexing theorem uses the convergence of spreads to prove that the performance of the index structure converges to linear scan.

3.1   Step 1 of Proof

Our first step is to show that the series of spreads created by a series of workloads with vanishing variance converges to the constant 1.

Lemma 1. *Let $W_1, W_2, ..$ be a series of workloads with vanishing variance and constant size n. Let $C_1, C_2, ..$ be the spreads associated with $W_1, W_2, ...$ respectively. Then $C_m \to_p 1$.*

The notation $C_m \to_p 1$ is a standard probability theory notation, specifying that the series $C_1, C_2, ..$ converges in probability to the constant 1. The convergence in probability is defined as

$$\forall \varepsilon > 0 \qquad \lim_{m\to\infty} P[1 - \varepsilon \le C_m \le 1 + \varepsilon] = 1$$

Since the minimal value for C_m is 1 we can restate this equation as

$$\forall \varepsilon > 0 \qquad \lim_{m \to \infty} P[C_m \leq 1 + \varepsilon] = 1$$

Outline of proof: We start with a series of workloads with vanishing variance and need to get to the convergence of a series of spreads. The vanishing variance property deals with convergence of a transformed version of the distance distribution. A spread is defined as a ratio of maximal distance distribution over minimal distance distribution. To get from one to the other we use the following steps:

1. Prove that vanishing variance implies convergence of a transformed distance distribution. The transformed version is $V_m = D_m^\alpha / \mathbf{E}[D_m^\alpha]$.
2. Next we get rid of the power of α from V_m, so we can deal with the actual distance distribution. We show that $V_m^{1/\alpha}$ converges as well.
3. To get to convergence of spread we show first that a vector of k instances of $V_m^{1/\alpha}$ also converges to a constant. Then we show that the minimum and maximum of the vector converges as well.
4. Finally, we show that the ratio of maximum over minimum (from the previous step) converges. By taking that ratio we conveniently get rid of the constants we carried all along–the division of the distance distribution by $\mathbf{E}[D_m^\alpha]$. After getting rid of these constants, the ratio of maximum over minimum is exactly the spread we were looking for.

Proof.
Step 1. Let $D_1, D_2, \ldots$ be the distance distributions of $W_1, W_2, \ldots$ Using the vanishing variance property we find $\alpha > 0$ such that

$$\lim_{m \to \infty} \mathrm{var}\left(\frac{D_m^\alpha}{\mathbf{E}[D_m^\alpha]}\right) = 0$$

We denote $V_m = D_m^\alpha / \mathbf{E}[D_m^\alpha]$.

The expected value of V_m is 1 because it is a random variable (D_m) divided by its expected value. For any $\varepsilon > 0$ we can calculate the variance of V_m as

$$\mathrm{var}(V_m) = \mathbf{E}\left[(V_m - \mathbf{E}[V_m])^2\right] = \mathbf{E}\left[(V_m - 1)^2\right] \leq$$

$$\leq 0 \cdot P[|V_m - 1| \leq \varepsilon] + \varepsilon^2 \cdot P[|V_m - 1| > \varepsilon] = \varepsilon^2 \cdot P[|V_m - 1| > \varepsilon]$$

We can insert the limit argument and get:

$$0 = \lim_{m \to \infty} \mathrm{var}(V_m) \leq \lim_{m \to \infty} \varepsilon^2 \cdot P[|V_m - 1| > \varepsilon]$$

Since ε is a constant for all m we have: $\lim_{m \to \infty} P[|V_m - 1| > \varepsilon] = 0$. This is the definition of convergence in probability so $V_m \to_p 1$.

Step 2. The function $f(x) = x^{(1/\alpha)}$ is continuous, so we can use it to transform V_m and still have convergence in probability (Slutsky's theorem). Therefore, $V_m^{(1/\alpha)} \to_p 1^{(1/\alpha)} = 1$.

Step 3. For each workload W_m we create a vector of distances of size $n(n+1)/2$ elements in the following way:

- Take $X_{m,1}, .., X_{m,n+1}$ independent random variables following the data distribution of W_m.
- Create vector $\boldsymbol{D_m} =< D_{m,1}, .., D_{m,k} >$ (where $k = n(n+1)/2$) by taking the distances between all possible distinct pairs of points $d(X_{m,i}, X_{m,j})$ where $i \neq j$.

Note, in the rest of the proof, whenever we apply a scalar function to a vector we mean that the result is a vector and the function is applied to each of the elements. In other words,

$$f(< A_1, .., A_k >) =< f(A_1), .., f(A_k) >$$

Let $\mu_m = \mathbf{E}\left[D_m^\alpha\right]^{1/\alpha}$. The vector $\boldsymbol{D_m}/\mu_m$ has k elements, each element is a random variable with the same distribution as $V_m^{(1/\alpha)}$. Therefore $\boldsymbol{D_m}/\mu_m \to_\mathrm{p} < 1, .., 1 >$.

Since the maximum (and minimum) of a vector are continuous functions, we can apply Slutsky's theorem again and get

$$\max\left\{\boldsymbol{D_m}/\mu_m\right\} \to_\mathrm{p} 1 \quad \text{and} \quad \min\left\{\boldsymbol{D_m}/\mu_m\right\} \to_\mathrm{p} 1$$

Step 4. Using Slutsky's theorem yet again we can divide two random variables and still have the convergence in probability property. Therefore,

$$\frac{\max\left\{\boldsymbol{D_m}/\mu_m\right\}}{\min\left\{\boldsymbol{D_m}/\mu_m\right\}} = \frac{\max\left\{\boldsymbol{D_m}\right\}}{\min\left\{\boldsymbol{D_m}\right\}} \to_\mathrm{p} 1$$

However, $\max\left\{\boldsymbol{D_m}\right\}$ is the maximum of all distances between $n+1$ independent points of W_m, and $\min\left\{\boldsymbol{D_m}\right\}$ is the minimum of these distances. Therefore their ratio is the spread C_m of W_m.

Therefore, $C_m \to_\mathrm{p} 1$.   □

3.2   Step 2 of Proof

The second step in our proof of the NN indexing theorem uses the convergence of spreads to prove that the performance of the index structure converges to linear scan.

Lemma 2. *Let $W_1, W_2, ..$ be a series of workloads with constant size n, associated spreads $C_1, C_2, ..$ and $C_m \to_p 1$. Let $\mathcal{I}$ be a convex description index structure and denote the performance of $\mathcal{I}$ over workload W_m as N_m. Then $\lim_{m\to\infty} \mathbf{E}\left[N_m\right] = n$.*

Proof.
Step 1. For this step we ignore the fact that we are dealing with random variables and convergence in probability. We will only look at a single instance of a workload–actual data points, an actual query, an actual index structure and absolutely no random variables. Our goal is to show that if the spread of the actual instance is very low, then the performance of the index structure is the

same as the performance of linear scan. It so happens that we can show this for spreads that are below $\sqrt{5/4}$.

So, suppose we have an instance of n data points $x_1, .., x_n$ and a query point $q = x_{n+1}$. Suppose the spread of the instance is below our threshold of $\sqrt{5/4}$. Note that the spread we use is the ratio of maximal distance over minimal distance, where the maximum and minimum is taken over all distances between distinct pairs of points from the set $\{x_1, .., x_{n+1}\}$ (i.e., we include the query point as part of the set). We also have a convex description index I. We will show that the distance of the query point q to any bucket B of the index is less than the distance of the query point to its nearest neighbor. This means that all index buckets are retrieved during query execution and therefore the performance of the index is exactly n.

Let B be any bucket of the index structure, containing two distinct data points x_i and x_j. (Obviously, x_i and x_j are not the query point x_{n+1}.) Since the boundary of B is convex it contains the midpoint between the two data points x_i and x_j. We denote this midpoint by $y = (x_i + x_j)/2$. The distance of q to the boundary of B is at most $d(q, y)$ (the distance of a point and a region is the minimum of all distances between the point and the points that belong to that region). Therefore, it is enough to show that $d(q, y)$ is lower than the distance of q to its nearest neighbor. The situation we just described is illustrated in Figure 1.

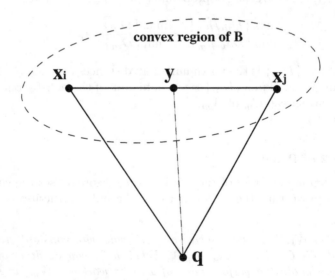

Fig. 1. Illustration of midpoint y for Lemma 2, Step 1

Let c_{min} be the minimal distance between all distinct pairs of points from the set $\{x_1, .., x_{n+1}\}$. Similarly, the maximal distance is c_{max}. By definition, the spread c is c_{max}/c_{min}. Let c_{nn} be the distance of q to its nearest neighbor. Obviously, $c_{min} \leq c_{nn}$. We will show that $d(q, y) < c_{min}$ and that will prove that $d(q, y) < c_{nn}$.

Consider the triangle created by the points x_i, x_j and q (see Figure 1). The distance $d(q, y)$ can be maximized by maximizing the distances $d(q, x_i)$ and $d(q, x_j)$ and by minimizing the distance $d(x_i, x_j)$. Since these three distances are between c_{min} and c_{max}, we can maximize the value of $d(q, y)$ by setting $d(q, x_i) = d(q, x_j) = c_{max}$ and $d(x_i, x_j) = c_{min}$. We can calculate the distance $d(q, y)$ (under this scenario) using Pythagoras' theorem: $d(q, y)^2 = c_{max}^2 - \left(\frac{1}{2}c_{min}\right)^2$.

We also know that the spread is less than $\sqrt{5/4}$ so $c_{max} < \sqrt{5/4}c_{min}$. Therefore,

$$d(q, y)^2 = c_{max}^2 - \left(\frac{c_{min}}{2}\right)^2 < \left(\sqrt{\frac{5}{4}}c_{min}\right)^2 - \left(\frac{c_{min}}{2}\right)^2 = c_{min}^2$$

Therefore we showed that $d(q, y) < c_{min} \leq c_{nn}$, so the bucket B is fetched during query execution. Since this holds for all buckets of the index, the performance of the index is exactly n (i.e., we fetch all buckets and therefore fetch all data points).

Step 2. We now know, for instances of workloads, how a very low value of spread causes the performance of an index structure to be the same as the performance of linear scan. We need to use that result to get the more general result about the convergence of the expected performance of the index structures to the performance of linear scan (i.e., now we deal with the probability theory aspect of the lemma).

We know that $C_m \to_p 1$ (a condition of the lemma). This means that the probability of the event $C_m < \sqrt{5/4}$ converges to 1 as m increases (by definition of convergence in probability). In mathematical notation:

$$\lim_{m \to \infty} P\left[C_m < \sqrt{5/4}\right] = 1$$

The event $C_m < \sqrt{5/4}$ implies that the performance of the index structure is exactly n. In other words, it implies the event $N_m = n$. (That is exactly what Step 1 proved.) Therefore, $P[N_m = n] \geq P\left[C_m < \sqrt{5/4}\right]$. Since a probability cannot exceed the value 1, we have: $\lim_{m \to \infty} P[N_m = n] = 1$. By definition of expectation we get:

$$\mathbf{E}[N_m] = \sum_{i=0}^{n} i \cdot P[N_m = i] \geq n \cdot P[N_m = n]$$

Since $\lim_{m \to \infty} P[N_m = n] = 1$ we also have,

$$\lim_{m \to \infty} \mathbf{E}[N_m] \geq \lim_{m \to \infty} \{n \cdot P[N_m = n]\} = n \cdot 1 = n$$

Since the upper bound on any N_m is n we have $\lim_{m \to \infty} \mathbf{E}[N_m] = n$.

Therefore, the performance of the index structure converges to the performance of a linear scan of the data set. □

Lemma 1 and Lemma 2 together constitute a complete proof of the nearest neighbors indexing theorem.

4   Rate of Convergence

The indexability theorem deals with convergence of the performance of an index structure to the performance of linear scan. A stronger result would tell us at what rate this convergence occurs. In this section, we explore the possibility of this stronger result.

First, we need to clarify the term *rate of convergence*. The simplest enhancement of our result is to be able to determine at what point in a series of workloads the performance of the index structure crosses an arbitrary threshold that we consider acceptable. For example, if we know that the index buckets are fetched using random I/O then a performance of $n/10$ (i.e., fetching 10% of the data point) will not compete with the sequential I/O of linear scan.

Let us define the problem in mathematical terms. Suppose we are given the conditions of the indexability theorem: a series of workloads $W_1, W_2, \dots$ with vanishing variance and a convex description index structures. Suppose we are also given an acceptable threshold for index performance t (where $0 < t < n$). Can we determine the first dimensionality value m such that the average performance of the index over W_m is greater than the threshold t?

The answer to the above problem is "no". We cannot find the first m because we have no information about the beginning of the series of workloads. All we know about the series is that some property (variance of a transformed distance distribution) converges in the limit. We can modify the beginning of the series (first m workloads, for any m we choose) to be whatever we want and the theorem's condition (vanishing variance) will not change. The problem is that our model deals with convergence in the limit and not with what happens at the beginning of the series.

We might have better results if we knew all the details of the vanishing variance property for a specific series. We need to know which $\alpha > 0$ is used to satisfy the vanishing variance property and for each m we should know the exact value of $\mathrm{var}\,(D_m^\alpha / \mathbf{E}\,[D_m^\alpha])$. All we knew before is that there exists some $\alpha > 0$ such that $\lim_{m \to \infty} \mathrm{var}\,(D_m^\alpha / \mathbf{E}\,[D_m^\alpha]) = 0$.

Based on this knowledge we should be able to find some bounds for the spreads $C_1, C_2, \dots$ of the workloads, and find a spread C_m with a median less than $\sqrt{5/4}$. This, in turn, will tell us that at least half the times we try a query for W_m we will end up fetching all data points.

Unfortunately, these approximations are very crude and will not tell us anything practical. For example, take the typical series of workloads using uniform data distribution (the first example in Section 2.2). Assume the number of points is $10,000$. Using simulation, we estimated the first dimensionality (i.e., first m) with a median spread of less than $\sqrt{5/4}$ at about four thousand. This means that a convex description index structure (e.g., an R-Tree) will fetch all data points at least for 50% of the queries if the number of dimensions is 4000. Some experimentation clearly showed that an R-Tree already starts to exhibit such performance at about forty dimensions (using a very low fanout of 10 points per data page).

Our approximation was two orders of magnitude off the mark, even when we started with knowledge about spread and not just about vanishing variance. Clearly, our model of an index structure and workloads is not sufficient for an analysis of rate of convergence. An open problem is how this framework can be strengthened (or an alternative developed) to enable such an analysis.

5   Discussion

5.1   Conclusion

In this paper we presented a mathematical analysis of the most common index scalability experiments performed for solving the nearest neighbors problem. The nearest neighbors indexing theorem shows that almost all known multidimensional index structures do not scale with dimensionality when used for a broad range of workloads. The failure to scale with dimensionality is inherent in the type of data sets used and in the use of convex descriptions for index "buckets" (leaf pages, in typical tree-structured indexes).

Our main conclusion is that the research community should no longer test index structures on uniform distributions, or more generally the types of workloads that exhibit vanishing variance. Beyer et al. [3] argued that these data sets are "meaningless" (i.e., have little practical value for real applications) and therefore should not be considered for indexing. We enhance this argument by showing that these data sets are not indexable by almost all index structures we know about.

5.2   Related Work

Our result is the next logical step after the Instability Theorem (Beyer et al. [3]). In fact, Lemma 1 is a modified version of the Instability Theorem. The main contribution of this paper is Lemma 2–applying the convergence of spreads to explain the performance of index structures–and its consequence, the Nearest Neighbors indexing theorem.

Hellerstein, Koutsoupias and Papadimitriou created a "framework for measuring the efficiency of an indexing scheme for a workload" (see [7]). They define a workload to consist of a set of objects (called data) and a set of subsets of the data (called queries). Each query is characterized only by the set of valid answers for the query (i.e., the query is indistinguishable from its result set). Hellerstein et al. use this basic definition in an analysis of various workloads while considering two main factors: "storage redundancy (how many times each item in the data set is stored) and access overhead (how many times more blocks then necessary does a query retrieve)". They ignore one major aspect of query complexity–the cost of gathering enough evidence to prove that the result of a query is the correct result. By ignoring this aspect of the solution, they get low bounds on the complexity of queries. Their justification for this approach is: "First, we are mostly interested in lower bounds, and therefore are free to disregard aspects of the complexity ... Second, these aspects do not seem to be the source of design difficulties or of complexity ...".

Unfortunately, the most important aspect of the complexity of nearest neighbors queries is the cost of gathering evidence to prove that a specific data point is the nearest neighbor. For a data set of size n there are at most n different queries, if we do not distinguish between the query and its result set (each query result is one point). However, sometimes the most efficient way to prove that we have the correct nearest neighbors is to measure the distance to all other data points. Therefore, the framework suggested by Hellerstein et al. is not suitable for the nearest neighbors problem.

5.3   Future Work

Interesting avenues for further work include: (1) identifying meaningful types of data sets (e.g., clustered data sets) and specialized problem scenarios (e.g., almost exact-match problems) for which high-dimensional indexing remains feasible, (2) techniques to determine if a real workload falls into one of the cases that we can index effectively, and (3) results about rates of convergence of indexing methods with increasing dimensionality.

The nearest neighbors indexing theorem does not tell us anything about the rate at which the performance of index structures converges to the performance of linear scan. It would be interesting to find at what dimensionality an index structure is supposed to fail. Unfortunately, the conditions of the theorem are too broad to describe a rate of convergence. Also, the argument used in the proof does not allow us to reason about the rate of convergence. For example, suppose we use the uniform data set with an R-Tree, and choose a size of 100,000 data points. The R-Tree will fail at about 15 dimensions, while the data sets will reach the average spread used by the theorem ($\sqrt{5}/2$) at more than a thousand dimensions. There is clearly much to be done to learn about the rate of convergence.

Another limitation of our result is the use of the Euclidean distance metric. The Euclidean distance is by far the most commonly used metric, but a good line of inquiry would be to find indexing theorems for other metrics. Robert R. Meyer suggested to us a variant of the theorem that shows that using rectangles for convex descriptions (e.g., an R-Tree) will fail to scale with dimensionality when using the L_1 metric. We do not have a corresponding result for the L_∞ metric. We suspect that rectangle shapes might work for such a metric even with vanishing variance (i.e., performance may not converge to the performance of linear scan).

References

1. Beckmann, N., Kriegel H.-P., Schneider, R. and Seeger, B.: The R*-Tree: An Efficient and Robust Access Method for Points and Rectangles. Proc. SIGMOD (1992) 322–331
2. Berchtold, S., Keim, D. A. and Kriegel H.-P.: The x-tree : An Index Structure for High-Dimensional Data. Proc. VLDB (1996) 28-39
3. Beyer, K., Goldstein, J., Ramakrishnan, R. and Shaft, U.: When Is Nearest Neighbors Meaningful? Proc. ICDT (1999)

4. Gionis, A., Indyk, P. and Motwani, R.: Similarity search in high dimensions via hashing. Proc. VLDB (1999) 518-529
5. Goldstein, J.: mproved Query Processing and Data Representation Techniques. Ph.D. Thesis, Univ. of Wisconsin-Madison (1999)
6. Guttman, A." R-Trees: A Dynamic Index Structure for Spatial Searching. Proc. SIGMOD (1984) 47-57
7. Hellerstein, J. M., Koutsoupias, E. and Papadimitriou, C. H.: On the analysis of indexing schemes. Proc. PODS (1997) 249-256
8. Katayama, N.,and Satoh, S.: The SR-tree: An Index Structure for High-Dimensional Nearest Neighbor Queries. Proc. SIGMOD (1997) 369-380
9. Lin K.-I., Jagadish, H. V. and Faloutsos, C.: The TV-Tree – An Index Structure for High-Dimensional Data. VLDB J.: Special Issue on Spatial Database Systems **3/4** (1994) 517-542
10. Robinson, J. T.: The K-D-B Tree: A Search Structure for Large Multi-dimensional Dynamic Indexes. Proc. SIGMOD (1981) 10-18
11. Sellis, T. K., Roussopoulos, N. and Faloutsos, C.: The R+-Tree: A Dynamic Index for Multi-Dimensional Objects. Proc. VLDB (1987) 507-518
12. Shaft, U.: Database Support for Queries by Image Content. Ph.D. Thesis, Univ. of Wisconsin-Madison (2002)
13. Smith, J. R.: Query vector projection access method. In Storage and Retrieval for Image and Video Databases VII (1998) 511-522
14. White, D. A. and Jain R. C.: Similarity Indexing with the SS-tree. Proc. ICDE (1996) 516-523

Nonmaterialized Motion Information in Transport Networks

Hu Cao and Ouri Wolfson

Department of Computer Science,
University of Illinois at Chicago,
851 S. Morgan Street, Chicago, IL, 60607, USA
{hcao2, wolfson}@cs.uic.edu

Abstract. The traditional way of representing motion in 3D space-time uses a trajectory, i.e. a sequence of (x,y,t) points. Such a trajectory may be produced by periodic sampling of a Global Positioning System (GPS) receiver. The are two problems with this representation of motion. First, imprecision due to errors (e.g. GPS receivers often produce off-the-road locations), and second, space complexity due to a large number of samplings. We examine an alternative representation, called a nonmaterialized trajectory, which addresses both problems by taking advantage of the a priori knowledge that the motion occurs on a transport network.

1   Introduction

Location management, i.e. the management of transient location information, is an enabling technology for location based service applications. It is also a fundamental component of other technologies such as fly-through visualization (the visualized terrain changes continuously with the location of the user), context awareness (location of the user determines the content, format, or timing of information delivered), augmented reality (location of both the viewer and the viewed object determines the type of information delivered to viewer), and cellular communication.

Usually, locations of a moving object are obtained by sensors and are given as a set of spatio-temporal points of the form (x, y, t). Such a point indicates that a moving object m (represented as a 2-dimensional point) was at geographic location with coordinates (x, y) at time t. These spatio-temporal points may be generated, for example, by a GPS receiver on board m. We will call such point a GPS point, although it may be generated by other means (e.g. PCS network triangulation, RFID).

The first problem arising in location management is that GPS receivers are imprecise, and thus this raw data is noisy and error prone. Indeed, a data point of a typical GPS receiver has an error that ranges from several feet to tens of meters. In most cases, the motion occurs on a road network, and thus the error of a GPS point can be corrected by "snapping" the point onto the road network. This correction is very important for many natural queries such as "retrieve the

T. Eiter and L. Libkin (Eds.): ICDT 2005, LNCS 3363, pp. 173–188, 2005.

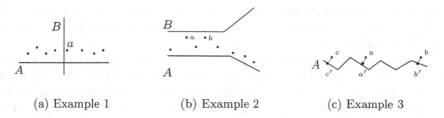

(a) Example 1   (b) Example 2   (c) Example 3

Fig. 1. Figure 1(a) and Figure 1(b) illustrate the problem with naive snapping; Figure 1(c) illustrates space saving of nonmaterialized trajectory

number of vehicles that traveled on the highway between exits 48 and 52 of I80 in the last hour". Such a query is impossible to answer precisely if the locations of moving objects are off-the-road, since vehicles traveling on parallel roads may seem to have traveled on the highway, and vice versa. Similarly, the query "What is the route taken by Bill today" requires translation of motion from raw GPS data into a higher level of abstraction.

One may be tempted to propose a simple solution to the error-correction problem, namely snap each GPS point to the closest road segment. However this is a simplistic solution that may produce incorrect results. For example, consider Figure 1(a) that illustrates a road network, and several GPS points. Clearly the vehicle traveled on road segment A, and thus GPS point a needs to be snapped to A, although B is the closest road segment to a. Another example is shown in Figure 1(b). Clearly the vehicle traveled on road A, but this is deduced only by examining the whole sequence of GPS points, and snapping GPS points a, b onto the closest road segment will produce an incorrect result.

As a <u>first result</u> of this paper, we propose an efficient algorithm that, given a trajectory T of a moving object[1], a road network, and a GPS receiver error bound ε, determines whether there exists another trajectory T', called the *road-snapped trajectory*, such that: (i) T' is on the road network, and (ii) the distance between T and T' is not higher than ε; and if so it finds T'. In other words, we find for a trajectory T, a possible route in the road-network that was followed by the moving object.

The second problem addressed in this paper is data volume. In principle, a GPS receiver can generate a new (x, y, t) point every second, and the number of moving objects may be hundreds of millions to billions. The problem is compounded by the fact that one is interested in historical spatio-temporal information for data mining.

Now consider that usually computation of the location at any point in time is enabled by linear interpolation between consecutive trajectory vertices[7, 14]. Then the road-snapped trajectory may have more points than the original trajectory, since it contains the snapped vertices of T, as well as the vertices of the

---

[1] The trajectory of a moving object is a polygonal line in 3D that represents a piece-wise linear function from time to location in two-dimensional space; the GPS points are the vertices of the polygonal line. Thus the trajectory models a trip.

route. For example, if the two consecutive GPS points a and b of Figure 1c are snapped onto the depicted road, the trajectory between a' and b' will consist of six vertices rather than two.

Thus one can immediately recognize the storage-space problem that location based services applications will face, as well as the computation burden for processing such large amount of information. Additionally, in online tracking where the spatio-temporal points are transmitted from a moving object to a server, this storage problem translates into a bandwidth and power problem.

Our nonmaterialized trajectory concept addresses this problem by separating the motion description into two components, namely the spatial component represented by the road network (i.e. the map) that is common to all the trajectories, and the temporal component that is specific to each trajectory. So, for example, assuming constant speed motion, the nonmaterialized trajectory representing the motion of Figure 1(c) consists of the street A and two time-points, the time at a' and the time at b' (rather than six points used by the materialized representation). Together with the coordinates of street A given by the map, this nonmaterialized trajectory can provide the location of the moving object at any point in time. And actually, the nonmaterialized trajectory has even fewer points because it is a bounded error approximation of the original trajectory. So, for example, assume that c' precedes a', and consider the nonmaterialized trajectory T': "on street A, at time point t_c at location c' and at time point t_b at location b'". If the distance of T' from the original trajectory is not higher than ε, then a' can be eliminated from the nonmaterialized trajectory. Thus the nonmaterialized representation is an abstraction that is concise because it encapsulates two mechanisms, namely: separation of the temporal component from the spatial one, and bounded error approximation. Obviously, the map will also need to be kept. However, the same map is shared among many trajectories.

The concept of a nonmaterialized trajectory can be demonstrated by the following analogy. When giving driving directions, one could indicate: starting from (x_1, y_1) drive in a straight line to (x_2, y_2), from there drive in a straight line to (x_3, y_3), etc. This would be analogous to a regular, i.e. materialized trajectory given as a function from time to space. Nobody uses this form of directions. Instead, directions are given as: drive on Halsted Street, make a left of Canal street, then make a right on Division street. This is equivalent to the concept of a nonmaterialized trajectory that gives the time $\rightarrow$ space function implicitly; using the map, the function can be made explicit.

As a second result of this paper, we provide an efficient algorithm that constructs a nonmaterialized trajectory T'' for a given road-snapped trajectory T' and an error bound ε, such that the distance between the original trajectory T and T'' is at most ε; furthermore, the size of T'' is minimum among all nonmaterialized trajectories that can be constructed based on T'. Why not find a minimum-size nonmaterialized trajectory that is at distance ε from the original trajectory T? We conjecture that this problem is NP-complete.

Then we analyze the errors to spatio-temporal queries introduced by the approximation, and we show that these errors are bounded. In other words, the nonmaterialized trajectory T'' (which is also a road-snapped trajectory) is an approximation of the original trajectory T. What is the "distance" in the answers of a given spatio-temporal query posed to T and T''? We show in this paper that this distance is bounded for all natural spatio-temporal queries. One may be tempted to discount these results, on the ground that it is intuitively clear that if the error of the approximation is bounded (i.e. the distance between T and T'' is bounded), then the error of the answer to each query is also bounded. However, we show that this is not necessarily the case. Specifically, we show that for every ε and δ there exists a trajectory T with a road-snapped trajectory T' such that the Euclidean distance between T and T' is at most ε, but the distance between the answers to the query "where is the moving object at time 2pm" on T and T' is higher than δ. Similarly, the error to other natural spatio-temporal queries is unbounded in a sense made precise in this paper. The reason the our snapping algorithm produces error-bounded approximations is that it does not use the Euclidean distance, but another, called time_uniform distance.

Trajectory snapping is supposed to correct location sensing errors, so one may wonder why we are concerned about queries on the original trajectory T. The answer is that one may never be sure what the actual motion function was, and so we want to limit the damage in case the snapping is to an incorrect route.

In summary, **the main results of this paper are as follows**. First, we provide an efficient algorithm that, given a trajectory T, a road network, and an error bound ε, determines whether there exists an ε-distant road-snapped trajectory; and if so it finds it. Second, we provide an algorithm that, for a road-snapped trajectory T'' and an original trajectory T and a bound ε, finds a nonmaterialized trajectory T'' that is at distance at most ε from T, and has minimum size among all nonmaterialized trajectories derived from T'. Third, we defined the notion of error boundness for spatio-temporal queries, and we show that the time_uniform distance used by our snapping algorithm is error-bounded with respect to the spatio-temporal query types: where is a moving object at a given time, range query, nearest neighbor, and join. We also show that the Euclidean distance is not error bounded w.r.t. these query types.

The rest of the paper is organized as follows. In section 2 we introduce the model. In sections 3, 4, and 5 we devise the first, second and third results discussed in the previous paragraph, respectively. In section 6 we compare our work to relevant literature, and in section 7 we conclude the paper.

2   The Model

Representing the *(location,time)* information of the moving object as a trajectory is a typical approach (c.f. [7, 14]). Point locations are represented as longitude-latitude (x, y)-coordinates. We do not discuss moving objects with a third altitude dimension, although our results can be extended to this case. Time is a real number t. Thus every *(location,time)* of a moving point object is given as a 3-dimensional (x, y, t) point. We do not discuss moving objects with an extent such as weather phenomena.

Definition 1. *A* <u>trajectory</u> *T is a piece-wise linear function from the time interval $[t_1, t_n]$ to $(\overline{X,Y})$ space. It is represented by the vertices of the function polygonal-line $T_1 = (x_1, y_1, t_1)$, $T_2 = (x_2, y_2, t_2)$, ..., $T_n = (x_n, y_n, t_n)$, such that for all $i \in \{1, \ldots, n-1\}$, $t_i < t_{i+1}$. For a given trajectory T, its projection on the (X, Y) plane is called the* <u>route</u> *of T, denoted as $R(T)$. The* <u>location</u> *of T at time t is the value of the function at t.*

A trajectory (or a *materialized trajectory*) defines the location of a moving object in the (X, Y) plane as a function of time t. The vertices of the trajectory are the known locations (e.g. the GPS points), and the trajectory function is obtained by straight-forward linear interpolation between these locations. An illustration of trajectory and its route is shown in Figure 2(a). Observe that this representation cannot model nonlinear motion such as acceleration, but can approximate it with arbitrary precision given enough trajectory vertices.

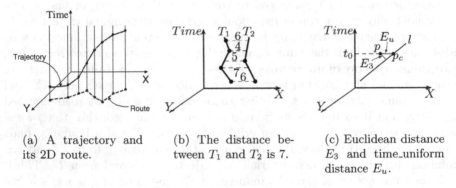

(a) A trajectory and its 2D route.

(b) The distance between T_1 and T_2 is 7.

(c) Euclidean distance E_3 and time-uniform distance E_u.

Fig. 2. Distance between trajectories and distance functions

Next, for the purpose of trajectory snapping, we define a map. A *map*, or a *road network*, is a directed graph; the nodes are labeled by (X, Y) coordinates and represent junctions[2] and the arcs represent straight-line road segments between junctions. Each arc has a length, which is the Euclidean distance between its two endpoints. The arcs of the map are partitioned into *streets*, where each street is a path in the map, the streets are disjoint (i.e. we assume that 42nd-st-going-east and 42nd-st-going-west are different streets), and every arc of the map belongs to some street. We assume without loss of generality that each street is acyclic.

Every point location on the map (node or point on an arc) can be also be defined in the *linear reference system*, i.e. the distance from the beginning of a street. Thus a point-location on the map can be defined in the Cartesian system as an (x, y) location, or in the linear reference system as *(street, distance)*.

---

[2] A junction is not necessarily intersection of two streets, but maybe the vertex of a polyline representing the geometry of the road.

Our objective is to construct a trajectory on the map that is an ε-approximation of the original trajectory, i.e. at ε distance from the original trajectory. For this purpose we need to define the distance between two trajectories. The Hausdorff distance[2] between trajectories is defined as follows. Let M be the distance between a 3D point and the 3D straight line between two consecutive trajectory vertices. Examples of two possible M's, the Euclidean and the time_uniform, are given at the end of this section. The distance $d_M(p, T)$ between a 3D point p and a trajectory T is the minimum (among all straight line segments of T) M-distance between p and a line segment of T. The Hausdorff M-distance from a trajectory T to another trajectory T' is defined as $\tilde{D}_M(T, T') = \max_{p \in T} d(p, T')$, i.e. the Hausdorff distance from T to T' is the maximum distance from a point of T, to T'. The symmetric Hausdorff distance between T and T' (or, for short, the Hausdorff distance between two trajectories) is defined as $D_M(T, T') = \max(\tilde{D}_M(T, T'), \tilde{D}_M(T', T))$; i.e. it is the maximum of the distances from T to T' and from T' to T (see Figure 2(b)).

Definition 2. *Given a trajectory T, a road network N, a tolerance $\varepsilon > 0$, and a distance M between a 3D point and a 3D line, the ε_M-road-snapped trajectory T' is a trajectory whose route is a path in the graph N, and $D_M(T, T') \leq \varepsilon$.*

In the above definition the tolerance ε is the sum of two maximum errors. One is the error of the location sensing device such as a GPS receiver, and the second is the error of the map. The ε-road-snapped trajectory is a possible actual trajectory of the moving object.

Now we take the inner distance function M to be the three dimensional *time_uniform* distance E_u defined as follows. For a point $p = (x_0, y_0, t_0)$ on one trajectory and a line segment l on the other, $E_u(p, l) = \sqrt{(x_0 - x_c)^2 + (y_0 - y_c)^2}$, where $p_c = (x_c, y_c, t_0)$ is the unique point on l which has the same *Time* value as p (see Figure 2(c)); if such a point does not exist, then the time_uniform distance between p and l is infinity.

Observe that the time_uniform distance is different than the Euclidean distance between p and l (see Figure 2(c)). Intuitively, the time_uniform distance between a trajectory point p and a trajectory line l is the distance between p and the point on l that has the same time as p. Whereas the Euclidean distance between p and l is the minimum distance between p and a point on l.

In section 5 we will discuss the Euclidean distance function, but until then we will always assume that M is the time_uniform distance and will omit M.

3   Road-Snapped Trajectory Construction

Assume that we are given a trajectory T, a map M, and a tolerance ε. In this section we devise an efficient algorithm that determines whether or not there exists an ε-road-snapped trajectory T'. If so, it finds it. The algorithm constructs a Snapping Configuration Graph (SCG), finds a certain path in SCG, and then extracts T' from this path.

The SCG construction uses the following definition. Given two polygonal lines in the (X, Y) coordinate system, the ε-*neighborhood* of a vertex p in one polygonal line is the set of 2D points on the other polygonal line that are at distance at most ε from p. The concept is illustrated in figure 4(b).

The snapping configuration graph is constructed as follows. For the trajectory T given as a sequence of vertices $T_1, \ldots, T_i, \ldots, T_n$, and a map with arcs $(l_1, \ldots, l_m)$, the nodes of SCG are of two types: (1) (T_i, l_j) for each trajectory vertex T_i and arc l_j for which the Euclidean distance between the 2D projection of T_i and l_j is at most ε. Intuitively, this indicates that T_i can be snapped onto l_j. And (2) $(l_j, \overrightarrow{T_i T_{i+1}})$, when the distance between the front end-point of l_j and the (X, Y) projection of $\overrightarrow{T_i T_{i+1}}$ is at most ε. Intuitively, this means that in the road-snapped trajectory, some point between T_i and T_{i+1} can be snapped onto the front endpoint of l_j.

The arcs of SCG indicate the possible pairwise sequences of individual nodes to construct a road-snapped trajectory. The arcs of SCG are of four types:

• (1) $(T_i, l_j) \rightarrow (T_{i+1}, l_j)$, if the ε-neighborhood of the 2D projection of T_{i+1} on directed line segment l_j is not totally behind (in l_j) the ε-neighborhood of the 2D projection of T_i on l_j. Intuitively, this arc indicates that if T_i is snapped onto l_j, then T_{i+1} can be snapped onto l_j as well. Observe that this can be done only if "not totally behind" restriction is satisfied. In other words, there must be a point p of l_j that is in the neighborhood of T_{i+1}; and p appears on l_j before another point q of l_j that is in the neighborhood of T_i.

• (2) $(T_i, l_j) \rightarrow (l_j, \overrightarrow{T_i T_{i+1}})$. Intuitively, this arc means that if one vertex of the road-snapped trajectory is T_i snapped onto l_j; then the next vertex of the road-snapped trajectory can be the point of the trajectory between T_i and T_{i+1} that is snapped onto the front endpoint of l_j. In this case, T_{i+1} is snapped onto another line segment of the map.

• (3) $(l_j, \overrightarrow{T_i T_{i+1}}) \rightarrow (T_{i+1}, l_{j'})$, where $l_{j'}$ is one of the adjacent arcs that follows l_j in the map. Intuitively, this arc means that if one vertex of the road-snapped trajectory is some point of the trajectory between T_i and T_{i+1} that is snapped onto the front endpoint of l_j; then the next vertex of the road-snapped trajectory can be T_{i+1} that is snapped onto an arc of the map that is adjacent to l_j.

• (4) $(l_j, \overrightarrow{T_i T_{i+1}}) \rightarrow (l_{j'}, \overrightarrow{T_i T_{i+1}})$, where $l_{j'}$ is one of the adjacent arcs that follows l_j in the map, and the ε-neighborhood of the front end-point of l'_j on the 2D projection $\overrightarrow{T_i T_{i+1}}$ is not totally behind that of l_j. Intuitively, this arc means that if one vertex of the road-snapped trajectory is some point of the trajectory between T_i and T_{i+1} that is snapped onto the front endpoint of l_j; then the following vertex can be be another point between T_i and T_{i+1} that is snapped onto the front endpoint of l'_j.

Intuitively, the four types of arcs represent four cases for adjacent vertices of the road-snapped trajectory TT, Tl, lT, ll; where T represents a vertex derived from the trajectory and l represents a vertex derived from the map.

Theorem 1. *Given a trajectory $T = T_1, \ldots, T_n$, a map M, and a tolerance ε, there exists an acyclic path π in SCG starting at a node (T_1, l) and ending at a node (T_n, l') if and only if there exists an ε-road-snapped trajectory T'.*

The above theorem provides the necessary and sufficient condition for the existence of an ε-road-snapped trajectory, and its proof[3] is constructive, i.e. it finds the trajectory. It is easy to see that the time complexity of the algorithm is $O(nm^2)$ for a trajectory with n vertices and a map with m arcs at distance ε from T. Observe that the complexity does not depend on the total number of arcs in the map, only on the ones that are at distance ε from the trajectory.

Assume now that there exists a trajectory T' whose route is on the map M, such that T' is at distance at most ε from T. A route R of such a trajectory is called a *feasible route* of T. Given the path π (see Theorem 1), its feasible route is: the set of arcs that appear in π, either in the first component of a node, or in the second. By construction of SCG, this is a path in the map. This procedure of constructing a SCG and finding a feasible route is illustrated in example 1.

Example 1. Consider the map M and the trajectory T shown in Figure 3(a). The map is drawn as a directed graph with 17 directed arcs $l_1, \ldots, l_{17}$. The trajectory consists of six trajectory vertices from T_0 to T_5, shown as the dashed polygonal line in Figure 3(a). The arrowed lines indicate that the corresponding vertex has an ε-neighborhood in the line segment to which it points.

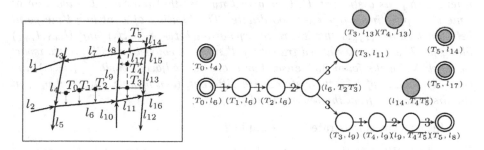

(a) The road network and trajectory.   (b) The snapping configuration graph.

Fig. 3. Example of snapping configuration graph

Figure 3(b) depicts the snapping configuration graph generated from the map and the trajectory in Figure 3(a). There are 15 nodes in the SCG. The labels of the SCG arcs indicate the arc types. The connected nodes are colored white and the isolated ones are in gray. Especially observe that $(T_3, l_{13}) \rightarrow (T_4, l_{13})$ is not a valid arc since the ε-neighborhood of the 2D projection of T_4 on l_{13} is behind that of T_3. The nodes that pertain to the start trajectory vertex and the end trajectory vertex are illustrated by double circles. According to Theorem 1, a

---

[3] The proof and the proofs of other theorems are omitted, due to space constraint.

road-snapped trajectory of T exists since there is a path π from (T_0, l_6) to (T_5, l_8) and it is the only one in the SCG. Thus, we can extract a road-snapped trajectory T' with eight vertices $T_0', T_1', T_2', \ldots, T_7'$ which correspond nodes (T_0, l_6) to (T_5, l_8) on π respectively. The feasible route R of T' is (l_6, l_9, l_8). $\square$

4   Nonmaterialized Trajectory Construction

In this section we devise an algorithm that, given a path π in SCG, constructs a nonmaterialized ε-road-snapped trajectory T'' of minimum size. The route R of T'' is the feasible route of π and T'' has minimum size among all nonmaterialized trajectories on R.

We start with the definition of a nonmaterialized trajectory. Intuitively, a nonmaterialized trajectory describes the motion in the linear reference system. For example, started at 0.2 mile-post of Broadway-north (the mile-post simply indicates location from the beginning of the street) at 2pm and drove to the 3.2 mile-post, then turned on 42nd street-west at 2.2 mile-post at 2:10pm, etc. Formally, a nonmaterialized trajectory is defined as follows.

Definition 3. (Trajectory, Nonmaterialized) *Consider a map M consisting of a set of streets P. A* <u>nonmaterialized trajectory</u> *T is a function from time to map locations represented as a sequence of tuples $(\langle p_1, l_1, t_1 \rangle, \ldots, \langle p_m, l_m, t_m \rangle)$, where each p_i is a street in P, l_i is a real number that indicates T's location at time t_i in p_i's linear reference coordinate. The location of T at any time-point between t_i and t_{i+1} is the linear interpolation between (l_i, t_i) and (l_{i+1}, t_{i+1}) along p_i. The nonmaterialized trajectory T must be consistent with the transport network N, in the following sense. For every two adjacent tuples (p_i, l_i, t_i) and $(p_{i+1}, l_{i+1}, t_{i+1})$ of T, if their streets are different, then p_i must intersect p_{i+1} at the distance l_{i+1} from the beginning of p_{i+1}.*

This concept is illustrated in example 2.

Example 2. What is the nonmaterialized view of trajectory T' in Example 1? Assume that we have constructed a road-snapped trajectory T' from the path π and the route $R = (l_6, l_9, l_8)$. Further assume that R is on two streets S_1 and S_2, where l_6 is on S_1 from the 3.2 mile-post to 3.6 mile-post, l_9 is on S_2 from the 0.3 mile-post to the 1 mile-post, and l_8 is on S_2 from the 1 mile-post to the 1.4 mile-post. The first vertex T_0' of T' is on l_6 at the 0.1 mile-post from the intersection of l_2 and l_6 at 1:00pm. The second vertex T_1' is on l_6 at the 0.2 mile-post from the intersection of l_2 and l_6 at 1:01pm. The third vertex T_2' is on l_6 at the 0.3 mile-post from the intersection of l_2 and l_6 at 1:03pm. The fourth vertex T_3' is at the intersection of l_6 and l_9 at 1:06pm. The fifth vertex T_4' is the snapping of T_3 on l_9 at the 0.2 mile-post from the intersection of l_6 and l_9 at 1:09pm. The sixth vertex T_5' is the snapping of T_4 on l_9 at the 0.5 mile point from intersection of l_6 and l_9 at 1:11pm . The seventh vertex T_6' is at the intersection of l_9 and l_8 at 1:14pm. The last vertex T_7' is on l_8 at the 0.2 mile-post from intersection of l_9 and l_8 at 1:16pm . Then, the nonmaterialized representation of T' is the sequence $(S_1, 3.3, 1:00\text{pm})$, $(S_1, 3.4, 1:01\text{pm})$, $(S_1, 3.5, 1:03\text{pm})$, $(S_2, 0.3, 1:06\text{pm})$, $(S_2, 0.5, 1:09\text{pm})$, $(S_2, 0.8, 1:11\text{pm})$,$(S_2, 1, 1:14\text{pm})$,$(S_2, 1.2, 1:16\text{pm})$. Note that the size of this representation is eight, longer than the size of the original trajectory, because, as mentioned in the introduction, it represents both the vertices of trajectory and the road network.   □

A nonmaterialized trajectory can easily be transformed to the equivalent materialized representation, in linear time, by traversing, in sequence, the tuples of the nonmaterialized representation, and for each one, interpolating the arrival time at every vertex of the route. Similarly, one can transform in linear time a road-snapped materialized trajectory T into a nonmaterialized one by creating a nonmaterialized tuple for each vertex of T.

The nonmaterialized trajectory is created based on the feasible route R and the SCG path π found in the previous section. The number of tuples in the nonmaterialized trajectory is minimum for the path π.

The Nonmaterialized Trajectory Construction (NTC) algorithm starts with a feasible route R and a trajectory T and constructs the nonmaterialized trajectory for each street S of R, i.e it works one street at a time, starting from the first to the last. If the same street appears on the feasible route more than once, then the procedure is repeated for each occurrence of the street on R. For ease of exposition assume that the feasible path consists of a single street S.

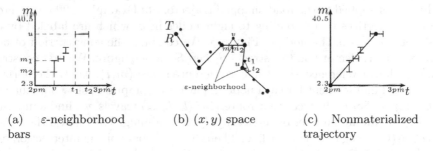

(a) ε-neighborhood bars

(b) (x, y) space

(c)   Nonmaterialized trajectory

Fig. 4. Nonmaterialized trajectory construction in the linear reference/time space

The NTC algorithm constructs the minimum size nonmaterialized trajectory in the (m, t) two-dimensional space. It uses the following result.

Theorem 2. *If there exists an acyclic path π in SCG starting at a node (T_1, l) and ending at a node (T_n, l'), then each vertex T_i of the trajectory T appears in π as the first component of a node, at most once.*

The procedure is as follows. In the (m, t) space the t axis is the time linear reference built based on trajectory T, and the m axis is the street linear reference. So if the trajectory starts at 2pm and ends at 3pm the t axis has these endpoints. And if the feasible route starts at the 2.3 milepost of S and ends at the 40.5 mile-post, the m axis has 2.3 and 40.5 as the endpoints (see Fig. 4). Observe that since each street is acyclic, each arc of the map appears in m at most once.

NTC then constructs an m-(vertical) line segment for each vertex v of T, and a t-(horizontal) line segment for each arc u represented in m (Fig. 4(a)).

The vertical line segment for v is constructed as follows. According to Theorems 1 and 2 there is exactly one node (v, l) in the SCG path π, and l is represented in m at most once. If l is represented in m, then consider the ε-neighborhood on l of the projection of v on the (X, Y) space. Assume that this neighborhood in the m coordinate is (m_1, m_2). Then we draw the vertical bar (m_1, m_2) at the time corresponding to v on t (see Figure 4(a)).

The horizontal line segment for the arc u is constructed as follows. Since there is a single street in the feasible path, in the SCG path π there is exactly one node $(u, \overrightarrow{T_i T_{i+1}})$. Then, in the (X, Y) space, compute the ε-neighborhood of the front-end point of u on the projection of $\overrightarrow{T_i T_{i+1}}$. Assume that this neighborhood in the t coordinate is $[t_1, t_2]$. Then we draw the horizontal bar of length $t_2 - t_1$ at the linear reference point which is the front-end of u (Fig. 4(a)).

To construct the nonmaterialized trajectory, we proceed as follows. Let $m = f(t)$ be some piecewise linear monotonic function that stabs all the line segments constructed by the above procedure. If the vertices of its polygonal line are $(t_1, m_1), (t_2, m_2), \dots (t_n, m_n)$, then this sequence is a nonmaterialized trajectory on the street S.

This NTC procedure is illustrated in example 3.

Example 3. Figure 5 illustrates the nonmaterialized trajectory construction procedure. It is applied to the road-snapped trajectory of Example 1. The trajectory is of eight vertices corresponding to eight nodes in π, which are labeled by the first components of the node in Figure 5. We combine the construction of nonmaterialized trajectory on two streets S_1 and S_2 in one figure. We first construct the time linear reference/street linear reference space (m, t). Next, the horizontal/vertical line segment for each node in path π is computed, shown as the bars in the figure. For each street that route $R = (l_6, l_9, l_8)$ travels, we find a minimal-size (i.e. minimum number of vertices) polyline stabbing. We stab all the bars of street $S_1(l_6)$ using one straight line. Then, from the bars of the intersection of l_6 and l_9, we stab the rest of the bars on street S_2 (l_9 and l_8) with a two piece polyline. Writing down the street name, the m and t value for each dot in the figure, we get the nonmaterialized representation of trajectory T on map M. Note that the size of the nonmaterialized trajectory is four and T has six vertices. In this sense, the figure shows the data reduction aspect of our approach.   □

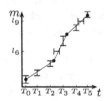

Fig. 5. Constructing the nonmaterialized trajectory

The question now is what ensures that a piece-wise linear function required by the above theorem exists? The answer is given by Theorem 1. Namely, if the path π exists there is a nonmaterialized trajectory, and therefore a stabbing. We are interested in a stabbing that has a minimum number of straight line segments, because this will ensure a minimum number of tuples in the nonmaterialized trajectory for π. This can be done using the results of [9, 12]. It provides a greedy algorithm for stabbing n line segments with a polygonal line of minimum size in linear time.

Theorem 3. *For every trajectory T, map M, and positive real number ε, a nonmaterialized trajectory T'' created with the above algorithm satisfies: (1) The route $R(T'')$ is a path in the map. (2) The distance between the original trajectory T and T'' at most ε. (3) It has minimum size among all nonmaterialized trajectories on $R(T'')$.*

The total number of vertical and horizontal bars is $O(n + m)$, each bar can be constructed in constant time, and the piecewise linear stabbing $m = f(t)$ can be constructed in linear time, using the approach in [9]. Therefore, the time complexity of the NTC algorithm is $O(n + m)$. Thus, the time complexity of finding the nonmaterialized trajectory is dominated by the previous step of the algorithm (finding π), and is $O(nm^2)$.

5   Bounded Error of Spatio-Temporal Queries

Our proposed nonmaterialized trajectory T'' is a road-snapped trajectory at distance ε from T. In this section we will analyze the relationship between a trajectory and its road-snapped trajectory with respect to the error in answering spatio-temporal queries. We show that in general, although the distance between a trajectory T and its road-snapped trajectory T' is bounded, the error of spatio-temporal queries may be unbounded. In other words, distance between the answer to a query on T and the same query on T' may be arbitrarily large. Particularly, even if the Euclidean distance between T and T' is bounded, then this undesirable phenomenon, namely unbounded query errors, may occur. We also show that this undesirable behavior does not occur for the road-snapped trajectories produced by the algorithm introduced in this paper. The reason is that the algorithm uses the time-uniform distance between T and T'.

We consider the following basic spatio-temporal *query types*, whose semantics for a trajectory $T = (x_1, y_1, t_1), (x_2, y_2, t_2), ..., (x_n, y_n, t_n)$, are as follows:

- *where_at(T, t)* – returns the location of the trajectory T at time t.
- *intersect(T, P, t_1, t_2)* – is *true* if the location of T is inside the convex polygon P sometime between t_1 and t_2. (This is also called a range query).

We first define the concept of query-error-boundedness for a distance-function between trajectories. The concept is defined for a query type. Then we show that the Euclidean distance is not query-error-bounded for the spatio-temporal query types, but the time-uniform distance is query-error-bounded for them.

Now we explain the notion of query-error-boundedness. So far we restricted the discussion to the time-uniform distance between a trajectory T and its ε-road-snapped trajectory T' (see def. 2). Here we relax this restriction. Let $q(T)$ denote the answer of some spatio-temporal query q with respect to a trajectory T. Similarly, let $q(T')$ denote the answer of the same query q when posed to an ε_D-road-snapped trajectory T' of T. We say that the distance function D is query-error-bounded for q when there exists a bound δ on the distance between the two answers. More precisely, if we let $dist(q(T),q(T'))$ denote the distance between the two answers, query-error-boundedness of D means that for every ε there exists a δ such that for every trajectory T, $dist(q(T),q(T')) \leq \delta$.

We formalize this notion for each of the query types, as follows. A distance function D is <u>error-bounded</u> with respect to query-type q if for every tolerance ε, there exists a positive number δ, called the <u>answer error bound</u>, such that for every trajectory T and a ε_D-road-snapped trajectory T' of T (the rest of the definition depends on the query-type as follows):

• <u>*where_at*</u> – For every t for which both T and T' are defined, let $(x,y) = where\_at(T,t)$ and let $(x',y') = where\_at(T',t)$. The distance between (x,y) and (x',y') is bounded by δ, namely $\sqrt{(x'-x)^2+(y'-y)^2} \leq \delta$.
• <u>*intersect*</u> – For any polygon P, if $intersect(T',P,t_1,t_2)$ is *true*, then there exists a time $t \in [t_1,t_2]$ such that the expected location of the original trajectory T at time t is no further than δ from $P \cup$ interior of P. Conversely, if $intersect(T',P,t_1,t_2)$ is *false*, then for every $t \in [t_1,t_2]$, the expected location of the original trajectory T at time t is either outside P, or, if inside, it is within δ of a side of P (i.e. it does not penetrate P by more than δ). Intuitively, this means that if the ε_D-road-snapped trajectory T' intersects P, then T is not further than δ from P; and if T' does not intersect P, then T does not intersect P, or intersects it "very little". Thus, the user, knowing that the query addresses road-snapped trajectories, may decide to adjust the polygon P accordingly.

The following subsumption relationship holds among query types.

Theorem 4. *Any distance function D is error-bounded w.r.t. the where_at query type if and only if it is error-bounded for the intersect query type.*

Interestingly, the Euclidean distance is not error-bounded w.r.t. where_at query type. While the time-uniform distance is error-bounded.

Theorem 5. *The 3D Euclidean distance is not error-bounded w.r.t the where_at query type.*

Theorem 6. *The time-uniform distance is error-bounded w.r.t. the where_at query type. Furthermore, for any tolerance ε, the answer-error-bound of the where_at query-type is ε.*

Together with Theorem 4, the above result implies that the time-uniform distance is also error-bounded w.r.t. the intersect type. It can also be shown that for the distance E_u, for any tolerance ε, the answer-error-bound of the intersect query type is equal to ε.

6   Related Work

Recently, modeling, management, and query processing of network confined movement has received significant attention[8, 14]. However, the required error-correction to make the work applicable has been ignored. Our study provides the necessary preprocessing step. Some papers adopted the similar idea of separating spatial and temporal components of trajectories [8]. However, their objective was to improve the performance of indexing, whereas our objective here is to correct errors, provide a higher level of motion abstraction, and reduce size.

Trajectory snapping is also studied for car navigation under the title *map matching*[11, 16]. Most of those works take a heuristic approach to snapping, and their main purpose is to determine in real time the current block the driver is on. In order to do so they only consider the last GPS point, or the last few GPS points. Therefore, when considering the snapped blocks one may obtain a route that is not connected. However, since the purpose is simply to determine the current location of a user in real-time, this drawback is not important for their purpose. The two-page paper [17] provides a heuristic for map matching. To the best of our knowledge, our road-snapped trajectory construction algorithm is the first complete map matching algorithm, which determinates whether a road-snapped trajectory exists for the given error bound.

Similar to map matching, researchers are also studying the matching problems between different spatial datasets[5], and the problem of robotic mapping[15]. However, the objectives of these papers are different than ours, and their techniques are probably not directly applicable here.

Nonmaterialized trajectory representation of motion is related to data reduction, a very popular topic in the database research. When it comes to generating the answers to the queries, there are two approaches: 1. The data is decompressed before answering a query [6]; and 2. The compressed data is used to answer the query, and the answer contains some error [4, 10]. Our approach is *lossy*, i.e we do not recover the original trajectories after snapping. Recently *wavelets* have become a popular paradigm for data reduction which provides fast and "reasonably approximate" answer to queries [4]. The original data is reduced to compact sets of coefficients (*wavelet synopses*) which are used to answer the queries. The main difference with our approach which provides deterministic error-bounds to queries, is that these works either do not ensure a bound on the error of query answers, or ensure an *asymptotic/probabilistic* bounds on the error. A similar observation holds for the works which use *histograms* or *sampling* to compress the data and provide a reasonably accurate answer to the queries (see [1]).

Finally, let us mention some previous work on data reduction by strong line-simplification ([3][13]). These work did not address road-snapping or nonmaterialized trajectories, thus the line simplified trajectories may still be off the road network. However, [3] did consider soundness of queries. The concept of error-boundedness in this paper is a generalization of soundness to the case where the vertices of the approximate trajectory are not necessarily a subset of those of the original trajectory (in contrast to line simplification which imposes such a restriction). [13] also used the time_uniform distance and studied the error and the compression ratio experimentally.

7 Conclusions

With the proliferation of location based services and mobile devices including sensors, computers, and GPS receivers, the importance of motion information will increase tremendously. In this paper we addressed the problem of producing a higher level of abstraction for motion data, based on constraints provided by road networks. We introduced an algorithm for "adjusting" a given trajectory T to fit the road network; the adjustment is called a road-snapped trajectory, T'', and it has several properties. First, it is within a distance ε (the location-sensor error) from T. Second, it is on the road network. Third, it is nonmaterialized, i.e. it provides the temporal information separately from the spatial information common to all the trajectories. Fourth, it is minimized in a local sense, i.e. for a given materialized snapped trajectory. Fifth, it is error bounded with respect to the spatio-temporal queries: where is a moving object at a given time, range query, nearest neighbor, and join. In other words, the answers to any such query posed on T and T' are close. We have shown that this property is not trivial even though T and T' are ε-close; i.e. the property holds for the time_uniform distance metric, but not for the Euclidean metric. The time-complexity of the algorithm is $O(nm^2)$, for a trajectory with n vertices and a map with m straight line segments at distance ε from T.

References

1. Special issue on data reduction techniques. *IEEE Data Engineering*, 20(4), 1998.
2. H. Alt and L. J. Guibas. Discrete geometric shapes: Matching, interpolation, and approximation A survey. Technical Report B 96-11, Institut für Informatik, Freie Universität Berlin, 1996.
3. H. Cao, O. Wolfson, and G. Trajcevski. Spatiotemporal data reduction with deterministic error bounds. In *DIALM-POMC'03*, pages 33–42, 2003.
4. K. Chakrabarti, M. Garofalakis, R. Rastogi, and K. Shim. Approximate query processing using wavelets. In *VLDB 2000*, Septermber 2000.
5. C. Chen, S. Thakkar, C. Knoblock, and C. Shahabi. Automatically annotating and integrating spatial datasets. In *SSTD'03*, 2003.
6. Z. Chen, J. Gehrke, and F. Korn. Query optimization in compressed database systems. In *ACM SIGMOD 2001*, pages 271–282. ACM Press, 2001.
7. L. Florizzi, R. H. Guting, E. Nardelli, and M. Schneider. A data model and data structures for moving objects databases. Technical Report 260-10, Fern-Universität Hagen, 1999.
8. E. Frentzos. Indexing objects moving on fixed networks. In *Proc. 8th Int'l Symposium on Spatial and Temporal Databases, SSTD'03*, 2003.
9. S. K. Ghosh. Computing the visibility polygon from a convex set and related problem. *Journal of Algorithms*, 12:75–95, 1991.
10. P. B. Gibbons, Y. Matias, and V. Poosala. Fast incremental maintenance of approximate histograms. In *VLDB*, 1997.

11. J. S. Greenfeld. Matching gps observations to locations on a digital map. In *The 81th Annual Meeting of the Transportation Research Board*, Washington D.C, 2002.
12. L. J. Guibas, J. E. Hershberger, J. S. B. Mitchell, and J. xS. Snoeyink. Approximating polygons and subdivisions with minimum link paths. In *ISAAC' 91*, 1991.
13. N. Meratnia and R. A. de By. Spatiotemporal compression techniques for moving point objects. In *EDBT*, pages 765–782, 2004.
14. D. Pfoser and C. S. Jensen. Indexing of network constrained moving objects. In *ACM GIS*, pages 25–32. ACM Press, 2003.
15. S. Thrun. Robotic mapping: a survey. In *Exploring artificial intelligence in the new millennium*, pages 1–35. Morgan Kaufmann Publishers Inc., 2003.
16. C. E. White, D. Bernstein, and A. L. Kornhauser. Some map matching algorithms for personal navigation assistants. *Transportation Research Part C*, 8:91–108, 2000.
17. H. Yin and O. Wolfson. A weight-based map matching method in moving objects databases. In *SSTDM*, 2004.

Algorithms for the Database Layout Problem

Gagan Aggarwal*, Tomás Feder**, Rajeev Motwani***, Rina Panigrahy,
and An Zhu†

Computer Science Department, Stanford University, Stanford, CA 94305
{gagan, rajeev, rinap, anzhu}@cs.stanford.edu,
tomas@theory.stanford.edu

Abstract. We present a formal analysis of the database layout problem, i.e., the problem of determining how database objects such as tables and indexes are assigned to disk drives. Optimizing this layout has a direct impact on the I/O performance of the entire system. The traditional approach of striping each object across all available disk drives is aimed at optimizing I/O parallelism; however, it is suboptimal when queries co-access two or more database objects, e.g., during a merge join of two tables, due to the increase in random disk seeks. We adopt an existing model, which takes into account both the benefit of I/O parallelism and the overhead due to random disk accesses, in the context of a query workload which includes co-access of database objects. The resulting optimization problem is intractable in general and we employ techniques from approximation algorithms to present provable performance guarantees. We show that while optimally exploiting I/O parallelism alone suggests uniformly striping data objects (even for heterogeneous files and disks), optimizing random disk access alone would assign each data object to a single disk drive. This confirms the intuition that the two effects are in tension with each other. We provide approximation algorithms in an attempt to optimize the trade-off between the two effects. We show that our algorithm achieves the best possible approximation ratio.

1 Introduction

As relational databases keep growing in size, good overall performance for queries and updates necessitates the optimization of I/O performance on secondary storage. A significant aspect of I/O performance is *database layout*, i.e., how database objects such as tables, indexes, materialized views, etc, are assigned to the available disk drives.

* Supported in part by a Stanford Graduate Fellowship, NSF Grants EIA-0137761 and ITR-0331640 and a grant from SNRC.
** 268 Waverley St., Palo Alto, CA 94301.
*** Supported in part by NSF Grant IIS-0118173 and EIA-0137761, an Okawa Foundation Research Grant, and grants from Microsoft and Veritas.
† Supported in part by a GRPW fellowship from Bell Labs, Lucent Technologies, and NSF Grant EIA-0137761.

T. Eiter and L. Libkin (Eds.): ICDT 2005, LNCS 3363, pp. 189–203, 2005.
© Springer-Verlag Berlin Heidelberg 2005

The traditional approach has been to spread out each database object uniformly over all available disk drives, called *full striping*, in order to obtain I/O parallelism. Full striping minimizes the transfer time of a database object to main memory. Thus, as long as only one object is accessed at a time, this solution can be shown to be optimal with respect to I/O performance. However, when dealing with a query workload which involves co-access of of two or more database objects, e.g., a merge join of two tables, there is a distinct possibility that uniform striping could lead to substantially suboptimal performance. The main reason is that if the concurrently-accessed (co-accessed) objects are co-located on a disk drive, then the seek time encountered switching access between these two objects begins to dominate the I/O cost instead. As a result, there is a trade-off between the benefit due to I/O parallelism and the overhead due to random I/O accesses. For queries co-accessing multiple objects, I/O performance might be improved by choosing a database layout which differs from full striping. For instance, consider the following example given in [1]. Consider queries Q_3 and Q_{10} of the TPC-H benchmark. The execution plan of both these queries accesses the tables *lineitem* and *orders* together and performs a Merge Join. The execution time of these queries were measured over the following two database layouts over a system of 8 disks: (1) Full striping: each table was spread uniformly across all 8 disks. (2) *lineitem* was spread uniformly on 5 disks, and *orders* was spread uniformly across the other 3 disks. Both Q_3 and Q_{10} executed about 40% faster on the database layout (2) as compared to (1). The main reason is that contrary to layout (1), layout (2) avoided a large number of random I/O accesses.

In our study of the database layout problem, we adopt the framework and cost model proposed by Agrawal, Chaudhuri, Das, and Narasayya [1], which combines the effects of both I/O parallelism and random disk access. Using their framework, we model the problem as follows. All database objects are referred to as *files*, each with a size r_i specified in terms of number of disk blocks. In addition, we are given a set of (heterogeneous) disk drives. The goal is to determine a layout of files on disks (specifying what fraction of each file is assigned to each disk), while minimizing the total I/O access time. Naturally, the optimal layout depends on the characteristics of the workload handled by the system. We assume that the workload is given as part of the input. From the query plans, we can extract the frequencies of accessing individual files as well as co-accessed files. For the sake of brevity, we focus our exposition on the case of two-object queries, i.e., queries co-accessing exactly two files. Note that single-object queries are trivially handled by viewing queries accessing a single file i as co-accessing files i and x, where x is an imaginary file of size zero. In general, if a query co-accesses more than two files, we can replace the query with a set of two-object queries [1]; the details are omitted for the purpose of this extended abstract.

For a query q that co-accesses files i and i', the total I/O access time is divided into two parts: the transfer time and the seek time. Transfer time measures the time it takes to sequentially access file blocks on a disk. Let r_{ij} be the number of blocks of file i assigned to disk j. Then, the *transfer time* of query q in disk j is given by $\alpha_j(r_{ij} + r_{i'j})$, where $1/\alpha_j$ is the transfer rate per disk block for disk j. Seek time measures the extra time it takes to re-position the disk head due to random accesses between files i and i'. Let T_j be the average time taken to re-position the disk head, and let B be the average number of blocks read before the system switches from reading one file to the other. We define the seek rate β_j of disk j to be $2T_j/B$. Then the *seek time* for disk j for query q is given by $\beta_j \min\{r_{ij}, r_{i'j}\}$. We justify it as follows: without loss of generality, let $r_{ij} \leq r_{i'j}$; then, the number of times the disk head switches to file i from file i' on disk j is bounded by r_{ij}/B, and the number of times it switches to file i' from file i on disk j is also bounded by the same number. So the total seek time is $T_j \cdot 2r_{ij}/N = \beta_j r_{ij}$. Finally, the total I/O access time of query q is the maximum I/O access time of query q over all disks.

Formally, the problem is defined as follows.

Definition 1. [Database Layout Problem]

INPUT: *Files $F = \{1, 2, \ldots, n\}$, with file i having size r_i. A set of disks $D = \{1, 2, \ldots, m\}$, where each disk j has transfer rate $1/\alpha_i$, seek rate β_j, and load capacity L_j. A query workload consisting of a set of queries $Q = \{q = (i, i') : i, i' \in F\}$, with each query $q = (i, i')$ having frequency weight $\phi(i, i')$.*

OBJECTIVE: *Determine a feasible (defined below) assignment of files to disks so as to minimize the overall query access time (defined below). Let r_{ij} denote the number of blocks of file i assigned to disk j. An assignment is said to be feasible if $\sum_{j \in D} r_{ij} = r_i$ for all files i and $\sum_{i \in F} r_{ij} \leq L_j$ for all disks j. The overall query access time is $\sum_{q \in Q} P(q)$, where the access time for query $q = (i, i')$ is $P(q) = \phi(i, i') \cdot \max_{j \in D}[\alpha_j \cdot (r_{ij} + r_{i'j}) + \beta_j \cdot \min\{r_{ij}, r_{i'j}\}]$.*

We present a formal analysis of this optimization problem. Our main contribution is to establish almost tight theoretical bounds in terms of approximation ratio for the above problem. Define $\gamma = \max_{j \in D} \frac{\beta_j}{\alpha_j}$. We show that the above problem is NP-hard to *approximate* within a factor of $\rho\gamma$, for some constant $0 < \rho < 1$. On a positive note, we present an $(1 + \gamma/2)$-approximation polynomial-time algorithm for the general objective function. By the preceding negative result, our approximation algorithm is optimal up to small constant factors. In establishing the positive $(1 + \gamma/2)$-approximation result, we relate our problem to the problem of minimizing the transfer time only. We show that, when seek time is ignored, a natural weighted variant of *full striping* gives the optimal solution, provided disk capacities are not a constraint. In order to take disk capacities into account, we formulate the problem as a linear program to find the optimal solution in polynomial time. To establish the negative result, we relate our problem to the problem of minimizing the seek time only. We show that, when the transfer time is ignored, there exists an optimal solution that assigns each file to a single disk, i.e., no files are split across disks. This observation helps us relate the problem to a well-studied NP-complete problem, allowing us to infer its intractability. We also consider single-object queries, i.e., queries which do not involve co-access of files. For a workload consisting of only such queries, we give a simple and fast greedy algorithm, and show that it always finds the optimal assignment of files to disks. This algorithm is much faster compared to the straightforward linear programming method.

The rest of this paper is organized as follows. Section 2 presents algorithms for single-object queries. Section 3 investigates the structure of database layout while minimizing only the transfer time, providing an optimal algorithm for this objective function. Section 4 investigates the structure of database layout while minimizing only the seek time. Section 5 deals with the problem of minimizing the combination of transfer and seek times. Finally, we conclude in Section 6 with an overview of some related work in this area.

2   A Fast Greedy Algorithm for Single Object Queries

In this section, we present an efficient algorithm to find the optimal assignment for single-object queries. Since each query consists of only one file, there is no random access cost, i.e., we have to consider only the transfer time for each file, and $P(q)$ reduces to $\max_{j \in D}\{r_{ij}\alpha_j\}$ for a query q accessing file i. Also, let ϕ_i denote the access frequency for file i.

If the disks are homogeneous, then it is clear that striping each file uniformly across all disks is an optimal solution. Instead, we analyze the general case where the disks are heterogeneous, and the files can be of different sizes. Notice that we could write a linear program (LP) to solve any single-object query instance, but here we present an optimal greedy algorithm, which is simpler and faster than the LP approach.

The greedy algorithm is as follows. Consider the files one by one, in decreasing order of their frequency ϕ_i. For file i, we first attempt to split file i across all m disks so the transfer time of file i is uniform across all disks. If such an assignment does not violate the capacity constraint for any disk, then assign file i accordingly and remove it from our consideration. We then proceed with the next file in order. Otherwise, let L'_j denote the currently available capacity of disk j and let $\kappa = \min_j \{L'_j\alpha_j\}$. Then we partially assign file i by setting $r_{ij} = \frac{\kappa}{\alpha_j}$ for each disk j. Clearly, the assigned portion of file i has uniform transfer time across all available disks, and no disk capacity is violated. In addition, there is at least one disk, whose load capacity is completely saturated after the partially assignment of i. The saturated disks are removed from further consideration, while the remainder of file i is considered at the next iteration. Notice that in each iteration, we either assign a file completely, or saturate the capacity of at least one of the disks. This implies that the algorithm terminates after at most $n + m$ such iterations. The pseudo-code of the greedy algorithm is presented in the Appendix.

We now show that the greedy algorithm produces an optimal assignment. We first prove the following lemma about the greedy algorithm.

Lemma 1. *After any iteration, let U be the current set of unsaturated disks. Then for each file i, $r_{ij}\alpha_j$ is a constant over all disks $j \in U$. Further, $r_{ij}\alpha_j \geq r_{ij'}\alpha_{j'}$ for any two disks $j \in U$ and $j' \notin U$.*

Proof. In the greedy algorithm, we always (partially) assign a file i to disks so that $r_{ij}\alpha_j$ is the same for all unsaturated disks. Moreover, once a disk gets saturated, no more files are assigned to it. This implies that for any file i, $r_{ij}\alpha_j$ for the saturated disks is no more than that for the unsaturated disks.   □

Let C_j denote the current load on disk j, i.e., the sum of all file sizes assigned to disk j. The above lemma gives us the following corollary.

Corollary 1. *After any iteration, let U be the set of unsaturated disks. $C_j\alpha_j$ is a constant over all disks $j \in U$. Further, $C_j\alpha_j \geq C_{j'}\alpha_{j'}$ for any two disk $j \in U$ and $j' \notin U$.*

Next, we prove the optimality of the greedy solution.

Theorem 1. *Let S be the assignment defined by the r_{ij}'s produced by the greedy algorithm. Let S' be any other assignment. Let Z be the total transfer time incurred by S and let Z' be the total transfer time incurred by S'. Then $Z \leq Z'$.*

Proof. Given an instance $\mathcal{I}$, let $\phi = \min_i \{\phi_i\}$. First consider the assignment S. For each file i, let z_i denote its transfer time weighted by its frequency, i.e., $z_i = \phi_i \cdot \max_j\{\alpha_j r_{ij}\}$. Let $z_i = z_i^A + z_i^B$, where $z_i^A = (\phi_i - \phi) \cdot \max_j\{\alpha_j r_{ij}\}$ and $z_i^B = \phi \cdot \max_j\{\alpha_j r_{ij}\}$. Further, let the total transfer time over all files be $Z = Z^A + Z^B$, where $Z^A = \sum_i z_i^A$ and $Z^B = \sum_i z_i^B$. Now consider any other assignment S'. Let r'_{ij} be the file assignments corresponding to S'. Define $z'_i = z'^A_i + z'^B_i$ in terms of the r'_{ij}, and $Z' = Z'^A + Z'^B$ as above.

We will show that $Z \leq Z'$ for all instances by induction on the number of files n. The hypothesis states that $Z \leq Z'$ for all instances with k files. The base case with $k = 0$ is clearly true. For the induction hypothesis, we assume that $Z \leq Z'$ for $k = m$. Consider an instance $\mathcal{I}$ with $m + 1$ files. Assume that the files are numbered in decreasing order of frequency ϕ_i. Notice that Z^A for instance $\mathcal{I}$ represents the total transfer time incurred by the greedy algorithm on an instance $\mathcal{I}_1$ consisting of files 1 through m in the original instance $\mathcal{I}$, with file i having frequency $\phi_i - \phi$. This is because each file's frequency is reduced uniformly by ϕ, so the relative order of the files remains unchanged. The greedy algorithm would consider these m files in the same order as in instance $\mathcal{I}$, and give exactly the same assignment of these m files to disks. Similarly, Z'^A represents the total transfer time on instance $\mathcal{I}_1$ under assignment S'. By the inductive hypothesis, we know that $Z^A \leq Z'^A$. Now we concentrate on Z^B. Consider an instance $\mathcal{I}_2$, consisting of all $m + 1$ files in $\mathcal{I}$, each with frequency ϕ. If we resolve ties such that the files are considered in the same order as for $\mathcal{I}$, then Z^B corresponds to the total transfer time incurred by the greedy algorithm on instance $\mathcal{I}_2$. Similarly, Z'^B corresponds to the total transfer time on the instance $\mathcal{I}_2$ under assignment S'.

Let l be the last disk that received some file assignment according to the greedy algorithm running on instance $\mathcal{I}_2$. By Lemma 1, we have that for any file i and disk j, $r_{ij}\alpha_j \leq r_{il}\alpha_l$, implying $\max_j\{r_{ij}\alpha_j\} = r_{il}\alpha_l$. Since the current load on disk l is $C_l = \sum_i r_{il}$, we have that the overall transfer time $Z^B = \phi\alpha_l C_l$. By

Corollary 1, in assignment $\mathcal{S}$, every disk j is either saturated, or has a current load C_j, such that $C_j \alpha_j = C_l \alpha_l$. Now consider the assignment $\mathcal{S}'$ that incurs Z'^B on instance $\mathcal{I}_2$. Let C_j' denote the final load on disk j in $\mathcal{S}'$. Then there exists a disk d, such that $C_d' \geq C_d$ for some disk d which is unsaturated in $\mathcal{S}$. This is because $C_d' < C_d$ for all unsaturated disks would imply that the total amount assigned by $\mathcal{S}'$ is less than the total amount assigned by $\mathcal{S}$. Thus, $Z'^B \geq \phi \alpha_d C_d' \geq \phi \alpha_d C_d = \phi \alpha_l C_l = Z^B$. Therefore $Z' = Z'^A + Z'^B \geq Z^A + Z^B = Z$. This completes the induction. □

This completes our discussion of single-object queries. In the rest of the paper, we will concentrate on the general model in which each query co-accesses two objects.

3   Algorithms for Minimizing Transfer Time

In this section, we develop algorithms that minimize the total transfer time only, while ignoring the seek time, for a workload consisting of queries that co-access two files. We show that the optimal assignment will spread files uniformly across all disks, if the disks have large enough storage capacity. We also present an algorithm to solve the more general case where disks have limited capacities. The following definitions will be used throughout the rest of the paper.

Definition 2. Let f_{ij} denote the fraction of file i assigned to disk j: $f_{ij} = r_{ij}/r_i$. Let $T(q)$ and $S(q)$ denote the maximum transfer and seek time, respectively, for query $q = (i, i')$: $T(q) = \max_{j \in D}\{r_{ij}\alpha_j + r_{i'j}\alpha_j\}$ and $S(q) = \max_{j \in D}(\min\{r_{ij}, r_{i'j}\} \cdot \beta_j)$.

By definition, $\phi(i, i') \cdot \max\{T(q), S(q)\} \leq P(q) \leq \phi(i, i')(T(q) + S(q))$, where $P(q)$ is the total disk access time for query q. In this section, minimizing the transfer time corresponds to minimizing the term $\sum_{q=(i,i')} \phi(i, i')T(q)$. We use superscripts to distinguish between different assignments, for instance, $S^{\mathcal{A}}(q)$ denotes the seek time of query q in assignment $\mathcal{A}$. When the context is clear, the superscripts are omitted.

Theorem 2. If disks have unlimited storage capacity, then each file should be split such that the transfer time is uniform across all disks, i.e., for each file i, $r_{ij}\alpha_j$ is the same for any disk j.

Proof. For each file i, let $\kappa_i = r_i \cdot (\sum_j \frac{1}{\alpha_j})^{-1}$ and $r_{ij} = \frac{\kappa_i}{\alpha_j}$. We first show that for a query $q = (i, i')$, $T(q) \geq \kappa_i + \kappa_{i'}$ in any assignment. The two files have a combined size of $r_i + r_{i'}$. Since we are only concerned with transfer time, it is equivalent to spreading a single file f of size $r_f = r_i + r_{i'}$ across disks. The best way is to set $\kappa_f = r_f \cdot (\sum_j \frac{1}{\alpha_j})^{-1}$ and $r_{fj} = \frac{\kappa_f}{\alpha_j}$. This implies that $\kappa_f = \kappa_i + \kappa_{i'}$, hence $T(q) = \kappa_f \geq \kappa_i + \kappa_{i'}$. The uniform assignment achieves this lower bound for each query, which implies its optimality. □

The above theorem applies as along as the disk capacities are large enough, i.e., $L_j \geq \sum_i r_{ij}$, $\forall j$. If some of the disks have smaller capacities, we can use linear programming to solve the instance optimally. Besides the variables r_{ij}, we introduce a new variable $x_{ii'}$, representing the transfer time $T(q)$ for each query $q = (i, i')$.

$$\min : \sum_{q=(i,i') \in Q} \phi(i, i') x_{ii'}$$
$$\text{subject to} : x_{ii'} \geq (r_{ij} + r_{i'j}) \alpha_j, \ \forall \ q = (i, i') \in Q, \ j \in D$$
$$L_j \geq \sum_{i \in F} r_{ij}, \ \forall \ j \in D$$
$$r_i = \sum_{j \in D} r_{ij}, \ \forall \ i \in F$$
$$r_{ij} \geq 0, \ \forall \ i \in F, \ j \in D$$

Clearly, the values r_{ij} obtained after solving the LP will be an optimal assignment of files to disks.

4 Algorithms for Minimizing Seek Time

Next we consider the problem of minimizing only the seek time, i.e., the term $\sum_{q=(i,i')} \phi(i, i') S(q)$. Our goal is to establish the fact that the problem of minimizing the total seek time is equivalent to the MINIMUM EDGE DELETION k-PARTITION problem, which is well studied. As shown at the end of this section, minimizing the total seek time for homogeneous disks is very hard to approximate, which implies that the general case of heterogeneous disks is at least as hard to approximate. The hardness result from this section will aid us in deriving a hardness result for the case of minimizing the combined access time.

Definition 3. [MINIMUM EDGE DELETION k-PARTITION PROBLEM]

INPUT: *A graph $G = (V, E)$, with weighted edges.*
OBJECTIVE: *Find a coloring of vertices with k colors $C : V \to \{k\}$ that minimizes the total weight of monochromatic edges (an edge is monochromatic iff its end points have the same color in C).*

In the next theorem, we show that if we insist that each file must be completely assigned to only one disk, then the problem of minimizing seek time is equivalent to the MINIMUM EDGE DELETION k-PARTITION (MEDP-k) problem. We define the INTEGRAL SEEK TIME (IST) problem as the one that forbids splitting files.

Theorem 3. *The MINIMUM EDGE DELETION m-PARTITION problem is equivalent to the INTEGRAL SEEK TIME problem, where each file must be assigned completely to only one of the m homogeneous disks.*

Proof. First, we reduce the IST problem with m homogeneous disks to the MEDP-m problem. Given files F, disks D and a query workload Q with query frequency $\phi(i, i')$'s, we create a graph $G = (V, E)$, where $V = F$ and $E = Q$. And the weight of the edge $e = (i, i')$, $w(e)$, is set to $\phi(i, i') \min\{r_i, r_{i'}\}$. Given a solution S to this created instance of the MEDP-m problem, we produce an assignment $\mathcal{A}$ for the IST problem as follows: a file i is assigned to disk j if and only if it was assigned color j in the MEDP-m solution. It is clear that the total weight of monochromatic edges in S is exactly the total seek time incurred by assignment $\mathcal{A}$.

We now reduce the MEDP-m problem to the IST problem. Given $G = (V, E)$ and $w(e)$, we create an instance, where $F = V$, $|D| = m$, $Q = E$, and $\phi(i, i') = w(e)$ for each edge $e = (i, i')$. Each file i has unit size, and each of the m disks has seek rate 1. Given any assignment $\mathcal{A}$ of the created instance, we then produce a solution S to the MEDP-m problem as follows: vertex i is assigned color j if and only if it was assigned to disk j in $\mathcal{A}$. Clearly, the total seek time in $\mathcal{A}$ is the same as the total weight of monochromatic edges in S. $\square$

However, in general an optimal assignment to the original problem of minimizing the total seek time need not be integral, i.e., a file could be split across multiple disks. We distinguish between these two types of assignment: *integral* and *fractional.*

Definition 4. *An integral assignment of files to disks is the one that assigns each file completely to one of the disks. A fractional assignment allows a file to be split across multiple disks.*

We aim to show that for every fractional assignment, one can find an integral assignment with equal or less total seek time. This will imply that the problem of minimizing the total seek time is equivalent to the IST problem. But we first show a weaker statement.

Lemma 2. *For any assignment $\mathcal{A}$ with total seek time $C_{\mathcal{A}}$, there exists an integral assignment $\mathcal{A}'$ with total seek time $C_{\mathcal{A}'}$, where $C_{\mathcal{A}'} \leq 2C_{\mathcal{A}}$.*

Proof. Recall that f_{ij} denotes the fraction of file i assigned to disk j in $\mathcal{A}$. Thus, $\sum_j f_{ij} = 1$ for all i. We create the *integral* assignment $\mathcal{A}'$ via a randomized algorithm. In $\mathcal{A}'$, we assign file i to disk j with probability f_{ij}. Next, we bound the total seek time incurred in $\mathcal{A}'$. Consider any query $q = (i, i')$. In $\mathcal{A}$, the seek time incurred in co-accessing files i and i' is $S^{\mathcal{A}}(q) = \max_j\{\min\{r_i f_{ij} \beta_j, r_{i'} f_{i'j} \beta_j\}\}$. Let $g = \max_j\{\min\{f_{ij} \beta_j, f_{i'j} \beta_j\}\}$, then $S^{\mathcal{A}}(q) \geq g \cdot \min\{r_i, r_{i'}\}$. In the assignment $\mathcal{A}'$, if files i and i' are assigned to different disks, then there is no seek time incurred in co-accessing files i and i'. If files i and i' are assigned to the same disk j, then the seek time becomes $\beta_j \cdot \min\{r_i, r_{i'}\}$. The probability of both the files i and i' being assigned to disks j is $f_{ij} \cdot f_{i'j}$. Observe that $f_{ij} \cdot f_{i'j} \cdot \beta_j \leq g \cdot (f_{ij} + f_{i'j})$. This implies the expected total seek time for $\mathcal{A}'$ is given by

$$S^{\mathcal{A}'}(q) = \min\{r_i, \ r_{i'}\} \cdot \sum_j f_{ij} \cdot f_{i'j} \cdot \beta_j$$

$$\leq \min\{r_i, \ r_{i'}\} \cdot \sum_j g \cdot (f_{ij} + f_{i'j})$$

$$= \min\{r_i, \ r_{i'}\} \cdot g \cdot (\sum_j f_{ij} + \sum_j f_{i'j})$$

$$= 2g \cdot \min\{r_i, \ r_{i'}\}$$

$$\leq 2S^{\mathcal{A}}(q)$$

Since $C_{\mathcal{A}} = \sum_{q=(i,i')\in Q} \phi(i,i')S^{\mathcal{A}}(q)$ and $C_{\mathcal{A}'} = \sum_{q=(i,i')\in Q} \phi(i,i')S^{\mathcal{A}'}(q)$, we conclude that $C_{\mathcal{A}'} \leq 2C_{\mathcal{A}}$. We just showed that the expected seek time for the integral solutions returned by the randomized algorithm is no more than $2C_{\mathcal{A}}$. This implies the existence of an integral assignment with seek time no more than $2C_{\mathcal{A}}$. □

We note that the factor 2 is tight for this randomized rounding procedure. Consider the following fractional assignment for two unit size files and two identical disks with seek rate 1: $r_{11} = r_{22} = \epsilon$ and $r_{12} = r_{21} = 1 - \epsilon$. Thus the seek time $S^{\mathcal{A}}$ for the query $q = (1,2)$ is ϵ. After randomized rounding of this fractional assignment, the two files collide with probability $2\epsilon(1-\epsilon)$, for an expected seek time $S^{\mathcal{A}'}$ of $2\epsilon(1-\epsilon)$. The ratio of $S^{\mathcal{A}}$ to $S^{\mathcal{A}'}$ approaches 2 as $\epsilon \to 0$.

Next, we will show that there exists an integral assignment which is as good as the optimal *fractional* assignment. We first prove a weaker property for which we need to introduce the following notation.

Definition 5. *Define $c_{ij} = r_{ij}\beta_j$, the potential seek time of file i on disk j. For each file i, define $c_i^{\min} = \min_j\{c_{ij} : c_{ij} \neq 0\}$ and $c_i^{\max} = \max_j\{c_{ij}\}$. Let U (for unequally split) denote the set of files i such that $c_i^{\max} \neq c_i^{\min}$. Define $\lambda = \min_{i \in U}\{c_i^{\min}\}$. Let $V = \{z_1, z_2, \ldots, z_k\} \subseteq U$ denote the set of files such that $c_i^{\min} = \lambda$, for $i \in V$. For an assignment $\mathcal{A}$, define the stretch of $\mathcal{A}$ as $R(A) = \max_{z_i \in V}\{c_{z_i}^{\max} - c_{z_i}^{\min}\}$.*

Lemma 3. *There exists an optimal fractional solution, such that each file is split uniformly in terms of potential seek time across a subset of disks, i.e., for each file i there exists a constant c_i, such that $c_{ij} \in \{0, c_i\}$ for all disks j.*

Proof. We prove this by contradiction. Suppose every optimal *fractional* assignment violates this property. Let $\mathcal{A}$ be the optimal fractional assignment with the minimum stretch $R(A)$. In $\mathcal{A}$, we count the total frequency Φ of queries of the form $q = (z_i, \star)$ with $z_i \in V, \star \in U$, and $S^{\mathcal{A}}(q) = c_{z_i}^{\min} = \lambda$, or of the form $q = (z_i, \star)$ with $z_i \in V, \star \notin U$, $S^{\mathcal{A}}(q) = \lambda$, and $c_\star^{\min} = c_\star^{\max} > \lambda$. Since queries are unordered pairs of files, in the case of a query of the form $q = (z_i, z_{i'})$ with $z_i, z_{i'} \in V$, we only increment Φ once if $S^{\mathcal{A}}(q) = \lambda$. For each $z_i \in V$, we also count the total frequencies Ψ_i of queries of the form $q = (z_i, \star)$ with $\star \notin V$ and $S^{\mathcal{A}}(q) = c_{z_i}^{\max}$, or of the form $q = (z_i, \star)$ with $\star \in V$, $S^{\mathcal{A}}(q) = c_{z_i}^{\max}$, and $c_\star^{\max} > c_{z_i}^{\max}$. In addition, for each query of the form $q = (z_i, z_{i'})$, we keep a counter $\Psi_{ii'}$, which is set to $\Psi_{ii'} = \phi(i, i')$ if $S^{\mathcal{A}}(q) = c_{z_i}^{\max} = c_{z_{i'}}^{\max}$, and is set to 0 otherwise.

Notice that for any query $q = (i, i')$, we have $S^{\mathcal{A}}(q) \leq c_i^{\max}$ and $S^{\mathcal{A}}(q) \leq c_{i'}^{\max}$. Another useful property is that for any query $q = (i, i')$, if we increase r_{ij} by ϵ/β_j for all j with $c_{ij} = S^{\mathcal{A}}(q)$, then the new seek time for q is no more than $S^{\mathcal{A}}(q) + \epsilon$. Consider the following two possible modifications to assignment $\mathcal{A}$:

1. Increase the value $\lambda = c_{z_i}^{\min}$ by a small amount $\epsilon > 0$ (as determined later). We achieve this by increasing the value $r_{z_i j}$ by ϵ/β_j on disks j with $c_{z_i j} = c_{z_i}^{\min}$, for each $z_i \in V$. To balance out the assignment for files in V, we decrease $c_{z_i j}$ by an appropriate amount $\epsilon_i > 0$, on disks j with $c_{z_i j} = c_{z_i}^{\max}$, for each $z_i \in V$. The ϵ_i's are chosen as described below, and this in turn determines the value of ϵ. Let the assignment obtained after this modification be $\mathcal{A}'$. If a query q was contributing to Φ, i.e., $q = (z_i, \star)$ with $S^{\mathcal{A}}(q) = \lambda$, then $S^{\mathcal{A}'}(q) \leq \lambda + \epsilon$.

   Claim 1: There exist ϵ_i's and ϵ small enough such that if the query $q = (z_i, \star)$ contributed to Ψ_i in assignment $\mathcal{A}$, then $S^{\mathcal{A}'}(q) \leq c_{z_i}^{\max} - \epsilon_i$.

   We argue this as follows. As long as $c_{z_i}^{\max} - \epsilon_i$ is the maximum potential seek time for file z_i in $\mathcal{A}'$, $S^{\mathcal{A}'}(q) \leq c_{z_i}^{\max} - \epsilon_i$. To ensure this, an ϵ_i should be no more than the difference between the maximum and second maximum potential seek time of file z_i in $\mathcal{A}$. This upper bound on ϵ_i determines a maximum allowed value for ϵ. For each file $z_i \in V$, we determine the upper bound Υ_i imposed by file z_i on ϵ. By setting $\epsilon \leq \Upsilon = \min_i \{\Upsilon_i\}$ and then picking the ϵ_i's based on this choice, we also ensure that for the query $q = (z_i, z_{i'})$ with $S^{\mathcal{A}}(q) = c_{z_i}^{\max} = c_{z_{i'}}^{\max}$, $S^{\mathcal{A}'}(q) \leq c_{z_i}^{\max} - \max\{\epsilon_i, \epsilon_{i'}\}$.

   Claim 2: There exists an ϵ small enough such that in addition to the conditions mentioned in claim 1, the seek time of all other[1] queries does not increase.

   We argue this as follows. For a query $q = (z_i, \star)$ with $S^{\mathcal{A}}(q) < \lambda$, since we didn't change the assignment of any file with potential seek time less than λ on any disk, $S^{\mathcal{A}'}(q) \leq S^{\mathcal{A}}(q)$. For a query $q = (z_i, \star)$ with $S^{\mathcal{A}}(q) = \lambda$ and not counted towards Φ, we know that $\star \notin U$ and $c_\star^{\min} = c_\star^{\max} = \lambda$, implying that $S^{\mathcal{A}'}(q) \leq \lambda$. For a query $q = (z_i, \star)$ with $S^{\mathcal{A}}(q) > \lambda$, we just need to make sure that $\epsilon \leq S^{\mathcal{A}}(q) - \lambda$. Thus, the overall upper bound on the value for ϵ is $\min\{\Upsilon, \min_{q:S^{\mathcal{A}}(q)>\lambda} S^{\mathcal{A}}(q) - \lambda\}$. By choosing such an ϵ and then choosing the ϵ_i's appropriately, the total seek time for $\mathcal{A}'$ compared to that of $\mathcal{A}$ is increased by at most $\epsilon\Phi$, and decreased by at least
   $$\sum_{1 \leq i \leq k} \epsilon_i \Psi_i + \sum_{q=(i,i') \in Q} \max\{\epsilon_i, \epsilon_{i'}\} \Psi_{ii'}.$$

2. Decrease the value $\lambda = c_{z_i}^{\min}$ by the same amount ϵ determined in the first modification. We do this by decreasing the value $r_{z_i j}$ by ϵ/β_j on disks j with $c_{z_i j} = c_{z_i}^{\min}$, for each $z_i \in V$. Correspondingly, we increase $c_{z_i j}$ by the appropriate amount ϵ_i, on those disks j with $c_{\{z_i\}j} = c_{z_i}^{\max}$, for each $z_i \in V$. Let $\mathcal{A}''$ be the assignment obtained after this modification.

---

[1] Queries that are not counted towards Φ, Ψ_i, or $\Psi_{i,i'}$. A query $q = (z_i, z_i')$ is counted towards $\Psi_{i,i'}$ only if $\Psi_{i,i'} = \phi(i, i')$.

Claim: If a query q contributed towards Φ, i.e., $q = (z_i, \star)$ with $S^{\mathcal{A}}(q) = \lambda$, then $S^{\mathcal{A}''}(q) = \lambda - \epsilon$.

We prove this claim by considering three situations. If $\star \notin U$, then by definition, $c_\star^{\max} = c_\star^{\min} > \lambda$. The fact that $S^{\mathcal{A}}(q) = \lambda$ implies that $\star$ resides only on those disks j where $c_{z_i j}^{\mathcal{A}} \in \{0, \lambda\}$. We know that for these disks j, $c_{z_i j}^{\mathcal{A}'} \in \{0, \lambda - \epsilon\}$, and hence the claim holds. Else if $\star \in U$ but $\star \notin V$, then $c_\star^{\min} > \lambda$. In this case, the claim holds by a reasoning similar to the one above. Otherwise, $\star = z_{i'} \in V$. In this case, $S^{\mathcal{A}}(q) = \lambda$ implies that in $\mathcal{A}$, there is no disk j for which both $c_{z_i j}$ and $c_{z_{i'} j}$ exceed λ, and again the claim holds with a similar reasoning.

Next, notice that if $q = (z_i, \star)$ was counted towards Ψ_i in $\mathcal{A}$, then $S^{\mathcal{A}''}(q) \leq c_{z_i}^{\max} + \epsilon_i$. And if $\Psi_{ii'} = \phi(i, i')$, then $S^{\mathcal{A}''}(q) = c_{z_i}^{\max} + \min\{\epsilon_i, \epsilon_{i'}\}$. Regardless of the above choice of ϵ, this modification does not increase the seek time of any other queries which do not contribute towards Φ, Ψ_i, or $\Psi_{i,i'}$, since only the $c_{z_i}^{\max}$'s are increased. Thus the total seek time is decreased by at least $\epsilon \Phi$, and increased by at most $\sum_{1 \leq i \leq k} \epsilon_i \Psi_i + \sum_{i \neq i'} \min\{\epsilon_i, \epsilon_{i'}\} \Psi_{ii'}$.

If the first modification does not increase the total seek time, then we have found an optimal assignment $\mathcal{A}'$ with a smaller stretch value than $\mathcal{A}$, contradicting the choice of $\mathcal{A}$. Otherwise, the second assignment $\mathcal{A}''$ must have smaller total seek time compared to $\mathcal{A}$, since $\min\{\epsilon_i, \epsilon_{i'}\} \leq \max\{\epsilon_i, \epsilon_{i'}\}$. In this case, we have found an assignment with a smaller total seek time than $\mathcal{A}$, contradicting the optimality of $\mathcal{A}$. $\qquad\square$

Using the previous lemma, we now show the following.

Theorem 4. *There exists an* integral *assignment that is optimal, i.e., no worse than any* fractional *assignment.*

Proof. We prove this by contradiction. Suppose every optimal assignment splits at least one file. Among all optimal *fractional* assignments that spread the files uniformly in terms of potential seek time (by the previous lemma, there exists at least one such assignment), let $\mathcal{A}$ be the assignment which minimizes the number of split files. Let c_i be the uniform potential seek time for file i. Consider the file z with the largest c_i among all the split files i. For convenience, reorder the disks so that $c_{zj} = c_z$ for $1 \leq j \leq k$, where $k \in \mathbb{N}$. Let Φ_j denote the total frequency of queries of the form $q = (z, \star)$ with $c_{\star j} > c_z$, for disks 1 through k. Note that $S^{\mathcal{A}}(q) = c_z$ for these queries. Since z is the file with the largest c_z among all split files, $c_{\star j} > c_z$ implies that $\star$ must be completely assigned to disk j. Thus, queries that contribute to different Φ_j's are disjoint, implying that the total seek time for these queries is $\sum_{1 \leq j \leq k} \Phi_j c_z = \sum_{1 \leq j \leq k} \Phi_j \beta_j r_{zj}$. We modify $\mathcal{A}$ by completely assigning z to disk y with the smallest $\Phi_j \beta_j$, for $1 \leq j \leq k$. Let $\mathcal{A}'$ be the assignment obtained after the modification. Under this assignment, the total seek time for the queries that contributed towards Φ_j's is $\Phi_y \beta_y r_z = \Phi_y \beta_y \sum_{1 \leq j \leq k} r_{zj} \leq \sum_{1 \leq j \leq k} \Phi_j \beta_j r_{zj}$. For any other query $q = (z, \star)$ with $c_{\star j} \leq c_z$, the seek costs do not increase in $\mathcal{A}'$. This is because if $c_{\star y} = c_\star$, then the seek cost remains $c_\star$ as before; otherwise it becomes zero. Thus, overall

$\mathcal{A}'$ has no more total seek time than the optimal assignment $\mathcal{A}$, with one less split file z, contradicting the choice of $\mathcal{A}$.   □

The preceding theorem proves the existence of an *integral* optimal assignment. Our next theorem gives a polynomial time algorithm converting any *fractional* assignment to an *integral* one with equal or less total seek time, improving Lemma 2.

Theorem 5. *There exists a polynomial time algorithm, which for any given fractional assignment $\mathcal{A}$, finds an integral assignment $\mathcal{A}'$ with equal or less total seek time.*

Proof. We utilize the proof of Lemma 3. At each step, we either perform Modification 1 or Modification 2, whichever doesn't increase the total seek time. The first modification requires us to pick an appropriate ϵ. For this, the two sufficient conditions are:

1. We need to ensure that for each file z_i, $c_{z_i}^{\max} - \epsilon_i$ is still the maximum potential seek time for file z_i in $\mathcal{A}'$. For this, each ϵ_i should be no more than the difference between the maximum and second maximum potential seek time of file z_i in $\mathcal{A}$. This determines an upper bound Υ_i on the value of ϵ. Enumerating over all such z_i's, set $\epsilon_1 = \min_i \Upsilon_i$. Note that choosing $\epsilon = \epsilon_1$ decreases the maximum potential seek time of at least one file z_i to its second maximum potential seek time in $\mathcal{A}$, thus reducing the total number of different potential seek costs for file z_i by at least 1.

2. We need to ensure that $\lambda + \epsilon$ does not exceed $S^{\mathcal{A}}(q)$, for every query q with $S^{\mathcal{A}}(q) > \lambda$. For this, we can pick $\epsilon \leq \epsilon_2 = \min_{q:S^{\mathcal{A}}(q)>\lambda} S^{\mathcal{A}}(q) - \lambda$. Note that choosing $\epsilon = \epsilon_2$ also decreases the number of different potential seek costs for some file by 1.

We set $\epsilon = \min\{\epsilon_1, \epsilon_2\}$, and each execution of the first modification reduces the number of different potential seek costs for some file by one.

If the second modification is chosen instead, then reducing λ by ϵ does not increase the total seek time. In this case, by an argument similar to the one in Lemma 3, reducing $c_{z_i}^{\min}$ from λ all the way down to 0 instead[2] would not increase the total seek time either. This variant of the second modification also reduces the number of different potential seek costs for some file by one.

We have a total of n files, each file having at most m different potential seek costs in $\mathcal{A}$. This implies that at most nm modifications are needed to produce a solution with uniform potential seek costs for all files.

Next we utilize Theorem 4 to reassign each split file to a unique disk. We need at most n such reassignments, since each reassignment decreases the number of split files by one. Overall, the total number of operations is polynomial.   □

The above theorem indicates that the problem of minimizing the total seek time is equivalent to the IST problem. Together with Theorem 3, we establish the following equivalence relation.

---

[2] We set $c_{z_ij}^{\mathcal{A}'}$ to 0 for all z_i's and j such that $c_{z_ij}^{\mathcal{A}} = c_{z_i}^{\min} = \lambda$.

Corollary 2. *The problem of minimizing the total seek time with m homogeneous disks is equivalent to the* MINIMUM EDGE DELETION m-PARTITION *problem.*

The next two theorems are direct implication of the previous corollary, using results from the MEDP-k problem.

Theorem 6. *For every fixed $\epsilon > 0$ and every $2 - \epsilon < \alpha \leq 2$, it is NP-hard to approximate the total seek time within a factor of $O(n^{2-\epsilon})$, over instances with n files, $|Q| = \Theta(n^{\alpha})$ queries, and $m \geq 3$ disks.*

Proof. This follows immediately from the result of Kann, Khanna, Lagergren, and Panconesi [6], which states that it is NP-hard to approximate the MEDP-k problem within a factor of $O(n^{2-\epsilon})$, with n vertices, $\Theta(n^{\alpha})$ edges and $k \geq 3$. □

Theorem 7. *With two disks, one can approximate the total seek time within a factor of $O(\log n)$, where n is the number of files. For the problem with three disks, one can approximate the total seek time within a factor of ϵn^2, for any constant $\epsilon > 0$.*

Proof. The result for two disks follows immediately by the approximation result for MEDP-2 in a paper by Garg, Vazirani, and Yannakakis [5]. The result for three disks follows immediately from Lemma 9 of the paper by Kann, Khanna, Lagergren, and Panconesi [6]. □

5   Combining Transfer and Seek Time

In this section, we consider the problem of minimizing the combined transfer and seek time, a.k.a., the DATA LAYOUT (DL) problem. Recall that $\gamma = \max_{j \in D}\{\frac{\beta_j}{\alpha_j}\}$.

Theorem 8. *The optimal assignment $\mathcal{A}$, which minimizes only the total transfer time, is a $(1 + \gamma/2)$-approximation to the problem of minimizing the total combined transfer and seek time.*

Proof. For any query $q = (i, i')$, recall that $T(q) = \max_j\{r_{ij}\alpha_j + r_{i'j}\alpha_j\}$ and $S(q) = \max_j\{\min\{r_{ij}\beta_j, r_{i'j}\beta_j\}\}$. Note that $\min\{r_{ij}\beta_j, r_{i'j}\beta_j\} \leq (r_{ij} + r_{i'j})/2 \cdot \beta_j \leq \gamma/2(r_{ij}\alpha_j + r_{i'j}\alpha_j)$. We thus conclude that $S(q) \leq \gamma/2 \cdot T(q)$ for any assignment. Comparing $\mathcal{A}$ with any other assignment $\mathcal{B}$, we see that $\sum_{q \in Q} T^{\mathcal{A}}(q) \leq \sum_{q \in Q} T^{\mathcal{B}}(q)$, by the optimality of $\mathcal{A}$ in terms of transfer time. Also $\sum_{q \in Q} S^{\mathcal{A}}(q) \leq \gamma/2\sum_{q \in Q} T^{\mathcal{A}}(q) \leq \gamma/2\sum_{q \in Q} T^{\mathcal{B}}(q)$. Since $\sum_{q \in Q} P^{\mathcal{A}}(q) \leq \phi(i, i')(\sum_{q \in Q} T^{\mathcal{A}}(q) + \sum_{q \in Q} S^{\mathcal{A}}(q))$, we get that $\sum_{q \in Q} P^{\mathcal{A}}(q) \leq \phi(i, i')(1 + \gamma/2)\sum_{q \in Q} T^{\mathcal{B}}(q) \leq (1 + \gamma/2)\sum_{q \in Q} P^{\mathcal{B}}(q)$. □

Theorem 9. *It is NP-hard to approximate the* DATABASE LAYOUT *problem within a factor of $\rho \cdot \gamma$, for some constant $0 < \rho < 1$.*

Proof. We use a hardness result for a special case of the MEDP-k problem shown in [9], which states that for the class of graphs with unit-weight edges, it is NP-hard to decide whether the number of the monochromatic edges is 0 or at least $\rho|E|$, for some constant $0 < \rho < 1$. We reduce this case of the MEDP-k problem to the DL problem as following. Similar to Theorem 3, given a graph $G = (V, E)$, we introduce a DL instance with $|V|$ unit-size files, k homogeneous disks, and $|E|$ queries with $\phi(i, i') = w(e) = 1$, for every edge $e = (i, i')$. And for each disk j, we set $\alpha_j = 1$ and $\beta_j = \gamma$. If there exists a coloring of G for which the number of the monochromatic edges is 0, then there exists a corresponding assignment $\mathcal{A}$ of files to disks, such that $S(q) = 0$ for all queries q. Notice that for this assignment $\mathcal{A}$, $T(q) \leq \max\{r_i, r_{i'}\} = 1$ for every query $q = (i, i')$. Thus, the overall access time of $\mathcal{A}$ is no more than $|E|$. On the other hand, if for any coloring of G, the number of the monochromatic edges is at least $\rho|E|$, then by Theorem 3, the total seek time for any assignment is at least $\gamma\rho|E|$. Thus, it is NP-hard to decide whether the total access time of the derived DL instance is at most $|E|$, or at least $\gamma\rho|E|$. The ratio of these two values implies the hardness result. $\qquad\square$

6   Related Work

To the best of our knowledge, there is no earlier theoretic work providing a formal analysis of models that take into consideration the cost of co-accessing data objects in determining a database layout. Our results indicate that no algorithm can achieve an approximation ratio better than $\rho\gamma$ on all instances, unless $P = NP$. However, this does not exclude the search for heuristics that perform well in practice. Indeed, our work was motivated by that of Agrawal, Chaudhuri, Das, and Narasayya [1], who studied some greedy heuristics and showed that empirically, they out-perform full striping. To this extent, our formal analysis complements the earlier work. On the other hand, our work indicates that striping files produce solutions that are close to the theoretical lower bound.

There has been a significant amount of work in the area of storage administration and management. Since workload and query plans change over time, dynamic load balancing has been the focus of numerous earlier papers [2, 3, 4, 7, 8, 10, 11]. Due to space constraints, we refer the reader to [1] for a detailed survey of this line of work.

References

1. S. Agrawal, S. Chaudhuri, A. Das, and V. Narasayya. Automating Layout of Relational Databases. In *Proceedings of 19th International Conference on Data Engineering*, 2003, pp. 607–618.
2. The AutoAdmin Project. *research.microsoft.com/dmx/AutoAdmin*.
3. G. Copeland, W. Alexander, E. Boughter, and T. Keller. Data Placement in Bubba. In *Proceedings of SIGMOD Conference*, 1988, pp. 99–108.

4. H. Dewan, M. Hernandez, K. Mok, and S. Stolfo. Predictive Dynamic Load Balancing of Parallel Hash-Joins Over Heterogeneous Processors in the Presence of Data Skew. In *Proceedings of PDIS*, 1994, pp. 40–49.

5. N. Garg,V.V. Vazirani, and M. Yannakakis. Multiway cuts in directed and node weighted graphs. In *Proceedings of 21st International Colloquium on Automata, Languages and Programming*, 1994, pp. 487–498.

6. V. Kann, S. Khanna, J. Lagergren, and A. Panconesi. On the Hardness of Approximating Max k-Cut and its dual. *Chicago Journal of Theoretical Computer Science*, 1997.

7. M. Lee, M. Kitsuregawa, B. Ooi, K. Tan, and A. Mondal. Towards Self-Tuning Data Placement in Parallel Database Systems. In *Proceedings of SIGMOD Conference*, 2000, pp. 225–236.

8. L. Lee, P. Scheuermann, and R. Vingralek. File Assignment in Parallel I/O Systems with Minimum Variance and Service Time. *IEEE Transactions on Computers*, 1998.

9. E. Petrank. The Hardness Of Approximation: Gap Location. In *Israel Symposium on Theory of Computing Systems*, 1993, pp. 275–284.

10. P. Scheuermann, G. Weikum, and P. Zabback. Data Partitioning and Load Balancing in Parallel Disk Systems. *The VLDB Journal*, 7(1998): 48–66.

11. R. Vingralek, Y. Breitbart, and G. Weikum. SNOWBALL: Scalable Storage on Networks of Workstations with Balanced Load. *Distributed and Parallel Databases*, 6(1998): 117-158.

Appendix: Pseudo-Code for the Greedy Algorithm

Algorithm 1 GREEDY

1: Sort files in decreasing order of their frequency ϕ_i.
2: Let $R_j = L_j$ for each disk j. {R_j denotes the available storage on disk j.}
3: Initialize each r_{ij} to be 0.
4: **while** There are files left unassigned **do**
5:    Consider the first file i in the list
6:    Set $\theta_i = r_i(\sum_j 1/\alpha_j)^{-1}$.
7:    Set $q_{ij} = \theta_i/\alpha_j$. {So $\sum_j q_{ij} = r_i$ and $q_{ij}\alpha_j = \theta_i$ for all j.}
8:    **if** $\forall j$, $q_{ij} \leq R_j$ **then** {In this case, file i is completely assigned.}
9:       $r_{ij} = r_{ij} + q_{ij}$
10:      Update $R_j = R_j - q_{ij}$, $\forall j$
11:      Delete file i from the list.
12:   **else** {In this case, there exists a disk with $R_j = 0$, i.e., saturated.}
13:      Find $\lambda = \min_j \frac{R_j}{q_{ij}}$
14:      Set $q_{ij} = \lambda q_{ij}$
15:      $r_{ij} = r_{ij} + q_{ij}$
16:      Update $R_j = R_j - q_{ij}$, $\forall j$. {Note one of the disks must be saturated.}
17:      Update $r_i = r_i - \sum_j q_{ij}$. {File i will be considered again in the next step.}
18:      Remove any saturated disks from consideration.
19:   **end if**
20: **end while**

Approximately Dominating Representatives⋆

Vladlen Koltun and Christos H. Papadimitriou

Computer Science Division, University of California, Berkeley, CA 94720-1776, USA
{vladlen, christos}@cs.berkeley.edu

Abstract. We propose and investigate from the algorithmic standpoint a novel form of fuzzy query called *approximately dominating representatives* or ADRs. The ADRs of a multidimensional point set consist of a few points guaranteed to contain an approximate optimum of *any* monotone Lipschitz continuous combining function of the dimensions. ADRs can be computed by appropriately post-processing Pareto, or "skyline," queries [14, 1]. We show that the problem of minimizing the number of points returned, for a user-specified desired approximation, can be solved in polynomial time in two dimensions; for three and more it is NP-hard but has a polynomial-time logarithmic approximation. Finally, we present a polynomial-time, constant factor approximation algorithm for three dimensions.

1 Introduction

In recent years there has been much interest in "fuzzy" queries in databases [5], in which a user seeks an object that is not maximal with respect to one criterion, but is "good" in several respects simultaneously. In a multimedia database, for example, we may want to find a document in the corpus that best matches specifications of color (such as "orange") and shape (perhaps "round"). In querying a restaurant database we may seek an establishment that is near our current location, of high quality, inexpensive, etc. MapQuest may want to return to a user a path that minimizes some combination of distance, delay, number of turns, tolls, fuel consumption, etc. Notice that, in the above examples, we assume that we know the precise valuations of the objects (documents, restaurants, paths) in various dimensions (shape score, color score, restaurant quality, tolls, etc.); the fuzzy part is that we do not know the exact objective that we wish to optimize—presumably some function combining all these criteria.

There has been much work within database research both in defining and implementing such queries. Among the approaches taken and subproblems attacked are these:

– Exploring principled, axiomatic ways that lead to the proper definition of the combining function (see, e.g., [5, 7, 8]). The main difficulty here (the interesting and elegant results in these papers notwithstanding) is that the combining function depends in crucial and complex ways on the application

---

⋆ Work on this paper was supported by an NSF ITR grant and a France-Berkeley Foundation grant.

T. Eiter and L. Libkin (Eds.): ICDT 2005, LNCS 3363, pp. 204–214, 2005.

and the intent of the query, and there are no universal rules to guide us here (except for some common-sense properties such as monotonicity).

- Assuming that we know a combining function, solving the algorithmic problem of retrieving *the k best items* with respect to this function [6]. The algorithms here are analyzed either in terms of an assumed distribution of the criteria values, or in a peculiar worst-case sense applicable to middleware algorithms. The k best goal is a reflection of the fact that, deep down, we are not sure about the combining function, and so we want enough results to cover as many possibilities as feasible.
- A more elaborate version of the latter method requests feedback from the user (such as singling out one of the k results as the "best," in a manner similar to Google's "more like this"), and uses this feedback to modify in a heuristic way the combining function and retrieve new, presumably subjectively better, results [4].
- A more radical and principled approach is to be completely agnostic about the combining function, and retrieve all objects that *could* be best under *some* monotonic combining function. This leads us directly to multi-objective optimization [12, 13] and to *Pareto sets*, most often known in the database literature as "skyline queries". These return any object that is not dominated (in all criteria) by some other object; it can be shown (see Proposition 1) that these are precisely the objects that could be best under some monotonic combining function. (If we know that the combining function is linear, then we have a convex, smaller variant of the skyline query, see Proposition 2.) There are algorithms that compute these sets as quickly as it can be hoped (see, e.g., [1]). The downside here is that the skyline set of a large multidimensional point set can be (and is typically) huge: The skyline set of a random n-point subset of $[0, 1]^d$ contains $\Theta(\log^{d-1} n)$ in expectation [2]. Hence, skyline queries will typically flood the user with a large portion of the whole database.

In this paper we introduce *approximately dominating representatives*, or *ADRs*, a refinement of the skyline queries that remedies the output volume problem at a small (and controlled) loss of accuracy. For any $\varepsilon \geq 0$ specified by the user, an ε-ADR query will return a set of objects $\{a_1, \ldots, a_k\}$ that has the following property: For any other object a in the database, there is an $i \leq k$ such that the vector $a_i \cdot (1 + \varepsilon)$ (i.e., a_i boosted by ε in all dimensions) dominates a in all dimensions.

The ADR concept was inspired by the work in [12] (see also [13] for a database-related application) on approximate multi-objective optimization, and our basic results are variants of results there. However, [12] focused on combinatorial optimization problems, where instead of a database of objects we have an implicitly represented exponential set of feasible solutions (say, all spanning trees of n nodes), evaluated by multiple cost functions. [12] did not consider the problem of minimizing the size of the set of ADRs, the focus of our technical results.

There are several variants of ADRs that could be advantageous under some conditions and could be offered as options in an implementation: Additive approximation instead of proportional; different approximations specifications for different criteria; the convex version alluded to in Proposition 2; and combinations of the above. In this paper we focus on the basic ADR (proportionate, uniform approximation of the whole skyline); our results can be extended painlessly to the other variants. The only exception is that, in a couple of our proofs we use the additive variant because it is simpler to explain (and is equivalent if one considers the logarithm of each criterion).

The skyline of a database (that is, the ε-ADR with $\varepsilon = 0$) is unique. For $\varepsilon > 0$, on the other hand, there may be many ADRs, varying significantly in size. However, an ADR can be considerably smaller than the exact skyline: We show that an ε-ADR has size $O((1/\varepsilon \log \frac{M}{m})^d)$—independent of n—where we assume that we have d criteria-dimensions, and that the values of each criterion are between m and M (Proposition 4). This is a worst-case estimate: Among the many ADRs of a database some will typically be much smaller, and our algorithms strive to find the smallest possible ADR for the given database and ε. For example, if the database has a "knee" or "sweet point" — that is, a point that approximately dominates all others — our ADR algorithms will find it and the query will return only this point. We show that an ADR is guaranteed to contain a close approximation of the optimum object under the (unknown) true combining function, as long as this function is monotonic and satisfies a Lipschitz continuity condition (Proposition 5).

Thus, the main problem that we attack in this paper is the following: *Given a set of n points in d dimensions and $\varepsilon > 0$, find the smallest possible ε-ADR.* We show that the problem can be solved in linear time in two dimensions by a greedy algorithm (Theorem 1), and is NP-hard in higher dimensions (Theorem 2). However, it can be approximated within a factor of $\ln n$ by a trivial reduction to the SET COVER problem. It is an open problem whether better approximation algorithms are possible; we conjecture that $\ln n$ is a lower bound for this problem (it is for the general set cover problem, see [10]).

We assume in general that we have computed the skyline query of the set, and our task is to post-process it to determine the smallest possible ADR (in the 2-dimensional case, our algorithm can be made optimal in the sense of [6], by running directly on the database).

Finally, we show that in three dimensions constant factor approximation is possible. The proof of this result extends to the present domain certain sophisticated results on coverings of two-dimensional geometric objects. A very sophisticated adaptation of those techniques is required, since the present situation is three-dimensional. The complexity of both the technique and the adaptation result in a huge approximation factor (currently about 200...). The point of our result is then that alternatives to the greedy algorithm exist in three dimensions (even though the current state of the art can prove only very conservative bounds for them), and thus the $\ln n$ lower bound conjectured above for unbounded dimension does not hold in three dimensions. Unfortunately, we know of no techniques that can establish an inapproximability results for lower approximation factors.

A final note: Very recently we became aware of independent work by Vassilvitskii and Yannakakis [15] which, even though on a different if related topic, reaches conclusions remarkably parallel to ours. They focus on multi-objective optimization problems, as opposed to static multi-dimensional skyline queries. Their goal is to obtain approximate Pareto curves with as few points as possible for the given ε. They approximate the optimum number of points within a factor of 3 in two dimensions; in three dimensions they show that no such approximation is possible, but they are able to obtain one if the ε is tripled or so. And in higher dimensions they show that even this is impossible.

2   Preliminaries

We assume that the database has been reduced to the values of n objects with respect to d criteria. Thus, a database A is a finite subset of $[m, M]^d$, with $|A| = n$, where $0 < m < M$ are assumed to be fixed. We say that $a \in A$ dominates $a' \in A$, written $a \succ a'$, if for all coordinates $i = 1, \ldots, d$ we have $a_i \geq a_i'$.

We further assume that all criteria are to be maximized. (Otherwise, a reversal of axis would do the trick.) The *skyline* (or *Pareto set*) of A is the set $\text{SKY}[A] = \{a \in A : \text{for all } a' \in A \setminus \{a\}, a' \not\succ a\}$.

We are not certain that the following justification of the skyline has been brought to the attention of the database community. Call a function $f : \Re^d \mapsto \Re$ *monotonic* if $a \succ a'$ implies $f(a) \geq f(a')$.

Proposition 1. *A point $a \in A$ is in $\text{SKY}[A]$ if and only if there is a monotonic function f such that $a = \arg\max_{a' \in A} f(a')$.*

Thus, $\text{SKY}[A]$ contains all possible optima of all possible monotonic combining functions. If we further know that f is linear, that is, of the form $f(a) = a \cdot c$ for some nonnegative vector c, then the possibilities are restricted in an interesting way: Define the *convex skyline* of A to be $\text{C-SKY}[A] = \{a \in A : \sum_{a' \in A \setminus \{a\}} \lambda_{a'} a' \not\succ a, \text{ for any } \lambda_{a'} \geq 0, \text{ for all } a' \in A\}$. The convex skyline omits certain points that are covered by convex combinations of others.

Proposition 2. *A point $a \in A$ is in $\text{C-SKY}[A]$ if and only if there is a linear function f such that $a = \arg\max_{a' \in A} f(a')$.*

$\text{SKY}[A]$ is typically quite large:

Proposition 3 ([2]). *If A consists of n points drawn uniformly at random from $[m, M]^d$, the expected size of $\text{SKY}[A]$ is $\Theta(\log^{d-1} n)$.*

Fix a database A and $\varepsilon \geq 0$. A *set of ε-approximate dominating representatives*, or an *ε-ADR*, is a subset D of A that has the following property: For every $a \in A$ there is a $d \in D$ such that $(1 + \varepsilon) \cdot d \succ a$. An ADR can be significantly smaller than $\text{SKY}[A]$:

Proposition 4. *There is always an ε-ADR of size $O((\frac{1}{\varepsilon} \log \frac{M}{m})^d)$.*

Proof Sketch. Subdivide $[m, M]^d$ into axis-parallel orthogonal domains as follows. Consider the set of values

$$V = \left\{ m(1+\varepsilon)^j \;\middle|\; 0 \le j \le \left\lceil \log_{1+\varepsilon} \frac{M}{m} \right\rceil \right\}.$$

V is a geometric progression with step $1 + \varepsilon$, minimal value m, maximal value above M and cardinality $|V| = O(\frac{1}{\varepsilon} \log \frac{M}{m})$. The j-th value of V is denoted by V_j. For any set of indices $1 \le j_i \le |V|-1$, for $1 \le i \le d$, consider the axis-parallel orthogonal domain

$$\left\{ a \in [m, M]^d \;\middle|\; \forall 1 \le i \le d \,.\, V_{j_i} \le a_i \le V_{j_i+1} \right\}.$$

The number of such domains is $O((\frac{1}{\varepsilon} \log \frac{M}{m})^d)$. We can create an ADR by picking one object in each undominated non-empty domain. ∎

Call a function $f : \Re^d \mapsto \Re$ *log-Lipschitz continuous with constant C* if $f((1+\varepsilon) \cdot a) \le (1+C\varepsilon) \cdot f(a)$. Most common combining functions (such as linear combinations, max, etc.) are log-Lipschitz continuous with constant one. The following generalization of Proposition 1 is a justification of ε-ADR:

Proposition 5 *Any ε-ADR contains a point whose value is within a factor of $(1+C\varepsilon)$ of the optimal, for any monotone combining function that is log-Lipschitz continuous with constant C.*

Proof Sketch. Let $a \in A$ be the optimum. There is an a' in the ADR that satisfies $(1 + \varepsilon)a' \succ a$, and thus $(1 + C\varepsilon)f(a') \ge f((1 + \varepsilon)a') \ge f(a)$. ∎

Finally, we point out a straightforward connection of ADRs with the SET COVER problem. For each $a \in A$ define $S_a = \{a' \in A : (1+\varepsilon) \cdot a \succ a'\}$. It is easy to see that, if D is an ε-ADR, then $\bigcup_{a \in D} S_a = A$. Hence, finding a good ε-ADR is tantamount to finding a small set cover. In fact, since all points in A are dominated by SKY[A], it suffices to consider the intersections of S_a with SKY[A]. This latter observation often yields faster algorithms, since we can pre-process A to compute SKY[A] [1] and select from this our ε-ADR.

3   Two Dimensions

Assume that the points are sorted in decreasing first coordinate. We introduce a greedy algorithm that, for a given ε, works as follows: Consider the point a with the highest a_1, and let $B[a]$ be the set of all points b such that $a \in S_b$.

Lemma 1. *There is a $b^* \in B[a]$ such that $S_{b^*} = \bigcup_{b \in B[a]} S_b$.*

Proof Sketch. Take b^* to be the point with $a_1/(1 + \varepsilon) \le b_1^* \le a_1$ with highest b_2^*; it is easy to check that S_{b^*} is a superset of all S_b's that contain a. ∎

This leads to the following greedy algorithm:

```
Input: Point set A ⊆ [m, M]², ε > 0
Output: Set of points D ⊆ A, the smallest ε-ADR of A
set b* = (M, 0) and D = ∅;
while there is a point a in A with a₁ ≤ b*₁ such that (1+ε)·b* ≱ a
do:
    select a to be the point with the highest a₁ among those;
    find the point b* with a₁/(1 + ε) ≤ b*₁ ≤ a₁ with highest b*₂;
    add b* to D;
```

Theorem 1. *The greedy algorithm computes in linear time the ε-ADR with the fewest points.*

Proof Sketch. It does compute an ε-ADR, because each chosen point b^* covers all points in A with first coordinate between the current a_1 (included) on the high end and the next a_1 (excluded) on the low side. Since a starts with the point with largest a_1 and in the end b^* dominates all points with first coordinate less than or equal to the current b_1^*, the collection D covers all of A. Optimality follows from Lemma 1, since b^* is always chosen to be the point whose S_{b^*} contains all other S_b's that cover the rightmost uncovered point in A. ∎

For efficiency, we can run this algorithm on the precomputed set SKY$[A]$, instead of A. Furthermore, it is not hard to see that a variant of this algorithm, alternating between the two coordinates, can be run directly on the set A and be optimized to stop at the earliest possible instant at which the ε-ADR has been found and validated, thus not examining large parts of A. This algorithm is optimal in the middleware sense of [6].

4   NP-Hardness

We show the following:

Theorem 2. *It is an NP-hard problem, given a point set $A \subseteq [m, M]^3$ and an ε > 0, to find the ε-ADR with the fewest points.*

Proof Sketch. For simplicity we shall consider the ε-ADR under the additive definition of approximate dominance; the multiplicative result follows trivially (either by imitating the proof or by considering the coordinates as logarithms).

The reduction is from 3SAT. We are given a Boolean formula with n clauses with 2 or 3 literals each. Set $\delta = 1/4n$ and $\varepsilon = \delta/n$. We shall create a set A of points, all lying just below the plane $x + y + z = 1$, such that the optimal ε-ADR of A reveals whether the formula is satisfiable.

The proof requires a number of gadgets. The *flip-flop* consists of the following points: $a = (-\delta, 0, 0)$, $b = (0, -\delta, 0)$, $t = (-2\varepsilon, -\varepsilon, -\varepsilon)$ and $f = (-\varepsilon, -2\varepsilon, -\varepsilon)$. The basic property of the flip-flop is this: $S_f = \{f, t, a\}$, $S_t = \{f, t, b\}$, and S_a, S_b are singletons. Thus a good cover will contain exactly one of S_t (which will mean a literal will be true) and S_f (false). Such flip-flops can be combined in tandem with the b point of one coinciding with the a point of the next to form paths that will propagate the values of the literals. There are six variants of the flip-flop, by permuting dimensions, and six more in which b is instead $(0, -\delta/2, -\delta/2)$. (These variants are needed for "bending" the paths.)

The *clause* gadget has points $c_1 = (-\delta/2, -\delta/2, 0)$, $c_2 = (0, -\delta/2, -\delta/2)$, $c_3 = (-\delta/2, 0, -d/2)$ plus other points $d_1 = (-\varepsilon, -\varepsilon, -2\varepsilon)$, $d_2 = (-2\varepsilon, -\varepsilon, -\varepsilon)$, $d_3 = (-\varepsilon, -2\varepsilon, -\varepsilon)$, and the non-singleton approximately dominated sets are now $S_{d_1} = \{d_1, d_2, d_3, c_2, c_3\}$, $S_{d_2} = \{d_1, d_2, d_3, c_1, c_3\}$, $S_{d_3} = \{d_1, d_2, d_3, c_1, c_2\}$. Thus if the three c_i points of a clause gadget coincide with the "true" endpoints of three literal chains, there is a way to cover all six points with one representative iff the truth assignment suggested by the choices in the literal chains satisfies the clause.

To complete the construction, we embed the set of clauses on the $x+y+z = 1$ plane as follows: We choose a point for every variable, a point for every clause, and a curve connecting each variable with each clause where it appears (we assume that each variable has one positive and two negative appearances). The curves are such that they are well-separated by at least δ, except of course for their endpoints and their crossovers. Then we have a flip-flop at every variable point (if the coordinates of the variable point are (x, y, z) then we add this vector to the coordinates of the points a, b, t, f of the gadget), repeat for the clauses, and we replace each curve with flip-flops in tandem.

Which brings us to the last gadget, the crossover. It consists of four points, $a = (-\delta/2, -\delta/2, 0)$, $b = (-\delta/2, 0, -\delta/2)$, $c = (-\varepsilon/2, -\varepsilon/3, -2\delta + \varepsilon)$, $d = (0, -\delta/2, -\delta/2)$, plus the points $tt = (-2\varepsilon, -\varepsilon, -\varepsilon)$, $tf = (-3\varepsilon/2, -\varepsilon, -2\varepsilon)$, $ff = (-\varepsilon, -3/2\varepsilon, -2\varepsilon)$, $ft = (-\varepsilon, -2\varepsilon, -\varepsilon)$. The coverage of these points is $S_{tt} = \{tt, ft, ff, tf, a, b\}$, $S_{tf} = \{tt, ft, ff, tf, b, c\}$, $S_{ff} = \{tt, ft, ff, tf, c, d\}$, $S_{ft} = \{tt, ft, ff, tf, d, a\}$, and thus represents a valid crossover between flip-flops (a, c) and (b, d). Placing this gadget where flip-flop paths cross completes the construction.

Let g be the total number of gadgets used in this construction. It is easy to see that the resulting set of points A has an ε-ADR with g points in it (that is, there is a way to choose a point from each gadget so that all of A is covered) iff the original formula was satisfiable. ∎

It is open whether the problem is MAXSNP-hard, that is, hard to approximate arbitrarily close. We conjecture that it is.

5   Approximation

As partial consolation for Theorem 2 we have:

Proposition 6. *There is a polynomial-time algorithm that approximates ADRs in any dimension within a factor of $\ln n$ of the optimum.*

Proof Sketch. By a reduction to the SET COVER problem, which is known to have this property. Recall the sets $S_a = \{a' \in A : (1+\varepsilon) \cdot a \succ a'\}$, one for each $a \in A$. It is easy then to see that ADRs are precisely covers of A by these sets. ∎

Three Dimensions

Moreover, when $d = 3$, a constant approximation ratio is possible:

Proposition 7. *There is a polynomial-time algorithm that approximates ADRs in three dimensions within a constant factor of the optimum.*

This is established using an adaptation of the SET COVER approximation algorithm of [3] that produces superior approximation factors in some geometric settings. The algorithm of [3] is actually an approximation scheme for the HITTING SET problem, which is dual to SET COVER. To describe the algorithm we first need to introduce some definitions.

A *negative octant* $O^-(a)$ (resp., *positive octant* $O^+(a)$) of a point $a \in \Re^3$ is the closed set $\{a' \in \Re^3 | a \succ a'\}$ (resp., $\{a' \in \Re^3 | a' \succ a\}$) of all points dominated by (resp., dominating) a. In more generality, the dominated region $D^-(T)$ of a set $T \subset \Re^3$ is the set $\{a' \in \Re^3 | a \succ a', a \in T\}$. Clearly, $D^-(T) = \bigcup_{a \in T} O^-(a)$. Define the dominating region $D^+(T) = \bigcup_{a \in T} O^+(a)$ symmetrically. Let $S = \text{SKY}[A]$ and let S^ε be the *ε-boosted* set $\{a \cdot (1+\varepsilon) | a \in S\}$. By definition, $D^-(S) \cap D^+(S) = S$. Denote the boundary of a closed set $\mathcal{R} \subset \Re^3$ by $\partial \mathcal{R}$.

For a set X and a set $R \subseteq 2^X$ of subsets of X, the pair (X, R) is said to be a *set system*. Given a set system (X, R) and a parameter r, a subset $N \subseteq X$ is said to be a $1/r$-net for (X, R) [9] if $N \cap X' \neq \emptyset$ for all $X' \in R$ such that $|X'| \geq |X|/r$. In other words, a $1/r$-net *hits* all sets of R whose size is at least $|X|/r$.

Theorem 3 ([3]). *Suppose (X, R) admits a $1/r$-net of size at most cr for a constant c, and such a $1/r$-net can be computed in time polynomial in $|X|$. Then a hitting set for (X, R) of size $4c \cdot OPT$ can be computed in polynomial time, where OPT is the size of the smallest hitting set for (X, R).*

Below we establish that the set system $(S^\varepsilon, \mathcal{O}^+)$ admits a $1/r$-net of size $O(r)$, where $\mathcal{O}^+$ is the set of all positive octants of the points of S: $\mathcal{O}^+ = \{O^+(a), a \in S\}$. Theorem 3 then implies that a HITTING SET for $(S^\varepsilon, \mathcal{O}^+)$ can be approximated within a constant factor in polynomial time. Due to the duality of HITTING SET and SET COVER, this yields a polynomial-time constant-approximation scheme for SET COVER on the system $(S, \mathcal{O}^-)$, where $\mathcal{O}^-$ is the set $\{O^-(a), a \in S^\varepsilon\}$. This doubles as an approximation scheme for ADRs in three dimensions, and implies Proposition 7.

It remains to derive a polynomial-time algorithm for computing $1/r$-nets of size $O(r)$ for $(S^\varepsilon, \mathcal{O}^+)$. It is clearly sufficient to solve this task when $\mathcal{O}^+$ is the set $\{O^+(a), a \in \Re^3\}$. We accomplish this by adapting the $1/r$-net construction scheme of Matoušek et al. [11]. Unfortunately, the size of the $1/r$-nets constructed using this scheme is close to $100r$. Improving the constant of proportionality in the construction is an interesting open problem.

Matoušek et al. [11] show how to construct a $1/r$-net of size $O(r)$ for a set system (X, F), such that X is a set of points in the plane and F is a *family of pseudo-disks*. A family F of compact sets in the plane is called a family of pseudo-disks if any three points $x, y, z \in \Re^2$ define a unique set $f \in F$, such that $x, y, z \in \partial f$. For instance, homothetic copies of a convex set are a family of pseudo-disks. Matoušek et al. [11] additionally require that the pseudo-disks are convex and smooth. To describe their construction further we need to define the F-*Delauney graph* of X. Two points $x, y \in X$ are F-Delauney neighbors if there exists a set $f \in F$, such that x, y are on the boundary of f and no point of X is contained in the interior of F. The geometric graph whose vertices are the points of X, such that F-Delauney neighbors are connected by straight edges, is the F-Delauney graph of X. When the pseudo-disks are convex and smooth, as assumed in [11], the F-Delauney graph is a triangulation.

The construction of [11] proceeds by considering a maximal collection $S_1, \ldots, S_k$ of sets of F, such that $|X \cap S_i| = n/6r$ and $(X \cap S_i) \bigcap (X \cap S_j) = \emptyset$ for $i, j \leq k$, $i \neq j$. (Special attention is given to the convex hull of X, but we do not expound on that in our brief overview.) Points of X contained in S_i are said to have color i. Now consider the F-Delauney graph of X and let its triangular face be called *bi-colored* if exactly two of its vertices are of the same color. Let an edge of the graph be called bi-colored if its vertices have distinct colors. Let a maximal connected chain of bi-colored triangles sharing bi-colored edges be called a *corridor*. Split all corridors into *subcorridors* of length at most $\lfloor n/6r \rfloor$ and let C denote the collection of these subcorridors. Every subcorridor of C is bounded by two bi-colored edges and two (potentially empty) chains of uni-colored edges. Let the (not necessarily distinct) end-points of these bi-colored edges be called the *corners* of the subcorridor. Let N denote the set of corners of the subcorridors of C. Matoušek et al. [11] prove that N has size $O(r)$ and is a $1/r$-net for (X, F). (Actually, they modify the above construction slightly to simplify the proof, but this is not essential here.)

We now show how to adapt the above construction to our setting. Consider a point $o \in \Re^3$, such that o is dominated by all points in S. Consider a horizontal plane Π that lies above all points of S^ε. Let Γ denote the surface $\partial D^+(S^\varepsilon)$. For a set $c \subseteq \Gamma$, define its projection c^* to be $\bigcup_{p \in c} l_{o,p} \cap \Pi$, where $l_{o,p}$ is the line spanned by o and p. Let S^* be the projection of S^ε. Let C be the family of curves $\{O^+(a) \cap \Gamma, a \in \Re^3\}$ on Γ. Let F be the set of projections of the curves of C. It is easy to see that the set system (S^ε, O^+) described above is equivalent to the set system (S^*, F), so it is sufficient to construct a $1/r$-net for the latter.

Consider the collection of bounded facets of Γ, projected onto Π. This region is called the *active region* of Π. It is easy to see that F is a family of pseudo-disks within the active region. We want to apply the construction of [11] in the context of the set system (S^*, F). However, the pseudo-disks under consideration are neither smooth nor convex, and the notions of "convex hull", "halfplane" and "Delauney graph", which are all essential in the construction and its analysis, have to be redefined in this context. We briefly sketch these adaptations below, defining the notions of F-*hull*, F-*halfplane* and F-*Delauney graph*.

Define the F-hull of the point set S^* to be the boundary of the active region. Given a point $a \in \Re^3$, consider moving this point in the negative x_1- (resp., x_2-, x_3-) direction. In the limit, the octant $O^+(a)$ becomes a quadrant Q. The projection of $Q \cap \Gamma$ is said to be an F-halfplane. It is easy to verify that any two points $a, b \in \Pi$ in general position span exactly two F-halfplanes. Consider now two points $a^*, b^* \in S^*$ that are projections of $a, b \in S^\varepsilon$, respectively. We say that a^* and b^* are F-*Delauney neighbors* if there exists an octant $O^+(x)$, for $x \in \Re^3$, such that $a, b \in \partial O^+(x)$ and no other point of S^ε is contained in the interior of $O^+(x)$. Fix any such octant, if one exists, and consider the line segments (a, x) and (b, x). Projecting these segments onto Π yields a two-segment polygonal path that connects a^* and b^*. We let this path be the F-Delauney edge of a^* and b^*. It is easy to verify that no two F-Delauney edges cross and thus the F-Delauney graph is planar.

With the above definitions we retrace the construction of [11] in the plane Π on the set system (S^*, F). A technical adaptation of the analysis in [11] shows that the construction correctly produces a $1/r$-net for (S^*, F) of size $O(r)$ in polynomial time. We can now plug this into Theorem 3 and finally complete the proof of Proposition 7.

6   Discussion and Open Problems

Can the lower bound for the set cover problem in [10] be extended to the high-dimensional ADR problem?

On the positive side, is there a better approximation ratio for 3-dimensional ADRs? We suspect that the answer is positive. Does the technique extend to more dimensions? The technique employed is very dimension-specific, and key insights in higher-dimensional computational geometry would be required for such progress. Are there limits to approximation of ADRs? We suspect that a more careful reduction would produce a minuscule such limit; larger lower bounds would probably require specialized PCPs (of which, by the way, none is known to us for geometric problems). In fact, we conjecture that a $\ln n$ lower bound is possible if the dimension is unbounded (by reversing the reduction to SET COVER).

This work also suggests some interesting experiments: How do our algorithms (exact and approximate ones) behave in practice? And are the results of ADR queries satisfactory to users in typical situations?

References

1. Wolf-Tilo Balke, Ulrich Güntzer, Jason Xin Zheng "Efficient Distributed Skylining for Web Information Systems," *EDBT 2004*, Heraklion, Crete, Greece, to appear in 2004.
2. J. L. Bentley, H. T. Kung, M. Schkolnick, C. D. Thompson "On the average number of maxima in a set of vectors and applications," *JACM 25*, pp. 536–543, 1978.
3. Hervé Brönnimann, Michael T. Goodrich "Almost Optimal Set Covers in Finite VC-Dimension," *DCG 14:4*, pp. 463–479, 1995.
4. Kaushik Chakrabarti, Kriengkrai Porkaew, Sharad Mehrotra "Refining Top-k Selection Queries based on User Feedback," *VLDB 2000*.
5. Ronald Fagin "Fuzzy Queries in Multimedia Database Systems," *PODS 1998*, pp. 1–10 (invited).

6. Ronald Fagin, Amnon Lotem, Moni Naor "Optimal Aggregation Algorithms for Middleware," *PODS 2001*.
7. Ronald Fagin "Combining Fuzzy Information from Multiple Systems," *JCSS 58:1*, pp. 83–99, 1999.
8. Ronald Fagin, Edward L. Wimmers "A formula for incorporating weights into scoring rules," *TCS 239:2*, pp. 309-338, 2000.
9. D. Haussler, Emo Welzl "Epsilon-nets and simplex range queries" *DCG 2*, pp. 127–151, 1987.
10. Carsten Lund, Mihalis Yannakakis "On the Hardness of Approximating Minimization Problems," *JACM, 41:5*, pp. 960-981, 1994.
11. J. Matoušek, R. Seidel, Emo Welzl "How to net a lot with little: small ε-nets for disks and halfspaces" *SoCG 1990*, pp. 16–22.
12. Christos H. Papadimitriou, Mihalis Yannakakis "On the Approximability of Trade-offs and Optimal Access of Web Sources," *FOCS 2000*, pp. 86–92.
13. Christos H. Papadimitriou, Mihalis Yannakakis "Multiobjective Query Optimization," *PODS 2001*.
14. Kian-Lee Tan, Pin-Kwang Eng, Beng Chin Ooi "Efficient Progressive Skyline Computation," *VLDB 2001*, pp. 301–310.
15. Sergei Vassilvitskii, Mihalis Yannakakis "Efficiently Computing Succinct Trade-Off Curves," *ICALP 2004*, pp. 1201-1213.

On Horn Axiomatizations for Sequential Data*

José L. Balcázar and Gemma Casas-Garriga

Departament de Llenguatges i Sistemes Informàtics,
Universitat Politècnica de Catalunya
{balqui, gcasas}@lsi.upc.es

Abstract. We propose a notion of deterministic association rules for ordered data. We prove that our proposed rules can be formally justified by a purely logical characterization, namely, a natural notion of empirical Horn approximation for ordered data which involves background Horn conditions; these ensure the consistency of the propositional theory obtained with the ordered context. The main proof resorts to a concept lattice model in the framework of Formal Concept Analysis, but adapted to ordered contexts. We also discuss a general method to mine these rules that can be easily incorporated into any algorithm for mining closed sequences, of which there are already some in the literature.

1 Introduction

According to a large number of sources, the field of Data Mining attempts at finding methods to extract from large masses of existing data, that was not gathered for that purpose, new, sound knowledge that allows to take actions with specific purposes. One natural way to interpret the last condition is to look for causal relationships, where the presence of some fact suggests that other facts follow from them. This is one of the reasons of the success of the association rules framework: in the presence of a community that tends to buy, say, sodas together with the less expensive spirits, a number of natural ideas to try to influence the behavior of the buyers and profit from the pattern easily come up.

However, association is not causality, even though it is frequently interpreted in that way (most of the times implicitly). As a token, one of the criticisms of the *lift* measure for the strength of association rules is its symmetry, which makes it impossible to "orient the rules", that is, disguise the association as causality. Along the same lines, criticisms of various sorts have been put forward for many other measures of the strength of implication such as confidence or correlation. The single case that would be beyond any such criticism is where the implication *always* holds. These cases have been named *deterministic association rules*, and are particularly interesting in domains coming from observations of scientific data, where underlying natural laws are actually causing the associations to appear in all cases [10].

An obvious criticism is that a single counterexample suffices to invalidate a deterministic association rule, and it could be due to data manipulation errors.

---

* This work is supported in part by MCYT TIC 2002-04019-C03-01 (MOISES).

T, Eiter and L. Libkin (Eds.): ICDT 2005, LNCS 3363, pp. 215–229, 2005.

However, this is not really an objection to the notion of deterministic association rules but simply a consideration that data cleaning techniques are necessary in any practical application of this notion; we come back to this point later on.

On the other hand, the central advantage of deterministic association rules is that they do not require to select, with little or no formal guidance, one single measure of strength of implication. Since they are pure standard implications, they can be studied in purely logical terms.

In fact, standard binary databases (as termed in data mining texts, even though they are rather just relations) of n attributes can be naturally viewed as sets of models (0/1 assignments to n propositional variables). Thus, from this perspective, association rules can be seen as propositional logic formulas capturing information contained in a set of models. Practically effective approaches to find such logical formulas have been proposed in the field of Knowledge Compilation ([3, 11]): among them, a prominent basic process is to "compile" the list of satisfying models, into a tractable set of Horn clauses ([8, 11]). Of course, it might happen that no Horn axiomatization exists for the given set of models; but then, a Horn approximation (the minimal Horn upper bound of the given theory, sometimes called the empirical Horn approximation) can always be computed.

In [2], the following is proved: if deterministic association rules are computed from data according to the published lattice-theoretic methods [9, 10, 14], the rules obtained axiomatize exactly the minimal Horn upper bound of the propositional theory given by the data. These lattice-theoretic methods are actually described in terms of *concept lattices* [7]; this framework allows also for the study of general association rules (see [15] and the references there) and functional dependencies (see e.g. [6]). Concept lattices are given by *closed* subsets of attributes and *closed* subsets of tuples, where all the tuples in a concept share the attributes of the same concept, and viceversa. The notion of closure can be defined in a number of equivalent ways.

However, mining closed sets of binary attributes is but the simplest closure-based data mining problem; our goal here is to extend these results into the case of ordered transactions [1]. In these applications, each input tuple no longer is a set of attributes, but rather a sequence of them. Standard examples, instead of typical market-basket data, are of a more structured sort, such as the sequence of actions on a single bank account. Recent work in [13] and [12] provides algorithmic solutions to discover closed sequential patterns, so that there exists indeed a notion of closure-based analysis for these sequences; but, so far, no notion of deterministic association rules for them. Our goal is to formulate a theory of associations for this ordered context, in such a way that

- it advances in the theory underlying the state of the art algorithms for closure-based analysis of sequences,
- it corresponds closely to the lattice-theoretic approach employed for the computation of deterministic association rules in the unordered case, and
- it allows for a precise logical characterization, similar in spirit to [2].

Our starting point is the model in [4], which formalizes a concept lattice of closed sets of sequences by means of a new Galois connection. Here, we contribute with the proposal of notions of deterministic association rules for ordered contexts, and we validate formally the proposal by exhibiting a logical characterization of the deterministic association rules with order that parallels the existing one for unordered contexts. We also discuss the integration of the computation of these rules with existing algorithms to mine closed sequences.

2   Preliminaries

Let $\mathcal{I} = \{i_1, \ldots, i_n\}$ be a finite set of items. These will be our atomic objects. *Itemsets* are subsets $I_i \subseteq \mathcal{I}$. Since actually n is unbounded, we could alternatively have an infinite set of items from which, at every moment, only the finitely many ones appearing in a given dataset are relevant.

Sequences are ordered lists of itemsets. The set of all the possible sequences will be noted by $\mathcal{S}$. Here we are following the same framework for modeling sequences or temporal data tuples as in [1] or [13], whose closed sequential patterns (that will be later introduced) were formally characterized in our previous work [4], and which we seek in this paper to complement with adequate notions of association rules. Thus, our data consists of a database of ordered transactions that we model as a set of sequences, $\mathcal{D} = \{s_1, s_2, \ldots s_n\}$. Our notation for the component itemsets of a given sequence will be $s = \langle (I_1)(I_2) \ldots (I_n) \rangle$, meaning that itemset I_i occurs before itemset I_j for $i < j$.

An alternative view of our data, borrowed from Formal Concept Analysis, is in the form of an ordered context; *objects* of the context are sequences, *attributes* of the context are items, and the database becomes a ternary relation, subset of $\mathcal{O} \times \mathcal{I} \times \mathbb{N}$, in which each tuple $\langle o, i, t \rangle$ indicates that item i appears in the t-th element of the object o. A simple example of the described data and the associated context can be found in figure 1, where each object o_i of the formal context represents the corresponding input sequence (or ordered transaction) s_i. The context for a set of data $\mathcal{D}$ is relevant to this work to see objects $o_i \in \mathcal{O}$ and input sequences $s_i \in \mathcal{D}$ as equivalent.

Seq id	Sequence
s_1	$\langle (A)(B)(C)(D) \rangle$
s_2	$\langle (B)(C)(D)(A) \rangle$
s_3	$\langle (B)(C)(A)(D) \rangle$

	A	B	C	D
o_1	1	2	3	4
o_2	4	1	2	3
o_3	3	1	2	4

(a)   Collection   of data $\mathcal{D}$

(b)   Context $\mathbb{K}$

Fig. 1. Example of ordered data $\mathcal{D}$ and its context $\mathbb{K}$

Sequence $s = \langle (I_1) \ldots (I_n) \rangle$ is a *subsequence* of sequence $s' = \langle (I_1') \ldots (I_m') \rangle$ if there exist integers $j_1 < j_2 \cdots < j_n$ such that $I_1 \subseteq I_{j_1}', \ldots, I_n \subseteq I_{j_n}'$. We note this case by $s \subseteq s'$. For example, the sequence $\langle (A)(D) \rangle$ is a subsequence of the first and third sequences in figure 1.

The *intersection* of a set of sequences $s_1, \ldots, s_n \in S$ is the set of maximal subsequences contained in all the s_i. Note that the intersection of a set of sequences, or even the intersection of two sequences, is not necessarily a single sequence. For example, the intersection of the two sequences $s = \langle (AD)(C)(B) \rangle$ and $s' = \langle (A)(B)(C) \rangle$ is the set of sequences $\{\langle (A)(C) \rangle, \langle (A)(B) \rangle\}$: both are contained in s and s', and among those having this property they are maximal; all other common subsequences are not maximal since they can be extended to one of these. The maximality condition discards redundant information since the presence of, e.g., $\langle (A)(B) \rangle$ in the intersection already informs of the presence of each of the itemsets (A) and (B).

We partially order also sets of sequences, as follows: $S \preceq S'$ if and only if $\forall s \in S \, \exists s' \in S' \, s \subseteq s'$.

2.1 Propositional Horn Logic

Assume a standard propositional logic language with propositional variables, noted by $\{v_i\}$. The number of variables is finite, and we note by $\mathcal{V}$ the set of all variables; but again, we could alternatively use an infinite set of variables provided that the propositional issues corresponding to a fixed dataset only involve finitely many of them (this is in fact the case of our application). A literal is either a propositional variable, called a positive literal, or its negation, called a negative literal. A clause is a disjunction of literals and can be seen simply as the set of the literals it contains. A clause is *Horn* if and only if it contains at most one positive literal. Horn clauses with a positive literal are called *definite*, and can be written as $H \rightarrow v$ where H is a conjunction of positive literals that were negative in the clause, whereas v is the single positive literal in the clause. Horn clauses without positive literals are called *nondefinite*, and can be written similarly as $H \rightarrow \square$, where $\square$ expresses unsatisfiability. A Horn formula is a conjunction of Horn clauses.

A *model* is a complete truth assignment, i.e. a mapping from the variables to $\{0, 1\}$. We note by $m(v)$ the value that the model m assigns to the variable v. The intersection of two models is the bitwise conjunction, returning another model. A model satisfies a formula if the formula evaluates to true in the model. The set of all models will be noted by $\mathcal{M}$.

A theory is a set of models. A theory is Horn if there is a Horn formula which axiomatizes it, in the sense that it is satisfied exactly by the models in the theory. When a theory contains another we say that the first is an upper bound for the second; for instance, by removing clauses from a Horn formula we get a larger or equal Horn theory. The following is known (see e.g. [8]):

Theorem 1. *Given a propositional theory T, there is exactly one minimal Horn theory containing it. Semantically, it contains all the models that are intersections of models of T. Syntactically, it can be described by the conjunction of all Horn clauses satisfied by all models from T.*

The theory obtained in this way is called sometimes the *empirical Horn approximation* of the original theory. Clearly, then, a theory T is Horn if and only if it is actually *closed under intersection*, so that it coincides with its empirical Horn approximation. These concepts are a cornerstone of the area of research known as Knowledge Compilation [3].

2.2 Closures and Galois Connections

The framework introduced previously allows us to cast our reasoning in terms of closure operators. A closure operator Γ on a lattice, such as the one formed by the subsets of any fixed universe, is one that satisfies the three basic closure axioms: monotonicity, extensivity and idempotency. It follows from these properties that the intersection of closed sets is a closed set.

In the main case of interest for data mining, the universe will be our set of items $\mathcal{I}$. Then, closure operators give rise to closed sets of items, generators, and deterministic association rules. *Closed sets* are those sets of items that coincide with their closure, that is, $\Gamma(Z) = Z$ where $Z \subseteq \mathcal{I}$. When $\Gamma(G) = Z$ for a set G and G is minimal for that resulting Z, we say that G is a *generator* of Z. One way for constructing closure operators is by composition of two derivation operators forming a Galois connection [7]. Implications of the form $G \rightarrow Z$ where G is a generator of Z, turn out to be the particular case of association rules where no support condition is imposed but confidence is 1 (or 100%) [10], [9]. Such rules in this unordered context are sometimes called *deterministic association rules*.

It turns out that it is possible to exactly characterize this set of deterministic association rules in terms of propositional logic: we can associate a propositional variable to each item; then transactions become models, and each association rule becomes a conjunction of Horn clauses with the same left hand side. Then:

Theorem 2. *[2] Given a set of transactions, the conjunction of all the deterministic association rules defines exactly the empirical Horn approximation of the theory formed by the given tuples.*

So, the theorem determines that the empirical Horn approximation of the unordered data can be computed through the Formal Concept Analysis method of constructing deterministic association rules, that is, constructing the closed sets of attributes and identifying minimal generators for each closed set.

In this paper we want to find a notion of deterministic association rules for the more complex case of sequential data (ordered context), and of course we would like to support our proposal by proving a similar characterization.

3   Deterministic Association Rules in Ordered Contexts

Of course, the first task is to make available a closure operator that fits ordered data and specifies sensible results on practical cases. The most relevant existing contributions on mining closed sequential patterns are given by the algorithms CloSpan [13] or BIDE [12]. The extracted closed patterns by those algorithms are said to be stable in terms of support, which means that the closed patterns are maximal sequences in the set of objects where they are contained. For instance, taking data from figure 1, we see that sequence $\langle (B)(D) \rangle$ is not a closed pattern since it can be extended to $\langle (B)(C)(D) \rangle$ in all the objects where it is contained. However, $\langle (B)(C)(D) \rangle$ or $\langle (A)(D) \rangle$ are closed (so, stable). We want to make sure that our theoretical notions fit appropriately these approaches. In fact, we do have already the closure operator set in place, through the Galois connection from [4], described below. There, two operators are defined in a formal context corresponding to sequences, and it is proved that they indeed enjoy the properties of a Galois connection so that their composition provides a closure operator.

Note that this task is nontrivial because it departs from the case of unordered transactions in the very definition of intersection. Whereas the intersection of two itemsets is another itemset, the intersection of two sequences (whether with or without the maximality condition we have imposed in the definition of intersection) does not in general result in a single sequence. So, the formal concept framework developed in [4] works with sets of sequences. Again, another difficulty arises, since ordering sets of sequences just by set inclusion does not give a Galois connection; using instead the ordering $S \preceq S'$ we have defined above does work, provided that the corresponding operators are defined adequately:

- For a set $O \subseteq \mathcal{O}$ of objects, $\phi(O) = \{s \in \mathcal{S} | \ s \ maximal \ contained \ in \ o, \ \forall o \in O\}$. This $\phi(O)$ is the set of maximal sequences common to all O, i.e., $\phi(O)$ represents the intersection of the input sequences equivalent to O.
- For a set $S \subseteq \mathcal{S}$ of sequences, $\psi(S) = \{o \in \mathcal{O} | \ s \ contained \ in \ o, \ \forall s \in S\}$. This $\psi(S)$ is the set of objects containing all the sequences in S.

As mentioned, these two maps form a Galois connection (proved in [4]), and so, we can get the corresponding closure operator from their composition. We will call $\Delta = \phi \cdot \psi$ the closure operator on sets of sequences; thus, by definition, a set of sequences S is *closed* if and only if $\Delta(S) = S$. Similarly to any other Galois connection, we can also consider the dual operator Δ^{-1} that operates on sets of objects (although this dual operator is irrelevant for our present contribution).

It is proved that this operator Δ can characterize the closed sequences of CloSpan or BIDE as those sequences s that belong to the closure of $\{s\}$. Indeed, the instrumental property that connects the closure operator with the CloSpan sequences is the following:

Proposition 1. *[4] All sequences in a closed set are maximal in it w.r.t. $\subseteq$.*

Then it follows that $s \in \Delta(\{s\})$ if and only if s belongs to some closed set, and therefore the result of a mining task for closed sets under our Galois connection is the same as the result of the CloSpan or BIDE algorithm.

As described in the preliminaries (and exemplified by figure 1), given the data sequences $\mathcal{S}$ on items $\mathcal{I}$ we can construct the relation R which contains the same information as the individual components of each input sequence; thus, from R we obtain the collection of all formal concepts each corresponding to a closed set of sequences, and partially ordered by $\preceq$. As in any other Galois connections (see [7]), it gives immediately a lattice $\mathfrak{B}(\mathcal{S}, \mathcal{I}, R)$ of formal concepts. For example, for the data in example 1(a), we depict graphically in figure 2 the corresponding lattice of closed sets of sequences. Together with each node S in

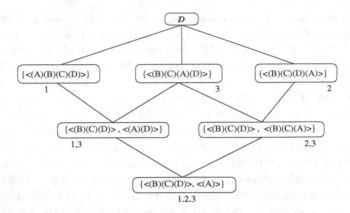

Fig. 2. Example of a concept lattice $\mathfrak{B}(\mathcal{S}, \mathcal{I}, R)$

the lattice, we have added as a label the list of object identifiers where S is maximally contained (thus, as happens in general in Galois connections, these lists form a dual view of the same lattice that, in our case, is ordered by set-theoretic inclusion downwards). We also can see in the figure that, for each input sequence $s_i \in \mathcal{D}$, the set $\{s_i\}$ is a closed set; this always happens in general, also.

The set of sequences contained in all the input sequences will be called the *bottom or infimum* of the lattice; in most cases it will happen to be a trivial, somewhat artificial, element containing only the empty sequence. Similarly, we can also add an artificial set of sequences not contained in any input sequence, so that it forms the *top* of the concept lattice. In the example showed in figure 2, an artificial top not belonging to any object is added to the lattice and we note it by the set of input sequences $\mathcal{D}$ (i.e. we assume that $\mathcal{D} \not\preceq \{s_i\}$ for all $s_i \in \mathcal{D}$). This artificial top is not actually necessary in the model, and it was not originally presented in [4]; however, we add it to the lattice just to the effect of our later arguments. We say that a closed set of sequences S' is an *immediate predecessor* of another closed set of sequences S if $S' \preceq S$ and no closed set S'' exists in the lattice with $S' \preceq S'' \preceq S$. For example, in figure 2 $\{\langle (B)(C)(D)\rangle, \langle (A)\rangle\}$ is an immediate predecessor of two closed sets of sequences: $\{\langle (B)(C)(D)\rangle, \langle (B)(C)(A)\rangle\}$ and $\{\langle (B)(C)(D)\rangle, \langle (A)(D)\rangle\}$. Notice that the Galois connection presented in this section may be extended to other kind of structured data such as graphs or trees; we are currently working towards this formalization.

3.1   Generators of the Closed Set of Sequences

We say that a set of sequences G is a *generator* of S if we have that $\Delta(G) = S$. We say that a generator G is *minimal* if there is no other G' s.t. $G' \preceq G$ and $G \neq G'$, such that $\Delta(G') = S$. We will only consider minimal generators. These will be graphically added to the concept lattice model by dashed lines, as showed in figure 3. Minimal generators of the top of the lattice are not considered here, but, for the sake of illustration, it is easily seen that $\{\langle (C)(B)\rangle\}$ is among them.

We can define a family of deterministic association rules for sequences.

222   J.L. Balcázar and G. Casas-Garriga

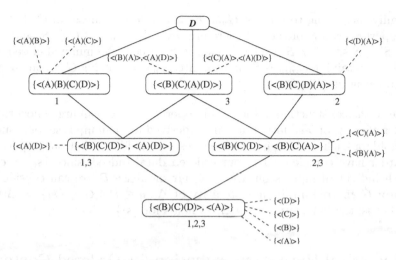

Fig. 3. Concept lattice $\mathfrak{B}(\mathcal{S}, \mathcal{I}, R)$ with minimal generators

Definition 1. *A deterministic association rule with order is a pair* (G, S), *usually denoted* $G \to S$, *where* $G, S \subseteq \mathcal{S}$ *and* $G \preceq S$ *s.t.* $\Delta(G) = S$. *We say that such a rule holds for a given set of sequences* $S' \subseteq \mathcal{S}$ *if either* $G \npreceq S'$ *or* $S \preceq S'$.

The following lemmas characterize exactly the relation between the generators and their associated closed set of sequences, and will be useful to prove our main result characterizing deterministic association rules in ordered contexts by means of Horn logic.

Lemma 1. *Let* $\Delta(G) = S$; *then* $G \preceq S$ *and, for all closed sets of sequences* S' *s.t.* $S' \preceq S$ *and* $S' \neq S$, *we have that* $G \npreceq S'$.

Proof. That $G \preceq \Delta(G)$ follows from the fact that Δ is a closure operator. We prove the following contrapositive of the rest: for closed sets S and S', if $\Delta(G) = S$ and $G \preceq S' \preceq S$ then $S' = S$. Indeed, by monotonicity of Δ, $\Delta(G) \preceq \Delta(S') \preceq \Delta(S)$ and, being S and S' closed, this translates into $S \preceq S' \preceq S$. Using here the fact that all sequences in all closed sets are maximal in them, it follows that $S = S'$. $\square$

Actually, this is just a rephrasing of the well-known fact that closure operators assign to each set the *minimal* closed set that is above it; in the standard case (unordered data) the comparison is by set inclusion, but here the peculiarity is that the comparison is according to $G \preceq S$.

Lemma 2. *Let* $G \preceq S$ *where* S *is a closed set of sequences, and assume that, for all closed* S', *if* $S' \preceq S$ *and* $S' \neq S$ *then* $G \npreceq S'$; *then* G *contains at least one minimal generator of* S.

Proof. Consider all subsets of G for which the same property indicated for G still holds. Since they are a finite family, at least one of them is minimal in the family (according to $\preceq$). Let G_{min} be this *minimal* subset of G that fulfills the property (or, any of them if there are several): $G_{min} \preceq G \preceq S$, and for all closed $S' \preceq S$ s.t. $S' \neq S$, we have $G_{min} \npreceq S'$. Then, the minimal closed set of sequences containing G_{min} is S, and so, $\Delta(G_{min}) = S$, being G_{min} one minimal generator contained in G. $\qquad\square$

Due to the construction of the closure operator Δ, we can argue now that all the rules of our proposed form that can be derived from an input set of sequences $\mathcal{D}$ do hold for each of those input sequences; we could say that our implications with order have confidence 1 in our ordered data. Indeed, since $\{s_i\}$ is closed for each individual input sequence s_i of our database $\mathcal{D}$, we can consider any generator G and obtain, by monotonicity of Δ, $s_i \in \mathcal{D} \wedge G \preceq \{s_i\} \Rightarrow \Delta(G) \preceq \{s_i\}$; that is, the implication $G \to \Delta(G)$ holds for $\{s_i\}$.

4   Empirical Horn Approximation for Ordered Contexts

This section comes back to the propositional logic framework and Horn theories and introduces background knowledge to define the empirical Horn approximation for ordered contexts. To motivate our choices, let us briefly discuss a feature of the analysis in [2].

Indeed, the first step there, is to see each unordered transaction as a propositional model, and this is easy to obtain since actually it suffices to see the items as propositional variables. We can see this conceptual renaming as an isomorphism, or, even further, by using as propositional variables the very set of items, the translation is a mere identity function.

But this is no longer the case in our ordered contexts. Taking as propositional variables simply the items would not provide a sufficiently structured translation of our data sequences into propositional models. Thus, our next goal is to propose a more specific mapping that considers the ordered context. The resulting empirical Horn approximation of the ordered data will allow us to characterize the association rules defined in the previous section.

By way of example, consider figure 1, where the first object consists explicitly of the sequence $\langle (A)(B)(C)(D) \rangle$; however, it also contains implicitly all the subsequences $s' \subseteq \langle (A)(B)(C)(D) \rangle$. Thus, each input sequence can be also seen as a tuple of all those subsequences contained in it. Now we assign *one propositional variable to each subsequence* of each input sequence; and restrict the family of possible models by this background knowledge, thus discarding all models that would pretend to include a given sequence s but simultaneously discard some subsequence of s.

More precisely, let m be a model: we impose on it the constraints that if $m(x) = 1$ for a propositional variable x, then $m(y) = 1$ for all those variables y such that y represents a subsequence of the sequence represented by x. For instance, if a propositional variable x corresponds to the sequence $\langle (A)(B)(C) \rangle$, then a model m assigning 1 to x should also assign 1 to the variable representing $\langle (A)(B) \rangle$, and similarly with other subsequences.

We define more specifically the interpretation of variables as sequences by an *injective* function $\xi : S \rightarrow \mathcal{V}$. For our convenience, we notationally extend this function with $\xi^{-1}(\square) = \mathcal{D}$, where $\square$ is the unsatisfiable boolean constant, and $\mathcal{D}$ is the notation for the set of sequences not belonging to any input sequence. Now, each input sequence s in the data corresponds to a model m_s: the one that sets to true exactly the variables $\xi(s')$ where $s' \subseteq s$; and we can find the empirical Horn approximation of the corresponding theory. It is important that the constraints we have imposed to the models, that when $s' \subseteq s$ then $\xi(s) \rightarrow \xi(s')$, are indeed Horn clauses, which we call *background Horn conditions*, and hold on all input models, so that they are imposed automatically unto the whole Horn approximation: the conjunction of all Horn clauses satisfied by all the models corresponding to input sequences. We call this conjunction the *empirical Horn approximation for ordered data*, and any model there can be mapped back into a set of sequences that is closed downwards under the subsequence relation.

4.1   Characterization

We are ready to present now the equivalence between the association rules extracted by the closure-based method presented in section 3, and the empirical Horn approximation for ordered data.

Theorem 3. *Given a set of input sequences S, the conjunction of all the deterministic association rules with order constructed as in section 3.1, seen as propositional formulas, and together with the background Horn conditions, axiomatizes exactly the empirical Horn approximation of the theory containing the set of models $M = \{m_s | s \in \mathcal{D}\} \subseteq \mathcal{M}$.*

Proof. We prove separately both directions for this theorem: 1/ that the deterministic association rules (that is, their corresponding propositional implications) are implied by the empirical Horn approximation; and 2/ that all the clauses in the empirical Horn approximation are implied by the conjunction of the (propositional implications corresponding to) deterministic association rules.

$\Rightarrow$/ Consider a deterministic association rule $G \rightarrow S$ s.t. $\Delta(G) = S$. By distribuitivity, we can rewrite the rule as a conjunction of different implications $G \rightarrow s_i$ where $S = \{s_1, \ldots, s_m\} \in 2^S$. As explained after lemma 1, all the input sequences having as subsequences all the elements of G must have also s_i, so that the translation of $G \rightarrow s_i$ is a Horn clause that is true for all the given models in M and, by the theorems in the previous section, it belongs to the empirical Horn approximation. Likewise, the background Horn conditions are also satisfied by all models and thus hold in the empirical Horn approximation.

$\Leftarrow$/ Let $F \rightarrow v$ be an arbitrary Horn clause where F is a set of variables, and v is a single variable. Assume this clause to be true for all the given models $M = \{m_s | s \in \mathcal{D}\}$ that correspond to the input sequences; note that these follow the constraints mentioned above: if $m \in M$, and $m(x) = 1$ for a propositional variable x, then $m(y) = 1$ for all those variables y such that $\xi^{-1}(y) \subseteq \xi^{-1}(x)$. In order to show that $F \rightarrow v$ is a consequence of the rules found from the concept lattice for S, we will find an association rule that, upon translation, and in the presence of the background Horn conditions, logically implies our Horn clause.

Looking at F as a set of variables, we can consider the set of corresponding sequences $S' = \{\xi^{-1}(v)|v \in F\}$; let $S'' = \Delta(S')$ be its closure. By previous lemmas 1 and 2, we know that S' will contain at least one minimal generator of S'', that is, $G \subseteq S'$ s.t. $\Delta(G) = S''$. Therefore, the rule $G \rightarrow S''$ will be one of the rules constructed by the FCA method.

On the other hand, we have assumed that the clause $F \rightarrow v$ holds for all the models M. By definition, it means that $S' \rightarrow \xi^{-1}(v)$ also holds in all the input sequences, in the sense that whenever $S' \preceq \{s\}$ for an input sequence s, also $\xi^{-1}(v) \subseteq s$; and this implies that $\{\xi^{-1}(v)\} \preceq \Delta(S') = S''$: so, for some sequence $s \in S''$ we have that $\xi^{-1}(v) \subseteq s$ or, equivalently, the Horn clause $\xi(s) \rightarrow v$ belongs to the background Horn conditions.

Finally, we have found that $G \rightarrow s$ is one of the rules composing $G \rightarrow S$, which is one of the association rules coming from the closure system. Since $G \subseteq S'$, the variables corresponding to sequences from G are all in F, and thus the clause $F' \rightarrow \xi(s)$ with $F' \subseteq F$ corresponds to one of the association rules. By subsumption, and one resolution step with $\xi(s) \rightarrow v$, we see that $F \rightarrow v$ follows indeed from the association rules plus the background Horn conditions. $\qquad \square$

Note that this proof works also well when the Horn clause is nondefinite, that is, when considering $F \rightarrow \square$. In this case no model from M satisfies all the variables in F, so, $S' \not\preceq \{s_i\}$ for all $s_i \in \mathcal{D}$; indeed we have that $\Delta(S') = \mathcal{D}$ (top of the lattice not included in any input sequence).

Our characterization brings meaning to the deterministic association rules extracted by the lattice method of ordered data. We have seen that they exactly correspond to the empirical Horn approximation under the necessary background Horn conditions. Next step is then to discuss the algorithmic consequences of calculating these implication rules with order, and to propose specific algorithms.

5   Computing Rules in Ordered Contexts

As mentioned before and proved in [4], the closure operator Δ characterizes the closed patterns of CloSpan [13] (which are closed in the sense of not being extendable in support, thus stable) as those that belong to a closed set. This fact makes CloSpan a good candidate algorithm to construct the concepts of our lattice model. Recently, a more efficient algorithm, BIDE [12], has been presented; according to the authors, it outperforms CloSpan being more than an order of magnitude faster; however, the output patterns mined by CloSpan or BIDE are exactly the same. To the best of our knowledge, these two algorithms are the only contributions to the mining of closed sequences up to now. The output of either can be used to construct the concepts of our model, just by appropriately organizing them.

However, computing the deterministic association rules in the ordered data (equivalently, the empirical Horn approximation for the ordered context) we seem to need as well all the minimal generators, in order to output all rules $G \rightarrow S$

where S is closed and G is a minimal generator of S. Thus, an important next step to add to any current algorithm for closed sequences is then the calculation of minimal generators for each closed set. We want to compute these minimal generators by means of a general method, so that it can be plugged into any underlying algorithm of mining closed sequential patterns such as either CloSpan or BIDE. In this way, after computing the closed sets of sequences, the chosen algorithm can directly calculate the minimal generators as well, without incurring in inconvenient overheads for intersecting sequences of the database. In this section we show how to compute minimal generators of a closed set of sequences S as a sort of transversal of appropriately defined differences between S and all proper closed predecessors in the lattice.

The difficulty of this proposal will rely on the formalization of both steps: 1/ what it is exactly the difference between two sets of sequences, and 2/ how to properly define the appropriate variant of transversal. The motivation to look for such an approach is that it can be seen that the concept lattice we have obtained is isomorphic to a standard concept lattice for which such a method of computing rules does already exist [10]; note however that it is not immediate to carry over the isomorphism into the generators, so that we prefer to develop our method fully within the closure operator on sets of sequences.

For comparison purposes, we quote here a result that we found in [10] and that we would like to export here, whereby the minimal generators of a closed set in the unordered context obtained by a closure operator Γ are characterized (the original statement differs from ours but their equivalence is readily seen.)

Theorem 4. *Let Z be a closed set of items $Z = \Gamma(Z)$; the minimal generators of Z are found as the minimal transversal hypergraph of the hypergraph of the differences $Z - Z'$ where Z' are the proper closed subsets of Z in the unordered lattice.*

The transversal hypergraph consists of sets that intersect each and every of the given differences (called *faces* in [10], a term that comes from related matroid-theoretic facts). Also, it is not difficult to see that it suffices to state that the generator intersects the differences with $Z - Z'$ for the closed immediate subsets of Z. For instance, let $Z = \{a, b, c\}$ be a closed set of items, whose immediate closed predecessors in the lattice are $Z'_1 = \{a, b\}$ and $Z'_2 = \{a, c\}$; then, the minimal generators of Z can be found by transversing the hypergraph of differences $H = \{Z - Z'_1, Z - Z'_2\}$, that is, $H = \{\{c\}, \{b\}\}$. The minimal transversal of H is $\{c, b\}$, and so it is the minimal generator of Z.

We would like to have a similar result as theorem 4 for the minimal generators of the closed sets of sequences.

5.1   Computing Minimal Generators for Closed Set of Sequences

We preserve here the term *faces* for our appropriate formalization of the differences between one closed set and its proper closed predecessors (according to $\preceq$); for closed S, each face of S is $S - S'$, where $S' \preceq S$ is a proper closed predecessor of S, and the difference is defined as

$$S - S' = \{s | \{s\} \preceq S \text{ but } \{s\} \npreceq S'\}$$

The main property now is:

Lemma 3. *Let S be a closed set of sequences and $G \preceq S$; then $\Delta(G) = S$ if and only if G intersects all the faces of S.*

Here by G intersecting a face $S - S'$ we understand set-theoretic intersection, that is, there must exist a common sequence in both. This corresponds to our notion of transversal for ordered data.

Proof. Assume first that G does not intersect the face $S - S'$, for some $S' \preceq S$; thus, no $s \in G$ fulfills the condition in the definition of the face. Since $G \preceq S$, for all such s, $\{s\} \preceq S$ as well, and this implies $\{s\} \preceq S'$, or actually $G \preceq S'$. Now, by monotonicity of Δ, from $G \preceq S' \preceq S$ and the fact that sequences in closed sets are maximal we obtain $S = S'$ just as in 1; and S' is not a proper predecessor so that $S - S'$ is not a face. Conversely, assume that G indeed intersects all the faces; from $G \preceq S$ and monotonicity again we have $\Delta(G) \preceq S$. Equality will follow as we need, if we prove that $\Delta(G)$ is not a proper predecessor. Indeed, by lemma 1, $G \preceq \Delta(G)$, so for all $s \in G$, $\{s\} \preceq \Delta(G)$, which negates the condition in the definition of $S - \Delta(G)$. Thus it can't happen that any s is both in G and in $S - \Delta(G)$, and this last difference cannot be a face because G intersects all of them. This implies that $\Delta(G)$ is not a proper predecessor.   □

Again, we only need to consider immediate predecessors: if G intersects the faces corresponding to immediate predecessors, it must also intersect the other faces, which are larger. Additionally, we may be only interested in minimal generators (according to $\preceq$) since non-minimal generators only yield redundant association rules. It is not difficult to see that this can be enforced by using only those subsequences of sequences in S that are minimal in their respective face for the construction of the generators as in lemma 3.

For a more graphical example of our method, let $S = \{\langle (B)(C)(A)(D) \rangle\}$ be a closed set of sequences, as showed in the lattice of figure 2; the proper predecessors of S are the closed set of sequences $S'_1 = \{\langle (B)(C)(D) \rangle, \langle (A)(D) \rangle\}$, and $S'_2 = \{\langle (B)(C)(D) \rangle, \langle (B)(C)(A) \rangle\}$. The minimal new subsequences in S not contained in S'_1 are $F_1 = \{\langle (B)(A) \rangle, \langle (C)(A) \rangle\}$, and the minimal new subsequences in S not contained in S'_2 are $F_2 = \{\langle (A)(D) \rangle\}$. Now, to find the minimal generators of S we must minimally transverse these differences, which are indeed the two faces of S, obtaining two generators: $G_1 = \{\langle (A)(D) \rangle, \langle (B)(A) \rangle\}$ and $G_2 = \{\langle (A)(D) \rangle, \langle (C)(A) \rangle\}$, which are exactly the minimal generators of S (see figure 3).

6   Conclusions

We have proposed a notion of deterministic association rules in ordered data, building on the fact that such rules for unordered data can be formally justified as implications in a propositional logic framework; our extension provides a way of mining facts where a set of subsequences implies another subsequence in the data, and proves that the mined rules can be formally justified as well by a purely logical characterization. We do that using the concept lattice model provided by the Galois connection and associated closure operator proposed in [4]: by means of minimal generators that imply a closed set of sequences of the concept lattice. Indeed, these deterministic association rules characterize exactly the natural notion of empirical Horn approximation for ordered data, which involves specifying a number of background Horn conditions that ensure consistency of the theory with the ordered context.

We have discussed as well the algorithmic consequences of deriving such implications with order. Since any current algorithm for mining closed sequences can be used for constructing the closed concepts of our lattice model, we just need to incorporate here the derivation of minimal generators. We consider the characterization of generators as transversals of faces, known in the unordered case, and we prove a parallel result in our ordered case. This provides a method that can be easily incorporated in any algorithm that constructs our closed sets in the appropriate order, such as the algorithms existing in fact for closed sequences, so that generators and association rules can be indeed inferred from just the system of closed sets. We are currently developing implementations of our methods to investigate their behavior in practice.

Other extensions of the basic itemset-based characterization are worth more research. A relevant property of the rules studied here is the need of absolute confidence; this can be inappropriate in two different ways. First, one may wish to take into account the possibility of small errors, such as miskeying, that make inapplicable a deterministic association rule; it is possible to adapt the case of itemsets to this consideration [15], which we consider a data cleaning problem rather than a data mining or relational problem. A second, inherently different case is the more usual application of association rules where more relaxed confidences are used. For this case, there is a large number of proposals of how to measure the strength of the implication; a survey and comparison, with appropriate references, is given in [5]. To our knowledge, there is no principled way to select one of them and know what one is actually doing through this choice; specific data mining software may allow only some of them, as a consequence mainly of research schools of their designers. In fact, most measures allow for examples of counterintuitive or misleading results.

We believe that it is possible to modify the definitions of Horn approximations so as to take into account the various forms of strength of implication, or at least some of them; so that, at the time of selecting one measure of strength of implication, we know more information about the specific bias we are introducing in the analysis, and maybe check the pertinence of such a bias against domain information that could be available to the data miner. This difficult but important extension of our work, which also will allow for consideration of sequential or more generally structured contexts, is to be pursued in the near future by the authors.

References

1. R. Agrawal and R. Srikant. Mining sequential patterns. In *Eleventh International Conference on Data Engineering*, pp. 3–14. IEEE Computer Society Press, 1995.
2. J.L. Balcázar and J. Baixeries. Discrete deterministic datamining as knowledge compilation. In *Workshop on Discrete Mathematics and Data Mining, in SIAM Int. Conf.*, 2003.
3. M. Cadoli. Knowledge compilation and approximation: Terminology, questions, references. In *AI/MATH-96, 4th. Int. Symposium on Artificial Intelligence and Mathematics*, 1996.
4. G. Casas-Garriga. Towards a formal framework for mining general patterns from structured data. In *Workshop Multi-relational Datamining, in KDD Int. Conf*, 2003.
5. G. Casas-Garriga. Statistical strategies to remove all the uniteresting association rules. In *Proc. 16th European Conf. on Artificial Intelligence*, pp. 430–435, 2004.
6. A. Day. The lattice theory of functional dependencies and normal decompositions. *Int. Journal of Algebra and Computation*, 2(4):409–431, 1992.
7. B. Ganter and R. Wille. *Formal Concept Analysis. Mathematical Foundations*. Springer, 1998.
8. H. Kautz, M. Kearns, and B. Selman. Horn approximations of empirical data. *Artificial Intelligence*, 74(1):129–145, 1995.
9. N. Pasquier, Y. Bastide, R. Taouil L., and Lakhal. Closed set based discovery of small covers for association rules. In *Proc. 15th Int. Conf. on Advanced Databases*, pp. 361–381, 1999.
10. J.L. Pfaltz and C.M. Taylor. Scientific knowledge discovery through iterative transformations of concept lattices. In *Workshop on Discrete Mathematics and Data Mining, in SIAM Int. Conf.*, pp. 65–74, 2002.
11. B. Selman and H. Kautz. Knowledge compilation and theory approximation. *Journal of the ACM*, 43(2):193–224, 1996.
12. J. Wang and J. Han. BIDE: Efficient mining of frequent closed sequences. In *Proc. 19th Int. Conference on Data Engineering*, pp. 79–90, 2003.
13. X. Yan, J. Han, and R. Afshar. Clospan: Mining closed sequential patterns in large datasets. In *Proc. Int. Conference SIAM Data Mining*, 2003.
14. M. Zaki. Generating non-redundant association rules. In *Proc. 6th Int. Conference on Knowledge Discovery and Data Mining*, pp. 34–43, 2000.
15. M. Zaki and M. Ogihara. Theoretical foundations of association rules. In *Workshop on Research Issues in Data Mining and Knowledge Discovery, in SIGMOD-DMKD Int. Conf.*, 1998.

Privacy in Database Publishing

Alin Deutsch* and Yannis Papakonstantinou**

Department of Computer Science and Engineering,
University of California, San Diego
{deutsch, yannis}@cs.ucsd.edu

Abstract. We formulate and study a privacy guarantee to data owners, who share information with clients by publishing views of a proprietary database. The owner identifies the sensitive proprietary data using a secret query against the proprietary database. Given an extra view, the privacy guarantee ensures that potential attackers will not learn any information about the secret that could not already be obtained from the existing views. We define "learning" as the modification of the attacker's a-priori probability distribution on the set of possible secrets. We assume arbitrary a-priori distributions (including distributions that correlate the existence of particular tuples) and solve the problem when secret and views are expressed as unions of conjunctive queries with non-equalities, under integrity constraints. We consider guarantees (a) for given view extents (b) for given domain of the secret and (c) independent of the domain and extents.

1   Introduction

Database publishing systems export a set of views of a proprietary database. Clients can access proprietary data only by formulating queries against the views. Data owners are subject to two conflicting requirements when designing a publishing system. On one hand, they need to publish appropriate views of the proprietary data to support the various types of interactions with the clients. On the other hand they must protect sensitive proprietary data. The purpose of this work is to provide a privacy guarantee as well as algorithms for checking it.

The Publishing Setting. We consider the following setting, which corresponds to the Global-As-View data integration scenario [12, 18]. We are given a proprietary relational database of schema $\mathcal{PR}$, a set of constraints Δ formulated in terms of $\mathcal{PR}$ and a set of relational views $\bar{V}$ over $\mathcal{PR}$. The public schema $\mathcal{PU}$ is the collection of all view names. The data owner identifies the sensitive proprietary data using a *secret query* S against $\mathcal{PR}$. Note that no client can ask such a query, as the system only accepts queries against $\mathcal{PU}$. Instead, the attacking client (from now on referred to as *attacker* or *client*) can try to formulate a series

---

* Supported by NSF/CAREER 0347968.
** Supported by NSF/ITR 0313384.

T. Eiter and L. Libkin (Eds.): ICDT 2005, LNCS 3363, pp. 230–245, 2005.

of legal queries against $\mathcal{PU}$ (which the system is bound to answer) and combine their results locally to obtain information on the secret answer to S, where the notion of "obtaining information" on the secret will be refined shortly. The data owner wants to defend against such attacks.

A Relativized Privacy Guarantee. We formulate and study a guarantee pertaining to the effect of adding new views in addition to the ones that are already posted. More specifically, we assume that the owner considers the publishing of a new view N. While the owner accepts the partial disclosure of the secret by the views $\bar{V}$, he is willing to add N only if it does not disclose any additional information. We view "disclosure" in its strongest, information-theoretic sense: we model the attacker's a priori beliefs about the secret by an assignment of probabilities to the possible secrets and guarantee that, regardless of the a priori beliefs/probabilities of the attacker, knowledge of the extent of view N does not lead to a revision of the a priori beliefs/probabilities, even if the attacker has unbounded computational resources. We first illustrate the key intuitions behind the proposed guarantee with examples.

Example 1 shows that in the common case when the owner cannot make assumptions on what the attacker already knows, the guarantee has to be quantified over all a-priori probability assignments to secrets assumed by the attacker

Example 1. Consider the proprietary relational schema

$$\mathcal{PR} = \{RS(reviewer, subcom) \; SP(subcom, paper) \; RP(reviewer, paper)\}$$

where RS associates reviewers with the program subcommittee they belong to, SP associates each paper to the subcommittee it was assigned to, and RP associates reviewers with the papers they reviewed.

The database satisfies the set of constraints $\Delta = \{C_1, C_2, C_3\}$:

$$C_1 : RP[reviewer] \subseteq RS[reviewer]$$
$$C_2 : RP[paper] \subseteq SP[paper]$$
$$C_3 : \forall r \forall p \; RP(r,p) \rightarrow \exists c \; RS(r,c) \land SP(c,p)$$

where C_1 states that there are no paper reviewers besides those listed in subcommittees and C_2 states that every reviewed paper belongs to a subcommittee, and C_3 states that papers submitted to subcommittee c can only be reviewed by reviewers associated to c.

RS	reviewer	subcom
	r_1	c_1
	r_2	c_1
	r_3	c_2
	r_4	c_2

SP	subcom	paper
	c_1	p_1
	c_1	p_2
	c_2	p_3
	c_2	p_4

RP	reviewer	paper
	r_1	p_1
	r_2	p_2
	r_3	p_3
	r_4	p_4

Fig. 1. Instance I for Example 1

The example instance I appears in Figure 1. Let the public data be described by the schema $\mathcal{PU} = \{V_R, V_S\}$ where the views V_R, V_S expose respectively the set of reviewers and subcommittees:

$$V_R(r) \leftarrow RS(r, s) \qquad V_S(s) \leftarrow RS(r, s)$$

with extents $\{r_1, r_2, r_3, r_4\}$ and $\{c_1, c_2\}$ respectively, when evaluated on I. We investigate the privacy breaches associated with posting the additional views

$$V_{RS}(r, s) \leftarrow RS(r, s) \qquad V_{SP}(s, p) \leftarrow SP(s, p).$$

Of course we want to prevent outsiders from obtaining information about who reviewed a given paper, i.e., from changing their a-priori belief on the likelihood of each fact of the form "a given reviewer reviewed p_1". Let's say we want to hide who reviewed paper p_1.[1] This can be stated precisely as the following secret query against the proprietary schema:

$$S(r) \leftarrow RP(r, p_1).$$

In the absence of knowledge besides V_R and V_S, any subset of V_R's extent could have reviewed paper p_1. The set of possible secrets therefore contains among others the candidates $s_1 = \{r_1, r_3\}$ $s_2 = \{r_1, r_2\}$, $s_3 = \{r_1, r_2, r_4\}$, etc.

Let's assume that the attacker's domain knowledge (e.g., his assumptions on who is likely to bid and who has declared conflict-of-interest) prompts him to assign a non-zero probability $\mathtt{prob}_1$ to s_1. If the owner now publishes the extent of V_{RS}, the attacker realizes (using constraint C_3) that p_1 must have been reviewed by somebody who serves on committee c_1, unlike r_3. The attacker thus adjusts $\mathtt{prob}_1$ and $\mathtt{prob}_3$ to 0, distributing their value among the probabilities of the remaining possible secrets (such as s_2). In other words, the remaining possible secrets are more likely after seeing the extent of the new views. This adjustment is due to learning something about the secret, namely that it cannot contain r_3 or r_4.

Notice that if the attacker had known this fact from outside sources, he would have set $\mathtt{prob}_1$ to 0 to begin with and hence not learned anything new from the additional view extents. However, if the owner cannot predict the attacker's prior knowledge, he must follow the conservative approach that the views breach privacy if they can be used to revise *some* a priori belief of the attacker.   □

The following example illustrates the point that privacy breaches depend on the proprietary database instance.

Example 2. In Example 1, the publishing of views V_{RS} and V_{SP} was breaching privacy on instance I. In contrast, consider an instance I' obtained from I by

---

[1] Note that in practice we would allow the owner to specify the secret as a parameterized query, i.e., have in the place of p_1 a parameter that stands for "any paper id". In the interest of simplifying the notation we assume that the secret involves a particular constant p_1. The generalization is straightforward.

replacing all subcommittees with the same value c_0. Then publishing V_{RS} and V_{SP} does not change the probability distribution on possible secrets since all values in the extent of V_R remain candidates for reviewers of paper p_1. In this case the privacy guarantee holds and the new views can be published.   □

Finally, note that integrity constraints can significantly boost the attacker's chances of defeating the privacy guarantee and must therefore be taken into account by the owner. We have seen in Example 1 how integrity constraint C_3 could be used by the attacker to revise his a priori probabilities for the secrets. Note that if the attacker did not know C_1, C_2, C_3 to hold, the set of possible secrets would not change after publishing the extra views. For instance, it does not matter what subcommittee a paper is assigned to if outside reviewers can also review it. Example 3 shows a scenario in which integrity constraints that specify cardinality constraints lead to much more dramatic privacy breaches, exposing the secret fully. Our results take into account such constraints.

Example 3. Let I'' be an instance that coincides with I on the extents of SP and RS and in which RP states that papers p_1 and p_2 are reviewed by both r_1 and r_2 and that papers p_3, p_4 are reviewed by both r_3 and r_4. Before seeing V_{RS}, V_{SP} the attacker considers any subset of reviewers as plausible, leading to 15 possible secrets to pick from. If the attacker now sees the extents of V_{RS} and V_{SP} corresponding to I'', he must conclude that only subsets of $\{r_1, r_2\}$ are plausible secrets, leading to 3 possibilities: $\{r_1\}, \{r_2\}, \{r_1, r_2\}$. Now assume that the attacker has the additional knowledge that each paper has exactly two reviewers. We express this prior knowledge in the form of integrity constraints stating that each paper has at most two (C_4) and at least two reviewers (C_5).

$$C_4 : \forall p \forall r_1 \forall r_2 \forall r \ RP(r_1, p) \land RP(r_2, p) \land RP(r, p) \to r = r_1 \lor r = r_2$$
$$C_5 : \forall p \forall c \ SP(c, p) \to \exists r_1 \exists r_2 \ RP(r_1, p) \land RP(r_2, p) \land r_1 \neq r_2$$

C_4 and C_5 further prune the set of possible secrets to only $\{r_1, r_2\}$, the probability of which is necessarily 1. In other words the secret is fully exposed!   □

Contributions. We formulate a novel privacy guarantee that ensures that, given existing views $\bar{V}$ and integrity constraints Δ, a new view N can be safely published. The guarantee does not assume any particular attack method; instead it checks that regardless of the attacker's a priori belief about the secret and computational resources, posting the extent of N can not lead to a revision of the attacker's belief. The owner specifies the secret by a query S over the proprietary database instance I. In that case we say that N is *safe* for S on I, denoted $safe_{\bar{V}}^{\Delta}(N, S, I)$. We formulate two versions of the safety guarantee. The first, $Gsafe_{\bar{V}}^{\Delta}(N, S, I)$, assumes that the attacker has domain knowledge about the possible worlds which witness (generate) the secret. Then we formulate a less strict guarantee, $Esafe_{\bar{V}}^{\Delta}(N, S, I)$, which applies when the attacker's domain knowledge pertains to the likelihood of secrets, and he has no opinion which distinguishes among the possible worlds witnessing the same secret.

We solve the problem of deciding both guarantees when S, N and all views in $\bar{V}$ are defined by unions of conjunctive queries with non-equalities (UCQ$^{\neq}$) and the constraints in Δ are equivalent to containment statements between UCQ$^{\neq}$ queries. These constraints extend classical embedded dependencies [2] with disjunction and non-equality, and they can express the standard key and foreign key constraints, but also cardinality constraints and beyond. All constraints in our motivating examples belong to this class. We consider three levels of strengthening for each guarantee.

1. We show that $Esafe_{\bar{V}}^{\Delta}(N, S, I)$ is decidable in **PSPACE** in the size of the instance I and that $Gsafe_{\bar{V}}^{\Delta}(N, S, I)$ is $\mathbf{\Pi_2^P}$-complete in the size of I.
2. We prove that for a fixed domain $\mathcal{D}$ we can check in **PSPACE** in the size of $\mathcal{D}$ that $Esafe_{\bar{V}}^{\Delta}(N, S, I)$ holds for all instances I over $\mathcal{D}$. The analogous problem for $Gsafe$ is $\mathbf{\Pi_2^P}$-complete in the size of $\mathcal{D}$.
3. For both kinds of safety, we show undecidability of checking safety on all instances I (regardless of their domain).

Our techniques shed additional light on the relationship between privacy and information integration. In particular, in the process of establishing our undecidability results, we expose an interesting connection with a problem from information integration, namely lossless answering of queries using views [4].

2   Two Formal Privacy Guarantees

Possible Worlds and Plausible Secrets. Let I be a proprietary database instance satisfying Δ. Denote with E the corresponding $\mathcal{PU}$-instance, which associates to each table $V \in \bar{V}$ the extent $V(I)$ (in short $\bar{V}(I) = E$). Given E, there is a set of $\mathcal{PR}$-instances w over an infinite domain, that satisfy the constraints Δ (denoted $w \models \Delta$) and on which the views yield E ($\bar{V}(w) = E$). These instances are known as *possible worlds* in the literature (see [11] and references therein). Denote their set with

$$Worlds_{\bar{V}}^{\Delta}(E) = \{w \mid w \models \Delta \wedge \bar{V}(w) = E\}.$$

Clearly, $I \in Worlds_{\bar{V}}^{\Delta}(E)$. We call a secret s *plausible* given E if it occurs in a possible world, i.e., there exists $w \in Worlds_{\bar{V}}^{\Delta}(E)$ such that $S(w) = s$. Observe that $S(I)$ is trivially plausible.

Attacker's Knowledge of Secret Assuming Zero Views. We model the attacker's general domain knowledge as a probability distribution $\mathbf{P} : \mathcal{S} \to [0, 1]$ defined over the set of outcomes $\mathcal{S}$ [17] that consists of all possible instances of the secret which are witnessed by some world that satisfies Δ. As usual, given an event, i.e., a set of outcomes $S \subseteq \mathcal{S}$, we denote by $\mathbf{P}(S)$ the probability $\Sigma_{s \in S} \mathbf{P}(s)$ of the event [17].

Note that we make no assumptions on $\mathbf{P}$, thus allowing for distributions that correlate particular tuples. For example, the distribution may model the knowledge that "reviewers r_1 and r_2 have the same research background and are likely to review the same papers" or that "a paper is very likely to have exactly three reviews and it is impossible that it has less than two or more than four". This modeling is in contrast to the one used in [15], which assumes independent probability of individual tuples appearing in the secret.

Induced Probability Distributions over Private Database. The attacker's knowledge of the secret, i.e., the distribution $\mathbf{P}$, induces possible compatible probability distributions $\mathbf{P}' : \mathcal{W} \to [0,1]$ over the set $\mathcal{W}$ of instances of the private database which satisfy Δ. Clearly, $Worlds_{\bar{V}}^{\Delta}(E) \subseteq \mathcal{W}$. Note that the attacker is often unaware of the details of those distributions since they may also involve data that are tangential or irrelevant to the secret, i.e., data that the attacker is unaware of or is not interested in. For example, though the attacker of Example 1 only cares about paper p_1 and its potential reviewers, the induced probability distribution assigns probabilities to the full set of data pertaining to the conference. Our work considers two assumptions for deducing the compatible probability distributions over the private database instance and produces corresponding results:

1. **General:** The distribution $\mathbf{P}$ induces the set $\mathcal{P}^g$ that consists of all distributions $\mathbf{P}^g$ that are defined on $\mathcal{W}$ and have the property

$$\forall s \in \mathcal{S} : \ \Sigma_{w \in \mathcal{W}, S(w)=s} \mathbf{P}^g(w) = \mathbf{P}(s) \tag{1}$$

   We will see that according to the general assumption, maintaining privacy requires that no possible world w that witnesses a secret instance s (i.e., $S(w) = s$) can be eliminated by the extra view. A less strict requirement, which is compatible with the fact that the attacker may not have an opinion on the non-secret data, is provided by the next assumption.

2. **Equiprobable Witnesses:** The distribution $\mathbf{P}$ induces the unique distribution $\mathbf{P}^e$, called *equiprobable witness*, that is defined on $\mathcal{W}$ and has the property

$$\forall s \in \mathcal{S}, w \in \mathcal{W} : \ S(w) = s \Rightarrow \mathbf{P}^e(w) = \frac{\mathbf{P}(s)}{|\{w' \mid w' \in \mathcal{W}, S(w') = s\}|}$$

   i.e., all witnesses w of a secret s have equal probability. Obviously $\mathbf{P}^e \in \mathcal{P}^g$.

Belief Based on a-priori Set of Views. With a slight abuse of notation, in the context of a distribution $\mathbf{P}^g : \mathcal{W} \to [0,1]$ a secret instance $s \in \mathcal{S}$ will also stand for the event $\{w \mid w \in \mathcal{W}, S(w) = s\}$ and E will also stand for the event $Worlds_{\bar{V}}^{\Delta}(E)$. Then the conditional probability $\mathbf{P}^g(s|E)$ denotes the probability of s being the secret once the view extents E have been observed, but before seeing the extent of the additional view N that the owner considers whether to publish or not. We will call $\mathbf{P}^g(s|E)$ the attacker's *a priori* belief, and according to the conditional probability definition [17] we have

$$\mathbf{P}^g(s|E) = \frac{\sum_{w \in Worlds_{\bar{V}}^{\Delta}(E), S(w)=s} \mathbf{P}^g(w)}{\sum_{w \in Worlds_{\bar{V}}^{\Delta}(E)} \mathbf{P}^g(w)} \tag{2}$$

Since $\mathbf{P}^e \in \mathcal{P}^g$, Equation (2) holds also for $\mathbf{P}^e$. Notice that (2) associates probability 0 to implausible secrets. Also, the more possible worlds witness a certain secret candidate s, the higher its probability. In particular, if all possible worlds yield the same secret s then $\mathbf{P}^g(s|E) = 1$.

A-Posteriori Belief. Now consider a new view N and let E' be the $\mathcal{PU} \cup \{N\}$-instance which extends E by associating to N the extent $N(I)$. E' is what the attacker would observe after the additional publishing of view N. As above, we denote with $Worlds^\Delta_{\bar{V},N}(E')$ the set of possible worlds of E' and the conditional probability $\mathbf{P}^g(s|E') = \mathbf{P}^g(s|Worlds^\Delta_{\bar{V},N}(E'))$ models the probability of each secret instance once the instance of N is also observed.

The Privacy Guarantees. We propose two privacy guarantees that correspond to the general and the equiprobable witness assumptions. Both guarantees ensure that N can be safely published by checking that, regardless of the attacker's domain knowledge, the a priori and a posteriori beliefs coincide.

Definition 1 (Instance-Dependent View Safety Under Equiprobable Witnesses). We say that view N is *safe* under equiprobable witnesses for the secret query S on $\mathcal{PR}$-instance I given views $\bar{V}$ and constraints Δ iff for each probability distribution $\mathbf{P}$ on the candidate secrets and for each s we have

$$\mathbf{P}^e(s|E) = \mathbf{P}^e(s|E')$$

where $E = \bar{V}(I)$ and $E' = (\bar{V}, N)(I)$. We denote this property as $Esafe^\Delta_{\bar{V}}(N, S, I)$.

Definition 2 (Instance-Dependent View Safety Under General Induced Probabilities). We say that view N is *safe* under general induced probabilities for the secret query S on $\mathcal{PR}$-instance I given views $\bar{V}$ and constraints Δ iff for each probability distribution $\mathbf{P}$ on the candidate secrets, for each s, and for each $\mathbf{P}^g \in \mathcal{P}^g$ we have

$$\mathbf{P}^g(s|E) = \mathbf{P}^g(s|E')$$

where $E = \bar{V}(I)$ and $E' = (\bar{V}, N)(I)$. We denote this property as $Gsafe^\Delta_{\bar{V}}(N, S, I)$.

Safety over Classes of Instances. As shown in Example 2, the satisfaction of the privacy guarantee depends on the proprietary database I. The owner is thus faced with the following dilemma. Checking the guarantee on a given instance I avoids being overly conservative and rejecting the publishing of many extra views because they breach privacy on another instance I'. On the other hand, this means re-checking the privacy guarantee upon each update to I. Alternatively, we consider the following two levels of strengthening the safety guarantees from Definitions 1 and 2 to take into account classes of instances.

$$Esafe^\Delta_{\bar{V}}(N, S, \mathcal{D}) := \forall I \in Inst(\mathcal{D}) : \ Esafe^\Delta_{\bar{V}}(N, S, I) \qquad (3)$$

$$Esafe^\Delta_{\bar{V}}(N, S) := \forall I : \ Esafe^\Delta_{\bar{V}}(N, S, I) \qquad (4)$$

$$Gsafe^\Delta_{\bar{V}}(N, S, \mathcal{D}) := \forall I \in Inst(\mathcal{D}) : \ Gsafe^\Delta_{\bar{V}}(N, S, I) \qquad (5)$$

$$Gsafe^\Delta_{\bar{V}}(N, S) := \forall I : \ Gsafe^\Delta_{\bar{V}}(N, S, I) \qquad (6)$$

(3) and (5) extend safety to a (finite) set $Inst(\mathcal{D})$ of $\mathcal{PR}$-instances over some given, finite domain $\mathcal{D}$ (useful when modeling dictionary attacks), while (4) and (6) extend safety to all $\mathcal{PR}$-instances.

Dictionary Attacks. It is often appropriate to assume that the attacker already knows the domain of the secret and hence is able to launch *dictionary attacks*, i.e., attacks that consist of potentially large numbers of queries that involve constants that have not been retrieved from the database; instead the attacker already knows those constants from his "dictionary knowledge". A typical example is an insurance database, in which we may want to assume that the list of potential patients and the list of diseases are publicly known (from the employee lists of the participating companies and a medical encyclopedia) but the data owner wants to hide the association between patients and diseases. When dictionary attacks are of concern, we model the dictionary knowledge of the attacker by including among the published views *dictionary views* which publish projections of the secret on those attributes whose domain is considered to be known to the attacker. Notice that in our running example dictionary views arise naturally and need not be added: V_R is already one.

3   Preliminaries: Queries and Constraints

Queries. A *term* is a variable or constant. By $\bar{x}$ we denote a finite sequence of terms $x_1, \ldots, x_k$. The language of conjunctive queries with non-equalities $(\mathrm{CQ}^{\neq})$ consists of expressions of the form $Q(\bar{z}) \leftarrow \ell_1(\bar{x}_1), \ldots, \ell_n(\bar{x}_n)$ where each $\ell_i(\bar{x}_i)$ in the rule *body* is a *literal*, i.e., an atom $R(\bar{x})$, an equality $x_i = x_j$ or an inequality $x_i \neq x_j$. Given $Q \in \mathrm{CQ}^{\neq}$, we define $\mathrm{head}(Q)$ and $\mathrm{body}(Q)$ to give the parts to the left and to the right of the arrow, respectively. A union of conjunctive queries with non-equalities $(\mathrm{UCQ}^{\neq})$ is an expression of the form $Q = \bigvee_{i=1}^{n} Q_i$ where $Q_i \in \mathrm{CQ}^{\neq}$ for each $1 \leq i \leq n$. We have $Q(\mathcal{D}) = \bigcup_i Q_i(\mathcal{D})$, where $Q(\mathcal{D})$ denotes the result of query Q on database $\mathcal{D}$. All queries and views in the motivating examples belong to $\mathrm{UCQ}^{\neq}$.

Constraints. For a given query language $\mathcal{L}$, we consider the corresponding constraint language

$$\mathrm{IC}(\mathcal{L}) := \{\forall \bar{x}(U \rightarrow V) : U, V \in \mathcal{L}\}$$

where $\bar{x}$ is the set of free variables in both U and V. These kinds of constraints express the containment of the queries U in V and are known as *embedded dependencies* when $\mathcal{L} = \mathrm{CQ}$ (conjunctive queries). Given a set of constraints $\Sigma \subseteq \mathrm{IC}(\mathrm{CQ})$, there is a well known procedure for extending a query $Q \in \mathrm{CQ}$ to another query Q' by an iterative procedure known as the *chase*. However, the constraints in Example 1 belong to the more expressive language $\mathrm{IC}(\mathrm{UCQ}^{\neq})$ (see also the cardinality constraints in Example 3). In [8,5], we extended the chase to $Q \in \mathrm{UCQ}^{\neq}$ and $\Sigma \subseteq \mathrm{IC}(\mathrm{UCQ}^{\neq})$. The extension is repeated in the full version of this paper [6]. We only give an example here, which illustrates that the chase produces unions of conjunctive queries with non-equalities (or, equivalently, queries whose body is in disjunctive normal form).

Example 4. Consider the query body $T(x, y)$ and the constraint

$$\sigma := \forall x \forall y T(x, y) \rightarrow (\exists z\ R(x, z)) \vee (x \neq y).$$

[2] A chase step of $T(x, y)$ with σ yields the following query body in disjunctive normal form: $T(x, y) \wedge R(x, z) \vee T(x, y) \wedge x \neq y$.   □

It is well-known that checking termination of the chase is undecidable even for the constraint language IC(CQ). In the full paper [6], we repeat a sufficient condition for termination introduced in [8], namely the property of a set of constraints having *stratified witnesses*. This condition is the most general termination condition we are aware of, and it is efficiently checkable (in PTIME in the size of the constraint set). Essentially, it ensures that only a finite number of new variables (such as z in Example 4) can be introduced into the chase result, which therefore must be finite.

Theorem 1 ([8]). *If $\Delta \subseteq \text{IC}(\text{UCQ}^{\neq})$ has stratified witnesses, then the chase with Δ of any $Q \in \text{UCQ}^{\neq}$ terminates. It yields a result $\bigvee_{i=1}^{n} Q_i$ where each $Q_i \in \text{CQ}^{\neq}$ has size polynomial in the size of Q and n is exponential in the size of Q.*

In this paper, we assume that all queries belong to $\text{UCQ}^{\neq}$ and that all constraints belong to $\text{IC}(\text{UCQ}^{\neq})$.

4   General Induced Probability

Privacy on Given Instance or Domain. The main difficulty we need to overcome when checking $Gsafe_{\overline{V}}^{\Delta}(N, S, I)$ is the fact that the guarantee is universally quantified over infinitely many probability distributions $\mathbf{P}$ on the secrets and over infinitely many induced probability distributions $\mathbf{P}^g$ on the possible worlds. The following result solves this problem partially, showing that we can ignore probability distributions altogether, reducing the problem to comparing possible worlds only. Recall that E' is E extended with the new materialized view N.

Lemma 1. $Gsafe_{\overline{V}}^{\Delta}(N, S, I)$ *holds if and only if* $Worlds_{\overline{V}}^{\Delta}(E) = Worlds_{\overline{V}, N}^{\Delta}(E')$.

What is left to do is to compute the sets of possible worlds, $Worlds_{\overline{V}}^{\Delta}(E)$ and $Worlds_{\overline{V}, N}^{\Delta}(E')$. The problem here is that these sets have potentially infinite cardinality. In the remainder of this section, we solve this problem as follows. First, we show that the infinite set of possible worlds is finitely representable by a set of *templates*, denoted $TWorlds_{\overline{V}}^{\Delta}(E)$. Then we show how do adapt Lemma 1 to compare only $TWorlds_{\overline{V}}^{\Delta}(E)$ and $TWorlds_{\overline{V}, N}^{\Delta}(E')$ (Theorem 3 below). Finally, we show how to compute $TWorlds_{\overline{V}}^{\Delta}(E)$.

---

[2] σ belongs to $\text{IC}(\text{UCQ}^{\neq})$ as it can be restated as the containment of $Q_1(x, y) \leftarrow T(x, y)$ in $Q_2(x, y) \leftarrow T(x, y) \wedge R(x, z) \vee T(x, y) \wedge x \neq y$.

Possible World Templates. It was shown in [11] that for conjunctive query views and in the absence of constraints, the infinite set of possible worlds is finitely representable by a set of *templates*. We extend this result to $\text{UCQ}^{\neq}$ views and in the presence of constraints. Let $\mathcal{D}$ be a set of constants and $\mathcal{V}$ a set of variables. A database over $\mathcal{D}$ associates to each relation in its schema a set of tuples of constants from $\mathcal{D}$. A database template over $\mathcal{D}$ and $\mathcal{V}$ associates to each relation a set of tuples of constants and variables from $\mathcal{D} \cup \mathcal{V}$ [11]. The notion of evaluating a $\text{UCQ}^{\neq}$ query over a database template extends in the obvious way. Given the views $\bar{V}$ of extent E, a *possible world template* is a database template T such that $\bar{V}(T) = E$.

Example 5. Consider a proprietary database of schema $R(A, B, C)$ and domain $\mathcal{D}$. Also consider the view $V(A, C) \leftarrow R(A, B, C)$ of extent $E = \{(a_1, c_1), (a_2, c_2)\}$. Then $T_1 = \{R(a_1, x_1, c_1), R(a_2, x_2, c_2)\}$ and $T_2 = \{R(a_1, x_3, c_1), R(a_2, x_3, c_2)\}$ are possible world templates since $V(T_1) = V(T_2) = E$. $Worlds_V(E)$ is represented by $\{T_1, T_2\}$ in the following sense: for any possible world $W \in Worlds_V(E)$, there is an injective homomorphic embedding from T into W. In particular, if we instantiate x_1, x_2, x_3 with constants from $\mathcal{D}$ in all possible ways (but never x_1 and x_2 with the same constant, as T_2 takes care of that case), we are sure to obtain only possible worlds (infinitely many if $\mathcal{D}$ is infinite). Notice that in general we need more than one template to represent the possible worlds. If in the above example we also exported the view $V'(B) \leftarrow R(A, B, C)$ of extent $\{b_1, b_2\}$ then the possible worlds would be given by the templates $T_1 = \{R(a_1, b_1, c_1), R(a_1, b_2, c_2)\}$, $T_2 = \{R(a_1, b_2, c_1), R(a_1, b_1, c_2)\}$, $T_3 = \{R(a_1, b_1, c_1), R(a_1, b_1, c_2)\}$, $T_4 = \{R(a_1, b_2, c_1), R(a_1, b_2, c_2)\}$, which happen to be full-fledged databases as they mention no variables.

Definition 3 (Reduced Universal Set of Possible World Templates). We say that a set $\mathcal{T}$ of possible world templates is *universal* for a view extent E if for any possible world W of E, there is an injective homomorphic embedding h from some $T \in \mathcal{T}$ into W, i.e. the images under h of distinct variables from T are distinct. $\mathcal{T}$ is *reduced* if (i) for each $T_1, T_2 \in \mathcal{T}$ with $T_1 \neq T_2$ there is no injective homomorphic embedding from T_1 into T_2 and (ii) for each $T \in \mathcal{T}$ there is no injective homomorphism from T into a proper subset of T's tuples.

Given the integrity constraints Δ and the published views $\bar{V}$ of extent E, there may be several universal sets of possible world templates, but only a single reduced one:

Theorem 2. *The reduced universal set of possible world templates is unique up to isomorphism. We denote this set with $TWorlds_{\bar{V}}^{\Delta}(E)$.*

It turns out that instead of comparing sets of possible worlds, we can compare their reduced universal sets of templates:

Theorem 3. $Gsafe_{\bar{V}}^{\Delta}(N, S, I)$ *holds iff* $TWorlds_{\bar{V}}^{\Delta}(E) = TWorlds_{\bar{V}, N}^{\Delta}(E')$.

We next provide an algorithm for finding $TWorlds_{\bar{V}}^{\Delta}(E)$. The algorithm is based on capturing the view definitions with a set of constraints Σ_V and *chasing* the extent E with Σ_V as well as the integrity constraints in Δ. All these constraints belong to $IC(UCQ^{\neq})$ and are described below.

Let $\bar{V} = V_1, \ldots, V_n$. We define Σ_V as the following set of constraints:

$$\Sigma_V := \{\forall \bar{x}_i \bar{y}_i (\text{body}(V_i) \to \text{head}(V_i)) \mid 1 \le i \le n\}$$
$$\cup \{\forall \bar{x}_i (\text{head}(V_i) \to \exists \bar{y}_i \text{body}(V_i)) \mid 1 \le i \le n\}$$

where $\bar{x}_i$ are the variables in $\text{head}(V_i)$, and where $\bar{y}_i$ are the variables in $\text{body}(V_i)$ which do not appear in $\text{head}(V_i)$.

For a given extent E of the views, we introduce the following set of constraints Σ_E. Let E associate to view V_i the set of tuples $\{t_1, \ldots, t_{n_i}\}$. Then define

$$\Sigma_E := \{\forall t \; V_i(t) \to \bigvee_{j=1}^{n_i} t = t_j \mid 1 \le i \le n\}$$

which states that for each i, the only tuples in V_i are the ones given by E.

Finally, define the following axiom about equality: $\sigma_{\neq} := \forall x \forall y \; true \to x{=}y \vee x{\neq}y$. Also, let the *canonical tableau* of E be the conjunction of all facts in E:

$$CanT(E) := \bigwedge_{i=1}^{n} \bigwedge_{j=1}^{n_i} V_i(t_j).$$

Function PWT below returns the desired set of possible world templates.

```
function PWT(E; V; Δ)
(1) Compute Σ := Δ ∪ Σ_V ∪ Σ_E ∪ {σ_≠}.
(2) Let ⋁_{l=1}^{m} T_l be the result of chasing CanT(E) with Σ.
(3) For each l, compute T'_l := T_l|_{PR} (that is, keep only the PR literals).
(4) Set T_1 := {T'_l | 1 ≤ l ≤ m}.
(5) Let T_2 be the reduced T_1, obtained by dropping each T from T_1
        for which there is another T' ∈ T_1 and a homomorphic embedding
        from T' into T.
(6) Return T_2.
```

Since function PWT is based on chasing, it is not a priori clear that it even terminates. Theorem 4 guarantees termination of PWT and implies the finiteness and computability of $TWorlds_{\bar{V}}^{\Delta}(E)$.

Theorem 4. *If Δ has stratified witnesses then:*

1. *Function* PWT *is guaranteed to terminate for any $\bar{V}$ and E.*
2. *The result of* PWT *is a template set of cardinality at most exponential in the size of E. Each template has size polynomial in the size of E.*
3. $PWT(E; \bar{V}; \Delta) = TWorlds_{\bar{V}}^{\Delta}(E)$.

Theorems 3 and 4 immediately suggest a decision procedure for $Gsafe_{\bar{V}}^{\Delta}(N, S, I)$:

Corollary 1. *If Δ has stratified witnesses, then $Gsafe_{\bar{V}}^{\Delta}(N, S, I)$ holds if and only if $PWT(\bar{V}; \Delta; E) = PWT(\bar{V}, N; \Delta; E')$.*

Notice that, by Theorem 4 (2), the naive algorithm which eagerly computes the results of PWT requires exponential space in the size of I. However, checking that $\text{PWT}(\bar{V}; \Delta; E) \neq \text{PWT}(\bar{V}, N; \Delta; E')$ is clearly in Σ_2^p: guess a template $T \in \text{PWT}(\bar{V}; \Delta; E)$ and then ask an NP oracle whether $T \in \text{PWT}(\bar{V}; \Delta; E')$. Hence $Gsafe_{\bar{V}}^{\Delta}(N, S, I)$ is in $\mathbf{\Pi_2^P}$, which turns out to be asymptotically optimal:

Theorem 5. *If Δ has stratified witnesses then*

1. *$Gsafe_{\bar{V}}^{\Delta}(N, S, I)$ is $\mathbf{\Pi_2^P}$-complete in the size of I.*
2. *$Gsafe_{\bar{V}}^{\Delta}(N, S, \mathcal{D})$ is $\mathbf{\Pi_2^P}$-complete in the size of $\mathcal{D}$.*

Unrestricted Privacy. We next show that the strongest level of *Gsafe*, namely $Gsafe_{\bar{V}}^{\Delta}(N, S) := \forall I \ Gsafe_{\bar{V}}^{\Delta}(N, S, I)$ is undecidable. Towards achieving this result, we expose an interesting connection with a problem that has recently received considerable attention in the area of information integration, namely lossless query answering using views.

Lossless Query Answering. Given a set of views $\bar{V}$ and a query Q (both formulated against the same schema) in data integration we are interested in answering Q using only the extents E of the views. Typical algorithms proposed in the literature (e.g. [9]) find the *certain* answers to Q, defined as $cert_Q(E) := \bigcap_{w \in Worlds_{\bar{V}}(E)} Q(w)$. Notice that regardless of which possible world I from $Worlds_{\bar{V}}(E)$ actually generated the view extents E, we have $cert_Q(E) \subseteq Q(I)$. [4] asks whether for each I and corresponding E, we can retrieve the exact answer to $Q(I)$ from E, i.e. $\forall I \ E = \bar{V}(I) \rightarrow cert_Q(E) = Q(I)$. If so we say that the views $\bar{V}$ can be used to losslessly answer Q, denoted $\bar{V} \models Q$. [4] identifies the decidable cases for regular path queries and views over semistructured data. In contrast, in the relational model [7] shows that even in the absence of constraints, if Q and $\bar{V}$ belong to UCQ, the problem is undecidable.

It turns out that the problem $\bar{V} \models Q$ reduces to $Gsafe_{\bar{V}}^{\emptyset}(Q, \text{id})$ where id is the identity secret query which returns the entire database. This implies:

Theorem 6. *$Gsafe_{\bar{V}}^{\Delta}(N, S)$ is undecidable, even under no constraints ($\Delta = \emptyset$).*

In some scenarios the $Gsafe_{\bar{V}}^{\Delta}(N, S, I)$ guarantee may turn out to be too strong. By Lemma 1, it requires the set of possible worlds not to change, which in turn means that $N(I)$ can be obtained solely from $\bar{V}(I)$. Depending on I, only few and non-interesting N's could pass this test. In the next section we relax this guarantee assuming that attackers treat witnesses for a secret as equiprobable.

5   Equiprobable Witnesses

Privacy on Given Instance or Domain. As was the case for the *Gsafe* guarantee, the main difficulty to overcome when checking $Esafe_{\bar{V}}^{\Delta}(N, S, I)$ is the universal quantification over infinitely many probability distributions $\mathbf{P}$ on the candidates for secrets. Again we solve this problem by showing that we can ignore probability distributions entirely. This time however we reduce the problem to *counting* possible worlds and *plausible* secrets. Denote the multiplicity of secret s when E is published as the number of possible worlds on which the secret query evaluates to s: $mult_E(s) = |\{w \mid w \in Worlds_{\bar{V}}^{\Delta}(E), S(w) = s\}|$ and $mult_{E'}(s) = |\{w' \mid w' \in Worlds_{\bar{V},N}^{\Delta}(E'), S(w') = s\}|$. Notice that s is plausible for E if and only if $mult_E(s) > 0$.

Lemma 2. *$Esafe_{\bar{V}}^{\Delta}(N, S, I)$ holds if and only if*

1. *each plausible secret for E stays plausible for E', and*
2. *all pairs s_1, s_2 of secrets that are plausible for E satisfy $\frac{mult_E(s_1)}{mult_E(s_2)} = \frac{mult_{E'}(s_1)}{mult_{E'}(s_2)}$.*

What is left to do is to compute the multiplicities of secrets, which requires computing the sets of possible worlds, $Worlds_{\bar{V}}^{\Delta}(E)$ and $Worlds_{\bar{V},N}^{\Delta}(E')$. We again use the finite representations of these sets $TWorlds_{\bar{V}}^{\Delta}(E)$, respectively $TWorlds_{\bar{V},N}^{\Delta}(E')$ and we show next (Theorem 7) that the privacy guarantee reduces to running the test of Lemma 2 on these template sets. We first introduce a notation for the multiplicity of templates witnessing s: $Tmult_E(s) = |\{t \in TWorlds_{\bar{V}}^{\Delta}(E) \mid S(t) = s\}|$ and $Tmult_{E'}(s) = |\{t' \in TWorlds_{\bar{V},N}^{\Delta}(E') \mid S(t') = s\}|$.

Theorem 7. *1. Assume that the set of views $\bar{V}$ contains dictionary views for each projection of the secret query S. Then every candidate secret s is plausible for E if and only if there exists $T \in TWorlds_{\bar{V}}^{\Delta}(E)$ with $S(T) = s$.*

2. $Esafe_{\bar{V}}^{\Delta}(N, S, I)$ holds if and only if for every pair of plausible secrets s_1, s_2 we have $\frac{Tmult_E(s_1)}{Tmult_E(s_2)} = \frac{Tmult_{E'}(s_1)}{Tmult_{E'}(s_2)}$.

Putting together Theorem 7 and Theorem 4, we obtain that algorithm ESAFE below is a decision procedure for $Esafe_{\bar{V}}^{\Delta}(N, S, I)$.

---

algorithm ESAFE $(\bar{V}, \Delta, N, S, I)$
(1) Compute $E := \bar{V}(I)$ and $E' := (\bar{V}, N)(I)$.
(2) Compute $TWorlds_{\bar{V}}^{\Delta}(E) := \mathrm{PWT}(\bar{V}; \Delta; E)$, and
        $TWorlds_{\bar{V},N}^{\Delta}(E') := \mathrm{PWT}(\bar{V}, N; \Delta; E')$.
(3) Compute $Secrets_{\bar{V}}^{\Delta}(E) := \{S(w) \mid w \in TWorlds_{\bar{V}}^{\Delta}(E)\}$.
(4) For each $s_1, s_2 \in Secrets_{\bar{V}}^{\Delta}(E)$ do
        if $\frac{Tmult_E(s_1)}{Tmult_E(s_2)} \neq \frac{Tmult_{E'}(s_1)}{Tmult_{E'}(s_2)}$ then return false.
(5) Return true.

Notice that, as presented, algorithm ESAFE needs exponential space in the size of I. Indeed, the two calls of function PWT yield results of size exponential in the size of E and E' (therefore exponential in the size of I). This presentation was chosen for the sake of simplicity. It turns out that we can do better.

Theorem 8. *If Δ has stratified witnesses then*

1. *$Esafe_{\bar{V}}^{\Delta}(N, S, I)$ is decidable in **PSPACE** in the size of I.*
2. *$Esafe_{\bar{V}}^{\Delta}(N, S, \mathcal{D})$ is decidable in **PSPACE** in the size of $\mathcal{D}$.*

The proof is based on the key idea that we do not need to first list the entire result of PWT, instead enumerating the possible world templates on demand. The technique extends straightforwardly to deciding $Esafe_{\tilde{V}}^{\Delta}(N, S, \mathcal{D})$: enumerate in **PSPACE** in the size of $\mathcal{D}$ all instances $I \in Inst(\mathcal{D})$ and check $Esafe_{\tilde{V}}^{\Delta}(N, S, I)$ using algorithm ESAFE.

We do not have a matching lower bound for these results. Indeed, we conjecture that the exact complexity lies in the counting complexity class $\mathbf{C_{=}P}$ [19] which is included in **PSPACE**.

Unrestricted Privacy. Using a reduction from the problem of lossless query answering, we show that $Esafe_{\tilde{V}}^{\Delta}(N, S) := \forall I \; Esafe_{\tilde{V}}^{\Delta}(N, S, I)$ is undecidable:

Theorem 9. $Esafe_{\tilde{V}}^{\Delta}(N, S)$ *is undecidable even under no constraints* $(\Delta = \emptyset)$.

6   Discussion

The key insight on which our framework for privacy diagnostics is based is the fact that the modeling of the attacker's knowledge should start from possible worlds or at least plausible secrets. The individual tuples in the secret are correlated by appearing together in possible worlds.

For a comparison of the two proposed flavors of privacy guarantees, assume that E has 200 possible worlds, on which the secret query evaluates to s_1 for 100 worlds and to s_2 for the remaining worlds. If after publishing E', only 100 worlds remain, of which none witnesses s_1, both guarantees will fail. The same happens if 101 world remain, of which 1 witnesses s_1 and the rest s_2. However, if a posteriori we are left with 100 secrets of which half witness s_1 and half witness s_2, *Gsafe* fails while *Esafe* holds. We leave it to the data owner to decide which guarantee is more appropriate for a specific application.

Notice that our framework can easily model and defend against collusion by multiple attackers. Suppose that access control mechanisms allow attacker a_1 to see a set of views $\bar{V}_1$ and attacker a_2 to access $\bar{V}_2$. Then defending against their collusion requires checking $safe_{\bar{V}_1, \bar{V}_2}^{\Delta}(E)$.

Also observe that since integrity constraints have the same effect as additional views, namely of ruling out possible worlds, the publishing of integrity constraints can also lead to privacy breaches. The publisher can employ the same framework to decide whether the publication of a constraint is safe.

In light of the high complexity bounds we obtained in terms of data complexity, our future work will focus on finding special cases for the view and secret definitions which yield tractability. We are also looking into further relaxations of the privacy guarantees.

7   Related Work

Prior work on privacy in databases has focused on implementing access control, i.e. allowing clients to see only those published views which they are authorized to. The techniques are based on cryptographically encoding the data (see [13, 14] and references within). Other techniques involve the authentication of users via credentials, as in the TrustBuilder project (see [20] for a comprehensive list of publications). Our work is orthogonal to work on access control, as it helps data owners design the views such that attackers cannot breach privacy using only *authorized* accesses.

[1] introduces *c*-tables, a compact formalism for finitely representing large (and potentially infinite) sets of possible worlds, and shows Π_2^p-complete data complexity for checking that the sets of possible worlds represented by two *c*-tables are the same. *c*-tables are not sufficiently expressive to model the set of possible worlds given by a view instance. [11] introduces *database templates* to this end and shows how to compute them using the chase, but does not address the comparison of the sets of possible worlds. Our approach for finding possible world templates coincides with the one in [11] when there are no constraints on the private database and the views are conjunctive queries.

[10] solves the problem of limiting privacy breaches in a scenario in which the aggregation of a set of private client data items is computed at the server. A privacy breach is essentially defined as a significant difference between the a posteriori and the a priori probability distributions. [10] provides not only a diagnostic tool, it also scrambles the data to improve privacy. The model assumes independence among the private values at the clients. Thus, the techniques do not apply directly to our scenario, where the secret tuples are not independent of each other (indeed they are correlated via the possible worlds in which they appear). On the other hand, we do not handle aggregation, which is at the center of the model in [10]. [3] takes aggregation into account and shows that exposing the result of counting queries allows the retrieval of an isomorphic copy of the structure of the database.

[16] takes a dual approach to ours. While we use queries to specify what cannot be disclosed, [16] uses conjunctive query views to specify what may be seen by outsiders. In this setting, conjunctive client queries asked against the proprietary database are answered only if they have a rewriting using the allowable views.

[15] is the closest work in spirit to ours. It pioneers the idea of specifying the secret as a conjunctive query and checking that the new view does not leak information about the secret by modifying the a priori probabilities of possible secrets. The most significant difference stems from the fact that [15] assumes that the tuples in the secret answer are *independent events*. This fails to defend against attackers who take into account correlations between tuples. This restriction is used to derive decidability even for the unrestricted guarantee. [15] lists as open the problem of deciding the guarantee when the independence assumption on secret tuples is lifted. This is the problem we address in this work. Not surprisingly, this problem is harder: the unrestricted guarantee becomes undecidable. Furthermore, we needed to refine the privacy guarantee in order to model whether the attacker knows or does not know anything about the witnesses of the secrets. Other differences are the fact that the guarantee is checked

in [15] only for restricted integrity constraints (functional dependencies) and a-priori views (only boolean views). Also, [15] does not address the case when the instance is given, focusing on given domain and unrestricted guarantee only. Extending the results to the instance-based guarantee when no finite domain is given would require generating the set of possible world templates.

References

1. S. Abiteboul, P. Kanellakis, and G. Grahne. On the representation and querying of sets of possible worlds. *Theoretical Computer Science*, 78:159–187, 1991.
2. Serge Abiteboul, Richard Hull, and Victor Vianu. *Foundations of Databases*. Addison-Wesley, 1995.
3. Michal Bielecki and Jan Van den Bussche. Database interrogation using conjunctive queries. In *ICDT*, pages 259–269, 2003.
4. Diego Calvanese, Giuseppe De Giacomo, Maurizio Lenzerini, and Moshe Y. Vardi. Lossless regular views. In *Symposium on Principles of Database Systems (PODS 2002)*, pages 247–258, 2002.
5. Alin Deutsch and Val Tannen. XML Queries and Constraints, Containment and Reformulation. To appear in *J. Theoretical Computer Science (TCS)*, 2005.
6. Alin Deutsch and Yannis Papakonstantinou. Privacy in Database Publishing. Technical report, Department of Computer Science and Engineering, UCSD, 2004. Extended version of this paper, available from http://www.db.ucsd.edu.
7. A. Deutsch, L. Sui, and V. Vianu. Queryies determined by views. Manuscript available from http://www.db.ucsd.edu/people/alin/papers/QdV.ps, 2004.
8. Alin Deutsch and Val Tannen. Reformulation of xml queries and constraints. In *ICDT*, 2003.
9. Oliver M. Duschka, Michael R. Genesereth, and Alon Y. Levy. Recursive query plans for data integration. *Journal of Logic Programming*, 43(1):49–73, 2000.
10. A. Evfimievski, J. Gehrke, and R. Srikant. Limiting privacy breaches in privacy preserving data mining. In *PODS*, 2003.
11. Gösta Grahne and Alberto O. Mendelzon. Tableau techniques for querying information sources through global schemas. In *ICDT*, 1999.
12. Alon Halevy. Logic-based techniques in data integration. In *Logic Based Artificial Intelligence*, 2000.
13. G. Miklau and D. Suciu. Cryptographically enforced conditional access for xml. In *WebDB*, 2002.
14. Gerome Miklau and Dan Suciu. Controlling access to published data using cryptography. In *VLDB*, 2003.
15. Gerome Miklau and Dan Suciu. A formal analysis of information disclosure in data exchange. In *SIGMOD Conf.*, 2004.
16. Shariq Rizvi, Alberto O. Mendelzon, S. Sudarshan, and Prasan Roy. Extending query rewriting techniques for fine-grained access control. In *SIGMOD Conf.*, 2004.
17. Murray R Spiegel, John J. Schiller, and R. Alu Srinivasan. *Schaum's Outline of Probability and Statistics*. MCGraw-Hill, 2000.
18. Jeffrey D. Ullman. Information integration using logical views. In *Proceedings of the Sixth International Conference on Database Theory*, 1997.
19. K. Wagner. The complexity of combinatorial problems with succinct input representation. *Acta Informatica*, 23:325–356, 1986.
20. Winslett et. al. The TrustBuilder Project. Publications Available from http://drl.cs.uiuc.edu/security/pubs.html.

Anonymizing Tables

Gagan Aggarwal, Tomás Feder, Krishnaram Kenthapadi, Rajeev Motwani,
Rina Panigrahy, Dilys Thomas, and An Zhu

Stanford University*

Abstract. We consider the problem of releasing tables from a relational database containing personal records, while ensuring individual
privacy and maintaining data integrity to the extent possible. One of
the techniques proposed in the literature is k-anonymization. A release
is considered k-anonymous if the information for each person contained
in the release cannot be distinguished from at least $k - 1$ other persons whose information also appears in the release. In the k-ANONYMITY
problem the objective is to minimally suppress cells in the table so as
to ensure that the released version is k-anonymous. We show that the
k-ANONYMITY problem is NP-hard even when the attribute values are
ternary. On the positive side, we provide an $O(k)$-approximation algorithm for the problem. This improves upon the previous best known
$O(k \log k)$-approximation. We also give improved positive results for the
interesting cases with specific values of k — in particular, we give a 1.5-
approximation algorithm for the special case of 2-ANONYMITY, and a
2-approximation algorithm for 3-ANONYMITY.

1 Introduction

The information age has witnessed a tremendous growth in the amount of personal data that can be collected and analyzed. This has led to an increasing
use of data mining tools with the basic goal of inferring trends in order to
predict the future. However, the protection of personal data against privacy
intrusions has restricted the direct usage of data containing personal information [Eur98, Tim97]. In many scenarios, access to large amounts of *personal
data* is essential in order for accurate inferences to be drawn. For example,
hospitals might wish to collaborate with each other in order to catch the out-
break of epidemics in their early stages. This requires them to allow outside
access to medical records of their patients, potentially violating the doctor-
patient privilege. In such cases, the remedy is to provide data in a manner
that enables one to draw inferences without violating the privacy of individual
records.

Different approaches to address this problem have emerged recently. One
approach is to use *perturbation* techniques in order to hide the exact values of

* Supported in part by NSF Grants IIS-0118173, EIA-0137761, and ITR-0331640, and
grants from Microsoft, SNRC, and Veritas.

the data [AS00, AA01, DN03, DN04, EGS03, AST03]. However, this may not be suitable if one wants to make inferences with 100% confidence. If the function to be evaluated is known in advance, we can use techniques from *secure multi-party computation* [LP00, AMP04, FNP04]. However interactive data-mining tasks are inherently ad-hoc and the queries are not known ahead of time.

Another approach is to *suppress* or *generalize* some of the sensitive data values. We consider the k-anonymity model which was proposed by Samarati and Sweeney [Swe02, SS98]. Suppose we have a table with n tuples and m attributes. Let $k > 1$ be an integer. We wish to release a modified version of this table, where we can suppress the values of certain cells in the table. *The objective is to minimize the number of cells suppressed while ensuring that for each tuple in the modified table, there are at least $k-1$ other tuples in the modified table identical to it.* For example, consider the following table which is part of a medical database, with the identifying attributes such as name and social security number removed.

Age	Race	Gender	Zip Code	Diseases
47	White	Male	94305	Common Cold
35	White	Female	94045	Flu
27	Black	Female	92010	Flu
27	White	Female	92010	Hypertension

By joining with public databases (such as a voter list), non-identifying attributes such as Age, Race, Gender and Zip Code in the above table can together be used to identify individuals. In fact, Sweeney [Swe00] observed that for 87% of the population in the United States, the combination of Date of Birth, Gender and Zip Code corresponded to a unique person. Hence, simply removing the identifying (or key) attributes from a database is not enough. Instead we would like to suppress some of these entries so that any (Age, Race, Gender, Zip Code) tuple corresponds to at least k individuals. Note that we do not suppress any entry in the column for "Diseases". Joining this anonymized table with public databases can, if at all, only identify an individual's disease to be one among k diseases. For instance, when $k = 2$, we could obtain the following anonymized table.

Age	Race	Gender	Zip Code	Diseases
*	White	*	*	Common Cold
*	White	*	*	Flu
27	*	Female	92010	Flu
27	*	Female	92010	Hypertension

We study the k-ANONYMITY problem: finding the *optimal* (in terms of minimizing the number of cells suppressed) k-anonymized table for any given table instance. We show that this problem is NP-hard even for the special case of ternary attribute values. This significantly strengthens the NP-hardness result in [MW04], which required the domain of attribute values to be larger than the number of tuples in the table. On the positive side, we give an $O(k)$-approximation algorithm for this problem (for arbitrary alphabet size) using a graph representation. This improves upon the previous best-known approximation guarantee of $O(k \log k)$ [MW04]. We also show that it is not possible to achieve an approximation factor better than $O(k)$ using the graph representation approach. In addition, for binary alphabets, we give a 1.5-approximation algorithm for $k = 2$ and a 2-approximation algorithm for $k = 3$.

The rest of the paper is organized as follows. In Section 2, we specify our model and formally state the problem of k-ANONYMITY. We establish the NP-hardness of k-ANONYMITY in Section 3. We then provide a 1.5 approximation algorithm for the 2-ANONYMITY problem for binary alphabet in Section 4, and follow this up with a brief sketch of the 2-approximation algorithm for 3-ANONYMITY (for binary alphabet) in Section 5. In Section 6, we present an $O(k)$-approximation algorithm for the k-ANONYMITY problem. In the Appendix, we present the details of the 2-approximation algorithm for 3-ANONYMITY.

2   Model and Main Results

Consider a database with n rows and m columns in which each entry comes from a finite alphabet Σ. For example, in a medical database, the rows represent individuals and the columns correspond to the different attributes. We would like to suppress some of the entries so that each row becomes identical to at least $k - 1$ other rows. A suppressed entry is denoted by the symbol $*$. Since suppression results in the release of *less information and hence less utility*, we would like to suppress as few entries as possible.

We can view the database as consisting of n m-dimensional vectors: $x_1, \ldots,$ $x_n \in \Sigma^m$. A *k-anonymous suppression* function t maps each x_i to $\tilde{x}_i$ by replacing some components of x_i by $*$, so that every $\tilde{x}_i$ is identical to at least $k - 1$ other $\tilde{x}_j$'s. This results in a partition of the n row vectors into *clusters* of size at least k each. The cost of the suppression, $c(t)$ is the total number of $*$'s in all the $\tilde{x}_i$'s.

---

k-ANONYMITY: *Given* $x_1, x_2, \ldots, x_n \in \Sigma^m$, *and an anonymity parameter* k, *obtain a k-anonymous suppression function* t *so that* $c(t)$ *is minimized.*

Clearly the decision version of k-ANONYMITY is in NP, since we can verify in polynomial time if the solution is k-anonymous and the suppression cost less than a given value. We show that k-ANONYMITY is NP-hard even when the alphabet size $|\Sigma| = 3$. This improves upon the NP-hardness result of [MW04] which required an alphabet size of n. On the positive side, we provide an $O(k)$-approximation algorithm for arbitrary k and arbitrary alphabet size. For a binary alphabet, we also provide 1.5-approximation for $k = 2$ and 2-approximation for $k = 3$.

3 NP-Hardness of k-ANONYMITY

Theorem 1. k-ANONYMITY *is NP-hard for a ternary alphabet* ($\Sigma = \{0, 1, 2\}$).

Proof Sketch: We show the NP-hardness of k-anonymity by reducing a specific instance of the problem from a known NP-hard graph problem. More specifically we show the hardness of k-anonymity for $k = 3$, by reduction from EDGE PARTITION INTO TRIANGLES [Kan94]: *Given a graph $G = (V, E)$ with $|E| = 3m$ for some integer m, can the edges of G be partitioned into m edge-disjoint triangles?*

Given an instance of the above problem, we create a database as follows. W.l.o.g., we assume that G is simple. The rows correspond to the $3m$ edges and the columns to the n vertices of G. The row corresponding to edge (a, b), r_{ab}, has 1's in the positions corresponding to a and b and 0's everywhere else. We first show that the cost of the optimal 3-ANONYMITY solution is at most $9m$ if and only if E can be partitioned into a collection of m disjoint triangles and 4-stars[1].

Suppose such a partition of edges is given. Consider any triangle (with a, b, c as the vertices). By suppressing the positions a, b and c in the rows r_{ab}, r_{bc} and r_{ca}, we get a cluster with three $*$'s in each modified row. Similarly, consider a 4-star with vertices a, b, c, d, where d is the center vertex. By suppressing the positions a, b and c in the rows r_{ad}, r_{bd} and r_{cd}, we get a cluster with three $*$'s in each modified row. Thus we obtain a solution to 3-ANONYMITY of cost $9m$.

On the other hand, suppose that there is a 3-ANONYMITY solution of cost at most $9m$. Since G is simple, any three rows are distinct and differ in at least 3 positions. Hence there should be at least three $*$'s in each modified row, so that the cost of the solution is at least $9m$. Thus the solution cost is exactly $9m$ and each modified row has exactly three $*$'s. Since any cluster of size > 3 will have at least four $*$'s in each modified row, it follows that each cluster has exactly three rows. There are exactly two possibilities: the corresponding edges form a triangle or a 4-star. Each modified row in a triangle has three $*$'s and zeros elsewhere while each modified row in a 4-star has three $*$'s, single 1 and zeros elsewhere. This corresponds to a partition of the graph edges into triangles or 4-stars, instead of only triangles.

Since we want a reduction from EDGE PARTITION INTO TRIANGLES, we "force" the 4-stars to pay more $*$'s by increasing the number of columns created in our k-ANONYMITY instance. Let $t = 1 + \lceil \log_2(3m) \rceil$. Consider an arbitrary ordering of E and express the rank of an edge $e = (a, b)$, in this ordering, in binary notation as $b_1 b_2 \ldots b_t$. Every row in the database now has t *blocks*, each of which has n columns. In the row corresponding to edge e, each block has zeros in all positions except a and b. Depending on the values in positions a and b, a block can be in two configurations: $conf_0$ has 1 in position a and 2 in position b while $conf_1$ has 2 in position a and 1 in position b. The ith block in this row has configuration $conf_{b_i}$. (For example, consider a

---

[1] By 4-star, we mean a tree on four vertices with a vertex of degree 3.

complete graph on four vertices: $\{v_1, v_2, v_3, v_4\}$. Suppose edge (v_1, v_2) has rank $5 = (0101)_2$. The corresponding row would have 4 blocks of 4 columns each: $1200 - 2100 - 1200 - 2100$.)

We will now show that the cost of the optimal 3-ANONYMITY solution is at most $9mt$ if and only if E can be partitioned into m disjoint triangles.

As earlier, every triangle in such a partition corresponds to a cluster with $3t$ $*$'s in each modified row. Thus we get a 3-ANONYMITY solution of cost $9mt$.

For the converse, suppose that we are given a 3-ANONYMITY solution of cost at most $9mt$. Again, any three rows differ in at least $3t$ positions so that the cost of any solution is at least $9mt$. Hence the solution cost is exactly $9mt$ and each modified row has exactly $3t$ $*$'s. Each cluster has exactly three rows. The corresponding edges should form a triangle: As any two of these edges differ in the configuration of at least one block, there would have been more than $3t$ $*$'s per row if they formed a 4-star instead. Thus we get a partition of E into disjoint triangles.

By reduction from EDGE PARTITION INTO r-CLIQUES [Kan94], we can extend the above proof for $k = \binom{r}{2}$, for $r \geq 3$. By replicating the graph in the above reduction, we can further extend the proof for $k = \alpha\binom{r}{2}$ for any integer α and $r \geq 3$. $\square$

4   Algorithm for 2-ANONYMITY

For a binary alphabet, we provide a polynomial time 1.5-approximation algorithm for 2-ANONYMITY, using a polynomial time algorithm for obtaining a minimum weight $[1, 2]$-factor of a graph. A $[1, 2]$-factor of an edge-weighted graph G is defined to be a spanning (i.e., containing all the vertices) subgraph F of G such that each vertex in F has degree 1 or 2. The weight of F is the sum of the weights of edges in F. Cornuejols [Cor88] showed that a minimum weight $[1, 2]$-factor of a graph can be computed in polynomial time.

Given an instance of the 2-ANONYMITY problem, we create an edge-weighted complete graph $G = (V, E)$ as follows. The vertex set V contains a vertex corresponding to each vector in the 2-ANONYMITY problem. The weight of an edge (a, b) is the Hamming distance between the vectors represented by a and b (i.e., the number of positions at which they differ). First we obtain a minimum weight $[1, 2]$-factor F of G. By optimality, F is a vertex-disjoint collection of edges and pairs of adjacent edges (If a $[1, 2]$-factor has a component which is either a cycle or a path of length ≥ 3, we can obtain a lesser weight $[1, 2]$-factor by removing edge(s).). We treat each component of F as a *cluster*, i.e., retain the bits on which all the vectors in the cluster agree and replace all other bits by $*$'s. Clearly this results in a 2-anonymized database.

Theorem 2. *The number of stars introduced by the above algorithm is at most 1.5 times the number of stars in an optimal 2-ANONYMITY solution.*

Proof Sketch: Let ALG and OPT denote the costs of the above solution and optimal 2-ANONYMITY solution respectively. Let $OFAC$ denote the weight of an optimal $[1, 2]$-factor. The optimal 2-ANONYMITY solution can be assumed to consist only of disjoint clusters of size 2 or 3 (as bigger clusters can be broken into such clusters without increasing the cost). We derive a $[1, 2]$-factor from this solution as follows. Include the edge between the two vertices in each 2-cluster. For 3-clusters, include the two edges of lesser weights amongst the three edges. Denote the weight of this $[1, 2]$-factor by FAC.

Consider three m-bit vectors x_1, x_2 and x_3 with pairwise Hamming distances α, β and γ as in Fig. 1. W.l.o.g, let $\gamma \geq \alpha, \beta$. Let x_{med} denote the "median" vector whose i^{th} bit is the majority of the ith bits of x_1, x_2 and x_3 and let p, q and r be the Hamming distances to x_{med} from the three vectors. Let x_s be the "star" vector obtained by minimal suppression of x_1, x_2 and x_3, i.e., it has the common bits where the three vectors agree and $*$'s elsewhere. Observe that $\alpha = q + r$, $\beta = r + p$ and $\gamma = p + q$. The other relevant distances are shown in the figure.

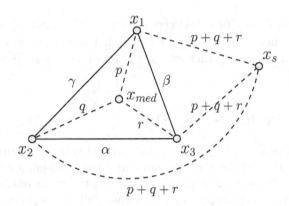

Fig. 1. Three vectors and their corresponding "median" and "star" vectors

Lemma 1. $ALG \leq 3 \cdot OFAC$

Proof Sketch: For a 2-cluster, we have to suppress all the bits at which the two vectors differ so that the total number of $*$'s is twice the Hamming distance (which is the edge weight). For a 3-cluster, say the one in the figure, the number of $*$'s is $(p + q + r)$ for each vector, so that the total is $3(p + q + r) = \frac{3}{2}(\alpha + \beta + \gamma) \leq 3(\alpha + \beta)$ (using triangle inequality). The optimal $[1, 2]$-factor would have contained two (lesser weight) edges, incurring a cost of $(\alpha + \beta)$ for this cluster. Considering all the clusters formed by the optimal $[1, 2]$-factor algorithm, we get $ALG \leq 3 \cdot OFAC$.   □

Lemma 2. $FAC \leq OPT/2$

Proof Sketch: For a 2-cluster, cost incurred in $FAC = \frac{1}{2}$(cost incurred in OPT). For a 3-cluster (in the figure), cost incurred in $FAC = \alpha + \beta \leq \frac{2}{3}(\alpha + \beta + \gamma) = \frac{4}{3}(p + q + r)$, where the inequality follows using $\gamma \geq \alpha, \beta$. Since the cost incurred in OPT is $3(p + q + r)$, cost incurred in $FAC < \frac{1}{2}$(cost incurred in OPT). By considering all the clusters, we get $FAC \leq OPT/2$.   □

Since $OFAC \leq FAC$, it follows from the above lemmas that $ALG \leq \frac{3}{2}OPT$.   □

For an arbitrary alphabet size, x_{med} is no longer defined. However as before it can be shown that $OPT \geq (\alpha+\beta+\gamma) \geq \frac{3}{2}(\alpha+\beta)$, proving $FAC \leq \frac{2}{3}OPT$. As $ALG \leq 3 \cdot OFAC$ holds as before, we get $ALG \leq 2 \cdot OPT$. Thus the algorithm achieves a factor 2 approximation for arbitrary alphabet size.

5   Algorithm for 3-ANONYMITY

We now present a 2-approximation algorithm for 3-ANONYMITY with a binary alphabet. The idea is similar to the algorithm for 2-ANONYMITY. We construct the graph G corresponding to the 3-ANONYMITY instance as in the previous algorithm. A 2-factor of a graph is a spanning subgraph with each vertex having degree 2 (in other words, a collection of vertex-disjoint cycles spanning all the vertices). We run the polynomial time algorithm to find a minimum-weight 2-factor F of the graph G [Cor88]. We first show that the cost of this 2-factor, say $OFAC$, is at most 2/3 times the cost of the optimal 3-ANONYMITY solution, say OPT. Then, we show how to transform this 2-factor F into a 3-ANONYMITY solution of cost at most $3 \cdot OFAC$, giving us a factor-2 approximation algorithm for 3-ANONYMITY. The details can be found in the appendix.

6   Algorithm for General k-ANONYMITY

In this section, we address the problem of k-ANONYMITY for general k and arbitrary alphabet size, and give an $O(k)$-approximation algorithm for the problem. Given an instance of the k-ANONYMITY problem, we create an edge-weighted complete graph $G = (V, E)$. The vertex set V contains a vertex corresponding to each vector in the k-ANONYMITY problem. The weight, $w(e)$ of an edge $e = (a, b)$ is the number of attributes along which the vectors represented by a and b differ.

As mentioned in the introduction, with this representation, we lose some information about the structure of the problem, and cannot achieve a better than $O(k)$ approximation factor for the k-anonymity problem. We show this by giving two instances whose k-anonymity cost differs by a factor of $O(k)$, but the corresponding graphs for both the instances are identical. Let $l = 2^{k-2}$. For the first instance, take k vectors with kl-dimensions each. The bit positions $(i-1)l+1$ to il are referred to as the i-th block of a vector. The i-th vector has ones in the i-th block and zeros everywhere else. The k-anonymity cost for this instance is k^2l. For the second instance, take k vectors with $4l = 2^k$ dimensions each. The i-th vector breaks up its 2^k dimensions into 2^i equal-sized blocks and has ones in the odd blocks and zeros in the even blocks. This instance incurs a k-anonymity cost of $4kl$. Note that the graph corresponding to both the instances is a k-clique with all the pairwise distances being $2l = 2^{k-1}$.

Next, we describe our $O(k)$-approximation algorithm for the k-anonymity problem.

For any given k-ANONYMITY solution, define the *charge* of a vertex to be the number of $*$'s introduced into the vector it represents. Let OPT denote the cost of an optimal k-ANONYMITY solution, i.e., OPT is the sum of charges of all vertices in an optimal k-ANONYMITY solution.

Let $F = \{T_1, T_2, \ldots, T_r\}$, a forest in which each tree T_i has at least k vertices, be a subgraph of G. This forest describes a feasible partition for the k-ANONYMITY problem. In the k-ANONYMITY solution as per this partition, the charge of each vertex is at most the cost of the tree, $W(T_i) = \Sigma_{e \in E(T_i)} w(e)$. This is because any attribute along which a pair of vertices differs appears on the path between the two vertices. Thus, the k-anonymity cost of such a partition is at most $\Sigma_i |V(T_i)| W(T_i)$. We will refer to this as the k-anonymity cost of the forest. Note that the cost of a forest is simply the sum of the costs of its trees. The ratio of the k-anonymity cost to the simple cost of a forest is at most the number of vertices in the largest tree in the forest. Thus, if we can find a forest with the size of the largest component at most L and cost at most OPT, then we have an L-approximation algorithm. Next, we present an algorithm that finds such a forest with $L \leq 3k - 3$. Actually, the forest that we obtain has dummy vertices that act as Steiner points, but this does not affect the result.

The algorithm has the following overall structure, which is explained in more detail in the next two subsections.

Outline:

1. Create a forest G with cost at most OPT. The number of vertices in each tree is at least k.
2. Compute a decomposition of this forest (we are allowed to delete edges) such that each component has between k and $3k - 3$ vertices. The decomposition is done in a way that does not increase the sum of the costs of the edges.

6.1   Algorithm for Producing a Forest with Components of Size Atleast k

The key observation is that since each partition in a k-ANONYMITY solution groups a vertex with at least $k - 1$ other vertices, the charge of a vertex is at least equal to its distance to its $(k - 1)^{st}$ nearest neighbor. The idea is to construct a directed forest such that each vertex has at most one outgoing edge and $(\overrightarrow{u, v})$ is an edge only if v is one of the $k - 1$ nearest neighbors of u.

Algorithm FOREST
Invariant:
 – The chosen edges do not create any cycle.
 – The out-degree of each vertex is at most one.

1. Start with an empty edge set so that each vertex is in its own connected component.
2. Repeat until all components are of size at least k:
    Pick any component T having size smaller than k. Let u be a vertex in T without any outgoing edges. Since there are at most $k - 2$ other vertices

in T, one of the $k-1$ nearest neighbors of u, say v, must lie outside T. We add the edge $(\overline{u,v})$ to the forest. Observe that this step does not violate any of the invariants.

Lemma 3. *The forest produced by algorithm* FOREST *has minimum tree size at least k and has cost at most OPT.*

Proof Sketch: It is evident from the algorithm description that each component of the forest it produces has at least k vertices.

Let the cost of an edge $(\overline{u,v})$ be paid by vertex u. Note that each vertex u pays for at most one edge to one of its $k-1$ nearest neighbors. As noted earlier, this is less than the charge of this vertex in any k-ANONYMITY solution. Thus, the sum of costs of all edges in the forest is less than the total charge of all vertices in an optimal solution. □

6.2   Algorithm to Decompose Large Components into Smaller Ones

We next show how to break any component with size greater than $3k-3$ into two components each of size at least k. Let the size of the component we are breaking be $s > 3k-3$.

Algorithm DECOMPOSE-COMPONENT

1. Pick any vertex as the candidate vertex.
2. Root the tree at the candidate vertex u. Let U be the set of subtrees rooted at the children of u. Let the size of the largest subtree of U be ϕ. If $\phi \le s-k$, then we do the following partition and terminate.

   If $\phi \ge k$, then partition the tree into the largest subtree and the rest. Clearly, the size of both components is at least k. Otherwise, all subtrees have size at most $k-1$. In this case, keep adding subtrees to a partition till the first time its size becomes at least k. Clearly, at this point, its size is at most $2k-2$. Put the remaining subtrees and u (at least k vertices in all) into the other partition. In order to keep the first partition connected, a dummy vertex corresponding to u is placed in the first partition which acts only as a Steiner point and does not contribute to the size of the component.
3. Otherwise, pick the root of the largest subtree as the new candidate vertex and go to Step 2.

Lemma 4. *The above algorithm terminates.*

Proof Sketch: We will show that the size of the largest component ϕ (in Step 2) decreases in each iteration. Consider moving from candidate vertex u in one iteration to candidate vertex v in the next iteration. Since the algorithm did not terminate with u, if we root the tree at v, then the size of the subtree rooted at u is less than $s-(s-k)=k$. When we consider the largest subtree under v, either it is rooted at u, in which case, it is smaller than $k < s-k$. Otherwise, the new largest subtree is a subtree of the previous largest subtree. □

Theorem 3. *There is a* $(3k-3)$-*approximation algorithm for the* k-ANONYMITY *problem.*

Proof Sketch: First, use Algorithm FOREST to create a forest with cost at most OPT and minimum tree size at least k. Then repeatedly apply Algorithm DECOMPOSE-COMPONENT to any component that has size larger than $3k - 3$. Note that both these algorithms terminate in polynomial time. □

This factor can be improved to $\max(2k - 1, 3k - 5)$ by appropriately choosing the partition for u in Step 2 of Algorithm DECOMPOSE-COMPONENT. This reduces to $3k - 5$ for $k \geq 4$.

We can easily extend the above algorithm and analysis to the version of the problem where we allow an entire row to be deleted from the published database, instead of forcing it to pair with at least $k - 1$ other rows. The cost of deleting an entire row is modelled as changing all the entries of that row to stars, while the objective remains to minimize the number of stars.

7   Conclusion and Further Research Directions

We showed that the k-ANONYMITY problem is NP-hard, even when the attribute values are ternary. Then we gave an $O(k)$-approximation algorithm for the general k-ANONYMITY problem with arbitrary alphabet size, improving upon the previous best known $O(k \log k)$-approximation. For binary alphabets, we achieve an approximation factor of 1.5 for $k = 2$ and a factor of 2 for $k = 3$. We also show that for k-ANONYMITY, it is not possible to achieve an approximation factor better than $k/4$ by using the graph representation. It would also be interesting to see a hardness of approximation result for k-ANONYMITY without assuming the graph representation.

Releasing a database after k-anonymization prevents definitive *record linkages* with publicly available databases [Swe02]. In particular, for each record in the public database, at least k records in the k-anonymized database could correspond to it, which hides each individual in a crowd of k other people. The privacy parameter k must be chosen according to the application in order to ensure the required level of privacy. One source of concern about the k-anonymization model is that for a given record in the public database, all the k records corresponding to it in the anonymized database might have the same value of the sensitive attribute(s) ("Diseases" in our examples), thus revealing the sensitive attribute(s) conclusively. To address this issue, we could add a constraint that specifies that for each cluster in the k-anonymized database, the sensitive attribute(s) should take at least r distinct values. This would be an interesting direction for future research.

Another interesting direction of research is to extend the basic k-ANONYMITY model to deal with changes in the database. A hospital may want to periodically release an anonymized version of its patient database. However, releasing several anonymized versions of a database might leak enough information to enable *record linkages* for some of the records. It would be useful to extend the k-ANONYMITY framework to handle inserts, deletes and updates to a database.

References

[AA01]   D. Agrawal and C. Aggarwal. On the design and quantification of privacy preserving datamining algorithms. In *Proc. of the ACM Symp. on Principles of Database Systems*, 2001.

[AMP04]   G. Aggarwal, N. Mishra, and B. Pinkas. Privacy preserving computation of the k-th ranked element. In *EUROCRYPT*, 2004.

[AS00]   R. Agrawal and R. Srikant. Privacy-preserving data mining. In *Proc. of the ACM SIGMOD Intl. Conf. on Management of Data*, pages 439–450, May 2000.

[AST03]   R. Agrawal, R. Srikant, and D. Thomas. Privacy preserving aggregates. Technical report, Stanford University, 2003.

[Cor88]   G. P. Cornuejols. General factors of graphs. In *Journal of Combinatorial Theory B 45*, pages 185–198, 1988.

[DN03]   I. Dinur and K. Nissim. Revealing information while preserving privacy. In *Proc. of the ACM Symp. on Principles of Database Systems*, pages 202–210, 2003.

[DN04]   C. Dwork and K. Nissim. Privacy-preserving datamining on vertically partitioned databases. In *CRYPTO*, 2004.

[EGS03]   A. Evfimievski, J. Gehrke, and R. Srikant. Limiting privacy breaches in privacy preserving data mining. In *Proc. of the ACM Symp. on Principles of Database Systems*, June 2003.

[Eur98]   European Union. *Directive on Privacy Protection*, October 1998.

[FNP04]   M. Freedman, K. Nissim, and B. Pinkas. Efficient private matching and set intersection. In *EUROCRYPT*, 2004.

[Kan94]   V. Kann. Maximum bounded H-matching is MAX SNP-complete. In *Information Processing Letters, 49*, pages 309–318, 1994.

[LP00]   Y. Lindell and B. Pinkas. Privacy preserving data mining. In *CRYPTO*, pages 36–54, 2000.

[MW04]   A. Meyerson and R. Williams. On the complexity of optimal k-anonymity. In *Proc. of the ACM Symp. on Principles of Database Systems*, June 2004.

[SS98]   P. Samarati and L. Sweeney. Generalizing data to provide anonymity when disclosing information (abstract). In *Proc. of the ACM Symp. on Principles of Database Systems*, page 188, 1998.

[Swe00]   L. Sweeney. Uniqueness of simple demographics in the U.S. population. In *LIDAP-WP4. Carnegie Mellon University, Laboratory for International Data Privacy, Pittsburgh, PA*, 2000.

[Swe02]   L. Sweeney. k-Anonymity: A model for protecting privacy. In *International Journal on Uncertainty Fuzziness Knowledge-based Systems*, June 2002.

[Tim97]   Time. *The Death of Privacy*, August 1997.

A   Detailed Algorithm for 3-ANONYMITY

Lemma 5. *The cost of the optimal 2-factor, $OFAC$ on graph G corresponding to the vectors in the 3-ANONYMITY instance is at most $2/3$ times the cost of the optimal 3-ANONYMITY solution, OPT.*

Proof Sketch: Note that the optimal 3-ANONYMITY solution will cluster 3, 4 or 5 vertices together (any larger groups can be broken up into smaller groups of size at least 3, without increasing the cost of the solution). Given an optimal solution to the 3-ANONYMITY problem, we construct a 2-factor solution as follows. For every cluster of the 3-ANONYMITY solution, pick the minimum-weight cycle involving the vertices of the cluster. Next, we analyze the cost FAC of this 2-factor. Define the *charge* of a vertex to be the number of $*$'s in the vector corresponding to this vertex in the 3-ANONYMITY solution. We consider the following three cases:

(a) If a cluster i is of size 3, the 2-factor contains a triangle on the corresponding vertices. Let a, b and c be the lengths of the edges of the triangle. Using an argument similar to Lemma 1, we get that $(a+b+c)$ is twice the charge of each vertex in this cluster. Thus, OPT pays a total cost of $OPT_i = 3(a+b+c)/2$ while FAC pays $FAC_i = a+b+c = \frac{2}{3}OPT_i$

(b) If a cluster i is of size 4, the 2-factor corresponds to the cheapest 4-cycle on the 4 vertices. Let τ be the sum of the weights of all the $\binom{4}{2} = 6$ edges on these four vertices. Then, by considering all 4-cycles and choosing the minimum weight 4-cycle, we ensure that the cost paid by FAC for these vertices $FAC_i \leq \frac{4}{6}\tau$. Also, the charge of any of these 4 vertices is at least half the cost of any triangle on (three of) these four vertices (again by using the argument of Lemma 1). Averaging over all triangles, we get that cost paid by OPT, $OPT_i \geq 4.\frac{1}{2}.\frac{3}{6}.\tau = \tau$. Thus, $FAC_i \leq \frac{2}{3}OPT_i$.

(c) If a cluster i is of size 5, let τ be the sum of weights of all $\binom{5}{2} = 10$ edges on these five vertices. Then, FAC pays $FAC_i \leq \frac{5}{10}\tau$. Also, the charge of any of these vertices is at least half the cost of any triangle on (three of) these vertices. Averaging over all triangles, we get that cost paid by OPT for cluster i, $OPT_i \geq 5.\frac{1}{2}.\frac{3}{10}.\tau = \frac{3}{4}\tau$. Thus, $FAC_i \leq \frac{2}{3}OPT_i$.

Thus, adding up over all clusters, we get $FAC \leq \frac{2}{3}OPT$. Thus, $OFAC \leq \frac{2}{3}OPT$.

$\square$

Lemma 6. *Given a 2-factor F with cost FAC, we can get a solution for 3-ANONYMITY of cost $SOL \leq 3 \cdot FAC$.*

Proof Sketch: To get a solution for 3-ANONYMITY, we make every cycle in F with size 3, 4 or 5 into a cluster. For each larger cycle C, if $|C| = 3x$ for x an integer, then we break it up into x clusters, each containing 3 adjacent vertices of C, such that the total cost of edges of the cycle within the clusters is minimized. Similarly, if $C = 3x + 1$, x an integer, we break it into x clusters, $x - 1$ of size 3, and one of size 4. If $C = 3x + 2$, x an integer, then we break it up into $x - 2$ clusters of size 3, and two clusters of size 4.

Let $len(C)$ denote the length of a cycle C in the 2-factor. Then depending on the size of the cycle C, we can show that the 3-ANONYMITY solution SOL pays as follows:

(a) For a triangle, SOL pays $3 \cdot \frac{1}{2} \cdot len(C) \leq 3 \cdot len(C)$.
(b) For a 4-cycle, SOL pays at most $4 \cdot \frac{1}{2} \cdot len(C) \leq 3 \cdot len(C)$.
(c) For a 5-cycle, SOL pays at most $5 \cdot \frac{1}{2} \cdot len(C) \leq 3 \cdot len(C)$.

This is so (for the above cases) because the number of attributes along which the vertices differ is at most $\text{len}(C)/2$.

(d) For a $3x$-cycle, $x > 1$, SOL pays at most $3 \cdot \frac{2x}{3x} \cdot \text{len}(C) \leq 3 \cdot \text{len}(C)$.

(e) For a $(3x+1)$-cycle, $x > 1$, SOL pays at most $\frac{2(x-1)\cdot 3 + 3\cdot 4}{3x+1} \cdot \text{len}(C) \leq 3\cdot\text{len}(C)$.

(f) For a $(3x+2)$-cycle, $x > 1$, SOL pays at most $\frac{2(x-2)\cdot 3 + 6\cdot 4}{3x+2} \cdot \text{len}(C) \leq 3\cdot\text{len}(C)$.
(Equality can hold in this case, when $x = 2$.)

Thus, adding over all clusters, SOL pays no more than 3 times the total cost of all cycles, i.e., $3 \cdot FAC$.   □

Combining the above lemmas, we obtain a factor-2 approximation for 3-ANONYMITY.

Authorization Views and Conditional Query Containment

Zheng Zhang and Alberto O. Mendelzon

University of Toronto,
Department of Computer Science
{zhzhang, mendel}@cs.toronto.edu

Abstract. A recent proposal for database access control consists of defining "authorization views" that specify the accessible data, and declaring a query valid if it can be completely rewritten using the views. Unlike traditional work in query rewriting using views, the rewritten query needs to be equivalent to the original query only over the set of database states that agree with a given set of materializations for the authorization views. With this motivation, we study conditional query containment, *i.e.*, containment over states that agree on a set of materialized views. We give an algorithm to test conditional containment of conjunctive queries with respect to a set of materialized conjunctive views. We show the problem is Π_2^p-complete. Based on the algorithm, we give a test for a query to be conditionally authorized given a set of materialized authorization views.

1 Introduction

Access control is an integral part of databases and information systems. Traditionally, access control has been achieved by presenting users with a set of views that their queries must operate on. An alternative approach achieves "authorization transparency" [13, 14, 15, 16] by using views in a different way. A set of "authorization views" specifies what information a user is allowed to access. The user writes the query in terms of the base relations, and the system tests the query for validity by determining whether it can be completely rewritten using the authorization views. For flexibility, views can be parameterized with information specific to a session, such as the user-id, location, date, time, etc., which are instantiated before access control is performed.

Example 1. Consider a database with the following relations: *Employees(**eid**, name, rank)*, *Projects(**pid**, name, headid)*, *EP(**eid**, **pid**)*, *Progress(**eid**, **pid**, prgs)*. The *EP* relation associates employees with projects, while a tuple in *Progress* represents a progress report by an employee on a project that the employee is working on. We use this schema as a running example here and in Section 4. The following authorization view V_1 states the policy that an employee can see the progress of his or her colleagues in the projects that the employee is working on.

$$V_1(eid, pid, prgs) \leftarrow Progress(eid, pid, prgs), EP(\$userid, pid).$$

T. Eiter and L. Libkin (Eds.): ICDT 2005, LNCS 3363, pp. 259–273, 2005.
© Springer-Verlag Berlin Heidelberg 2005

For simplicity, we assume that a user's id is the same as his or her employee-id. The parameter $user-id is instantiated to the actual user-id before access control is performed. The set of authorization view definitions resulting from instantiating all the parameters that occur in them is called the *instantiated authorization views*. These define exactly what information is accessible to the user in the current session.

Now suppose employee '88' wants to see the progress in all the projects that he or she is associated with, using the following query q.

$$q(eid, pid, prgs) \leftarrow Progress(eid, pid, prgs), EP(88, pid).$$

The instantiated authorization view V_1 is as follows.

$$V_1(eid, pid, prgs) \leftarrow Progress(eid, pid, prgs), EP(88, pid).$$

The following query q' is an equivalent rewriting of q in terms of the instantiated view V_1, showing that q is authorized.

$$q'(eid, pid, prgs) \leftarrow V_1(eid, pid, prgs).$$

Now suppose the same employee wants to see who are the employees who have reported progress in both projects 'XP1' and 'XP2', using the following query q.

$$q(eid) \leftarrow Progress(eid, XP1, prgs_1), Progress(eid, XP2, prgs_2).$$

Since it is the same employee, the instantiated authorization view remains the same. It is easy to see that there is no rewriting q' of q in terms of V_1 such that q' is equivalent to q over all database states; hence, the query will be rejected. But this is unnecessarily harsh. Intuitively, if EP says that employee '88' is working on projects 'XP1' and 'XP2', then q should be authorized. The problem is that the requirement that there be a rewriting q' that is equivalent to q *over all database states* is too strong. For example, the following q' is equivalent to the last query q, not over all database states, but only over those states where employee '88' is working on projects 'XP1' and 'XP2'.

$$q'(eid) \leftarrow V_1(eid, XP1, prgs_1), V_1(eid, XP2, prgs_2).$$

In sum, we adopt the definition of [14]: a query q is *conditionally valid* with respect to a set of views V and a set of materializations of these views MV if there is a rewriting q' of q using the views V such that, for all database states where the values of the views V agree with MV, q agrees with q'.

Note that unconditional authorization (*i.e.*, with equivalence required over all database states) reduces to the well-known problem of whether a query can be rewritten using views [10, 11]. Just as query containment plays a crucial role in the theory of rewriting queries using views, the problem of *conditional query containment* with respect to a set of view materializations must be solved in order to solve the problem of conditional authorization. We study conditional containment of conjunctive queries with respect to a set of materialized conjunctive views. We show that this problem is Π_2^p-complete and use it to give a test for conditional query authorization.

The rest of the paper is organized as follows. Section 2 is the preliminaries. Section 3 presents the test for conditional containment between conjunctive queries. Section 4 presents our solution to conditional query authorization. Section 5 describes related work, and Section 6 concludes the paper and gives directions for future work.

2 Preliminaries

We consider the usual class of conjunctive queries, CQ. The *conjunctive queries with arithmetic comparisons* (CQ^{AC}) extend the conjunctive queries CQ by allowing subgoals with built-in predicates of the form $x_j\theta x_k$, where x_j and x_k are either variables or constants and θ is $\neq, =, <,$ or $\leq$. Every variable occurring in an equality or inequality must also occur in a regular subgoal. The predicates used in the regular subgoals are called *EDB* (extensional database) predicates. In particular, denote by $CQ^{\neq}$ the subclass of CQ^{AC} with only disequations $(\neq)$.

The *normalization* of a query q in CQ^{AC} creates a new query nq from q in two steps: first replace each occurrence of a shared variable x in the regular subgoals, except the first occurrence, by a new distinct variable x_i and add $x = x_i$ to nq; then replace each constant c by a new distinct variable t, and add $t = c$ to nq.

Given an instance d, a valuation ρ from a query CQ into d is a total function ρ from the variables of Q to the domain of constants from d such that $\rho(X_i) \in d(p_i)$ for each regular subgoal $p_i(X_i)$ of Q. The answer to a query Q on instance d is denoted by $Q(d)$ and defined as follows.

$Q(d) = \{\rho(X) \mid \rho$ is a valuation for Q into $d, q(X)$ is the head predicate of $Q\}$.

A query Q is *satisfiable* if there exists a database instance d such that $Q(d)$ is nonempty. Unlike the CQ's, which are always satisfiable, a query in CQ^{AC} is unsatisfiable when its equality and inequality subgoals are unsatisfiable.

For any two queries Q_1 and Q_2, Q_1 is said to be *unconditionally contained* in Q_2, denoted by $Q_1 \subseteq Q_2$, if for all database instances d, $Q_1(d) \subseteq Q_2(d)$. Many algorithms exist to test containment of CQ's and their extensions under set semantics [2, 4, 8, 17]. Among them, the concept of *containment mapping* is widely used. A containment mapping from query Q_2 to query Q_1 is a function from the variables and constants of Q_2 to those of Q_1 that is the identity on constants and that induces a mapping from the subgoals of Q_2 to those of Q_1.

Theorem 1. *[4] For any two CQ's Q_1 and Q_2, $Q_1 \subseteq Q_2$ if and only if there exists a containment mapping ρ from Q_2 to Q_1 such that ρ maps the head of Q_2 to the head of Q_1.*

This theorem remains true when Q_1 contains built-in predicates [10]. We say a query Q_r is a *complete rewriting* of Q using V if Q_r is written using only the views in V and is equivalent to Q. The paper just cited also gives an algorithm to determine whether a query Q has a complete rewriting in a set of views V.

3   Conditional Query Containment

This section presents our solution to the conditional query containment problem. We assume a fixed set of view definitions $V = \{v_1, \ldots v_n\}$. For each view v_i, we are given an instance of it called mv_i. The set of all materialized view instances is called MV. The set of database instances $D = \{d \mid v_j(d) = mv_j, 1 \leq j \leq n\}$ is called the set of *valid instances* for V and MV. Note that it is possible for the set of materializations to be inconsistent, *i.e.* , the set D can be empty. Although our methods work in this case also, we do not treat it explicitly in this paper for lack of space.

The default variable set is $\{x, y, z, \ldots\}$ while $\{X, Y, Z, \ldots\}$ are tuples of variables and constants. We only consider queries and views in CQ (*i.e.* , no arithmetic comparisons) in the following sections, unless otherwise noted.

Definition 1. *For any two queries Q_1 and Q_2, Q_1 is said to be conditionally contained in Q_2 w.r.t. V and MV, denoted by $Q_1 \sqsubseteq_{V,MV} Q_2$, if for every d in D, $Q_1(d) \subseteq Q_2(d)$. Q_1 is said to be conditionally equivalent to Q_2 w.r.t. V and MV, denoted by $Q_1 \equiv_{V,MV} Q_2$, if $Q_1 \sqsubseteq_{V,MV} Q_2$ and $Q_2 \sqsubseteq_{V,MV} Q_1$.*

Definition 2. *A query Q is conditionally empty w.r.t. V and MV if $Q(d)$ is empty for every d in D.*

3.1   A Necessary Condition

Given two CQ's Q_1 and Q_2 such that $Q_1 \subseteq Q_2$, by Theorem 1, the set of EDB predicates appearing in Q_2 must be contained in the set of those appearing in Q_1. This, however, may not be the case for conditional containment.

Example 2. Given a view $v(x) \leftarrow r_2(x)$ and two queries $Q_1 : q_1() \leftarrow r_1(x), r_2(x)$, $Q_2 : q_2() \leftarrow r_2(x), r_3(x)$. If mv is empty, Q_1 and Q_2 are conditionally empty. Hence, $Q_1 \equiv_{v,mv} Q_2$ even though their sets of EDB predicates do not contain each other.

If mv is nonempty, query results depend on r_1 and r_3, respectively. The materialized view does not have r_1 and r_3 in its body, so there is no conditional containment relationship between the two queries.

Theorem 2. *If $Q_1 \sqsubseteq_{V,MV} Q_2$, then either Q_1 is conditionally empty w.r.t. V and MV, or the set of EDB predicates of Q_2 is contained in the set of EDB predicates appearing either in Q_1 or in the definition of some view whose materialization is nonempty.*

Thus, we know that if Q_1 is not conditionally empty, and the set of EDB predicates of Q_2 is not contained in the set of EDB predicates appearing in Q_1 or in the definition of one or more nonempty materialized views, then we can conclude $Q_1 \not\sqsubseteq_{V,MV} Q_2$. We will discuss testing conditional emptiness in Section 3.5. From now on, we assume that the condition of the Theorem holds.

Our plan for testing conditional containment is as follows. First, for any conjunctive query Q we shall construct a query Q' that has the property that Q' agrees with Q on the valid instances and is empty on the invalid ones. Given two CQ's Q_1 and Q_2, it will follow that $Q_1 \subseteq_{V,MV} Q_2$ if and only if $Q'_1 \subseteq Q_2$. That is, we have transformed the problem of conditional containment to one of standard, unconditional containment. Unfortunately, we are not done yet, because Q'_1 is not a conjunctive query, or even a union of queries in CQ^{AC}; it is a nonrecursive Datalog program with negation. The second step therefore is to transform Q'_1 into a query Q''_1 that is a union of queries in CQ^{AC} and still has the property that $Q_1 \subseteq_{V,MV} Q_2$ if and only if $Q''_1 \subseteq Q_2$.

3.2   Construction of Q'

For each view v_i and materialization mv_i, such that mv_i is not empty, we create a set of subgoals P_i that we will add to the body of Q. Abusing notation slightly, we say that P_i is true on instance d when there is a valuation that embeds P_i in d. Intuitively, P_i is true on instance d if and only if every tuple in mv_i is in $v_i(d)$. Suppose that view v_i is given by

$$v_i(x_1, x_2, \ldots, x_{s_i}) \leftarrow r_s(\ldots, x_1, \ldots), \ldots, r_t(\ldots, x_2, \ldots), \ldots$$

and its nonempty materialization mv_i consists of tuples: $t_1 = (x_1^1, x_2^1, \ldots, x_{s_i}^1), \ldots,$ $t_{K_i} = (x_1^{K_i}, x_2^{K_i}, \ldots, x_{s_i}^{K_i})$ where $s_i \geq 0$ is the size of the head predicate of v_i and $K_i \geq 1$ is the cardinality of mv_i. For $(1 \leq j \leq K_i)$, let

$$c_{i_j} = \{r_s(\ldots, x_1, \ldots), \ldots, r_t(\ldots, x_2, \ldots), \ldots, x_1 = x_1^j, x_2 = x_2^j, \ldots, x_{s_i} = x_{s_i}^j\}.$$

Rename the variables in each c_{i_j} so that they are disjoint from every other c_{i_j} and also disjoint from those in Q. Let $P_i = \bigcup_{j=1}^{K_i} c_{i_j}$.

Lemma 1. *There is a valuation from P_i into d if and only if $mv_i \subseteq v_i(d)$.*

In addition to the P_i's, we define a set of negated subgoals called N_i's, one for each view v_i. Each N_i is the negation of a subgoal $c_i()$, where c_i is a new intensional predicate. Intuitively, $c_i()$ will be true (nonempty) on instance d if and only if $v_i(d)$ contains some tuple not in mv_i; so that N_i will be true on instance d if and only if $v_i(d) \subseteq mv_i$. The rule that defines c_i is the following.

$$c_i() \leftarrow r_s(\ldots, x_1, \ldots), \ldots, r_t(\ldots, x_2, \ldots), \ldots,$$
$$\bigwedge_{k=1}^{K_i} \neg(x_1 = x_1^k, x_2 = x_2^k, \ldots, x_{s_i} = x_{s_i}^k). \ (*)$$

Note that the rule for c_i is expressed for convenience with a negated conjunction of subgoals in the body; this is a shorthand for the union c_i of all the rules whose body contains one disequation from each of the negated subgoals.

Lemma 2. *N_i is true on instance d if and only if $v_i(d) \subseteq mv_i$.*

Now we can rewrite Q as a nonrecursive Datalog program by adding all the P_i and N_i subgoals to its body, and attaching the rules that define the c_i's.

$$Q' : q(X) \leftarrow p_1(X_1), p_2(X_2), \ldots, p_n(X_n), P_1, \ldots, P_m,$$
$$N_1, \ldots, N_m, N_{m+1}, \ldots, N_{m'}.$$
$$c_i() \leftarrow r_s(\ldots, x_1, \ldots), \ldots, r_t(\ldots, x_2, \ldots), \ldots,$$
$$\bigwedge_{k=1}^{K_i} \neg(x_1 = x_1^k, x_2 = x_2^k, \ldots, x_{s_i} = x_{s_i}^k).$$

where m' is the number of views and m is the number of views with nonempty materializations. Q' has the following properties.

Lemma 3. $Q'(d) = Q(d)$ *for all valid database instances* d*, and* $Q'(d') = \emptyset$ *for all invalid database instances* d'*.*

Example 3. Consider three views $v_1() \leftarrow r(x)$ with mv_1 containing just the one tuple $()$ (*i.e.* , true), $v_2(x) \leftarrow s(x)$ with mv_2 containing just the tuple (e), and $v_3(x) \leftarrow t(x)$ with empty materialization, as well as a CQ $Q : q(x) \leftarrow r(x)$. The Datalog program is

$$Q' : q(x) \leftarrow r(x), r(x_1), s(e), \neg c_2, \neg c_3.$$
$$c_2() \leftarrow s(x), x \neq e.$$
$$c_3() \leftarrow t(x).$$

Proposition 1. *Given two CQ's* Q_1 *and* Q_2 *as well as a set of conjunctive views* V *with materializations* MV*,* $Q'_1 \subseteq Q_2$ *if and only if* $Q_1 \subseteq_{V,MV} Q_2$*.*

Proof. (only if) Suppose $Q'_1 \subseteq Q_2$. Let d be a valid database instance. Then $Q'_1(d) = Q1(d)$ by Lemma 3. Therefore, $Q1(d) \subseteq Q_2(d)$.

(if) Suppose $Q_1 \subseteq_{V,MV} Q_2$. Let d be any database instance. If d is valid, from $Q_1(d) \subseteq Q_2(d)$, it follows that $Q'_1(d) \subseteq Q_2(d)$. If d is not valid, $Q'_1(d) = \emptyset$, so $Q'_1(d) \subseteq Q_2(d)$. Therefore, $Q'_1 \subseteq Q_2$. $\square$

3.3   Construction of Q''

With the above proposition, we are on our way to transform the conditional containment problem into an unconditional problem. We would like to eliminate the c_i's and replace the corresponding N_i's to create a CQ or one of its extensions. Consider a c_i whose mv_i is nonempty. Query (*) is equivalent to a union c_i of queries c_{ik} in $CQ^{\neq}$ which share the same regular subgoals. Given a database instance e, $N_i = true$ for e means there is no valuation over the regular subgoals of c_i into e such that $(x_1, x_2, \ldots, x_{s_i})$ is mapped to a tuple not in mv_i. We will relax this restriction by replacing N_i with N'_i, where $N'_i = true$ for e means that, if d is any sub-instance obtained by some valuation ρ of the regular subgoals in Q' over e, then there is no valuation over the regular subgoals of c_i into d such that $(x_1, x_2, \ldots, x_{s_i})$ is mapped to a tuple not in mv_i. To obtain N'_i, we first normalize each query c_{ik} in c_i (see Section 2) and obtain a rule whose body has three parts: the regular subgoals nc^+_{ik}, a set of equalities Eq_{ik}, and a set of negations Neq_{ik} in c_{ik}. Since c_{ik}'s share the regular subgoals, nc^+_{ik}'s are the same, denoted by nc^+_i. So are Eq_{ik}'s, denoted by Eq_i. Clearly, $\bigcup_k Neq_{ik}$ is equivalent to the disequations in c_i,

$$Neq_i = \bigwedge_{k=1}^{K_i} \neg(x_1 = x_1^k, x_2 = x_2^k, \ldots, x_{s_i} = x_{s_i}^k).$$

Consider all the containment mappings $\{mp_{i1}, mp_{i2}, \ldots, mp_{ig}\}$ from nc^+_i to Q'. Since we are assuming that mv_i is nonempty, $\bigcup_k Neq_{ik}$ is nonempty. Let N'_i be:

$$\bigwedge_{j=1}^{g} \neg mp_{ij}(Eq_i) \vee \neg mp_{ij}\Big(\bigcup_k Neq_{ik}\Big).$$

Notice all subgoals in $mp_{ij}(nc^+_i)$ exist in Q', hence they are redundant and omitted here. Furthermore, $\bigcup_k Neq_{ik}$ is just Neq_i, hence $\neg mp_{ij}(\bigcup_k Neq_{ik})$ can be simplified to $\neg mp_{ij}(Neq_i)$ which is equivalent to its positive form, say $mp_{ij}(Peq_i)$,

$$\bigvee_{l=1}^{K_i} (mp_{ij}(x_1) = x_1^l, mp_{ij}(x_2) = x_2^l, \ldots, mp_{ij}(x_{s_i}) = x_{s_i}^l).$$

Example 4. Given a view $v(x) \leftarrow r_1(x, y, y)$ with mv containing only the tuple (1) and a query $Q : q(x, y) \leftarrow r_1(x, y, z), r_2(z)$, the Datalog program Q' is

$$Q' : q(x, y) \leftarrow r_1(x, y, z), r_2(z), r_1(1, y_1, y_1), \neg c_1,$$
$$c_1() \leftarrow r1(x_2, y_2, y_2), x_2 \neq 1.$$

The normalization of c_1 is $nc_1 \leftarrow r1(x_2, y_2, y_3), y_2 = y_3, x_2 \neq 1$. There are two containment mappings from nc_1^+ to Q':

$$\{mp_{11} : r1(x_2, y_2, y_3) \rightarrow r_1(x, y, z), \quad mp_{12} : r1(x_2, y_2, y_3) \rightarrow r_1(1, y_1, y_1)\}.$$

So $\neg mp_{11}(y_2 = y_3)$ is $(y \neq z)$, $mp_{11}(x_2 = 1)$ is $(x = 1)$ and $\neg mp_{12}(y_2 = y_3)$ is $(y_1 \neq y_1)$, $mp_{12}(x_2 = 1)$ is $(1 = 1)$. Thus, $(y \neq z \vee x = 1) \wedge (y_1 \neq y_1 \vee 1 = 1)$ can replace the $\neg c_1$ in Q'. Thus, Q'' is a union of queries in $CQ^{\neq}$.

$$Q'' : q(x, y) \leftarrow r_1(x, y, z), r_2(z), r_1(1, y_1, y_1), y \neq z.$$
$$q(1, y) \leftarrow r_1(1, y, z), r_2(z), r_1(1, y_1, y_1).$$

We would also like to replace N_i's with empty mv_i in a similar fashion. Since in this case there is no P_i in Q', we cannot guarantee that every subgoal in nc^+_i can be mapped to a regular subgoal in Q'. Consider all the containment mappings $\{mp_{i1}, mp_{i2}, \ldots, mp_{ig}\}$ from nc_i^+ to Q', where if a subgoal $p(X)$ in nc_i^+ cannot be mapped to a subgoal in Q' (*i.e.* , the EDB predicate p does not appear in Q'), then $p(X)$ is mapped to itself. We define N_i' in this case as:

$$\bigwedge_{j=1}^{g} \neg mp_{ij}(nc_i^+) \vee \neg mp_{ij}(Eq_i).$$

If every EDB predicate in v_i appears in Q or in some view with a nonempty materialization, then for a containment mapping mp_{ij}, all subgoals in $mp_{ij}(nc_i^+)$ are in Q', and if Eq_i is nonempty, we can replace N_i by $\bigwedge_{j=1}^{g} \neg mp_{ij}(Eq_i)$. If Eq_i is empty, we can conclude that Q is conditionally empty with respect to V and MV (See Section 3.5). For all other cases, we simply delete N_i from Q'.

In sum, we rewrite Q' into the following:

$$Q'' : q(X) \leftarrow p_1(X_1), \ldots, p_n(X_n), P_1, \ldots, P_m,$$
$$\bigwedge_{k,j} \neg mp_{kj}(Eq_k), \bigwedge_{i,j} \neg mp_{ij}(Eq_i) \vee mp_{ij}(Peq_i)$$

where each P_i and $\bigwedge_j \neg mp_{ij}(Eq_i) \vee mp_{ij}(Peq_i)$ represent a view v_i with nonempty materialization, and each $\bigwedge_j \neg mp_{kj}(Eq_k)$ represents a view v_k whose EDB predicates appear in Q or in the views with nonempty materializations, and whose mv_k is empty. Q'' is equivalent to a union of queries in $CQ^{\neq}$. Let the view definitions be fixed. The number of queries in the union is exponential in the sizes of the query and the view materializations. Notice that Example 3 covers all possible cases in the construction of Q'; Example 4 shows how to replace N_i when mv_i is nonempty in the construction of Q''. Before we show more examples to cover different cases when mv_i is empty in the construction of Q'', we state that Q'' has the following properties.

Lemma 4. *Given a CQ Q and a set of conjunctive views V with materializations MV, let ρ be a valuation of Q'' on any input database instance. Then the set $\{\rho(p(X)) \mid p(X)$ is a regular subgoal of $Q''\}$ is a valid database instance.*

Lemma 5. *Given a CQ Q and a set of conjunctive views V with materializations MV, $Q(d) = Q'(d) = Q''(d)$ for all valid database instances d.*

Lemma 6. *Given a CQ Q and a set of conjunctive views V with materializations MV, $Q'(d) \subseteq Q''(d)$ for all database instances d.*

Theorem 3. *Let Q_1 and Q_2 be two CQ's, V be a set of conjunctive views with materializations MV. $Q_1'' \subseteq Q_2$ if and only if $Q_1 \subseteq_{V,MV} Q_2$.*

Example 5. Given two queries $Q_1 : q_1(x) \leftarrow r(x), s(y)$; $Q_2 : q_2(x) \leftarrow r(x)$ and a view $v() \leftarrow r(x), s(x)$ with no tuple. The set of EDB predicates of Q_2 is contained in the set of Q_1's EDB predicates. All EDB predicates in v appear in Q_1. Therefore, $Q_1'' : q_1(x) \leftarrow r(x), s(y), x \neq y$. Clearly, Q_1'' is unconditionally contained in Q_2, which implies $Q_1 \subseteq_{V,MV} Q_2$. If the view is $v() \leftarrow r(x)$ with no tuple, then its Eq is empty and all EDB predicates in v appear in Q_1. Thus, Q_1 is conditionally empty with respect to V and MV.

Example 6. Given two queries $Q_1 : q_1(x) \leftarrow s(x), t(x); \ Q_2 : q_2(x) \leftarrow s(x)$ and a view $v() \leftarrow r(x)$ with no tuple. View v has no effect over the containment relationship between Q_1 and Q_2. $Q_1'' : q_1(x) \leftarrow s(x), t(x)$ is unconditionally contained in Q_2. Thus, $Q_1 \subseteq_{V,MV} Q_2$.

Example 7. Given two queries $Q_1 : q_1(x) \leftarrow s(x), t(x); \ Q_2 : q_2(x) \leftarrow s(x)$ and a view $v() \leftarrow r(x), t(x)$ with no tuple. The EDB predicate r does not appear in Q_1 and Q_2. Q_1'' is Q_1. For any valuation ρ of Q_1'', the valuation of the regular subgoals in Q_1'' is a valid database instance since the empty r makes mv empty. $Q_1'' \subseteq Q_2$ implies $Q_1 \subseteq_{V,MV} Q_2$.

The construction of Q'', and Theorem 3, can in fact be generalized to the case when Q_1 and Q_2 are unions of queries in $CQ^{\neq}$. First, consider the case when Q is in $CQ^{\neq}$. Then Q' and Q'' are constructed as before, *i.e.*, we leave the disequations of Q untouched. Notice a valuation of Q'' satisfies all the equality and inequality subgoals in Q.

When Q is a union of queries in $CQ^{\neq}$, let q be one of them in the union. We can create q' and q'' as above. Then Q'' is a union of such q'''s. In particular, consider Q'' for some CQ Q. Q'' is a union of queries in $CQ^{\neq}$. Since the views and their materializations are unchanged, the P_i's in $(Q'')'$ are the same as the P_i's in Q'. So are N_i's in $(Q'')'$ and Q'. Since Q'' contains P_i's of Q' as its subgoals, adding another set of P_i's does not change the semantics of Q''. Thus, the P_i's in $(Q'')'$ can be deleted. Next, we would like to replace the N_i's in $(Q'')'$ to create $(Q'')''$. Since Q' shares the regular subgoals with Q'', which has the same regular subgoals of $(Q'')'$ (after deleting the extra P_i's), the containment mappings from nc_i^+'s to Q' are the same as those from nc_i^+'s to $(Q'')'$. Thus, the replacement of N_i's in Q' is the same as the one for $(Q'')'$ (Notice all the equations and disequations only depend on the view definitions and materializations, which are not changed). Hence $(Q'')''$ is Q''. We conclude that the Q'' construction can be generalized to unions of queries in $CQ^{\neq}$.

Theorem 4. *Let Q_1 and Q_2 be two unions of queries in $CQ^{\neq}$, V be a set of conjunctive views with materializations MV. Then $Q_1'' \subseteq Q_2$ if and only if $Q_1 \subseteq_{V,MV} Q_2$.*

3.4 Complexity of Conditional Query Containment

For standard containment, complexity is given as a function of query size. However, for conditional containment, the sizes of the queries, the view definitions, and the view materializations are all important factors on the problem's complexity. In our analysis, we chose to assume that the view definitions change much more slowly than the underlying database instance and the user queries, so the view definitions are fixed and we measured the combined complexity as a function of query size and materialization size.

Let Q_1 and Q_2 be two CQ's, V be a set of conjunctive views with materializations MV. As described in the previous sections, we can construct a query

Q_1'', a union of queries in $CQ^{\neq}$, such that $Q_1'' \subseteq Q_2$ if and only if $Q_1 \subseteq_{V,MV} Q_2$. This idea provides the following upper bound on the complexity of conditional query containment.

Theorem 5. *Let Q_1 and Q_2 be two CQ's, V be a set of conjunctive views with materializations MV. Determining whether $Q_1 \subseteq_{V,MV} Q_2$ is in Π_2^p.*

Proof (Sketch). By Theorem 3, $Q_1'' \subseteq Q_2$ if and only if $Q_1 \subseteq_{V,MV} Q_2$. Thus, if for all queries q in the union Q_1'', there exists a containment mapping from Q_2 to q such that the head of Q_2 is mapped to the head of q, then $Q_1 \subseteq_{V,MV} Q_2$. Let g_i be the number of containment mappings from nc_i^+ to Q_1'. Since the sizes of views are constants, g_i is polynomial in the sizes of Q_1 and the view materializations. The number of equality and inequality subgoals in q is the sum of all g_i's. Therefore, the size of q is polynomial in the sizes of Q_1 and the view materializations. The size of a containment mapping from Q_2 to q is polynomial in the sizes of the queries and the view materializations. Thus, the complexity is Π_2^p.   □

Theorem 6. *Let Q_1 and Q_2 be two CQ's, V be a set of conjunctive views with materializations MV. Determining whether $Q_1 \subseteq_{V,MV} Q_2$ is Π_2^p-hard.*

Proof (Sketch). To reduce from the $\forall\exists$-CNF problem to our problem, we use a similar construction to the one in [12]. Our construction is slightly modified from the one in the paper just cited, because we assume the queries and the materializations can vary and the view definitions are fixed while Millstein *et al.* assumed the queries and the view definitions can vary.   □

The above two theorems show that the problem is Π_2^p-complete when the queries and the materializations can vary. In comparison, the certain answer containment problem of [12] is Π_2^p-complete when the queries and the view definitions can vary. In terms of unconditional query containment where the input consists of just the two queries, determining the containment between two $CQ^{\neq}$'s is also Π_2^p-complete [18]. In contrast, unconditional CQ containment is NP-complete [4] in terms of the sizes of the input queries.

3.5   Testing Conditional Emptiness

So far we have assumed Q_1 and Q_2 are not conditionally empty queries and the set of EDB predicates of Q_2 is contained in the set of EDB predicates appearing either in Q_1 or in the definition of some view whose materialization is nonempty. Thus, we need to determine whether a query Q is conditionally empty with respect to a set of conjunctive views V with materializations MV. We first create Q'' from Q as before. From Lemma 4, we get the following result.

Proposition 2. *A CQ Q is conditionally empty w.r.t. a set of conjunctive views V with materializations MV if and only if Q'' is unsatisfiable.*

Example 8. Given $v_1(x) \leftarrow r_2(x)$ with one tuple (2) and $v_2(x) \leftarrow r_4(x)$ with one tuple (4); two queries $Q_1 : q_1(x) \leftarrow r_1(x), r_2(x), r_4(x)$ and $Q_2 : q_2(x) \leftarrow r_2(x), r_3(x), r_4(x)$. Note that the set of EDB predicates of Q_2 is not contained in the set of the EDB predicates appearing in Q_1 or the views with nonempty materializations, and similarly for Q_1. By Theorem 2, if the two queries are nonempty with respect to V and MV, then there is no conditional containment relationship between the two queries. To check if the queries are conditionally empty, we construct Q_1'' and Q_2'':

$$Q_1'' : q_1(x) \leftarrow r_1(x), r_2(x), r_4(x), r_2(2), r_4(4), x = 2, x = 4.$$

Clearly, Q_1'' is not satisfiable. Similarly, Q_2'' is unsatisfiable:

$$Q_2'' : q_2(x) \leftarrow r_2(x), r_3(x), r_4(x), r_2(2), r_4(4), x = 2, x = 4.$$

Therefore, we conclude the two queries are conditionally empty.

Theorem 7. *Given a CQ Q and a set of conjunctive views V with materializations MV, checking whether Q is conditionally empty w.r.t. V and MV is coNP-complete.*

Proof. Checking whether Q is conditionally empty with respect to V and MV is equivalent to checking whether Q'' is unsatisfiable. Satisfiability of Q'' can be checked in time polynomial in the sizes of V and MV by guessing a valuation for one of the disjuncts in Q'' and checking it is satisfied by that valuation. Therefore, the problem of checking whether Q is conditionally empty with respect to V and MV is in *coNP*.

The *coNP*-hardness is obtained by adapting the following result of Abiteboul and Duschka [1]. Let V be a set of conjunctive views with materializations MV, checking whether there exists a database instance d such that $MV = V(d)$ is NP-hard. We assume that MV is not empty, since when MV is empty, there is trivially an instance I (the empty instance) such that $V(I) = MV$. We reduce the complement of this problem to our problem.

Since MV is nonempty, there exists some nonempty mv_i. Let $r(X)$ be a subgoal in v_i. Define a CQ $Q : q() \leftarrow r(X)$. If for all database instances d, $MV \neq V(d)$, then Q'' is unsatisfiable. Otherwise, by Lemma 4, there exists a d such that $MV = V(d)$. Therefore, by Proposition 2, Q is conditionally empty with respect to V and MV.

If Q is conditionally empty with respect to V and MV, there does not exist a database instance d such that $MV = V(d)$. Otherwise, since mv_i is nonempty, $Q(d)$ is nonempty for the valid database instance d.

Thus, checking conditionally emptiness is also *coNP*-hard.   □

4   Conditional Authorization

In the Introduction, we discussed parameterized authorization views. Given a user query, our approach always first instantiates the parameterized views using the parameter values associated with the user and the session, before we determine whether a query should be conditionally authorized. Thus, we can assume in this section that the views have already been instantiated. First, we define conditional authorization.

Definition 3. *A query Q is conditionally authorized w.r.t. authorization views V with materializations MV, if there is a query Q_r that is written using only the views in V, and that is conditionally equivalent to Q.*

We have shown how to construct Q'' for a CQ Q. We know Q is conditionally empty if and only if Q'' is unsatisfiable. If Q is conditionally empty, there are many complete rewritings of Q'' using views V. Therefore, Q should be authorized.

When Q is not conditionally empty, we have shown that $Q(d) = Q''(d)$ for all valid database instances d. Therefore, if there is a complete rewriting of Q'' using V, the query Q is conditionally authorized. We would like to show that if there is no complete rewriting of Q'' using V, then Q is not conditionally authorized. Suppose Q'' does not have a complete rewriting and Q is still conditionally authorized. Then there exists a query Q_1 that is conditionally equivalent to Q and that can be rewritten using only the views in V. Let us abuse notation and call Q_1 also the query obtained by expanding the view subgoals in this rewriting.

Lemma 7. *1. Every EDB predicate of Q'' occurs in Q_1 or in the definition of some view with nonempty materialization.*
2. Every EDB predicate of Q_1'' occurs in Q'' or in the definition of some view with nonempty materialization.

Since $Q(d) = Q''(d)$ for all valid database instances d, $Q_1 \equiv_{V,MV} Q''$. Thus, by the above lemma and Theorem 4, $Q_1 \subseteq_{V,MV} Q''$ implies $Q_1'' \subseteq Q''$. On the other hand, we know $Q_1'' \equiv_{V,MV} Q_1 \equiv_{V,MV} Q \equiv_{V,MV} Q''$. Since $(Q'')''$ is still Q'', $Q'' \subseteq_{V,MV} Q_1''$ implies $Q'' \subseteq Q_1''$. Then, we have $Q'' \equiv Q_1''$. However, we know Q_1'' is completely rewritable in V, yet Q'' does not have a complete rewriting using V, which is a contradiction.

Theorem 8. *Let Q be a CQ and V be a set of conjunctive views with materializations MV. Q is conditionally authorized if and only if there is a complete rewriting of Q'' using V.*

Similar to the discussion of Theorem 3, the above theorem also applies when Q is a union of queries in $CQ^{\neq}$. Since the query contains inequalities while the views are conjunctive, the algorithm in [10] can be used here to check whether Q'' has a complete rewriting in V.

In the paper just cited, the algorithm depends on a bound for the number of view literals that need to appear in a complete rewriting. The same bound applies for conditional complete rewritings.

Corollary 1. *Let Q be a CQ with n subgoals, and V be a set of conjunctive views with materializations MV. If there is a query Q_r that is written using only the views in V, and that is conditionally equivalent to Q, then it has such a rewriting with at most n subgoals.*

Example 9 (Example 1 continued). Recall the query q is

$$q(eid) \leftarrow Progress(eid, XP1, prgs_1), Progress(eid, XP2, prgs_2),$$

and the instantiated authorization view is

$$V_1(eid, pid, prgs) \leftarrow Progress(eid, pid, prgs), EP(88, pid).$$

We consider the following four cases of the materialization of the instantiated authorization view.

1. MV_1 is not empty, and in the current database state, employee '88' is working on projects 'XP1' and 'XP2', and some other employee has reported progress for both projects. Let MV_1 be { $(99, XP1, P_1), (99, XP2, P_2)$ }.

$$q''(99) \leftarrow Progress(99, XP1, P_1), Progress(99, XP2, P_2),$$
$$Progress(99, XP1, P_1), EP(88, XP1),$$
$$Progress(99, XP2, P_2), EP(88, XP2).$$

   Thus, the complete rewriting is $q''(99) \leftarrow V_1(99, XP1, P_1), V_1(99, XP2, P_2)$. Therefore, we authorize this query q.

2. MV_1 is not empty, and in the current database state, employee '88' is not working on both projects, say only on project 'XP2', and some other employee has reported progress for 'XP2'. Let MV_1 be $\{(99, XP2, P_2)\}$.

$$q''(eid) \leftarrow Progress(eid, XP1, prgs_1), Progress(99, XP2, P_2),$$
$$Progress(99, XP2, P_2), EP(88, XP2).$$

   There is no containment mapping from the body of V_1 to the body of q'' such that $Progress(eid, XP1, prgs_1)$ is the image of $Progress(eid, pid, prgs)$, since that requires $EP(88, XP1)$ to occur in q''. There is no complete rewriting of q'' using V_1. Therefore, we reject the query q. In fact, the materialization can contain other information, such as employee '88' works on project 'XP3' and there is a report for 'XP3' from some employee. As long as the materialization does not contain $(99, XP1, P_1)$, the above analysis applies. Similarly, when employee '88' does not work on any of the two projects and MV_1 is not empty, the query should be rejected.

3. MV_1 is empty, but there is one more authorization view that allows any user to know who is working on which project: $V_2(eid, pid) \leftarrow EP(eid, pid)$. Suppose the materialization of V_2 is $(88, XP1), (88, XP2)$.

$$q''(eid) \leftarrow Progress(eid, XP1, prgs_1), Progress(eid, XP2, prgs_2),$$
$$EP(88, XP1), EP(88, XP2), XP1 \neq XP1, XP2 \neq XP2.$$

   This is a conditionally empty query, hence, we accept it.

4. MV_1 is empty. From the information of other materialized authorization views, employee '88' cannot infer that he or she is associated with projects

'XP1' and 'XP2'. There are no containment mappings to show $EP(88, XP1)$ and $EP(88, XP2)$ exist in all valid database states. Suppose there are no other authorization views. Then we have

$$q''(eid) \leftarrow Progress(eid, XP1, prgs_1), Progress(eid, XP2, prgs_2).$$

There is no complete rewriting of q'' using V_1 since there is no containment mapping from the view to q''. Therefore, we reject the query q.

5   Related Work

Chaudhuri et al. [5] considered the problem of optimizing queries in the presence of materialized views. They gave an incomplete set of query rewriting rules that generate conditionally equivalent queries under bag semantics. Rizvi et al. [14] gave an incomplete set of inference rules for conditional authorization of SQL queries using bag semantics.

Millstein et al. introduced the notion of *certain answer containment* with respect to a set of global views in a Data Integration System [12]. Our setting can be viewed as a Data Integration System with base relations as the global schema and authorization views as the local sources, using Local-As-View semantics [9]. However, our notion of conditional containment is different from Millstein et al.'s, which is based on the set of certain answers of one query being contained in the set of certain answers of the other one.

Instead of defining authorized queries in terms of rewritings, we could use Calvanese et al.'s notion of *lossless query* [3] and say a query is authorized if it is lossless with respect to the views V and their materializations MV, that is, for any two valid instances d and e with respect to V and MV, $Q(d) = Q(e)$. Existence of rewritings is a special case of this. Losslessness has been studied for regular path queries and materialized regular views in [3].

An alternative approach to solve the problem of conditional query containment could be to reduce it to the problem of deciding containment under a set of embedded or disjunctive dependencies, which is decidable under disjunctive chase [7]. Similarly, conditional query authorization could be solved as rewriting a query using views in the presence of embedded or disjunctive dependencies [6].

6   Conclusions and Future Work

We studied the problem of conditional query authorization. We showed that conditional query containment plays a crucial role in it and proposed an algorithm to test conditional containment for unions of queries in $CQ^{\neq}$. Then, we solved the problem of conditional authorization for a conjunctive query with respect to a set of conjunctive authorization views with materializations.

Given the high complexity of the conditional containment and authorization problems, we need to study heuristics or tractable classes of queries and views. For applying our results to the SQL setting, we would also like to solve conditional query authorization under bag semantics.

Acknowledgements

We thank the Natural Sciences and Engineering Research Council of Canada and the Institute for Robotics and Intelligent Systems for their support, and the anonymous reviewers for their careful comments.

References

1. S. Abiteboul and O. Duschka. Complexity of answering queries using materialized views. In *Proc. ACM PODS*, pages 254–263, 1998.
2. A. Aho, Y. Sagiv, and J. D. Ullman. Equivalence of relational expressions. *SIAM Journal of Computing*, (8)2:218–246, 1979.
3. D. Calvanese, D. G. Giuseppe, M. Lenzerini, and M. Y. Vardi. Lossless regular views. In *Proc. ACM PODS*, pages 247–258, 2002.
4. A. K. Chandra and P. M. Merlin. Optimal implementations of conjunctive queries in relational databases. In *Proc. STOC*, pages 77–90, 1977.
5. S. Chaudhuri, R. Krishnamurthy, S. Potamianos, and K. Shim. Optimizing queries with materialized views. In *Proc. ICDE*, pages 190–200, 1995.
6. A. Deutsch and V. Tannen. Reformulation of xml queries and constraints. In *Proc. ICDT*, pages 225–241, 2003.
7. G. Grahne and A. Mendelzon. Tableau techniques for querying information sources through global schema. In *Proc. ICDT*, pages 332–347, 1999.
8. A. Klug. On conjunctive queries containing inequalities. *Journal of the Association for Computing Machinery*, 35(1):146–160, 1998.
9. M. Lenzerini. Data integration: a theoretical perspective. In *Proc. ACM PODS*, pages 233–246, 2002.
10. A. Levy, A. Mendelzon, Y. Sagiv, and D. Srivastava. Answering queries using views. In *Proc. ACM PODS*, pages 95–104, 1995.
11. A. Levy, A. Rajaraman, and J. J. Ordille. Querying heterogeneous information sources using source descriptions. In *Proc. VLDB*, pages 251–262, 1996.
12. T. Millstein, A. Levy, and M. Friedman. Query containment for data integration systems. *Journal of Computer and System Sciences*, pages 67–75, 2002.
13. A. Motro. An access authorization model for relational databases based on algebraic manipulation of view definitions. In *Proc. ICDE*, pages 339–347, 1989.
14. S. Rizvi, A. Mendelzon, S. Sudarshan, and P. Roy. Extending query rewriting techniques for fine-grained access control. In *Proc. ACM SIGMOD*, pages 551–562, 2004.
15. A. Rosenthal and E. Sciore. View security as the basis for data warehouse security. In *Intl. Workshop on Design and Management of Data Warehouses*, 2000.
16. A. Rosenthal, E. Sciore, and V. Doshi. Security administration for federations, warehouses, and other derived data. In *IFIP WG11.3 Conf. on Database Security*, 1999.
17. Y. Sagiv and M. Yannakakis. Equivalence among relational expressions with the union and difference operations. *Journal of the ACM*, 27(4):633–655, 1980.
18. Ron van der Meyden. The complexity of querying indefinite data about linearly ordered domains (extended version). In *Proc. ACM PODS*, pages 331–345, 1992.

PTIME Queries Revisited

Alan Nash[1], Jeff Remmel[2], and Victor Vianu[3]

[1] Mathematics and CSE Departments,
[2] Mathematics Department,
[3] CSE Department,
UC San Diego, La Jolla, CA 92093, USA

Abstract. The existence of a language expressing precisely the PTIME queries on arbitrary structures remains the central open problem in the theory of database query languages. As it turns out, two variants of this question have been formulated. Surprisingly, despite the importance of the problem, the relationship between these variants has not been systematically explored. A first contribution of the present paper is to revisit the basic definitions and clarify the connection between these two variants. We then investigate two relaxations to the original problem that appear as tempting alternatives in the absence of a language for the PTIME queries. The first consists in trying to express the PTIME queries using a richer language that can also express queries beyond PTIME, but for which there exists a query processor evaluating all PTIME queries in PTIME. The second approach, studied by many researchers, is to focus on PTIME properties on restricted sets of graphs. Our results are mostly negative, and point out limitations to both approaches. Finally, we turn to a natural class of languages that we call finitely generated, whose syntax is obtained by applying a fixed set of constructors to a given set of building blocks. We identify a broad class of such languages that cannot express all the PTIME queries.

1   Introduction

The existence of a language expressing precisely the PTIME queries on arbitrary structures remains the most tantalizing open problem in the theory of database query languages. This question was first raised by Chandra and Harel [3] and later reformulated by Gurevich [9] who also stated the conjecture (now widely accepted) that no such language exists.

To reason about the existence of a language for the PTIME queries, one has to first come up with a very broad definition of query language (or logic), then define what it means for a logic to express the PTIME queries. It turns out that two such definitions have been proposed. To our knowledge, despite the importance of the problem, the relationship between these variants has not been systematically explored. We show that these two variants are different and may conceivably have distinct answers.

It is generally accepted that a query language specifies queries using expressions consisting of strings of symbols over some alphabet. We call these the

T. Eiter and L. Libkin (Eds.): ICDT 2005, LNCS 3363, pp. 274–288, 2005.

programs of the language. A first requirement is that a language should have effective syntax, meaning that its syntactically correct programs can be effectively enumerated. The semantics of a language L associates to each program in L a particular query. For simplicity, and since arbitrary structures can be efficiently represented as graphs [9], we focus in this paper on queries that are properties of graphs. Thus, we consider languages whose semantics associates to each program in the language a property of graphs. We say that L *expresses* the set of PTIME properties of graphs, denoted by P_G, if the set of graph properties associated to programs in L by its semantics is precisely P_G.

It is clear that simply having a language L expressing P_G is not satisfactory. At a minimum, we would like to be able to effectively and uniformly evaluate the programs in L. In other words, we would like to have a Turing machine E that, given as input a program p in L and a graph G, decides whether G satisfies the property defined by p. We call E an *evaluator* for L. Intuitively, an evaluator corresponds to a query processor for L. If such an evaluator exists, we call the language L *computable*. Since we are targeting the PTIME properties, we would further like E to uniformly evaluate every fixed program p in L in polynomial-time with respect to G. If such E exists, we call L *P-bounded*. The first formulation of the problem of the existence of a language for PTIME, by Chandra and Harel [3], asks whether there exists a P-bounded language expressing the PTIME queries. Most other definitions (e.g. [9,5]) further require that an explicit polynomial bound for the number of steps of each program in L as evaluated by the evaluator be effectively computable. In this case, we call L *effectively P-bounded*. The above notions extend naturally to properties of graphs: we call a set of PTIME properties of graphs computable, P-bounded, or effectively P-bounded iff there exists such a language expressing it.

Our first set of results shows that these two notions are distinct. In terms of languages, we show that:

(i) there exists a computable language for P_G that is not P-bounded and
(ii) if P_G is P-bounded, then there exists a P-bounded language for P_G that is not effectively P-bounded.

We also show that (i) and (ii) above hold for any computable subset of P_G that includes all finite properties.

It is legitimate to wonder whether P-bounded languages that are not effectively P-bounded are mere curiosities that can be avoided: given a P-bounded language, is it always possible to find an effectively P-bounded language for the same set of properties? We answer this question (and the corresponding one for computable vs. P-bounded) in the negative by showing the following:

(iii) there exist sets of PTIME graph properties that are computable, but not P-bounded and
(iv) there exist sets of PTIME graph properties that are P-bounded, but not effectively P-bounded.

In the special case of P_G, it remains open whether the existence of a P-bounded language for P_G implies the existence of an effectively P-bounded one.

In the absence of a language for the PTIME properties, various relaxations to the problem appear to offer tempting alternatives. We examine two natural approaches. The first consists in trying to capture P_G using a richer language allowing to express properties that likely lie beyond PTIME. Suppose we have a language L that expresses all of P_G, and possibly more. For example, such a language is Existential Second-Order logic ($\exists$SO), that is known to express the NP properties [6]. Assuming that P $\neq$ NP, some of the formulas in $\exists$SO express polynomial-time properties, while others do not. Furthermore, under the same assumption, it is easily shown, using Trakhtenbrot's theorem, that it is undecidable whether a given formula expresses a PTIME property. However, it is conceivable that $\exists$SO has an evaluator E that happens to evaluate every polynomial-time property in polynomial time. This would mean that a user could not only express all polynomial-time properties using $\exists$SO, but such properties could actually be evaluated uniformly in polynomial time. Short of an actual language for P_G, this would seem like a good alternative. Unfortunately, this solution is not a real alternative to a language for P_G. Indeed, we show that, if $\exists$SO (or any language that can express all of P_G) has an evaluator that computes all P_G properties in polynomial time, then there exists a P-bounded language expressing *exactly* P_G. Thus, the alternative formulation is no easier than the original problem of finding a language for P_G.

The second alternative to finding a language for P_G is to focus on interesting subsets of graphs rather than all graphs. For example, a beautiful result by Grohe shows that the PTIME properties of planar graphs can be expressed by a P-bounded language, specifically FO+LFP augmented with counting [8]. Such results raise the hope that the PTIME properties on larger and larger subsets of graphs can be captured and perhaps that, once a certain threshold is overcome, this might be extended to any set of PTIME properties. However, we prove a result that suggests there is no such threshold. It states that, for every PTIME-recognizable class $\mathcal{G}$ of graphs with infinite complement there exists a set of PTIME properties of graphs that includes all the PTIME properties of graphs in $\mathcal{G}$ and for which there is a computable, yet not P-bounded language. We also show an analogous result for effectively P-bounded languages. Of course, this does not invalidate the program of finding increasingly large sets of graphs whose PTIME properties have an (effectively) P-bounded language.

The notion of language used above is extremely general and may allow for very artificial constructs, not acceptable in real query languages. Given the difficulty in settling the question of the existence of a language for the PTIME queries in this general setting, it is tempting to wonder if additional criteria of naturalness may render the problem easier. Motivated by this, we consider here *finitely generated languages* (FGLs). These capture a wide array of languages in which queries are defined from finitely many "building blocks" using a fixed finite set of constructors. The classical example of an FGL is FO (the constructors implement $\exists, \forall, \vee, \wedge$, and $\neg$). However, our notion of FGL is much more powerful, since it allows for the individual building blocks and constructors to perform arbitrary PTIME computations. In fact, building blocks are formalized as polynomial-time properties, and constructors as polynomial-time Turing machines with oracle calls to other constructors or building blocks. The restricted structure of FGLs immediately removes some of the issues discussed above: all FGLs are effectively P-bounded. One might naturally wonder if the additional structure of FGLs allows to prove that there is no such language expressing exactly the PTIME properties of arbitrary graphs. This question remains open. However, we exhibit a broad class of FGLs, called *Set* FGLs (SFGLs), for which this can be proven. Informally, SFGLs are FGLs restricted in the way the constructors and building blocks in a program exchange information. Calls to oracles are made on hereditarily finite sets. The information exchanged does not break automorphisms of the input and is subject to restrictions on size and depth of nesting. Hereditarily finite sets can easily represent complex values used in many concrete database query languages [1]. SFGLs capture a natural programming paradigm, shared by many languages. One way to view SFGL's is as a generalization of FO with finitely many polynomially-computable Lindström quantifiers (see [5]). It is known that fixpoint logics with finitely many polynomially-computable Lindström quantifiers cannot express P$_G$ (see [4, 5]).

The paper is organized as follows. In Section 2 we formalize the notions of language, evaluator, and (effectively) P-bounded language and property. Section 3 presents our results comparing these notions. In Section 4 we discuss the two alternatives to obtaining a language for the PTIME properties: considering richer languages, and focusing on restricted sets of graphs. Finally, Section 5 presents the results on SFGLs.

2 Preliminaries

In this section we review some of the basic concepts related to query languages and their complexity, and introduce notation used throughout the paper.

We assume familiarity with Turing machines. We also assume a fixed effective enumeration of all Turing machines and denote by M_e the e-th Turing machine. We also assume knowledge of usual query languages such as first-order logic (FO), and FO extended with a least fixpoint operator, denoted FO+LFP (e.g., see [1, 5]). For a positive integer k, FO^k denotes the FO sentences using at most k variables, and similarly for (FO+LFP)^k.

Properties and Their Complexity. For simplicity, we focus here on PTIME *properties* rather than output-producing queries. A relational signature is a finite set of relation symbols together with associated arities. A finite structure over a given signature consists of a finite domain D and interpretations of the relation symbols in the signature as finite relations of appropriate arities over D. A property of structures over some signature is a set of finite structures over that signature, closed under isomorphism. We denote properties by $Q, R, S...$ and sets of properties by $\mathcal{Q}, \mathcal{R}, \mathcal{S}...$. Since structures over an arbitrary signature can be efficiently encoded as graphs (e.g., see [9, 5]), we will only consider in the sequel the relational signature consisting of a single binary relation representing the edges of a directed graph whose nodes are the elements of the domain. We denote this signature by γ, and the set of all finite graphs (finite structures over γ) by $\mathcal{G}$.

The *complexity* of a property is defined using classical complexity classes. To do this, we need to talk about the resources used by a Turing Machine "implementing" an algorithm for checking that a structure has the desired property. Since Turing Machines do not take structures as inputs, we need to use instead encodings of structures as strings. We use the following simple encoding for structures over signature γ. Suppose the structure represents a graph G whose set of nodes is D of size n. Let λ be a one-to-one mapping from D onto $\{1,\dots,n\}$, and let $\chi_G : \{1,\dots,n\}^2 \to \{0,1\}$ be the characteristic function of the set of edges in G via λ (so $\chi_G(\lambda(u),\lambda(v)) = 1$ iff (u,v) is an edge). The encoding of G is a string over alphabet $\{0,1\}$ consisting of all $\chi_G(i,j)$ listed in lexicographic order of the pairs (i,j). This encoding clearly depends on the labeling λ and is denoted by $enc_\lambda(G)$. The length of $enc_\lambda(G)$ is denoted by $|enc_\lambda(G)|$, and note that $|enc_\lambda(G)| = n^2$, where n is the number of nodes in the graph. As a shorthand, we also denote $|enc_\lambda(G)|$ by $|G|$.

Let $\mathcal{Q}$ be a property of graphs. We say that a Turing machine M decides $\mathcal{Q}$ iff for every graph G and labeling λ of its nodes, M halts on input $enc_\lambda(G)$ and accepts iff G has property $\mathcal{Q}$. Note that there is no requirement on inputs that are not correct encodings of graphs. Also observe that, since $\mathcal{Q}$ is closed under isomorphism, acceptance by M must be independent of the particular labeling λ. That is, for all labellings λ_1, λ_2, M accepts $enc_{\lambda_1}(G)$ iff M accepts $enc_{\lambda_2}(G)$.

We can now relate properties and complexity. We say that a property $\mathcal{Q}$ of graphs is a PTIME property iff there exists a Turing machine M deciding the property, and $k \in \mathbb{N}$, such that M halts on input $enc_\lambda(G)$ in at most $|enc_\lambda(G)|^k$ steps. We denote the set of PTIME properties of graphs by P_G.

Languages and Evaluators. To reason about the existence of a language for the PTIME properties, we need a very broad definition of query language (or logic). It is generally accepted that a query language specifies queries using expressions consisting of strings of symbols over some alphabet, which we call its *programs*. Moreover, the language should have effective syntax, meaning that its syntactically correct programs can be effectively enumerated. As a useful side effect, this allows us to ignore the specific syntax of a language, and simply refer to its programs by their index in the enumeration (1st program, 2nd program, etc). Since we will only be interested in data complexity and not query complexity, the cost of the translation between an index and the corresponding program is irrelevant. Thus, we can simply assume that the programs of the language are the indexes themselves, consisting of all strings in $\{0,1\}^*$. Whenever needed, we interpret such strings as positive natural numbers as follows: the string w corresponds to the natural number whose binary representation is $1w$ (this eliminates the problem of leading zeros and renders the mapping bijective). We denote the set of all such strings in $\{0,1\}^*$ by $\mathcal{E}$.

Given that the syntax of languages consists of the expressions in $\mathcal{E}$ and can be assumed fixed, we can define a language by the semantics associated to the expressions in $\mathcal{E}$. Thus, a language L for graph properties is a mapping associating to each expression $e \in \mathcal{E}$ a property $L(e)$ of graphs. We write $[L]$ for the set of properties defined by L. Of course, two different languages may express the same set of properties.

Observe that the semantics of a language is an abstract mapping, independent of any notion of computability or complexity. To capture the latter, we consider the notion of *evaluator* of a language. Intuitively, an evaluator corresponds to a query processor: it takes as input a program in the language together with a graph, and evaluates the program on the graph. More formally, an evaluator for a language L is a Turing machine E that takes as input a program e and the encoding of a graph G and evaluates e on G. To make this more precise, let us first fix a PTIME-computable pairing function $\langle -, - \rangle$ for $\mathbb{N}$, that is, a bijection $\langle -, - \rangle : \mathbb{N}^2 \to \mathbb{N}$ such that both $\langle -, - \rangle$ and π_1, π_2 satisfying $\pi_1(\langle x, y \rangle) = x$ and $\pi_2(\langle x, y \rangle) = y$ are PTIME computable (e.g., such a pairing function is provided in [10]). The tape alphabet of E is $\{0, 1\}$ and e and G are encoded as the binary representation of the integer $\langle e, enc_\lambda(G) \rangle$ for some labeling λ of the nodes of G. On any input of the form $\langle e, enc_\lambda(G) \rangle$, E halts and outputs 1 if G has property $L(e)$ and 0 otherwise. Note that a given language can have many different evaluators.

Languages and Complexity. What does it mean to have a language for the PTIME properties? We consider several notions that relate languages to properties of a given complexity, most of which have been proposed before. One of the contributions of the paper is to clarify the relationship between the different notions in a systematic way.

Consider a language L, defining a set of properties $[L]$. A first attempt at relating L to the polynomial-time properties is to look at the connection between $[L]$ and P_G. We say that L expresses P_G iff $[L] = P_G$. However, it is clear that this alone is not satisfactory. At a minimum, we would like to be able to effectively evaluate the queries in L. In other words, we would like to have, at the very least, an evaluator for L. If such is the case, we call the language L *computable*. We would also like to actually evaluate the queries of L in polynomial time. This is formalized as follows. We say that L has a P-bounded evaluator if it has some evaluator E that, for every *fixed* program e, runs in polynomial time on input $\langle e, enc_\lambda(G) \rangle$. The fact that we fix e means that our definition captures data rather than query complexity. Of course, a language that has a P-bounded evaluator only expresses polynomial-time properties.

Next, suppose we are given a P-bounded evaluator E for a language. The evaluator runs in polynomial time, but we do not necessarily know ahead of time the bounding polynomial. However, for many specific languages, such as FO+LFP, we are able to infer an explicit polynomial bound from the syntax. This is a nice property to have. We call an evaluator E effectively P-bounded if there exists a computable total mapping $B : \mathcal{E} \to \mathbb{N}$ that produces, for every program e, a number k such that E runs in time $|G|^k$ on input $\langle e, enc_\lambda(G) \rangle$.

We say that a language is (effectively) *P-bounded* if it has an (effectively) P-bounded evaluator. Similarly, a set of properties $\mathcal{P}$ is (effectively) P-bounded if there exists some (effectively) P-bounded language defining $\mathcal{P}$.

In considering the existence of a language L for the polynomial-time properties, two alternative requirements for such a language have been proposed. (1)
requires L to express precisely P_G, and have a P-bounded evaluator [3]. (2) additionally requires L to have an *effectively* P-bounded evaluator [9,5]. That is, (1)
requires P_G to be P-bounded and (2) requires P_G to be effectively P-bounded.

3   Computable, P-Bounded, and Effectively P-Bounded Languages

What is the connection between the notions of computable, P-bounded, and
effectively P-bounded language? We consider this question next. As we shall
see, these notions are generally distinct. This says that there are different flavors
of the question of the existence of a language for PTIME and that the answers
may be distinct for different flavors.

Obviously, every effectively P-bounded language is P-bounded and every
P-bounded language is computable. Consider now the converse inclusions. Of
course, a computable language L may express properties that are not in P_G, in
which case it cannot be P-bounded. However, suppose L expresses only properties in P_G. Is it the case that L must also be P-bounded? We next show this is
not the case. In fact, we exhibit a computable language expressing *precisely* the
properties in P_G, that has no P bounded evaluator.

Before we state the result, note that it is easy to find a computable language
for P_G. We recall such a language, defined in slightly different form by Andreas
Blass and Yuri Gurevich [9], that we denote L_Y. The syntax of L_Y consists of all
FO+LFP sentences φ over signature $\gamma \cup \{\leq\}$. Recall that an FO+LFP sentence
φ over this signature is order-invariant on a graph H iff its value on H and an
ordering $\leq$ of the nodes of H is independent of the choice of $\leq$. Furthermore, φ
is order invariant iff it is order invariant on all graphs. The semantics of L_Y is
defined next. Although we are considering sentences φ using $\leq$ in addition to γ,
we define $L_Y(\varphi)$ as a property of graphs alone, as follows. Let φ be a sentence
and G a graph. If φ (viewed as a usual FO+LFP sentence) is order-invariant for
all graphs H of size at most that of G, then G has property $L_Y(\varphi)$ iff φ evaluated
as an FO+LFP sentence on G with some arbitrarily chosen ordering $\leq$ is true.
Otherwise, G does not have property $L_Y(\varphi)$. Note that, if φ is order invariant
on all graphs, then $L_Y(\varphi)$ defines the same property as φ, so is a property in
P_G. If φ is not order invariant, then $L_Y(\varphi)$ contains only finitely many graphs,
so it is again in P_G. Finally, since order-invariant FO+LFP sentences express all
P_G properties [11,12], it follows that L_Y expresses precisely the P_G properties.
Clearly, L_Y has an evaluator, so it is a computable language for P_G. That is,

Remark 1. P_G is computable.

Remark 2. Note that the language L_Y is coNP-bounded. One might naturally
wonder if it can be proven that L_Y has no P-bounded evaluator. Clearly, such
a result must be conditional upon assumptions such as $P \neq NP$. However, we
are not aware of any proof that L_Y has no P-bounded evaluator even under

such complexity-theoretic assumptions. Thus, L_Y remains, for the time being, a candidate language for P_G.

As an intriguing aside, we mention a connection to another problem that appears to be similarly open:

(†) Input: A non-deterministic Turing machine M and a string 1^n.
Question: Does M accept ϵ (the empty string) in at most n steps?

It can be shown that L_Y is P-bounded iff there exists some algorithm solving (†) in $\text{TIME}(n^{f(M)})$ for some arbitrary function f. In other words, the problem can be solved by a (uniform) algorithm that is polynomial in n for fixed M (note that the non-uniform version of the problem is trivial: for each fixed M there exists an algorithm that is polynomial in n and solves (†)). Interestingly, the (non)-existence of such an algorithm for (†) appears to be open, and does not immediately follow from usual complexity-theoretic assumptions.

Theorem 1. *Every computable set of properties P that includes all finite properties has a computable language L which is not P-bounded.*

Proof. Since P is computable, it has a computable language L_C; we use L_C to build L. The semantics of L is defined as follows. We view the expressions in $\mathcal{E}$ as natural numbers. Let $L(2n+1) = L_C(n)$. Next, let $L(2n)$ be defined as follows. Let G be a graph and $\bar{G}$ the complete graph with the same nodes as G. Run the n-th Turing machine M_n on input $\langle 2n, enc_\lambda(\bar{G}) \rangle$ for some arbitrary λ (note that the encoding of $\bar{G}$ is independent of λ). If M_n does not stop in $2^{|G|}$ steps, then $G \notin L(2n)$. If $|\bar{G}|$ is the smallest size for which M_n stops in $2^{|G|}$ steps, then $G \in L(2n)$ iff M_n rejects $\bar{G}$. If $|\bar{G}|$ is not the smallest such size, then $G \notin L(2n)$. Note that $L(2n)$ contains only finitely many graphs, so is in P_G.

Next, suppose L has a P-bounded evaluator E, and suppose E is M_e. Since E is P-bounded, M_e runs in polynomial time with respect to $|\bar{G}|$ on every input of the form $\langle f, enc_\lambda(G) \rangle$ for fixed f. In particular, M_e runs in polynomial time with respect to $|\bar{G}|$ on input $\langle 2e, enc_\lambda(\bar{G}) \rangle$. It follows that there exists some $\bar{G}$ such that M_e stops in at most $2^{|G|}$ steps. By definition of $L(2e)$, the smallest such $\bar{G}$ has property $L(2e)$ iff M_e rejects. This contradicts the assumption that E is an evaluator for L.

Since P_G is computable,

Corollary 1. *P_G has a computable language that is not P-bounded.*

We next consider the connection between the notions of P-bounded language and effectively P-bounded language.

Theorem 2. *Every P-bounded set of properties P that includes all finite properties has a P-bounded language L which is not effectively P-bounded.*

Proof. Let K be some P-bounded language defining P. We define a language L as follows. First, $L(2n+1) = K(n)$. This ensures that L expresses all properties expressed by K. Next, we define $L(2n)$ as follows. Suppose $n = \langle e, b \rangle$. Intuitively, we define $L(2n)$ so that M_e cannot be an evaluator for L with bounding function

M_b. To this end, let G be a graph. To determine if $G \in L(2n)$, proceed as follows. First, run M_b on input $2n$ for $|G|$ steps. If M_b does not halt in $\leq |G|$ steps, then $G \notin L(2n)$. Otherwise, suppose that $|G| = t^2$. Then if $M_b(2n)$ halts in $\leq (t-1)^2$ steps, then $G \notin L(2n)$. Finally, if $M_b(2n)$ halts in s steps where $(t-1)^2 < s \leq t^2$, then let k be the output of $M_b(2n)$. Next, run M_e on input $\langle 2n, enc_\lambda(\bar{G}) \rangle$ for $|G|^k$ steps. If M_e halts, then $G \in L(2n)$ iff M_e rejects. Otherwise, $G \notin L(2n)$. Note that $L(2n)$ is a finite property, so it is already expressed by K. Clearly, L expresses precisely $\mathcal{P}$ and is P-bounded.

Now suppose L is effectively P-bounded. Then L has an evaluator E with bounding function B. Let $E = M_e$ and $B = M_b$. Let $n = \langle e, b \rangle$ and consider $L(2n)$. Since M_b halts on input $2n$, there exists a graph G such that M_b halts on $2n$ in at most $|G|$ steps. Consider the smallest such G. Let $k = M_b(2n)$. Since M_b computes the bounding function for M_e, it follows that M_e stops on input $\langle 2n, enc_\lambda(\bar{G}) \rangle$ in at most $|G|^k$ steps. However, by the definition of $L(2n)$, $G \in L(2n)$ iff M_e rejects on input $\langle 2n, enc_\lambda(\bar{G}) \rangle$. This contradicts the assumption that M_e is an evaluator for L.

Example 1. Consider the fixpoint queries defined by the FO+LFP sentences. The language FO+LFP is effectively P-bounded, and the properties it defines includes all finite properties. By Theorem 2, there exists some other language defining the fixpoint queries, that is P-bounded but not effectively P-bounded.

Corollary 2. *If P_G is P-bounded,[1] then it has a P-bounded language that is not effectively P-bounded.*

Remark 3. Theorem 2 states *the existence* of P-bounded languages that are not effectively P-bounded, for all P-bounded sets of properties that include the finite ones. A natural question is whether there are P-bounded sets of properties that do not have *any* effectively P-bounded language. The answer is affirmative: Theorem 5 in the next section shows the existence of many such classes of properties.

Clearly, it would be of interest to know if the existence of a P-bounded language expressing P_G implies the existence of an effectively P-bounded one. This remains open.

4   PTIME from Above and from Below

In the absence of a language expressing precisely the polynomial-time queries, various relaxations to the problem of capturing P_G can be useful. We describe here two natural approaches. The first consists in trying to capture the PTIME queries using a richer language allowing to express queries possibly not in PTIME, but that has an evaluator that evaluates every PTIME query in PTIME. The second approach, studied by many researchers, is to focus on PTIME

---

[1] Recall that it is not known whether P_G is P-bounded.

properties on restricted sets of graphs. Our results are mostly negative and point out limitations to both approaches.

4.1   P-Faithful Evaluators

Suppose we have a language L that expresses all of P_G and possibly more. For example, such a language is Existential Second-Order logic ($\exists$SO), that is known to express the NP properties [6]. Assuming that $P \neq NP$, some of the formulas in $\exists$SO express polynomial-time properties, while others do not. Furthermore, under the same assumption, it is easily shown using Trakhtenbrot's theorem that it is undecidable whether a given formula expresses a PTIME property. However, it is conceivable that $\exists$SO has an evaluator E that happens to evaluate every polynomial-time property in polynomial time. This means that a user can not only express all polynomial-time properties using $\exists$SO, but such properties can actually be evaluated in polynomial time. Short of an actual language for P_G, this would seem like a tempting alternative.

Unfortunately, this solution is not a real alternative to a language for P_G. Indeed, we show that, if $\exists$SO (or any language that can express all of P_G) has an evaluator that computes all P_G properties in polynomial time, then there exists a P-bounded language expressing *exactly* P_G. Thus, the alternative formulation is no easier than the original problem of finding a language for P_G.

We first formalize the above notions.

Definition 1. *Let L be a language expressing all properties in P_G. An evaluator E for L is* P-faithful *iff $E(\langle e, enc_\lambda(G) \rangle)$ runs in polynomial time with respect to G for every fixed e such that $L(e) \in P_G$. Furthermore, E is* effectively P-faithful *iff there exists a computable mapping $B : \mathcal{E} \to \mathbb{N}$ that produces, for every e for which $L(e) \in P_G$, a number k such that $E(\langle e, enc_\lambda(G) \rangle)$ runs in time $|G|^k$.*

We can now show the following.

Theorem 3. *If there is an (effectively) P-faithful language L for P_G, then there is an (effectively) P-bounded language K for P_G.*

Proof. The syntax of K consists of pairs (e, φ) where $e \in \mathcal{E}$ is interpreted with the semantics of L and φ is in L_Y (recall L_Y, the computable language expressing P_G, from Section 3). Suppose L has a P-faithful evaluator E_L, and let E_Y be an evaluator for L_Y. Let us define an evaluator E_K for K as follows. E_K on input (e, φ) and G does the following. First, start computing $E_L(e, H)$ and $E_Y(\varphi, H)$ on all graphs H smaller than G for $|G|$ steps. If in this number of steps $E_L(e, H)$ and $E_Y(\varphi, H)$ both halt for some H and one accepts while the other rejects, then reject G (so G does not have property $K(e, \varphi)$). Otherwise, run E_L on input (e, G) and accept iff E_L accepts. Note that, if $L(e)$ and $L_Y(\varphi)$ define different properties, then $K(e, \varphi)$ is finite (and is evaluated in polynomial time by the evaluator E_K). Otherwise, K is evaluated on input (e, φ) and G in polynomial time with respect to G, using the evaluator E_L applied to e and G, which takes polynomial time with respect to G because $L(e)$ is in P_G and E_L is P-faithful. An analogous argument shows that if E_L is effectively P-faithful then K is an effectively P-bounded language for P_G.

4.2   PTIME Properties with No (Effectively) P-Bounded Language

A productive alternative approach to the problem of finding a language for the PTIME queries has been to focus on interesting subsets of graphs rather than all graphs. We briefly mention two results that provide some insight into this approach. The results, proven by diagonalization, show that every "well-behaved" class of graphs can be extended to a class of graphs whose PTIME properties do not have an (effectively) P-bounded language (we omit the details).

Theorem 4. *For every PTIME-recognizable set of graphs $\mathcal{G}_0$ with infinite complement there exists a computable set of graph properties $\mathcal{H} \subset P_G$ that is not P-bounded and includes all PTIME properties of $\mathcal{G}_0$.*

Theorem 5. *For every PTIME-recognizable set of graphs $\mathcal{G}_0$ with infinite complement such that its set of PTIME properties is P-bounded, there exists a P-bounded set of graph properties $\mathcal{H} \subset P_G$ that is not effectively P-bounded and includes all PTIME properties of $\mathcal{G}_0$.*

5   Finitely Generated Languages

In this section we turn to *finitely generated languages* (FGLs). These capture a wide array of languages in which queries are defined from finitely many "building blocks" using a finite set of constructors. The classical example of an FGL is FO. However, our notion of FGLs is much more powerful.

Since we will be focusing on languages expressing PTIME queries, we require each of the building blocks and each constructor to be computable in polynomial time. We formalize this as follows. The syntax of an FGL L is given by all terms that can be built by using a finite set C of constant symbols and a finite set F of function symbols with associated finite arities. The semantics of L is as follows:

- to each $c \in C$ we associate a property K_c (a "building block") defined by a polynomial-time Turing machine M_c and
- to each $f \in F$ of arity k, we associate a polynomial-time Turing machine M_f (a "constructor") with access to k oracles.

The evaluator E for L is defined recursively as follows:

- If $t \in C$, then E on input $\langle t, enc_\lambda(G) \rangle$ runs M_t on input $enc_\lambda(G)$.
- If $t = f(t_1, \ldots, t_k)$ then E on input $\langle t, enc_\lambda(G) \rangle$ runs M_f on input $enc_\lambda(G)$ with oracles $E(t_1, -), \ldots, E(t_k, -)$.

Clearly, FGLs can be viewed as languages according to our general definition, since there exists an effectively computable bijection between the terms providing the syntax of FGLs and the set of strings $\mathcal{E}$ used for arbitrary languages. The following is immediate from the definition of FGLs.

Remark 4. Every FGL is effectively P-bounded.

One might naturally wonder if the additional structure of FGLs allows to prove that there is no such language expressing exactly the PTIME properties of graphs. This question remains open, even for ordered structures. To gain some intuition into the difficulties involved in settling this question, let us consider FGLs on ordered structures. Let FO+LFP^r consist of FO+LFP sentences using second-order variables (inductively defined relations) of arity at most r. We can show the following using an extension of the standard simulation of PTIME Turing machines on ordered structures by FO+LFP:

Lemma 1. *On ordered structures:*

(i) Each FGL is included [2] in FO+LFP^r for some r.
(ii) For every r, FO+LFP^r is included in some FGL.

It is known that on ordered structures, (a) if FO+LFP^r = PTIME for some r then PTIME $\neq$ PSPACE, and (b) if FO+LFP$^r \neq$ PTIME for some $r > 1$ then LOGSPACE $\neq$ PTIME [5, 7]. This together with Lemma 1 implies the following:

Theorem 6. *(i) If there exists an FGL expressing PTIME on ordered structures then PTIME $\neq$ PSPACE.*
(ii) If no FGL expresses PTIME on ordered structures then LOGSPACE $\neq$ PTIME.

Theorem 6 shows that settling the question of whether an FGL can express PTIME on ordered structures would resolve long-standing open problems in complexity theory. The question remains open for arbitrary structures. This leads us to consider a restriction of FGLs for which this question can be settled. We introduce *set FGLs (SFGLs)*, which are FGLs that operate on hereditarily finite sets under some restrictions. Before we do this, we introduce some terminology related to sets.

Sets. Given x and y, the pairing of x and y is $\{x, y\}$ and the union of x and y is $x \cup y$. For any finite set A, the *set of hereditarily finite sets over A*, HF(A), is the smallest set containing all elements in A (*atoms*), the empty set, and closed under the operations of pairing and binary union. Consider $x \in$ HF(A). The *transitive closure* of x, tc(x), is the smallest set y satisfying $x \subseteq y$ and $\forall u, v(u \in v \in y \rightarrow u \in y)$. We write $\|x\|$ for $|\text{tc}(x)|$. We set atoms$(x) := \text{tc}(x) \cap A$ and say that x is *atomless* if atoms$(x) = \emptyset$. We can think of x as a directed acyclic graph with $|\text{tc}(x)|+1$ nodes. Given an order of the atoms A, we can encode x as a string of length $\|x\|^2$. The *rank* of an atom is 0, the rank of the empty set is 0, and the rank of any other set x, rank(x), is $\max(1 + \text{rank}(y) : y \in x)$. We encode the ordered pair $\langle x, y \rangle$ in the standard way as $\{\{x\}, \{x, y\}\}$ and we encode tuples inductively by $\langle x, y, z \rangle = \langle \langle x, y \rangle, z \rangle$. As an aside, note that hereditarily finite sets can represent the complex values common in databases, obtained by nested application of set and tuple constructors (e.g., see [1]).

---

[2] Inclusion refers to the sets of properties expressed by each language.

Every permutation σ of A induces an automorphism of $\mathrm{HF}(A)$ (which we also call σ) in the obvious way. We say that $S \subseteq A$ A-*supports* x if every permutation σ of A which fixes S pointwise fixes x. We set $\mathrm{supp}_A(x) := S$ where $S \subseteq A$ is the smallest set S which A-supports x if there is such S satisfying $|S| < |A|/2$. Otherwise, we set $\mathrm{supp}_A(x) := A$. It is not obvious, but $\mathrm{supp}_A(x)$ is well-defined. We set $\mathrm{supp}(x) := \mathrm{supp}_{\mathrm{atoms}(x)}(x)$. Notice that $\mathrm{supp}(x) \subseteq \mathrm{supp}_A(x) \cap \mathrm{atoms}(x)$.

We say that $x, y \in \mathrm{HF}(A)$ are isomorphic, $x \cong y$, if there is a bijection $\sigma : \mathrm{atoms}(x) \to \mathrm{atoms}(y)$ such that $\sigma(x) = y$.

A set FGL (SFGL) is an FGL for which all inputs are (encodings of) sets $x \in \mathrm{HF}(\mathrm{atoms}(x))$ and for which there is a number m and a function g such that for each term $t = f(t_1, \ldots, t_k)$, every input set q to an oracle call made by the constructor M_f in the evaluation of t on input x satisfies:

1. $\mathrm{atoms}(q) \subseteq \mathrm{atoms}(x)$
2. $\|q\| \in O(\mathrm{atoms}(x)^m)$, and
3. $\mathrm{rank}(q) \leq g(t, \mathrm{rank}(x))$.

In addition, for each oracle t_i, the set $Q_t^i(x)$ consisting of all input sets q to calls to t_i made by M_f in the evaluation of t on input x is independent of the encoding of x (so is well defined). This requirement implies that $Q_t^i(x)$ is fixed by all automorphisms of x, a fact that is critical to the proof of Lemma 2 below. Finally, we require closure under isomorphism. That is, if $x \cong y$, then for all terms t, $x \models t$ iff $y \models t$.[3]

SFGLs are powerful enough to simulate FO with finitely many Lindström quantifiers $\mathbf{Q}$ [4, 5]. We briefly outline the simulation on a structure $\mathcal{A}$. We need

- one constant c_R for every relation symbol of $\mathcal{A}$,
- function symbols $f_\neg$ of arity 2 and $f_\vee$, $f_\wedge$ of arity 3,
- one function symbol f_Q of arity 2 for every Lindström quantifier Q,
- a constant $c_\emptyset$ corresponding to $\emptyset$, and
- function symbols f_p and f_u of arity 2 corresponding to pairing and union.

The term t_ϕ providing the simulation mimics the structure of $\phi \in \mathrm{FO}(\mathbf{Q})$: each logical operator corresponds to a constructor, which makes calls to its oracles on inputs $\mathcal{A}\bar{a}$ consisting of $\mathcal{A}$ extended with a tuple $\bar{a}$ providing a valuation for a subset $\bar{z}$ of the variables. There is one subtlety: the constructors calling oracles corresponding to sub-formulas must decide what components of $\bar{a}$ to pass to each sub-formula, which is determined by its free variables. This information is specified by an additional oracle defined by a term using $c_\emptyset$, f_p, and f_u and accepting precisely one atomless set that encodes the needed information. We write $t_{\bar{v}}$ for the term that accepts precisely the set representing $\bar{v}$. We define:

- If ϕ is an atomic formula $R\bar{x}$, then $t_\phi := c_R$.
- If $\phi(\bar{z})$ is $\alpha(\bar{x}) \wedge \beta(\bar{y})$, then $t_\phi := f_\wedge(t_\alpha, t_\beta, t_{\langle \bar{x}, \bar{y} \rangle})$ (similarly for $\vee$ and $\neg$).
- If $\phi(\bar{z})$ is $Q\bar{x}\alpha(\bar{x}\bar{z})$, then $t_\phi := t_{f_Q}(t_\alpha, t_{\langle \bar{x} \rangle})$.

---

[3] We write $x \models t$ if t accepts x.

To illustrate, consider the simulation of a conjunction $\alpha(\bar{x}) \wedge \beta(\bar{y})$. On input $\mathcal{A}\bar{a}$, $M_{f_\wedge}$ first queries its last oracle on atomless sets in their canonical order until some set s is accepted. If s does not encode appropriate tuples of variables, the constructor rejects. Otherwise, $M_{f_\wedge}$ uses $\bar{x}$ and $\bar{z}$ to obtain from $\bar{a}$ the tuples on which to issue queries to t_α and t_β: Notice that in the simulation of FO(**Q**), requirements (2) and (3) in the definition of SFGL are satisfied: constructors call oracles on inputs of the form $\mathcal{A}\bar{a}$ where $\bar{a}$ is a tuple of variables whose rank increases by at most a constant at each call. Thus, (2) and (3) can be viewed as generalizing this mode of computation.

Theorem 7. *There is no SFGL that expresses all PTIME properties of graphs.*

Proof. (outline) By Proposition 1 below, there is some b so that we can decide $x \models t$ in time $O(\|x\|^b)$ for x satisfying $x = \text{atoms}(x)$ (i.e. a "naked" set). In this case we can set $r = 1$ and $s = 0$ and we have $\|x\| = |\text{atoms}(x)|$. The result follows by a straightforward adaptation of the Time Hierarchy theorem [10].

Proposition 1. *If every building block of an SFGL runs in time $O(n^{t_c})$ and every constructor runs in time in time $O(n^{t_f})$ and has arity at most k, then for every term t, for every fixed r, s, m and for every x satisfying*

$$|\text{supp}(x)| \le s, \quad \|x\| \in O(|\text{atoms}(x)|^m), \quad \text{and rank}(x) \le r,$$

we can decide $x \models t$ in time $O(|\text{atoms}(x)|^b)$, where $b := m \cdot \max(t_c, t_f, 4)$.

Proof. (outline) Assume we have t_c, t_f, k, r, s and m satisfying the hypotheses. We show by induction on term depth d that the statement holds for each x satisfying the hypotheses. This is clear for $d = 0$; for the inductive step we use the following simulation to evaluate term $t = f(t_1, \ldots, t_j)$. We compute as M_f does on input x, except for each query q to oracle i we first look for q' isomorphic to q within an internal table T_i (initially empty). If such q' is found, we do not issue the query and instead use the answer obtained for q'. Otherwise, we issue the query and add q and the result of the query to the table T_i. We can divide the running time of this simulation into three parts: time spent in (1) the body of M_f, (2) table lookup, (3) queries. We set $n_x = \|x\|$, $a_x = |\text{atoms}(x)|$, $r_x = \text{rank}(x)$, $s_x = |\text{supp}(x)|$, $s_q := s + b$, and $r_q := g(t, r)$.

1. The time spent in the body of M_f is $O(n_x^{t_f}) \subseteq O(a_x^{m t_f}) \subseteq O(a_x^b)$.
2. To do the table lookup for a query q, we first compute its support, which we can do in time $O(a_x^2 n_x^2)$. To check for isomorphism against q' in the table, we try all possible bijections $\sigma : \text{supp}(q) \to \text{supp}(q')$. By Lemma 2 below we know that $|\text{supp}(q)| \le s_q$ for large enough x, so this adds a factor of $s_q!$. Finally, also by Lemma 2 below we know that the number of isomorphism classes of q depends only on r_q and s_q. Since $\|x\| \in O(|\text{atoms}(x)|^m)$, we can do the table lookup in time $O(a_x^{2+2m}) \subseteq O(a_x^b)$.

3. We know from above that the total number of queries we need to make depends on k, r_q, and s_q, but not on n_x. We can show that $|\text{atoms}(q)| \leq s_q$ or $|\text{atoms}(q)| \geq a_x - s_q$. If the former holds, $\|q\|$ is bounded by a constant depending only on r_q and s_q If the latter holds we have $O(a_x^m) = O(|\text{atoms}(q)|^m)$. Either way, $\|q\| \in O(|\text{atoms}(q)|^m)$ so we can apply the induction hypothesis using r_q and s_q in place of r and s. Therefore, we can answer all queries in time $O(|\text{atoms}(q)|^b) \subseteq O(a_x^b)$.

Lemma 2. *If every constructor runs in time $O(n_x^{b/m})$, then for fixed s and large enough x satisfying 1, 2, and 3 of Proposition 1 every query $q \in Q_x^t$ must satisfy $|\text{supp}_A(q)| \leq s + b$ where $A = \text{atoms}(x)$ and therefore also $|\text{supp}(q)| \leq s + b$. The number of isomorphism classes in Q_x^t depends only on $g(t, r)$ and $s + b$.*

Lemma 2 is an extension of Theorem 24 in [2]. The (difficult!) proof is omitted.

References

1. S. Abiteboul, R. Hull, and V. Vianu. *Foundations of databases*. Addison Wesley, 1995.
2. A. Blass, Y. Gurevich, and S. Shelah. Choiceless polynomial time. *Annals of Pure and Applied Logic*, 100:141–187, 1999.
3. A. Chandra and D. Harel. Structure and complexity of relational queries. *J. Comput. Syst. Sci*, 25(1):09–128, 1982.
4. A. Dawar and L. Hella. The expressive power of finitely many generalized quantifiers. *Inf. Comput.*, 123(2):172–184, 1995.
5. H.-D. Ebbinghaus and J. Flum. *Finite Model Theory*. Springer, 2nd edition, 1999.
6. R. Fagin. Generalized first-order spectra and polynomial-time recognizable sets. In R. Karp, editor, *Complexity of Computation*, pages 43–73. SIAM-AMS Proceedings, 1974.
7. M. Grohe. *The structure of fixed-point logics*. PhD thesis, Albert-Ludwigs Universität Freiburg, 1994.
8. M. Grohe. Fixed-point logics on planar graphs. In *Proc. Symp. on Logic in Computer Science*, 1998.
9. Y. Gurevich. Logic and the challenge of computer science. In E. Borger, editor, *Trends in Theoretical Computer Science*, pages 1–57. Computer Science Press, 1988.
10. J. Hopcroft and J. D. Ullman. *Introduction to Automata Theory, Languages, and Computation*. Reading, MA: Addison Wesley, 1979.
11. N. Immerman. Relational queries computable in polynomial time. *Information and Control*, 68:86–104, 1986.
12. M. Y. Vardi. The complexity of relational query languages. In *Proc. ACM SIGACT Symp. on the Theory of Computing*, pages 137–146, 1982.

Asymptotic Conditional Probabilities for Conjunctive Queries

Nilesh Dalvi, Gerome Miklau, and Dan Suciu

University of Washington

Abstract. We study the asymptotic probabilities of conjunctive queries on random graphs. We consider a probabilistic model where the expected graph size remains constant independent of the number of vertices. While it has been known that a convergence law holds for conjunctive queries under this model, we focus on the calculation of conditional probabilities. This has direct applications to database problems like query-view security, i.e. evaluating the probability of a sensitive query given the knowledge of a set of published views. We prove that a convergence law holds for conditional probabilities of conjunctive queries and we give a procedure for calculating the conditional probabilities.

1 Introduction

Two seemingly unrelated applications call for a renewed study of probabilistic properties of logical formulas. One is the study of information about a sensitive query which is disclosed by a public view [10]. The other is a study of queries with uncertain predicates [1]. Both have been studied using a certain probabilistic model, which, as we show here has some limitations. In this paper we propose a new probabilistic model of databases, considered before for random graphs [12, 9] but not for databases, and study properties of conjunctive queries under this new model. This model provides a characterization of information disclosure between a query and view, with query answerability at one end of the spectrum, and logical independence (or perfect security) at the other.

Motivation 1: Information Disclosure. We start by illustrating the limitation of the probabilistic model in [10]. The owner of a database I wishes to publish a view $V(I)$ over the database, and would like to determine whether certain sensitive information is disclosed by the view. The sensitive data is expressed in terms of a query, called the *sensitive query*, $Q(I)$. The *query-view security problem* requires one to check whether the view V does not leak any secret information about the query. In [10] this problem is modeled by comparing the *a priori* knowledge an adversary possesses about $Q(I)$, with the knowledge about $Q(I)$ given $V(I)$. The adversary's knowledge is described as the probability of $Q(I)$ attaining a certain value, when I is chosen randomly. If both the view and the sensitive query are boolean, the *a priori* probability is $\mathbf{P}(Q)$, while the *a posteriori* probability is the conditional probability $\mathbf{P}(Q \mid V)$. When the

T. Eiter and L. Libkin (Eds.): ICDT 2005, LNCS 3363, pp. 289–305, 2005.

two values are identical, then the query is said to be *perfectly secure* w.r.t. the view. The work in [10] is focused on deciding, for conjunctive queries Q and V, when perfect security holds. Notice that the definition is for one fixed domain and probability distribution, although the results in [10] show that it is largely independent of both.

The problem is that perfect security is often too restrictive for practical purposes, rejecting as insecure query-view pairs that are probably acceptable in practice. This is illustrated in the following example:

Example 1. Suppose we have a sensitive database *Employee*(*name, department, email*), and suppose we would like to publish a view V consisting of all departments but hiding all employee names. Limiting our discussion to boolean queries and views, suppose we want to publish that one of the departments is called *Amateur Astronomy*, but would like to hide the fact that one of the employees is *John Smith*. Then Q and V would be defined as follows:

$$V \leftarrow Employee(-, \text{``Amateur Astronomy''}, -)$$
$$Q \leftarrow Employee(\text{``John Smith''}, -, -)$$

Here Q is not perfectly secure w.r.t. to the view V. For a quick justification, consider the case where the domains for *name, department,* and *email* each consist of a single value (say *js@mystartup.com* for *email*). Then there are only two database instances, $\emptyset$ and $\{(\text{``John Smith''}, \text{``Amateur Astronomy''}, \text{``js@mystart-up.com''})\}$, and assume each has probability 0.5, hence $\mathbf{P}(Q) = 0.5$. By contrast, $\mathbf{P}(Q \mid V) = 1$. In fact, it can be shown that for every domain and probability distribution[1] $\mathbf{P}$ we have $\mathbf{P}(Q \mid V) > \mathbf{P}(Q)$, and therefore the query is not perfectly secure w.r.t. the view. However, the difference between the two probabilities is tiny for large domains, and for practical purposes the information disclosure should be considered negligible. In practice, users are usually willing to publish the set of *department*'s, even if the employee *name*'s are sensitive. Thus, the notion of *perfect security* is a higher standard than what is currently used in practice.

Capturing *practical security*, as opposed to *perfect security*, was left open in [10].

Motivation 2: Query Answering in the Presence of Uncertainties. For integrating large numbers of data sources the Local As View (LAV) approach has been proposed [7]. A global data instance I is specified indirectly, through a number of view definitions $V(I)$, one corresponding to each local data source. Only the materialized views $v = V(I)$ are known, but not the instance I, and any instance J is considered *possible* as long as[2] $v = V(J)$. A tuple t is a *certain answer* to a query $Q(I)$ if $t \in Q(J)$ for every possible instance J.

---

[1] We require $\mathbf{P}$ to be $\neq 0$ everywhere.
[2] Or $v \subseteq V(J)$ for the Open World Assumption.

When integrating and querying unfamiliar data sources however, one often needs to deal with uncertainties. Uncertain facts in databases have been addressed for example in [5], where they have been modeled as *probabilistic databases*. A probabilistic database is a probability distribution $\mathbf{P}(I)$ over all instances I. There are several ways in which one can derive such a probability distribution. In one application, for example, predicates in a user query are interpreted as uncertain, and the degree to which a tuple in the database matches the predicate is transformed into a probability [1].

We propose to use probabilistic databases for query answering using views, thus allowing uncertainties to be handled during data integration. We still have local sources described as views, and are given the materialized views only. But now we have a probability distribution $\mathbf{P}(J)$ on all possible database instances J, and the probability of a tuple t is the sum of $\mathbf{P}(J)$ over all J's for which $t \in Q(J)$. All certain tuples will have probability 1, but other tuples may have probability close to 1, and should be considered as probable answers.

Example 2. Continuing Example 1, suppose the company publishes two views, one with all *(name, department)* pairs in the database, and the other with all *(department, email)* pairs. Suppose we receive an email from *js@mystartup.com*, and would like to use these two views to find out the name of the person who sent out that email. As before, we restrict the discussion to boolean views and queries, and model the problem with the two boolean views below, and a boolean query (asking whether *"John Smith"* is the sender):

$$V' \leftarrow Employees(\text{``John Smith''}, \text{``Amateur Astronomy''}, -)$$
$$V'' \leftarrow Employees(-, \text{``Amateur Astronomy''}, \text{``js@mystartup.com''})$$
$$Q \leftarrow Employees(\text{``John Smith''}, -, \text{``js@mystartup.com''})$$

In order for Q to be a certain answer we need to have the logical implication $V'V'' \rightarrow Q$, which does not hold in this example. That is, Q is not a certain answer given V. We argue, however, that a system should report *"John Smith"* as a possible answer to the query. To see why, assume for the moment that there are, on average, 5 employees per department. Then *"John Smith"* is an answer with probability 20%. Clearly, in some applications it is critical to return it as an answer. Assume now that we know nothing about the database, except that V' and V'' are true, and that the *Employees* table has a number of records which is much smaller than the size of the domains for the three attributes. Then, if the domain size is very large, the probability of *"John Smith"* being an answer approaches 1. Indeed, if we populate a fixed (say 100) number of tuples in *Employee* with random values from a huge domain, the probability that two tuples have the same *department* value is close to 0. Hence, the probability that the two tuples satisfying V' and V'' are in fact the same tuple approaches 1, and *"John Smith"* is an answer with a probability close to 1.

This surprising example justifies our quest for an investigation of the asymptotic conditional probability of queries.

Contributions. In this paper we show that a certain new probability model provides a reasonable definition for both practical security and probable answers. In this model individual tuples have a uniform probability of occurring in the database, but the probability of each tuple t is now such that the expected size of the relation instance R is a given constant S (different constants may be used for different relation names). As the domain size n grows to ∞, the expected database size remains constant. Hence, in the case of directed graphs (i.e. a single, binary relation R), the probability that two given nodes are connected by an edge is S/n^2. Denoting by $\mu_n[Q]$ the probability that a boolean query Q is true on a domain of size n, our goal is to compute $\mu_n[Q \mid V]$ as $n \to \infty$.

For Information Disclosure we will propose, as a definition of practical security, the condition $\lim_n \mu_n[Q \mid V] = 0$. This is justified as follows. The adversary faces a large domain. For example, if he is trying to guess whether *"John Smith"* is an employee, then he has only a tiny probability of success: $1/n$ where n is the size of the domain. On the other hand, the size of the database is much smaller, and the adversary often knows a good approximation. This definition relaxes the previous definition of perfect security for sensitive queries Q (see Sec. 3).

For Query Answering we will propose, as a definition of probable answer, the condition $\lim_n \mu_n[Q \mid V] = 1$. Again, this relaxes the definition of certain answers (see Sec. 3).

The key technical contribution in this paper is to show that $\lim_n \mu_n[Q \mid V]$ for *conjunctive queries* Q and V always exists and to provide an algorithm for computing it. The key technical lemma is to show that, for each conjunctive query Q there exists two number c, d s.t. $\mu_n[Q] = c/n^d + O(1/n^{d+1})$. Moreover, both d and c can be computed algorithmically. Since $\mu_n[Q \mid V] = \mu_n[QV]/\mu_n[V]$, the main result follows easily.

Our main result leads to the following classification for query Q and view V, describing a spectrum of information disclosure and answerability.

Perfect Query-View Security $\mu_n[Q \mid V] = \mu_n[Q]$ for all n large enough. Here V provides no information about Q. This is the condition studied in [10].

Practical Query-View Security $\lim_{n\to\infty} \mu_n[Q \mid V] = 0$. This implies that the difference of probabilities is zero in the limit (since $\lim_n \mu_n[Q] = 0$ for all practical purposes). For finite n, V may in fact contain some information for answering Q, but it is considered negligible under our model.

Practical Disclosure $0 < \lim_{n\to\infty} \mu_n[Q \mid V] < 1$. Disclosure is non-negligible in this case. Our main result allows us to compute this quantity in terms of expected database size S.

Probable Query Answer $\lim_{n\to\infty} \mu_n[Q \mid V] = 1$. For any n, the answer to Q is not determined by V. However as $n \to \infty$, Q is almost surely true.

Certain Query Answer $\mu_n[Q \mid V] = 1$ for all n. Here V determines the answer to Q. That is, true is a certain answer to boolean query Q, given V.

Related Work. When restricted to graphs, our random database model is an instance of the random graphs introduced by Erdös and Rényi [2]. A random graph on n is a graph on n vertices where each edge is chosen randomly and independently with probability $p(n)$. The study of convergence laws on random graphs was initiated independently by Fagin [3] and Glebskiĭ et al. [6]. They consider random graphs with $p(n)$ a constant and proved a 0-1 law for statements of first order logic, i.e. the asymptotic probabilities always converge to either 0 or 1. These results hold for a pure relational vocabulary, without constants or function symbols.

The work was later extended to a class of edge probabilities of the form $p(n) = \beta n^{-\alpha}$, where $\alpha, \beta \geq 0$. The results of Shelah and Spencer [12] and Lynch [9] show that a convergence law holds for all $\alpha \geq 1$ and for all irrational α between 0 and 1, although the limit need not be 0 or 1. For the case of one binary predicate our random databases correspond to the case $\alpha = 2$ and $\beta = S$ (the expected size).

The problem of evaluating asymptotic conditional probabilities has received relatively less attention. Fagin [3] shows that conditional probabilities do not always converge for first order probabilities. Liogon'kiĭ [8] proves that even the problem of determining if conditional probabilities converge is undecidable for first order logic, but is decidable when restricted to only unary predicates.

Paper Organization. In Sec. 2 we review probability distributions for databases. In Sec. 3 we introduce the probabilistic model analyzed here. Sec. 4 contains the main theorems, with proofs deferred to the Appendix. We illustrate our main results on several examples in Sec. 5. We conclude in Sec. 6.

2 Basic Definitions and Background

We fix a vocabulary of relation names $R_1, R_2, \ldots R_m$. The number of attributes in relation R_i is its arity, denoted $A(R_i)$. For a finite domain D, a tuple for R_i is an element of $D^{A(R_i)}$, and we denote Tup the disjoint union of $D^{A(R_i)}$, for $i = 1, \ldots, m$. A database instance I over D is any subset of Tup, and $inst(D)$ denotes the set of all database instances over D.

The probability distributions over database instances that we consider are always derived by choosing tuples independently. Each tuple $t \in Tup$ is assigned a probability $\mathbf{P}[t]$ that it will occur in the database instance. This induces the following probability distribution on instances $I \in inst(D)$:

$$\mathbf{P}[I] = \prod_{t \in I} \mathbf{P}[t] \cdot \prod_{t \notin I} (1 - \mathbf{P}[t]) \tag{1}$$

The problem considered in this paper concerns the probability of a query. Our discussion will be restricted to *conjunctive queries*, possibly with the inequality operators $\neq$. Thus, a query is a conjunction of predicates, where each predicate is either a relational predicate $R(t_1, \ldots, t_k)$, called a *subgoal*, or an inequality predicate $x \neq t$; here x is a variable, while $t, t_1, \ldots, t_k$ are either variables or constants. We use letters from the end of the alphabet for variables, e.g. x, y, z, u, v, and from the beginning of the alphabet for constants, e.g. a, b, c.

Our results are presented only for boolean queries. They also apply to non-boolean queries under the Open World Assumption (OWA), using the simple transformation illustrated for the query below:

$$q(x, y) \leftarrow R(x, a, z), S(z, y)$$

Here q is non-boolean. Suppose its answer includes the tuples (a, b) and (c, b). This is expressed as $q(a, b) \wedge q(c, b)$, which becomes the following boolean query:

$$Q \leftarrow R(a, a, z_1), S(z_1, b), R(c, a, z_2), S(z_2, b)$$

Statements about q and the fact that its answers include (a, b) and (c, b) are thus rephrased into statements about the boolean query Q. In the rest of this paper we will consider only boolean queries, unless otherwise stated.

Given a boolean query Q and a probability distribution over database instances, the following expression represents the probability that Q is true on a randomly chosen database instance I:

$$\mathbf{P}[Q] = \sum_{\{I \in inst(D) | Q(I) = true\}} \mathbf{P}[I] \tag{2}$$

3   Probabilistic Model

We now introduce our new twist to the probabilistic model, in which we let the domain size tend to ∞ while keeping the expected size of each relation instance fixed. Let D_n denote a domain of size n.

For each relation R_i in the vocabulary, fix a number S_i representing the expected size of R_i. We then define a specific probability distribution, denoted μ_n (instead of $\mathbf{P}$), having the following properties:

1. For each relation R_i, each tuple (element of $(D_n)^{A(R_i)}$) belongs to R_i independently and with equal probability.
2. For each relation R_i, the expected size of R_i is S_i, independent of n.

It follows that, for every tuple t of R_i, $\mu_n[t] = S_i/n^{A(R_i)}$.

Given a boolean query Q, its probability, $\mu_n[Q]$ given by the formula (2), is the probability that Q is true on an instance I randomly chosen from $inst(D_n)$. Similarly, define $\mu_n[Q_1 \mid Q_2]$ to be the conditional probability that a database chosen randomly from $inst(D_n)$ satisfies Q_1, given that it satisfies Q_2. It is equal to $\mu_n[Q_1 Q_2]/\mu_n[Q_2]$. We are concerned with the following two asymptotic probabilities:

Definition 1. *For conjunctive query Q, the **asymptotic probability** of Q is $\mu[Q] = \lim_{n \to \infty} \mu_n[Q]$, if the limit exists.*

*For conjunctive queries Q_1, Q_2, the **conditional asymptotic probability** is $\mu[Q_1 \mid Q_2] = \lim_{n \to \infty} \mu_n[Q_1 \mid Q_2]$, if the limit exists.*

It is known[12] that $\mu[Q]$ exists for every pure relational FO formula Q (and, hence, for any conjunctive query without constants), and that it is not necessarily 0 or 1 (hence this model does not have a 0/1-law). To see the latter, consider the vocabulary of a single binary relation R, and the query $Q \leftarrow R(x, y)$. The query checks $R \neq \emptyset$. For each $n > 0$, $\mu_n[t] = S/n^2$ for any tuple t, and $\mu_n[Q] = 1 - (1 - S/n^2)^{n^2}$. Hence, $\mu[Q] = 1 - e^{-S}$.

Queries like the above are not interesting in database applications. More generally, call a subgoal of Q_1 *trivial* if it has no constants, and all its variables are distinct and do not occur in any other subgoals of Q_1 (they may occur however in inequality predicates). Trivial subgoals can be eliminated from a query Q_1, by splitting it into into a query Q without trivial subgoals, and several statements of the form $R \neq \emptyset$. For example, if $Q_1 \leftarrow R(x, y), T(u, a, b)$ (where $R(x, y)$ is a trivial subgoal), then $\mu_n[Q_1] = \mu_n[R \neq \emptyset]\mu_n[Q]$ where $Q \leftarrow T(u, a, b)$, and we have computed $\mu_n[R \neq \emptyset]$ above. For that reason we will assume throughout the paper that queries do not have trivial subgoals. It follows from our main results that in that case $\mu[Q] = 0$; conversely, $\mu[Q] > 0$ only if Q is a conjunction of queries of the form "R_i is non-empty".

Finally, we can define:

Definition 2. *Let Q and V be two boolean conjunctive queries.*

1. *Q is practically secure w.r.t. V if $\mu[Q \mid V] = 0$.*
2. *Q is a probable answer given V if $\mu[Q \mid V] = 1$.*

This definition relaxes previous definitions from the literature. Indeed, if Q has no trivial subgoals then $\mu[Q] = 0$; hence, if it is perfectly secure w.r.t V (i.e. $\mu_n[Q \mid V] = \mu_n[Q]$ for all n) then it is practically secure w.r.t V ($\mu[Q \mid V] = 0$). Similarly, if Q is a certain answer given V ($\mu_n[Q \mid V] = 1$ for all n) then it is a probable answer ($\mu[Q \mid V] = 1$).

4   Main Results

Throughout this section we consider conjunctive queries with inequality predicates $\neq$, and without trivial subgoals.

4.1   Main Result: Part I

Half of our main result is captured by the following theorem:

Theorem 1. *For every conjunctive query Q, there exists two numbers c, d such that:*

$$\mu_n(Q) = c(1/n)^d + O((1/n)^{d+1})$$

where d is an integer, $d \geq 1$. We denote c and d by $c_Q = \text{coeff}(Q)$ and $d_Q = \exp(Q)$ respectively.

It follows that $\mu[Q] = 0$. The number $exp(Q)$ depends only on the query Q, while $coeff(Q)$ depends both on the query Q and on $S_1, \ldots, S_m$, the expected cardinalities of the database relations. The second half of our main result shows how to compute $exp(Q)$ and $coeff(Q)$: we postpone it until we introduce the necessary notations.

Theorem 1 also implies the existence of the *conditional asymptotic probability* of formulas Q_1 and Q_2:

Corollary 1. *For any two boolean conjunctive queries* Q_1, Q_2 *the conditional asymptotic probability,* $\mu(Q_1|Q_2)$, *always exists and is as follows:*

$$\mu(Q_1|Q_2) = \begin{cases} 0 & \exp(Q_1Q_2) < \exp(Q_2) \\ \text{coeff}(Q_1Q_2)/\text{coeff}(Q_2) & \exp(Q_1Q_2) = \exp(Q_2) \end{cases}$$

We next show how to compute $coeff(Q)$ and $exp(Q)$.

4.2   Intuition

Here we illustrate the main intuition behind Theorem 1 and also motivate the notations needed to express $exp(Q)$ and $coeff(Q)$. We use a relational schema consisting of two tables, R and T, with arities 2 and 3 respectively, and expected sizes S_1 and S_2. Thus, given a domain $D_n = \{a_1, \ldots, a_n\}$, the probability of a tuple $R(a_i, a_j)$ is $p_1 = S_1/n^2$ and the probability of a tuple $T(a_i, a_j, a_k)$ is $p_2 = S_2/n^3$. We consider the following three queries:

$$Q_1 \leftarrow R(a, x)$$
$$Q_2 \leftarrow R(a, x), T(x, y, b), R(y, c)$$
$$Q_3 \leftarrow T(a, b, x), T(a, y, c)$$

Here a, b, c are constants and we will assume that they occur in the domain D_n (hence $n \geq 3$). For each query Q, our goal is to express its probability as $\mu_n[Q] = c/n^d + O(1/n^{d+1})$, focusing on computing $c_Q = exp(Q)$ and $d_Q = coeff(Q)$.

Let's start with Q_1. There are n possible ways to substitute it's variable x with constants in the domain D_n, and, for each substitution $\{a_i/x\}$, the probability of the tuple (a, a_i) is $p_1 = S_1/n^2$, hence:

$$\mu_n[Q_1] \approx n \times p_1 = n \times \frac{S_1}{n^2} = \frac{S_1}{n} \tag{3}$$

suggesting $d_Q = 1$, $c_Q = S_1$. Of course, this is not a rigorous calculation, since we have approximated the probability of $R(a, a_1) \vee \ldots \vee R(a, a_n)$ with the sum of their probabilities. A rigorous calculation confirms the values for c_Q and d_Q:

$$\mu_n[Q_1] = 1 - (1 - p_1)^n = np_1 + \frac{n(n-1)}{2}p_1^2 + \ldots = \frac{S_1}{n} + O(\frac{1}{n^2})$$

Consider now Q_2. Using the same informal reasoning, there are n^2 possible substitutions for the variables x, y, and for each substitution $\{a_i/x, a_j/y\}$, the probability that all three tuples $R(a, a_i)$, $T(a_i, a_j, b)$, and $R(a_j, c)$ appear in the database is $S_1/n^2 \cdot S_2/n^3 \cdot S_1/n^2$. Thus:

$$\mu_n[Q_2] \approx n^2 \times \frac{S_1 S_2 S_1}{n^{2+3+2}} = \frac{S_1^2 S_2}{n^5} \tag{4}$$

which suggests $d_Q = 5$ and $c_Q = S_1^2 S_2$. A rigorous, but much more complex calculation (which is omitted) confirms that $\mu_n[Q_2] = S_1^2 S_2/n^5 + O(1/n^6)$.

Formulas (3) and (4) suggest the following definition:

Definition 3. *Let Q be a conjunctive query, and let goals(Q) denote the set of its subgoals. We define several parameters, for each subgoal $g \in goals(Q)$ and for the entire query Q. For a subgoal g, we assume g is a predicate on the relation R_i, i.e. $g = R_i(t_1, \ldots, t_k)$. Recall that S_i is the expected cardinality of R_i.*

$$A(g) = A(R_i) \quad \text{the "arity" of subgoal } g$$
$$C(g) = S_i \quad \text{the "coefficient" of subgoal } g$$
$$V(Q) = \quad \text{the number of distinct variables in } Q$$
$$A(Q) = \sum \{A(g) \mid g \in goals(Q)\}$$
$$D(Q) = A(Q) - V(Q) \quad \text{the "exponent" of } Q$$
$$C(Q) = \prod \{C(g) \mid g \in goals(Q)\} \quad \text{the "coefficient" of } Q$$

For our running example we have:

$$D(Q_1) = 2 - 1 = 1 \qquad C(Q_1) = S_1$$
$$D(Q_2) = (2 + 3 + 2) - 2 = 5 \quad C(Q_2) = S_1 S_2 S_1 = S_1^2 S_2$$
$$D(Q_3) = (3 + 3) - 2 = 4 \qquad C(Q_3) = S_2^2$$

Generalized to any query Q, our informal argument says that there are $n^{V(Q)}$ substitutions of its variable, each leading to an event with probability $C(Q)/n^{A(Q)}$; thus $\mu_n[Q] \approx C(Q)/n^{D(Q)}$. This suggests $exp(Q) = D(Q)$ and $coeff(Q) = C(Q)$. However, this is not true on Q_3, i.e. $\mu_n[Q_3] \neq S_2^2/n^4 + O(1/n^5)$, because the two subgoals in Q_3 unify to $T(a, b, c)$, hence $\mu_n[Q_3] \geq \mu_n[T(a, b, c)] = S_2/n^3$. We will show that $\mu_n[Q_3] = S_2/n^3 + O(1/n^4)$. The example Q_3 suggests that we need to consider unifications between subgoals in the query. We do that next.

4.3   Unifications

We assume here a conjunctive query Q with $\neq$ predicates. From Q, we generate a set of queries Q_0 by unifying some of the subgoals. Each Q_0 is obtained by (1) applying some substitution to Q, (2) dropping all $\neq$ predicates and (3) eliminating duplicate subgoals. While generate this set, we do not consider two Q_0 which are isomorphic. The steps are formally defined below.

Substitutions. A *substitution*, η, is a mapping from variables to variables and constants. Importantly, we restrict substitutions to use only constants already in Q, thus, formally $\eta : Var(Q) \to Var(Q) \cup Const(Q)$. A substitution may not be defined on Q, if it violates some of the $\neq$ predicates. We denote $Q \models \eta$ if the substitution is defined on Q, and in that case $\eta(Q)$ denotes the result of applying η to the subgoals of Q (we drop the $\neq$ predicates). For example, if $Q \leftarrow R(a,x), R(x,y), R(y,z), x \neq y$ then the substitution $\eta = \{b/x, y/y, y/z\}$ is defined on Q and by applying it we obtain the query $Q_0 = \eta(Q)$, $Q_0 \leftarrow R(a,b), R(b,y), R(y,y)$. By contrast, the substitution $\eta' = \{x/x, x/y, z/z\}$ is not defined on Q.

Each substitution η defines a partition P on $goals(Q)$, such that two subgoals g, g' are in the same equivalence class if $\eta(g) = \eta(g')$. We call η a *unifier* for the partition P. Notice that $\eta(Q)$ has exactly $|P|$ subgoals, i.e. one for each equivalence class in P. For a trivial illustration, consider the query $Q \leftarrow R(a,x,b), R(x,y,v), R(z,z,w)$ and the substitution $\eta = \{z/x, z/y, b/v, b/w\}$. Then $\eta(Q) \leftarrow R(a,z,b), R(z,z,b)$, and η defines the partition $P = \{ \{R(a,x,b)\}, \{R(x,y,v), R(z,z,w)\}\}$, since the last two subgoals are mapped to the same subgoal by η.

A substitution η_0 is called the *most general unifier* for a partition P if for any other unifier η for P there exists a substitution θ s.t. $\eta = \theta \circ \eta_0$. In this case we call $\eta(Q)$ a *most general unifying query* of Q. Continuing our example, η is not a most general unifier for Q. The mgu is given by $\eta_0 = \{z/x, z/y, w/v\}$, which results in $\eta_0(Q) \leftarrow R(a,z,b), R(z,z,w)$. Indeed, η is obtained as $\theta \circ \eta_0$, for $\theta = \{b/w\}$.

Dropping $\neq$. All the $\neq$ predicates are dropped from the unifying query $Q_0 = \eta(Q)$. However, the $\neq$ predicates in Q are not ignored: they determine which substitutions we may apply to obtain all unifying queries.

Eliminate Duplicate Subgoals. Since $goals(Q_0)$ is a set, this is an obvious operation. Considering again $Q \leftarrow R(a,x,b), R(x,y,v), R(z,z,w)$ and the substitution $\eta = \{z/x, z/y, b/v, b/w\}$, if we apply mechanically η to Q we obtain $Q_0 \leftarrow R(a,z,b), R(z,z,b), R(z,z,b)$. The subgoal $R(z,z,b)$ is a duplicate, however, and should be eliminated, i.e. $Q_0 \leftarrow R(a,z,b), R(z,z,b)$. While this sounds evident, we insist on it because the functions $D(-)$ and $C(-)$ return different (and wrong) results if we fail to eliminate duplicates.

Drop Isomorphic Queries. When generating all unifying queries Q_0, we do not include two queries that are identical up to variable renaming.

We now formally define the set of unifying queries.

Definition 4. *Let Q be a conjunctive query. Define:*

$$UQ(Q) = \text{ the set of all unifying queries } Q_0 \text{ of } Q, \; Q_0 = \eta(Q)$$
$$MGUQ(Q) = \{Q_0 \mid Q_0 \in UQ(Q) \text{ and } Q_0 \text{ is a most general unifying query}\}$$

Note that any two distinct queries $Q_0, Q_0' \in UQ(Q)$ are not isomorphic.

4.4   Main Result: Part II

The second half of our main result, complementing Theorem 1 is:

Theorem 2. *Let Q be a conjunctive query possibly with $\neq$ predicates, and without trivial subgoals. Then the exponent $\exp(Q)$ and the coefficient $\mathrm{coeff}(Q)$ in Theorem 1 are given by:*

$$\exp(Q) = \min\{D(Q_0) \mid Q_0 \in UQ(Q)\} \tag{5}$$

$$\mathrm{coeff}(Q) = \sum\{C(Q_0) \mid Q_0 \in UQ(Q), D(Q_0) = \exp(Q)\} \tag{6}$$

Thus, to compute $exp(Q)$ we have to iterate over all unifying queries Q_0 and take the minimum value of $D(Q_0)$. To compute $coeff(Q)$ we have to iterate over all unifying queries Q_0 that achieve the minimum $D(Q_0)$. While this is an exponential time algorithm, as the next section shows, this cannot be avoided. Before illustrating the theorem, we prove that in both formulas (5) and (6) it suffices to iterate over $MGUQ(Q)$ rather than $UQ(Q)$. The algorithm becomes much more efficient, but remains exponential in the worst case. The correctness follows easily from the following:

Lemma 1. *Let $Q_0 \in UQ(Q) - MGUQ(Q)$. Then there exists $Q_1 \in MGUQ(Q)$ s.t. $D(Q_1) < D(Q_0)$.*

Proof. Let $Q_0 = \eta(Q)$, and let η define a partition P with k sets. Let η_1 be the most general unifier for the same partition, and denote $Q_1 = \eta_1(Q)$; $Q_1 \in MGUQ(Q)$. There exists θ s.t. $Q_0 = \theta(Q_1)$. Both Q_0 and Q_1 have exactly k distinct subgoals, hence $A(Q_0) = A(Q_1)$. Moreover, θ is not an isomorphism (since $Q_0 \notin MGUQ(Q)$), hence it either maps at least one variable to a constant, or it maps two distinct variables to the same variable. In both cases $V(Q_0) < V(Q_1)$, hence $D(Q_0) = A(Q_0) - V(Q_0) > D(Q_1) = A(Q_1) - V(Q_1)$.

In all examples below we will compute $exp(Q)$ and $coeff(Q)$ by using $MGUQ(Q)$ instead of $UQ(Q)$ in Theorem 2. The proof, however, will be for $UQ(Q)$.

We now illustrate Theorem 2 on several examples. For our three queries above, we have $MGUQ(Q_1) = \{Q_1\}$, $MGUQ(Q_2) = \{Q_2\}$, and $MGUQ(Q_3) = \{Q_3, Q_3'\}$ where $Q_3' \leftarrow T(a, b, c)$. This confirms the values for $exp(Q_i)$, $coeff(Q_i)$ we have found above for $i = 1, 2$. For Q_3, we have $D(Q_3') = 3 < D(Q_3) = 4$, hence $exp(Q_3) = 3$ and $coeff(Q_3) = C(Q_3') = S_2$.

For a slightly more complex example, consider the following two queries:

$$Q_4 \leftarrow R(a, x), R(y, b)$$
$$Q_5 \leftarrow R(a, x), R(y, b), x \neq b$$

Here $MGUQ(Q_4) = \{Q_4, Q_4'\}$, where $Q_4' \leftarrow R(a, b)$. We have $D(Q_4) = D(Q_4') = 2 = exp(Q_4)$, hence $coeff(Q_4) = C(Q_4) + C(Q_4') = S_1^2 + S_1$, according to Equation (6). By contrast, $MGUQ(Q_5) = \{Q_4\}$, since Q_4' is not a unifying query for Q_5. It follows:

$$\mu_n[Q_4] = \frac{S_1^2 + S_1}{n^2} + O(\frac{1}{n^3}) \qquad \mu_n[Q_5] = \frac{S_1^2}{n^2} + O(\frac{1}{n^3})$$

4.5   Complexity of Evaluating *coeff* and *exp*

Theorem 3. *Given a conjunctive query Q expected sizes of the relations, and a number k, deciding $\exp(Q) \leq k$ is NP-hard and evaluating $\mathrm{coeff}(Q)$ is #P-hard in the size of the query.*

The proof is omitted. Although evaluating these parameters is hard in the general case, there are several cases where its very efficient. An example is a query where no two sub-goals can be unified. For instance, a query with no relation occuring multiple times, or same relation always occuring with different constants.

5   Applications

We illustrate here our main results with five examples, corresponding to the five classes of query-view pairs described in Sec. 1. Recall that $\mu[Q \mid V] = \lim_{n \to \infty} \mu_n[Q \mid V]$

Perfect Query-View Security. This class is defined by $\mu_n[Q \mid V] = \mu_n[Q]$ for all n large enough. An example is:

$$V \leftarrow R(a, x); \quad Q \leftarrow R(b, x)$$

We showed[10] that $\mathbf{P}(Q \mid V) = \mathbf{P}(Q)$ for all domains D and tuple-independent probability distributions $\mathbf{P}$. The view leaks absolutely nothing about the query.

Practical Query-View Security. This class is defined by $\mu[Q \mid V] = 0$. Consider the following example:

$$V \leftarrow R(a, y); \quad Q \leftarrow R(x, b)$$

We have $exp(V) = 2 - 1 = 1$, and $exp(QV) = 2$ (see query Q_4 in Sec. 4.4). Hence $\mu[Q \mid V] = 0$. Example 1 in Sec. 1 is a variation. There:

$$V \leftarrow R(x, b, z); \quad Q \leftarrow R(a, y', z')$$

and we have $exp(V) = 3 - 2 = 1$, and $exp(QV) = 2$, since $UQ(QV) = \{ \{ R(x, b, z), R(a, y', z') \}, \{R(a, b, z)\} \}$. Again, $\mu[Q \mid V] = 0$. In both cases, although V leaks a tiny amount of information about Q, it is safe to publish V while keeping Q secret as long as the domain D is very large.

Practical Disclosure. This class is defined by $0 < \mu[Q \mid V] < 1$. For an illustration, consider

$$V \leftarrow R(a, y), R(x, b); \quad Q \leftarrow R(a, b)$$

We have $exp(V) = 2$, $coeff(V) = S + S^2$ (see query Q_4 in Sec. 4.3). For QV we note that $MGUQ(QV) = \{\{ R(a, y), R(x, b), R(a, b)\}, \{R(a, b), R(x, b)\},$

$\{R(a,b),R(a,y)\}$, $\{R(a,b)\}\}$, and that the minimum $D(-)$ is attained only by the last query, $R(a,b)$. Hence $exp(QV) = 2$, $coeff(QV) = S$. It follows that $\mu[QV] = 1/(1+S)$. Depending on the application, this may be considered to be an important leakage. For example, if the database has $S = 1000$ tuples, then an attacker has a chance of 0.1% of guessing the answer to Q.

This is an important example in practice. Suppose $R(name, phone)$ represents names and phone numbers, and the owner wants to publish all names, then separately all phone numbers, and wonders if the association between names and phone numbers remains secret. Clearly, it does not, since an attacker can pick a random name and phone number and associate them with about $1/S$ chance of success. Unless S is huge, this is an important leakage.

Probable Query Answering. Recall that this class is defined by $\mu_n[Q \mid V] = 1$. We illustrate this with an abstraction of Example 2 in Sec. 1:

$$V \leftarrow R(a,b,z), R(x,b,c); \quad Q \leftarrow R(a,y,c)$$

Here $MGUQ(V) = \{\{R(a,b,z), R(x,b,c)\}, \{R(a,b,c)\}\}$ and the minimum $D(-)$ is attained only by $R(a,b,c)$, hence $exp(V) = 3$ and $coeff(V) = S$. In a similar way, $MGUQ(QV) = \{\{R(a,b,z),R(x,b,c),R(a,y,c)\}, \{R(a,b,c),R(a,b,z)\}, \{R(a,b,c), R(a,y,c)\}, \{R(a,b,c), R(x,b,c)\}, \{R(a,b,c)\}\}$, and the minimum $D(-)$ is also attained only by the last query, hence $exp(QV) = 3$, $coeff(QV) = S$. It follows that $\mu[Q \mid V] = 1$.

This may also be important in practice. Although V does not logically imply Q, one may argue that for practical purposes if we know that V is true then we also know Q. For example, suppose we integrate two data sources $R_1(name, phone)$ and $R_2(phone, email)$, by describing them as projections of a global relation $R(name, phone, email)$. Suppose a user wants to find the email address of "John Smith", and that R_1 contains ("John Smith", 1234) and R_2 contains $(1234, js@com)$. The tuple ("John Smith", js@com) is not a certain answer, however it is a very probable answer, and should normally be returned to the user.

Certain Answers. Recall that this class is defined by $\mu_n[Q \mid V] = 1$ for all n. An example is:

$$V \leftarrow R(a,x,x); \quad Q \leftarrow R(a,y,z)$$

6   Conclusion

Our results show that for conjunctive queries, asymptotic conditional probabilities always exist, and can be evaluated algorithmically. Our results also hold when constants are allowed in the logic, which is required when queries need to refer to specific objects, and when converting non-boolean queries to boolean queries. We have shown that this model has interesting applications both to information disclosure and query answering.

References

1. N. Dalvi and D. Suciu. Efficient query evaluation on probabilistic databases. In *Conference on Very Large Data Bases*, 2004.
2. P. Erdös and A. Rényi. On the evolution of random graphs. *Magyar Tud. Akad. Mat. Kut. Int. Kozl.*, 5:17–61, 1960.
3. R. Fagin. Probabilities on finite models. *Journal of Symbolic Logic*, 41(1):50–58, 1976.
4. C. Fortuin, P. Kasteleyn, and J. Ginibre. Correlation inequalities on some partially ordered sets. *Comm.in Math. Physics*, 22:89–103, 1971.
5. N. Fuhr and T. Rlleke. A probabilistic relational algebra for the integration of information retrieval and database systems. *ACM Transactions on Information Sysytems*, 15(1):32–66, 1997.
6. Y. V. Glebskiĭ, D. I. Kogan, M. I. Liogon'kiĭ, and V. A. Talanov. Range and degree of realizability of formulas in the restricted predicate calculus. *Kibernetika*, 2:17–28, 1969. [Engl. Transl. Cybernetics, vol. 5, 142–154 (1972)].
7. A. Halevy. Answering queries using views: A survey. *VLDB Journal*, 10(4):270–294, 2001.
8. M. I. Liogon'kiĭ. On the conditional satisfyability ratio of logical formulas. *Mathematical Notes of the Academy of the USSR*, 6:856–861, 1969.
9. J. F. Lynch. Probabilities of sentences about very sparse random graphs. *Random Struct. Algorithms*, 3(1):33–54, 1992.
10. G. Miklau and D. Suciu. A formal analysis of information disclosure in data exchange. In *ACM SIGMOD International Conference on Management of Data*, pages 563–574, June 2004.
11. C. E. Shannon. Communication theory of secrecy systems. In *Bell System Technical Journal*, 1949.
12. J. Spencer and S. Shelah. Zero-one laws for sparse random graphs. *J. Amer. Math. Soc.*, pages 97–115, 1988.

A   Appendix

We prove here Theorems 1 and 2.

An *event* is a set of tuples, $e \subseteq Tup$, and we denote $\mu_n[e]$ the probability that all tuples are in a randomly chosen database instance. Since all tuples are independent events, we have $\mu_n[e] = \prod_{t \in e} \mu_n[t]$. If $e_1, \ldots, e_m$ are events then $e_1 \vee \ldots \vee e_m$ denotes the event that at least one of them happens, i.e. a randomly chosen database instance contains all tuples in e_i, for some $i = 1, \ldots, m$. The proof of theorems 1 and 2 relies on the following inequalities, representing a lower bound and an upper bound for $\mu_n[e_1 \vee \ldots \vee e_m]$, and which are standard in probability theory:

$$\sum_{i=1,m} \mu_n[e_i] - \sum_{1 \leq i < j \leq m} \mu_n[e_i e_j] \leq \mu_n[e_1 \vee \ldots \vee e_m] \leq \sum_{i=1,m} \mu_n[e_i] \qquad (7)$$

The event $e_i e_j$ represents the fact that all tuples in e_i and e_j are chosen; it is equivalent to the event $e_i \cup e_j$.

Given a conjunctive query Q_0, denote $Q_0^{\neq}$ the query obtained by adding all possible $\neq$ predicates, between any two distinct variables in Q_0, and between any variable and constant in Q. For example, if $Q_0 \leftarrow R(a,x), R(x,y)$ then $Q_0^{\neq} \leftarrow R(a,x), R(x,y), x \neq y, x \neq a, y \neq a$. The proof of the main result consists proving the following two equalities, then applying Eq.(7) to each of them.

$$Q \equiv \bigvee \{Q_0^{\neq} \mid Q_0 \in UQ(Q)\} \tag{8}$$

$$Q_0^{\neq} \equiv \bigvee \{\theta(Q_0^{\neq}) \mid Q_0^{\neq} \models \theta\} \tag{9}$$

In Eq.(9) the substitution θ ranges over all substitutions of the variables in Q_0 with constants[3] in D_n. This equation is the standard semantics of conjunctive queries, and we will not illustrate or discuss it further. Instead, we focus on Eq.(8). We first illustrate it on $Q \leftarrow R(a,x), R(x,y)$. This query has five unifiers, $UQ(Q) = \{Q, Q_1, Q_2, Q_3, Q_4\}$:

$$Q_1 \leftarrow R(a,a), R(a,y), \quad Q_2 \leftarrow R(a,x), R(x,a),$$
$$Q_3 \leftarrow R(a,z), R(z,z), \quad Q_4 \leftarrow R(a,a)$$

We have seen $Q^{\neq}$; similarly $Q_1^{\neq} \leftarrow R(a,a), R(a,y), y \neq a$, etc. Eq.(8) says:

$$Q \equiv Q^{\neq} \vee Q_1^{\neq} \vee Q_2^{\neq} \vee Q_3^{\neq} \vee Q_4^{\neq}$$

Now we prove (8). The containment in one direction is easy: $Q_0 \subseteq Q$ for $Q_0 \in UQ(Q)$ follows from the standard homomorphism theorem (since $Q_0 = \eta(Q)$), and $Q_0^{\neq} \subseteq Q_0$ is also immediate. For the other direction, consider one database instance I where Q is true, and let θ be the substitution that makes Q true. We will find some $Q_0 \in UQ(Q)$, s.t. $Q_0^{\neq}$ is also true in I. Let $const(Q)$ be all constants in Q, and $C = \{c_1, \ldots, c_m\}$ be all constants in $\theta(Q)$ that are not in $const(Q)$. Let $z_1, \ldots, z_m$ be m fresh variables, one for each constant in C. Define the following substitution η on Q's variables. If $\theta(x) \in const(Q)$, then $\eta(x) = \theta(x)$; otherwise, if $\theta(x) = c_i, i = 1, \ldots, m$, then $\eta(x) = z_i$. Let $Q_0 = \eta(Q)$. By definition $UQ(Q)$ contains some isomorphic copy of Q_0, so assume w.l.o.g. $Q_0 \in UQ(Q)$. The valuation θ_0 defined by $\theta_0(z_i) = c_i, i = 1, m$ is defined on $Q_0^{\neq}$, and $\theta_0(Q_0) = \theta(Q)$, proving that $Q_0^{\neq}$ is true on the instance I.

We now sketch the proof of Theorems 1 and 2, by proving an upper bound and a lower bound for $\mu_n[Q]$.

Upper Bound. We apply the upper bound in (7) twice: first to Eq.(8), then, for each unifying query $Q_0 \in UQ(Q)$, to Eq.(9). We obtain:

$$\mu_n[Q] \leq \sum_{Q_0 \in UQ(Q)} \sum_{\theta: Q_0^{\neq} \models \theta} \mu_n[\theta(Q_0^{\neq})]$$

For each substitution θ that is defined on $Q_0^{\neq}$ we have $\mu_n[\theta(Q_0^{\neq})] = C(Q_0)/n^{A(Q_0)}$ (see Definition 3 for notations). This is because $\theta(Q_0^{\neq})$ is a set of tuples having

---

[3] Unlike our definition in Sec. 4.3, here we do allow the substitution θ to use constants that do not appear in the query.

one distinct tuple for each subgoal in Q_0: the $\neq$ predicates prevent θ from mapping two subgoals to the same tuple. Moreover, there are $n^{V(Q_0)} - O(n^{V(Q_0)-1})$ substitutions θ that are defined on $Q_0^{\neq}$. Hence, for each unifier Q_0, the inner sum above is $C(Q_0)/n^{D(Q_0)} - O(1/n^{D(Q_0)+1})$. When summing up over all unifiers, the dominant terms are those with the lowest $D(Q_0)$, hence we have proven the following upper bound (see Theorem 2 for $exp(Q)$ and $coeff(Q)$):

$$\mu_n[Q] \leq \frac{coeff(Q)}{n^{exp(Q)}} + O(\frac{1}{n^{exp(Q)+1}})$$

Lower Bound. This is harder, because we have to prove that the second order terms in the lower bound of Eq.(7) are negligible: more precisely we show that the total contribution of these terms is $O(1/n^{exp(Q)+1})$. We first apply the lower bound to Eq.(8). The second order terms are here expressions of the form $\mu_n[Q_0^{\neq}Q_1^{\neq}]$, where $Q_0, Q_1 \in UQ(Q)$. Here $Q_0^{\neq}Q_1^{\neq}$ represents the conjunction of the two boolean queries, and is obtained by first renaming all variables in Q_0 and Q_1 to make them disjoint, and then taking the union of all predicates in the two queries, both subgoals and $\neq$ predicates. The number of such expressions depends only on Q, not on n, so it suffices to show that each such expression is $O(1/n^{exp(Q)+1})$. This follows from the following lemma, and our already proven upper bound:

Lemma 2. Let Q_0 and Q_1 be two non-isomorphic conjunctive queries, without $\neq$ predicates. Then $exp(Q_0^{\neq}Q_1^{\neq}) \geq \min(D(Q_0), D(Q_1)) + 1$.

Indeed, for $Q_0, Q_1 \in UQ(Q)$ the upper bound we have already shown gives us $\mu_n[Q_0^{\neq}Q_1^{\neq}] = O(1/n^{exp(Q_0^{\neq}Q_1^{\neq})})$, and the lemma implies that $exp(Q_0^{\neq}Q_1^{\neq}) \geq exp(Q) + 1$. We now prove the lemma. Assume the contrary, that $exp(Q_0^{\neq}Q_1^{\neq}) \leq D(Q_0)$ and $exp(Q_0^{\neq}Q_1^{\neq}) \leq D(Q_1)$. The first assumption implies that there exists a unifier $Q_0' = \eta(Q_0^{\neq}Q_1^{\neq})$ s.t. $D(Q_0') \leq D(Q_0)$. Since $goals(\eta(Q_0^{\neq})) \subseteq goals(\eta(Q_0^{\neq}Q_1^{\neq}))$ we have $D(\eta(Q_0^{\neq})) \geq D(\eta(Q_0^{\neq}Q_1^{\neq}))$; with the equality holding only if $goals(\eta(Q_0^{\neq})) = goals(\eta(Q_0^{\neq}Q_1^{\neq}))$, because there are no trivial subgoals in $\eta(Q_0^{\neq}Q_1^{\neq})$. (One can verify that if Q has no trivial subgoals, then $\eta(Q)$ has no trivial subgoals either.) Moreover, η maps all subgoals of $Q_0^{\neq}$ to distinct subgoals, because of the $\neq$ predicates, hence $D(Q_0) \geq D(\eta(Q_0^{\neq}))$, and equality holds only if η is an isomorphism. We have thus shown that $D(Q_0) \geq D(\eta(Q_0^{\neq}Q_1^{\neq})) \geq exp(Q_0^{\neq}Q_1^{\neq})$ and, given our first assumption, all three numbers are equal. This implies that $\eta(Q_0^{\neq}Q_1^{\neq})$ is an isomorphic copy of Q_0, which means that η is an injective function from Q_1 to (an isomorphic copy of) Q_0. Similarly, using the second assumption we prove the existence of an injective function from Q_0 to Q_1, implying that Q_0 and Q_1 are isomorphic, and contradicting the lemma's assumption.

We have shown so far $\sum_{Q_0 \in UQ(Q)} \mu_n[Q_0^{\neq}] - O(1/n^{expQ+1}) \leq \mu_n[Q]$. Given the upper bound, it suffices to consider in the sum only unifiers Q_0 for which $D(Q_0) = exp(Q)$: the others result in lower order terms. We apply now Eq.(9) to $Q_0^{\neq}$, and then the lower bound in (7). The higher order terms are now of the form

$\mu_n[\theta(Q_0^{\neq})\theta'(Q_0^{\neq})]$, and we will show that their combined effect is $O(1/n^{exp(Q)+1})$. The number of such terms is now dependent on n. Denote $e = \theta(Q_0^{\neq})$ and $e' = \theta'(Q_0^{\neq})$. Both e and e' are sets of tuples, and they have both the same number of tuples, namely equal to the number of subgoals in Q_0, because both θ and θ' are injective (due to the $\neq$ predicates). We examine their overlap. Consider two tuples $t \in e$ and $t' \in e'$ s.t. $t = t'$. They cannot come from two distinct subgoals in Q_0, because in that case those two subgoals were unifiable, and, after unifying them, one obtains $Q_1 \in UQ(Q)$ s.t. $D(Q_1) < D(Q_0)$, contradicting the fact that $D(Q_0) = exp(Q)$. So t and t' correspond to the same subgoal in Q_0. Consider all subgoals in Q_0 that are mapped to the same tuples by θ and θ'. Define a new boolean query Q_1 consisting of precisely these subgoals; hence $goals(Q_1) \subset goals(Q_0)$ (we cannot have equality because $\theta \neq \theta'$). The intuition here is that, when Q_1 has few subgoals (or, e.g., is empty), then $\mu_n[ee']$ is very small, since e and e' are largely independent; when Q_1 has many subgoals, then we use the fact that there cannot be too many pairs of valuations θ, θ' that agree on all subgoals in Q_1. For these we need the following inequalities, which are easily checked. (1) $\mu_n[\theta(Q_0^{\neq})\theta'(Q_0^{\neq})] = O(1/n^{2A(Q_0)-A(Q_1)})$, and (2) the number of pairs of substitutions θ, θ' which agree precisely on the subgoals in Q_1 is $O(n^{2(V(Q_0)-V(Q_1))})$. Now we can add the second order terms and obtain:

$$\sum_{Q_0(\neq)\models\theta,\theta'} \mu_n[\theta(Q_0^{\neq})\theta'(Q_0^{\neq})] = \sum_{Q_1:goals(Q_1)\subset goals(Q_0)} O(\frac{n^{2(V(Q_0)-V(Q_1))}}{1/n^{2A(Q_0)-A(Q_1)}})$$

$$= \sum_{Q_1:goals(Q_1)\subset goals(Q_0)} O(\frac{1}{n^{2D(Q_0)-D(Q_1)}})$$

$$\leq O(1/n^{D(Q_0)+1})$$

For the last inequality we have used the fact that $D(Q_1) < D(Q_0)$, since $goals(Q_1) \subset goals(Q_0)$ and Q_0 has no trivial subgoals.

Magic Sets and Their Application to Data Integration*

Wolfgang Faber**, Gianluigi Greco, and Nicola Leone

Mathematics Department, University of Calabria, 87030 Rende, Italy
{faber, ggreco, leone}@mat.unical.it

Abstract. We propose a generalization of the well-known Magic Sets technique to Datalog¬ programs with (possibly unstratified) negation under stable model semantics. Our technique produces a new program whose evaluation is generally more efficient (due to a smaller instantiation), while preserving soundness under cautious reasoning. Importantly, if the original program is consistent, then full query-equivalence is guaranteed for both brave and cautious reasoning, which turn out to be sound and complete.

In order to formally prove the correctness of our Magic Sets transformation, we introduce a novel notion of modularity for Datalog¬ under the stable model semantics, which is relevant per se. We prove that a module can be evaluated independently from the rest of the program, while preserving soundness under cautious reasoning. For consistent programs, both soundness and completeness are guaranteed for brave reasoning and cautious reasoning as well.

Our Magic Sets optimization constitutes an effective method for enhancing the performance of data-integration systems in which query-answering is carried out by means of cautious reasoning over Datalog¬ programs. In fact, preliminary results of experiments in the EU project INFOMIX, show that Magic Sets are fundamental for the scalability of the system.

1 Introduction

Datalog¬ programs are function-free logic programs where negation may occur in the bodies of rules [1]. Datalog¬ with stable model semantics [2, 3] [1] is a very expressive query language in a precise mathematical sense: under brave (cautious) reasoning Datalog¬ allows to express every query that is decidable in the complexity class NP (co-NP) [4]. In the 90s, Datalog¬ was not considered very much in the database community, mainly because of the high complexity of its evaluation (NP or co-NP depending on the reasoning modality [5, 6, 7]). However, the emerging of important database applications strictly requiring the co-NP expressiveness of Datalog¬ (see below and Sect. 5), along with the availability of a couple of effective Datalog¬ systems, like DLV [8] and Smodels [9], has renewed the interest in this language.

---

* This work was supported by the European Commission under projects IST-2002-33570 IN-FOMIX, and IST-2001-37004 WASP.

** Funded by an APART grant of the Austrian Academy of Sciences.

[1] Unless explicitly specified, Datalog¬ will always denote Datalog with negation under stable model semantics in this paper.

T. Eiter and L. Libkin (Eds.): ICDT 2005, LNCS 3363, pp. 306–320, 2005.

Our motivation to study optimization techniques for Datalog¬, comes from the data-integration area that we are investigating within the EU project "INFOMIX: Boosting Information Integration". INFOMIX is a powerful data-integration system, which is able to deal with both inconsistent and incomplete information. Following many recent proposals (see, e.g., [10, 11, 12, 13, 14, 15]), query answering in the INFOMIX data-integration system is reduced to cautious reasoning on Datalog¬ programs under stable model semantics. This reduction is possible since query answering in data-integration systems is co-NP-complete (in our setting and also in many other data-integration frameworks [15, 13]) like cautious reasoning on (unstratified) Datalog¬ programs under the stable model semantics [5, 6, 7].

Dealing with a co-NP-complete problem can appear unfeasible, or even crazy in a database setting where input may be very large. However, our present results show that suitable optimization techniques can "localize" the computation and limit the inefficient (co-NP) computation to a very small fragment of the input, obtaining fast query-answering, even in a powerful data-integration framework. The main contribution of the paper is the following.

▷ We define the new notions of *independent set* and *module* for Datalog¬, allowing us to identify program fragments which can be evaluated "independently", disregarding the rest of the program. The new notion of module is crucial for proving the correctness of our magic set method. It is strictly related to the splitting sets of [16], and to the modules of [17]; but we demonstrate that our notion has stronger semantic properties, which are useful for the computation.

▷ We design an extension of the Magic Set algorithm for general Datalog¬ programs (MS¬ algorithm for short). We show that different to stratified Datalog¬, where bindings are propagated only head-to-body in a rule, unstratified negation requires bindings to be propagated also body-to-head in general, in order to guarantee query equivalence. Such a body-to-head propagation, which has been carefully incorporated in our MS¬ method, allows us to properly deal with those rules (called *dangerous* rules) which may be the source of semantic problems. And, in fact, we prove that the rewriting generated by MS¬ is query equivalent to the input program $\mathcal{P}$ (under both brave and cautious semantics), provided that $\mathcal{P}$ is consistent. Even if the program is inconsistent soundness under cautious semantics and completeness under brave semantics are guaranteed by our transformation.

▷ We show that our method can be profitably exploited for query optimization in powerful data integration systems, where also incompleteness and inconsistency of data is dealt with; and we apply MS¬ in the EU project INFOMIX. Specifically, we show that our Magic Set technique can be employed for the optimization of the logic programs specifying the database repairs [2] [10, 11, 12, 13, 14, 15] (the queries on the data-integration system are eventually evaluated on these programs). MS¬ always ensures the full query equivalence of the optimized program w.r.t. the original one, since such programs are guaranteed to be consistent (a database repair always exists). Preliminary results of experiments, that we carried out on a real application scenario,

---

[2] Note that no previous magic-set technique is applicable, since these programs are unstratified and are to be evaluated under stable models semantics.

confirmed the viability and the effectiveness of our approach: the application of the Magic Set method allows us to "localize" the computation, and to obtain fast query-answering, even in a powerful data-integration framework.

2   Preliminaries and Notations

2.1   Datalog⁻ Queries

An *atom* $p(t_1,\ldots,t_k)$ is composed of a predicate symbol p of *arity* k and terms $t_1,\ldots,t_k$, which can either be constants or variables. A (*Datalog⁻ rule*) r is of the form $h \text{ :- } b_1,\ldots,b_m, \text{not } b_{m+1},\ldots, \text{not } b_n.$, where $h, b_1, \cdots, b_n$ are atoms and $0 \le m \le n$. $H(r) = h$ is the *head* of r, while $B(r) = B^+(r) \cup B^-(r)$ is the body of r, where $B^+(r) = \{b_1,\ldots,b_m\}$ is the positive and $B^-(r) = \{b_{m+1},\ldots,b_n\}$ the negative body of r. Finally, let $Atoms(r) = \{H(r)\} \cup B(r)$ denote the set of atoms in r, and $Atoms(\mathcal{P}) = \{Atoms(r) \mid r \in \mathcal{P}\}$ for a program $\mathcal{P}$.

A rule r with $H(r) = p(t_1,\ldots,t_k)$ is a defining rule for predicate p. If for a rule r, $B(r) = \emptyset$ holds, the rule is a *fact*. If all defining rules of a predicate p are facts, then p is an *EDB predicate*, otherwise it is an *IDB predicate*. A rule r is *positive* if $B^-(r) = \emptyset$. Throughout this paper, we assume that rules are *safe*, that is, each variable of a rule r appears in $B^+(r)$ [1].

A *datalog program with negation* (Datalog⁻ program for short) $\mathcal{P}$ is a finite set of rules. A *query* $\mathcal{Q}$ is simply an atom. We call an atom, rule, program, or query *ground*, if they do not contain variables. Given a program $\mathcal{P}$, we denote by $Ground(\mathcal{P})$ the set of all the rules obtained by applying to each rule $r \in \mathcal{P}$ all possible substitutions from the variables in r to the set of all the constants in $\mathcal{P}$.

Let the *base* $B_{\mathcal{P}}$ of $\mathcal{P}$ be the set of ground atoms constructible from predicates and constants in $\mathcal{P}$. A set of atoms $I \subseteq B_{\mathcal{P}}$ is an *interpretation* for $\mathcal{P}$. Given an interpretation I and set of rules T, let the restriction of I to T be defined as $I/_T = I \cap Atoms(T)$. In a similar way, let the restriction of a set S of interpretations to T be defined as $S/_T = \{I/_T \mid I \in S\}$, and let the restriction of a rule r to T ($R/_T$) be defined by dropping all body literals which are not in $Atoms(T)$. Given a positive rule $r \in Ground(\mathcal{P})$, an interpretation I satisfies r if $B(r) \subseteq I$ implies $H(r) \in I$. An interpretation I is a *model* of a Datalog program $\mathcal{P}$ if I satisfies all rules in $Ground(\mathcal{P})$. The *stable model* of a Datalog program $\mathcal{P}$ is the unique subset-minimal model $\mathrm{MM}(\mathcal{P})$.

Given a Datalog⁻ program $\mathcal{P}$ and an interpretation I, the *Gelfond-Lifschitz transform* $\mathcal{P}^I$ is defined as $\{H(r) \text{ :- } B^+(r) \mid r \in Ground(\mathcal{P}) : I \cap B^-(r) = \emptyset\}$. The set of *stable models* of a Datalog⁻ program $\mathcal{P}$, denoted by $\mathrm{SM}(\mathcal{P})$, is the set of interpretations I, such that $I = \mathrm{MM}(\mathcal{P}^I)$. $\mathcal{P}$ is *consistent* if $\mathrm{SM}(\mathcal{P}) \neq \emptyset$, otherwise *inconsistent*.

Let a be a ground atom and a program $\mathcal{P}$, then a is *cautious consequence* of $\mathcal{P}$, denoted by $\mathcal{P} \models_c a$, if $\forall M \in \mathrm{SM}(\mathcal{P}) : a \in M$; a is a *brave consequence* of $\mathcal{P}$, denoted by $\mathcal{P} \models_b a$, if $\exists M \in \mathrm{SM}(\mathcal{P}) : a \in M$. Given a query $\mathcal{Q} = b$, $Ans_c(\mathcal{Q}, \mathcal{P})$ denotes the set of substitutions ϑ, such that $\mathcal{P} \models_c b\vartheta$; $Ans_b(\mathcal{Q}, \mathcal{P})$ denotes the set of substitutions ϑ, such that $\mathcal{P} \models_b b\vartheta$.

Let $\mathcal{P}$ be a Datalog⁻ program and let $\mathcal{F}$ be a set of facts. Then, we denote by $\mathcal{P}_{\mathcal{F}}$ the program $\mathcal{P}_{\mathcal{F}} = \mathcal{P} \cup \mathcal{F}$. Let $\mathcal{P}$ and $\mathcal{P}'$ be Datalog⁻ programs and $\mathcal{Q}$ be a query. Then, $\mathcal{P}$ is *brave-sound* w.r.t. $\mathcal{P}'$ and $\mathcal{Q}$, denoted $\mathcal{P} \subseteq_{\mathcal{Q}}^b \mathcal{P}'$, if $Ans_b(\mathcal{Q}, \mathcal{P}_{\mathcal{F}}) \subseteq$

$Ans_b(Q, P'_F)$ is guaranteed for all set of facts F; P is *cautious-sound* w.r.t. P' and Q, denoted $P \subseteq^c_Q P'$, if $Ans_c(Q, P_F) \subseteq Ans_c(Q, P'_F)$ for all F. P is *brave-complete* (resp., *cautious-complete*) w.r.t. P' and Q, if $P \supseteq^b_Q P'$ (resp., $P \supseteq^c_Q P'$). Finally, P and P' are *brave-equivalent* (resp., *cautious-equivalent*) w.r.t. Q, denoted by $P \equiv^b_Q P'$ (resp. $P \equiv^c_Q P'$), if $P \subseteq^b_Q P'$ and $P \supseteq^b_Q P'$ (resp., $P \subseteq^c_Q P'$ and $P \supseteq^c_Q P'$).

With every program P, we associate a marked directed graph $DG_P = (N, E)$, called the *predicate dependency graph* of P, where (i) each predicate of P is a node in N, and (ii) there is an arc (a, b) in E directed from node a to node b if there is a rule $r \in P$ such that two predicates b and a of literals appear in $H(r)$ and $B(r)$, respectively. Such an arc is marked if a appears in $B^-(r)$. An *odd cycle* in DG_P is a cycle comprising an odd number of marked arcs. One can also define the *atom dependency graph* DG_P^A of a ground program P, by considering atoms rather than predicates.

3   Modularity Results

The backbone of optimizations techniques like Magic Sets is to (automatically) identify a part of the (ground) program, which can be used instead of the entire program to single out the *query program* (the part which is sufficient to answer the query). In the negation-free or stratified setting it is sufficient to examine reachability in the head-to-body direction. Negation under the stable semantics also gives rise to (partial) inconsistency, which may be triggered by activating an inconsistent part of the program in the body-to-head direction. To this end we will first present a way to identify possibly inconsistent parts of a program. Note that in this section we deal with ground programs.

Definition 1. Let P be a program (resp., ground program), and d be an predicate (resp., atom) of P. Then, we say that d is *dangerous* if either (i)d occurs in an odd cycle of DG_P (resp., DG_P^A), or (ii) d occurs in the body of a rule with a dangerous head predicate (resp., atom). A rule r is *dangerous*, if it contains a dangerous predicate (resp., atom) in the head. □

In principle, one can differentiate between conditional and unconditional sources of inconsistencies. In the approach we present here, we are concerned with the first type. In particular, that "isolated" inconsistencies are not covered, though one could easily come up with a modified definition to account also for these. Intuitively, an *independent atom set* of a ground program P is a set S of atoms whose semantics is not affected (apart from unconditional inconsistencies) by the remaining atoms of P, and can therefore be evaluated by disregarding the other atoms. Independent atom sets induce a corresponding module of P.

Definition 2. An *independent atom set* of a program P is a set $S \subseteq B_P$ such that for each atom $a \in S$ the following holds: (1) if $a = H(r)$ for a rule $r \in P$ then $Atoms(r) \subseteq S$, and (2) if a appears in the body of a dangerous rule $r \in P$ then $Atoms(r) \subseteq S$. A subset T of a program P is a *module* if $T = \{r \mid H(r) \in S\}$ for some independent set S. □

Example 1. Consider the following program P_1:

$z :- y, \text{not } z. \quad y :- q. \quad p :- \text{not } q. \quad q :- \text{not } p. \quad a :- p, \text{not } b. \quad b :- p, \text{not } a.$

Independent sets for $\mathcal{P}_1$ are $\{p, q, y, z\}$, $\emptyset$ and $\{p, q, y, z, a, b\}$, of which the first is the only non-trivial one. The corresponding module T of $\mathcal{P}_1$ is

$$z :\text{-}\, y, \text{not}\, z. \quad y :\text{-}\, q. \quad p :\text{-}\, \text{not}\, q. \quad q :\text{-}\, \text{not}\, p. \qquad\qquad \square$$

We next state the relationships between stable models of a program and its modules.

Theorem 1. *Let T be a module of a program $\mathcal{P}$, then (i) $\mathrm{SM}(\mathcal{P})/_T \subseteq \mathrm{SM}(\mathrm{T})$. Moreover, if $\mathcal{P}$ is consistent, then (ii) $\mathrm{SM}(\mathrm{T}) = \mathrm{SM}(\mathcal{P})/_T$.*

Proof. (i) If $\mathcal{P}$ is inconsistent, then the statement trivially holds as $\mathrm{SM}(\mathcal{P})/_T = \emptyset$. So in the following we will assume that $\mathcal{P}$ is consistent.

We show that if any interpretation I is a stable model of $\mathcal{P}$, then $I/_T$ is also a stable model of T: Recall that $T \subseteq \mathcal{P}$ and note that all rules contain only atoms of $Atoms(T)$, by item 1 of Definition 2. Next, observe that $T^{I/_T} = \mathcal{P}^I/_T$, hence $T^{I/_T} \subseteq \mathcal{P}^I$, and therefore since I is a model of $\mathcal{P}^I$, it is also a model of $T^{I/_T}$. $I/_T$ can be shown to be the minimal model of $T^{I/_T}$ by observing that if a model $J \subset I$ of $T^{I/_T}$ would exist, one could construct $I_J = J \cup \{H(r) \mid r \in (\mathcal{P}^I - T^I) \wedge B(r) \subseteq (I - I/_T) \cup J\}$ (J extended with the part of I which is not from T, which still follows from J). Clearly, $I_J \subset I$ is then a model of $\mathcal{P}^I$, contradicting the assumption that $I \in \mathrm{SM}(\mathcal{P})$.

(ii, Sketch) Since (i) holds also for consistent programs, what remains to show is $\mathrm{SM}(\mathrm{T}) \subseteq \mathrm{SM}(\mathcal{P})/_T$ for consistent $\mathcal{P}$. We show that for any stable model I of T, a stable model J exists such that $J/_T = I$. It has been shown that any odd-cycle-free Datalog$^\neg$ program is consistent [18]. Now observe that the only odd cycles in $\mathcal{P} - T$ are independent of T by item 2 of Definition 2. Since $\mathcal{P}$ is assumed to be consistent, such odd cycles can be deactivated by the presence of some atoms of $\mathcal{P} - T$, which, by Definition 2, are completely independent of T, such that a set of appropriate atoms K of $\mathcal{P} - T$ exists such that $K \cup I = J$. $\qquad\qquad \square$

Corollary 1. *Let T be a module of a consistent program $\mathcal{P}$. Then, each stable model of $\mathcal{P}$ can be obtained by enlarging a stable model of T.*

From Thm. 1, we can obtain similar results for query answering:

Theorem 2. *Given a ground atom q belonging to a module T of $\mathcal{P}$, then (1) $(T \models_c q) \Rightarrow (\mathcal{P} \models_c q)$, and (2) $(T \models_b q) \Leftarrow (\mathcal{P} \models_b q)$. Moreover, if $\mathcal{P}$ is consistent, then (1) $(T \models_c q) \Leftrightarrow (\mathcal{P} \models_c q)$, and (2) $(T \models_b q) \Leftrightarrow (\mathcal{P} \models_b q)$.*

Proof. If $\mathrm{SM}(\mathcal{P}) = \emptyset$ then $\mathcal{P} \models_c q$ for any $q \in Atoms(T)$, while $\mathcal{P} \models_b q$ for no $q \in Atoms(T)$. Therefore in this case, the implications are trivially satisfied. So from now on, consider $\mathrm{SM}(\mathcal{P}) \neq \emptyset$. In this case, the set of cautious consequences is $\bigcap \mathrm{SM}(\mathcal{P})$ and the set of brave consequences is $\bigcup \mathrm{SM}(\mathcal{P})$ in any case. Using Thm. 1 we can obtain the following:

1. We have to show that if q is in all stable models of T, then it is also in all stable models of $\mathcal{P}$. Clearly, we have $(\bigcap \mathrm{SM}(\mathrm{T})) \subseteq (\bigcap \mathrm{SM}(\mathcal{P})/_T)$ and therefore the result follows.
2. We have to show that if q is in some stable models of $\mathcal{P}$, then it is also in some stable model of T. Symmetrically, $(\bigcup \mathrm{SM}(\mathcal{P})/_T) \subseteq (\bigcup \mathrm{SM}(\mathrm{T}))$ and therefore the result follows.

The equivalence result then follows directly from Thm. 1, since in this case both $(\bigcap \mathrm{SM}(\mathrm{T})) = (\bigcap \mathrm{SM}(\mathcal{P})/_T)$ and $(\bigcup \mathrm{SM}(\mathcal{P})/_T) \subseteq (\bigcup \mathrm{SM}(\mathrm{T}))$ hold. $\qquad\qquad \square$

4   Magic Set Method for Datalog$^\neg$ Programs

In this section we present the Magic Set algorithm for general non-ground Datalog$^\neg$ programs (MS$^\neg$ algorithm for short). After recalling the Magic Set algorithm for positive Datalog queries, we discuss the key issues arising when dealing with Datalog$^\neg$ programs with unstratified negation. We then present the resulting MS$^\neg$ method, and finally we show some query equivalence results.

4.1   Datalog Programs

We will illustrate how the Magic-Set method simulates the top-down evaluation of a query by considering the program consisting of the rules path(X, Y) :- edge(X, Y). and path(X, Y) :- edge(X, Z), path(Z, Y). together with query path(1, 5)?.

Adornment Step: The key idea is to materialize, by suitable *adornments*, binding information for IDB predicates which would be propagated during a top-down computation. These are strings of the letters b and f, denoting bound or free for each argument of an IDB predicate. First, adornments are created for query predicates. The adorned version of the query above is path^{bb}(1, 5).

The query adornments are then used to propagate their information into the body of the rules defining it, simulating a top-down evaluation. Obviously various strategies can be pursued concerning the order of processing the body atoms and the propagation of bindings. These are referred to as Sideways Information Passing Strategies (*SIPS*), cf. [19]. Any SIPS must guarantee an iterative processing of all body atoms in r. Let q be an atom that has not yet been processed, and v be the set of already considered atoms, then a SIPS specifies a propagation v $\rightarrow_\chi$ q, where χ is the set of the variables bound by v, passing their values to q. In this paper we consider the SIPS which propagates binding only through EDB atoms; IDB atoms *receive* the bindings, but do not bound any further variable.

In the first rule of the example (path(X, Y) :- edge(X, Y).) a binding is only passed to the EDB predicate edge (which is not adorned), yielding the adorned rule path^{bb}(X, Y) :- edge(X, Y). In the second rule, path^{bb}(X, Y) passes its binding information to edge(X, Z) by path^{bb}(X, Y) $\rightarrow_{\{X\}}$ edge(X, Z). edge(X, Z) itself is not adorned, but it gives a binding to Z. Then, we consider path(Z, Y), for which we obtain the propagation path^{bb}(X, Y), edge(X, Z) $\rightarrow_{\{Y,Z\}}$ path(Z, Y). This causes the generation of the adorned atom path^{bb}(Z, Y), and the resulting adorned rule is path^{bb}(X, Y) :- edge(X, Z), path^{bb}(Z, Y).

In general, adorning a rule may generate new adorned predicates. This step is repeated until all adorned predicates have been processed, yielding the *adorned program*, in our example it consists of the rules path^{bb}(X, Y) :- edge(X, Y). and path^{bb}(X, Y) :- edge(X, Z), path^{bb}(Z, Y).

Generation Step: The adorned program is used to generate *magic rules*, which simulate the top-down evaluation scheme. Let the *magic version* *magic*(p$^\alpha$) for an adorned atom p$^\alpha$ be defined as magic_p$^\alpha$ in which all arguments labelled f in α are eliminated.

Then, for each adorned atom p in the body of an adorned rule r_a, a magic rule r_m is generated such that (i) the head of r_m consists of *magic*(p), and (ii) the body of r_m consists of the magic version of the head atom of r_a, followed by all of the

predicates of r_a which can propagate the binding on p. In our example we generate
magic_path^{bb}(Z, Y) :- magic_path^{bb}(X, Y), edge(X, Z).

Modification Step: The adorned rules are subsequently modified by including magic atoms generated in Step 2 in the rule bodies. The resulting rules are called *modified rules*. For each adorned rule the head of which is h, we extend its rule body by inserting ***magic***(h) and by stripping off the adornments of the other predicates[3]. In our example, path(X, Y) :- magic_path^{bb}(X, Y), edge(X, Y). and path(X, Y) :- magic_path^{bb}(X, Y), edge(X, Z), path(Z, Y). are generated.

Processing of the Query: For each adorned atom g^α of the query the *magic seed* ***magic***(g^α). is asserted. In our example we generate magic_path^{bb}(1, 5).

The complete rewritten program consists of the magic, modified, and query rules. Given a Datalog program $\mathcal{P}$, a query $\mathcal{Q}$, and the rewritten program $\mathcal{P}'$, it is well known (see e.g. [1]) that $\mathcal{P}$ and $\mathcal{P}'$ are equivalent w.r.t. $\mathcal{Q}$, i.e., $\mathcal{P}\equiv^b_\mathcal{Q}\mathcal{P}'$ and $\mathcal{P}\equiv^c_\mathcal{Q}\mathcal{P}'$ hold (since brave and cautious semantics coincide for Datalog programs).

4.2   Binding Propagation in Datalog$^\neg$ Programs: Some Key Issues

As argued in Sect. 3, different to positive Datalog, in which bindings are propagated only head-to-body in a rule, the problem with unstratified negation is that any rewriting for Datalog$^\neg$ programs, has to propagate bindings also body-to-head in general, in order to achieve query equivalence.

Example ?. Consider the program $\mathcal{P}_2$

z(X) :- y(X),not z(X).	y(X) :- q(X,Y).
p(X,Y) :- d(X,Y),not q(X,Y).	q(X,Y) :- d(X,Y),not p(X,Y).
a(X) :- p(X,Y),not b(X).	b(X) :- p(X, Y), not a(X).

together with the query $\mathcal{Q}_2 = p(a, X)$?, and the set of facts $F_2 = \{d(a, b)\}$. The stable models of $\mathcal{P}_2$ are $\{p(a, b), a(a), d(a, b)\}$ and $\{p(a, b), b(a), d(a, b)\}$, so we get $Ans_c(\mathcal{Q}_2, \mathcal{P}_{2,F_2}) = Ans_b(\mathcal{Q}_2, \mathcal{P}_{2,F_2}) = \{\{X/b\}\}$. Note that q(a, b) cannot occur in any stable model.
When applying the Magic Set technique,[4] we obtain as adorned program:

p^{bf}(X,Y) :- d(X,Y),not q^{bb}(X,Y).	q^{bb}(X,Y) :- d(X,Y),not p^{bb}(X,Y).
p^{bb}(X,Y) :- d(X,Y),not q^{bb}(X,Y).	

Then, the generation step produces the following magic program $Magic(\mathcal{Q}_2, \mathcal{P}_2)$:

magic_p^{bf}(a).	magic_q^{bb}(X,Y) :- magic_p^{bf}(X),d(X,Y).
magic_p^{bb}(X,Y) :- magic_q^{bb}(X,Y).	magic_q^{bb}(X,Y) :- magic_p^{bb}(X,Y).

Finally, the original rules are modified to $Modified(\mathcal{Q}_2, \mathcal{P}_2)$:

p(X,Y) :- magic_p^{bf}(X),d(X,Y),not q(X,Y).	q(X,Y) :- magic_q^{bb}(X,Y),d(X,Y),not p(X,Y).
p(X,Y) :- magic_p^{bb}(X,Y),d(X,Y),not q(X,Y).	

---

[3] We do this only for facilitating the equivalence proofs, one can alternatively adorn the query.

[4] We do not consider any special technique for negative literals. We adorn negative literals last, since they receive bindings, but do not bind any further variables.

```
Input:  A Datalog⁻ program P, and a query Q = g(t̄).
Output:  The optimized program MS⁻(Q, P).
var   S: stack of adorned predicates; modifiedRules,magicRules: set of rules;
begin
   1.  modifiedRules:= ∅; magicRules:=BuildQuerySeeds(Q, S);
   2.  while S ≠ ∅ do
   3.      pᵅ := S.pop();
   4.      for each rule r ∈ P with H(r) = p(t̄ₚ) do
   5.          rₐ :=Adorn(r,pᵅ,S);
   6.          magicRules := magicRules ⋃ Generate(rₐ);
   7.          modifiedRules := modifiedRules ⋃ {Modify(rₐ)};
   8.      end for
   9.      for each dangerous rule d ∈ P of the form h(t̄ₕ) :− q₁(t̄₁),...,qₘ(t̄ₘ) where qᵢ = p do
  10.          let dₛ be the rule qᵢ(t̄ᵢ) :− h(t̄ₕ), q₁(t̄₁),...,qᵢ₋₁(t̄₁),qᵢ₊₁(t̄₁),...,qₘ(t̄ₘ);
  11.          let dₐ:=Adorn(dₛ,pᵅ,S);
  12.          magicRules := magicRules ⋃ Generate(dₐ);
  13.      end for
  14. end while
  15. MS⁻(Q, P):=magicRules ⋃ modifiedRules;
  16. return MS⁻(Q, P);
end.
```

Fig. 1. Magic Set Algorithm

Together with the fact $d(a, b)$, $MS(\mathcal{P}_2) = Magic(\mathcal{Q}_2, \mathcal{P}_2) \cup Modified(\mathcal{Q}_2, \mathcal{P}_2)$ admits two stable models, say M_1 and M_2, such that $M_1/\mathcal{P}_2 = \{p(a, b)\}$ and $M_2/\mathcal{P}_2 = \{q(a, b)\}$. Therefore, $Ans_c(\mathcal{Q}_2, MS(\mathcal{P}_{2,F_2})) = \emptyset$, and $Ans_b(\mathcal{Q}_2, MS(\mathcal{P}_{2,F_2})) = \{\{X/b\}\}$. Hence, $MS(\mathcal{P}_2)$ is not cautious-complete w.r.t. $\mathcal{P}_2$.   □

In general the application of the traditional Magic Set method on unstratified programs would guarantee cautious-soundness and brave-completeness, but it would not ensure cautious-completeness and brave-soundness.

The reason for this semantic problem lies in the fact that the first rule of $\mathcal{P}_2$ acts as a constraint imposing any atom of the form $y(X)$ to be not entailed in any model. Then, from the second rule we also conclude that we cannot derive any fact of the form $q(X, Y)$. It follows that the constraint "indirectly" influences the query on predicate p, since the model M_2 of the rewritten program such that $M_2/\mathcal{P}_2 = \{q(a, b)\}$ cannot be extended to be a model for program $\mathcal{P}_2$.

In order to overcome this semantic problem, we next present a Magic Set rewriting which deals correctly with dangerous rules. In the above example, our method recognizes that the second rule is *dangerous* and propagates the binding coming from q (in the body) to y (in the head).

4.3   MS⁻ Algorithm

We next describe the peculiarities of our rewriting technique. We assume the existence of four auxiliary functions: *BuildQuerySeeds*$(\mathcal{Q}, S)$ adorns the given query $\mathcal{Q}$, creates an appropriate fact, and pushes newly adorned predicates onto the stack S, which is a variable parameter. *Adorn*(r,p^α,S) adorns the rule r using p^α and pushes new adorned predicates onto S. *Generate*(r_a) creates the magic rules for the adorned rule r_a, and *Modify*(r_a) creates the modified rule for r_a. These functions implement what was informally described in Sect. 4.1 for the Magic Set method. In particular, we assume that these functions implement the *basic* Magic Set method, propagating bindings only through

EDB predicates [22, 1] (as stated above, we do not consider any special technique for negative literals, which are simply adorned last in the rule).

The algorithm MS¬, reported in Fig. 1, implements the Magic Set method for Datalog¬ programs. Its input is a Datalog¬ program $\mathcal{P}$ and a query $\mathcal{Q}$. (Note that the algorithm can be used for positive rules as a special case.) If the query contains some constants, MS¬ outputs a (optimized) program MS¬$(\mathcal{Q}, \mathcal{P})$ consisting of a set of *modified* and *magic* rules (denoted by *modifiedRules* and *magicRules*, respectively). The algorithm generates modified and magic rules on a rule-by-rule basis. To this end, it exploits a stack S of predicates for storing all the adorned predicates that are still to be used for propagating the query binding (the **Adorn** function pushes on S each adorned predicates it generates, which has not been previously rewritten). At each step, an element p^α is removed from S, and the rules defining p are processed one-at-a-time.

The main steps of the algorithm MS¬ are illustrated by means of the program $\mathcal{P}_2$ in Example 2, and the query $\mathcal{Q}_2 = \mathsf{p(a, X)}$.

The computation starts in step 2 by initializing *modifiedRules* to the empty set. Then, the function **BuildQuerySeeds** is used for storing in *magicRules* the magic seeds, and pushing on the stack S the adorned predicates of $\mathcal{Q}$. For instance, given the query $\mathcal{Q}_2$ and the program $\mathcal{P}_2$, **BuildQuerySeeds** creates $\mathsf{magic\_p^{bf}(a).}$ and pushes $\mathsf{p^{bf}}$ onto the stack S.

The core of the technique (steps 2-13) is repeated until the stack S is empty, i.e., until there is no further adorned predicate to be propagated. Specifically, an adorned predicate p^α is removed from the stack S in step 3, and its binding is propagated.

In the steps 4-8, the binding of p^α is propagated in a traditional way, to each rule r of $\mathcal{P}$ having an atom $\mathsf{p}(\overline{\mathsf{t}})$ in the head. This propagation is as in the standard Magic Set method for stratified Datalog¬ programs.

Example 3. Consider again Example 2. Taking the predicate $\mathsf{p^{bf}}$ from the stack entails the adornment of the rule $\mathsf{p(X, Y) :- d(X, Y), not\ q(X, Y).}$. This yields the rule $\mathsf{p^{bf}(X, Y) :- d(X, Y), not\ q^{bb}(X, Y).}$, and the predicate $\mathsf{q^{bb}}$ is eventually pushed on the stack. Then, we can proceed (by using the standard algorithms) with the generation of one magic ($\mathsf{magic\_q^{bb}(X, Y) :- magic\_p^{bf}(X), d(X, Y).}$) and one modified rule ($\mathsf{p(X, Y) :- magic\_p^{bf}, d(X, Y), not\ q(X, Y).}$).   □

Steps 9-13 performs the propagation of the binding through each *dangerous* rule d in $\mathcal{P}$ of the form $\mathsf{h(\overline{t}_h) :- p(\overline{t}_p), q_1(\overline{t}_1), \ldots, q_m(\overline{t}_m).}$, having an atom $\mathsf{p}(\overline{\mathsf{t}}_p)$ in the body. These steps are, in fact, required for avoiding the semantic problems that we have described in the previous section. In this case, in order to simulate the body-to-head propagation, the rule d is first replaced by an "inverted" rule d_s of the form $\mathsf{p(\overline{t}_p) :- h(\overline{t}_h), q_1(\overline{t}_1), \ldots, q_m(\overline{t}_m).}$, which has been obtained by swapping the head predicate with the body predicate propagating the binding. Then, the adornment can be carried out as usual by means of the function **Adorn**. Since this "inverted" rule was not part of the original program and its only purpose is generating binding information, it will not give rise to a modified rule, but only to magic rules.

Example 4. When $\mathsf{q^{bb}}$ is removed from the stack, it can be used for adorning the body of the dangerous rule $\mathsf{y(X) :- q(X, Y)}$. Hence, we obtain first the "inverted" rule

$q(X, Y) :- y(X)$. and adorn it, obtaining $q^{bb}(X, Y) :- y^b(X)$. which gives rise to one magic rule: $\texttt{magic\_y}^b(X) :- \texttt{magic\_q}^{bb}(X, Y)$. $\qquad\square$

Finally, after all the adorned predicates have been processed the algorithm outputs the program $MS^-(\mathcal{Q}, \mathcal{P})$.

Example 5. The complete rewriting of program $\mathcal{P}_2$ w.r.t. query $\mathcal{Q}_2$ ($MS^-(\mathcal{Q}_2, \mathcal{P}_2)$) consists of the magic rules:

```
magic_p^bf(a).                        magic_q^bb(X,Y) :- magic_p^bf(X),d(X,Y).
magic_p^bb(X,Y) :- magic_q^bb(X,Y).   magic_y^b(X) :- magic_q^bb(X,Y).
magic_q^bf(X) :- magic_y^b(X).        magic_z^b(X) :- magic_y^b(X).
magic_z^b(X) :- magic_y^b(X),z(X).    magic_p^bb(X,Y) :- magic_q^bf(X),d(X,Y).
magic_q^bb(X,Y) :- magic_p^bb(X,Y).
```

plus the rewritten rules:

```
p(X,Y) :- magic_p^bf(X),d(X,Y),not q(X,Y).   q(X,Y) :- magic_q^bb(X,Y),d(X,Y),not p(X,Y).
y(X) :- magic_y^b(X),q(X,Y).                  z(X) :- magic_z^b(X),y(X),not z(X).
q(X,Y) :- magic_q^bf(X),d(X,Y),not p(X,Y).   p(X,Y) :- magic_p^bb(X,Y),d(X,Y),not q(X,Y).
```

It is worth noting that the rewritten program does not contain rules for predicates a and b, since they are not relevant for answering $\mathcal{Q}_2$. $MS^-(\mathcal{Q}_2, \mathcal{P}_2)$ admits only one stable model M, such that $M/_{\mathcal{P}_2} = \{p(a, b)\}$. Hence, $Ans_c(\mathcal{Q}_2, \mathcal{P}_{2,F_2}) = Ans_b(\mathcal{Q}_2, \mathcal{P}_{2,F_2}) = X/b$.the original semantics is preserved. $\qquad\square$

4.4 Query Equivalence Results

We conclude the presentation of the MS algorithm by formally proving its soundness. The result is shown by establishing correspondences between a program $\mathcal{P}$ and its transformed program $MS^-(\mathcal{Q}, \mathcal{P},)$ with respect to some query $\mathcal{Q}$.

To show this result, we will employ the notion of *simplification*: Given a ground program $\mathcal{P}$ and a subprogram $U \subseteq \mathcal{P}$, which admits exactly one stable model S. Then simplify$(\mathcal{P}, U)$ denotes the program $\{r/_{\mathcal{P}-U} \mid r \in (\mathcal{P} - U) \wedge B^+(r)/_U \subseteq S \wedge B^-(r)/_U \cap S = \emptyset\}$, which can be thought of as the partial evaluation w.r.t. S. This is needed to get rid of the magic predicates, which are not present in the original program.

Lemma 1. *Let $\mathcal{P}$ be a Datalog$^-$ program $\mathcal{P}$, $\mathcal{Q}$ a query. Furthermore, we denote by* magic$(\mathcal{Q}, \mathcal{P})$ *the set of magic rules in* $MS^-(\mathcal{Q}, \mathcal{P})$. *Then it holds that* $\mathcal{P}'' = $ simplify$(Ground(MS^-(\mathcal{Q}, \mathcal{P})), $ magic$(\mathcal{Q}, \mathcal{P}) \cup EDB(\mathcal{P}))$ *is a module of* $\mathcal{P}' = $ simplify$(Ground(\mathcal{P}), EDB(\mathcal{P}))$.

Proof (Sketch). Observe that $\mathcal{P}'' \subseteq \mathcal{P}'$ holds. Assume that $\mathcal{P}''$ is not a module of $\mathcal{P}'$. Then at least one of the following condition holds: (1) $\exists r' \in \mathcal{P}' - \mathcal{P}'', r'' \in \mathcal{P}''$: $H(r') = H(r'')$ (2) $\exists r'' \in \mathcal{P}''$: $\exists b \in B(r'')$: $\exists r' \in \mathcal{P}' - \mathcal{P}''$: $b = H(r')$ (3) $\exists r'' \in \mathcal{P}''$: $\exists r' \in \mathcal{P}' - \mathcal{P}''$: $H(r'') \in B(r')$ and r' is dangerous. One can show that all of (1), (2), and (3) lead to contradictions, and hence the result follows.

(1) For all rules in $\mathcal{P}$ with head predicate h, in $MS^-(\mathcal{Q}, \mathcal{P})$ there exists a copy for each adornment that was generated for h. So for any simplified ground instance r of

such a rule with head atom $h(c_1, \ldots, c_n)$, either $magic\_h^a(c_1, \ldots, c_m)$ holds for at least one adornment a of h, or it does not hold for any adornment of h. In the former case, for each rule in $\mathcal{P}$ with h in its head, a corresponding rule with $magic\_h^a$ in its body exists in $\mathrm{MS}^\neg(\mathcal{Q}, \mathcal{P})$. If $magic\_h^a(c1, \ldots, cm)$ holds for no adornment a, no simplified ground version of r is in $\mathcal{P}''$. In total, for each ground atom $h(c1, \ldots, cn)$ in $\mathcal{P}'$, either all or none of its defining rules are in $\mathcal{P}''$.

(2) Assume that r'' (the head of which is $h(c_1, \ldots, c_h)$) stems from a rule r_o'', which was adorned by a, such that $magic\_h^a(c_1, \ldots, c_{h_1})$ follows from the magic rules. Each IDB body atom of r_o'' has received some adornment based on a, in which bound arguments either directly share bound variables (w.r.t. a) with h, or via some EDB atoms. For any body predicate b, this gives rise to a magic rule $r_m : magic\_b^{a_1}(\bar{t}_{b_1}) :- magic\_h^a(\bar{t}_a), B.$ where B contains in particular all EDB atoms relevant for bound arguments of b. Concerning r' it contains some $b(d_1, \ldots, d_b)$ of the body of r'' in its head, and its originating rule r_o' is adorned by a_1. So in $\mathrm{MS}^\neg(\mathcal{Q}, \mathcal{P})$ a rule $r_m' : b(\bar{t}_{b_2}) :- magic\_b^{a_1}(\bar{t}_{b_3}), B'.$ occurs. Note that for all bound arguments $d_1, \ldots, d_k$ of $b(d_1, \ldots, d_b)$ w.r.t. a_1, $magic\_b^{a_1}(d_1, \ldots, d_k)$ follows from the magic rules because of r_m. So whenever a simplified ground instance of r_o' with $b(d_1, \ldots, d_b)$ in the head exists, so does one of r_m', which is hence in $\mathcal{P}''$.

(3) Observe first that the set of instantiations of dangerous rules in $\mathcal{P}$ is a superset of the set of dangerous rules in $Ground(\mathcal{P})$, which is in turn a superset the set of dangerous rules in any simplification of $Ground(\mathcal{P})$. So any dangerous rule in $\mathcal{P}'$ is also dangerous in $\mathcal{P}$. Therefore, the originating rule $r_o' \in \mathcal{P}$ of r' must have been adorned and "inverted", adorning in the following also the head of r_o'. So the dangerous rule r_o' eventually also gives rise to a modified rule in $\mathrm{MS}^\neg(\mathcal{Q}, \mathcal{P})$. Then, by the same argument as in (2), a magic rule obtained from the "inverted" rule must exist in $\mathrm{MS}^\neg(\mathcal{Q}, \mathcal{P})$, such that one of its instantiations matches the bound arguments of $H(r')$. So r' is in $\mathcal{P}''$ iff it is in $\mathcal{P}'$. $\square$

Theorem 3. *Let $\mathcal{P}$ be a Datalog$^\neg$ program, let $\mathcal{Q}$ be a query. Then, it holds that (1) $\mathrm{MS}^\neg(\langle\mathcal{Q}, \mathcal{P}\rangle) \subseteq_\mathcal{Q}^c \mathcal{P}$ and $\mathrm{MS}^\neg(\langle\mathcal{Q}, \mathcal{P}\rangle) \supseteq_\mathcal{Q}^b \mathcal{P}$, and (2) if $\mathrm{SM}(\mathcal{P}) \neq \emptyset$, $\mathrm{MS}^\neg(\langle\mathcal{Q}, \mathcal{P}\rangle) \equiv_\mathcal{Q}^b \mathcal{P}$ and $\mathrm{MS}^\neg(\langle\mathcal{Q}, \mathcal{P}\rangle) \equiv_\mathcal{Q}^c \mathcal{P}$.*

5   An Application to Data Integration

In this section we show an application of the Magic Set method for optimizing query answering in data integration systems, and report on the experience we are doing in the EU project INFOMIX on data integration. Let us first recall some basic notions.

A data integration system $\mathcal{I}$ is a triple $\langle \mathcal{G}, \mathcal{S}, \mathcal{M} \rangle$, where $\mathcal{G}$ is the global (relational) schema of the form $\mathcal{G} = \langle \Psi, \Sigma \rangle$, $\mathcal{S}$ is the source (relational) schema of the form $\mathcal{S} = \langle \Psi', \emptyset \rangle$, i.e., there are no integrity constraints on the sources, and $\mathcal{M}$ is the mapping between $\mathcal{G}$ and $\mathcal{S}$.

Example 6. Consider the data integration system $\mathcal{I}_0 = \langle \mathcal{G}_0, \mathcal{S}_0, \mathcal{M}_0 \rangle$, a simplification of the Demo Scenario in the EU project INFOMIX described below. The global schema $\mathcal{G}_0$ consists of the relations $professor(IDP, Pname, Phomepage)$, $student(IDS, Sname, Saddress)$, $exam\_data(IDP, IDS, Exam, Mark)$. The associated constraints in Σ_0 state that: (i) (*key constraints*) the keys of *professor*, *student*, and $exam\_data$ are the attributes IDP, IDS, and $(IDP, IDS, Exam)$, respectively, (ii) (*exclusion dependency*) a professor cannot be a student, and (iii) (*inclusion dependencies*) the identifiers of professors and students in the relation $exam\_data$ must be in the relations *professor* and *student*, respectively. The source schema S_0 comprises the relations s_1, s_2, s_3, and s_4. Finally, the mapping $\mathcal{M}_0$ is defined by the datalog program formed by $professor(X, Y, Z) :\!- s_1(X, Y, Z).$, $professor(X, Y, Z) :\!- s_4(Z, Y,, X).$, $student(X, Y, Z) :\!- s_2(Y, X, Z).$, $exam\_data(X, Y, Z, W) :\!- s_3(Y, X, Z, W).$ □

Given a database $\mathcal{D}$ for the source schema S, the user might issue a query q on the global schema which is populated by retrieving the data from $\mathcal{D}$ according to the mapping $\mathcal{M}$. However, while carrying out such an integration, it often happens that the retrieved (global) database, denoted by $ret(\mathcal{I}, \mathcal{D})$, is inconsistent w.r.t. Σ since data stored in local and autonomous sources are not in general required to satisfy constraints expressed on the global schema.

To remedy this problem, several approaches (see, e.g., [10, 11, 12, 13, 14, 15, 20]) defined the semantics of a data integration system $\mathcal{I}$ in terms of the repairs $rep(\mathcal{I}, \mathcal{D})$ of the database $ret(\mathcal{I}, \mathcal{D})$. Intuitively, each repair $\mathcal{R} \in rep(\mathcal{I}, \mathcal{D})$ is obtained by properly adding and deleting facts from $ret(\mathcal{I}, \mathcal{D})$ in order to satisfy constraints in Σ, as long as we "minimize" such additions and deletions.

These repairs depend on the interpretation of the mappings in $\mathcal{M}$, which, in fact, impose restrictions or preferences on the possibility of adding or removing facts from $ret(\mathcal{I}, \mathcal{D})$ to repair constraint violations. In the INFOMIX project, we have considered the *loosely-sound* semantics according to which mappings might retrieve only a subset of the tuples needed for answering the query. Hence, we can add an unbounded number of tuples to repair violations of inclusion dependencies; nonetheless, the semantics is loose in the sense that, in order to repair keys and exclusion dependencies, we are also allowed to delete a minimal set of tuples.

Given a data integration system $\mathcal{I}$ and a source database $\mathcal{D}$, a *query* q for $\mathcal{I}$ is an atom comprising a global relation in $\mathcal{I}$. Then, the answer to q is defined as the set $ans(q, \mathcal{I}, \mathcal{D})$ of all substitutions ϑ, such that, for each $1 \leq i \leq k$, $b_i\vartheta$ is true in each repair $\mathcal{R}$ in $rep(\mathcal{I}, \mathcal{D})$.

In order to design effective systems for query answering in data integration settings, the repair semantics has been formalized in the INFOMIX project (as well as in other approaches) by using logic programs, i.e., by encoding the constraints Σ of $\mathcal{G}$ and the mapping assertions $\mathcal{M}$ into a logic program, $\Pi(\mathcal{I}, \mathcal{D})$, using unstratified negation, such that the stable models of this program yield the repairs of the global database. The correctness of the rewriting is shown by the following theorem.

Theorem 4 ([13]). *Let $\mathcal{I} = \langle \mathcal{G}, S, \mathcal{M} \rangle$ be a data integration system, $\mathcal{D}$ be a database for S, and q be a query over $\mathcal{G}$. Then, $ans(q, \mathcal{I}, \mathcal{D})$ coincides with $Ans_c(q, \Pi(\mathcal{I}, \mathcal{D}))$.*

An attractive feature of this approach is that logic programs serve as executable logical specifications of repairs, and thus allow to state repair policies in a declarative rather than a procedural manner. However, a drawback of this approach is that with current implementations of stable model engines, such as DLV or Smodels, the evaluation of queries over large data sets quickly becomes infeasible, which calls for suitable optimization methods that help in speeding up the evaluation of queries expressed as logic programs [14].

To this aim, the binding propagation techniques proposed in this paper can be profitably exploited to isolate the relevant part of a database by "pushing down" the query constants to the sources. Importantly, our optimization fully preserves the original semantics of the data-integration query. Indeed, the loosely-sound semantics for data integration always guarantees the existence of a database repair no matter of the types of constraints in Σ, provided that the schema is *non-key-conflicting* [21]. Consequently, $\Pi(\mathcal{I}, \mathcal{D})$ is guaranteed to be consistent, and the correctness of the application of the Magic Set technique follows immediately from Thm. 3.

Theorem 5. *Let* $\mathcal{I} = \langle \mathcal{G}, \mathcal{S}, \mathcal{M} \rangle$ *be a data integration system,* $\mathcal{D}$ *be a database for* $\mathcal{S}$, *and* q *be a query over* $\mathcal{G}$. *Then,* $ans(q, \mathcal{I}, \mathcal{D})$ *coincides with* $Ans_c(q, \text{MS}^-(q, \Pi(\mathcal{I}, \mathcal{D})))$.

In order to test the effectiveness of the Magic Set technique for query optimization in data integration systems, we have carried out some experiments on the demonstration scenario of the INFOMIX project, which refers to the information system of the University "La Sapienza" in Rome. The global schema consists of 14 global relations with 29 constraints, while the source schema includes 29 relations (in 3 legacy databases) and 12 web wrappers (generating relational data) for more than 24MB of data.

Once a query q on $\mathcal{I}$ is submitted, a number of wrappers are executed to retrieve the data from the relevant sources for q, storing it in a Postgres database. Then, the Datalog¬ system DLV imports the Postgres data, and computes the answers for q w.r.t. $\Pi(\mathcal{I}, \mathcal{D})$. We measured the execution times of DLV for $\Pi(\mathcal{I}, \mathcal{D})$ and its magic-set rewritten version $\text{MS}^-(q, \Pi(\mathcal{I}, \mathcal{D}))$. Several experiments confirmed that on various practical queries, the performance is greatly improved by Magic Sets (in some cases, the query evaluation time passes from more than 20 minutes to a few seconds), while in the other cases we have observed no or only a minor overheads.

We finally observe that similar arguments can be also used to prove that our magic set technique can be profitably exploited in other approaches to data integration such as [10, 11, 12, 14]. In fact, all these approaches reduce answering a user query, q, to cautious reasoning over a logic program $\Pi(\mathcal{I}, \mathcal{D})$ which is guaranteed to be consistent.

Some of these approaches actually use disjunctive datalog programs, possibly with unstratified negation. We point out that the algorithm of this paper can be coupled with the method in [30], which is defined on positive disjunctive programs, obtaining a magic set method for arbitrary disjunctive programs.

6   Related Work and Conclusions

The Magic-Set method [22, 19, 1, 23] is one of the best known techniques for the optimization of Datalog queries. Many extensions and refinements of Magic-Sets have been proposed, addressing e.g. query constraints [24], modular stratification and well-founded semantics [25, 26], integration into cost-based query optimization [27]. The research on enhancements to the Magic-Set method is still going on. For instance, in the last-year ACM-PODS conference a magic-set technique for the class of *soft-stratifiable* programs was presented [28], and in [29, 30] magic sets techniques for disjunctive programs were proposed.

An extension of the Magic Set technique for *positive* Datalog programs with integrity constraints has been presented in [31]. The proposed method is shown to be *brave complete* and *cautious sound*. Comparing this method to our approach, we observe that: (1) Our method is more general than the method in [31], since the latter deals only with a strict subset of Datalog¬ (recall that an integrity constraint $:- C$. is just a shorthand for $p :- C$, not p); while our method supports full Datalog¬, allowing for unstratified negation. (2) Our method has much better semantic properties than [31]. Indeed, [31] do not ensure query equivalence in any case; while we guarantee full query equivalence, unless the input program is inconsistent (see Thm. 3). Such a query equivalence is in fact very relevant for data integration applications (see the previous Section).

Our modularity results are strictly related to splitting sets, as defined in [16], or equivalently to modules as defined in [17]. The main difference is that our notion of modules and independent sets guarantee query equivalence for consistent programs, which does not hold for these previous notions. In fact, in general, one can prove that only the first two items of Thm. 2 hold for splitting-set modules.

A different kind of query optimization for data integration has been done in [32]. This approach does not exploit constants that appear in the query, but only inconsistent (w.r.t. constraints of the global schema) portions of the retrieved database. In fact, no systematic technique for query optimization in data integration systems exploiting binding propagations has been proposed in the literature so far.

Concluding, we believe that our results are relevant to both theory and practice. On the theory side, our modularity results provide a better understanding of the structural properties of Datalog¬, complementing and advancing on previous works on modularity properties of this language. Moreover, the MS¬ algorithm generalizes Magic Sets, enlarging significantly their range of applicability to the full class of Datalog¬ programs under the stable model semantics. Importantly, our work can be profitably exploited for data-integration systems. Preliminary results of experiments show that the application of our techniques allows us to solve very advanced data-integration tasks.

References

1. Ullman, J.D.: Principles of Database and Knowledge Base Systems. Computer Science Press (1989)
2. Gelfond, M., Lifschitz, V.: The Stable Model Semantics for Logic Programming. In: ICLP/SLP'88, Cambridge, Mass., MIT Press (1988) 1070–1080
3. Bidoit, N., Froidevaux, C.: Negation by Default and Unstratifiable Logic Programs. Theoretical Computer Science **78** (1991) 85–112
4. Dantsin, E., Eiter, T., Gottlob, G., Voronkov, A.: Complexity and Expressive Power of Logic Programming. ACM Computing Surveys **33** (2001) 374–425
5. Bidoit, N., Froidevaux, C.: General Logical Databases and Programs: Default Logic Semantics and Stratification. Information and Computation **91** (1991) 15–54
6. Marek, V.W., Truszczyński, M.: Autoepistemic Logic. JACM **38** (1991) 588–619
7. Schlipf, J.: The Expressive Powers of Logic Programming Semantics. JCSS **51** (1995) 64–86 Abstract in Proc. PODS 90, pp. 196–204.
8. Leone, N., Pfeifer, G., Faber, W., Eiter, T., Gottlob, G., Perri, S., Scarcello, F.: The DLV System for Knowledge Representation and Reasoning. ACM TOCL (2004) To appear.
9. Niemelä, I., Simons, P., Syrjänen, T.: Smodels: A System for Answer Set Programming. In: NMR'2000 (2000)

10. Arenas, M., Bertossi, L.E., Chomicki, J.: Specifying and querying database repairs using logic programs with exceptions. In: Proc. of FQAS 2000, Springer (2000) 27–41
11. Greco, G., Greco, S., Zumpano, E.: A logic programming approach to the integration, repairing and querying of inconsistent databases. In: Proc. of ICLP'01, Springer (2001) 348–364
12. Barceló, P., Bertossi, L.: Repairing databases with annotated predicate logic. In: Proc. the 10th Int. Workshop on Non-Monotonic Reasoning (NMR 2002). (2002) 160–170
13. Calì, A., Lembo, D., Rosati, R.: Query rewriting and answering under constraints in data integration systems. In: Proc. of IJCAI 2003. (2003) 16–21
14. Bravo, L., Bertossi, L.: Logic programming for consistently querying data integration systems. In: Proc. of IJCAI 2003. (2003) 10–15
15. Chomicki, J., Marcinkowski, J.: Minimal-Change Integrity Maintenance Using Tuple Deletions. Information and Computation (2004) to Appear.
16. Lifschitz, V., Turner, H.: Splitting a Logic Program. In Van Hentenryck, P., ed.: ICLP'94, MIT Press (1994) 23–37
17. Eiter, T., Gottlob, G., Mannila, H.: Disjunctive Datalog. ACM TODS 22 (1997) 364–418
18. Dung, P.M.: On the Relations between Stable and Well-Founded Semantics of Logic Programs. Theoretical Computer Science 105 (1992) 7–25
19. Beeri, C., Ramakrishnan, R.: On the power of magic. JLP 10 (1991) 255–259
20. Calì, A., Calvanese, D., De Giacomo, G., Lenzerini, M.: Data integration under integrity constraints. Information Systems 29 (2004) 147–163
21. Calì, A., Lembo, D., Rosati, R.: On the decidability and complexity of query answering over inconsistent and incomplete databases. In: PODS '03. (2003) 260–271
22. Bancilhon, F., Maier, D., Sagiv, Y., Ullman, J.D.: Magic Sets and Other Strange Ways to Implement Logic Programs. In: PODS'86. (1986) 1–16
23. Mumick, I.S., Finkelstein, S.J., Pirahesh, H., Ramakrishnan, R.: Magic is relevant. In: SIGMOD Conference 1990. (1990) 247–258
24. Stuckey, P.J., Sudarshan, S.: Compiling query constraints. In: PODS'94, ACM Press (1994) 56–67
25. Ross, K.A.: Modular Stratification and Magic Sets for Datalog Programs with Negation. JACM 41 (1994) 1216–1266
26. Kemp, D.B., Srivastava, D., Stuckey, P.J.: Bottom-up evaluation and query optimization of well-founded models. Theoretical Computer Science 146 (1995) 145–184
27. Seshadri, P., Hellerstein, J.M., Pirahesh, H., Leung, T.Y.C., Ramakrishnan, R., Srivastava, D., Stuckey, P.J., Sudarshan, S.: Cost-based optimization for magic: Algebra and implementation. In: SIGMOD Conference 1996, ACM Press (1996) 435–446
28. Behrend, A.: Soft stratification for magic set based query evaluation in deductive databases. In: PODS 2003, ACM Press (2003) 102–110
29. Greco, S.: Binding Propagation Techniques for the Optimization of Bound Disjunctive Queries. IEEE TKDE 15 (2003) 368–385
30. Cumbo, C., Faber, W., Greco, G.: Enhancing the magic-set method for disjunctive datalog programs. In: Proc. of ICLP'04, Saint-Malo, France (2004) Forthcoming.
31. Greco, G., Greco, S., Trubitsyna, I., Zumpano, E.: Optimization of Bound Disjunctive Queries with Constraints. TPLP (to appear (CoRR report cs.LO/0406013))
32. Eiter, T., Fink, M., Greco, G., Lembo, D.: : Efficient evaluation of logic programs for querying data integration systems. In: Proc. of ICLP'03. (2003) 163–177

View-Based Query Processing:
On the Relationship Between Rewriting, Answering and Losslessness*

Diego Calvanese[1], Giuseppe De Giacomo[2],
Maurizio Lenzerini[2], and Moshe Y. Vardi[3]

[1] Facoltà di Scienze e Tecnologie Informatiche
Libera Università di Bolzano/Bozen, Italy
`calvanese@inf.unibz.it`
[2] Dipartimento di Informatica e Sistemistica "Antonio Ruberti"
Università di Roma "La Sapienza", Italy
{`degiacomo, lenzerini`}`@dis.uniroma1.it`
[3] Department of Computer Science
Rice University, Houston, U.S.A.
`vardi@cs.rice.edu`

Abstract. As a result of the extensive research in view-based query processing, three notions have been identified as fundamental, namely rewriting, answering, and losslessness. *Answering* amounts to computing the tuples satisfying the query in all databases consistent with the views. *Rewriting* consists in first reformulating the query in terms of the views and then evaluating the rewriting over the view extensions. *Losslessness* holds if we can answer the query by solely relying on the content of the views. While the mutual relationship between these three notions is easy to identify in the case of conjunctive queries, the terrain of notions gets considerably more complicated going beyond such a query class. In this paper, we revisit the notions of answering, rewriting, and losslessness and clarify their relationship in the setting of semistructured databases, and in particular for the basic query class in this setting, i.e., two-way regular path queries. Our first result is a clean explanation of the relationship between answering and rewriting, in which we characterize rewriting as a "linear approximations" of query answering. We show that applying this linear approximation to the constraint-satisfaction framework yields an elegant automata-theoretic approach to query rewriting. As for lossless-ness, we show that there are indeed two distinct interpretations for this

---

* This research has been partially supported by the EU funded Projects INFOMIX (IST-2001-33570) and SEWASIE (IST-2001-34825), by MIUR - Fondo Speciale per lo Sviluppo della Ricerca di Interesse Strategico - project "Società dell'Informazione", subproject SP1 "Reti Internet: Efficienza, Integrazione e Sicurezza", by MIUR - Fondo per gli Investimenti della Ricerca di Base (FIRB) - project "MAIS: Multichan-nel Adaptive Information Systems", by project HYPER, funded by IBM through a Shared University Research (SUR) Award grant, by NSF grants CCR-9988322, CCR-0124077, CCR-0311326, IIS-9908435, IIS-9978135, EIA-0086264, and ANI-0216467, by US-Israel BSF grant 9800096, by Texas ATP grant 003604-0058-2003, and by a grant from the Intel Corporation.

T. Eiter and L. Libkin (Eds.): ICDT 2005, LNCS 3363, pp. 321–336, 2005.

notion, namely with respect to answering, and with respect to rewriting. We also show that the constraint-theoretic approach and the automata-theoretic approach can be combined to give algorithmic characterization of the various facets of losslessness. Finally, we deal with the problem of coping with loss, by considering mechanisms aimed at explaining lossiness to the user.

1   Introduction

View-based query processing is the problem of computing the answer to a query based on a set of views [27, 31, 3]. This problem has recently received much attention in several application areas, such as mobile computing, query optimization, data warehousing, and data integration. A large number of results have been reported in the last years, and several methods have been proposed (see [25] for a recent survey).

As a result of the extensive research in this area, there is proliferation of notions whose relationship to each other is not clear. Fundamentally, there seems to be two basic approaches to view-based query processing. The first approach, originating with [27], is the *query-rewriting* approach, which is based on the idea of first reformulating the query in terms of the views and then evaluating the rewriting over the view extensions. The other approach, originating with [18], is the *query-answering* approach, which takes a more direct route, trying to compute the so-called *certain tuples*, i.e., the tuples satisfying the query in all databases consistent with the views, on the basis of the view definitions and the view extensions. The relationship between the two approaches has been discussed (e.g., [8, 14]), but not completely clarified, and is often ignored, see for example [27, 5, 21].

A related issue that has been studied in several papers is whether the information content of the views is sufficient to answer completely a given query. We say that a set of views is *lossless* with respect to a query, if, no matter what the database is, we can answer the query by solely relying on the content of the views. This concept has several applications, for example, in view selection [15], where we have to measure the quality of the choice of the views to materialize in the data warehouse, or in data integration, where we may be interested in checking whether the relevant queries can be answered by accessing only a given set of sources [28]. Several papers have addressed the issue of losslessness implicitly [27, 24, 28] or explicitly [11]. It should be noted, however, that losslessness is relative to the manner in which view-based query processing is performed, since the goal is lossless query processing. Thus, there ought to be two distinct notions of losslessness, with respect to query rewriting or with respect to query answering. Recent discussions of losslessness, such as [28, 11], do not reflect this distinction.

One reason for the confusion is that much of the work in this area has focused on using conjunctive queries for both target queries and view definitions, cf. [25]. This setting turns out to be extremely well behaved. In particular, query rewriting and query answering coincide, if we allow the target query to be written as a union of conjunctive queries. Furthermore, losslessness with respect to query rewriting and with respect to query answering also coincide, even if we require rewriting by conjunctive queries (disallowing unions). These results, implicit or explicit in [27], give the impression of a simple "terrain" of notions. Once, however, one goes even slightly beyond conjunctive queries or slightly modifies the view model, the terrain of notions gets considerably more complicated, as has already been observed in [3].

In this paper, we revisit the notions of query answering, query rewriting, and losslessness and clarify their relationship in the setting of semistructured databases, which capture data that do not fit into rigid, predefined schemas, and are best described by graph-based data models [6, 1, 22, 2]. The prevalent model for semistructured data is that of edge-labeled graphs, in which nodes describe data elements and edges describe relationships or values. (Extensions to node-labeled graphs or to node-edge-labeled graphs are straightforward.)

Methods for extracting information from semistructured data necessarily incorporate special querying mechanisms that are not common in traditional database systems. One such basic mechanism is that of *regular-path queries* (RPQs), which retrieves all pairs of nodes in the graph connected by a path conforming to a regular expression [7, 4]. We allow in our regular path queries also the inverse operator. The inverse operator is essential for expressing navigations in the database that traverse the edges both backward and forward [16]. We call such queries *two-way regular path queries* (2RPQs). Such path queries are useful in real settings (see for example [6, 7, 29]), and are part of the core of many query languages for semistructured data [4, 20, 17]. In our earlier work we studied both query answering and query rewriting for 2RPQs [9]. For an introductory survey on 2RPQs, see [13].

Our first result is a clean explanation of the relationship between query rewriting and query answering. We view query answering as the more robust notion among the two, since its definition is in terms of the information content of the view extensions. The certain tuples are the tuples whose presence in the answer logically follows from the view extension. In contrast, query rewriting is motivated by the pragmatic need to access the view extensions using a query language that is close, if not identical, to the language in which the target query and the views were formulated. For example, [27] considered rewriting of conjunctive queries by means of unions of conjunctive queries, [12] considered rewriting of RPQs by means of RPQs, and [9] considered rewriting of 2RPQs using 2RPQs.

The setup we use in this paper is that of *sound views*, in which view extension need not reflect global data completely. Thus, all we require from a view V_i defined in terms of a query Q_i is that its extension E_i with respect to a global database $\mathcal{B}$ is such that $E_i \subseteq Q_i(\mathcal{B})$. This setting corresponds to the long-standing *open-world approach* for querying incomplete information [30]. In this setting query answering can be characterized in terms of constraint satisfaction (or, equivalently, the homomorphism problem [19]), with a constraint template derived from the target query and view definition [14].

It now turns out that rewriting 2RPQs by means of 2RPQs amounts for seeking a "linear approximation" of query answering. That is, we retrieve a pair (c, d) from the view extension only if its inclusion in the answer is logically implied by a single path between c and d in the view extension. (For 2RPQs two-way paths are considered, while for RPQs one-way paths are considered.) We show that applying this linear approximation to the constraint-satisfaction framework yields the elegant automata-theoretic approach to query rewriting of [12], extended naturally to 2RPQs.

Once the relationship between query answering and query rewriting is clarified, we show that there are indeed two distinct notions of losslessness. Losslessness with respect to query rewriting is what has been called *exactness* in [12], while losslessness with respect to query answering, which we view as the more fundamental notion, is what has been studied in [11]. Since query rewriting is an approximation of query answering, exactness is a stronger notion than losslessness; exactness implies losslessness, but not vice versa. Exactness was taken in [12] to be a measure of quality of query rewriting, but we now see that it conflates query rewriting with losslessness. A better way to measure the quality of query rewriting is to measure its quality as an approximation. We say that query rewriting is *perfect* if it is equivalent to query answering. Thus, exactness is the conjunction of perfectness and losslessness (with respect to query answering). We also show that the constraint-theoretic approach and the automata-theoretic approach can be combined to give algorithmic characterization of the three notions: perfectness, losslessness, and exactness.

Finally, we consider lossiness, which we view as the central challenge of view-based query processing, as lossiness is more likely to be the norm rather than the exception. Once a schema designer has learned that a view decomposition is lossy with respect to a certain query, how should this "loss" be dealt with? We believe that database design tools should help users to "cope with loss". In particular, we believe that it would be useful to the user to understand what information is lost by view-based query answering. We discuss a variety of mechanisms aimed at explaining such lossiness to the user.

The paper is organized as follows. In Section 2 we recall the basic notions related to view-based query processing, and in Section 3 we recall the relationship between query answering and constraint satisfaction. In Section 4 we discuss the relationship between answering and rewriting. In Section 5 we study losslessness with respect to rewriting for 2RPQs and in Section 6 losslessness with respect to answering. For the latter we introduce the notion of linear fragment of certain answers. In Section 7 we discuss the relationship between exactness, perfectness, losslessness, and lossiness and conclude the paper.

2   Preliminaries

Following the usual approach in semistructured data [2], we define a *semistructured database* as a finite directed graph whose edges are labeled by elements from a given finite alphabet Σ. Each node represents an objects and an edge from object x to object y labeled by r, denoted $r(x, y)$, represents the fact that relation r holds between x and y. Observe that a semistructured database can be seen as a (finite) relational structure over the set Σ of binary relational symbols. A *relational structure* (or simply *structure*) $\mathcal{B}$ over Σ is a pair $(\Delta^{\mathcal{B}}, \cdot^{\mathcal{B}})$, where $\Delta^{\mathcal{B}}$ is a finite domain and $\cdot^{\mathcal{B}}$ is a function that assigns to each relation symbol in $r \in \Sigma$ a binary relation $r^{\mathcal{B}}$ over $\Delta^{\mathcal{B}}$, also denoted by $r(\mathcal{B})$.

A query is a function from relational structures to relations, assigning to each relational structure over a given alphabet a relation of a certain arity. In this paper we deal mainly with binary queries. A *regular-path query* (RPQ) over Σ is defined in terms of a regular language over Σ. The *answer* $Q(\mathcal{B})$ *to an RPQ* Q *over a database* $\mathcal{B}$ is the set of pairs of objects connected in $\mathcal{B}$ by a directed path traversing a sequence of edges forming a word in the regular language $L(Q)$ defined by Q.

RPQs allow for navigating the edges of a semistructured databases only in the forward direction. RPQs extended with the ability of navigating database edges backward are called *two-way regular-path queries* (2RPQs) [9]. Formally, we consider an alphabet $\Sigma^{\pm} = \Sigma \cup \{r^- \mid r \in \Sigma\}$ which includes a new symbol r^- for each relation symbol r in Σ. The symbol r^- denotes the *inverse* of the binary relation r. If $p \in \Sigma^{\pm}$, then we use p^- to mean the inverse of p, i.e., if p is r, then p^- is r^-, and if p is r^-, then p^- is r. A 2RPQ over Σ is defined in terms of a regular language over $\Sigma^{\pm}$. The *answer* $Q(\mathcal{B})$ *to a 2RPQ* Q *over a database* $\mathcal{B}$ is the set of pairs of objects connected in $\mathcal{B}$ by a semipath that conforms to the regular language $L(Q)$. A *semipath* in $\mathcal{B}$ from x to y (labeled with $p_1 \cdots p_n$) is a sequence of the form $(x_0, p_1, x_1, \ldots, x_{n-1}, p_n, x_n)$, where $n \geq 0$, $x_0 = x$, $x_n = y$, and for each x_{i-1}, p_i, x_i, we have that $p_i \in \Sigma^{\pm}$, and, if $p_i = r$ then $(x_{i-1}, x_i) \in r(\mathcal{B})$, and if $p_i = r^-$ then $(x_i, x_{i-1}) \in r(\mathcal{B})$. Intuitively, a semipath $(x_0, p_1, x_1, \ldots, x_{n-1}, p_n, x_n)$ corresponds to a navigation of the database from x_0 to x_n, following edges forward or backward, according to the sequence of edge labels $p_1 \cdots p_n$. Note that the objects in a semipath are not necessarily distinct. A semipath is said to be *simple* if no object in it appears more than once. A *linear database* with endpoints x and y is a database constituted by a single simple semipath from x to y. We say that a semipath $(x_0, p_1, \ldots, p_n, x_n)$ *conforms to* a 2RPQ Q if $p_1 \cdots p_n \in L(Q)$. Summing up, a pair (x, y) of objects is in the answer $Q(\mathcal{B})$ if and only if, by starting from x, it is possible to reach y by navigating on $\mathcal{B}$ according to one of the words in $L(Q)$. The notions above can be extended to *two-way path queries*, which are defined similarly to 2RPQs, but without requiring the language to be regular.

Consider now a semistructured database that is accessible only through a collection of views expressed as 2RPQs, and suppose we need to answer a 2RPQ over the database only on the basis of our knowledge on the views. Specifically, the collection of views is represented by a finite set $\mathcal{V}$ of *view symbols*, each denoting a binary relation. Each view symbol $V \in \mathcal{V}$ has an associated *view definition* V^{Σ}, which is a 2RPQ over Σ. A $\mathcal{V}$-*extension* $\mathcal{E}$ is a relational structure over $\mathcal{V}$. We consider views to be *sound* [3, 23], i.e., we model a situation where the extension of the views provides a subset of the results of applying the view definitions to the database. Formally, given a set $\mathcal{V}$ of views and a database $\mathcal{B}$, we use $\mathcal{V}^{\Sigma}(\mathcal{B})$ to denote the $\mathcal{V}$-extension $\mathcal{E}$ such that $V(\mathcal{E}) = V^{\Sigma}(\mathcal{B})$, for each $V \in \mathcal{V}$. We say that a $\mathcal{V}$-extension $\mathcal{E}$ is *sound wrt a database* $\mathcal{B}$ if $\mathcal{E} \subseteq \mathcal{V}^{\Sigma}(\mathcal{B})$. In other words, for a view $V \in \mathcal{V}$, all the tuples in $V(\mathcal{E})$ must appear in $V^{\Sigma}(\mathcal{B})$, but $V^{\Sigma}(\mathcal{B})$ may contain tuples not in $V(\mathcal{E})$.

Given a set $\mathcal{V}$ of views, a $\mathcal{V}$-extension $\mathcal{E}$, and a query Q over Σ, the set of *certain answers* (under sound views) to Q with respect to $\mathcal{V}$ and $\mathcal{E}$ is the set of pairs (x, y) of objects such that $(x, y) \in Q(\mathcal{B})$ for every database $\mathcal{B}$ wrt which $\mathcal{E}$ is sound, i.e., $\mathcal{E} \subseteq \mathcal{V}^{\Sigma}(\mathcal{B})$. *View-based query answering* consists in deciding whether a given pair of objects is a certain answer to Q with respect to $\mathcal{V}$ and $\mathcal{E}$. Given a set $\mathcal{V}$ of views and a query Q, we denote by $cert_{Q,\mathcal{V}}$ the query that, for every $\mathcal{V}$-extension $\mathcal{E}$, returns the set of certain answers to Q with respect to $\mathcal{V}$ and $\mathcal{E}$.

View-based query answering has also been tackled using an indirect approach, called *view-based query rewriting*. According to such an approach, a query Q over the database alphabet is processed by first reformulating Q into an expression of a fixed query language over the view alphabet $\mathcal{V}$ (called *rewriting*), and then evaluating the rewriting over the view extensions. Formally, let Q be a query over the database alphabet, and let Q_r be a query over the view alphabet $\mathcal{V}$. We say that Q_r is a *rewriting of Q under sound views* $\mathcal{V}$ (or simply, with respect to views $\mathcal{V}$), if for every database $\mathcal{B}$ and for every $\mathcal{V}$-extension $\mathcal{E}$ with $\mathcal{E} \subseteq \mathcal{V}^{\Sigma}(\mathcal{B})$, we have that $Q_r(\mathcal{E}) \subseteq Q(\mathcal{B})$. Since 2RPQs are monotone, by results in [14] (Proposition 13 and 24), rewritings admit the following simpler characterization. A 2RPQ Q_r is a rewriting of a 2RPQ Q if, for every database $\mathcal{B}$, we have that $Q_r(\mathcal{V}^{\Sigma}(\mathcal{B})) \subseteq Q(\mathcal{B})$. We make use of this characterization in the following.

Obviously, in view-based query rewriting, we are not interested in arbitrary rewritings, but we aim at computing rewritings that capture the original query at best. Let $\mathcal{C}$ be a query class in which rewritings are expressed. A query Q_r in $\mathcal{C}$ is a $\mathcal{C}$-*maximal rewriting* of Q under $\mathcal{V}$ if (i) it is a rewriting of Q under $\mathcal{V}$, and (ii) for each query Q_r' in $\mathcal{C}$ that is a rewriting of Q under $\mathcal{V}$ and for each database $\mathcal{B}$ and each $\mathcal{V}$-extension $\mathcal{E}$ with $\mathcal{E} \subseteq \mathcal{V}^{\Sigma}(\mathcal{B})$, we have that $Q_r'(\mathcal{E}) \subseteq Q_r(\mathcal{E})$. Since in this paper we are focusing on 2RPQs, we are interested in the case where also rewritings are 2RPQs over the view alphabet $\mathcal{V}$, i.e., rewritings are expressed in the same language as queries over the database.

Throughout the paper, we will assume that RPQs are expressed as finite state automata over an appropriate alphabet. Besides standard (one-way) deterministic and non-deterministic finite state automata over words (1DFAs and 1NFAs, respectively), we assume familiarity with two-way automata (2NFAs) [26].

3   Answering and Constraint Satisfaction

In this work we make use of the tight relationship between view-based query answering for RPQs and 2RPQs and constraint satisfaction, which we recall here.

A *constraint-satisfaction problem (CSP)* is traditionally defined in terms of a set of variables, a set of values, and a set of constraints, and asks whether there is an assignment of the variables with the values that satisfies the constraints.

A characterization of CSP can be given in terms of homomorphisms between relational structures [19]. Here we consider relational structures whose relations are of arbitrary arity.

A *homomorphism* $h : A \to B$ between two relational structures A and B over the same alphabet is a mapping $h : \Delta^A \to \Delta^B$ such that, if $(c_1, \ldots, c_n) \in r(A)$, then $(h(c_1), \ldots, h(c_n)) \in r(B)$, for every relation symbol r in the alphabet. Let $\mathcal{A}$ and $\mathcal{B}$ be two classes of structures. The *(uniform) constraint-satisfaction problem* $CSP(\mathcal{A}, \mathcal{B})$ is the following decision problem: given a structure $A \in \mathcal{A}$ and a structure $B \in \mathcal{B}$ over the same alphabet, is there a homomorphism $h : A \to B$? When $\mathcal{B}$ consists of a single structure B and $\mathcal{A}$ is the set of all structures over the alphabet of B, we get the so-called *non-uniform* constraint-satisfaction problem, denoted by $CSP(B)$, where B is fixed and the input is just a structure $A \in \mathcal{A}$. As usual, we use $CSP(B)$ also to denote the set of structures A such that there is a homomorphism from A to B. From the very definition of CSP it follows directly that every $CSP(\mathcal{A}, \mathcal{B})$ problem is in NP.

A tight relationship between non-uniform CSP and view-based query answering for RPQs and 2RPQs has been developed in [10, 14]. Such a relationship is based on the notions of constraint template, associated to the query and view definitions, and constraints instance, associated to the view extension. Formally, given a 2RPQ Q and a set $\mathcal{V}$ of 2RPQ views, the *constraint template* $CT_{Q,\mathcal{V}}$ of Q with respect to $\mathcal{V}$ is the relational structure C defined as follows.

- The alphabet of C is $\mathcal{V} \cup \{U_i, U_f\}$, where each view denotes a binary relation symbol, and U_i and U_f are unary relation symbols.
- Let $A^Q = (\Sigma^\pm, S^Q, S_0^Q, \varrho^Q, F^Q)$ be a 1NFA for Q, where $\Sigma^\pm$ is the alphabet, S^Q is the set of states, S_0^Q is the set of initial states, ϱ^Q is the transition relation, and F^Q is the set of final states. The structure $C = (\Delta^C, \cdot^C)$ is given by:

  - $\Delta^C = 2^{S^Q}$;
  - $\sigma \in U_i(C)$ iff $S_0^Q \subseteq \sigma$;
  - $\sigma \in U_f(C)$ iff $\sigma \cap F^Q = \emptyset$;
  - for a view $V \in \mathcal{V}$, we have that $(\sigma_1, \sigma_2) \in V^C$ iff there exists a word $q_1 \cdots q_k \in L(V^\Sigma)$ and a sequence $T_0, \ldots, T_k$ of subsets of S^Q such that the following hold:
    1. $T_0 = \sigma_1$ and $T_k = \sigma_2$,
    2. if $s \in T_i$ and $(s, q_{i+1}, t) \in \varrho^Q$ then $t \in T_{i+1}$, for $0 \leq i < k$, and
    3. if $s \in T_i$ and $(s, q_i^-, t) \in \varrho^Q$ then $t \in T_{i-1}$, for $0 < i \leq k$.

Intuitively, the constraint template represents for each view V how the states of A^Q (i.e., of the 1NFA for Q) change when we follow database edges according to what specified by words in $L(V^\Sigma)$. Specifically, the last condition above corresponds to saying that a pair of sets of states (σ_1, σ_2) is in $V(C)$ if and only if there is some word w in $L(V^\Sigma)$ such that the following holds: if we start from a state in σ_1 on the left edge of w and move back and forth on w according to the transitions in A^Q, then, if we end up at the left edge of w we can be only in states in σ_1, and if we end up at the right edge of w we can be only in states in

σ_2; similarly, if we start from a state in σ_2 on the right edge of w. Moreover, the sets of states in $U_i(C)$ contain all initial states of A^Q, while the sets of states in $U_f(C)$ do not contain any final state of A^Q. This takes into account that we aim at characterizing counterexamples to view-based query answering, and hence we are interested in not getting to a final state of A^Q, regardless of the initial state from which we start and how we follow transitions.

Observe that, to check the existence of a word $q_1 \cdots q_k \in L(V^\Sigma)$ and of a sequence $T_0, \ldots, T_k$ of subsets of S such that conditions 1–3 above are satisfied, we can resort to a construction analogous to the one in [32]. Hence, such a check can be done in polynomial space in the size of Q, and in fact in nondeterministic logarithmic space in the size of V^Σ.

Given a $\mathcal{V}$-extension $\mathcal{E}$ and a pair of objects c, d, the *constraint instance* $\mathcal{E}^{c,d}$ is the structure $I = (\Delta^I, \cdot^I)$ over the alphabet $\mathcal{V} \cup \{U_i, U_f\}$ defined as follows:

- $\Delta^I = \Delta^\mathcal{E} \cup \{c, d\}$;
- $V(I) = V(\mathcal{E})$, for each $V \in \mathcal{V}$;
- $U_i(I) = \{c\}$, and $U_f(I) = \{d\}$.

The following theorem provides the characterization of view-based query answering in terms of CSP.

Theorem 1 ([14]). *Let Q be a 2RPQ, $\mathcal{V}$ a set of 2RPQ views, $\mathcal{E}$ a $\mathcal{V}$-extension, and c, d a pair of objects. Then, $(c,d) \notin cert_{Q,\mathcal{V}}(\mathcal{E})$ if and only if there is a homomorphism from $\mathcal{E}^{c,d}$ to $CT_{Q,\mathcal{V}}$.*

4   Relationship Between Rewriting and Answering

The relationship between answering and rewriting in view-based query processing is not always well understood. As we said before, one reason for the confusion is that much of the work in this area has focused on a setting based on conjunctive queries, where answering and rewriting coincide. Indeed, if we allow the target query to be written as a union of conjunctive queries (UCQs), then the UCQ-maximal rewriting of the query computes exactly the certain answers. Things get more complicated with RPQs and 2RPQs. Interestingly, we show next that we can use the above characterization of view-based query answering in terms of CSP, to characterize also query rewriting, thus providing a clean explanation of the relationship between answering and rewriting.

A preliminary observation is that one can restrict the attention to linear databases when looking for counterexamples to rewritings.

Lemma 1 ([9]). *Let Q be a 2RPQ, $\mathcal{V}$ a set of 2RPQ views, and w a word over $\mathcal{V}^\pm$. Then w is not a rewriting (note that w can be viewed as a 2RPQ) of Q with respect to $\mathcal{V}$ if and only if there exists a linear database $\mathcal{B}$ with endpoints c and d, and a view extension $\mathcal{E}$ with $\mathcal{E} \subseteq \mathcal{V}^\Sigma(\mathcal{B})$, such that $(c,d) \in w(\mathcal{E})$ but $(c,d) \notin Q(\mathcal{B})$.*

Making use of this result, we are able to exploit the constraint template itself as a 1NFA that recognizes the words that do not belong to a rewriting. However, we have first to take care of the fact that only direct view symbols appear in the constraint template, while a rewriting is a 1NFA over direct and inverse view symbols. To do so, we extend the constraint template by adding to the alphabet, for each symbol $V \in \mathcal{V}$, also the inverse symbol V^-. Then we define $(\sigma_1, \sigma_2) \in V^{-C}$ if and only if $(\sigma_2, \sigma_1) \in V^C$. We denote the resulting constraint template with $CT^{\pm}_{Q,\mathcal{V}}$. Observe that the construction of $CT^{\pm}_{Q,\mathcal{V}}$ from $CT_{Q,\mathcal{V}}$ takes into account the perfect symmetry that we have when moving along direct and inverse database and view symbols.

Now, $C = CT^{\pm}_{Q,\mathcal{V}}$ can be viewed directly as a 1NFA A^{nr} over $\mathcal{V}^{\pm}$, by taking the domain of C as the set of states of A^{nr}, the extension of U_i and U_f in C respectively as the set of initial and final states, and by deriving the transition relation of A^{nr} from the extension of the various $v \in \mathcal{V}^{\pm}$ as follows: A^{nr} has a transition (σ_1, v, σ_2) if and only if $(\sigma_1, \sigma_2) \in v^C$.

Let A^{rew} be a 1NFA accepting the complement of A^{nr}. Then the following characterization of the 2RPQ-maximal rewriting holds.

Theorem 2. *Let Q be a 2RPQ and $\mathcal{V}$ a set of 2RPQ views. Then A^{rew} is the 2RPQ-maximal rewriting of Q with respect to $\mathcal{V}$.*

The above characterization provides a nice combination of the constraint based [10] and automata theoretic [9] approaches to view-based query processing for 2RPQs, and goes into the heart of view-based rewriting. A (language) rewriting accepts a pair (c, d) if there is a path between c and d such that, if we view this path as a linear view extension, then (c, d) is in the certain answer with respect to this view extension. That means that there is no homomorphism from this path into the constraint template. Indeed, for a path, the existence of a homomorphism into the constraint template means that the path is accepted by the template, viewed as an automaton. Naturally, the difference with view-based query answering, is that we are not limited to linear view extensions only. Suppose that V_i and V_j connect the same pair of objects in a view extension. In rewriting we have to ignore this and allow the choice of distinct pairs of objects for the two views in a counterexample database. Query answering instead takes into account that the two pairs of objects are the same. Thus, query answering is more precise than query rewriting. On the other hand, the simplification introduced by query rewriting allows to have polynomial time evaluation in the size of the data, while query answering is coNP-complete [8].

Finally, observe that the above construction provides also optimal upper bounds for the problems of computing the 2RPQ-maximal rewriting and of determining whether such a rewriting is nonempty [9]. Indeed, the constraint template, and hence the 1NFA A^{nr} can be constructed in EXPTIME and is of exponential size [14]. Hence, its complement A^{rew}, which provides the 2RPQ-maximal rewriting, is of double exponential size and can be constructed in 2EXPTIME. On the other hand, if we only want to check its emptiness, we can complement A^{nr} on the fly, getting an EXPSPACE upper bound. All these bounds are tight [12].

5   Losslessness with Respect to Rewriting

We deal now with the problem of analyzing the loss of information in view-based query processing, and of characterizing the quality of certain answers and of rewritings. For this purpose, we make use of the following basic notions.

- To determine whether the information content of a set of views is sufficient to answer completely a given query, we make use of the notion of losslessness [24, 11]. In [11], a set of views $\mathcal{V}$ is said to be *lossless* with respect to a query Q, if for every database $\mathcal{B}$ we have that $Q(\mathcal{B}) = cert_{Q,\mathcal{V}}(\mathcal{V}^\Sigma(\mathcal{B}))$.
- As for rewritings, equivalence of a rewriting to the original query, modulo the view definitions, is called exactness (cf. [27, 12]). Formally, a rewriting Q_r in a certain query class $\mathcal{C}$ is *an exact rewriting* of Q with respect to views $\mathcal{V}$, if for every database $\mathcal{B}$ we have that $Q(\mathcal{B}) = Q_r(\mathcal{V}^\Sigma(\mathcal{B}))$.
- Finally, to determine whether we lose answering power by resorting to rewriting, we can compare rewritings with the certain answers, with the aim of checking whether the two are actually equivalent. A rewriting Q_r in a certain query class $\mathcal{C}$ is *a perfect rewriting* of Q with respect to views $\mathcal{V}$, if for every database $\mathcal{B}$ and every view extension $\mathcal{E}$ with $\mathcal{E} \subseteq \mathcal{V}^\Sigma(\mathcal{B})$ we have that $cert_{Q,\mathcal{V}}(\mathcal{E}) = Q_r(\mathcal{E})$.

The first notion aims at determining possible loss with respect to view-based query answering, and will be discussed in the next section. The other two notions deal with the loss of information in the case of rewritings, and are discussed below.

In the case of conjunctive queries, the best rewriting of a conjunctive query Q is a union of conjunctive queries. Therefore, checking exactness amounts to verifying whether Q is contained in the UCQ-maximal rewriting. The latter is a, possibly exponential, union of conjunctive queries, each of linear size. Since a conjunctive query is contained in a union of conjunctive queries only if it is contained in one of its disjuncts, it suffices to check whether there is a single conjunctive query in the rewriting that is equivalent to Q, after substituting the view definitions. This can be done in NP in the size of Q. As for perfectness, we already observed that the maximal rewriting computes exactly the certain answers. Therefore, the maximal rewriting is always perfect.

In the case of 2RPQs, things are more complicated. Exactness is studied in [9], where it is shown that verifying the existence of an exact rewriting is 2EXPTIME-complete. On the other hand, perfectness is a new notion, and we provide here a method for checking perfectness of the 2RPQ-maximal rewriting A^{rew} of a query Q. Exploiting the fact that 2RPQs are monotone, by results in [14], this amounts to check whether for all databases $\mathcal{B}$ we have that $cert_{Q,\mathcal{V}}(\mathcal{V}^\Sigma(\mathcal{B})) \subseteq A^{rew}(\mathcal{V}^\Sigma(\mathcal{B}))$. To do this check, we can in principle directly use the technique in [14] based on *view-based containment* (see [14] for definitions): the 2RPQ-maximal rewriting A^{rew} is a 1NFA of double exponential size in Q, and checking whether for all databases $\mathcal{B}$ we have that $cert_{Q,\mathcal{V}}(\mathcal{V}^\Sigma(\mathcal{B})) \subseteq A^{rew}(\mathcal{V}^\Sigma(\mathcal{B}))$ amounts to checking whether Q is view-based contained in A^{rew}, which can be done in NEXPTIME in Q and A^{rew} [14]. This gives us a N3EXPTIME upper bound. However, we can do better, by making use of the fact that we have obtained the 1NFA A^{rew} for the rewriting by complementation, and thus by application of the subset construction. This allows us to characterize non-membership in the answer set to A^{rew} by homomorphism into a structure $C = (\Delta^C, \cdot^C)$, called the *rewriting constraint template* $CTR_{A^{rew}, \mathcal{V}}$ of A^{rew}, defined as follows:

- The alphabet of C is $\mathcal{V}^{\pm} \cup \{U_i, U_f\}$, where U_i and U_f denote unary relation symbols.
- Let $A^{nr} = (\mathcal{V}^{\pm}, S, S_0, \varrho, F)$ be a 1NFA for the complement of the rewriting (see Section 4). Then
  - $\Delta^C = 2^S$;
  - $\sigma \in U_i^C$ iff $S_0 \subseteq \sigma$;
  - $\sigma \in U_f^C$ iff $\sigma \subseteq F$;
  - $(\sigma_1, \sigma_2) \in r^C$ iff $\varrho(\sigma_1, r) \subseteq \sigma_2$ and $\varrho(\sigma_2, r^-) \subseteq \sigma_1$.

To characterize perfectness of the rewriting in terms of CSP, we need to introduce proper constraint templates (see also [14]). Given the rewriting constraint template $CT_{A^{rew}, \mathcal{V}}$, a *proper constraint template* $CT^{\alpha, \beta}_{A^{rew}, \mathcal{V}}$ is obtained by eliminating from $\mathcal{U}_i$ all but one element α and from $\mathcal{U}_f$ all but one element β.

Lemma 2. *Let Q be a 2RPQ and $\mathcal{V}$ be a set of 2RPQ views. Then the 2RPQ-maximal rewriting of Q with respect to $\mathcal{V}$ is perfect if and only if for every proper constraint template $CTR^{\alpha, \beta}_{A^{rew}, \mathcal{V}}$ of $CTR_{A^{rew}, \mathcal{V}}$, there exists a homomorphism from $CTR_{A^{rew}, \mathcal{V}} \alpha, \beta$ to $CT_{Q, \mathcal{V}}$.*

The above characterization provides us with a tighter upper bound than the one discussed above.

Theorem 3. *Let Q be a 2RPQ and $\mathcal{V}$ be a set of 2RPQ views. Then checking whether the 2RPQ-maximal rewriting of Q with respect to $\mathcal{V}$ is perfect can be done in N2EXPTIME in the size of Q and in NEXPTIME in the size of $\mathcal{V}^{\Sigma}$.*

We conjecture that such an upper bound is tight.

6   Losslessness with Respect to Answering

We now turn to verifying losslessness with respect to answering. We want to verify whether a set of views $\mathcal{V}$ is lossless with respect to a query Q, i.e., verifying whether $cert_{Q, \mathcal{V}}$ is equivalent to Q (cf. [11]).

In the case of conjunctive queries, we already observed that the maximal rewriting computes exactly the certain answers. Therefore, losslessness with respect to answering and losslessness with respect to rewriting coincide. The case of RPQs and 2RPQs is much more involved. Losslessness with respect to answering for RPQs was studied in [11]. In the rest of this section we study losslessness with respect to answering for 2RPQs.

The main step toward this goal is to characterize the linear fragment of certain answers. Formally, the *linear fragment of certain answers* $clin_{Q, \mathcal{V}}$ for a 2RPQ

Q with respect to a set $\mathcal{V}$ of 2RPQ views is the maximal two-way path query[1] Q' over Σ such that, for every database $\mathcal{B}$ we have that $Q'(\mathcal{B}) \subseteq cert_{Q,\mathcal{V}}(\mathcal{V}(\mathcal{B}))$. The following result shows that, in order to characterize the linear fragment of certain answers it is sufficient to restrict the attention to linear databases, i.e., databases constituted by a single semipath.

Lemma 3. *Let Q' be two-way path query. Then, if there is a database $\mathcal{B}$ and a pair of objects (c,d) in $\mathcal{B}$ such that $(c,d) \in Q'(\mathcal{B})$ and $(c,d) \notin cert_{Q,\mathcal{V}}(\mathcal{V}^{\Sigma}(\mathcal{B}))$, then there is a linear database $\mathcal{B}_\ell$ with endpoints c' and d' such that $(c',d') \in Q'(\mathcal{B}_\ell)$ and $(c',d') \notin cert_{Q,\mathcal{V}}(\mathcal{V}^{\Sigma}(\mathcal{B}_\ell))$.*

Hence, to construct the linear fragment of certain answers, we characterize the set of linear databases of the form $\mathcal{B} = (x_0, q_1, x_1, q_2, \ldots, q_m, x_m)$, for some m, such that $(x_0, x_m) \notin cert_{Q,\mathcal{V}}(\mathcal{V}(\mathcal{B}))$. By Theorem 1, this holds if and only if there is a homomorphism from the constraint instance $\mathcal{V}(\mathcal{B})^{x_0,x_m}$ to the constraint template $CT_{Q,\mathcal{V}}$. In other words, $(x_0, x_m) \notin cert_{Q,\mathcal{V}}(\mathcal{V}(\mathcal{B}))$ if and only if there is a function $\ell(\cdot)$ (i.e., the homomorphism) that labels $x_0, \ldots, x_m$ with sets of states of the 1NFA $A^Q = (\Sigma^{\pm}, S^Q, S_0^Q, \varrho^Q, F^Q)$ for Q such that the following conditions (which we call *CT-conditions*) hold:

- $S_0^Q \subseteq \ell(x_0)$;
- $\ell(x_m) \cap F^Q = \emptyset$;
- for each pair of objects x_j and x_h in $\mathcal{B}$ and each view V in $\mathcal{V}$, we have that, if $(x_j, x_h) \in V^\Sigma(\mathcal{B})$ then there exists a word $q_1 \cdots q_k \in L(V^\Sigma)$ and a sequence $T_0, \ldots, T_k$ of subsets of S^Q such that the following hold:
  1. $T_0 = \ell(x_j)$ and $T_k = \ell(x_h)$,
  2. if $s \in T_i$ and $(s, q_{i+1}, t) \in \varrho^Q$ then $t \in T_{i+1}$, for $0 \le i < k$, and
  3. if $s \in T_i$ and $(s, q_i^-, t) \in \varrho^Q$ then $t \in T_{i-1}$, for $0 < i \le k$.

Thus, we are looking for words of the form $\ell_0, q_1, \ldots, q_m, \ell_m$, where each ℓ_i is a set of states of A^Q, representing $\ell(x_i)$, and that satisfies the above conditions. As shown by the following lemma, we can construct a 1NFA that accepts such words, and then project away the ℓ_i transitions.

For a word $w \in \Sigma^{\pm*}$, we denote with $\mathcal{B}_w^{a,b}$ the linear database constituted by a path from a to b spelled by w (with arbitrary intermediate nodes).

Lemma 4. *Let Q be a 2RPQ and $\mathcal{V}$ be a set of 2RPQ views. Then we can construct in double exponential time in Q and $\mathcal{V}^{\Sigma}$ two 1NFAs A^{nlin} and A^{lin} such that:*

- *A^{nlin} accepts all words $w \in \Sigma^{\pm*}$ such that $(a,b) \notin cert_{Q,\mathcal{V}}(\mathcal{V}(\mathcal{B}_w^{a,b}))$.*
- *A^{lin} accepts all words $w \in \Sigma^{\pm*}$ such that $(a,b) \in cert_{Q,\mathcal{V}}(\mathcal{V}(\mathcal{B}_w^{a,b}))$.*

Both 1NFAs A^{nlin} and A^{lin} have a number of states that is doubly exponential in both Q and $\mathcal{V}^{\Sigma}$. Obviously, the two automata accept complementary languages. However, in the proof of the above lemma we show how to construct A^{lin} directly, instead of complementing A^{nlin}, to avoid an additional exponential blowup.

---

[1] Recall from Section 2 that two-way path queries are a generalization of 2RPQs in which the language used to define a query is not required to be regular.

Theorem 4. *Let Q be a 2RPQ and $\mathcal{V}$ be a set of 2RPQ views, and A^{nlin} and A^{lin} the 1NFAs defined as above. Then A^{lin} is the linear fragment $clin_{Q,\mathcal{V}}$ of the certain answers of Q with respect to $\mathcal{V}$.*

Corollary 1. *The linear fragment of a 2RPQ with respect to a set of 2RPQ views is a 2RPQ.*

Now we can deal with checking losslessness with respect to answering. To check whether a set $\mathcal{V}$ of 2RPQ views is lossless with respect to a 2RPQ query Q, we have to check whether for all databases $\mathcal{B}$, we have that $Q(\mathcal{B})$ is contained in the certain answers $cert_{Q,\mathcal{V}}(\mathcal{V}^\Sigma(\mathcal{B}))$. Since Q is itself a 2RPQ, and hence a path query, it suffices to check whether Q is contained in the linear fragment of the certain answers, i.e., whether for all databases $\mathcal{B}$ we have that $Q(\mathcal{B}) \subseteq clin_{Q,\mathcal{V}}(\mathcal{B})$. By exploiting the characterization of the linear fragment of the certain answers in terms of 1NFAs provided above, we get the following upper bound, which is tight already for RPQs [11].

Theorem 5. *Let Q be a 2RPQ and $\mathcal{V}$ be a set of 2RPQ views. Then checking whether $\mathcal{V}$ is lossless with respect to Q can be done in EXPSPACE in the size of Q and $\mathcal{V}^\Sigma$.*

Observe that when we have that a set of views is lossless with respect to a query, we have also, as side effect, that the linear fragment of certain answers is equivalent to the certain answers, since both are equivalent to the query. Now it is natural to try to understand when the linear fragment of certain answers is equivalent to the certain answers, independently of losslessness with respect to answering. Indeed, in this case, since the certain answers are actually expressible as a 2RPQ over the database, we directly get a characterization of the certain answers in the same language used for expressing the query and thus in terms that are understandable to the user.

Given a 2RPQ Q and a set of 2RPQ views $\mathcal{V}$, checking whether the linear fragment of certain answers is equivalent to the certain answers amounts to checking whether for every database $\mathcal{B}$ we have that $cert_{Q,\mathcal{V}}(\mathcal{V}^\Sigma(\mathcal{B})) \subseteq clin_{Q,\mathcal{V}}(\mathcal{B})$. Consider the 1NFA A^{lin}, constructed above, recognizing the linear fragment $clin_{Q,\mathcal{V}}$ of the certain answers of Q. One can verify that the certain answers $cert_{A^{lin},\mathcal{V}}$ of A^{lin} with respect to $\mathcal{V}$ are actually equivalent to A^{lin} itself. Hence, the above check amounts to verifying whether for all databases $\mathcal{B}$, we have that $cert_{Q,\mathcal{V}}(\mathcal{V}^\Sigma(\mathcal{B})) \subseteq cert_{A^{lin},\mathcal{V}}(\mathcal{V}^\Sigma(\mathcal{B}))$. This is a form of view-based containment, and by [14] it can done in NEXPTIME in the size of Q and A^{lin}. Considering that A^{lin} has a number of states that is doubly exponential in the size of Q and $\mathcal{V}^\Sigma$, we get the following upper bound.

Theorem 6. *Let Q be a 2RPQ and $\mathcal{V}$ be a set of 2RPQ views. Then checking whether the certain answers $cert_{Q,\mathcal{V}}$ of Q with respect to $\mathcal{V}$ is equivalent to its linear fragment can be done in N3EXPTIME in the size of Q and $\mathcal{V}^\Sigma$.*

We conjecture that such an upper bound can be improved.

7 Discussion

In this paper, we have revisited the notions of answering, rewriting and lossless-ness in the context of view-based query processing in semistructured databases. In particular the richness of RPQs and 2RPQs allows us to uncover several sub-tle distinctions between the notions of rewriting and answering, and losslessness with respect to them. Such distinctions are completely blurred when focusing on conjunctive queries, due to the fact that rewriting and answering collapse.

Let Q be a 2RPQ, $\mathcal{V}$ a set of 2RPQ views, and let $R_{Q,\mathcal{V}}^{max}$ denote the 2RPQ-maximal rewriting of Q with respect to $\mathcal{V}$. Then, by definition and by results in [14] exploiting the fact that 2RPQs are monotone, we know that for every database $\mathcal{B}$, the following holds:

$$R_{Q,\mathcal{V}}^{max}(\mathcal{V}^{\Sigma}(\mathcal{B})) \subseteq^{(1)} clin_{Q,\mathcal{V}}(\mathcal{B}) \subseteq^{(2)} cert_{Q,\mathcal{V}}(\mathcal{V}^{\Sigma}(\mathcal{B})) \subseteq^{(3)} Q(\mathcal{B})$$

Notice that we start from a database $\mathcal{B}$ and are evaluating $cert_{Q,\mathcal{V}}$ and $R_{Q,\mathcal{V}}^{max}$ over a particular view extension, namely $\mathcal{V}^{\Sigma}(\mathcal{B})$, instead of an arbitrary view extension $\mathcal{E}$ that is sound with respect to $\mathcal{B}$, i.e., such that $\mathcal{E} \subseteq \mathcal{V}^{\Sigma}(\mathcal{B})$. This is due to the fact that our aim is to understand whether there is loss. It is clear that when $\mathcal{E}$ is a strict subset of $\mathcal{V}^{\Sigma}(B)$ then loss may occur, but this has nothing to do with the "quality" of the views.

It is now of interest to consider the cases in which some or all of the above inclusions are actually equalities, since these correspond to the notions studied in this paper.

1. If $R_{Q,\mathcal{V}}^{max}$ is exact, i.e., is equivalent to Q (modulo the view definitions), then all three inclusions are actually equalities. Hence, not only we have losslessness with respect to rewriting but we also have both that the views are lossless with respect to answering and that $R_{Q,\mathcal{V}}^{max}$ is perfect. Thus exactness of the maximal rewriting is the strongest notion, combining both losslessness of the views and perfectness of the rewriting.
2. If $R_{Q,\mathcal{V}}^{max}$ is perfect, i.e., is equivalent to $cert_{Q,\mathcal{V}}$, then inclusions (1) and (2) are actually equalities. In this case, we also get that $cert_{Q,\mathcal{V}}$ has to coincide with $clin_{Q,\mathcal{V}}$. By Corollary 1 we can conclude that the certain answers are expressible as a 2RPQ over $\mathcal{B}$.
3. If $\mathcal{V}$ is lossless with respect to Q, i.e., we have losslessness with respect to answering, then inclusion (3) is actually an equality. Moreover, in this case, since Q is itself a 2RPQ, and hence is linear, then $cert_{Q,\mathcal{V}}$ has also to be linear and has to coincide with $clin_{Q,\mathcal{V}}$. Hence inclusion (2) is also an equality. In this case we know that there is not loss of information related to the fact that we are answering the query based on a set of views.
4. Finally, if $\mathcal{V}$ is lossy with respect to Q, i.e., we have lossiness with respect to answering, we can check whether inclusion (2) is actually an equality, i.e., whether the certain answers are actually expressible as a 2RPQ over the database. If this is the case, we directly get a characterization of the certain answers in the same language used for expressing the query, namely 2RPQs over the database, and thus in terms that are understandable to the user.

More generally, if $\mathcal{V}$ is lossy with respect to Q and inclusion (2) is a proper inclusion, we would like to provide an explanation for the answers that are actually returned or, equivalently, for the loss of information. Indeed, in this case, we know that there will be at least one view extension such that, in order to show that a tuple is not a certain answer, we need to resort to a non-linear database. It remains to be investigated whether the techniques we provide for doing the check allow one also to extract such a counterexample database to exhibit to the user.

References

1. S. Abiteboul. Querying semi-structured data. In *Proc. of the 6th Int. Conf. on Database Theory (ICDT'97)*, pages 1–18, 1997.
2. S. Abiteboul, P. Buneman, and D. Suciu. *Data on the Web: from Relations to Semistructured Data and XML*. Morgan Kaufmann, Los Altos, 2000.
3. S. Abiteboul and O. Duschka. Complexity of answering queries using materialized views. In *Proc. of the 17th ACM PODS Symp.*, pages 254–265, 1998.
4. S. Abiteboul, D. Quass, J. McHugh, J. Widom, and J. L. Wiener. The Lorel query language for semistructured data. *Int. J. on Digital Libraries*, 1(1):68–88, 1997.
5. F. N. Afrati, C. Li, and P. Mitra. Answering queries using views with arithmetic comparisons. In *Proc. of the 21st ACM PODS Symp.*, pages 209–220, 2002.
6. P. Buneman. Semistructured data. In *Proc. of the 16th ACM PODS Symp.*, pages 117–121, 1997.
7. P. Buneman, S. Davidson, G. Hillebrand, and D. Suciu. A query language and optimization technique for unstructured data. In *Proc. of the ACM SIGMOD Int. Conf. on Management of Data*, pages 505–516, 1996.
8. D. Calvanese, G. De Giacomo, M. Lenzerini, and M. Y. Vardi. Answering regular path queries using views. In *Proc. of the 16th IEEE Int. Conf. on Data Engineering (ICDE 2000)*, pages 389–398, 2000.
9. D. Calvanese, G. De Giacomo, M. Lenzerini, and M. Y. Vardi. Query processing using views for regular path queries with inverse. In *Proc. of the 19th ACM PODS Symp.*, pages 58–66, 2000.
10. D. Calvanese, G. De Giacomo, M. Lenzerini, and M. Y. Vardi. View-based query processing and constraint satisfaction. In *Proc. of the 15th IEEE Symp. on Logic in Computer Science (LICS 2000)*, pages 361–371, 2000.
11. D. Calvanese, G. De Giacomo, M. Lenzerini, and M. Y. Vardi. Lossless regular views. In *Proc. of the 21st ACM PODS Symp.*, pages 58–66, 2002.
12. D. Calvanese, G. De Giacomo, M. Lenzerini, and M. Y. Vardi. Rewriting of regular expressions and regular path queries. *J. of Computer and System Sciences*, 64(3):443–465, 2002.
13. D. Calvanese, G. De Giacomo, M. Lenzerini, and M. Y. Vardi. Reasoning on regular path queries. *SIGMOD Record*, 32(4):83–92, 2003.
14. D. Calvanese, G. De Giacomo, M. Lenzerini, and M. Y. Vardi. View-based query containment. In *Proc. of the 22nd ACM PODS Symp.*, pages 56–67, 2003.
15. R. Chirkova, A. Y. Halevy, and D. Suciu. A formal perspective on the view selection problem. In *Proc. of the 27th Int. Conf. on Very Large Data Bases (VLDB 2001)*, pages 59–68, 2001.
16. J. Clark and S. DeRose. XML Path Language (XPath) version 1.0 – W3C recommendation 16 november 1999. Technical report, World Wide Web Consortium, 1999.

17. A. Deutsch, M. F. Fernandez, D. Florescu, A. Levy, and D. Suciu. XML-QL: A query language for XML. Submission to the World Wide Web Consortium, 1998. Available at http://www.w3.org/TR/NOTE-xml-ql.

18. O. M. Duschka and M. R. Genesereth. Answering recursive queries using views. In *Proc. of the 16th ACM PODS Symp.*, pages 109–116, 1997.

19. T. Feder and M. Y. Vardi. The computational structure of monotone monadic SNP and constraint satisfaction. *SIAM J. on Computing*, 28:57–104, 1999.

20. M. F. Fernandez, D. Florescu, J. Kang, A. Y. Levy, and D. Suciu. Catching the boat with Strudel: Experiences with a web-site management system. In *Proc. of the ACM SIGMOD Int. Conf. on Management of Data*, pages 414–425, 1998.

21. S. Flesca and S. Greco. Rewriting queries using views. *IEEE Trans. on Knowledge and Data Engineering*, 13(6):980–995, 2001.

22. D. Florescu, A. Levy, and A. Mendelzon. Database techniques for the World-Wide Web: A survey. *SIGMOD Record*, 27(3):59–74, 1998.

23. G. Grahne and A. O. Mendelzon. Tableau techniques for querying information sources through global schemas. In *Proc. of the 7th Int. Conf. on Database Theory (ICDT'99)*, volume 1540 of *LNCS*, pages 332–347. Springer, 1999.

24. S. Grumbach and L. Tininini. On the content of materialized aggregate views. In *Proc. of the 19th ACM PODS Symp.*, pages 47–57, 2000.

25. A. Y. Halevy. Answering queries using views: A survey. *Very Large Database J.*, 10(4):270–294, 2001.

26. J. E. Hopcroft and J. D. Ullman. *Introduction to Automata Theory, Languages, and Computation*. Addison Wesley, 1979.

27. A. Y. Levy, A. O. Mendelzon, Y. Sagiv, and D. Srivastava. Answering queries using views. In *Proc. of the 14th ACM PODS Symp.*, pages 95–104, 1995.

28. C. Li, M. Bawa, and J. D. Ullman. Minimizing view sets without losing query-answering power. In *Proc. of the 8th Int. Conf. on Database Theory (ICDT 2001)*, pages 99–113, 2001.

29. T. Milo and D. Suciu. Index structures for path expressions. In *Proc. of the 7th Int. Conf. on Database Theory (ICDT'99)*, volume 1540 of *LNCS*, pages 277–295. Springer, 1999.

30. R. Reiter. On closed world data bases. In H. Gallaire and J. Minker, editors, *Logic and Databases*, pages 119–140. Plenum Publ. Co., 1978.

31. J. D. Ullman. Information integration using logical views. In *Proc. of the 6th Int. Conf. on Database Theory (ICDT'97)*, volume 1186 of *LNCS*, pages 19–40. Springer, 1997.

32. M. Y. Vardi. A temporal fixpoint calculus. In *Proc. of the 15th ACM POPL Symp.*, pages 250–259, 1988.

First-Order Query Rewriting for Inconsistent Databases

Ariel D. Fuxman and Renée J. Miller

Department of Computer Science,
University of Toronto
{afuxman, miller}@cs.toronto.edu

Abstract. We consider the problem of retrieving consistent answers over databases that might be inconsistent with respect to some given integrity constraints. In particular, we concentrate on sets of constraints that consist of key dependencies. Most of the existing work has focused on identifying intractable cases of this problem. In contrast, in this paper we give an algorithm that computes the consistent answers for a large and practical class of conjunctive queries. Given a query q, the algorithm returns a first-order query Q (called a *query rewriting*) such that for every (potentially inconsistent) database I, the consistent answers for q can be obtained by evaluating Q directly on I.

1   Introduction

Consistent query answering is the problem of retrieving "consistent" answers over databases that might be inconsistent with respect to some given integrity constraints. Applications that have motivated the study of this problem include data integration and data exchange. In data integration, the goal is to provide "a uniform interface to multiple autonomous data sources" [Hal01]. In data exchange, "data structured under one (source) schema must be restructured and translated into an instance of a different (target) schema" [FKMP03]. In both contexts, it is often the case that the source data does not satisfy the integrity constraints of the global or target schema. The traditional approach to deal with this situation involves "cleaning" the source instance in order to remove data that violates the target constraints. However, data cleaning is supported by semi-automatic tools at best, and it is necessarily a human-labor intensive process. An alternative approach would be to exchange an inconsistent instance, and employ the techniques of consistent query answering to resolve inconsistencies at query time. Of course, this approach becomes viable only if efficient tools for consistent query answering are available. In this paper, we present a number of results that are a step in this direction.

In addition to these long-standing problems, the trend toward autonomous computing is making the need to manage inconsistent data more acute. In autonomous environments, we can no longer assume that data are married with a single set of constraints that define their semantics. As constraints are used in an increasing number of roles (from modelling the query capabilities of a system, to defining mappings between independent sources), there is an increasing number

T. Eiter and L. Libkin (Eds.): ICDT 2005, LNCS 3363, pp. 337–351, 2005.

of applications in which data must be used with a set of independently designed constraints. In such applications, a static approach where consistency (with respect to a fixed set of constraints) is enforced by cleaning the database may not be appropriate. Rather, a dynamic approach in which data is not changed, but consistency is taken into account at query time, permits the constraints to evolve independently from the data.

The input to the consistent query answering problem is: a schema **R**, a set Σ of integrity constraints, and a database instance I over **R**. The database I might be *inconsistent*, in the sense that it might violate some of the constraints of Σ. In this work, we draw upon the concept of *repairs*, defined by Arenas et al. [ABC99], to give semantics to the problem. A repair $\mathcal{I}$ of I is an instance of **R** such that $\mathcal{I}$ satisfies the integrity constraints of Σ, and $\mathcal{I}$ differs minimally from I (where minimality is defined with respect to the symmetric difference between I and $\mathcal{I}$). Under this definition, repairs need not be unique. Intuitively, each repair corresponds to one possible way of "cleaning" the inconsistent database.

The notion of repairs is used to give semantics to consistent query answering in the following way. Given an instance I, a tuple t is said to be a *consistent answer* for q on I if $\mathcal{I} \models q[t]$, *for every* repair $\mathcal{I}$ of I. This concept is similar to that of *certain answers* used in the context of data integration [AD98], but for consistent answers the set of possible worlds are the repairs of the inconsistent database, rather than the legal instances of a global database.

In this work, we focus on sets of integrity constraints that consist of key dependencies. The most commonly used constraints in database systems are keys and foreign keys. Of these, keys pose a particular challenge since instances that are inconsistent with respect to a set of key dependencies admit an exponential number of repairs in the worst case. This potentially large number of repairs leads to the question of whether it is possible to compute consistent answers efficiently. The answer to this question is known to be negative in general [CM04, CLR03a]. However, this does not necessarily preclude the existence of classes of queries for which the problem is easier to compute. Hence, we consider the following question: for what queries is the problem of computing consistent answers in polynomial time (in data complexity)?

In general, given a query q, it does not suffice to evaluate q directly on a (possibly inconsistent) instance I in order to get the consistent answers. Therefore, a related question is: does there exist some other query Q such that for every instance I, the consistent answers for q can be obtained by just evaluating Q on I? If Q is a first-order query, we say that q is *first-order rewritable*. Since first-order queries can be written in SQL, if the query is first-order rewritable, then its consistent answers can be retrieved (at query time) using existing commercial database technology. Given the desirability of such an approach, we consider the question of identifying classes of queries that are first-order rewritable.

Summary of Results. The main contribution of this paper is an algorithm that produces a first-order query rewriting for the problem of computing consistent answers. The algorithm, which is presented in Section 3, runs in polynomial time in the size of the query. We prove the correctness of the algorithm for a large class of conjunctive queries. The class is defined in terms of the *join graph* of the query. The join graph is a directed graph such that: its vertices are the literals of the query; and it has an arc for each join in the query that involves some variable that is at the position of a non-key attribute. Our algorithm works for conjunctive queries without repeated relation symbols (but with any number of literals and variables) whose join graph is a forest. The class contains most queries that usually arise in practice. For example, 20 out of 22 queries in TPC-H [TPC03], the industry standard for decision support systems, are in this class.

In Section 4, we present a class of queries for which the conditions of applicability of the algorithm (which can be verified in polynomial time in the size of the query) are necessary and sufficient. That is, we show a class such that the problem of computing the consistent answers is coNP-complete for *every* query of the class whose join graph is not a forest. Notice that this type of result is much stronger than the usual approach taken in the consistent query answering literature, which consists of showing intractability of a class by exhibiting *at least one* query for which the problem is intractable. As a corollary of our result, we get a dichotomy for this class of queries: given a query q, either the problem of computing the consistent answers for q is first-order rewritable (and thus it is in PTIME), or it is a coNP-complete problem.

2   Formal Framework

A *schema* **R** is a finite collection of relation symbols, each of which has an associated arity. A set of *integrity constraints* Σ consists of sentences in some logical formalism over **R**. An *instance* I over **R** is a function that associates to each relation symbol R of **R** a relation $I(R)$. Given a tuple t occurring in relation $I(R)$, we denote by $R(t)$ the association between t and R. An instance I is *consistent* with respect to a set of integrity constraints Σ if I satisfies Σ in the standard model-theoretic sense, that is $I \models \Sigma$.

We adopt a semantics for consistent query answering that was originally introduced by Arenas et al. [ABC99], and relies upon the concept of *repairs*. A repair is an instance that satisfies the integrity constraints, and which has a minimal distance to the inconsistent database. The *distance* between two database instances I and I' is defined as their symmetric difference, i.e., $\Delta(I, I') = (I - I') \cup (I' - I)$. The formal definition of repair is the following.

Definition 1 (Repair [ABC99]). *Let I be an instance. We say that an instance $\mathcal{I}$ is a **repair** of I with respect to Σ if:* [1]

– $\mathcal{I} \models \Sigma$, *and*
– *there is no instance I' such that $I' \models \Sigma$ and $\Delta(I, I') \subset \Delta(I, \mathcal{I})$ (i.e., $\Delta(I, \mathcal{I})$ is minimal under set inclusion in the class of instances that satisfy Σ).*

Example 1. Let **R** be a schema with one relation symbol R. Assume that R has two attributes: E (Employee) and S (Salary), and that the only constraint in Σ

---
[1] Whenever Σ is clear from the context, we will just say that $\mathcal{I}$ is a repair of I.

is that the attribute E is the key of R. Let $I = \{R(John, 1000), R(John, 2000),$ $R(Mary, 3000)\}$. We can see that I is inconsistent with respect to Σ. There are two repairs: $\mathcal{I}_1 = \{(John, 1000), (Mary, 3000)\}$ and $\mathcal{I}_2 = \{(John, 2000),$ $(Mary, 3000)\}$. We use the term "repair", as opposed to "minimal repair", because it is standard in the literature [ABC99]. However, notice that, by definition, all repairs have a minimal distance to the inconsistent database. For example, $\{(John, 2000)\}$ and $\{(Mary, 3000)\}$ are not repairs because their distance with respect to I is not minimal under set inclusion. The minimality condition for the repairs is crucial in the definition. Otherwise, the empty set would trivially be a repair of every instance.

The semantics for query answering is given in terms of *consistent answers* [ABC99], which we define next.

Definition 2 (Consistent Answer [ABC99]). *Let* **R** *be a schema. Let* Σ *be a set of integrity constraints. Let* I *be an instance over* **R** *(possibly inconsistent with respect to* Σ*). Let* q *be a query over* **R**. *We say that a tuple* **t** *is a* consistent answer *with respect to* Σ *if* $\mathcal{I} \models q[\boldsymbol{t}]$, *for every repair* $\mathcal{I}$ *of* I *with respect to* Σ. *We denote this as* $\boldsymbol{t} \in$ **consistent**$_\Sigma(q, I)$.

Example 1 (continued). Let $q_1(e) = \exists s : R(e, s)$. The consistent answers for q_1 on I are the tuples $(John)$ and $(Mary)$. Let $q_2(e, s) = R(e, s)$. The only consistent answer for q_2 on I is $(Mary, 3000)$. Notice that the tuples $(John, 1000)$ and $(John, 2000)$ are not consistent answers. The reason is that neither of them are present in *both* repairs. Intuitively, this reflects the fact that John's salaries are inconsistent data.

For convenience, we will use the following notation for the consistent answers to Boolean queries.

Definition 3. *Let* **R** *be a schema. Let* Σ *be a set of integrity constraints. Let* I *be an instance over* **R**. *Let* q *be a Boolean query over* **R**. *We say that* **consistent**$_\Sigma(q, I) = $ **true** *if for every repair* $\mathcal{I}$ *of* I *with respect to* Σ, $\mathcal{I} \models q$. *We say that* **consistent**$_\Sigma(q, I) = $ **false** *if there exists* at least one *repair* $\mathcal{I}$ *of* I *with respect to* Σ *such that* $\mathcal{I} \not\models q$.

Notice the asymmetry between the case for **consistent**$_\Sigma(q, I) = $ **true** and **consistent**$_\Sigma(q, I) = $ **false**. While, for the former, every repair must satisfy the query, for the latter it suffices to have just one (non-satisfying) repair. This is not intrinsic to Boolean queries: by Definition 2, it is also the case that $\boldsymbol{t} \notin$ **consistent**$_\Sigma(q, I)$ if there exists at least one repair $\mathcal{I}$ such that $\mathcal{I} \not\models q[\boldsymbol{t}]$.

We will denote the problem of computing consistent answers as CONSISTENT(q, Σ), and define it as follows.

Definition 4. *Let* **R** *be a schema. Let* q *be a query over* **R**. *Let* Σ *be a set of integrity constraints. The* consistent query answering problem CONSISTENT(q, Σ) *is the following: given an instance* I *over* **R**, *and tuple* **t**, *is it the case that* $\boldsymbol{t} \in$ **consistent**$_\Sigma(q, I)$?

We will design an algorithm that computes consistent answers *directly* from the inconsistent database, without explicitly building the repairs. In fact, given a query q, the algorithm will return a first-order query Q such that, for every instance I, the consistent answers for q can be obtained by just evaluating Q on I. We call Q a *first-order query rewriting*, and define it next.

Definition 5 (First-Order Query Rewriting). *Let* $\mathbf{R}$ *be a schema. Let* Σ *be a set of integrity constraints. Let* q *be a query over* $\mathbf{R}$. *We say that the problem* CONSISTENT(q, Σ) *is* first-order rewritable *if there is a first-order query* Q *such that* $I \models Q[\mathbf{t}]$ *iff* $\mathbf{t} \in$ consistent$_\Sigma(q, I)$, *for every instance* I *over* $\mathbf{R}$. *We also say that* Q *is a* first-order rewriting *of the problem* CONSISTENT(q, Σ). [2]

Notice that if CONSISTENT(q, Σ) is first-order rewritable, then it is tractable. This is because the data complexity of first-order logic is in PTIME (actually, in AC^0). Thus, it can be tested in polynomial time whether $I \models Q[\mathbf{t}]$. Besides this, an approach based on query rewriting is attractive because first-order queries can be written in SQL. Therefore, if the query is first-order rewritable, the consistent answers can be retrieved using existing database technology.

Throughout the paper, we will assume that the set Σ of integrity constraints consists of at most one key dependency per relation of the schema. To facilitate specifying the set of constraints each time that we give a query, we will underline the positions in each literal that correspond to key attributes. Furthermore, by convention, the key attributes will be given first. For example, the query $q = \exists x, y, z : R_1(\underline{x}, y) \wedge R_2(\underline{y}, z)$ indicates that literals R_1 and R_2 represent binary relations whose first attribute is the key. We will use bold letters (e.g., $\mathbf{x}$, $\mathbf{y}$) to denote vectors of variables or constants from a query or tuple. In addition, when we give a tuple, we will underline the values that appear at the position of key attributes. For instance, for a tuple $R(\underline{c}, d)$, we will say that $\underline{c}$ is a *key value*, and d is a *non-key value*. Using this notation, the key constraints of Σ that are relevant to the query are denoted directly in the query expression.

The results in this paper concern (classes of) conjunctive queries. We will adopt the convention of using $\mathbf{x}$ to denote variables and constants that appear at the position of key attributes, and $\mathbf{y}$ for variables and constants that appear at the position of non-key attributes. Thus, conjunctive queries will be of the form:

$$q(w_1, \ldots, w_m) = \exists z_1, \ldots, z_l : R_1(\underline{\mathbf{x}_1}, \mathbf{y}_1), \ldots, R_n(\underline{\mathbf{x}_n}, \mathbf{y}_n)$$

where $w_1, \ldots, w_m, z_1, \ldots, z_l$ are all the variables that appear in the literals of q. We will say that $w_1, \ldots, w_m$ are the *free variables* of q. Notice that even though there are no equality symbols in q, their effect is achieved by having variables that appear in q more than once. The queries may also contain constants, which we will denote with bold letters from the beginning of the alphabet (e.g., **a** and **b**). We will say that there is a *join* on a variable w if w appears in two literals $R_i(\underline{\mathbf{x}_i}, \mathbf{y}_i)$ and $R_j(\underline{\mathbf{x}_j}, \mathbf{y}_j)$ such that $i \neq j$. If w occurs in $\mathbf{y}_i$ and $\mathbf{y}_j$, we say that there is a *non-key join* on w.

---

[2] On occasion, we will simply say that q is *first-order rewritable*, and that Q is a *first-order rewriting* of q.

Throughout the paper, we will focus on the class of conjunctive queries *without repeated relation symbols*. A conjunctive query without repeated relation symbols is a conjunctive query such that every relation symbol of the schema appears in q at most once. Notice that, in spite of this restriction, the query can still have any arbitrary number of literals and relation symbols, and there are no constraints on the occurrence of variables in the query.

3   A Query Rewriting Algorithm

3.1   A Class of Tractable Queries

The problem of computing consistent answers for conjunctive queries over databases that might violate a set of key constraints is known to be coNP-complete in general [CM04, CLR03a]. This is the case even for queries with no repeated relation symbols, which is the focus of this section. However, this does not necessarily preclude the existence of classes of queries for which the problem is easier to compute. In fact, in this section we characterize a large and practical class of conjunctive queries for which the problem of computing consistent answers is indeed tractable. Even more so, we show that all queries in this class are first-order rewritable, and we give a polynomial-time algorithm that computes the first-order rewriting.

Before presenting the tractable class, let us consider the following queries for which the problem of computing consistent answers is coNP-complete, as will be shown in Section 4.

- $q_1 = \exists x, x', y : R_1(\underline{x}, y) \wedge R_2(\underline{x'}, y)$
- $q_2 = \exists x, y, z : R_1(\underline{z}, \underline{x}, y) \wedge R_2(\underline{y}, x)$
- $q_3 = \exists x, y, z, w : R_1(\underline{x}, y) \wedge R_2(\underline{z}, w) \wedge R_3(\underline{y}, \underline{w})$

The queries presented above are rare in practice. The first consists of a join between *non-key* attributes; the second involves a cycle; and the third, a join with part, but not the entire key of a relation. We use these queries to provide insight into when a query is intractable. In particular, we will show in Section 4 a class of queries for which the presence of cycles and non-key joins are in fact necessary conditions for intractability. Notice that such conditions are concerned with the joins in the query where at least one non-key variable is involved. In order to define such conditions precisely, we will state them in terms of what we call the *join graph* of the query.

Definition 6 (Join Graph). *Let q be a conjunctive query. The join graph G of q is a directed graph such that:*

- *the vertices of G are the literals of q;*
- *there is an arc from R_i to R_j if $i \neq j$ and there is some variable w such that w occurs at the position of a non-key attribute in R_i and w occurs in R_j;*
- *there is a self-loop at R_i (i.e., an arc from R_i to R_i) if there is some variable w such that w occurs at the position of a non-key attribute of R_i, and w occurs at least twice in R_i.*

As we can see in Figure 1, the join graphs of q_1 and q_2 have a cycle. The join graph of q_3 does not have a cycle, but it is not a tree because the node for relation R_3 has two incoming arcs. Therefore, we will focus on queries whose join graph is a tree (or a forest). For example, the join graph of the following query is a tree. The graph is shown in Figure 1.

$$q_4 = \exists x, y, z, w : R_1(\underline{x}, y) \wedge R_2(\underline{y}, z) \wedge R_3(\underline{z}, w) \wedge R_4(\underline{y}, \mathbf{a})$$

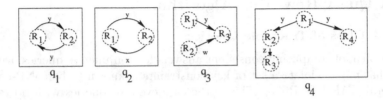

Fig. 1. Join graphs

An additional condition that we will impose on the query is that the joins from non-key to key attributes involve the *entire* key of a relation. We will call such joins *full*. For example, all the non-key to key joins of query q_4 are full. On the other hand, in the query $q = \exists x, y, z, w : R_1(\underline{x}, y) \wedge R_2(\underline{z}, y, w)$ the join between R_1 and R_2 is not full since it does not involve the entire key of R_2.

Definition 7. *Let q be a conjunctive query. Let $R_i(\underline{x}_i, y_i)$ and $R_j(\underline{x}_j, y_j)$ be a pair of literals of q. We say that there is a full non-key to key join from R_i to R_j if every variable of x_j appears in y_i.*

Considering queries with only full non-key to key joins, the class $\mathcal{C}_{tree}$ that we define next consists of the queries whose join graph is a forest.

Definition 8. *Let q be conjunctive query without repeated relation symbols. Let G be the join graph of q. We say that $q \in \mathcal{C}_{tree}$ if G is a forest (i.e., every connected component of G is a tree) and every non-key to key join of q is full.*

A fundamental observation about $\mathcal{C}_{tree}$ is that it is a very common, practical class of queries. Arguably, the most used form of joins are from a set of non-key attributes of one relation (which may be a foreign key)[3] to the key of another relation (which may be a primary key). Furthermore, such joins typically involve the *entire* primary key of the relation (and, hence, they are full joins in our terms). Finally, cycles are rarely present in the queries used in practice. Admittedly, the restriction not to have repeated relation symbols does rule out some common queries (those in which the same relation appears twice in the FROM clause of an SQL query). Still, many queries used in practice do not have

---

[3] Notice that in this work we are not dealing with the problem of inconsistency with respect to foreign keys, but with respect to key dependencies.

repeated relation symbols. As an empirical observation, we point out that 20 out of 22 queries in the TPC-H standard [TPC03] are in class $\mathcal{C}_{tree}$. [4]

3.2   Algorithm

The following examples highlight some of the intuition underlying our query rewriting algorithm.

Example 2. Let $q = \exists x : R_1(\underline{x}, \mathbf{a})$. First of all, notice that q itself is not a query rewriting of $\mathrm{CONSISTENT}(q, \Sigma)$. Consider the instance $I_1 = \{R_1(\underline{c_1}, a), R_1(\underline{c_1}, b)\}$. It is easy to see that $I_1 \models q$. However, $\mathbf{consistent}_\Sigma(q, I_1) = \mathtt{false}$ because the repair $\mathcal{I} = \{R_1(\underline{c_1}, b)\}$ is such that $\mathcal{I} \not\models q$. Now, consider $I_2 = \{R_1(\underline{c_1}, a), R_1(\underline{c_1}, b), R_1(\underline{c_2}, a)\}$. It is easy to see that $\mathbf{consistent}_\Sigma(q, I_2) = \mathtt{true}$. This is because there is a key value in R_1 (c_2 in this case) that appears with a as its non-key value, and does not appear with any other constant a' such that $a' \neq a$. This can be checked with a formula $Q_{consist} = \forall y' : R_1(\underline{x}, y') \rightarrow y' = \mathbf{a}$. In fact, we will show that a query rewriting Q for q can be obtained as the conjunction of q and $Q_{consist}$:

$$Q = \exists x : R_1(\underline{x}, \mathbf{a}) \wedge \forall y' : R_1(\underline{x}, y') \rightarrow y' = \mathbf{a}$$

Example 3. Let $q = \exists x, y, z : R_1(x, y) \wedge R_2(y, z)$. As in the previous example, q itself is not a query rewriting of $\mathrm{CONSISTENT}(q, \Sigma)$. For, consider the instance $I_1 = \{R_1(\underline{c_1}, d_1), R_1(\underline{c_1}, d_2), R_2(\underline{d_1}, e_1)\}$. It is easy to see that $I_1 \models q$. However, $\mathbf{consistent}_\Sigma(q, I_1) = \mathtt{false}$ because the repair $\mathcal{I} = \{R_1(\underline{c_1}, d_2), R_2(\underline{d_1}, e_1)\}$ is such that $\mathcal{I} \not\models q$. Now, consider $I_2 = \{R_1(\underline{c_1}, d_1), R_1(\underline{c_1}, d_2), R_2(\underline{d_1}, e_1), R_2(\underline{d_2}, e_2)\}$. It is easy to see that $\mathbf{consistent}_\Sigma(q, I_2) = \mathtt{true}$. This is because *every* non-key value that appears together with c_1 in some tuple (in this case, d_1 and d_2) joins with a tuple of R_2. This can be checked with a formula $Q_{consist} = \forall y' : R_1(\underline{x}, y') \rightarrow \exists z' : R_2(\underline{y'}, z')$. We will soon show that a query rewriting Q for q can be obtained as the conjunction of q and $Q_{consist}$, as follows:

$$Q = \exists x, y, z : R_1(\underline{x}, y) \wedge R_2(\underline{y}, z) \wedge \forall y' : (R_1(\underline{x}, y') \rightarrow \exists z' : R_2(\underline{y'}, z'))$$

We now proceed to present $\mathtt{RewriteConsistent}$, our query rewriting algorithm. For convenience, it is split into three modules, which are shown in Figures 2, 3, and 4. Given a query q such that $q \in \mathcal{C}_{tree}$, and a set of key constraints Σ, $\mathtt{RewriteConsistent}(q, \Sigma)$ returns a first-order rewriting Q for the problem of obtaining the consistent answers for q with respect to Σ. The algorithm $\mathtt{RewriteConsistent}$ is shown in Figure 2. The first-order rewriting Q that it returns is obtained as the conjunction of the input query q, and a new query called $Q_{consist}$. The query $Q_{consist}$ is used to ensure that q is satisfied in *every* repair (and, hence, $\mathbf{consistent}_\Sigma(q, I) = \mathtt{true}$). It is important to notice that $Q_{consist}$ will be applied directly to the inconsistent database (i.e., we will never generate

---

[4] This is considering the Select-Project-Join structure of the queries, not additional features such as aggregation or arithmetical operators. The reason that two of the queries are outside the class is just because they have repeated relation symbols.

the repairs). The query $Q_{consist}$ is obtained by recursion on the tree structure of each of the components of the join graph of q (recall that since $q \in \mathcal{C}_{tree}$, the join graph is a forest). The recursive algorithm is called RewriteTree, and is shown in Figure 3.

In the query $Q_{consist}$, some of the variables of q are renamed. Let us illustrate this with the query $q = \exists x, y, z : R_1(\underline{x}, y) \wedge R_2(\underline{y}, z)$ from Example 3. In this case, $Q_{consist} = \forall y' : R_1(\underline{x}, y') \rightarrow \exists z' : R_2(\underline{y}, z')$. Notice that the variable y of q is renamed to y' in $Q_{consist}$. In order to keep track of the renaming during the execution of the algorithm, we use a substitution δ for the variables of q.

The variables that will be renamed in $Q_{consist}$ by the substitution δ are those that are involved in some join from a non-key to a key position. Notice that these are the joins that create arcs in the join graph. The renamed variables are universally quantified in $Q_{consist}$. The intuition behind this is that the renamed variable denotes a non-key position in a literal and, as we illustrated in Example 3, the query must be satisfied by all the non-key values of a given key.

In the algorithm RewriteConsistent, the substitution δ is initialized to be just the identity on the variables that do not appear in non-key positions of any literal. These are the variables in the set $IdentityVars$ of the algorithm. During the recursive execution of RewriteTree(T_i, Σ, δ), the literal $R(\underline{x}, y)$ at the root of T_i is selected, and the variables of y are renamed to newly-created variables from a vector y^*. The substitution δ is used here to record such renamings.

At each step, RewriteTree produces a rewriting Q_{local} for the literal $R(\underline{x}, y)$ at the root of the tree. This rewriting is done independently of the rest of the query, and produced by the algorithm RewriteLocal. We show this algorithm in Figure 4. The query Q_{local} deals with the constants that appear in y in the same way as we illustrated in Example 2.

Notice that we have presented the algorithm only for Boolean queries, but this is just for notational simplicity. In order to apply the algorithm to queries with free variables, it suffices to treat the free variables as if they were constants (using the algorithm RewriteLocal). For example, consider the query $q(y) = \exists x : R_1(\underline{x}, y)$. Notice that the only difference with the query of Example 2 is that the constant $\mathbf{a}$ is replaced by the free variable y. The query rewriting for q is the following:

$$Q(y) = \exists x : R_1(\underline{x}, y) \wedge \forall y' : R_1(\underline{x}, y') \rightarrow y' = y$$

The next example illustrates the application of the algorithm.

Example 4. Let q be the query q_4 introduced in Section 3.1.

$$q = \exists x, y, z, w : R_1(\underline{x}, y) \wedge R_2(\underline{y}, z) \wedge R_3(\underline{z}, w) \wedge R_4(\underline{y}, \mathbf{a})$$

The join graph T of q is shown in Figure 1. In this case, T consists of one connected component, which is a tree. Let T_2 be the subtree of T that consists of the nodes for literals R_2 and R_3. Let T_3 be a tree that consists of exactly one node, for literal R_3. Let T_4 be a tree that consists of exactly one node, for literal R_4. The first-order query rewriting Q of q is obtained by applying the algorithm RewriteConsistent(q, Σ) as follows.

Algorithm RewriteConsistent(q, Σ)
  Let G be the join graph of q
  Let $T_1, \ldots, T_m$ be the connected components of G
  Let $IdentityVars = \{x :$ there is a literal $R(\underline{x}, y)$ in q such that x occurs in $\underline{x}$,
                     and for every literal $R'(\underline{x}', y')$ in q, x does not occur in $y'\}$
  Let δ be the identity substitution for the variables of $IdentityVars$
  for $i := 1$ to m **do**
    Let $Q_i = $ RewriteTree(T_i, Σ, δ)
  end for
  Let $Q_{consist} = \bigwedge_{i=1\ldots m} Q_i$
  Let $Q = q \wedge Q_{consist}$
  return Q

Fig. 2. Query rewriting algorithm

$Q = $ RewriteConsistent$(q, \Sigma) = q \wedge Q_{consist}$
$Q_{consist}(x) = $ RewriteTree$(T, \Sigma, \langle x/x \rangle) = \forall y' : R_1(\underline{x}, y') \rightarrow (Q_2 \wedge Q_4)$
$Q_2(y') = $ RewriteTree$(T_2, \Sigma, \langle x/x, y/y' \rangle) = \exists z' : R_2(\underline{y}', z') \wedge \forall z' : R_2(\underline{y}', z') \rightarrow Q_3$
$Q_3(z') = $ RewriteTree$(T_3, \Sigma, \langle x/x, y/y', z/z' \rangle) = \exists w' : R_3(\underline{z}', w')$
$Q_4(y') = $ RewriteTree$(T_4, \Sigma, \langle x/x, y/y' \rangle) = \exists u' : R_4(\underline{y}', u') \wedge \forall u' : (R_4(\underline{y}', u') \rightarrow u' = \mathsf{a})$

3.3   Correctness Proof

For the correctness proof, we will refer to the query associated to a join graph. The *query q_G for a join graph G* is a conjunctive query such that the literals of q_G are the literals that appear in the nodes of G; all the variables of q_G that occur at a non-key position in a literal of q_G are existentially quantified; and the rest of the variables of q_G are free. Notice that if a variable of q_G is the cause of the existence of an arc in the join graph G (e.g., variables y and z from Example 4), then the variable is existentially-quantified in q_G.

Definition 9. *Let G be a join graph. Let $R_1(\underline{x}_1, y_1), \ldots, R_n(\underline{x}_n, y_n)$ be the literals that appear in the nodes of G. Let $W = \{w : w$ is a variable that appears in y_j, for some j such that $1 \leq j \leq n\}$. Let w be the variables of W. Let z be the variables of $R_1, \ldots, R_n$ that are not in W. We say that q_G is the query for G if q_G is of the following form:*

$$q_G(z) = \exists w : R_1(\underline{x}_1, y_1) \wedge \ldots \wedge R_n(\underline{x}_n, y_n)$$

The correctness proof of RewriteTree is by induction on the size of the input tree, and relies on the following lemma.

Lemma 1. *Let T be a join graph such that T is a tree. Let q_T be the query for T, as in Definition 9. Let δ be a substitution for the free variables of q_T. Let Q be the first-order query returned by RewriteTree(T, Σ, δ).*

Let I be an instance. Let ν_q be a valuation for the free variables of q_T such that $I \models q_T[\nu_q]$. Let ν_Q be a valuation for the free variables of Q such that

---

Algorithm RewriteTree(T, Σ, δ)
  Let $R(\underline{x}, y)$ be the literal at the root node of T
  Let $x^* = x[\delta]$
  Let l be the arity of y
  Let $y^* = y'_1, \ldots, y'_l$, where $y'_1, \ldots, y'_l$ are newly created variables
  if T consists of exactly one node **then**
    Let $Q_{local} = $ RewriteLocal($R, x^*, y, y^*, \Sigma, \delta$)
    return Q_{local}
  end if
  Let T_{local} be a tree that consists of exactly one node with literal R
  Let $Q_{local} = $ RewriteTree($T_{local}, \Sigma, \delta$)
  Let $R_1, \ldots, R_m$ be the children of R in T
  Let $\delta' = \delta \cup \{y/y' : $ there exists p such that y and y' are variables that occur at
                        position p in y and y^*, respectively$\}$
  for $i := 1$ to m **do**
    Let T_i be the subtree of T rooted at R_i
    Let $Q_i = $ RewriteTree(T_i, Σ, δ')
  end for
  Let $Q_{subtrees} = \bigwedge_{i=1 \ldots m} Q_i$
  Let $Q = Q_{local} \wedge \forall y^* : (R(\underline{x}^*, y^*) \rightarrow Q_{subtrees})$
  return Q

Fig. 3. Recursive algorithm on the tree structure of the join graph

$\nu_Q(w) = \nu_q(w)$ if $\delta(w) = w$. Then, $I \models Q[\nu_Q]$ iff $\mathcal{I} \models q_T[\delta][\nu_Q]$ for every repair $\mathcal{I}$ of I.

From the previous lemma, we obtain the main result of the section proving that the rewriting algorithm is correct for all queries in $\mathcal{C}_{tree}$.

Theorem 1. *Let* $\mathbf{R}$ *be a schema. Let* Σ *be a set of integrity constraints, consisting of one key dependency per relation of* $\mathbf{R}$. *Let* q *be a conjunctive query over* $\mathbf{R}$ *such that* $q \in \mathcal{C}_{tree}$. *Let* t *be a tuple. Let* Q *be the first-order query returned by* RewriteConsistent(q, Σ).
Then, for every instance I *over* $\mathbf{R}$, $I \models Q[t]$ *iff* $t \in$ **consistent**$_\Sigma(q, I)$.

4   A Dichotomy Result

In the previous section, we presented a query rewriting algorithm which works on queries with full joins whose join graph is a forest. Clearly, this is a sufficient condition for a query to be first-order rewritable. In this section, we address the following question: for which class of queries is it also a necessary condition? In particular, we show a class of queries such that the problem of computing the consistent answers is coNP-complete for *every* query of the class which does not satisfy the conditions of our query rewriting algorithm. Notice that this establishes a dichotomy between first-order rewritability and coNP-completeness, and

---

Algorithm RewriteLocal($R, \boldsymbol{x}^*, \boldsymbol{y}, \boldsymbol{y}^*, \Sigma, \delta$)

  if there is at least one constant in $\boldsymbol{y}$ **then**

    Let l be the arity of $\boldsymbol{y}$

    for $i := 1$ to l **do**

      Let y' be the variable that appears at position i of $\boldsymbol{y}^*$

      if there is a constant c at position i of $\boldsymbol{y}$ **then**

        Let E_i be the equality $y' = c$

      end if

    end for

    $EqualityPos = \{i : \text{ there is a constant a position } i \text{ in } \boldsymbol{y}\}$

    Let $Q_{const} = \bigwedge_{i \in EqualityPos} E_i$

    if δ is the identity substitution on all variables of $\boldsymbol{x}$ **then**

      Let $Q_{local} = \forall \boldsymbol{y}^* : (R(\underline{\boldsymbol{x}}^*, \boldsymbol{y}^*) \rightarrow Q_{const})$

    else

      Let $Q_{local} = \exists \boldsymbol{y}^* : R(\underline{\boldsymbol{x}}^*, \boldsymbol{y}^*) \wedge \forall \boldsymbol{y}^* : (R(\underline{\boldsymbol{x}}^*, \boldsymbol{y}^*) \rightarrow Q_{const})$

    end if

  end if

  if there are no constants in $\boldsymbol{y}$ **then**

    if δ is the identity substitution on all variables of $\boldsymbol{x}$ **then**

      Let Q_{local} be an empty string

    else

      Let $Q_{local} = \exists \boldsymbol{y}^* : R(\underline{\boldsymbol{x}}^*, \boldsymbol{y}^*)$

    end if

  end if

  return Q_{local}

Fig. 4. Query rewriting for given literal

is therefore much stronger than the complexity results present in the consistent query answering literature [CM04, CLR03a]. In the literature, a class $\mathcal{C}$ is said to be coNP-hard if there is *at least one* query $q \in \mathcal{C}$ such that CONSISTENT(q, Σ) is a coNP-hard problem. Under such a definition, it suffices to exhibit just *one* intractable query in order to conclude that the entire class is coNP-complete. In contrast, in this section we will present a class of queries such that for *every* query q in the class, CONSISTENT(q, Σ) is coNP-complete.

As a first step towards proving a dichotomy for the class of conjunctive queries, we will focus on a subclass for which we can establish such a result. We call this subclass $\mathcal{C}^*$, and define it in Definition 10. In the definition, we give three conditions that are meant to rule out of the class the *only* cases of the dichotomy that we leave open. We illustrate the conditions as follows. Consider the query $q_5 = \exists x, y : R_1(\underline{x}, y) \wedge R_2(\underline{x}, y)$. The join graph of this query is not a forest; yet, it is not difficult to find a rewriting for it. What is particular about q_5 is the fact that its two literals have the *same* key. We rule out this case with the first condition of Definition 10. Now, consider the query $q_6 = \exists x : R_1(\underline{x}, x)$. Although it is easy to find a rewriting for this query, its join graph contains a self-loop. We rule out the queries whose join graph is a self-loop with the second condition of Definition 10. Finally, our query rewriting algorithm assumes that queries have full non-key to key joins. For the moment, the case in which such joins are partial, but the join graph is still a forest, remains open. Therefore, we rule this case out of C^* with the third condition of the definition.

Definition 10. *We say that a conjunctive query q without repeated relation symbols is in class C^* if:*

 - *for every literal $R(\underline{x}, y)$ of q, there is some variable x such that x occurs in $\underline{x}$, and x does not appear in any literal R' of q such that $R' \neq R$, and*
 - *the join graph of q has no self-loops.*
 - *if the join graph of q is a forest, then every non-key to key join of q is full.*

We will consider a class, called C_{hard}, of all queries of C^* whose join graph is not a forest. We prove that the problem of computing the consistent answers for every query of C_{hard} is coNP-complete as follows. In Lemma 2, we prove that, given a query q such that $q \in C_{hard}$, the problem of obtaining the consistent answers for q can be reduced from the problem of obtaining the consistent answers for one of three particular query families. Queries q_1, q_2, and q_3 shown in Figure 1 are in fact examples of these three query families. In Lemma 3, we prove that the problem CONSISTENT(q, Σ) is coNP-complete for each such query.

Definition 11. *We say that a query q is in class C_{hard} if $q \in C^*$ and $q \notin C_{tree}$.*

Lemma 2. *Let q be a query such that $q \in C_{hard}$. Then, there is a polynomial-time reduction from CONSISTENT(q', Σ') to CONSISTENT(q, Σ), where q' is one of the following queries:*

 - $\exists w_1, \ldots, w_{m+1} : S_1(\underline{w}_{m+1}, \underline{w}_m, w_1) \wedge S_2(\underline{w}_1, w_2) \wedge S_3(\underline{w}_2, w_3) \wedge \ldots$
   $\wedge S_m(\underline{w}_{m-1}, w_m)$
 - $\exists x, x', y : S_1(\underline{x}, y) \wedge S_2(\underline{x}', y)$
 - $\exists x, x', w_1, w_2 : S_1(\underline{x}, w_1) \wedge S_2(\underline{x}', w_2) \wedge S_3(\underline{w}_1, \underline{w}_2)$

Lemma 3. *The problem CONSISTENT(q, Σ) is coNP-complete for the following queries:*

 - $\exists w_1, \ldots, w_{m+1} : S_1(\underline{w}_{m+1}, \underline{w}_m, w_1) \wedge S_2(\underline{w}_1, w_2) \wedge S_3(\underline{w}_2, w_3) \wedge \ldots$
   $\wedge S_m(\underline{w}_{m-1}, w_m)$
 - $\exists x, x', y : S_1(\underline{x}, y) \wedge S_2(\underline{x}', y)$
 - $\exists x, x', w_1, w_2 : S_1(\underline{x}, w_1) \wedge S_2(\underline{x}', w_2) \wedge S_3(\underline{w}_1, \underline{w}_2)$

Theorem 2. *Let q be a query such that $q \in C_{hard}$. Then, CONSISTENT(q, Σ) is coNP-complete in data complexity.*

In general, by Ladner's Theorem [Lad75], there are classes of coNP problems for which there is no dichotomy between P and coNP-complete problems. However, this is not the case for the class of queries that is the focus of this section. In fact, as a corollary of Theorems 1 and 2, we get a dichotomy between membership in P and coNP-completeness. Notice that, given a query q such that $q \in C^*$, it can be decided in polynomial time on which side of the dichotomy the query q falls. Under a complexity-theoretic assumption, we also get a dichotomy between first-order rewritability and coNP-completeness. An alternative approach, which we leave as future work, would be to avoid complexity-theoretic assumptions, and appeal to games arguments in order to prove first-order inexpressibility.

Corollary 1. *Let q be a query such that $q \in C^*$. Then, CONSISTENT(q, Σ) is either in P, or it is coNP-complete.*

Corollary 2. *Let q be a query such that $q \in C^*$. Assuming $P \neq coNP$, the problem CONSISTENT(q, Σ) is first-order rewritable iff $q \in C_{tree}$.*

5   Related Work

The main difference between this work and others in the consistent query answering literature is our focus on producing a *first-order* rewriting. Instead of rewriting into first-order formulas, most work in the literature is based on rewriting into logic programs (e.g., [CLR03b] and [BB03]). Their focus is on obtaining correct disjunctive logic programs for (usually large) classes of queries and constraints. However, given the high complexity of disjunctive logic programming, none of these approaches focus on tractability issues.

There are two proposals in the consistent query answering literature that are based on first-order query rewriting, but they apply to very restricted classes of queries. Arenas et al. [ABC99] consider quantifier-free conjunctive queries (i.e., queries without existential quantifiers). Chomicki and Marcinkowski [CM04] propose a rewriting for *simple* conjunctive queries, which are queries where no variables are shared between literals (and therefore, there are no joins). We have presented a query rewriting for a much larger, and practical, class of queries.

Chomicki and Marcinkowski [CM04] and Calì et al. [CLR03a] thoroughly study the decidability and complexity of consistent query answering for several classes of queries and integrity constraints. In order to show intractability of a class, they take the usual approach of exhibiting one particular query of the class for which the problem is intractable. To the best of our knowledge, ours is the first dichotomy result in the area of consistent query answering.

The work on disjunctive databases [vdM98] is relevant in our context. In particular, if Σ is a set of key dependencies, the set of all repairs of an inconsistent database can be represented as a disjunctive database D in such a way that each repair corresponds to a minimal model of D. However, there are no results in the literature for first-order query rewriting over disjunctive databases. The only tractability results in this context have been given for OR-databases [IvdMV95], which are a restricted type of disjunctive databases. However, in general, given a database I possibly inconsistent with respect to a set of key dependencies, there may be no OR-database D such that all the models of D are repairs of I.

6 Conclusions and Future Work

We presented a query-rewriting algorithm for computing consistent answers. The algorithm works on a large and practical class of conjunctive queries without repeated relation symbols. We are currently extending the algorithm in order to take into account queries with repeated relation symbols. Our algorithm works on queries with full joins whose join graph is a forest. We showed a class of queries C^* in which this is in fact a necessary and sufficient condition for a query to be first-order rewritable. For this class of queries, our algorithm covers all queries which are first-order rewritable. We have mentioned that, outside the class C^*, there are some queries whose join graph is not a forest, yet they are first-order rewritable. We are working on an extension of the algorithm that considers such queries.

In this work, we assumed that the set Σ of constraints that might be violated consists of key dependencies. It would be interesting to consider foreign key dependencies as well. In this way, we would be covering the most common constraints that are supported by commercial database systems.

Acknowledgments. We would like to thank Leonid Libkin, Marcelo Arenas, Pablo Barcelo, and Ken Pu for their comments and feedback.

References

[ABC99]   M. Arenas, L. Bertossi, and J. Chomicki. Consistent query answers in inconsistent databases. In *PODS*, pages 68–79, 1999.

[AD98]   S. Abiteboul and O. M. Duschka. Complexity of answering queries using materialized views. In *PODS*, pages 254–263, 1998.

[BB03]   L. Bravo and L. Bertossi. Logic programs for consistently querying data integration systems. In *IJCAI*, pages 10–15, 2003.

[CLR03a] A. Calì, D. Lembo, and R. Rosati. On the decidability and complexity of query answering over inconsistent and incomplete databases. In *PODS*, pages 260–271, 2003.

[CLR03b] A. Calì, D. Lembo, and R. Rosati. Query rewriting and answering under constraints in data integration systems. In *IJCAI*, pages 16–21, 2003.

[CM04]   J. Chomicki and J. Marcinkowski. Minimal-change integrity maintenance using tuple deletions. To appear in Information and Computation, 2004.

[FKMP03] R. Fagin, P. Kolaitis, R. J. Miller, and L. Popa. Data exchange: Semantics and query answering. In *ICDT*, pages 207–224, 2003.

[Hal01]   A. Halevy. Answering queries using views: A survey. *VLDB Journal*, 10(4):270–294, 2001.

[IvdMV95] T. Imielinski, R. van der Meyden, and K. Vadaparty. Complexity tailored design: A new design methodology for databases with incomplete information. *J. Computer and System Sciences*, 51(3):405–432, 1995.

[Lad75]   R. E. Ladner. On the structure of polynomial time reducibility. *J. of the ACM*, 22(1):155–171, 1975.

[TPC03]   Transaction Processing Performance Council: TPC. TPC Benchmark H (Decision Support). Standard Specification Revision 2.1.0, 2003.

[vdM98]   R. van der Meyden. Logical approaches to incomplete information: A survey. In *Logics for Databases and Inf. Systems*, pages 307–356. Kluwer, 1998.

Rewriting Queries Using Views with Access Patterns Under Integrity Constraints*

Alin Deutsch[1], Bertram Ludäscher[2], and Alan Nash[3]

University of California, San Diego

deutsch@cs.ucsd.edu, ludaesch@sdsc.edu, anash@math.ucsd.edu

Abstract. We study the problem of rewriting queries using views in the presence of access patterns, integrity constraints, disjunction, and negation. We provide asymptotically optimal algorithms for finding minimal containing and maximal contained rewritings and for deciding whether an exact rewriting exists. We show that rewriting queries using views in this case reduces (a) to rewriting queries with access patterns and constraints without views and also (b) to rewriting queries using views under constraints without access patterns. We show how to solve (a) directly and how to reduce (b) to rewriting queries under constraints only (semantic optimization). These reductions provide two separate routes to a unified solution for all three problems, based on an extension of the relational chase theory to queries and constraints with disjunction and negation. We also handle equality and arithmetic comparisons.

1 Introduction

We study the problem of rewriting a query Q in terms of a given set of views $\mathcal{V}$ with limited access patterns $\mathcal{P}$, under a set Σ of integrity constraints. More precisely, we are interested in determining whether there exists a query plan Q', expressed in terms of the views $\mathcal{V}$ only, that is executable (i.e., observes $\mathcal{P}$) and equivalent to Q for all databases satisfying Σ. We say that Q is *feasible* if such Q' exists. For infeasible Q we seek the minimal containing and maximal contained executable queries, which provide the "best possible" executable query plans for approximating the answer to Q from above and below. Our results unify and extend a number of previous results in data integration (see related work). In particular, they apply to queries, views, and constraints over unions of conjunctive queries with negation (UCQ⁻), equality and arithmetic comparisons.

The following example shows the common case of a query that has no equivalent executable rewriting (i.e., is not feasible) in the absence of constraints, but that can yield such a rewriting when constraints are given.

Example 1. Consider the following set of relations with access patterns: conference $C^{io}(a,t)$, journal $J^{io}(a,t)$, magazine $M^{oo}(a,t)$, PC-magazine $P^{ioo}(a,t,p)$,

---

* Supported by NSF/CAREER 0347968, NSF/ITR 0225673 (GEON), NSF/ITR 0225674 (SEEK), DOE SciDAC DE-FC02-01ER25486 (SDM), NIH/NCRR 1R24 RR019701-01 Biomedical Informatics Research Network Coordinating Center (BIRN-CC).

T. Eiter and L. Libkin (Eds.): ICDT 2005, LNCS 3363, pp. 352–367, 2005.

the set of listed publishers $L^i(p)$, repository $R^{oo}(a,t)$, ACM anthology $A^{iii}(a,t,o)$, and DBLP conference article $D^{ooo}(a,t,c)$. The relation symbols are annotated with access patterns, indicating which arguments must be given as inputs (marked 'i') and which ones can be retrieved as outputs (marked 'o') when accessing the relation. For example $C^{io}(a,t)$ means that an author a has to be given as input before one can retrieve the titles t of a's conference publications from $C(a,t)$.

Let Q be the query which asks for pairs of authors and titles of conference publications, journal publications, and magazines which are not PC-magazines:

$$Q(a,t) \leftarrow \underline{C(a,t)} \tag{1}$$
$$Q(a,t) \leftarrow \underline{J(a,t)} \tag{2}$$
$$Q(a,t) \leftarrow \underline{M(a,t)}, \neg P(a,t,p), \underline{L(p)} \tag{3}$$

Q cannot be executed since no underlined literal is answerable: e.g., the access patterns require a to be bound before invoking $C(a,t)$ but no such binding is available. Worse yet, Q is not even feasible, i.e., there is no executable query Q' equivalent to Q. However, if the following set Σ of integrity constraints is given, an executable Q' can be found that is equivalent under Σ:

$$\forall a \forall t \ C(a,t) \rightarrow \exists c \ D(a,t,c) \tag{4}$$
$$\forall a \forall t \ J(a,t) \rightarrow \exists p \ R(a,t) \wedge \neg P(a,t,p) \wedge L(p) \vee \exists o \exists c \ A(a,t,o), D(a,t,c) \tag{5}$$
$$\forall a \forall t \ M(a,t) \rightarrow \exists p \ \neg P(a,t,p), L(p) \tag{6}$$

Constraint (4) states that every conference publication is a DBLP conference publication; (5) states that every journal publication is available from a repository, comes from a listed publisher and is not a PC magazine, or is available from the ACM anthology and from DBLP; and (6) states that magazine articles are not PC-magazine articles. We are only interested in databases which satisfy these constraints Σ. On those databases, Q is equivalent to Q^Σ, obtained by "chasing" Q with Σ:

$$Q^\Sigma(a,t) \leftarrow C(a,t), D(a,t,c)$$
$$Q^\Sigma(a,t) \leftarrow J(a,t), R(a,t), \neg P(a,t,p), \underline{L(p)}$$
$$Q^\Sigma(a,t) \leftarrow J(a,t), \underline{A(a,t,o)}, D(a,t,c)$$
$$Q^\Sigma(a,t) \leftarrow \underline{M(a,t)}, \neg P(a,t,p), \underline{L(p)}$$

Again, unanswerable literals are underlined. The *answerable part* $\text{ans}(Q^\Sigma)$ is obtained (roughly) by removing unanswerable parts:

$$\text{ans}(Q^\Sigma)(a,t) \leftarrow C(a,t), D(a,t,c) \tag{7}$$
$$\text{ans}(Q^\Sigma)(a,t) \leftarrow J(a,t), R(a,t) \tag{8}$$
$$\text{ans}(Q^\Sigma)(a,t) \leftarrow J(a,t), D(a,t,c) \tag{9}$$
$$\text{ans}(Q^\Sigma)(a,t) \leftarrow M(a,t) \tag{10}$$

In general, the answerable part is not equivalent to Q: e.g., the subquery (10) is not contained in (3) and thus $\text{ans}(Q^\Sigma)$ might produce more answers than

Q. However the equivalence may still hold under Σ, i.e., for all databases satisfying Σ. This can be checked (cf. Corollary 2) and is indeed the case here. Then $\text{ans}(Q^\Sigma)$ is the desired executable plan, equivalent to Q for all databases satisfying the constraints Σ.

As we will show, if there is an equivalent query Q' under Σ, our algorithm will find it, and if no such Q' exists, we can find the minimal containing and the maximal contained plans, providing least overestimate and greatest underestimate queries for Q under Σ, respectively.

Example 2. This example illustrates that our techniques can also rewrite queries in terms of views with access patterns. For example, the rules

$$V_1^{oo}(a,t) :- C(a,t), R(a,t)$$
$$V_2^{io}(a,t) :- C(a,t), \neg R(a,t)$$

state that the view V_1 has conference articles that are also in the repository R, while V_2 has those that are not in R. The access patterns indicate that at least a must be given when accessing $V_2(a,t)$, while no inputs are required for accessing V_1. We will show that if we want to rewrite a query in terms of the views only, this can be achieved by considering constraints and access patterns only. To this end, we model views as constraints and also include "negation constraints" of the form $\forall a \forall t (\mathtt{true} \rightarrow (R(a,t) \vee \neg R(a,t)))$. Chasing the query $Q(a,t) \leftarrow C(a,t)$ with the latter yields

$$Q'(a,t) \leftarrow C(a,t), R(a,t)$$
$$Q'(a,t) \leftarrow C(a,t), \neg R(a,t)$$

which then rewrites in terms of V_1 and V_2 to

$$Q''(a,t) \leftarrow V_1(a,t)$$
$$Q''(a,t) \leftarrow V_2(a,t).$$

Here, Q'' is not executable (the access pattern for V_2 requires a to be bound). Under the constraint $\forall a \forall t (C(a,t) \rightarrow R(a,t))$, our algorithm can discard the unanswerable second rule, resulting in the executable rewriting $Q'''(a,t) \leftarrow V_1(a,t)$.

Contributions. We solve the problem of rewriting queries using views with limited access patterns under integrity constraints (denoted $\{Q, \mathcal{V}, \mathcal{P}, \Sigma\}$) and prove that feasibility is **NP**-complete for queries, views, and constraints over[1] UCQ and Π_2^P-complete for UCQ$^\neg$. These results hold in those cases when the chase terminates and its result is not too large (Theorem 10). A fairly general sufficient condition for this (undecidable) behavior of the chase is given by Theorem 8. We present an algorithm, VIEWREWRITE, which is guaranteed to find an exact plan (if one exists) or at least the minimal containing plan (unique if it exists) (Theorem 9). We also give an algorithm for finding the maximal contained executable plan (Theorem 11).

---

[1] A constraint *over* $\mathcal{L}$ is an implication $\forall \bar{x}(U \rightarrow V)$ with $U, V \in \mathcal{L}$ (cf. Section 2).

One side effect of our results is a unified treatment for three flavors of rewriting problems which have been introduced and solved separately. We show that $\{Q, V, P, \Sigma\}$ reduces to $\{Q, P, \Sigma\}$, i.e., rewriting queries with access patterns and constraints without views (Theorem 9) and also to $\{Q, V, \Sigma\}$, i.e. rewriting queries under constraints using views without access patterns (Theorem 15).

We show how to solve $\{Q, P, \Sigma\}$ and $\{Q, V, \Sigma\}$ by reduction to rewriting queries under constraints only (semantic optimization, denoted $\{Q, \Sigma\}$). These reductions provide two separate routes $\{Q, V, P, \Sigma\} \rightsquigarrow \{Q, P, \Sigma\} \rightsquigarrow \{Q, \Sigma\}$ and $\{Q, V, P, \Sigma\} \rightsquigarrow \{Q, V, \Sigma\} \rightsquigarrow \{Q, \Sigma\}$ to a unified solution for all three problems, based on our extension of the relational chase theory to queries and constraints with disjunction and negation. Specifically we show that a minimal containing query in the $\{Q, P, \Sigma\}$ case can be obtained by chasing Q with Σ and computing the answerable part. Similarly, in the presence of views, we can compute the minimal containing query by chasing with Σ and the constraints corresponding to V and again computing the answerable part.

We also extend the above results to handle equality and arithmetic comparisons by modeling them with constraints (Section 7).

Related Work. There is a large body of related work that deals with one or more of the following three aspects: (i) query rewriting under *limited access patterns*, see [22, 20, 14, 9, 23, 16, 15, 19, 18] and references within; (ii) query rewriting under *integrity constraints* (a.k.a. semantic query optimization), see for instance [12, 5] and references within; and (iii) query rewriting and answering *using views* [6, 7, 11]. These all have important applications in data integration and query optimization [13, 17, 10]. All of the above mentioned work on rewriting has focused on either of two flavors: *maximal contained* or *exact* rewritings.

In this paper, we introduce algorithms which deal uniformly with all three aspects of rewriting and find exact, maximal contained and *minimal containing* rewritings.

In the category of maximal contained rewritings, the closest related results are those of [7], which considers the most expressive queries and views, and of [12], which handles the most expressive constraints. [7] shows how to obtain a maximal contained rewriting for recursive Datalog queries using conjunctive query views. [7] also considers access patterns on the views as well as very restricted constraints (which can express the standard key but not all foreign key constraints) and it shows how to construct a recursive plan which is guaranteed to be maximal contained. As opposed to [7], we do not consider recursive queries but we allow negation and disjunction in queries, views and constraints (our constraints express key, foreign key, join, multi-valued, and embedded dependencies and beyond). Moreover, we provide decision procedures for the existence of an *exact* plan and, in its absence, we show how to obtain not only the best *contained* but also the best *containing* approximations. [12] finds the maximal contained rewriting of CQ queries under more expressive constraints than [7] (embedded dependencies), provided the predicate dependency graph is acyclic. However, views, access patterns and negation (in either query or constraints) are not handled.

With respect to finding exact rewritings, [5] shows how to treat views and integrity constraints uniformly for UCQ queries. The present paper extends these results to UCQ¬ queries, constraints, views with limited access patterns, and maximal contained and minimal containing rewritings. [16, 15] shows **NP**-completeness for deciding feasibility of UCQ queries over relations with limited access patterns (i.e. no negation, no views and no constraints are considered). Still in the absence of views and constraints, [19] shows that if negation is added then deciding feasibility becomes Π_2^P-complete; [18] further extends the notion of feasibility to all first-order queries and characterizes the complexity of many first-order query classes.

Outline. The preliminaries in Section 2 include earlier results on containment and feasibility under access patterns. Section 3 presents our results on feasibility and rewriting with access patterns under constraints. In Section 4 we generalize these results to include views. In Section 5 we establish our results on maximal contained executable queries. Section 6 provides an alternative method for deciding feasibility: Instead of handling access patterns via the answerable part, we show that they too can be reduced to constraints and the chase. Section 7 shows how other extensions such as equality and arithmetic comparisons can all be treated uniformly via constraints.

2   Preliminaries

Queries. A *term* is a variable or constant. By $\bar{x}$ we denote a finite sequence of terms $x_1, \ldots, x_k$. We use lowercase letters $x, y, z, \ldots$ for terms and uppercase letters $P, Q, R, \ldots$ for relation symbols and queries. A *datalog rule* is an expression of the form $P(\bar{z}) \leftarrow \ell_1(\bar{x}_1), \ldots, \ell_n(\bar{x}_n)$ where each $\ell_i(\bar{x}_i)$ in the rule *body* is a *literal*, i.e., a *positive* atom $R(\bar{x})$ or a *negative* literal $\neg R(\bar{x})$. Given a rule Q, we define head(Q) and body(Q) to be the parts to the left and to the right of the arrow, respectively. A datalog *program* is a finite set of datalog rules. We only consider nonrecursive programs and we further require that all rules have the same head. Therefore, head(P) is well-defined for the programs P we consider.

We represent queries by programs unless otherwise specified. If a query Q is given by multiple rules $Q_1, \ldots, Q_n$, we denote this by $Q = \bigvee_i Q_i$ and we have $Q(\mathcal{D}) = \bigcup_i Q_i(\mathcal{D})$, where $Q(\mathcal{D})$ denotes the result of query Q on database $\mathcal{D}$.

Queries given by a single rule are *conjunctive queries* (CQ) if all literals are positive and *conjunctive queries with negation* (CQ¬) otherwise. Queries given by multiple rules are *unions of conjunctive queries* (UCQ) if all literals are positive and *conjunctive queries with negation* (UCQ¬) otherwise.

A query $Q \in$ CQ¬ is *safe* if every variable which appears in the rule (whether in the head or in the body) appears positively in its body. A query $Q = \bigvee_i Q_i$ with $Q_1, \ldots, Q_n \in$ CQ¬ is *safe* if every Q_i is safe. In the definition of ans(Q) below, we will need to consider two special kinds of queries. A query $Q \in$ CQ¬ given by head(Q) $\leftarrow \perp$ is unsatisfiable and is always safe (this is an extension of the definition above). A query $Q \in$ CQ¬ given by a rule with an empty body is safe if there are no variables in the head (i.e., if the query is boolean).

Unless otherwise specified, all queries are UCQ¯ and safe. Furthermore, E, P, and Q always denote queries.

Containment. P is *contained* in Q ($P \sqsubseteq Q$) if, for all databases $\mathcal{D}$, $P(\mathcal{D}) \subseteq Q(\mathcal{D})$. P is *equivalent* to Q ($P \equiv Q$) if $P \sqsubseteq Q$ and $Q \sqsubseteq P$. Given a set of constraints Σ, P is Σ-*contained* in Q ($P \sqsubseteq_\Sigma Q$) if, for all $\mathcal{D}$ which satisfy Σ, $P(\mathcal{D}) \subseteq Q(\mathcal{D})$. P is Σ-*equivalent* to Q ($P \equiv_\Sigma Q$) if $P \sqsubseteq_\Sigma Q$ and $Q \sqsubseteq_\Sigma P$.

CONT($\mathcal{L}$) is the decision problem: for $P, Q \in \mathcal{L}$ determine whether $P \sqsubseteq Q$ ($\mathcal{L}$ is a class of queries). CONT$_\Sigma$($\mathcal{L}$) is the problem: for $P, Q \in \mathcal{L}$ decide whether $P \sqsubseteq_\Sigma Q$.

Theorem 1. *a)* CONT(CQ) *and* CONT(UCQ) *are* **NP**-*complete [2]*.
b) CONT(CQ¯) *and* CONT(UCQ¯) *are* $\mathbf{\Pi_2^P}$-*complete [21]*.

Access Patterns. An *access pattern* for a k-ary relation R is an expression R^α where α is word of length k over the alphabet $\{\mathrm{i}, \mathrm{o}\}$. 'i' denotes a required *input slot* and 'o' denotes an *output slot* (no value required). Given access patterns $\mathcal{P}$, an *annotation* of Q assigns to each occurrence of a relation symbol a pattern from $\mathcal{P}$.

Definition 1 (Executable). Q *is* executable *if it can be annotated so that every variable of a rule appears first positively in an output slot in the body of that rule.*

Definition 2 (Feasible). Q *is* feasible *if it is equivalent to an executable query Q'.* FEASIBLE($\mathcal{L}$) *is the decision problem: for $Q \in \mathcal{L}$, determine whether Q is feasible.*

For $Q \in$ CQ¯, we say that a literal $\ell(\bar{x})$ (not necessarily in Q) is Q-*answerable* if there is an executable $Q' \in$ CQ¯ which is a conjunction of $\ell(\bar{x})$ and literals in Q. The *answerable part* of a query Q is another query ans(Q) defined below. ans(Q) may be undefined for some queries Q, but when defined it is executable.

Definition 3 (Answerable Part). *If $Q \in$ CQ¯ is unsatisfiable we set the body of* ans(Q) *to* $\perp$*; otherwise we set the body of* ans(Q) *to the conjunction of the Q-answerable literals in Q in the order specified by the algorithm in the proof of Lemma 1. We set* head(ans(Q)) $:=$ head(Q). *However, if the resulting query* ans(Q) *is unsafe, we say that* ans(Q) *is undefined. If $Q = \bigvee_i Q_i$ with $Q_1, \ldots, Q_n \in$ CQ¯, we set* ans(Q) $:= \bigvee_i$ ans(Q_i). *In this case* ans(Q) *is defined iff every* ans(Q_i) *is defined.*

Lemma 1. ans(Q) *can be computed in quadratic time.*

Proof. We consider the case when $Q \in$ CQ¯; the case $Q \in$ UCQ¯ is handled the same way, one rule at a time. Give ans(Q) the same head as Q and build its body one literal at a time as follows. Start with $\mathcal{B}$, the set of bound variables, empty. Find the first literal $\ell(\bar{x})$ in Q not yet added to ans(Q) such that,

- $\ell(\bar{x})$ is positive and there is some access pattern for it in $\mathcal{P}$ such that all variables in $\bar{x}$ which appear in input slots in $\ell(\bar{x})$ are in $\mathcal{B}$, or
- $\ell(\bar{x})$ is negative and its variables are in $\mathcal{B}$.

If there is no such literal, stop. Otherwise, add $\ell(\bar{x})$ to ans(Q), set $\mathcal{B} := \mathcal{B} \cup \{\bar{x}\}$, and repeat. Clearly, this algorithm adds to the body of ans(Q) all the Q-answerable literals in Q and no others.

The main results on testing feasibility for $\mathrm{UCQ}^{\neg}$ queries are [19]: if defined, ans(Q) is the minimal executable query containing Q (Theorem 2); checking feasibility of $\mathrm{UCQ}^{\neg}$ queries can be reduced to checking $\mathrm{UCQ}^{\neg}$ query containment (Corollary 1), and is in fact as hard as checking query containment of $\mathrm{UCQ}^{\neg}$ queries (Theorem 3b). Checking feasibility of UCQ queries is **NP**-complete (Theorem 3a) [20].

Theorem 2. *If $Q \sqsubseteq E$ and E is executable then* ans(Q) *is defined and it holds that $Q \sqsubseteq$ ans(Q) $\sqsubseteq E$.*

Corollary 1. *Q is feasible iff* ans(Q) *is defined and* ans(Q) $\sqsubseteq Q$.

Theorem 3. *a)* FEASIBLE(UCQ) *is **NP**-complete.*
b) FEASIBLE($\mathrm{UCQ}^{\neg}$) *is $\mathbf{\Pi_2^P}$-complete.*

Chase. We consider constraints of the form $\mathrm{IC}(\mathcal{L}) := \{\forall \bar{x}\,(U \to V) \mid U, V \in \mathcal{L}\}$ where $\bar{x}$ is the set of free variables in both U and V. Such constraints express the containment of U in V and are known as *embedded dependencies* when $\mathcal{L} = \mathrm{CQ}$.

Unless otherwise specified, we assume all constraints are subsets of $\mathrm{IC}(\mathrm{UCQ}^{\neg})$. **Furthermore Σ always denotes a set of constraints.**

Given a set of constraints $\Sigma \subseteq \mathrm{IC}(\mathrm{UCQ})$, there is a well known procedure for extending a query $Q \in \mathrm{UCQ}$ to another query Q' by an iterative procedure known as the *chase* which depends on the order O of the constraints. That is, we set $Q' := \mathrm{chase}(Q, \Sigma, O) \in \mathrm{UCQ}$. In [3] we extend this procedure to $Q \in \mathrm{UCQ}^{\neg}$ and $\Sigma \subseteq \mathrm{IC}(\mathrm{UCQ}^{\neg})$.

The chase does not always terminate (even in the case with no negation) and its syntactic form depends on the order O. However if the chase terminates for any two orders O_1 and O_2, then $\mathrm{chase}(Q, \Sigma, O_1) \equiv \mathrm{chase}(Q, \Sigma, O_2)$.

Definition 4 (Negation Constraints). *$\Sigma_{\neg}^{\tau} \subseteq \mathrm{IC}(\mathrm{UCQ}^{\neg})$ is the smallest set of constraints which contains, for each k, each k-ary relation R in the schema τ and some k-tuple $\bar{x}$ of variables, the constraint $\forall \bar{x}\,(\mathbf{true} \to (\,R(\bar{x}) \vee \neg R(\bar{x})\,))$.*

We allow unsafe sentences as constraints (we need them for $\Sigma_{\neg}^{\tau}$); however if Q is safe, then $\mathrm{chase}(Q, \Sigma, O)$ is also safe, even when Σ includes unsafe sentences.

Definition 5 (Chase Result Q^{Σ}). *$Q^{\Sigma} := \mathrm{chase}(Q, \Sigma \cup \Sigma_{\neg}^{\tau}, O)$ for some order on which the chase terminates (if there is such order).*

Notice that Q^{Σ} is defined only up to equivalence. The following two results extend previous results which do not handle negation.

Theorem 4 (Chase Completeness). *If Q^Σ is defined, then $Q^\Sigma \sqsubseteq P$ iff $Q \sqsubseteq_\Sigma P$.*

Theorem 5. *If $\Sigma \subseteq \mathrm{IC}(\mathrm{UCQ}^\neg)$ and there is a polynomial p such that for all Q, $Q^\Sigma (= \bigvee_i Q'_i) \in \mathrm{UCQ}^\neg$ and all i: $|Q'_i| \leqslant p(|Q|)$, then $\mathrm{CONT}_\Sigma(\mathrm{UCQ}^\neg)$ is Π_2^P-complete.*

We write $Q^{\Sigma,\Sigma'}$ for $(Q^\Sigma)^{\Sigma'}$ which in general is not equivalent to $Q^{\Sigma \cup \Sigma'}$.

3 Integrity Constraints

We consider $\{Q, \mathcal{P}, \Sigma\}$, i.e., the problem of answering a query Q in the presence of access patterns $\mathcal{P}$ and integrity constraints Σ.

Definition 6 (Σ-Feasible). *Q is Σ-feasible if it is Σ-equivalent to an executable query Q'. $\mathrm{FEASIBLE}_\Sigma(\mathcal{L})$ is the decision problem: for $Q \in \mathcal{L}$, decide whether Q is Σ-feasible.*

The main results in this section are that, if defined, $\mathrm{ans}(Q^\Sigma)$ is the minimal executable query Σ-containing Q (Theorem 6), that checking Σ-feasibility of $\mathrm{UCQ}^\neg$ queries can be reduced to checking containment of $\mathrm{UCQ}^\neg$ queries (Corollary 2), and that in those cases where Q^Σ is well-defined (i.e., the chase terminates) and not too large its complexity is the same as that of checking containment of $\mathrm{UCQ}^\neg$ queries (Theorem 7b). Corresponding results hold for CQ, $\mathrm{CQ}^\neg$, and UCQ (Theorem 7a). We outline the algorithms REWRITE and FEASIBLE which use the following functions:

- $\mathrm{ans}(Q)$, which given a query Q, produces the query $\mathrm{ans}(Q)$. A quadratic time algorithm for this function is outlined in the proof of Lemma 1.
- $\mathrm{chase}(Q, \Sigma, O)$, which given a query Q, a set of constraints Σ, and an order on the constraints O, produces the query $\mathrm{chase}(Q, \Sigma, O)$. An algorithm for this function is outlined in [3]. No guarantees are given for the running time or space of $\mathrm{chase}(Q, \Sigma, O)$; in fact, it may not even terminate.
- $\mathrm{contained}(P, Q)$, which given queries P and Q, returns true if $P \sqsubseteq Q$, false otherwise (its complexity is given in Theorem 1).

Note that algorithm REWRITE(Q, Σ) may return **undefined** or may not terminate; similarly, FEASIBLE(Q, Σ) may not terminate. Theorem 6 and Corollary 2 below show that algorithms REWRITE and FEASIBLE are correct and complete, in those cases in which the chase terminates regardless of the order O.

---

function REWRITE(Q, Σ)
(1) Compute $\Sigma' := \Sigma \cup \Sigma_\neg^\tau$ and pick some order O for Σ';
(2) $Q^1 := \mathrm{chase}(Q, \Sigma', O)$;
(3) $Q^2 := \mathrm{ans}(Q^1)$;
(4) **return** Q^2.

Here we give a simplified version of FEASIBLE which gives an exponential time algorithm. This algorithm can be parallelized to give a $\mathbf{\Pi_2^P}$ algorithm when Q and Σ satisfy the assumptions of Theorem 7b, as outlined in the proof of that theorem.

---

function FEASIBLE(Q, Σ)
(1-3) *same as (1-3) of* REWRITE(Q, Σ);
  (4) **if** $Q^2 =$ undefined **then return** false;
  (5) $Q^3 :=$ chase(Q^2, Σ', O);
  (6) **return** contained(Q^3, Q).

Theorem 6. *If* $Q \sqsubseteq_\Sigma E$, E *is executable, and* Q^Σ *is defined, then* ans(Q^Σ) *is defined and* $Q \sqsubseteq_\Sigma$ ans$(Q^\Sigma) \sqsubseteq E$.

Proof. Assume $Q \sqsubseteq_\Sigma E$ and E executable; by Theorem 4, $Q^\Sigma \sqsubseteq E$. Thus, by Theorem 2, ans(Q^Σ) is defined and $Q^\Sigma \sqsubseteq$ ans$(Q^\Sigma) \sqsubseteq E$. By Theorem 4, $Q \sqsubseteq_\Sigma$ ans$(Q^\Sigma) \sqsubseteq E$.

Corollary 2. *The following are equivalent:*

1. Q *is* Σ-*feasible.*
2. ans(Q^Σ) *is defined and* ans$(Q^\Sigma) \sqsubseteq_\Sigma Q$.
3. ans$(Q^\Sigma)^\Sigma$ *is defined and* ans$(Q^\Sigma)^\Sigma \sqsubseteq Q$.

Theorem 7. *a) If* $\Sigma \subseteq$ IC(UCQ) *and there is a polynomial p such that for all* Q, $Q^\Sigma \in$ UCQ: $|Q^\Sigma| \leqslant p(|Q|)$, *then* FEASIBLE$_\Sigma$(UCQ) *is* **NP**-*complete.*
b) If $\Sigma \subseteq$ IC(UCQ$^\neg$) *and there is a polynomial p such that for all* Q, $Q^\Sigma (= \bigvee_i Q'_i) \in$ UCQ$^\neg$ *and for all* i: $|Q'_i| \leqslant p(|Q|)$, *then* FEASIBLE$_\Sigma$(UCQ$^\neg$) *is* $\mathbf{\Pi_2^P}$-*complete.*

The fact that Q^Σ is defined only up to equivalence is not a concern for our needs, due to the following result.

Lemma 2.

a) If $P \sqsubseteq Q$ *and* ans(Q) *is defined, then* ans(P) *is defined and* ans$(P) \sqsubseteq$ ans(Q).
b) If $P \equiv Q$ *and* ans(Q) *is defined, then* ans(P) *is defined and* ans$(P) \equiv$ ans(Q).

Proof. (a) If ans(Q) is defined then it is executable and $P \sqsubseteq Q \sqsubseteq$ ans(Q). By Theorem 2, ans(P) is defined and ans$(P) \sqsubseteq$ ans(Q). (b) follows from (a).

In general it is undecidable whether the chase terminates. [5] introduces a sufficient condition, checkable in **P**, for termination of the chase with IC(UCQ) constraints. It is fairly wide and generalizes the notions of full and acyclic dependencies [1]. The condition requires a set of constraints to have *stratified witnesses*.[2] We recall the definition in [3], where we extend the notion to sets of IC(UCQ$^\neg$) constraints and also provide a proof of the following result.

Theorem 8. *For any* $Q \in$ UCQ$^\neg$, *any* $\Sigma \subseteq$ IC(UCQ$^\neg$) *with stratified witnesses (this is checkable in* **P***) and any total order* O *on* Σ, *the chase terminates. Moreover,* Q^Σ *satisfies the assumptions in Theorem 7.*

---

[2] The notion first arose in a conversation between the first author and Lucian Popa. It was then independently used in [8] under the term *weakly acyclic*.

4   Views

We now consider the problem $\{Q, \mathcal{V}, \mathcal{P}, \Sigma_c\}$: given a query Q, a set of views $\mathcal{V}$ given as $\mathrm{UCQ}^\neg$ queries $V_1, \ldots, V_n$ with access patterns $\mathcal{P}$ on the view heads, and a set of constraints Σ_c, we are interested in finding an executable Σ_c-rewriting of Q in terms of $V_1, \ldots, V_n$. That is, we want a query E over $\mathcal{V}$ that is Σ_c-equivalent to Q.

We reduce this case to the case of integrity constraints alone covered in the previous section as follows. Assume the views are over the schema τ. We can express the views as "forward" and "backward" constraints

$$\Sigma_f^{\mathcal{V}} := \{\forall \bar{x}_i \bar{y}_i \, (\mathrm{body}(V_i) \to \mathrm{head}(V_i)) \mid V_i \in \mathcal{V}, 1 \leqslant i \leqslant n\}$$

$$\Sigma_b^{\mathcal{V}} := \{\forall \bar{x}_i \, (\mathrm{head}(V_i) \to \exists \bar{y}_i \mathrm{body}(V_i)) \mid V_i \in \mathcal{V}, 1 \leqslant i \leqslant n\}$$

over the schema $\tau \cup \tau_V$, where $\tau_V := \bigcup_i \mathrm{head}(V_i)$ consists of all view heads; $\bar{x}_i$ are the variables in $\mathrm{head}(V_i)$, and $\bar{y}_i$ are the variables in $\mathrm{body}(V_i)$ which do not appear in $\mathrm{head}(V_i)$. Clearly, $\Sigma_f^{\mathcal{V}}, \Sigma_b^{\mathcal{V}} \subseteq \mathrm{IC}(\mathrm{UCQ}^\neg)$. Set $\Sigma := \Sigma_c \cup \Sigma_f^{\mathcal{V}} \cup \Sigma_b^{\mathcal{V}}$.

The main results in this section are that we can reduce $\{Q, \mathcal{V}, \mathcal{P}, \Sigma_c\}$, the case of views with constraints, to $\{Q, \mathcal{P}, \Sigma\}$, the case without views via $\Sigma := \Sigma_c \cup \Sigma_f^{\mathcal{V}} \cup \Sigma_b^{\mathcal{V}}$, where the views $\mathcal{V}$ are captured by the constraints $\Sigma_f^{\mathcal{V}}$ and $\Sigma_b^{\mathcal{V}}$ above. In fact, it is enough to consider $Q^{\Sigma_c, \Sigma_f^{\mathcal{V}}}$ instead of Q^{Σ} for computing the answerable part (but for testing feasiblity we also need $\Sigma_b^{\mathcal{V}}$). If defined, $\mathrm{ans}(Q^{\Sigma_c, \Sigma_f^{\mathcal{V}}}|\tau_V)$ is the minimal executable query over $\mathcal{V}$ Σ_c-containing Q (Theorem 9) where $Q|\tau$ is the query with the same head as Q and with body given by the literals in Q which have relation symbols in schema τ. It follows that the problem of whether there is a Σ_c-equivalent rewriting of a query Q over $\mathcal{V}$ can be reduced to checking containment (Corollary 3). We also show that we can stratify the chase and that we only need special conditions on Σ_c (but not on $\Sigma_f^{\mathcal{V}}$ or $\Sigma_b^{\mathcal{V}}$) to guarantee that Q^{Σ} is well-defined and suitably small (Theorem 10). We outline the algorithms VIEWREWRITE and VIEWFEASIBLE which use the functions $\mathrm{ans}(Q)$, $\mathrm{chase}(Q, \Sigma, O)$, and $\mathrm{contained}(P, Q)$.

---

function VIEWREWRITE$(Q, \Sigma_c, \mathcal{V})$
(1) Compute $\Sigma_c' := \Sigma_c \cup \Sigma_\neg^\tau$ and pick some order O_c for Σ_c';
(2) Compute $\Sigma_f^{\mathcal{V}'} := \Sigma_f^{\mathcal{V}} \cup \Sigma_\neg^\tau$ and pick some order O_f for $\Sigma_f^{\mathcal{V}'}$;
(3) $Q^1 := \mathrm{chase}(Q, \Sigma_c', O_c)$;
(4) $Q^2 := \mathrm{chase}(Q^1, \Sigma_f^{\mathcal{V}}, O_f)$;
(5) $Q^3 := Q^2|\tau_V$ (that is, drop all τ literals);
(6) $Q^4 := \mathrm{ans}(Q^3)$;
(7) **return** Q^4.

VIEWREWRITE$(Q, \Sigma_c, \mathcal{V})$ may return **undefined** or may not terminate. Similarly, VIEWFEASIBLE$(Q, \Sigma_c, \mathcal{V})$ may not terminate. Theorem 9 and Corollary 3 show that these algorithms are correct and complete, provided the chase terminates regardless of the order O. The simplified version of VIEWFEASIBLE below results in an exponential time algorithm; however, it can be parallelized to give a $\mathbf{\Pi_2^P}$ algorithm when Q and Σ satisfy the assumptions of Theorem 10.

---

function VIEWFEASIBLE($Q, \Sigma_c, \mathcal{V}$)

(1–6) *same as (1–6) of* VIEWREWRITE($Q, \Sigma_c, \mathcal{V}$);

(7) **if** $Q^4 = $ undefined **then return** false;

(8) Compute $\Sigma_b^{\mathcal{V}'} := \Sigma_b^{\mathcal{V}} \cup \Sigma_\rightharpoondown^\tau$ and pick some order O_b for $\Sigma_b^{\mathcal{V}'}$;

(9) $Q^5 := \text{chase}(Q^4, \Sigma_b^{\mathcal{V}'}, O_b)$;

(10) $Q^6 := \text{chase}(Q^5, \Sigma_c', O_c)$;

(11) $Q^7 := Q^6|\tau$ (that is, drop all τ_V literals);

(12) **return** contained(Q^7, Q).

Theorem 9. *If defined,* ans($Q^{\Sigma_c, \Sigma_f^{\mathcal{V}}}|\tau_V$) *is the minimal executable query over* $\mathcal{V}$ Σ_c-*containing Q (otherwise there is no such executable query).*

Corollary 3. *There is an executable Σ_c-rewriting of Q over $\mathcal{V}$ iff* ans($Q^{\Sigma_c, \Sigma_f^{\mathcal{V}}}|\tau_V$) *is defined and* ans($Q^{\Sigma_c, \Sigma_f^{\mathcal{V}}}|\tau_V$)$^{\Sigma_b^{\mathcal{V}}, \Sigma_c}|\tau \sqsubseteq Q$.

Theorem 10. a) *If $\Sigma \subseteq$ IC(UCQ), $\mathcal{V} \subseteq$ UCQ and there is a polynomial p such that for all $Q, Q^{\Sigma_c} \in$ UCQ: $|Q^{\Sigma_c}| \leqslant p(|Q|)$, then* VIEWFEASIBLE *is* NP-*complete.*

b) *If $\Sigma \subseteq$ IC(UCQ$^\neg$), $\mathcal{V} \subseteq$ UCQ$^\neg$ and there is a polynomial p such that for all Q, $Q^{\Sigma_c} (= \bigvee_i Q_i') \in$ UCQ$^\neg$ and all i: $|Q_i'| \leqslant p(|Q|)$, then* VIEWFEASIBLE *is* $\mathbf{\Pi_2^P}$-*complete.*

These results follow from the corresponding results in the previous section and the following considerations. Notice that Q' is a Σ_c-rewriting of Q over $\mathcal{V}$ iff $Q'|\tau_V = Q'$ and $Q' \equiv_\Sigma Q$ (the first part simply says that Q' is a query over $\mathcal{V}$). Since Σ includes the definitions of the views in $\mathcal{V}$, the second part expresses the desired equivalence under both Σ_c and the view definitions.

We know by Theorem 6 that ans($Q^\Sigma|\tau_V$) is the minimal executable query over τ_V Σ-containing Q. Since $\Sigma_f^{\mathcal{V}}$ and $\Sigma_b^{\mathcal{V}}$ express the equivalence of the views with their definitions over τ, this is the same as the minimal executable query over $\mathcal{V}$ Σ_c-containing Q. It follows that there is an executable Σ_c-rewriting of Q over $\mathcal{V}$ iff ans($Q^\Sigma|\tau_V$) $\sqsubseteq_\Sigma Q$ iff ans($Q^\Sigma|\tau_V$)$^\Sigma \sqsubseteq Q$.

The effect of chasing twice with Σ can be roughly described as follows:

- In Q^Σ we introduce the view heads.
- In ans($Q^\Sigma|\tau_V$) we remove the original literals in Q and the view bodies.
- In ans($Q^\Sigma|\tau_V$)$^\Sigma$ we expand the view heads to again include their bodies.

At this point, we have a query over $\tau \cup \tau_V$, but since Q is over τ, only the τ part matters. Therefore ans($Q^\Sigma|\tau_V$)$^\Sigma \sqsubseteq Q$ iff ans($Q^\Sigma|\tau_V$)$^\Sigma|\tau \sqsubseteq Q$. Furthermore, ans($Q^\Sigma|\tau_V$)$^\Sigma|\tau \sqsubseteq Q$ iff ans($Q^{\Sigma_c, \Sigma_f^{\mathcal{V}}}|\tau_V$)$^{\Sigma_b^{\mathcal{V}}, \Sigma_c}|\tau \sqsubseteq Q$ since $Q^{\Sigma_c, \Sigma_f^{\mathcal{V}}, \Sigma_b^{\mathcal{V}}} \equiv Q^{\Sigma_c, \Sigma_f^{\mathcal{V}}}$. This is because $\Sigma_f^{\mathcal{V}}$ only introduces atoms with relation symbols from τ_V and these in turn can only "fire" constraints from $\Sigma_b^{\mathcal{V}}$ which reintroduce bodies that have already been matched (with new quantified variables). Such chase steps never apply.

The chases with $\Sigma_f^{\mathcal{V}}$ and $\Sigma_b^{\mathcal{V}}$ can be done in a one step since new atoms added by $\Sigma_f^{\mathcal{V}}$ constraints have relation symbols in τ_V, whereas $\Sigma_f^{\mathcal{V}}$ constraints must match atoms with relation symbols in τ; similarly for $\Sigma_b^{\mathcal{V}}$ with the roles of τ and τ_V reversed. Only chasing with Σ_c may result in an infinite chase or in Q being too large.

Notice that, by Theorem 8, we can test in polynomial time whether Σ_c meets sufficient (and fairly wide) conditions that satisfy the assumptions of Theorem 10.

5   Maximal Contained Rewritings

Since exact rewritings of a query Q do not always exist, we want to approximate Q as best as possible. In Sections 3 and 4 we have shown how to obtain the minimal containing rewritings, which are the best overestimates of Q. In this section we consider maximal contained rewritings of Q, which are the best underestimates of Q.

Given a schema τ, let D_τ be the unary recursive query given by rules of the form $D_\tau(x_j) \leftarrow D_\tau(x_{i_1}), \ldots, D_\tau(x_{i_k}), R(\bar{x})$ for every relation $R \in \tau$ and every access pattern R^α where $x_{i_1}, \ldots, x_{i_k}$ are the input slots of R^α and j is an output slot in R^α.

Definition 7 (Domain Extension). *The* domain extension *of* $Q \in \text{CQ}^\neg$ *is another query* $\text{dext}(Q)$ *given by the rules with head* $D_\tau(x_j)$ *mentioned above and the rule*

$$\text{dext}(Q)(\bar{x}) \leftarrow D_\tau(y_1), \ldots, D_\tau(y_k), \text{body}(Q)$$

where y_i *are the variables in* $\text{body}(Q)$.

For $Q(= \bigvee_i Q_i) \in \text{UCQ}^\neg$, *we define* $\text{dext}(Q) := \bigvee_i \text{dext}(Q_i)$.

Notice that D_τ and $\text{dext}(Q)$ are recursive queries; in particular, here we deviate from the convention in Section 2 that all the rules of a query have the same head. Clearly, $\text{dext}(Q)$ is executable.[3] D_τ, $\text{dext}(Q)$, and the following result are given in [7] for CQ.

Theorem 11. *If* $E \sqsubseteq Q$, E *is executable, and* E *contains no constants, then* $E \sqsubseteq \text{dext}(Q) \sqsubseteq Q$.

We must disallow constants since they can be used to partially enumerate the domain. If we allow constants and '=', we can add rules of the form $D_\tau(x) \leftarrow (x = c)$ for every constant c. Notice that nothing special needs to be done here to handle negation since negative literals do not contribute towards enumerating the domain.

Theorem 12. *If* $E \sqsubseteq_\Sigma Q$, E *is executable,* E *contains no constants, and* E^Σ *is defined, then* $E \sqsubseteq_\Sigma \text{dext}(Q) \sqsubseteq Q$.

---

[3] We have not defined "executable" for recursive queries, but the extension is straightforward.

Proof. If E is executable, then E^Σ is also executable and satisfies $E^\Sigma \sqsubseteq Q$. Therefore, $E^\Sigma \sqsubseteq \text{dext}(Q)$ holds, which is equivalent to $E \sqsubseteq_\Sigma \text{dext}(Q)$.

Now assume that as in Section 4 we have a query Q, a set of constraints Σ_c, and a set of views $\mathcal{V}$ given by UCQ⁻ queries $V_1, \ldots, V_n$ with access patterns on the heads of the views. We express the views as constraints $\Sigma_f^{\mathcal{V}}$ and $\Sigma_b^{\mathcal{V}}$ as in Section 4. We are interested in finding a maximal Σ_c-contained executable rewriting of Q in terms of $V_1, \ldots, V_n$. That is, we want a query over $\mathcal{V}$ that is maximally Σ-contained in Q.

Theorem 13. *If E is a maximal Σ_c-contained rewriting of Q over $\mathcal{V}$ (regardless of access patterns), then* $\text{dext}(E)$ *is a maximal contained executable Σ_c-rewriting of Q.*

Proof. Assume E is as in premise and P is an executable query over $\mathcal{V}$ and $P \sqsubseteq_\Sigma Q$. Then $P \sqsubseteq_\Sigma E$ by the maximality of E. Since P is executable, by Theorem 12, $P \sqsubseteq_\Sigma \text{dext}(E)$.

[7] shows how to compute such a maximal Σ_c-contained rewriting of Q in the absence of negation using a recursive plan. But it is easy to see that such recursive plans can be transformed into a union of conjunctive queries: we simply take the union of all minimal CQ queries over $\mathcal{V}$ which are Σ_c-contained in Q (the results of [7] imply that this union is finite when the chase terminates) The extension to handle negation is straightforward and we omit it in view of our results in the next section.

6   Reducing Access Patterns to Constraints

In this section, we show that the problem $\{Q, \mathcal{P}, \Sigma\}$ of deciding feasibility in the presence of access patterns reduces to the problem $\{Q, \Sigma\}$ of deciding equivalence in the presence of constraints only (Theorem 14). Furthermore, we reduce the problem $\{Q, \mathcal{V}, \mathcal{P}, \Sigma\}$ of finding rewritings using views with access patterns to one of finding rewritings using views and constraints in the absence of access patterns $\{Q, \mathcal{V}, \Sigma\}$ (Theorem 15). These results enable alternative proofs for the complexity of answering queries in the presence of access patterns. They also facilitate an alternative implementation of algorithms REWRITE, FEASIBLE, VIEWREWRITE etc. using a chase-based module for rewriting under constraints such as the **C&B** implementation in [4].

The reduction is based on the observation that the domain enumeration program D_τ from Section 5 is a view (albeit recursive) and can therefore be captured with integrity constraints, as shown in Section 4. Call the set of resulting constraints Σ_D; notice that $\Sigma_D \subseteq \text{IC}(\text{UCQ}^-)$.

Theorem 14. *Q is Σ-feasible iff $Q \sqsubseteq_{\Sigma_D \cup \Sigma} \text{dext}(Q)$.*

Since $\text{dext}(Q) \sqsubseteq Q$, we only need to check $Q \sqsubseteq_{\Sigma_D} \text{dext}(Q)$ in Theorem 14. We thus retrieve the complexity results for checking feasibility from the complexity of checking containment. If $\Sigma = \emptyset$ we can show that (a) $\text{chase}(Q, \Sigma_D, O)$

terminates for any order O on Σ_D, (b) the chase result is unique regardless of O (denote it Q^{Σ_D}), and (c) if we restrict Q^{Σ_D} to only those atoms $R(\bar{x})$ for which $D(\bar{x})$ appears in Q^{Σ_D}, we obtain ans(Q). This and Theorem 15 below enable an alternative implementation of algorithm VIEWREWRITE, which does not compute ans(Q^3) in step (6) but instead uses $\mathcal{V}^D$ for $\mathcal{V}$ and $\Sigma \cup \Sigma_D$ for Σ.

We now reduce the rewriting problem $\{Q, \mathcal{V}, \mathcal{P}, \Sigma\}$ to $\{Q, \mathcal{V}, \Sigma\}$. First, define D_τ as in Section 5, but using view symbols instead of relation symbols from τ. Next capture D_τ with constraints Σ_D. For any $V \in \mathcal{V}$ and access pattern V^α, define a new view $V^D(\text{free}(V)) := \text{body}(V), D(x_{i_1}), \ldots, D(x_{i_k})$ where the $x_{i_j} \in \text{free}(V)$ are the free variables of V which appear in input slots. Each V^D is a view without access patterns. Denoting $\mathcal{V}^D := \{V^D \mid V \in \mathcal{V}\}$, we have the following result.

Theorem 15. *a) Q has an executable Σ-rewriting over $\mathcal{V}$ iff it has a $\Sigma \cup \Sigma_D$-rewriting over $\mathcal{V}^D$.*

b) For each exact (minimal containing) $\Sigma \cup \Sigma_D$-rewriting of Q over $\mathcal{V}^D$, we can derive in polynomial time an exact (minimal containing) Σ-rewriting of Q over $\mathcal{V}$.

7   Extensions

The key technique that allows us to treat negation, views, and access patterns uniformly is modeling with constraints (recall $\Sigma_\neg^\tau$, $\Sigma_f^\mathcal{V} \cup \Sigma_b^\mathcal{V}$, respectively Σ_D). This approach enables the straightforward implementation of our algorithms by reusing an already existing chase module [4]. It turns out that we can extend our solution to handling equality and arithmetic comparisons by capturing them with constraints as well.

Handling Equality. Equality can be modeled as a binary relation E with access patterns 'io' and 'oi' subject to the following constraints $\Sigma_{\doteq}^\tau \subseteq \text{IC}(\text{CQ})$:

- $\forall x \ \text{true} \to E(x, x)$,
- $\forall x, y \ E(x, y) \to E(y, x)$, and,
- for every $R \in \tau$: $\forall \bar{x}, \bar{y} \ R(\bar{x}) \wedge E(x_1, y_1) \wedge \ldots \wedge E(x_k, y_k) \to R(\bar{y})$.

Handling Arithmetic Comparisons. The comparison '$\leq$', which gives UCQAC$^\neg$, can be handled as a binary relation LE with access pattern 'ii' subject to the following constraints $\Sigma_\leq \subseteq \text{IC}(\text{CQ}^\neg)$ which say that LE is an unbounded dense total ordering:

- $\forall x, y, z \ LE(x, y) \wedge LE(y, z) \to LE(x, z)$,
- $\forall x, y \ LE(x, y) \wedge LE(y, x) \to E(x, y)$,
- $\forall x, y \ \neg LE(x, y) \to LE(y, x)$, and
- $\forall x, y \ L(x, y) \to \exists u, v, w \ (L(u, x) \wedge L(x, v) \wedge L(v, y) \wedge L(y, w))$,

where $L(x, y)$ stands for $LE(x, y) \wedge \neg E(x, y)$.

Notice that the chase with the last axiom (the density axiom) is non-terminating, yielding chains of $<$ comparisons of arbitrary length. However, we can show that if in each integrity constraint all variables that appear in a $\leq$ atom also appear in some relational atom other than a $\leq$ atom, then there is no need to chase with the density axiom. In this case, all of our results extend to unions of conjunctive queries with negation, equality and arithmetic comparisons as well as the corresponding constraints. All we need to do is replace Σ with $\Sigma' := \Sigma \cup \Sigma_\leq \cup \Sigma_=^\tau$ and run algorithms FEASIBLE, VIEWREWRITE, REWRITE, VIEWFEASIBLE on Σ'.

Even if the restriction above does not hold, it can be shown that the chase with the density axiom can be truncated so as to generate $<$ chains of length bounded by the number of variables in the original query. All we need to do is run algorithms FEASIBLE,VIEWREWRITE,REWRITE,VIEWFEASIBLE using the truncating chase.

References

1. Serge Abiteboul, Richard Hull, and Victor Vianu. *Foundations of Databases*. Addison Wesley, 1995.
2. A. K. Chandra and P. M. Merlin. Optimal implementation of conjunctive queries in relational data bases. In *ACM Symposium on Theory of Computing (STOC)*, pages 77–90, 1977.
3. Alin Deutsch, Bertram Ludäscher, and Alan Nash. Rewriting queries using views with access patterns under integrity constraints. Technical report, Department of Computer Science and Engineering, UCSD, 2004. extended version of this paper: http://www.db.ucsd.edu:8080/root/index.jsp?pageStr=publications.
4. Alin Deutsch and Val Tannen. Mars: A system for publishing xml from mixed and redundant storage. In *Intl. Conf. on Very Large Data Bases (VLDB)*, 2003.
5. Alin Deutsch and Val Tannen. Reformulation of xml queries and constraints. In *Intl. Conf. on Database Theory (ICDT)*, 2003.
6. Oliver M. Duschka and Michael R. Genesereth. Answering recursive queries using views. In *PODS*, 1997.
7. Oliver M. Duschka, Michael R. Genesereth, and Alon Y. Levy. Recursive query plans for data integration. *Journal of Logic Programming*, 43(1):49–73, 2000.
8. Ronald Fagin, Phokion G. Kolaitis, Renée J. Miller, and Lucian Popa. Data exchange: Semantics and query answering. In *Intl. Conf. on Database Theory (ICDT)*, 2003.
9. Daniela Florescu, Alon Y. Levy, Ioana Manolescu, and Dan Suciu. Query optimization in the presence of limited access patterns. In *SIGMOD*, pages 311–322, 1999.
10. J. Grant and J. Minker. A logic-based approach to data integration. *Theory and Practice of Logic Programming*, 2(3):323–368, 2002.
11. Alon Halevy. Answering queries using views: A survey. *VLDB Journal*, 10(4):270–294, 2001.
12. Christoph Koch. Query rewriting with symmetric constraints. *AI Communications*, 17(2), 2004. to appear.
13. Alon Y. Levy. Logic-based techniques in data integration. In Jack Minker, editor, *Workshop on Logic-Based Artificial Intelligence, Washington, DC*, 1999.
14. Alon Y. Levy, Anand Rajaraman, and Joann J. Ordille. Querying heterogeneous information sources using source descriptions. In *22nd Intl. Conf. on Very Large Data Bases (VLDB)*, pages 251–262, Bombay, India, 1996.

15. Chen Li. Computing complete answers to queries in the presence of limited access patterns. *Journal of VLDB*, 12:211–227, 2003.
16. Chen Li and Edward Y. Chang. On answering queries in the presence of limited access patterns. In *Intl. Conference on Database Theory (ICDT)*, 2001.
17. Todd D. Millstein, Alon Y. Levy, and Marc Friedman. Query containment for data integration systems. In *PODS*, pages 67–75, 2000.
18. Alan Nash and Bertram Ludäscher. Processing first-order queries under limited access patterns. In *PODS*, Paris, France, 2004.
19. Alan Nash and Bertram Ludäscher. Processing unions of conjunctive queries with negation under limited access patterns. In *Intl. Conference on Extending Database Technology (EDBT)*, Heraklion, Crete, Greece, 2004.
20. A. Rajaraman, Y. Sagiv, and J. D. Ullman. Answering queries using templates with binding patterns. In *PODS*, pages 105–112, 1995.
21. Yehoshua Sagiv and Mihalis Yannakakis. Equivalences among relational expressions with the union and difference operators. *Journal of the ACM*, 27(4):633–655, 1980.
22. Jeffrey Ullman. The complexity of ordering subgoals. In *PODS*, 1988.
23. Vasilis Vassalos and Yannis Papakonstantinou. Expressive capabilities description languages and query rewriting algorithms. *Journal of Logic Programming*, 43(1):75–122, 2000.

Optimal Workload-Based Weighted Wavelet Synopses

Yossi Matias and Daniel Urieli

School of Computer Science
Tel-Aviv University
{matias, daniel1}@tau.ac.il

Abstract. In recent years wavelets were shown to be effective data synopses. We are concerned with the problem of finding efficiently wavelet synopses for massive data sets, in situations where information about query workload is available. We present linear time, I/O optimal algorithms for building optimal workload-based wavelet synopses for point queries. The synopses are based on a novel construction of weighted inner-products and use weighted wavelets that are adapted to those products. The synopses are optimal in the sense that the subset of retained coefficients is the best possible for the bases in use with respect to either the mean-squared absolute or relative errors. For the latter, this is the first optimal wavelet synopsis even for the regular, non-workload-based case. Experimental results demonstrate the advantage obtained by the new optimal wavelet synopses, as well as the robustness of the synopses to deviations in the actual query workload.

1 Introduction

In recent years there has been increasing attention to the development and study of data synopses, as effective means for addressing performance issues in massive data sets. Data synopses are concise representations of data sets, that are meant to effectively support approximate queries to the represented data sets [10]. A primary constraint of a data synopsis is its size. The effectiveness of a data synopsis is measured by the accuracy of the answers it provides, as well as by its response time and its construction time. Several different synopses were introduced and studied, including random samples, sketches, and different types of histograms. Recently, wavelet-based synopses were introduced and shown to be a powerful tool for building effective data synopses for various applications, including selectivity estimation for query optimization in DBMS, approximate query processing in OLAP applications and more (see [17, 21, 22, 2, 6, 9, 8], and references therein).

The general idea of wavelet-based approximations is to transform a given data vector of size N into a representation with respect to a wavelet basis (this is called a *wavelet transform*), and approximate it using only $M \ll N$ wavelet basis vectors, by retaining only M coefficients from the linear combination that spans the data vector (*coefficients thresholding*). The linear combination that uses only M coefficients (and assumes that all other coefficients are zero) defines

T. Eiter and L. Libkin (Eds.): ICDT 2005, LNCS 3363, pp. 368–382, 2005.

a new vector that approximates the original vector, using less space. This is called *M-term approximation*, which defines a *wavelet synopsis* of size M.

Wavelet Synopses. Wavelets were traditionally used to compress some data sets where the purpose is to reconstruct, in a later time, an approximation of the *whole* data using the set of retained coefficients. The situation is a little different when using wavelets for building synopses in database systems [17]: in this case only *portions* of the data are reconstructed each time, in response to user queries, rather than the whole data at once. As a result, portions of the data that are used for answering frequent queries are reconstructed more frequently than portions of the data that correspond to rare queries. Therefore, the approximation error is measured over the *multi-set of actual queries*, rather than over the data itself. For more wavelet synopses basics see [17].

Another aspect of the use of wavelets in database systems is that due to the large data-sizes in databases (giga-, tera- and peta-bytes), the efficiency of building wavelet synopses is of primary importance. Disk I/Os should be minimized as much as possible, and non-linear-time algorithms may be unacceptable.

Optimal Wavelet Synopses. The main advantage of transforming the data into a representation with respect to a wavelet basis is that for data vectors containing similar values, many wavelet coefficients tend to have very small values. Thus, eliminating such small coefficients introduces only small errors when reconstructing the original data, resulting in a very effective form of lossy data compression.

Generally speaking, we can characterize a wavelet approximation by three attributes: how the approximation error is measured, what wavelet basis is used and how coefficient thresholding is done. Many bases were suggested and used in traditional wavelets literature. Given a basis with respect to which the transform is done, the selection of coefficients that are retained in the wavelet synopsis may have significant impact on the approximation error. The goal is therefore to select a subset of M coefficients that minimizes some approximation-error measure. This subset is called an *optimal wavelet synopsis*, with respect to the chosen error measure.

While there has been a considerable work on wavelet synopses and their applications [17, 21, 22, 2, 6, 14, 9, 8], so far there were only a few optimality results. The first one is a linear-time Parseval-based algorithm, which was used in traditional wavelets literature (e.g [12]), where the error was measured over the *data*. This algorithm minimizes the L_2 norm of the error vector, and equivalently it minimizes the mean-squared-absolute error over all possible point queries [17]. No algorithm that minimizes the mean-squared-relative error over all possible point queries was known. The second one, introduced recently [9], is a polynomial-time ($O(N^2 M \log M)$) algorithm that minimizes the max relative or max absolute error over all possible point queries. Another optimality result is a polynomial time dynamic-programming algorithm that obtains an optimal wavelet synopsis over multiple measures [6]. The synopsis is optimal w.r.t. an error metric defined as weighted combination of L_2 norms over the multiple measures (this weighted combination has no relation with the notion of weighted wavelets of this paper).

Workload-Based Wavelet Synopses. In recent years there is increased interest in workload-based synopses – synopses that are adapted to a given query workload, with the assumption that the workload represents (approximately) a probability distribution from which future queries will be taken. Chaudhuri et al [4] argue that identifying an appropriate precomputed sample that avoids large errors on an *arbitrary* query is virtually impossible. To minimize the effects of this problem, previous studies have proposed using the *workload* to guide the process of selecting samples [1, 3, 7]. By picking a sample that is tuned to the given workload, we can reduce the error over frequent (or otherwise "important") queries in the workload.

In [4], the authors formulate the problem of pre-computing a sample as an *optimization* problem, whose goal is to pick a sample that minimizes the error for the given workload.

Recently, *workload-based wavelet synopses* were proposed by Portman and Matias [14, 19]. Using an adaptive-greedy algorithm, the query-workload information was used during the thresholding process in order to build a wavelet synopsis that reduces the error w.r.t. to the query workload. These workload-based wavelet synopses demonstrate significant improvement with respect to prior synopses. They are, however, not optimal w.r.t. the query workload.

In this paper, we address the problem of finding efficiently *optimal* workload-based wavelet synopses.

1.1   Contributions

We introduce efficient algorithms for finding optimal workload-based wavelet synopses using *weighted Haar (WH)* wavelets, for workloads of point queries. Our main contributions are:

- Linear-time, I/O optimal algorithms that find optimal Workload-based Weighted Wavelet (WWW) synopses[1]:
  - An optimal synopsis w.r.t. workload-based mean-squared *absolute*-error (*WB-MSE*).
  - An optimal synopsis w.r.t. workload-based mean-squared *relative*-error (*WB-MRE*).
  Equivalently, the algorithms minimize the *expected* squared, absolute or relative errors over a point query taken from a given distribution.
- The *WB-MRE* algorithm, used with uniform workload, is also the first algorithm that minimizes the mean-squared-relative-error over the *data values*, with respect to a wavelet basis.
- Both WWW synopses are also optimal with respect to *enhanced wavelet synopses*, which allow changing the values of the synopses coefficients to arbitrary values.

---

[1] No relation whatsover to the world-wide-web.

- Experimental results show the advantage of our synopses with respect to existing synopses.
- The synopses are robust to deviation from the pre-defined workload, as demonstrated by our experiments.

The above results were obtained using the following novel techniques.

- We define the problem of finding optimal workload-based wavelet synopses in terms of a *weighted norm*, a *weighted-inner-product* and a *weighted-inner-product-space*. This enables linear time I/O optimal algorithms for building optimal workload-based wavelet synopses.
  The approach of using a weighted inner product can also be used to the general case in which each data point is given different priority, representing its significance. This generalization is used to obtain the optimal synopses for max relative error, where the weight of each point is normalized by its value. Using these weights, one can find a weighted-wavelet basis, and an optimal weighted wavelet synopsis in linear time, with $O(N/B)$ I/Os.
- We introduce the use of *weighted wavelets* for data synopses. Using weighted wavelets [5, 11] enables finding optimal workload-based wavelet synopses efficiently. In contrast, it is not known how to obtain optimal workload-based wavelet synopses with respect to the Haar basis efficiently. If we ignore the efficiency of finding a synopsis, the Haar basis is as good as the weighted Haar basis for approximation.

In the wavelets literature (e.g., [12]), wavelets are used to approximate a given signal, which is treated as a vector in an inner-product space. Since an inner-product defines an L_2 norm, the approximation error is measured as the L_2 norm of the error vector, which is the difference between the approximated vector and the approximating vector. Many wavelet bases were used for approximation, as different bases are adequate for approximating different collections of data vectors. By using an orthonormal wavelet basis, an optimal coefficient thresholding can be achieved in linear time, based on Parseval's formula. When using non-orthogonal wavelet basis, or measuring the error using other norms (e.g., L_∞), it is not known whether an optimal coefficient thresholding can be found efficiently, so usually non-optimal greedy algorithms are used in practice.

A weighted Haar (WH) basis is a generalization of the standard Haar basis, which is typically used for wavelet synopses due to its simplicity. There are several attributes by which a wavelet basis is characterized, which affects the quality of the approximations achieved using this basis (for full discussion, see [12]). These attribute are: the set of nested spaces of increasing resolution which the basis spans, the number of vanishing moments of the basis, and its compact support (if exists). Both Haar basis and a WH basis span the same subsets of nested spaces, have one vanishing moment, and a compact support of size 1.

Haar basis is orthonormal for uniform workload of point queries. Hence it is optimal for the MSE error measure. The WH basis is orthonormal with respect to the *weighted* inner-product defined by the problem of finding optimal workload-based wavelet synopses. As a result, an optimal workload-based synopses with respect to WH basis is achieved efficiently, based on Parseval's formula, while for the Haar basis no efficient optimal thresholding algorithm is known, in cases other than uniform workload.

1.2 Paper Outline

The rest of the paper is organized as follows. In Sec. 2 we describe our basic approach, including the workload-based error metrics and optimal thresholding in orthonormal bases. In Sec. 3 we define the problem of finding optimal workload-based wavelet synopses in terms of weighted inner product, and solve it using an orthonormal basis. In Sec. 4 we describe the optimal algorithm for minimizing *WB-MSE*, which is based on the construction of Sec. 3. In Sec. 5 we extend the algorithm to work for the *WB-MRE*, and in Sec. 6 we draw our conclusions. Due to space limitations, some technical proofs and additional experiments can be found in the full paper [16].

2 Basics

2.1 Workload-Based Error Metrics

Let $D = (d_0, ..., d_{N-1})$ be a sequence with $N = 2^j$ values. Denote the set of point queries as $Q = (q_0, ..., q_{N-1})$, where q_i is a query which its answer is d_i. Let a workload $W = (c_0, ..., c_{N-1})$ be a vector of weights that represents the probability distribution from which future point queries are to be generated. Let $(u_0, ..., u_{N-1})$ be a basis of R^N, than $D = \sum_{i=0}^{N} \alpha_i u_i$. We can represent D by a vector of coefficients $(\alpha_0, ..., \alpha_{N-1})$.

Suppose we want to approximate D using a subset of the coefficients $S \subset \{\alpha_0, ..., \alpha_{N-1}\}$ where $|S| = M$. Then, for any subset S we can define a weighted norm WL_2 with respect to S, that provides a measure for the errors expected for queries drawn from the probability distribution represented by W, when using S as a synopsis. S is then referred to as a *workload-based wavelet synopsis*.

Denote $\hat{d}_i$ as an approximation of d_i using S. There are two standard ways to measure the error over the i'th data value (equivalently, *point query*): *The absolute error*: $e_a(i) = e_a(q_i) = |d_i - \hat{d}_i|$; and *the relative error*: $e_r(i) = e_r(q_i) = \frac{|d_i - \hat{d}_i|}{max\{|d_i|, s\}}$, where s is a positive bound that prevents small values from dominating the relative error.

While the standard (non-workload-based) approach is to reduce the L_2 norm of the vector of errors $(e_1, ..., e_N)$ (where $e_i = e_a(i)$ or $e_i = e_r(i)$), here we would generalize the L_2 norm to reflect the query workload. Let W be a given *workload* consisting of a vector of queries' probabilities $c_1, ..., c_N$, where c_i is the probability that q_i occurs; that is, $0 < c_i \leq 1$, and $\sum_{i=0}^{N-1} c_i = 1$. The *weighted-L_2 norm* of the vector of (absolute or relative) errors $e = (e_1, ..., e_N)$ is defined as:

$$WL_2(e) = \|e\|_w = \sqrt{\sum_{i=0}^{N-1} c_i \cdot e_i^2}$$

where $0 < c_i \leq 1$, $\sum_{i=0}^{N-1} c_i = 1$. Thus, each data value d_i, or equivalently each point query q_i, is given some weight c_i that represents its significance. Note that WL_2 norm is the square-root of the mean squared error for a point query that is drawn from the given distribution. Thus, minimizing that norm of the error is equivalent to minimizing the *mean squared error of an answer to a query*.

In general, the weights given to data values need not necessarily represent a probability distribution of point queries, but any other significance measure. For example, in Sec. 5 we use weights to solve the problem of minimizing the mean-squared relative error measured over the *data values* (the non-workload-based case).

Notice that it is a generalization of the MSE norm: by taking equal weights for each query, meaning $c_i = \frac{1}{N}$ for each i and $e_i = e_a(i)$, we get the standard MSE norm. We use the term *workload-based error* for the WL_2 norm of the vector of errors e. When e_i are absolute (resp. relative) errors the workload-based error would be called the *WB-MSE* (resp. *WB-MRE*).

2.2 Optimal Thresholding in Orthonormal Bases

The construction is based on Parseval's formula, and a known theorem that results from it (Thm. 1).

Parseval's Formula. Let V be a vector space, where $v \in V$ is a vector and $\{u_0, ..., u_{N-1}\}$ is an orthonormal basis of V. We can express v as $v = \sum_{i=0}^{N-1} \alpha_i u_i$. Then

$$\|v\|^2 = \sum_{i=0}^{N-1} \alpha_i^2 \tag{1}$$

An M-term approximation is achieved by representing v using a subset of coefficients $S \subset \{\alpha_0, ..., \alpha_{N-1}\}$ where $|S| = M$. The error vector is than $e = \sum_{i \notin S} \alpha_i u_i$. By Parseval's formula, $\|e\|^2 = \sum_{i \notin S} \alpha_i^2$. This proves the following theorem.

Theorem 1 (Parseval-Based Optimal Thresholding). *Let V be a vector space, where $v \in V$ is a vector and $\{u_0, ..., u_{N-1}\}$ is an orthonormal basis of V. We can represent v by $\{\alpha_0, ..., \alpha_{N-1}\}$ where $v = \sum_{i=0}^{N-1} \alpha_i u_i$. Suppose we want to approximate v using a subset $S \subset \{\alpha_0, ..., \alpha_{N-1}\}$ where $|S| = M \ll N$. Picking the M largest coefficients to S minimizes the L_2 norm of the error vector, over all possible subsets of M coefficients.*

Given an inner-product, based on this theorem one can easily find an optimal synopses by choosing the largest M coefficients.

2.3 Optimality over Enhanced Wavelet Synopses

Notice that in the previous section we limited ourselves to picking subsets of coefficients with original values from the linear combination that spans v (as is usually done). In case $\{u_0, ..., u_{N-1}\}$ is a wavelet basis, these are the coefficients that results from the wavelet transform. We next show that the optimal thresh-olding according to Thm. 1 is optimal even according to an enhanced definition of M-term approximation. We define *enhanced wavelet synopses* as wavelet syn-opses that allow *arbitrary values* to the retained wavelet coefficients, rather than the original values that resulted from the transform. The set of possible standard synopses is a subset of the set of possible *enhanced* synopses, and therefore an optimal synopsis according to the standard definition is not necessarily optimal according to the enhanced definition.

Theorem 2. *When using an orthonormal basis, choosing the largest M coeffi-cients with original values is an optimal enhanced synopses.*

Proof. The proof is based on the fact that the basis is orthonormal. It is enough to show that given some synopsis of M coefficients with original values, any change to the values of some subset of coefficients in the synopsis would only make the approximation error larger:
Let $u_1, ..., u_N$ be an orthonormal basis and let $v = \alpha_1 u_1 + ... + \alpha_N u_N$ be the vector we would like to approximate by keeping only M wavelet coefficients. Without loss of generality, suppose we choose the first M coefficients and have the following approximation for v: $\tilde{v} = \sum_{i=1}^{M} \alpha_i u_i$. According to Parseval's for-mula $\|e\|^2 = \sum_{i=M+1}^{N} \alpha_i^2$ since the basis is orthonormal. Now suppose we would change the values of some subset of j retained coefficients to new values. Let us see that due to the orthonormality of the basis it would only make the error larger. Without loss of generality we would change the first j coefficients, mean-ing, we would change $\alpha_1, ..., \alpha_j$ to be $\alpha'_1, ..., \alpha'_j$. In this case the approximation would be $\tilde{v}' = \sum_{i=1}^{j} \alpha'_i u_i + \sum_{i=j+1}^{M} \alpha_i u_i$. The approximation error would be $v - \tilde{v}' = \sum_{i=1}^{j} (\alpha_i - \alpha'_i) u_i + \sum_{i=M+1}^{N} \alpha_i u_i$. It is easy to see that the error of ap-proximation would be: $\|e\|^2 = \langle v - \tilde{v}', v - \tilde{v}' \rangle = \sum_{i=1}^{j} (\alpha_i - \alpha'_i)^2 + \sum_{i=M+1}^{N} \alpha_i^2 > \sum_{i=M+1}^{N} \alpha_i^2$.

3   The Workload-Based Inner Product

In this section, we define the problem of finding an optimal workload-based synopses in terms of a weighted-inner-product space, and solve it relying on this construction. Here we deal with the case where e_i are the absolute errors (the algorithm minimizes the *WB-MSE*). An extension to relative errors (*WB-MRE*) is introduced in Sec. 5
Our development is as follows:

1. Transforming the data vector D into an equivalent representation as a func-tion f in a space of piecewise constant functions over $[0, 1)$. (Sec. 3.1)
2. Defining the *workload-based inner product*. (Sec. 3.2)
3. Using the inner product to define an L_2 norm, showing that the newly defined norm is equivalent to the *weighted L_2 norm* (*WL_2*). (Sec. 3.3)

4. Defining a *weighted Haar basis* which is orthonormal with respect to the new inner product. (Sec. 3.4)

Based on Thm. 1 and Thm. 2 one can easily find an optimal workload-based wavelet synopses with respect to a weighted Haar wavelet basis.

3.1 Transforming the Data Vector into a Piecewise Constant Function

We assume that our approximated data vector D is of size $N = 2^j$. As in [20], we treat sequences (vectors) of 2^j points as piecewise constant functions defined on the half-open interval $[0, 1)$. In order to do so, we will use the concept of a vector space from linear algebra. A sequence of one point is just a function that is constant over the entire interval $[0, 1)$; we'll let V_0 be the space of all these functions. A sequence of 2 points is a function that has two constant parts over the intervals $[0, \frac{1}{2})$ and $[\frac{1}{2}, 1)$. We'll call the space containing all these functions V_1. If we continue in this manner, the space V_j will include all piecewise constant functions on the interval $[0, 1)$, with the interval divided equally into 2^j different sub-intervals. We can now think of every one-dimensional sequence D of 2^j values as being an element, or vector f, in V_j.

3.2 Defining a Workload-Based Inner Product

The first step is to choose an inner product defined on the vector space V_j. Since we want to minimize a *workload based error* (and not the regular L_2 error), we started by defining a new *workload based inner product*. The new inner product is a generalization of the standard inner product. It is a sum of $N = 2^j$ weighted standard products; each of them is defined over an interval of size $\frac{1}{N}$:

$$\langle f, g \rangle = N \cdot \left(\sum_{i=0}^{N-1} c_i \int_{\frac{i}{N}}^{\frac{i+1}{N}} f(x)\, g(x)\, dx \right) \ \textit{where } 0 < c_i \le 1, \ \sum_{i=0}^{N-1} c_i = 1 \quad (2)$$

Lemma 1. $\langle f, g \rangle$ *is an inner product.*

The proof of the lemma can be found in the full paper. As mentioned before, a coefficient c_i represents the probability (or a weight) for the i'th point query (q_i) to appear. Notice that the answer of which is the ith data value, which is function value at the i'th interval. When all coefficients c_i are equal to $\frac{1}{N}$ (a uniform distribution of queries), we get the standard inner product, and therefore this is a generalization of the standard inner product.

3.3 Defining a Norm Based on the Inner Product

Based on that inner product we define an inner-product-based (IPB) norm:

$$\|f\|_{\text{IPB}} = \sqrt{\langle f, f \rangle} \quad (3)$$

Lemma 2. *The norm* $\|f\|_{\text{IPB}}$ *measured over the vector of absolute errors is the weighted L_2 norm of this vector, i.e* $\|e\|^2_{\text{IPB}} = \sum_{i=0}^{N-1} c_i e_i^2 = \|e\|^2_{\text{w}}$.

The proof of the lemma can be found in the full paper. Notice that when all coefficients are equal to $\frac{1}{N}$ we get the regular L_2 norm, and therefore this is a generalization of the regular L_2 norm (MSE).
Our goal is to minimize the *workload based error* which is the WL_2 norm of the vector of errors.

3.4   Defining an Orthonormal Basis

At this stage we would like to use Thm. 1. The next step would thus be finding an orthonormal (with respect to a workload based inner product) wavelet basis for the space V_j. The basis is a *Weighted Haar Basis*. For each workload-based inner product (defined by a given query workload) there is corresponding orthonormal weighted Haar basis, and our algorithm finds this basis in linear time, given the workload of point queries. We describe the bases here, and see how to find a basis based on a given workload of point queries. We will later use this information in the algorithmic part.

In order to build a weighted Haar basis, we take the Haar basis functions and for the k'th basis function we multiply its positive (resp. negative) part by some x_k (resp. y_k). We would like to choose such x_k and y_k so that we get an orthonormal basis with respect to our inner product. Thus, instead of using Haar basis functions (Fig. 1), we use functions of the kind illustrated in Fig. 2, where x_k and y_k are not necessarily (and probably not) equal, so our basis looks like the one in (Fig. 3). One needs to show how to choose x_k and y_k.

Let u_k be some Haar basis function as described above. Let $[a_{k_0}, a_{k_1})$ be the interval over which the basis function is positive and let $[a_{k_1}, a_{k_2})$ be the interval over which the function is negative. Recall that a_{k_0}, a_{k_1} and a_{k_2} are both multiples of $\frac{1}{N}$ and therefore the interval precisely contains some number of continuous intervals of the form $[\frac{i}{N}, \frac{i+1}{N}]$ (also $a_{k_1} = \frac{a_{k_0}+a_{k_2}}{2}$). Moreover, the size of the interval over which the function is positive (resp. negative) is $\frac{1}{2^i}$ for some $i < j$ (As we remember, $N = 2^j$). Recall that for the i'th interval of size $\frac{1}{N}$, meaning $[\frac{i}{N}, \frac{i+1}{N})$ there is a corresponding weight coefficient c_i which is the coefficient that is used in the inner product. Notice that each Haar basis func-

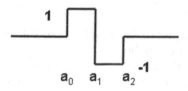

Fig. 1. An example for a Haar basis function

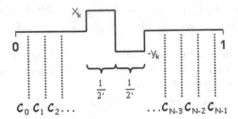

Fig. 2. An example for a Weighted Haar Basis function

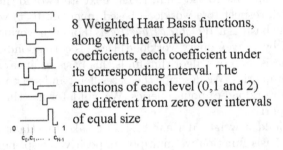

8 Weighted Haar Basis functions, along with the workload coefficients, each coefficient under its corresponding interval. The functions of each level (0,1 and 2) are different from zero over intervals of equal size

Fig. 3. The weighted Haar Basis along with the workload coefficients

tion is positive (negative) over some number of (whole) such intervals. We can therefore associate the sum of coefficients of the intervals "under" the positive (negative) part of the function with the positive (negative) part of the function. Let us denote the sum of weight coefficients (c_i's) corresponding to intervals that are under the positive (resp. negative) as l_k (resp. r_k).

Lemma 3. *Suppose for each Haar basis function v_k we choose x_k and y_k such that*

$$x_k = \sqrt{\frac{r_k}{l_k r_k + l_k^2}} \quad y_k = \sqrt{\frac{l_k}{l_k r_k + r_k^2}}$$

and multiply the positive (resp. negative) part of v_k by x_k (resp. y_k); by doing that we get an orthonormal set of $N = 2^j$ functions, meaning we get an orthonormal basis.

The proof of the lemma can be found in the full paper. Again, notice that had all the workload coefficients been equal ($c_i = \frac{1}{N}$) we would get the standard Haar basis used to minimize the standard L_2 norm.

As we have seen, this is an orthonormal basis to our function space. In order to see that it is a wavelet basis, we can notice that for each $k = 1, ..., j$, the first 2^k functions are an orthonormal set belonging to V_k (its dimension is 2^k) and which is therefore a basis of V_k.

4   The Algorithm for the WWW Transform

In this section we describe the algorithmic part. Given a workload of point queries and a data vector to be approximated, we build workload-based wavelet synopses of the data vector using a weighted Haar basis. The algorithm has two parts:

1. Computing efficiently a *Weighted Haar basis*, given a workload of point queries. (Sec. 4.1)
2. Computing efficiently the *Weighted Haar Wavelet Transform* with respect to the chosen basis. (Sec. 4.2)

4.1   Computing Efficiently a Weighted Haar Basis

Note that at this point we already have a method to find an orthonormal basis with respect to a given workload based inner product. Recall that in order to know x_k and y_k for every basis function we need to know the corresponding l_k and r_k. We are going to compute all those partial sums in linear time. Suppose that the basis functions are arranged in an array like in a binary tree representation. The highest resolution functions are at indexes $\frac{N}{2}, ..., N - 1$, which are the lowest level of the tree. The next resolution level functions are at indexes $\frac{N}{4}, ..., \frac{N}{2} - 1$, and so on, until the constant basis function is in index 0. Notice that for the lowest level (highest resolution) functions (indexes $\frac{N}{2}, ..., N - 1$) we already have their l_k's and r_k's. These are exactly the workload coefficients. It can be easily seen in Fig. 3 for the lower four functions. Notice that after computing the accumulated sums for the functions at resolution level i, we have all the information to compute the higher level functions: let u_k be a function at resolution level i and u_{2k}, u_{2k+1} be at level $i + 1$, where their supports included in u_k's support (u_k is their ancestor in the binary tree of functions). We can use the following formula for computing l_k and r_k:

$$l_k = l_{2k} + r_{2k} \quad r_k = l_{2k+1} + r_{2k+1}$$

See Fig. 3. Thus, we can compute in one pass only the lowest level, and build the upper levels bottom-up (in a way somewhat similar to the Haar wavelet transform). The algorithm consists of phases, where in each phase the functions of a specific level are computed. At the end of a phase, we keep a temporary array holding all the pairwise sums of all the l_k's and r_k's from that phase and use them for computing the next phase functions. Clearly, the running time is $\frac{N}{2} + \frac{N}{4} + ... + 1 = O(N)$. The number of I/Os is $O(N/B)$ I/Os (where B is the block size of the disk) – since the process is similar to the computation Haar wavelet transform. Recall that given r_k and l_k, one can easily compute the k'th basis function (its positive and negative parts) using the following formula:

$$x_k = \sqrt{\frac{r_k}{l_k r_k + l_k^2}} \quad y_k = \sqrt{\frac{l_k}{l_k r_k + r_k^2}}$$

4.2   Computing a Weighted Haar Wavelet Transform

Given the basis we would like to efficiently perform the wavelet transform with respect to that basis. Let us look at the case of $N = 2$ (Fig. 4). Suppose we would like to represent the function in Fig. 5. It is easy to compute the following result (denote α_i as the coefficient of f_i):

$$\alpha_0 = \frac{yv_0 + xv_1}{x + y} \qquad \alpha_1 = \frac{v_0 - v_1}{x + y}$$

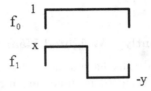

Fig. 4. An example for the Weighted Haar Transform

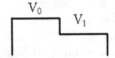

Fig. 5. A simple function with 2 values over $[0, 1)$

(by solving 2x2 matrix). Notice that the coefficients are weighted averages and differences, since the transform generalizes the standard Haar transform (by taking $x = y = \sqrt{2^i}$ we get the standard Haar transform). It's easy to reconstruct the original function from the coefficients:

$$v_0 = \alpha_0 + x\alpha_1 \qquad v_1 = \alpha_0 - y\alpha_1$$

This implies a straightforward method to compute the wavelet transform (which is I/O efficient as well) according to the way we compute a regular wavelet transform with respect to the Haar basis: we go over the data, and compute the weighted differences which are the coefficients of the bottom level functions. We keep the weighted averages, which can be represented *solely* by the rest of the basis functions (the "lower resolution" functions - as in the regular Haar wavelet transform), in another array. We repeat the process over the averages time and time again until we have the overall average, which is added to our array as the coefficient of the constant function ($v_0(x) = const$). While computing the transform, in addition to reading the values of the signal, we need to read the proper basis function that is relevant for the current stage (in order to use the x_k and y_k of the function that is employed in the above formula). This is easy to do, since all the functions are stored in an array F and the index of a function is determined by the iteration number and is identical to the index of the corresponding currently computed coefficient. A pseudo code of the algorithm can be found in the full paper.

The steps of our algorithm are identical to the steps of the Haar algorithm, with the addition of reading the data at $F[i]$ (the x_k and y_k of the function) during the i'th iteration. Therefore the I/O complexity of that phase remains $O(N/B)$ (B is the disk block size) with $O(N)$ running time.

After obtaining the coefficient of the orthonormal basis we keep the largest M coefficients, along with their corresponding M functions, and throw the smallest coefficients. This can be done efficiently using an *M-approximate quantile algorithm* [13]. Based on Thm. 1 we obtain an optimal synopsis.

5   Optimal Synopsis for Mean Relative Error

We show how to minimize the weighted L_2 norm of the vector of *relative* errors, weighted by the query workload, by using weighted wavelets. As a special case, this minimizes the mean-squared-relative-error measured over the data values.

Recall that in order to minimize the weighted L_2 norm of relative errors, we need to minimize $\sum_{i=1}^{N} c_i \left(\frac{|d_i - \hat{d}_i|}{max\{d_i, s\}} \right)^2$. For simplicity, we show instead how to minimize $\sum_{i=1}^{N} c_i \left(\frac{|d_i - \hat{d}_i|}{d_i} \right)^2$; the extension to the above is straightforward. Since $n - d_1, ..., d_N$ is part of the input of the algorithm, it is fixed throughout the algorithm's execution. We can thus divide each c_i by d_i^2 and get a new vector of weights: $W = \left(\frac{c_1}{d_1^2}, ..., \frac{c_N}{d_N^2} \right)$. Relying on our previous results, and using the new vector of weights we minimize $\sum_{i=1}^{N} \frac{c_i}{d_i^2} \left(|d_i - \hat{d}_i| \right)^2 = \sum_{i=1}^{N} c_i \left(\frac{|d_i - \hat{d}_i|}{d_i} \right)^2$, which is the WL_2 norm of relative errors. Notice that in the case $b_i = \frac{1}{N}$ (the uniform case) the algorithm minimizes the mean-relative-error over all *data values*. As far as we know, this is the first algorithm that minimizes the mean-relative-error over the data values.

6   Conclusions

In this paper we introduce the use of weighted wavelets for building optimal workload-based wavelet synopses. We present two time-optimal and I/O-optimal algorithms for workload-based wavelet synopses, which minimize the WB-MSE and and the WB-MRE error measures, with respect to any given query workload. The advantage of optimal workload-based wavelet synopses, as well as their robustness, were demonstrated by experimentations (in the full paper).

Recently, and independently of our work, Muthukrishnan [18] presented an optimal workload-based wavelet synopsis with respect to the standard *Haar* basis. The algorithm for building the optimal synopsis is based on dynamic programming and takes $O(N^2 M / \log M)$ time. As noted above, standard Haar basis is not orthonormal w.r.t. the workload-based error metric, and an optimal synopsis w.r.t. this basis is not necessarily also an optimal enhanced wavelet synopsis. Obtaining optimal enhanced wavelet synopses for the standard Haar wavelets may be an interesting open problem. Also, as quadratic time is too costly for massive data sets, it may be interesting to obtain a time efficient algorithm for such synopses. As far as approximation error is concerned, although in general optimal synopses w.r.t. the standard Haar and the weighted Haar bases are incomparable, both bases have the same characteristics. It would be interesting to compare the actual approximation errors of the two synopses for various data sets. This may indeed be the subject of a future work.

In a recent related paper [15], we show how to find optimal wavelet synopses for range-sum queries, using a framework similar to the one used in this paper. We define the problem of finding an optimal synopsis for range-sum queries in terms of a proper inner-product, and find an optimal synopsis, which minimizes the MSE measured over all possible range-sum queries, in linear time, with $O(N/B)$ I/Os.

Acknowledgments. We thank Leon Portman for helpful discussions and for his assistance in setting up the experiments on the τ-synopses system. We also thank Prof. Nira Dyn for helpful discussions regarding the wavelets theory.

References

1. A. Aboulnaga and S. Chaudhuri. Self-tuning histograms: Building histograms without looking at data. In *Proceedings of the 1999 ACM SIGMOD International Conference on Management of Data*, pages 181–192, 1999.
2. K. Chakrabarti, M. Garofalakis, R. Rastogi, and K. Shim. Approximate query processing using wavelets. In *VLDB 2000, Proceedings of 26th International Conference on Very Large Data Bases, 2000*, pages 111–122.
3. S. Chaudhuri, G. Das, M. Datar, R. Motwani, , and V. R. Narasayya. Overcoming limitations of sampling for aggregation queries. In *ICDE*, pages 534–542, 2001.
4. S. Chaudhuri, G. Das, and V. Narasayya. A robust, optimization-based approach for approximate answering of aggregate queries. In *Proceedings of the 2001 ACM SIGMOD international conference on on Management of data*, 2001.
5. R. R. Coifman, P. W. Jones, , and S. Semmes. Two elementary proofs of the l2 boundedness of cauchy integrals on lipschitz curves. *J. Amer. Math. Soc.*, 2(3):553–564, 1989.
6. A. Deligiannakis and N. Roussopoulos. Extended wavelets for multiple measures. In *Proceedings of the 2003 ACM SIGMOD International Conference on Management of Data*, pages 229–240.
7. V. Ganti, M.-L. Lee, and R. Ramakrishnan. Icicles: Self-tuning samples for approximate query answering. *The VLDB Journal*, pages 176–187, 2000.
8. M. Garofalakis and P. B. Gibbons. Wavelet synopses with error guarantees. In *Proceedings of the 2002 ACM SIGMOD International Conference on Management of Data*, 2002.
9. M. Garofalakis and A. Kumar. Deterministic wavelet thresholding for maximum-error metrics. In *Proceedings of the 2004 ACM SIGMOD international conference on on Management of data*, pages 166–176.

10. P. B. Gibbons and Y. Matias. Synopsis data structures for massive data sets. In *DIMACS: Series in Discrete Mathematics and Theoretical Computer Science: Special Issue on External Memory Algorithms and Visualization, A*, 1999.

11. M. Girardi and W. Sweldens. A new class of unbalanced Haar wavelets that form an unconditional basis for L_p on general measure spaces. *J. Fourier Anal. Appl.*, 3(4), 1997.

12. S. Mallat. *A Wavelet Tour of Signal Processing*. Academic Press, 2nd edition, 1999.

13. G. S. Manku, S. R., and B. G. Lindsay. Approximate medians and other quantiles in one pass and with limited memory. In *Proceedings of the 1998 ACM SIGMOD International Conference on Management of Data*, pages 426–435, New York, 1998.

14. Y. Matias and L. Portman. Workload-based wavelet synopses. Technical report, Department of Computer Science,Tel Aviv University, 2003.

15. Y. Matias and D. Urieli. Optimal wavelet synopses for range-sum queries. Technical report, Department of Computer Science, Tel-Aviv University, 2004.

16. Y. Matias and D. Urieli. Optimal workload-based weighted wavelet synopses. Technical report, Department of Computer Science, Tel-Aviv University, 2004.

17. Y. Matias, J. S. Vitter, and M. Wang. Wavelet-based histograms for selectivity estimation. In *Proceedings of the 1998 ACM SIGMOD International Conference on Management of Data*, pages 448–459, Seattle, WA, June 1998.

18. S. Muthukrishnan. Workload-optimal wavelet synopsis. Technical report, May 2004.

19. L. Portman. Workload-based wavelet synopses. M.sc thesis, Tel Aviv University, 2003.

20. E. J. Stollnitz, T. D. Derose, and D. H. Salesin. *Wavelets for Computer Graphics*. Morgan Kaufmann, 1996.

21. J. S. Vitter and M. Wang. Approximate computation of multidimensional aggregates of sparse data using wavelets. In *Proceedings of the 1999 ACM SIGMOD International Conference on Management of Data*, pages 193–204, Phildelphia, June 1999.

22. J. S. Vitter, M. Wang, and B. Iyer. Data cube approximation and histograms via wavelets. In *Proceedings of Seventh International Conference on Information and Knowledge Management*, pages 96–104, Washington D.C., November 1998.

Selecting and Using Views
to Compute Aggregate Queries
(Extended Abstract)

Foto Afrati[1] and Rada Chirkova[2]

[1] Electrical and Computing Eng., National Technical University of Athens,
157 73 Athens, Greece
[2] Computer Science Department, North Carolina State University,
Raleigh, NC 27695, USA**

Abstract. We consider a workload of aggregate queries and investigate
the problem of selecting views that (1) provide equivalent rewritings for
all queries, and (2) are optimal, in that the cost of evaluating the query
workload is minimized. We consider conjunctive views and rewritings,
with or without aggregation; in each rewriting, only one view contributes
to computing the aggregated query output. We look at query rewriting
using existing views and at view selection. In the query-rewriting problem, we give sufficient and necessary conditions for a rewriting to exist.
For view selection, we prove complexity results. Finally, we give algorithms for obtaining rewritings and selecting views.

1   Introduction

The problem of using materialized views to answer queries is of interest in many
applications. Using materialized views to compute aggregate queries results in
potentially greater benefits than for purely conjunctive queries, as a view with aggregation precomputes some of the grouping/aggregation on some of the query's
subgoals. Because aggregate queries are often computed on large volumes of
stored data, in many applications it is beneficial to use previously cached results
as views to answer a new query [1, 2, 3].

We consider the problem of selecting views to minimize query-evaluation
costs, for aggregate queries and rewritings. In solving this problem, the first issue we need to address is what types of query rewritings using views should be
considered. As it turns out, finding rewritings for aggregate queries introduces
additional complications when compared to finding rewritings for conjunctive
queries without aggregation. Thus, in this paper we address two problems: first,
how to answer aggregate queries using aggregate views by constructing equivalent rewritings; second, how to optimally select aggregate views to materialize,
for use in those rewritings. In taking the first problem, we consider central rewritings, that is, rewritings that use at most one aggregate view. This is a natural

** This author's work on this material has been supported by the National Science
Foundation under Grant No. 0307072.

T. Eiter and L. Libkin (Eds.): ICDT 2005, LNCS 3363, pp. 383–397, 2005.

choice in many applications; for instance, in the star-schema framework the fact table provides the aggregate view and the dimension tables provide the other views in the rewritings [1, 4]. In the second problem, we base our view selection on a cost model that has been used in various previous work for restricted types of rewritings (see, e.g., [2, 5]). We now illustrate our approach with an example.

Example 1. Consider a database with three relations, relation P that stores transactions and relations T and W that store information about store branches: *P(storeId, product, salePrice, profit, dayOfSale, monthOfSale, yearOfSale);* *T(storeId, storeChain); W(storeId, storeCity)*. Suppose query Q_1 gives maximal profit per store chain per product for the year 2004, and Q_2 gives total sales per product per year per city, for all stores. Here is a SQL definition of Q_2:

```
SELECT product, yearOfSale, storeCity, sum(salePrice)
FROM P, W
WHERE P.storeId = W.storeId
GROUP BY product, yearOfSale, storeCity;
```

These two queries can be rewritten using a single multiaggregate view. In our datalog rule notation the queries, the view and the rewritings can be written as:

$$q_1(S, Y, max(T)) \qquad :- p(X, Y, Z, T, N, L, 2004), t(X, S).$$
$$q_2(Y, M, U, sum(Z)) \qquad :- p(X, Y, Z, T, N, L, M), w(X, U).$$
$$v_1(X, Y, M, sum(Z), max(T)) :- p(X, Y, Z, T, N, L, M).$$
$$q_1'(S, Y, max(K)) \qquad :- v_1(X, Y, 2004, F, K), t(X, S).$$
$$q_2'(Y, M, U, sum(J)) \qquad :- v_1(X, Y, M, J, K), w(X, U).$$

In each rewriting, multiaggregate view V_1 is the only subgoal that contributes to the computation of the aggregation; we call it *central view*. Note that V_1 can be used as a central view to rewrite both queries.

In this paper, we first establish how to obtain rewritings that use one central view — we call them *central rewritings*. Then we study how to select a central view given a query workload, such that the view can be used to rewrite as many workload queries as possible, such as view V_1 in the above example. We study the complexity of the view-selection problem under a very general cost model.

Our formalism uses datalog to express aggregate queries, views, and rewritings, but note that it is only a convenience. It is easy and straightforward to translate any SQL query with aggregation to a datalog query with aggregation; the semantics also carry over trivially. Thus, all our results are about standard SQL aggregate queries and can be extended to queries with HAVING.

In constructing rewritings, we use a uniform framework for aggregate functions *sum, count, max,* and *min*. The framework is extensible to other aggregate functions with general algebraic properties, such as duplicate insensitive or distributive [6, 7]. We show that conjunctive views can be used in rewritings, and we explore when bag-set or bag semantics are needed. By obtaining both positive and negative results, we present a complete characterization of the cases where "simple" rewritings can be obtained — that is, conjunctive rewritings without aggregation. For the view-selection problem, we study the complexity of the problem for our rewritings and rewritings in the literature. We present algorithms for constructing rewritings and for selecting views to materialize. Both algorithms are based on our results obtained on properties of rewritings.

The structure of this paper is as follows. Section 2 defines aggregate queries and equivalence among aggregate queries. Section 3 presents our framework, in particular the types of rewritings we consider and the cost model for view selection. In Section 4 we prove necessary and sufficient conditions for a type of rewriting to exist and provide negative results. In Section 5 we prove that the view-selection problem is NP-complete for *sum*, *count*, and provide an exponential-time lower bound on the complexity of view selection for *max*, *min*. In Section 6 we give algorithms for obtaining rewritings given a query and views and for selecting central views given a query workload.

Related Work

Recent work [8, 9] has considered the problem of rewriting a query with aggregation and arithmetic comparisons using multiple views with aggregation. Complete algorithms are obtained for constructing rewritings that use multiplication within an aggregate operator and use aggregate views in the body of the rewritings. Our central rewritings have a simpler syntax and can be translated into the rewriting templates of [8, 9] using straightforward transformations. The major differences in our rewritings are that (1) we do not consider comparisons, and (2) we use bag-valued views in our rewritings, while [8, 9] use count-views in their rewritings. Difference (2) allows us to simplify the heads of our rewritings and to avoid the multiplication needed in the heads of the rewritings of [8, 9]. In addition, we show negative results and use them to argue that our algorithms find a rewriting with a simple syntax whenever there exists one.

On view selection, considerable work has been done in efficiently selecting views in the datacube context (e.g., [1, 2]), where the focus is on getting efficient algorithms for selecting views to materialize for important special cases of the problem; thus, rewritings using a single view subgoal were considered. In this paper we focus on obtaining results on the complexity of the view-selection problem for central rewritings. Complexity results for the view-selection problem for conjunctive queries and views without aggregation were presented in [5]. To the best of our knowledge, our approach is the first to address the problem of view selection for aggregate queries considering rewritings with multiple view subgoals and multiaggregate views.

The problems of rewriting queries using views and of view selection for aggregate queries have been considered in the context of data warehousing and data cubes [7, 10]. In most cases, the problem considered was to answer each query (or part of a query) using a single view [1, 2, 3, 6, 11]. Other related work on aggregate query rewriting includes [12], which considers rewriting aggregate queries using multiple aggregate views over a single relation, and [13], which presents fast algorithms for computing the cube operator. [14] considers the problem of using aggregate views to compute queries in temporal databases. Work related to query languages with aggregate capabilities includes [15, 16, 17, 18].

Finally, it is known that the problem of query rewriting is closely related to query containment and equivalence. Results on equivalence of aggregate queries are presented in [8, 19], which establish that checking the equivalence of unions of *sum* or *count*-queries is GI-hard and in PSPACE. (GI is the class of problems that are many-one reducible to the graph isomorphism problem.) [8] shows that checking equivalence of unions of *max*-queries is Π_2^p-complete, whereas checking equivalence of unions of conjunctive queries without aggregation is NP-complete.

2   Preliminaries

In this section we provide definitions and technical background for our framework. Many of the definitions are taken from [8], which introduced aggregate queries in a datalog syntax.

A *relational database* is a collection of stored relations. Each relation R is a collection of tuples; each tuple is a list of values of the attributes in the *relation schema* of R. The schemas of the relations in a database constitute its *database schema*. A relation is viewed as either a set or a bag (a.k.a. multiset) of tuples. A bag can be thought of as a set of elements (the *core-set* of the bag) with multiplicities attached to each element. In a *set-valued database*, all stored relations are sets; in a *bag-valued database*, multiset stored relations are allowed.

A *query* is a mapping from databases to databases, usually specified by a logical formula on the schema S of the input databases. Typically, the output database (the *query answer*) is a database with a single relation. A *conjunctive query* is definable by a positive existential first-order formula, with conjunctions as its only Boolean connective. Conjunctive queries are usually written as rules of this form: $q(\bar{s}) \; : - \; p_1(\bar{s}_1), \ldots, p_k(\bar{s}_k)$, where $q(\bar{s})$ is the *head* of the query, and the conjunction $p_1(\bar{s}_1), \ldots, p_k(\bar{s}_k)$ is its *body*. In each subgoal (or *atom*) $p_i(\bar{s}_i)$, predicate p_i corresponds to a stored relation with schema in S, and every argument is either a variable or a constant. The variables in $\bar{s}$ are called *head* (or *distinguished*) *variables* of q, and the variables in each $\bar{s}_i$ are called *body variables* of q. The body variables of q that are not its head variables are called *nondistinguished variables* of q. We consider *safe* queries; a conjunctive query q is safe if all its distinguished variables are also among its body variables.

We denote the body of a conjunctive query by A. An *assignment* γ for A is a mapping of the variables appearing in A to constants, and of the constants appearing in A to themselves. Assignments are naturally extended to tuples and atoms; for instance, for a tuple of variables $\bar{s} = (s_1, \ldots, s_k)$ we let $\gamma\bar{s}$ denote the tuple $(\gamma(s_1), \ldots, \gamma(s_k))$. *Satisfaction* of atoms by an assignment w.r.t a database is defined as follows: $p_i(\gamma\bar{s})$ is satisfied if the tuple $\gamma\bar{s}$ is in the relation that corresponds to the predicate of subgoal p_i. This definition is naturally extended to that of satisfaction of conjunctions of atoms.

Under *set semantics*, a conjunctive query $q(\bar{s}) \leftarrow A$ defines a new relation $q^{\mathcal{D}}$, for a given set database $\mathcal{D}$, as follows: $q^{\mathcal{D}} := \{\gamma\bar{s} \mid \gamma \text{ satisfies } A \text{ w.r.t. } \mathcal{D}\}$. Under *bag-set semantics* [20], a conjunctive query $q(\bar{s}) \leftarrow A$ defines a new bag (multiset) relation $\{\!\{q\}\!\}^{\mathcal{D}}$, for a given set database $\mathcal{D}$, as follows: $\{\!\{q\}\!\}^{\mathcal{D}} := \{\!\{\gamma\bar{s} \mid \gamma$ satisfies A w.r.t. $\mathcal{D}\}\!\}$. We say that the query is computed under *bag semantics* [20] if both the input database and the answer are bags. In this case, the collection of satisfying assignments is viewed as a multiset. We say that a query is *set-valued* if it is computed under set semantics, and is *bag-valued* otherwise.

We define query equivalence under each of the three types of semantics. Two queries are *set-equivalent* (*bag-set-equivalent*, *bag-equivalent*, respectively) if they produce the same set (bag, respectively) of answers on every database (every set database for the first two cases, every bag database for the third case). When we compute a query, we will say whether we compute it *as a bag* or *as a set*, unless obvious from the context.

We assume that the data we want to aggregate are real numbers, $\mathbf{R}$. If S is a set, then $\mathcal{M}(S)$ denotes the set of finite multisets over S. A *k-ary aggregate function* is a function $\alpha : \mathcal{M}(\mathbf{R}^k) \rightarrow \mathbf{R}$ that maps multisets of k-tuples of real numbers to real numbers. An *aggregate term* is an expression built up using variables and aggregate functions. Every aggregate term with k variables gives rise to a k-ary aggregate function in a natural way.

We use $\alpha(y)$ as an abstract notation for a unary aggregate term, where y is the variable in the term. The aggregate queries that we consider here have the (unary or 0-ary) aggregate functions *count*, *count*(∗), *sum*, *max*, and *min*. Note that *count* is over an argument whereas *count*(∗) is the only function that we consider here that takes no argument. (There is a distinction in SQL semantics between *count* and *count*(∗).) In the rest of the paper, we will not refer again to the distinction between *count* and *count*(∗), as our results carry over.

An *aggregate query* [8, 19] is a conjunctive query augmented by an aggregate term in its head. For a query with a k-ary aggregate function α, the syntax is:

$$q(\bar{s}, \alpha(\bar{y})) \leftarrow A . \tag{1}$$

Here, A is a conjunction of atoms, see definition of conjunctive query; $\alpha(\bar{y})$ is a k-ary aggregate term; $\bar{s}$ are the *grouping attributes* of q; none of the variables in $\bar{y}$ appears among $\bar{s}$. Finally, q is *safe*: all variables in $\bar{s}$ and $\bar{y}$ occur in A. In this paper we consider aggregate queries with unary aggregate functions *sum*, *count*, *max*, and *min*.

With each aggregate query q (Eq. 1) we associate its conjunctive *core* $\check{q}$:[1]

$$\check{q}(\bar{s}, \bar{y}) \leftarrow A . \tag{2}$$

We define the semantics of an aggregate query as follows: Let $\mathcal{D}$ be a database and q an aggregate query as in Equation 1. When q is applied on $\mathcal{D}$ it yields a relation $q^{\mathcal{D}}$ that is defined by the following three steps: First, we compute the core $\check{q}$ on $\mathcal{D}$ as a bag B. We then form equivalence classes in B. Two tuples belong to the same equivalence class if they agree on the values of the grouping arguments of q. This is the *grouping* step. The third step is *aggregation*; it associates with

---

[1] The core of a *count*(∗)-query has just the grouping arguments $\bar{s}$ in the head.

each equivalence class a value that is the aggregate function computed on a bag which contains all values of the input argument(s) of the aggregated attribute(s) in this class. For each class, it returns one tuple which contains the values of the grouping arguments of q and the computed aggregated value.

An aggregate function α is *duplicate-insensitive* [6] if the result of α computed over a bag of values is the same as the result of α computed over the core set of the bag. Otherwise α is *duplicate-sensitive*. We say that an aggregate function α is *distributive* [7] if there is a function γ such that $\alpha(\{\!\{X_{ij}\}\!\}) = \gamma(\{\!\{\alpha(\{\!\{X_{ij}\}\!\}) \mid i = 1,\ldots,I) \mid j = 1,\ldots,J\}\!\})$. All the functions we consider are distributive. In fact, for all α, $\gamma = \alpha$, except that for *count*, $\gamma = sum$.

Now we define equivalence between aggregate queries. In general, two aggregate queries with different aggregate functions may be equivalent [8]. In this paper we consider equivalence between queries with the same aggregate function only; we define this case of equivalence using the notion of compatible queries.

Definition 1. *(Compatible queries [19]) Two queries are compatible if the tuples of arguments in their heads are identical.*

Definition 2. *(Equivalence of compatible aggregate queries [19]) For two compatible aggregate queries $q(\bar{x}, \alpha(y)) \leftarrow B(\bar{s})$ and $q'(\bar{x}, \alpha(y)) \leftarrow B'(s')$, $q \equiv q'$ if $q(\mathcal{D}) = q'(\mathcal{D})$ for every database $\mathcal{D}$.*

Equivalence of compatible aggregate queries is investigated in [8, 19] where it is shown that: (1) Two conjunctive queries are bag-set equivalent iff they are isomorphic after duplicate subgoals are removed; (2) equivalence of *sum*-queries and *count*-queries can be reduced to bag-set equivalence of their cores; (3) equivalence of *max*-queries can be reduced to set-equivalence of their cores.

3   Our Framework

In this section we present our framework, in particular the types of rewritings we consider and the cost model for view selection.

3.1   Rewriting Templates for Aggregate Queries

Let $\mathcal{V}$ be a set of views (which are queries, conjunctive or aggregated[2]) defined on a database schema $\mathcal{S}$; let $\mathcal{D}$ be a database with schema $\mathcal{S}$. Then by $\mathcal{D}_\mathcal{V}$ we denote the database obtained by computing all the view relations in $\mathcal{V}$ on $\mathcal{D}$.

Definition 3. *(Equivalent rewriting) Let Q be a query defined on database schema $\mathcal{S}$, and let $\mathcal{V}$ be a set of views defined on $\mathcal{S}$; let R be a query defined using the views in $\mathcal{V}$. Then Q and R are equivalent, denoted $Q \equiv R$, if and only if for any database $\mathcal{D}$, $Q(\mathcal{D}) = R(\mathcal{D}_\mathcal{V})$.*

---

[2] We consider *multiaggregate views*, that is, views defined by queries with possibly more than one aggregate term in the head.

We say that a view V is *set-valued* if V is computed and stored to be accessed as a set, and that V is *bag-valued* if V is computed and stored to be accessed as a bag. In rewritings, a bag-valued view V will be denoted by an adornment as V^b. The following example shows that equivalence of a rewriting to a query depends on whether conjunctive views are set- or bag-valued.

Example 2. Consider a query Q and a view V which is the core of Q.

$q(X, count(*)) \ : - \ p(X, Y, Z).$
$v(X) \qquad\qquad : - \ p(X, Y, Z).$
$r(X, count(*)) \ : - \ v^b(X).$

The rewriting R is equivalent to the query Q when the view V is bag-valued. However, if the view V is set-valued, then there is no equivalence, as evidenced by a database $\mathcal{D} \ = \ \{ \ p(1,3,4), \ p(1,5,6) \ \}$. On $\mathcal{D}$, the answer to the query Q has one tuple $(1, 2)$. At the same time, the answer to the view V computed as a set has one tuple (1), and therefore the answer to the rewriting R has one tuple $(1, 1)$.

3.2   Central Rewritings

Finding rewritings for aggregate queries introduces additional complications when compared to finding rewritings for conjunctive queries without aggregation. Now a decision has to be made on the following: (1) What kinds of queries are the views, and what kind of query is the rewriting; we consider conjunctive views and rewritings with or without aggregation. (2) Whether the views are computed under set, bag, or bag-set semantics; we consider this issue in detail in Section 4. (3) Moreover, as a consequence of the choices we make, the aggregate function in the head of the rewriting may or may not depend on some aggregated attributes of the views. Our choice here is to depend only on one aggregated attribute of a single view, which we call *central* view. The other (conjunctive or aggregate) views in the rewriting are called *noncentral views*.

Aggregate queries (and views that are defined by aggregate queries) are not symmetrical with respect to all their attributes. We call the aggregated attribute(s) of a query (or view) its *output argument(s)*. We do not consider rewritings whose join conditions involve output arguments of aggregate views; this is a natural choice taken by all similar work in the literature.

Thus we make the following assumptions on the rewritings we consider:

1. The argument of aggregation in the head of the rewriting comes from exactly one (central) view in the body of the rewriting. We use the term *central aggregate operator* to denote:
   (a) in the case the central view is aggregated, the aggregate operator of the central view that contributes to the aggregation in the head, or
   (b) in the case the central view is conjunctive, the aggregate operator in the head of the rewriting.
2. Aggregated outputs of noncentral views are not used in the head of the rewriting.

3. We do not consider rewritings whose join conditions involve output arguments of any participating views.

We call such rewritings *central rewritings*. In all our results, we consider only central rewritings.

We may now view the rewritings we consider as belonging to one of the following three classes: CQ/CQA when the central view is purely conjunctive and the rewriting has aggregation, CQA/CQ when the central view has aggregation and the rewriting is purely conjunctive, and CQA/CQA when both the central view and the rewriting have aggregation. It is easier to state our results for each class separately. Our rewriting template R for all three rewritings is

$$r(\bar{x}, \alpha(y)) \leftarrow v_0(\bar{x}_0, y), v_1^b(\bar{x}_1, y_1), \dots, v_k^b(\bar{x}_k, y_k) \ . \tag{3}$$

where α is a nontrivial aggregate operator in cases CQ/CQA and CQA/CQA, and is an identity in case CQA/CQ (i.e., the head is $r(\bar{x}, y)$). In cases CQA/CQ and CQA/CQA, the output argument y in the central view v_0 is the result of applying a (non-identity) aggregate function to one of the arguments in the body of the view; in the case CQ/CQA, we assume a central view without aggregation which covers all subgoals that contain the variable y. In Section 4 we give conditions under which noncentral views $v_1, \dots, v_k$ can be computed under set semantics (and, in particular, can be defined by aggregate queries).

3.3   Unfoldings of Rewritings

We now consider *unfoldings* of central rewritings; similarly to [8], we use unfoldings to reason about equivalence of queries and their rewritings. Unlike the case of rewriting conjunctive queries without aggregation, where it is straightforward how to define and use expansions [21], in presence of aggregation unfoldings may present complications. As we show in Section 4, central rewritings are not always equivalent to their unfoldings. Here we define unfoldings.

We are given a set of views $v_0, v_1^b \dots, v_k^b$ defined as conjunctive queries, possibly with aggregation, over the base predicates, and are given a query R over the views, defined as in Equation 3. We refer to R as a "rewriting" even in the case where we have not associated it with any particular query (whose rewriting is to be obtained). The *unfolding* R^u of R is a join of all the subgoals of the views in R, followed by some grouping and aggregation. If we denote by B_{v_i} the body of a view v_i, then an unfolding R^u of R is defined as follows:

$$r^u(\bar{x}, \beta(y)) \leftarrow B_{v_0} \ \& \ B_{v_1} \ \& \ \dots \ \& \ B_{v_k} \ . \tag{4}$$

where (1) β is the aggregate operator of the central view v_0 of R, if v_0 is aggregated, or else is the aggregate operator in the head of R; (2) the variables in the B_{v_i}'s ($i \geq 0$) that are also contained in the $\bar{x}_i$ are retained the same as in the rewriting, whereas the other (nondistinguished) variables in the view definitions are replaced by fresh variables that are not used in any other B_{v_j} with $j \neq i$. Moreover, y is the output argument of the central view v_0; if v_0 has aggregation, then y is the unaggregated argument in the definition of v_0. In the conjunctive case, the unfolding is equivalent to the expansion [21] of the rewriting.

3.4 View Selection and Cost Model

Our goal is to design minimal-cost views, that is, views whose use in the rewriting of a query results in the cheapest computation of the query. We assume that the view relations have been precomputed and stored in the database. Thus, we don't assume any cost of computing the views. We assume that the size of a database relation is the number of tuples in it, and that the cost of computing a join is the sum of the sizes of the input relations and of the output relation (this faithfully models the cost of, e.g., hash joins). For conjunctive queries, we measure the cost of query evaluation as the sum of the costs of all the joins in the evaluation [2, 5]. (We assume that all selections are pushed down as far as they go, and consider only left-linear query trees for joins.) For aggregate queries, our *sum-cost model* measures the cost of evaluating a query as the sum of the costs of three steps in the evaluation: computation of the conjunctive core, grouping, and aggregation. The *total cost* of evaluating a query workload is the sum of the costs of evaluating all individual queries in the workload. (The sum can be weighted using frequency values for individual workload queries.)

We assume that we must satisfy a bound (*storage limit*) on the sum of the sizes of the relations for the views that will be selected to be materialized. Our formulation of the view-selection problem is as follows.

Definition 4. *(View-selection problem) Given a query workload Q, an oracle O that gives view sizes,[3] and a storage limit L (a positive integer), return a set V of view definitions, such that:*

(1) the views in V give an equivalent central rewriting of each query in Q,
(2) the view relations satisfy L on all databases defined by O, and
(3) the total cost of evaluating Q using V, for the size estimates given by the oracle O, is minimum among all sets of views that satisfy (1) and (2).

4 Results on Equivalence of Unfoldings and Rewriting

In this section we present necessary and sufficient conditions for central rewritings to exist.[4] More precisely, we present results that prove that the unfoldings defined in Section 3 are equivalent to the rewritings (see Theorems 1–3). In fact, these three theorems follow from the results in [8]; we need to state them in order to emphasize that the conditions are not only sufficient but are necessary as well. As a consequence, equivalence of a rewriting to a query is reduced to equivalence between two aggregate queries, which has a solution [19]. Then we present negative results (Propositions 1–2), which prove that the unfolding technique cannot provide rewritings in the cases where the conditions of any of Theorems 1–3 are not met. Results on the CQA/CQA case and proofs can be found in [22]. Based on the results in this section, we present in Section 6

---

[3] Instead of an oracle, we can be given a database D.

[4] The extended version [22] of the paper has the proofs for the results in Sections 4–6.

an algorithm for constucting equivalent central rewritings that are either CQ (if possible) or CQA rewritings. The intuition is the same as for the algorithm in [9], which can be tailored to create our candidate rewritings too. At the same time, our algorithm is less complicated, as it treats only central rewritings and, in addition, tries to provide CQ rewritings whenever possible.

4.1   Case CQ/CQA: Central View CQ and Rewriting CQA

In this section we consider central rewritings with aggregation (CQA) whose central views do not have aggregation (CQ). We distinguish between two cases, one where the aggregate operator may be duplicate sensitive and the second where it is duplicate insensitive [6].

Theorem 1. *Suppose that all views in a CQ/CQA rewriting R are bag-valued, or that the aggregate operator in the head of R is max or min. Then $R \equiv R^u$.*

If a rewriting R with aggregate function *sum* or *count* in the head has views that are set-valued or have aggregation, it could be that R is not equivalent to its unfolding R^u.

Example 3. We use three views:

$$w_1(A, B) \qquad\qquad :\text{-} \; p(A, B).$$
$$w_2(B, C) \qquad\qquad :\text{-} \; s(B, C, D), t(C, G).$$
$$w_3(B, C, count(D)) \;\; :\text{-} \; s(B, C, D), t(C, G).$$

to construct the following three rewritings and their respective unfoldings:

$$r_1(B, C, sum(A)) \quad :\text{-} \; w_1(A, B), w_2(B, C).$$
$$r_1^u(B, C, sum(A)) \quad :\text{-} \; p(A, B), s(B, C, D), t(C, G).$$
$$r_2(B, count(C)) \qquad :\text{-} \; w_2(B, C).$$
$$r_2^u(B, count(C)) \qquad :\text{-} \; s(B, C, D), t(C, G).$$
$$r_3(B, count) \qquad\quad :\text{-} \; w_3(B, C, H).$$
$$r_3^u(B, count) \qquad\quad :\text{-} \; s(B, C, D), t(C, G).$$

If the relation for the view W_2 is computed as a set (W_2^s), R_1 and its unfolding R_1^u are not equivalent, and neither are R_2 and R_2^u, as evidenced by a database $\mathcal{D} = \{ \; p(6,1), \; p(7,1), \; s(1,2,3), \; s(1,2,4), \; t(2,5) \; \}$. Because R_3 uses a view with aggregation, R_3 and R_3^u are not equivalent (we use the same database $\mathcal{D}$); at the same time, if we rewrite R_3 to use a bag-valued view W_2^b instead of W_3, the new rewriting will be equivalent to its unfolding, which is still R_3^u.

This negative result shows that the results in Theorem 1 are tight:

Proposition 1. *Let R be a CQ/CQA rewriting with central aggregation sum or count. Suppose that R has either a view with (any nontrivial) aggregation, or a set-valued view with at least one nondistinguished variable. Then the unfolding R^u of R is not set-equivalent to R.*

4.2   Case CQA/CQ: Central View CQA and Rewriting CQ

In this section we consider central rewritings without aggregation (CQ) whose central views have aggregation (CQA). We first present a restriction on the relationship between the grouping arguments in the head of rewritings of this type and in the central view of the rewriting.

Lemma 1. *For any CQA/CQ rewriting R, if R is equivalent to its unfolding R^u, then the tuple of attributes in the head of R contains all grouping attributes of R's central view.*

Intuitively, if the conditions of Lemma 1 are not satisfied, then on at least one database the answer to the rewriting will have multiple tuples that agree on all values of the grouping arguments. This effect is caused by the grouping arguments of the central view that do not go to the head of the rewriting. It is interesting to note that among the three central rewriting types, only CQA/CQ has a connection between the attributes in the head of the rewriting and the attributes of the central view. (The other two rewriting types may use in the head a proper subset of the grouping attributes of the view or none at all.)

Theorem 2. *Consider a CQA/CQ rewriting R. Suppose that (i) all noncentral views of R have no aggregation, (ii) R does not have nondistinguished attributes in its body (except possibly noncentral aggregated arguments in R's central view – in case of multiaggregate views), (iii) noncentral views do not have nondistinguished attributes in their definitions, and (iv) all grouping attributes of the central view appear in the head of R. Then R is equivalent to its unfolding R^u on set-valued databases.*

Although none of the conditions in Theorem 2 can be relaxed for *sum* or *count* queries, see Proposition 2, they can be relaxed for *max* and *min* queries:

Theorem 3. *Let R be a CQA/CQ rewriting with central aggregation max or min. Suppose that all the grouping arguments of the central view of R appear in the head of R. Then R is equivalent to its unfolding R^u on set-valued databases, provided R is evaluated under set semantics.*

Proposition 2. *Consider a CQA/CQ query R with central aggregation sum or count. Suppose at least one of the following holds: (1) A noncentral view in R is defined by an aggregate query, with any aggregate function. (2) A noncentral view in R is defined by a query with nondistinguished variables. (3) R has nondistinguished variables, other than noncentral aggregation in the central view of R. Then R is not equivalent to its unfolding R^u.*

5   View Selection

In this section we discuss the view-selection problem for aggregate queries and views, assuming central rewritings. In this setting, we prove that the view-selection problem is NP-complete for *sum*, *count*, and provide an exponential-time lower bound on the complexity of view selection for *max*, *min*. In Section 6 we give an algorithm for selecting central aggregate views.

5.1   Decidability

Theorem 4. *The view-selection problem under the storage limit is decidable for finite workloads of conjunctive queries with aggregation and for conjunctive views and rewritings, with or without aggregation, for the three central rewriting types we consider.*

The query workloads may contain queries both with and without aggregation.

5.2   NP-Completeness for *Sum* or *Count* Queries

In this section we present an NP-completeness result for the view-selection problem for workloads of *sum* or *count* queries. It follows from the proof that the view-selection problem for conjunctive queries, views, and rewritings under *bag* semantics is also NP-complete.

Theorem 5. *The decision version of the view-selection problem under the storage limit is NP-complete for finite workloads of conjunctive queries with sum or count aggregation and for conjunctive views and rewritings, with or without aggregation, for the three central rewriting types we consider.*

5.3   Lower Bound for *Max* or *Min* Queries

We prove an exponential-time lower bound for view selection under a storage limit for *max* and *min* queries.

Theorem 6. *The view-selection problem under the storage limit has an exponential-time lower bound for finite workloads of conjunctive queries with max or min aggregation and for conjunctive views and rewritings, with or without aggregation, for the three central rewriting types we consider.*

Intuitively, the number of views that can be used in equivalent rewritings of *max* and *min* queries is up to exponential in the number of subgoals of the queries. This result does not hold for *sum* and *count* queries, for which equivalence of queries and rewritings stems from the isomorphism of the bodies (in datalog) of the queries and of the unfoldings of the rewritings.

6   Algorithms

In this section we give algorithms for obtaining rewritings given a query and views and for selecting central views given a query workload. Using the results in Section 4, we base our algorithms on the following observations.

Proposition 3. *In a CQA/CQ rewriting, the set of all grouping attributes of the central view is a subset of the set of all grouping attributes of the rewriting. We call this central view* grouping-complete.

In a CQA/CQA rewriting, the set of the grouping attributes of the rewriting is a union of subsets of the grouping attributes in the central view and of the non-aggregated attributes in noncentral views. We call this central view grouping-incomplete.

Given an aggregate view V, we define its *reduced-core view V^r* to be a view whose body is the body of V and whose head is a new predicate name V^r; the arguments in the head of V^r are all the grouping attributes of V. For a rewriting R, its *reduced-core rewriting R^r* is a conjunctive rewriting whose head attributes are R's grouping attributes only and whose body uses only reduced-core views. The reduced-core rewriting is a conjunctive query, and the following holds:

Proposition 4. *Let R be an equivalent central rewriting of a query Q using views $\mathcal{V}$, and let the central view of R be CQA. Let R^r be a reduced-core rewriting of R, and $\mathcal{V}'$ the reduced-core views of $\mathcal{V}$. Then R^r is an equivalent rewriting of the reduced-core query of Q using $\mathcal{V}'$.*

6.1   Constructing Rewritings

In this section we give an algorithm that, given a query and a set of views, constructs all equivalent rewritings of the query using the views. We reduce this problem to the problem of obtaining rewritings for purely conjunctive queries. Due to lack of space, we describe only the case for *max* queries and CQA/CQA or CQA/CQ rewritings. The other cases are similar with the additional observation that, in the duplicate-sensitive cases, we find rewritings for the purely conjunctive queries whose unfolding is isomorphically mapped on the query.

In the following algorithm, Q^r and V^r are the reduced-core queries of a query Q and of views, respectively. We use an algorithm in the literature [23] to find all rewritings Q^r using V^r.

Procedure *Find-R.* Input: query Q, set of views V
Consider Q^r ,V^r.
Find all rewritings of Q^r using V^r.
 For each rewriting R^r do:
 Consider the expansion R^{r-exp}
  For each containment mapping from Q^r to R^{r-exp} do:
  If there is a view in the rewriting such that its aggregated attribute is the image of
   the aggregated attribute of the query, do:
   Call this the central view.
   If the central view is grouping-incomplete then construct CQA/CQA rewriting
   If the central view is grouping-complete then construct CQA/CQ rewriting
  end
 end
end

The following theorem is a consequence of Proposition 4.

Theorem 7. *If there is a central rewriting of a query Q using views $\mathcal{V}$, then procedure Find-R will find it.*

6.2   Selecting Views

We present an algorithm that selects multiaggregate views to be used as central views, given a query workload. The algorithm selects all *maximal* multiaggregate views; for a query workload, a view is maximal if there does not exist another multiaggregate view with more aggregated arguments which can replace it in all the rewritings in the workload. The algorithm is based on the following result.

Proposition 5. *Let R be a central (CQ or CQA) rewriting of a query Q. Then all the subgoals in Q which contain the aggregated attribute of Q are also subgoals of the central view of R, and each grouping attribute of Q is a grouping attribute of the central view of R or is in the head of one of the noncentral views in R.*

Based on Proposition 5, we observe that there is a subset of subgoals of the query which are also contained in the body of the definition of any central view which rewrites this query. We refer to a view whose body is exactly this subset of subgoals as a *central minimal view* for the query.

The algorithm considers each query Q in the workload and constructs a pair of views (V_c^Q, V_n^Q) that essentially represent a central minimal view and a collective noncentral view. We may think of the pair (V_c^Q, V_n^Q) as providing a rewriting for Q with the minimum number of subgoals in the central view V_c^Q. We call (V_c^Q, V_n^Q) *characteristic views* of the query Q. For each query Q, its characteristic views are found as follows: First we find the central minimal view V_c^Q for each pair (V_c^Q, V_n^Q) by selecting head arguments for the subset of the query subgoals that can serve as the body of the definition of V_c^Q based on Proposition 5(1). Then based on Proposition 5(2), we find the view V_n^Q.

In the next step, the algorithm finds multiaggregate views for the given query workload, by considering all combinations of characteristic views for the workload queries and finding compatible pairs of characteristic views. Two pairs are *compatible* if (1) the two central views can be combined in a single multiaggregate view V_m, and (2) V_m can be used to rewrite both queries. Finally, the algorithm finds a maximal set of characteristic central views from the characteristic pairs based on compatibility of the pairs.

The correctness of the algorithm is based on the following result.

Proposition 6.   *1. Each query has a bounded number of characteristic views.*
  2. In any central rewriting of a query Q, the views used in the rewriting can also be used to produce central rewritings of characteristic views.
  3. It is decidable to tell whether two pairs of characteristic views are compatible.

Theorem 8. *Given a query workload $\mathcal{Q}$, the algorithm finds all maximal multiaggregate views for $\mathcal{Q}$.*

References

1. Harinarayan, V., Rajaraman, A., Ullman, J. Implementing data cubes efficiently. In: Proceedings of SIGMOD (1996) 205–216
2. Gupta, H., Harinarayan, V., Rajaraman, A., Ullman, J. Index selection for OLAP. In: Proceedings of ICDE (1997) 208–219
3. Agrawal, S., Chaudhuri, S., Narasayya, V. Automated selection of materialized views and indexes in SQL databases. In: Proceedings of VLDB (2000) 496–505
4. Ullman, J.D. Efficient implementation of data cubes via materialized views. In: Proceedings of KDD (1996) 386–388
5. Chirkova, R., Halevy, A., Suciu, D. A formal perspective on the view selection problem. VLDB Journal **11** (2002) 216–237
6. Gupta, A., Harinarayan, V., Quass, D. Aggregate-query processing in data warehousing environments. In: Proceedings of VLDB (1995) 358–369
7. Gray, J., Chaudhuri, S., Bosworth, A., Layman, A., Reichart, D., Venkatrao, M. Data cube: A relational aggregation operator generalizing Group-by, Cross-Tab, and Sub Totals. Data Mining and Knowledge Discovery. **1** (1997) 29–53
8. Cohen, S., Nutt, W., Serebrenik, A. Rewriting aggregate queries using views. In: Proceedings of PODS (1999) 155–166
9. Cohen, S., Nutt, W., Serebrenik, A. Algorithms for rewriting aggregate queries using views. In: Proceedings of ADBIS-DASFAA (2000) 65–78
10. Widom, J. Research problems in data warehousing. In: Proceedings of CIKM (1995)
11. Srivastava, D., Dar, S., Jagadish, H., Levy, A. Answering queries with aggregation using views. In: Proceedings of VLDB (1996) 318–329
12. Grumbach, S., Tininini, L. On the content of materialized aggregate views. Journal of Computer and System Sciences **66** (2003) 133–168
13. Agarwal, S., Agrawal, R., Deshpande, P., Gupta, A., Naughton, J., Ramakrishnan, R., Sarawagi, S. On the computation of multidimensional aggregates. In: Proceedings of VLDB (1996) 506–521
14. Yang, J., Widom, J. Incremental computation and maintenance of temporal aggregates. In: Proceedings of ICDE (2001) 51–62
15. Benedikt, M., Libkin, L. Aggregate operators in constraint query languages. Journal of Computer and System Sciences **64** (2002) 628–654
16. Ross, K., Srivastava, D., Stuckey, P., Sudarshan, S. Foundations of aggregation constraints. Theoretical Computer Science **193** (1998) 149–179
17. Özsoyoglu, G., Özsoyoglu, Z., Matos, V. Extending relational algebra and relational calculus with set-valued attributes and aggregate functions. ACM Transactions on Database Systems (TODS) **12** (1987) 566–592
18. Lechtenbörger, J., Shu, H., Vossen, G. Aggregate queries over conditional tables. Journal of Intelligent Information Systems **19** (2002) 343–362
19. Nutt, W., Sagiv, Y., Shurin, S. Deciding equivalences among aggregate queries. In: Proceedings of PODS (1998) 214–223
20. Chaudhuri, S., Vardi, M. Optimization of real conjunctive queries. In: Proceedings of PODS (1993) 59–70
21. Ullman, J.D. Information integration using logical views. In: Proceedings of ICDT (1997)
22. Afrati, F., Chirkova, R. Selecting and using views to compute aggregate queries. http://www4.ncsu.edu/~rychirko/Papers/aggregAquv.pdf (2004)
23. Afrati, F., Li, C., Ullman, J. Generating efficient plans for queries using views. In: Proceedings of SIGMOD (2001)

Efficient Computation of Frequent and Top-k Elements in Data Streams*

Ahmed Metwally**, Divyakant Agrawal, and Amr El Abbadi

Department of Computer Science,
University of California, Santa Barbara
{metwally, agrawal, amr}@cs.ucsb.edu

Abstract. We propose an integrated approach for solving both problems of finding the most popular k elements, and finding frequent elements in a data stream. Our technique is efficient and exact if the alphabet under consideration is small. In the more practical large alphabet case, our solution is space efficient and reports both top-k and frequent elements with tight guarantees on errors. For general data distributions, our top-k algorithm can return a set of k' elements, where $k' \approx k$, which are guaranteed to be the top-k' elements; and we use minimal space for calculating frequent elements. For realistic Zipfian data, our space requirement for the frequent elements problem decreases dramatically with the parameter of the distribution; and for top-k queries, we ensure that only the top-k elements, in the correct order, are reported. Our experiments show significant space reductions with no loss in accuracy.

1 Introduction

Recently, online monitoring of data streams has emerged as an important data management problem. This new key research topic has its foundations and applications in many domains, including databases, data mining, algorithms, networking, theory and statistics. However, new challenges have emerged. Due to their vast sizes, some stream types should be mined fast before being deleted forever. Generally, the alphabet is too large to keep exact information for all elements. Conventional database, and mining techniques, though effective with stored data, are deemed impractical in this setting.

This work was primarily motivated by the setting of Internet advertising commissioners, who represent the middle persons between Internet publishers, and Internet advertisers. The file systems are bombarded continuously by streams of various types: advertisement rendering, clicks, sales, and leads; and each type is handled differently. For instance, before rendering an advertisement for a user, the clicks stream summary structure should be queried to determine what advertisements would suit the user's profile. If the user's profile indicates that

---

* This work was supported in part by NSF under grants EIA 00-80134, NSF 02-09112, and CNF 04-23336.
** Part of this work was done while the first author was at ValueClick, Inc.

T. Eiter and L. Libkin (Eds.): ICDT 2005, LNCS 3363, pp. 398–412, 2005.

(s)he is not a *frequent* "clicker", then this user, most probably, will not click any displayed advertisement. Thus, it can be more profitable to show Pay-Per-Impression advertisements, which generate revenue on rendering them. On the other hand, if the user's profile was found to be one of the *frequent* profiles, then, there is a good chance that this user will click some of the advertisements shown and potentially generate a sale/lead transaction. In this case, Pay-Per-Click advertisements should be displayed. Choosing what advertisements to display entails retrieving the *top* advertisement categories for this specific user profile.

From the above example we need to solve two problems. We would like to know if the user's profile is *frequent* in the click stream, and we need to identify the *top* advertisements for this specific profile. The problems of finding frequent[1] and top-k elements are closely related, yet, to the best of our knowledge, no integrated solution has been proposed. In this paper, we propose an integrated approach for solving both problems of finding the top-k elements, and finding frequent elements in a data stream. Our *Space-Saving* algorithm reports both top-k and frequent elements with tight guarantees on errors. For general data distributions, our algorithm answers top-k queries by returning a set of k' elements, where $k' \approx k$, which are guaranteed to be the top-k' elements; and we use minimal space for calculating frequent elements. For realistic Zipfian data, our space requirement for the frequent elements problem decreases dramatically with the parameter of the distribution; and for top-k queries, we ensure that only the top-k elements, in the correct order, are reported.

The rest of the paper is organized as follows. Section 2 highlights the related work. In Section 3, we introduce our *Space-Saving* algorithm, and its associated data structure, followed by a discussion of query processing in Section 4. We comment on our experimental results in Section 5, and conclude in Section 6.

2   Background and Related Work

Formally, given an alphabet, A, a *frequent element*, e_i, is an element whose frequency, f_i, in a stream S of a given size N, exceeds a user specified support ϕN, where $0 \leq \phi \leq 1$; whereas the *top-k elements* are the k elements with highest frequencies. Since the space requirements for exact solutions of these problems are impractical, other relaxations of the original problems were proposes. The FindCandidateTop(S, k, l) problem was proposed in [3] to ask for l elements among which the top-k elements are concealed, with no guarantees on the rank of the remaining $(l-k)$ elements. The FindApproxTop(S, k, ϵ) [3] is a more practical approximation for the top-k problem. The user asks for a list of k elements such that every element, e_i, in the list has $f_i > (1 - \epsilon)f_k$, where ϵ is a user-defined error, and $f_1 \geq \ldots \geq f_{|A|}$, such that e_k is the element with k^{th} rank. The Hot Items[2] problem is a special case of the frequent elements problem, proposed in [15], that asks for k elements, each of which has $f_i > \frac{N}{k+1}$. This extends the early

---

[1] The term "Heavy Hitters" was also used in [4].

[2] The term "Hot Items" was coined later in [5].

work done in [2], and [8] for identifying a majority element. The most popular variation of the frequent elements problem, ϵ-Deficient Frequent Elements [13], asks for all the elements with fequency greater than $(\phi - \epsilon)N$.

Several algorithms [3], [5], [6], [7], [10], [11], [13] have been proposed to handle the top-k, the frequent elements problems, and their variations. These techniques can be classified into *counter-based*, and *sketch-based* techniques.

Counter-Based Techniques keep an individual counter for each element in the monitored set, a subset of A. The counter of a monitored element, e_i, is updated when e_i occurs in the stream. If there is no counter kept for the observed ID, it is either disregarded, or some algorithm-dependent action is taken.

For solving the ϵ-Deficient Frequent Elements, algorithms *Sticky Sampling*, and *Lossy Counting* were proposed in [13]. The algorithms cut the stream into rounds. Though simple and intuitive, they suffer from zeroing too many counters at rounds' boundaries, and thus, they free space before it is really needed. In addition, answering a frequent elements query entails scanning all counters.

Demaine *et al.* proposed the *Frequent* algorithm to solve the Hot Items problem in [6]. Their algorithm, a re-discovery of the algorithm in [15], outputs a list of k elements with no guarantee on which elements, if any, have frequency more than $\frac{N}{k+1}$. The same algorithm was proposed independently by Karp *et al.* in [11]. *Frequent* extends the early work done in [2], and [8] for finding a majority item, using only one counter. *Frequent* [6] keeps k counters to monitor k elements. If a monitored element is observed, its counter is incremented, else all counters are decremented. In case any counter reaches 0, it is assigned the next observed element. When the algorithm terminates, the monitored elements are the candidate frequent elements. [6] proposed a lightweight data structure that can decrement all counters in $O(1)$ operations. The sampling algorithm *Probabilistic-InPlace* [6], which is similar to *Sticky Sampling* [13], solves FindCandidateTop(S, k, $2k$). When queried, the algorithm returns the upper half of the counters, in the hope that they are the correct top-k. Again, the algorithm deletes half the counters at rounds' boundaries, which is $\Omega(|\text{distinct values of the deleted counters}|)$. In general, counter-based techniques exhibit fast per-item processing.

Sketch-Based Techniques do not monitor a subset of elements, rather provide, with less stringent guarantees, frequency estimation for all elements using bit-maps of counters. Usually, each element is hashed into the space of counters using a family of hash functions, and the hashed-to counters are updated for every hit of this element. Those "representative" counters are then queried for the element frequency with less accuracy, due to hashing collisions.

The *CountSketch* algorithm, proposed in [3], solves the FindApproxTop(S, k, ϵ) problem, with success probability $(1 - \delta)$. Its bottleneck is estimating the frequency of the element by finding the median of its representative counters.

The *GroupTest* algorithm, proposed in [5], answers queries about Hot Items, with a constant probability of failure, δ. A novel algorithm, *FindMajority*, was first devised to detect the majority element, assuming elements' IDs to be $1 \ldots |A|$. Then *GroupTest*, a probabilistic generalization, was devised that employs several independent copies of *FindMajority*. *GroupTest* is generally accurate. However, its space complexity is large, and it offers no information about elements' frequencies or relative order. The *Multistage filters* approach proposed in [7], which was also independently proposed in [10], is very similar to *GroupTest*.

Sketch-based techniques monitor all elements. However, a hit entails expensive calculations. They do not offer guarantees about relative order or estimated frequencies, and their space usage are not bounded by the size of the alphabet.

3   Summarizing the Data Stream

The main difficulty in devising an integrated solution is that queries of one type cannot serve as a pre-processing step for the other type of queries. For instance, the frequent elements receiving 1% or more of the total hits might constitute the top-100 elements, some of them, or none. In order to use frequent elements queries to pre-process the stream for a top-k query, several frequent elements queries have to be issued to reach a lower bound on the frequency of the kth element; and in order to use top-k queries to pre-process the stream for a frequent elements query, several top-k queries have to be issued to reach an upper bound on the number of frequent elements. To offer an integrated solution, we generalized both problems to *accurately estimate the number of hits for significant elements, and store these frequencies in an always-sorted structure.* We, then, devised a generalized algorithm for the generalized problem.

3.1   The *Space-Saving* Algorithm

In this section, we propose our counter-based *Space-Saving* algorithm and its associated Stream-Summary data structure. The underlying idea is to maintain partial information of interest; i.e., we monitor only m elements. If we observe an element that is monitored, we just increment its counter. If we observe an element, e_{new}, that is not monitored, give it the benefit of doubt, and replace the element that currently has the least hits, min, with e_{new}. Assign $count_{new}$ the value $min+1$. For each element e_i, we keep track of its maximum over-estimation, ε_i, resulting from the initialization of its counter when it was inserted into the list. That is, when starting to monitor e_i, set ε_i to the counter value that was evicted. The algorithm is sketched in Figure 1.

In general, the top elements among non-skewed data are of no great significance. Hence, we concentrate on skewed datasets. The basic intuition is to make use of the skewed property of the data, since we expect a minority of the elements, the more frequent ones, to get the majority of the hits. Frequent elements will reside in the counters of bigger values, and will not be distorted by the ineffective hits of the infrequent elements, and thus, will never be replaced out of the monitored counters. Meanwhile, the numerous infrequent elements will be striving to reside on the smaller counters, whose values will grow slower than those of the larger counters.

In addition, if the skew remains, but the popular elements change overtime, the algorithm adapts automatically. The elements that are growing more popular

```
Algorithm: Space-Saving(m counters, stream S)
begin
   for each element, e_i, in S{
      If e_i is monitored,
         increment count_i;
      else{
         let e_min be the element with least hits, min
         replace e_min with e_i;
         Assign count_i the value min + 1;
         Assign ε_i the value min;
      }
   }// end for
end;
```

Fig. 1. The *Space-Saving* Algorithm

will gradually be pushed to the top of the list as they receive more hits. If one of the previously popular elements lost its popularity, it will receive less hits. Thus, its relative position will decline, as other counters get incremented, until it eventually gets dropped from the list.

Even if the data is not skewed, the errors in the counters will be inversely proportional to the number of counters, as shown later. Keeping only a moderate number of counters will guarantee very small errors. This is because the more counters we keep, the less it is probable to replace elements, and thus, the smaller the over-estimation errors in counters' values.

To implement this algorithm, we need a data structure that cheaply increments counters without violating their order, and that ensures constant time retrieval. We propose the *Stream-Summary* data structure for these purposes.

In a Stream-Summary, all elements with the same counter value are linked together in a linked list. They all point to a parent bucket. The value of the parent bucket is the same as the counters' value of all of its elements. Every bucket points to exactly one element among its child list, and buckets are kept in a doubly linked list, sorted by their values. Initially, all counters are empty, and are attached to a single parent bucket with value 0.

The elements can be stored in a hash table for constant amortized access cost, or in an associative memory for constant worst case access cost. The Stream-Summary can be sequentially traversed as a sorted list, since the buckets' list is sorted. In case it is feasible to keep counters for all elements in A, Stream-Summary can be used to report both the most and the least significant elements.

The algorithm for counting elements' hits using *Stream-Summary* is straightforward. When an element's counter is updated, its bucket's neighbor with the larger value is checked. If it has a value equal to the new value of the element, then the element is detached from its current list, and is inserted in the child list of this neighbor. Otherwise, a new bucket with the correct value is created, and is attached to the bucket list in the right place; and this element is attached to this new bucket. The old bucket is deleted if it points to an empty child list. The worst case scenario costs 10 pointer assignments, and one heap allocation.

Stream-Summary is motivated by the work done in [6]. However, to look up a value of a counter using the data structure in [6], it takes $O(m)$, while Stream-Summary looks values up in $\Theta(1)$, for online queries about specific elements.

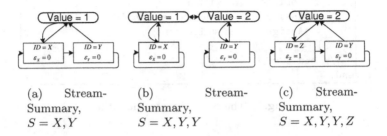

(a)   Stream-Summary, $S = X, Y$

(b)   Stream-Summary, $S = X, Y, Y$

(c)   Stream-Summary, $S = X, Y, Y, Z$

Fig. 2. *Space-Saving* updates to a Stream-Summary data structure as elements are observed

Example 1. Assuming $m = 2$, and $A = \{X, Y, Z\}$. The stream $S = X, Y$ will yield the Stream-Summary in Figure 2(a), after the two counters accommodate the observed elements. When another Y arrives, a new bucket is created with value 2, and Y gets attached to it, as shown in Figure 2(b). When Z arrives, the element with the minimum counter, X, is replaced by Z. Z has $\varepsilon_Z = 1$, since that was the count of X when evicted. The final Stream-Summary is shown in Figure 2(c).

3.2   Properties of the *Space-Saving* Algorithm

To prove the space bounds in the following sections, we analyze some properties of the *Space-Saving* algorithm, which will help us establish our space bounds. For space limitations, all proofs of lemmas and theorems are omitted, and the reader is referred to the full version [14].

Lemma 1. $N = \sum_{\forall i | e_i \in Stream-Summary} (count_i)$

A pivotal factor in our analysis is the value of min. min is highly dynamic since it is dependent on the permutation of elements in S. We give an example for this. If $m = 2$, and $N = 4$. $S = X, Z, Y, Y$ yields $min = 1$, while $S = X, Y, Y, Z$ yields $min = 2$. Although it would be very useful to quantify min, we do not want to involve the order in which hits were received in our analysis, because predicating the analysis on all possible stream permutations will be intractable. Thus, we establish an upper bound on min.

We assume that the number of distinct elements in S is greater than m. Thus, all m counters are occupied. Otherwise, all counts are exact, and the problem is trivial. Hence, from Lemma 1 we deduce the following.

Lemma 2. *Among all counters, the minimum counter value, min, is less than or equal to $\lfloor \frac{N}{m} \rfloor$.*

We are interested in *min* since it represents an upper bound on the over-estimation in any counter in Stream-Summary. Moreover, any element e_i, with frequency $f_i > min$, is guaranteed to be monitored, as shown next.

Theorem 1. *An element e_i with $f_i > min$, must exist in the Stream-Summary.*

The strength behind our simple algorithm is that we keep the information until the space is absolutely needed, and we do not initialize counters in batches like other counter-based algorithms. This is what allowed us to prove these properties about the proposed algorithm. In the next section, we use these properties to derive a bound on the space requirements for solving different problems.

4   Processing Queries

In this section, we discuss query processing using the Stream-Summary data structure. We also analyze the space requirements for both the general case, where no data distribution is assumed, and the more interesting Ziptian case.

4.1   Frequent Elements

In order to answer queries about the frequent elements, we sequentially traverse Stream-Summary as a sorted list until an element with frequency less than the user support is reached. Thus, we report frequent elements in $\Theta(|\text{frequent elements}|)$. If for each reported element e_i, $count_i - \varepsilon_i > \phi N$, then the algorithm **guarantees that all, and only the frequent elements** are reported. This guarantee is conveyed through the boolean parameter **guaranteed**. The number of counters, m, should be specified by the user according to the data properties

```
Algorithm: QueryFrequent(m counters, support φ)
begin
  Bool guaranteed = true;
  Integer i = 1;
  while (count_i > φN){
     output e_i;
     If ((count_i - ε_i) < φN)
        guaranteed = false;
     i++;
  }// end while
  return( guaranteed )
end;
```

Fig. 3. Reporting Frequent Elements

or the available memory on the server. The *QueryFrequent* algorithm is given in Figure 3. Next, we determine the relationship between m and the user specified error, ϵ.

The General Case. We will analyze the space requirements for the general case of the data distribution.

Theorem 2. *Assuming no specific data distribution, or user-supplied support, to find all frequent elements with error ϵ, the* Space-Saving *algorithm uses a number of counters that is bounded by* $\min(|A|, \frac{1}{\epsilon})$. *Any element, e_i, with frequency $f_i > \epsilon N$ is guaranteed to be in the Stream-Summary.*

Zipf Distribution Analysis. Assuming Zipfian data [16], with parameter α, $f_i = \frac{N}{i^\alpha \zeta(\alpha)}$, where $\zeta(\alpha) = \sum_{i=1}^{|A|} \frac{1}{i^\alpha}$ converges to a small constant inversely proportional to α, except for $\alpha \leq 1$. For instance, $\zeta(1) \approx \ln(1.78|A|)$. We assume $\alpha \geq 1$, to ensure that the data is worth analyzing. As noted before, we do not expect the popular elements to be of great importance if the data is uniform or weakly skewed.

Theorem 3. *Assuming Zipfian data with parameter α, to calculate the frequent elements with error rate ϵ, the* Space-Saving *algorithm uses only* $\min(|A|, \left(\frac{1}{\epsilon}\right)^{\frac{1}{\alpha}})$ *counters. This is regardless of the stream permutation.*

Comparison with Similar Work. The bound of Theorem 2 is tight. For instance, this can happen if all the IDs in S are distinct. However, this bound is much better than those guaranteed by the algorithms in [13]. The *Sticky Sampling* algorithm has a space bound of $\frac{2}{\epsilon} \log(\frac{1}{\phi\delta})$, where ϕ is the user given support, and δ is the failure probability. The *Lossy Counting* algorithm has a bound of $\frac{1}{\epsilon} \log(\epsilon N)$. Furthermore, our algorithm has better bounds than *GroupTest* [5], whose bound is $O(\frac{1}{\phi} \log(\frac{1}{\delta\phi}) \log(|A|))$, which is less scalable than ours. For example, for $N = 10^6$, $|A| = 10^4$, $\phi = 10^{-1}$, $\epsilon = 10^{-2}$, and $\delta = 10^{-1}$, we need only 100 counters, while *Sticky Sampling* needs 700 counters, *Lossy Counting* needs 1000 counters, and *GroupTest* needs $C * 930$ counters, where $C \geq 1$.

Frequent [6] has a similar bound in the general case. Using m counters, the elements' under-estimation error is bounded by $\frac{N-1}{m}$. Although this is close to the theoretical under-estimation error bound, as proved in [1], there is no straightforward feasible extension of the algorithm to track the under-estimation error for each counter. In addition, every observation of a non-monitored element increases the errors for all the monitored elements, since their counters get decremented. Therefore, elements of higher frequency are more error prone, and thus, it is still difficult to guess the frequent elements, which is not the case for our algorithm. Even more, the structure [6] is built and queried in a way that does not allow the user to specify an error threshold, ϵ. Thus, the algorithm has only one parameter, the support ϕ, which increases the number of false positives dramatically, as will be clear from the experimental results in Section 5.

The number of counter used in *GroupTest* [5] depends on the failure probability, δ, as well as the support, ϕ. Thus, it does not suffer from the single-threshold drawback of *Frequent*. However, it does not output frequencies at all, and reveals nothing about the relative order of the elements. In addition, its assumption that elememts' IDs are $1 \ldots |A|$ can only be enforced by building an indexed lookup table that maps every ID to a unique number in the range $1 \ldots |A|$. Thus, practically, *GroupTest* needs $O(|A|)$ space, which is infeasible in most cases. Meanwhile, we only require the m IDs to fit in memory.

For the Zipfian case, we make no comparison to other works, since we are not aware of a similar analysis. For the numerical example given above, if $\alpha = 2$, we would need 10 counters instead of 100, to guarantee the same error of 10^{-2}.

4.2 Top-k Elements

For the top-k elements, the algorithm outputs the first k elements. We call the results to have **guaranteed top-k** if by looking at the results only, we can tell that the reported top-k elements are correct. The *Space-Saving* algorithm reports a guaranteed top-k if $\forall_{i \leq k}, count_i - \varepsilon_i \geq count_{k+1}$. That is, the guaranteed number of hits for each reported element is greater than the over-estimated number of hits for the element in position $k + 1$. All guaranteed top-i subsets, for all i, can be reported in $\Theta(m)$, by iterating on all the counters $1 \ldots m - 1$. At each iteration, i, the $\min_{\forall_{j \leq i}}(count_j - \varepsilon_j)$ is compared to $count_{i+1}$. The first i elements are guaranteed to be the top-i elements if this minimum is greater than or equal to $count_{i+1}$. The algorithm guarantees the top-m if in addition to this condition, $\varepsilon_m = 0$.

Similarly, we call the top-k to have **guaranteed order** if $\forall_{i \leq k}, count_i - \varepsilon_i \geq count_{i+1}$. That is, in addition to having guaranteed top-k, the order of elements among the top-k elements are guaranteed to hold, if the guaranteed hits for every element in the top-k are greater than the over-estimated hits of the next element.

This is the first algorithm that can give guarantees about its output. For top-k queries, even if we cannot guarantee the top-k, we output the top-k candidates, and can extend our output to include guaranteed top-k' elements, where k' is practically very close to k. For the case of Zipfian data, we guarantee that $k' = k$, as shown later in the section. The algorithm *QueryTop-k* is given in Figure 4.

The algorithm consists of two loops. The first loop outputs the top-k candidates. At each iteration the order of the elements reported so far is checked. If the order is violated, `order` is set to false. At the end of the loop, the top-k candidates are checked to be the guaranteed top-k, by checking that all of these candidates have guaranteed hits that exceed the overestimated counter of the $k + 1$ element. If this does not hold, the second loop is executed to search for the next k', where k' is slightly greater than k, such that top-k' are guaranteed. Next, we look at the space requirements for solving this problem.

The General Case. We start by considering data which is not as skewed as Zipf of parameter 1. We deal with skewed data later. We also look at the relaxed

```
Algorithm: QueryTop-k(m counters, Integer k)
begin
    Bool order = true;
    Bool guaranteed = false;
    Integer min-guar-freq = ∞;
    for i = 1...k{
        output e_i;
        If ((count_i − ε_i) < min-guar-freq)
            min-guar-freq = (count_i − ε_i);
        If ((count_i − ε_i) < count_{i+1})
            order = false;
    }// end for
    If (count_{k+1} ≤ min-guar-freq){
        guaranteed = true;
    }else{
        output e_{k+1};
        for i = k + 2...m{
            output e_i;
            If ((count_{i-1} − ε_{i-1}) < min-guar-freq)
                min-guar-freq = (count_{i-1} − ε_{i-1});
            If (count_i ≤ min-guar-freq){
                guaranteed = true;
                break;
            }
        }
    }
    return( guaranteed, order )
end;
```

Fig. 4. Reporting Top-k

version of the problem defined in [3], which is finding a list of k elements, among which every element e_i has $f_i > (1 - \epsilon)f_k$.

Theorem 4. *Regardless of the data distribution, to calculate the relaxed top-k elements with error ϵ, the Space-Saving algorithm uses $\min(|A|, \frac{N}{\epsilon f_k})$ counters. Any element, e_i, whose $f_i > (1 - \epsilon)f_k$ is guaranteed to be monitored.*

Zipf Distribution Analysis. To answer exact top-k queries, ϵ can be automatically set less than $f_k - f_{k+1}$. Thus, we guarantee correctness, and order.

Theorem 5. *Assuming the data is Zipfian with parameter $\alpha > 1$, to calculate the exact top-k, the Space-Saving algorithm uses $\min(|A|, O((\frac{k}{\alpha})^{\frac{1}{\alpha}}k))$ counters. When $\alpha = 1$, the space complexity is $\min(|A|, O(k^2 \log(|A|)))$. This is regardless of the stream permutation. Also, the order among the top-k elements is preserved.*

Comparison with Similar Work. These bounds are better than the bounds guaranteed by the best known algorithm, *CountSketch* [3], for a good range of practical values of the parameters $|A|$, ϵ, and k. *CountSketch* solves the relaxed version of the problem, FindApproxTop(S, k, ϵ), with failure probability δ, using space of $O(\log(\frac{N}{\delta})(k + \frac{1}{(\epsilon f_k)^2} \sum_{i=k+1}^{|A|} f_i^2))$, with a a large constant hidden in the big-O notation, according to [3], and [5]. Our bound for the relaxed problem is $\frac{N}{\epsilon f_k}$, with a 0-failure probability. For instance, for $N = 10^6$, $|A| = 10^4$, $k = 100$, and $\epsilon = \delta = 10^{-1}$, and a uniformly distributed data, we require 10^3 counters, while *CountSketch* needs $C * 2.3 * 10^7$ counters, where $C \gg 1$, which is more than the entire stream. In addition, our algorithm guarantees that any element, e_i, whose $f_i > (1 - \epsilon)f_k$ does belong to the Stream-Summary, and does not simply output a random k selection of these elements.

In case of a non-Zipf distribution, or a weakly skewed Zipf distribution with $\alpha < 1$, for all $i \geq k$, we will assume that $f_i \geq \frac{N}{\zeta(1)} * \frac{1}{i}$. This assumption is justified. Since we are assuming a non-skewed distribution, the top few elements have a less significant share in S than in the case of Zipf(1), and less frequent elements will have a higher share in S than they would have had if the distribution is Zipf(1). Using this assumption, we rewrite our bound as $O(\frac{k*\log(N)}{\epsilon})$; while the bound in [3] can be rewritten as $O(\log(\frac{N}{\delta}) * (k + \frac{k^2}{\epsilon^2}\left(\frac{1}{k+1} - \frac{1}{|A|}\right))) \approx O(\frac{k}{\epsilon^2}\log(\frac{N}{\delta}))$. Even more, depending on the data distribution, our algorithm can guarantee the reported top-k to be correct, with weak data skew; while *CountSketch* does not offer any guarantees.

We can assume that field experts know whether the data is skewed enough to be considered Zipf(1) or not. Even if this is not applicable, we can start by analyzing a sample from the data, and then resizing the structure accordingly.

In the case of Zipf Distribution, the bound of [3] is $O(k\log(\frac{N}{\delta}))$. For $\alpha > 1$, our bound is $O((\frac{k}{\alpha})^{\frac{1}{\alpha}}k)$. Only when $\alpha = 1$, the space complexity is $O(k^2\log(|A|))$, and thus, our bound is better for cases of skewed data, long streams/windows, and has a 0-failure probability. In addition, we preserve the order of the top-k elements. To show the difference in space requirements, we give an example. For $N = 10^6$, $|A| = 10^4$, $k = 10$, $\alpha = 2$, and $\delta = 10^{-1}$ our space requirements are only 66 counters, while [3] needs $C * 230$ counters, where $C \gg 1$.

5   Experimental Results

We conducted a set of experiments, using both real and synthetic data. For space constraints, we summarize our synthetic data results here. The real data experimental results agree with those presented here, and the reader is referred to [14] for a full analysis on both the synthetic and real data experimental results. We generated several synthetic Zipfian datasets with the zipf parameter, α, varying from 0, which is uniform, to 3, which is highly skewed, on a fixed interval of $\frac{1}{2}$. The size of each dataset, N, is 10^7 hits. This set of experiments measure how the algorithms adapt to, and make use of data skew.

The algorithms were run on a PentiumIV 2.66 GHz, with 1.0 GB RAM. The stream was input and processed by each algorithm, and then a query was issued, and we recorded the *recall*, the number of correct elements found as a percentage

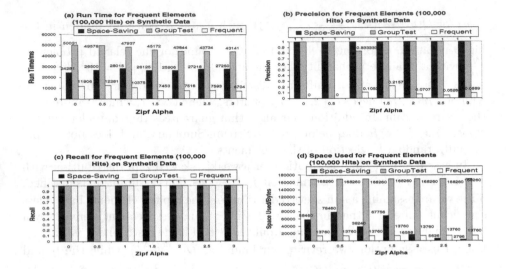

Fig. 5. Performance Comparison for the Frequent Elements Problem Using Synthetic Zipfian Data

of the number of actual correct elements; and the *precision*, the number of correct elements found as a percentage of the entire output [5]. We also measured the run time and space used by each algorithm, which indicates the capability to deal with high-speed streams, and to reside on servers with limited memories.

For the frequent elements problem, we compared our results with those of *GroupTest* [5], and *Frequent* [6]. For *GroupTest*, and *Frequent*, we used the C code available on the web-site of the first author of [5]. *Space-Saving*, *GroupTest*, and *Frequent* were queried for the frequent elements with support, ϕ, of 10^{-2}. We set ϵ, the error, to be one hundredth of ϕ, the required support; and δ, the failing probability, to be 0.01. Although *Frequent* ran up to four times faster than *Space-Saving*, as clear from Figure 5(a), its results were not competitive in terms of precision. Since it is not possible to specify an ϵ parameter for the algorithm, its precision was very low in all the runs. When the Zipf parameter was 0.0, and 0.5, the algorithm reported 28, and 19 elements, respectively, and actually there were no elements satisfying the support. For the rest of the experiments in Figure 5(b), the precision achieved by *Frequent* ranged from 0.053 to 0.216. The space used ranged from one fifth to five times the space of *Space-Saving*, as shown in Figure 5(d). It is interesting to note that as the data became more skewed, the space advantage of *Space-Saving* increased, while *Frequent* was not able to exploit the data skew to reduce its space requirements. Compared to *GroupTest*, from Figure 5(a), *Space-Saving* ran 1.5 to 2 times faster than *GroupTest*. The precision of the proposed algorithm was always 1; while *GroupTest* precision depended on α, with a precision of 0.83 when $\alpha = 1$, as sketched in Figure 5(b). The recalls of both algorithms were constant at 1, as clear from Figure 5(c). The

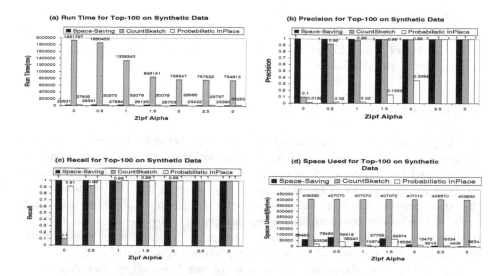

Fig. 6. Performance Comparison for the Top-k Problem Using Synthetic Zipfian Data

advantage of *Space-Saving* is clear in Figure 5(d), which shows that *Space-Saving* achieved a reduction in the space used by a factor ranging from 2 up to 60.

For the top-k problem, we implemented *Probabilistic-InPlace* [6], and *CountSketch* [3]. For the *CountSketch* [3] algorithm, we implemented the median algorithm by Hoare [9] with Median-of-three partition, which has a linear run time, in the average case [12]. Instead of maintaining a heap as suggested in [3], we kept a stream-summary of fixed length k. This guarantees constant time update for elements in the stream-summary, while the heap would entail $O(\log(k))$ operations. The difference in the space usage between the heap and the stream-summary of size k is negligible, when compared to the space used by the *CountSketch* algorithm. For the hidden constant of the *CountSketch* [3], we ran the algorithm several times, and we estimated that a factor of 16 would enable *CountSketch* to achieve results comparable to *Space-Saving* in terms of precision and recall. The *Space-Saving*, *CountSketch*, and *Probabilistic-InPlace* algorithms were used to identify the top-100 elements. For *CountSketch*, we set the probability of failure, δ, to 0.01. Both the *Space-Saving*, and the *Probabilistic-InPlace* were allowed the same number of counters; and thus, their run time and space usages were comparable, as clear from Figure 6(a), and Figure 6(d), respectively. The precision of *Probabilistic-InPlace* increased from 0.02 to 0.36 as the skew increased; and finally reached 1, when $\alpha \geq 2.5$, as indicated in Figure 6(b). On the contrary, from Figure 6(c), the recall of *Probabilistic-InPlace* was very high throughout the entire range of α. The precision and recall of *Space-Saving* were constant at 1. From Figure 6(a), the time reductions of *Space-Saving* over *CountSketch* ranged from a factor of 30, to 82. Although we used a hidden factor of 16, as indicated earlier, *CountSketch* failed to attain a recall and precision of 1, for all the experiments. *CountSketch* had a very low precision and recall for uniform data. From Figure 6(b), and Figure 6(c), the precision and recall of *CountSketch* did not reach 1 except for $\alpha \geq 2.5$. The space reductions of *Space-Saving* ranged from a factor of 5, to 117, as manifested in Figure 6(d). The performance gap increased with the data skew.

6   Discussion

This paper has devised an integrated approach for solving an interesting family of problems in data streams. The Stream-Summary data structure was proposed, and utilized by the *Space-Saving* algorithm to guarantee strict error bounds for approximate counts of elements, using very limited space. We showed that the *Space-Saving* algorithm can handle both the frequent elements and top-k problems because it efficiently estimates the elements' frequencies. The memory requirements were analyzed with special attention to the case of skewed data. We validated the theoretical analysis by experimental evaluation.

This is the first algorithm, to the best of our knowledge, that guarantees the order of the top-k elements. Even when it cannot guarantee the top-k, the algorithm outputs guaranteed top-k' elements, where $k' \approx k$.

In practice, if the alphabet is too large, like in the case of IP addresses, only a subset of this alphabet is observed in the stream, and not all the 2^{32} addresses. Our space bounds are actually a function of the number of distinct elements which have occurred in the stream. However, in our analysis, we have assumed that the entire alphabet is observed in the stream, which is the worst case for our algorithm. Yet, our space bounds are still better than those of other algorithms.

The main practical strengths of the *Space-Saving* algorithm is that it can use whatever space is available on the server to estimate the elements' frequencies, and provide guarantees on its results whenever possible. Even when analysts are not sure about the appropriate parameters, the algorithm can run in the available memory, and the results can be analyzed for further adaptation. It is interesting that running the algorithm on the available space ensures that more important elements are less susceptible to noise. It can be easily shown that the expected value of the over-estimation, ε_i, is proportional to the summation of the length of the stream sections when e_i was not monitored, which is inversely proportional to f_i.

References

1. P. Bose, E. Kranakis, P. Morin, and Y. Tang. Bounds for frequency estimation of packet streams. In *Proceedings of the 10th International Colloquium on Structural Information and Communication Complexity*, pages 33–42, 2003.
2. R. Boyer and J. Moore. A fast majority vote algorithm. Technical Report 1981-32, Institute for Computing Science, University of Texas, Austin, February 1981.
3. M. Charikar, K. Chen, and M. Farach-Colton. Finding frequent items in data streams. In *Proceedings of the 29th International Colloquium on Automata, Languages and Programming*, pages 693–703. Springer-Verlag, 2002.

4. G. Cormode, F. Korn, S. Muthukrishnan, and D. Srivastava. Finding hierarchical heavy hitters in data streams. In *Proceedings of the 29th International Conference on Very Large Databases*, pages 296–306, 2003.
5. G. Cormode and S. Muthukrishnan. Whats hot and whats not: Tracking most frequent items dynamically. In *Proceedings of the 22nd Symposium on Principles of Databse Systems*, pages 296–306, June 2003.
6. E. D. Demaine, A. Lopez-Ortiz, and J. I. Munro. Frequency estimation of internet packet streams with limited space. In *Proceedings of the 10th Annual European Symposium on Algorithms*, pages 348–360, 2002.
7. C. Estan and G. Varghese. New directions in traffic measurement and accounting: Focusing on the elephants, ignoring the mice. *ACM Trans. Comput. Syst.*, 21(3):270–313, 2003.
8. M. J. Fischer and S. L. Salzberg. Finding a majority among n votes: Solution to problem 81-5. *Journal of Algorithms*, 3:376–379, 1982.
9. C. A. R. Hoare. Algorithm 65: Find. *Communications of the ACM*, 4(7):321–322, 1961.
10. C. Jin, W. Qian, C. Sha, J. X. Yu, and A. Zhou. Dynamically maintaining frequent items over a data stream. In *Proceedings of the twelfth international conference on Information and knowledge management*, pages 287–294. ACM Press, 2003.
11. R. Karp, S. Shenker, and C. Papadimitriou. A simple algorithm for finding frequent elements in streams and bags. *ACM Transactions on Database Systems*, 28(1):51–55, 2003.
12. P. Kirschenhofer, H. Prodinger, and C. Martinez. Analysis of Hoare's FIND algorithm with median-of-three partition. *Random Structures Algorithms*, 10(1-2):143–156, 1997.
13. G. Manku and R. Motwani. Approximate frequency counts over data streams. In *Proceedings of the 28th International Conference on Very Large Data Bases*, pages 346–357, 2002.
14. A. Metwally, D. Agrawal, and A. El Abbadi. Efficient computation of frequent and top-k elements in data streams. Technical Report 2005-23, University of California, Santa Barbara, September 2005.
15. J. Misra and D. Gries. Finding repeated elements. *Science of Computer Programming*, 2:143–152, November 1982.
16. G.K. Zipf. *Human Behavior and The Principle of Least Effort*. Addison-Wesley, 1949.

Author Index